WHO'S WHO IN THE MART~~~~
SPECIAL EDITION THIRD SERIES

AMERICAN MARTIAL ARTS ALLIANCE FOUNDATION

HONORING
CYNTHIA ROTHROCK
QUEEN OF MARTIAL ARTS CINEMA

BY GRAND MASTER JESSIE BOWEN

Elite
PUBLICATIONS

An Elite Publications Book

Greenville, NC 27858

Tel: 919-618-8075

info@elitepublications.org

www.elitepublications.org

All attempts have been made to ensure the accuracy of the information presented in this book, but this is not a guarantee.

Publisher: Elite Publications

First Printing: July 2023

Language: English

Paperback ISBN-13: 9798851755699

Hardcover ISNB-13: 9798851755880

Kindle Version Available

Cover & interior design by Tiger Shark, Inc.

Ordering Information: Special discounts are available on quantity purchases by corporations, associations, educators, and others. For details, contact the publisher at the above address U.S. trade bookstores and wholesalers: Please contact Jessie Bowen. Tel: (919) 618-8075 or email info@elitepublications.org.

PRINTED IN THE UNITED STATES OF AMERICA

MEET THE AMAA BOOK PROJECT TEAM

PUBLISHER:

Elite Publications

2120 E. Firetower Rd #107-58

Greenville, NC 27858

www.elitepublications.org

CONTENT EDITORS:

Jessica C. Phillips

Krystal Harvey

ASSOCIATE EDITOR:

Dr. Gwendolyn Bowen

DIRECTOR OF MARKETING:

Jessica C. Phillips

INTERIOR DESIGN & BOOK COVER:

Krystal Harvey

Tiger Shark, Inc.

www.tigersharkmediausa.com

CONTRIBUTORS:

Dr. Robert Goldberg

Grand Master Cynthia Rothrock

TABLE OF
CONTENTS

TABLE OF
CONTENTS

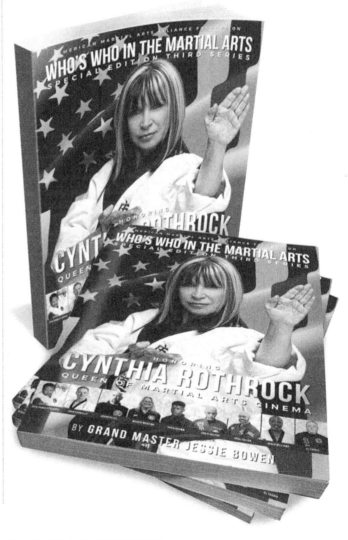

ACKNOWLEDGEMENTS

"Who's Who in the Martial Arts" biography book series, including Grandmasters Cynthia Rothrock, Pat Johnson, Bill "Superfoot" Wallace, Jhoon Rhee, Stephen K. Hayes, Ernie Reyes, Sr., Bill Clark, and others.

Back in 2015, we could never have imagined that this book series would evolve into an international brand with its own publishing company. I owe a debt of gratitude to my wife, Dr. Gwendolyn Bowen, for believing in the idea that we could create something from nothing. I would also like to express my appreciation to my daughter, Jessica C. Phillips, and Krystal Harvey, the head of the management and graphics team at Elite Publications, for their hard work, discipline, and creative vision.

My hope is that this book will serve as a source of inspiration and motivation for its readers and ignite a passion for martial arts through the eyes of the authors featured on its pages.

Grand Master Jessie Bowen

Founder & President
American Martial Arts Alliance Foundation
Elite Publications
www.whoswhointhemartialarts.com
www.elitepublications.org

I feel incredibly thankful to the individuals who played a crucial role in creating a book series that profoundly impacted the world of martial arts literature. I would like to express my special gratitude towards my teacher, Grandmaster Jan Wellendorf, and my friends and mentors, Grandmasters Joe Corley and Jeff Smith. I would also like to acknowledge the martial artists who have lent their reputation and prestige to the

WHO'S WHO IN THE MARTIAL ARTS
HONORING OUR MARTIAL ARTS LEGENDS & LEADERS
FOREWORD BY DR. ROBERT GOLDMAN

The "Who's Who in the Martial Arts Tribute to Cynthia Rothrock" biography book is a compilation of inspiring stories shared by true legends, leaders, and teachers in the martial arts industry. One of the featured martial artists is Grand Master Cynthia Rothrock, who has achieved a level of greatness that few (male or female) martial artists have reached. Despite her remarkable accomplishments, she remains humble, kind, and always willing to give back to her students and fellow practitioners worldwide. She is a true role model for aspiring grandmasters, following the highest levels of tradition.

As martial artists, we are committed to inspiring and motivating others, promoting sports participation, and encouraging a healthy and fit lifestyle. When we give back to others, we also benefit ourselves. By making a difference in the lives of others, we can improve our own lives as well. This book highlights the inspiring stories of martial artists who have positively impacted their students and communities worldwide.

The martial artists featured in this book all share a common experience of adversity, challenges, obstacles, failures, and successes. It's important to understand that failure is a part of the journey to greatness. How we handle failure defines our character and determines how our story will end.

The champions in this book have demonstrated an unstoppable spirit throughout their lives, never allowing their minds to negotiate with their will to succeed. The key to success is having inner strength, an unbreakable will, an unstoppable spirit, and persistence. Winners never quit, and quitters never win. Achieving greatness takes years of focus, discipline, commitment, and hard work ethic. Perfection may not be attainable, but by chasing it, we can catch excellence.

Our legacy is determined by the positive impact we make on the lives of others. We must be the change we wish to see in the world and strive to do better than our previous best. By sharing our art and becoming lifelong teachers, mentors, and leaders, we can leave a lasting impact on the martial arts industry and the lives we touch.

Let us honor and cherish Grand Master Cynthia Rothrock for her outstanding contributions to the martial arts industry, including the featured inductees and readers worldwide.

Dr. Robert Goldman, MD, PHd

Anti-Aging & Sports Medicine Pioneer
https://drbobgoldman.com/

WHO'S WHO IN THE MARTIAL ARTS

INTRODUCTION TO THE WHO'S WHO BOOK SERIES

The Who's Who Book Series is not your typical martial arts book. It aims to inspire and motivate readers by sharing the stories of martial artists whose lives have been transformed through studying and applying the principles taught in martial arts.

For over 1500 years, martial arts have been essential to personal development training. In the pages of this book, you will read about the journeys of hundreds of martial artists who share how martial arts has impacted their lives.

Grandmaster Bowen's Who's Who Biography Book Series showcases the global recognition of individual accomplishments rather than glorifying the martial artists themselves. By reading about the martial arts leaders, you will be amazed by the magnitude of individual effort and sacrifices made from grassroots activities to global media and organizational results. Instead of debating which blocks, strikes, or styles are better, this book celebrates the individual strengths of those who share the marital arts bond. Their legacies have impacted martial arts in America and around the world.

Regardless of where you are in life, martial arts can be a powerful tool to improve your physical, mental, and spiritual well-being. It helps individuals find their purpose and let go of negativity and things that hold them back. Dive into the journeys of Who's Who in the Martial Arts and discover the transformative power of martial arts.

GET YOUR WHO'S WHO SERIES TODAY!

THE AMERICAN MARTIAL ARTS ALLIANCE FOUNDATION
WHO'S WHO IN THE MARTIAL ARTS HONORS
GRAND MASTER
Cynthia Rothrock
THE QUEEN OF MARTIAL ARTS CINEMA

WHO'S WHO IN THE MARTIAL ARTS HONORS
GRAND MASTER CYNTHIA ROTHROCK
THE QUEEN OF MARTIAL ARTS CINEMA
WORLD CHAMPION. MOVIE STAR. ROLE MODEL. ADVENTURE SEEKER.

Her Journey

Cynthia Rothrock is among the world's greatest martial arts/action film stars. Few other performers can match her presence and energy on the silver screen. She is the undisputed "Queen of Martial Arts Cinema." Cynthia Rothrock is an incredibly accomplished martial artist and action star. She holds five black belts in various Far Eastern martial arts disciplines. These arts include; Tang Soo Do (Korean), Tae Kwon Do (Korean), Eagle Claw (Chinese), Wu Shu (contemporary Chinese), and Northern Shaolin (classical Chinese).

When she was a 13-year-old growing up in Scranton, Pennsylvania, she started taking lessons at her parent's best friend's private gym. Little did she know then that this casual interest would lead to a full-time professional career. Her martial arts teachers quickly recognized her natural abilities and encouraged her to enter an open karate competition. By the time she had earned her first black belt, she was well on her way to becoming a martial arts champion. By 1982 Cynthia was one of the premier Kata (forms) and weapon competitors in the United States. Competing in divisions not segregated by male-female categories, she captured every title in open and closed karate competitions.

From 1981-1985 she was the undefeated World Karate Champion in both forms and weapon competition. She established a legacy of wins and accumulated hundreds of trophies for her martial arts prowess, an unparalleled feat even today! She is a consummate performer with Chinese weapons like the Chinese Double Broad Swords, Staff, Chinese Nine-section Steel Whip Chain, Chinese Iron Fan, and an assortment of Okinawan Kobudo and Japanese Bugei Weapons.

As a Forms and Weapon Champion, Cynthia Rothrock has traveled the world performing the intricacies of her martial arts arsenal. With precision flare and panache, she has demonstrated before hundreds of thousands of spectators across the globe. Her "action-packed" self-defense and fight scenario performances garnered her a reputation as a consummate professional in martial arts.

This international exposure soon propelled her to martial arts celebrity status, and within a mere period of less than two years, Cynthia became a household name in martial arts circles. In addition to being featured on virtually every martial arts magazine cover worldwide, Cynthia appears in over 300 stories and articles in national and international publications. Some of these magazines include Black Belt Magazine (United States), Inside Kung-Fu (United States), Martial Arts Training (United States), Martial Arts Stars (United States), Inside Karate (United States), Sensei (Spanish Argentina), Australian Fighting Arts, China Sports (Beijing, China), Budo (Brazil), Combat Sport (Spanish-Brazil), Combat Magazine (England), Sushido (French), Kung-Fu Wu Shu (French), Karate Budo Journal (Germany), Australian Tae Kwon Do, The Fighters (England), Martial Arts Illustrated (England), Michael De Pasquale Jr.'s Karate International (United States), Budo Karate (Japan), Banzai International (Italy), Czarny Pas (Poland), Cinturon Negro (Spain), Ninja Weapons (United States), El Budoka (Spain), Kicksider (Germany), Impact Magazine (Germany), Karate Illustrated (United States), Ninja Weapons (United States), El Budoka (Spain), Kicksider (Germany), Impact Magazine

a stick of dynamite after "starring" in a Kentucky Fried Chicken commercial in the early 1980s. Soon after, notable producers and directors like Fred Weintraub and Robert Clouse (Enter the Dragon) recognized her martial arts skills, and her career steadily climbed. Cynthia's first full-length motion picture was Yes Madam, where she co-starred with Michelle Yeoh. The movie turned out to be a hit and broke all box office records in Hong Kong. Cynthia and Michelle were on their way to becoming two of the world's most successful female action stars. When Cynthia was invited to Hong Kong to appear in motion pictures, she didn't know what to expect. Initially, she imagined they would do period pieces where she would wear tight pigtails and traditional Chinese costuming. Surprisingly, she soon

(Germany), Karate Illustrated (United States), The Swedish Fighter's International (Sweden), Master (United States), Kung-Fu Illustrated (United States), The Fighter (Thailand), Masters Series (United States), The Martial Arts Gazette (United States), Karate Proþles (United States), Sport Karate International (United States), The World of Martial Arts (United States), The Dojo (United States), and hundreds of national and international newspapers.

Cynthia Rothrock is also one of the very select individuals inducted into the Black Belt Hall of Fame and Inside Kung-Fu Hall of Fame. Inclusions in renowned organizations include the Martial Arts Gallery of Fame, MARTIAL ARTS, Traditions, History, People, The Martial Arts Sourcebook, and dozens of other historical reference books of martial significance.

Cinematically, Cynthia burst onto the scene like

discovered that she would star in Chinese action films set in modern times with contemporary themes. As a result, Cynthia Rothrock spent five years in Hong Kong, starring in Asian-produced motion pictures. She starred with Kung-fu greats Samo Hung and Yuen Biao during that time.

She was even offered a role opposite Jackie Chan in Armour of Gods, but Jackie got injured, so the company put her in Righting Wrongs with superstar Yuen Biao. During that Asian tenure, she, unbeknownst to her, has set a record of becoming the very first non-Chinese Westerner to carry an action movie single-handedly in Hong Kong. She left Hong Kong as one of the most celebrated action stars in Hong Kong's cinematic history! Cynthia Rothrock's movie career "shooting schedule" has taken her

to some of the most exotic locations on the planet. Paradoxically, she has also endured some of the worse climatic conditions that anyone in the motion picture could ever anticipate – all in the name of making "action-adventure" motion pictures.

Publicity has followed Cynthia Rothrock through every stage of her illustrious career. She is the "media darling" of virtually every reporter, writer, and martial arts magazine worldwide. They know that she draws readers by the thousands to their publication. Her "image" and "career" is perhaps followed more closely (by martial arts enthusiast) than any other "martial arts" actors except Chuck Norris or Jackie Chan.

GRAND MASTER CYNTHIA ROTHROCK
THE QUEEN OF MARTIAL ARTS CINEMA
WORLD CHAMPION. MOVIE STAR. ROLE MODEL. ADVENTURE SEEKER.

Rothrock on Film

Cynthia Rothrock is a martial arts expert and athlete who became a film actress, starring in several highly successful action movies. She first made a name as an action actress in Hong Kong before going on to wow audiences on her home turf. At the time of her popularity, she was well-known as the "Queen of Martial Arts Films."

Upon completing her goal of being undefeated in competition, she began her martial arts acting career, starring in movies produced and filmed in Hong Kong. Her first movie, Yes, Madam, alongside Michelle Yeoh, broke box office records making her a massive star in Hong Kong. After three years of living in Hong Kong and finishing seven films, she returned to the United States to continue her acting career.

Today she has starred in over 60 movies and is, for the first time, developing and producing her very own action film titled Black Creek.

Black Creek is a dark, gritty, dystopian, western action martial arts film featuring a strong 'no-holds-barred' female protagonist portrayed by Cynthia. The plot centers around a sheriff's sister who seeks revenge against the terrifying leader of a group of outlaws after discovering he brutally murdered her brother, his wife, and other family members in a gritty southwestern town. Black Creek promises to deliver an adrenaline-packed ride from start to finish.

To learn more, visit BlackCreekMovie.com.

GRAND MASTER CYNTHIA ROTHROCK
THE QUEEN OF MARTIAL ARTS CINEMA
WORLD CHAMPION. MOVIE STAR. ROLE MODEL. ADVENTURE SEEKER.

Filmography

1. Yes, Madam! (1985)
2. 24 Hours to Midnight (1985)
3. The Millionaires' Express (1986)
4. Magic Crystal (1986)
5. Righting Wrongs (1986)
6. Fight to Win (1987)
7. No Retreat, No Surrender 2 (1987)
8. Top Squad (1988)
9. Rapid Fire (1988)
10. Jungle Heat (1988)
11. Female Reporter (1989)
12. Miao tan shuang long (1989)
13. China O'Brien (1990)
14. China O'Brien II (Video) (1990)
15. Martial Law (Video) (1990)
16. Prince of the Sun (1990)
17. No Witnesses (1990)
18. Fast Getaway (Video) (1991)
19. Martial Law II: Undercover (Video) (1991)
20. Tiger Claws (1991)
21. Angel of Fury (1992)
22. Lady Dragon (1992)
23. Rage and Honor (1992)
24. Honor and Glory (1993)
25. Rage and Honor II (1993)
26. Irresistible Force (TV Movie) (1993)
27. Lady Dragon 2 (1993)

GRAND MASTER CYNTHIA ROTHROCK
THE QUEEN OF MARTIAL ARTS CINEMA
WORLD CHAMPION. MOVIE STAR. ROLE MODEL. ADVENTURE SEEKER.

Filmography

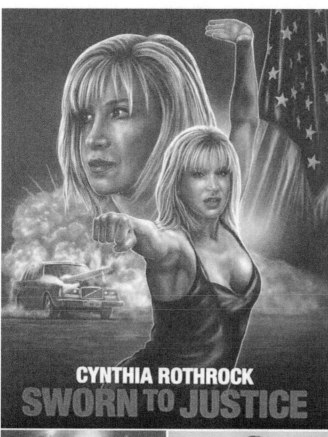

28. Undefeatable (1993)
29. Fast Getaway II (Video) (1994)
30. Guardian Angel (Video) (1994)
31. Fatal Passion (1995)
32. Eye for an Eye (1996)
33. Tiger Claws II (1996)
34. Hercules: The Legendary Journeys (TV Series) (1996)
35. Sworn to Justice (1996)
36. The Dukes of Hazzard: Reunion! (TV Movie) (1997)
37. Deep Cover (1997)
38. Night Vision (1997)
39. The Hostage (1998)
40. Tiger Claws III (2000)
41. Manhattan Chase (2000)
42. The Untouchable 2 (Video Game) (2001)
43. Set Me Free (2001)
44. Redemption (Video) (2002)
45. Outside the Law (2002)
46. Sci-Fighter (2002)
47. Lost Bullet (2007)
48. Santa's Summer House (2012)
49. Badass Showdown (2013)
50. Mercenaries (2014)
51. The Martial Arts Kid (2015)
52. Showdown in Manila (2016)

GRAND MASTER CYNTHIA ROTHROCK
THE QUEEN OF MARTIAL ARTS CINEMA
WORLD CHAMPION. MOVIE STAR. ROLE MODEL. ADVENTURE SEEKER.

Filmography

53. Beyond the Game (2016)

54. Asian Ghost Story (The Narrator: Voiceover) (2016)

55. Mr. and Mrs. Smit (TV Series) (2016)

56. Star Raiders: The Adventures of Saber Raine (2017)

57. A Doggone Hollywood (2017)

58. Death Fighter (2017)

59. B-Team (Video Game: General Rothrock) (2018)

60. Fury of the Fist and the Golden Fleece (2018)

61. Cool Cat Kids Superhero (2018)

62. Mrs. Cloudover: Episode 2.6, Episode 1.3, Episode 1.2

63. Diary of a Lunatic (TV Mini-Series) (completed)

64. Anadellia Rises (completed)

65. No Way Back (pre-production)

66. Operation Dagon (pre-production)

67. Prey of Wrath (pre-production)

68. Darkness of Man (completed)

69. The Last Kumite (post-production)

70. Black Creek (pre-production)

THE AMERICAN MARTIAL ARTS ALLIANCE FOUNDATION
WHO'S WHO IN THE MARTIAL ARTS

AMAAF
Future Leaders

Sophia LEACH

> " Martial arts helped with my confidence; when testing, teaching, or presenting for tournaments, the most important thing is to be confident.

WHY THE *Martial Arts?*

When I was younger, my parents had a requirement that I was involved in at least one sport. While I tried everything from ballet to soccer, Taekwondo was the only sport I ever really enjoyed. I enjoyed the sport so much more than the others because it made sense to me. There are specific movements and rules to follow, and they do not change. I also like how practical the sport is overall; each move was explained to me, and I understood how it could be used in real life. When I first began martial arts, I was not very good, but through my teachers, I learned and was able to enjoy martial arts.

TRAINING INFORMATION

- School: Desert Taekwondo
- Martial Arts Styles & Rank: ITF Taekwondo (Jun Tong Taekwondo Federation), 3rd Dan Black Belt
- Instructors/Influencers: Master Mel Tompson, Grand Master Malm, Grand Master Mark Plante
- Birthplace/Growing Up: Columbus, OH / Tucson, AZ
- Year started training: 2012

PROFESSIONAL ORGANIZATIONS

- Desert Taekwondo
- National Junior Honor Society

How MARTIAL ARTS HELPS ME IN *My Life!*

Martial arts helped with my confidence; when testing, teaching, or presenting for tournaments, the most important thing is to be confident. This confidence has also bled into my whole life. It helps that through Taekwondo. I believe I should be able to get myself out of any situation if necessary. It has also helped me think quickly and come up with fast solutions because sparring requires you to do what is necessary depending on what your opponent throws. Having the skill of quick thinking makes your life easier.

What's your favorite martial arts technique and why?

The sidekick because it is a strong kick and can be sneaky when used properly. It can easily be used for both attacks and defenses.

Who has influenced you most in your Martial Arts study?

My head instructor, Grand Master Brian Malm, was the most influential because of his constant encouragement.

What do you love most about the martial arts study?

I love how universal martial arts are. When taught right, it teaches you about everything you might need, both physical and mental. It can teach you control, confidence, determination, and different ways to defend yourself and others.

PERSONAL ACHIEVEMENTS

- I think that something I have achieved is the ability to teach. I have learned how to teach others in Taekwondo and help new people enjoy it as much as I do. When I tried mountain bike racing, I earned a podium spot. I have also been able to grow outside of sports and sell some of the art that I have made. Lastly, I have received almost straight A's throughout my school career.

MAJOR ACHIEVEMENTS

- I think that a major achievement for me was earning my third-degree black belt in Taekwondo. During the testing for my third degree, I could break three boards with my elbow and another three with my sidekick. This is important because I was afraid to break boards for a long time. I broke all three boards on the first try for both breaks. This took years of practice, discipline, coaching, and guidance from my instructors. I also learned how to use a few weapons, which are not in the normal curriculum for my school. I was able to learn the bo staff and the tonfa bo. I also won first place overall in a recent (2023) tournament, meaning that the 'points' I received for the wins I had earned in the tournament were higher than anyone else's. I enjoy tournaments and the challenge they present.

Final Thoughts?

I think it is important to find something you like to do that keeps you happy and stick with it. Find at least one thing in your life to work out your body and your brain that you enjoy and live life.

Michael MELE

> Martial arts have allowed me to maintain discipline and self-control in all areas of my life, especially in school.

WHY THE *Martial Arts?*

I began because my older brothers did Tae Kwon Do, and I looked up to them so much. I would always beg my mother to sign me up for Tae Kwon Do classes, and when she did, I instantly fell in love with it.

TRAINING INFORMATION

- School: Taecole Tae Kwon Do
- Martial Arts Styles & Rank: ITF Tae Kwon Do, 3rd Degree Black Belt
- Instructors/Influencers: Master Maggie Messina
- Birthplace/Growing Up: Albertson, NY
- Year started training: 2012

PROFESSIONAL ORGANIZATIONS

- Taecole Tae Kwon Do

~~How~~ MARTIAL ARTS HELPS ME IN *My Life!*

Martial arts have allowed me to maintain discipline and self-control in all areas of my life, especially in school. Without martial arts, I would have had a lot of trouble focusing in school and doing my best in all my classes. The focus that I have built doing Tae Kwon Do for all my life has transferred to school and sports. The physical assets that come with learning martial arts enhance your understanding of how to generate power with techniques and equilibrium, which has directly affected my ability to play sports as best as possible. Martial arts have helped me with so much in my life, mentally and physically.

What's your favorite martial arts technique and why?

The sidekick is my all-time favorite martial arts technique because this kick is one of if not the most powerful kicks in all of the martial arts. The force you can generate while doing a proper side kick is equivalent to being hit by a car going 30 mph. Not only is it so powerful, but it is also enjoyable. The sidekick is my favorite kick to do any time, especially when hitting targets.

Who has influenced you most in your Martial Arts study?

Master Maggie Messina is the most influential person during my martial arts study. Master Messina has taught me ever since I was five years old, and she taught me everything I know. She teaches in such a way that unless you try to be bored, you will never get bored while

PERSONAL ACHIEVEMENTS

- Chosen to be on the Top 25 Nassau County Lacrosse Showcase team as a rising freshman

MAJOR ACHIEVEMENTS

- Varsity Lacrosse as a freshman
- Competed in World Cup Open Martial Arts Championship 2023 and received two silver medals,
- AP Spanish and AP World History
- Honors Chemistry
- TV Studio Club
- Herricks Choir Rookie of the Year award.

HOW MARTIAL ARTS (CONTINUED)

learning under her. Her teaching style is unique, and she explains everything in context with the real world, so it is extremely easy to understand. She has also guided me through my entire life and helped me make the best decisions for myself.

What do you love most about the martial arts study?

I love how martial arts is a physical and mental sport and an art. Martial art is such a beautifully crafted art/sport that allows people to better themselves physically and mentally, stay in shape, and also paint their picture with their techniques.

Final Thoughts?

I hope one day I can be even half as successful and outstanding as Master Maggie Messina is. She is the person I look up to most, not only as my master instructor and mentor but also as a second mother. She has helped me through every challenging situation in my life, and I would never ask anyone else in the world to help me because she helps me better than anyone else.

James
SHORTS

"

Martial arts has given me the self-confidence and ability to help others as I've always wanted to do.

WHY THE *Martial Arts?*

I started martial arts because I was tired of being the weak one. When I was young, I was always down in the dumps, thinking nothing I did mattered. Important stuff seemed like it didn't make any difference. But a point hit when I just couldn't ignore it anymore. Growing up, I realized that talk and grit alone wouldn't cut it. There were times when I had to step up and help people I cared about who needed looking after. I wanted to be their rock, their shield. But how could I do that if I couldn't even stand up for myself? So I decided to bust out of my comfort zone, telling myself over and over if I wanted things to change, I had to do it myself. If not, I'd be stuck in my own head, unable to do anything for anyone. That's when I found Guardian Fist Kung Fu. It was like a lifeline thrown at me. It gave me a reason to feel good about myself. I became confident and started growing as a person. Now, I can say I'm strong enough to be someone others can rely on. I can

TRAINING INFORMATION

- School: Cloud Forest Chin Woo Martial Arts Academy
- Martial Arts Styles & Rank: Wei Shi Chuan (Guardian Fist Kung Fu)-1st Duan Black Sash
- Instructors/Influencers: Michael Johnson
- Birthplace/Growing Up: Chicago, IL / Greensboro, NC
- Year started training: 2015

PROFESSIONAL ORGANIZATIONS

- Cloud Forest Chin Woo Association
- Overseas Chinese Martial Arts Federation
- Dragon Society International
- Wei Family Tai Chi Chuan Association
- Order of Dragon's Bane Discipleship

be the guardian I always wanted to be. And that's not the end. I'm gonna keep pushing, keep growing stronger and smarter, until I'm someone that would make the old me burst with pride. I'm ready to be a guardian, to protect those I care about, no matter what. After all, I'm a martial artist and won't stop at anything.

How MARTIAL ARTS HELPS ME IN My Life!

Martial arts has given me the self-confidence and ability to help others as I've always wanted to do. When you don't have the ability to fight or defend yourself, this world seems to run you over, and it takes from you what it wants. My Sifu taught me that to live the kind of life I want to live, I must be like a sleeping dragon. No one walks up to the dragon and kicks it awake because it's a dragon. I train in the external and internal arts because I want to understand more about power. Why people want it bad enough to step on others, and what it means to hold such power. The more I know about it, the more I'll understand their motivations and will be able to open communication with those around me. But I will always be the dragon, and people close to me will know that I intend to live a peaceful life, so they should just let me do that.

What's your favorite martial arts technique and why?

My favorite martial arts technique is definitely the Monkey Palm Wave Strikes. They are versatile strikes and always have been my favorite movement to practice in our form sets.

PERSONAL ACHIEVEMENTS

- In martial arts, I can do a zero-distance punch with an egg in my hand without breaking it or pulling my fist away from the board.
- Proud to be an online social influencer and soon-to-be-released YouTube Channel.

MAJOR ACHIEVEMENTS

- 1st Duan Black Sash in Wei Shi Chuan (Guardian Fist Kung Fu) Discipled under the Wei Family Lineage
- National Honors Society of High School Scholars
- Accepted into the GAP program
- International Martial Arts Federation
- Wei Family Tai Chi Association
- Golden Lion Kuo Shu

Who has influenced you most in your Martial Arts study?

I will give the credit to Michael Johnson, Shifu. He has influenced me the most during my martial arts study. I have always been able to go to him when I have a problem that needs solving. And it can honestly be 'any problem.' He's never judged me and has only helped me understand my own feelings more. Those early years of training in Guardian Fist were rough emotionally. I had a lot going on, so being able to go to Michael Johnson Shifu and talk things through was exactly what I needed. Oh, and he's an incredible martial arts teacher so that also was a big influence!

What do you love most about the martial arts study?

The perfection of power and speed. It's exhilarating how good it feels to see the movement in your mind's eye, then bring it to life with my own power and ability.

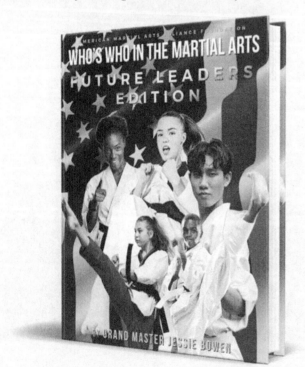

Final Thoughts?

It's only been five years since I first stepped into Cloud Forest Chin Woo Martial Arts Academy, my Kung Fu Home. There was a time I didn't understand things well enough to know if I would live to see five years later. But Kung Fu became my anchor, and from my anchor, I found the strength to love life and to know that no matter what comes my way, I have family, my Shifu, and my martial arts family there to back me up. Thank you for giving me the chance to let my voice and story be heard!

19

WHO'S WHO IN THE MARTIAL ARTS

PKA WORLDWIDE
Honorees

Bobby S. BRIGGS

> **"** The Martial Arts has always, and continues to teach me valuable lessons in life.

WHY THE Martial Arts?

As a small, poor farm kid, I was always fascinated with martial arts mainly because it was something that was so mysterious to me. And I also loved anything physical for as long as I can remember (like football, boxing, martial arts, etc.).

I was a huge Bruce Lee and Chuck Norris fan at the same time. I played all kinds of sports throughout school. I had an elementary boxing coach recommend to me at one time that I should also take Karate to help with my coordination. Little did he know that I had already gone to some Karate classes as often as my family could afford to let me go. But when my boxing mentor said this to me, I became more serious about martial arts. Since my family could not afford my Karate classes, I worked harder to try and find ways to make money so I could attend Karate classes as often as possible. Since I also loved sports so much, it

TRAINING INFORMATION

- Martial Arts Styles & Ranks: Kidokime-ryu Karate-do, 10th Degree, JuDan; Okinawa-te, 9th Degree, KuDan; Kenpo Karate, 5th Degree, GoDan; Shotokan, 1st Degree, ShoDan; Shito-ryu, 1st Degree, ShoDan; American Gojo-ryu, 1st Degree, Shodan; Isshin-ryu Karate, 1st Degree; American Karate, 1st Degree, ShoDan; Hapkido, 1st Degree; Tae Kwon Do, 1st Degree

- Instructors/Influencers: Hanshi James White, Hanshi Bill Daniels, Kyoshi David Ray, Kyoshi Rick Sparks, Kyoshi Ken Herfurth, Sensei Chuck Taylor, Sensei Greg McMahan, Sensei Arvin Pearson, Sensei Ernest Watkins, Sensei Ronnie Delfino, Sensei Tony Simmons

- Birthplace/Growing Up: Spruce Pine, NC / Burnsville, NC

- Yrs. In the Martial Arts: 54-55 years

- Yrs. Instructing: 45 years

- School Owner, Manager & Instructor at Kidokime-ryu Karate-do Hombu Dojo, Ranking Black Belt Instructor (Soke) for Kidokime-ryu Karate-do Worldwide

soon became apparent that my Karate was very helpful in my excelling in that also.

Karate seemed to greatly enhance my athletic ability in the sports I played. But very soon, I discovered that as much as I loved sports, Karate quickly became my life's love. I never gave up on sports. As a matter of fact, my Karate and the sports that I played throughout school complimented each other very well. In the area where I was raised, there were very, very few places where I could go to find a martial arts school. Luckily for me, I did find some that had awesome instructors that led me in the right direction and became a very important figure in my life, and that's where and how my martial arts career began.

~~How~~ MARTIAL ARTS CHANGED *My Life!*

Martial arts has taught me a great deal. Most importantly, I believe it taught me to persevere and overcome any difficult obstacles I may face in my life. It's taught me that hard work ALWAYS pays off. It's taught me that where there's a will, there's a way.

Martial arts has always and continues to teach me valuable life lessons. One of my favorite lessons (quotes) is, "Success is never owned; it is rented. And the rent is due each and every day."

PROFESSIONAL ORGANIZATIONS

- National Universal Karate Association (N.U.K.A.) Lifetime Member
- American Martial Arts Association (AMAA) Lifetime Member
- Professional Karate Association Worldwide Lifetime Member (PKA)
- Kenpo Karate Institute Lifetime Member (KKI)

PERSONAL ACHIEVEMENTS

Soke Briggs has competed, won, and placed in hundreds of both sport Karate (point fighting, Kata, Weapons, and Self-Defense), as well as, full-contact kickboxing all across the world, and has won numerous times, and defending Champion in many different categories.

MAJOR ACHIEVEMENTS

- Promoted to KuDan (9th Deg Black Belt) by the Okinawan Karate-do on Mar 22, 2014, in Okinawa-te Karate
- Promoted to JuDan (10th Deg Black Belt) by N.U.K.A. on Aug 4, 2018, in Kidokime-ryu Karate-do
- Inducted into the Martial Arts Legends Hall of Fame as the Karate Grandmaster of the Year
- Inducted into the Action Martial Arts Hall of Honors/Hall of Heroes for "Outstanding Achievements in the Martial Arts as a GrandMaster"
- Inducted into the Action Martial Arts Magazine World History Book, Action Martial Arts Magazine Hall of Honors, Official 20th Anniversary Issue
- Has been in multiple Martial Arts Magazines, Books, and Newspaper articles
- Has been in Multiple "Changing Lives" Series Martial Arts Books
- Martial Arts Extraordinaire Bio book (for Martial Artists with more than 50 yrs of experience)
- Three "Who's Who in the Martial Arts" inductions
- Author of Kidokime-ryu Karate-do book
- AMAA Who's Who in the Martial Arts Hall of Honors
- AMAA Legends "Golden Achievement Award" (50 Years)
- Recipient of the Who's Who Legends Award, AMAA Hall of Honors
- Inducted in the Action Martial Arts Hall of Honors 2022 for the "Platinum Lifetime Achievements"

How has Grandmaster CYNTHIA ROTHROCK Influenced me?

I had the pleasure of meeting Cynthia Rothrock in person several years ago at a martial arts event. I had seen her in movies and different magazines over the years and had become a big fan of hers. We have become friends over the past several years, but I'm still a fan. Cynthia is one of the most loving, caring, down-to-earth, sweetest human beings on this earth. She's a great instructor as well. I've been to several of her seminars and was invited to be one of the four inaugural Instructors at her First Annual Hall of Honors weekend in Cherry Hill, NJ, last year in Oct of 2022. My wife and I also have pledged support for her new movie that she is producing and starring in, "Black Creek." Cynthia is a role model to all of my female martial arts students and all female martial artists worldwide. I'm proud to have GM Cynthia Rothrock as a friend.

Become an AMAA MEMBER!

MAJOR ACHIEVEMENTS

- Action Martial Arts Hall of Honors as "Esteemed Martial Artist"
- Bushido Championship Instructor Award
- AMAA Changing Lives Legacy Award featuring GM Bill "Superfoot" Wallace, and inducted in the Who's Who in the Martial Arts Hall of Honors, 2022
- Inducted into the Cynthia Rothrock Premier Hall of Honors for "Platinum Lifetime Achievement", 2022
- Action Martial Arts Hall of Honors Inductee for 2023 for "Diamond Lifetime Contributions"
- Has been interviewed and featured on Numerous Radio talk shows, as well as, TV News stories featured on the Far East Network (FEN) for military personnel throughout Japan, Okinawa, and the Philippines
- Numerous Military (both Peacetime and Combat) Awards, Decorations, and Medals.
- Numerous Civilian Police Awards and Recognition
- Numerous Civic Awards and Recognitions

Mary
BRIGGS

"

Martial Arts has made an impact on my life in multiple ways, and in ways I never thought about...

WHY THE *Martial Arts?*

I started in Martial Arts late in life, more out of curiosity than anything else. I did not know anyone that was involved in Martial Arts and what little I saw of it was on TV or in the movies. Which means I didn't really know anything about it. I moved to Charlotte in 2000 to work for The Hartford Insurance Company, and met Soke Briggs in 2008. Shortly after we met and got to know each other I learned he was in Martial Arts. He talked to me quite a bit about Martial Arts and I had a lot of questions. He told me about the style he practiced, telling me that it was very disciplined. He explained some of the things that he had learned, told me about his instructors and all the places he had been able to practice and teach all over the world. And he told me about his current rank at that time and what other styles he had studied and held black belts in. He asked if I would be interested in taking Martial Arts classes and I said I would

TRAINING INFORMATION

- Martial Arts Styles & Rank: Kidokime-ryu Karate-do, YonDan (4th Degree), Okinawa-te, Shodan (1st Degree)
- Instructors/Influencers: Soke Bobby S. Briggs, Kyoshi Kenneth L. Herfurth
- Birthplace/Growing Up: Roanoke, VA / Bedford, VA
- Yrs. In the Martial Arts: 15 years
- Yrs. Instructing: 11 years
- School owner & Instructor at Kidokime-ryu Karate-do Hombu Dojo, PKA Worldwide Member, AMAA Lifetime member

PROFESSIONAL ORGANIZATIONS

- Professional Karate Association (PKA)
- American Martial Arts Alliance (AMAA)

like to give it a try. Soon after, I took my first class with Soke Briggs as my instructor. I was in my forties at the time. I decided I wanted to see what it was really all about. It was tough in the beginning and I wasn't sure about it at all. But I kept coming back to class. After a couple of months, I tested and earned my yellow belt. I still wasn't sure if I wanted to continue, but something just kept pulling me back to class. So as the weeks and months passed, I was training and learning, testing and passing belt tests. When I reached the intermediate level was when all the different pieces of Kidokime-ryu Karate-do began to slowly fit together. And then it seemed that all of a sudden, I was training for my Shodan. After 4 ½ years I was facing the toughest test of my Martial Arts journey. So, starting Martial Arts out of curiosity led to one of my greatest achievements, the 1st female Shodan in Kidokime-ryu Karate-do.

How MARTIAL ARTS CHANGED My Life!

Martial arts has made an impact on my life in multiple ways, and in ways I never thought about. It has helped me gain and be more confident in my personal life and job, in my interactions with people I teach, and with people I work with. It has made me stronger, both mentally and physically. It has taught me how to defend myself. It has taught me the true meaning of character, of being disciplined in training, being more disciplined in everyday tasks, and again with my job.

Martial arts has taught me perseverance – striving to reach your goal no matter how

PERSONAL ACHIEVEMENTS

- Numerous Employee of the Quarter Awards
- Numerous Employee of the Month Awards
- Numerous Civic Awards and Recognitions

MAJOR ACHIEVEMENTS

- Inducted into the Martial Arts Legends Hall of Fame as the 2019 Karate Instructor of the Year in Mt. Laurel, NJ (October 26, 2019)
- Promoted to YonDan (4th Degree Black Belt, Aug 8 2020 by Kyoshi Kenneth L. Herfurth, endorsed by Soke Bobby S.Briggs, Hanshi James White, & Hanshi Bill Daniels)
- The first female to ever be promoted to Black Belt in Kidokime-ryu Karate-do
- Honored to be recognized as "The Ladies of PKA Worldwide"
- Has been in multiple Martial Arts Books
- Former Undefeated Kata (Forms) Champion, and Grand Champion
- Received the Who's Who Legends Award AMAA Hall of Honors in Las Vegas, NV 2021
- Inducted in the Action Martial Arts Hall of Honors 2022 for Outstanding Achievements in the Martial Arts
- AMAA Changing Lives Legacy Award featuring GM Bill "Superfoot" Wallace, and inducted in the Who's Who in the Martial Arts Hall of Honors, 2022
- Inducted into the Cynthia Rothrock Premier Hall of Honors for "Instructor of the Year", 2022
- Action Martial Arts Hall of Honors Inductee for 2023 for "Esteemed Elite Warrior"

tough it gets. It has taught me about self-control and what that means in the dojo, and I have found that it has also helped me maintain self-control in many different situations. Martial arts brought to the forefront the things that parents strive to teach their children – respect for themselves and others, discipline, integrity and what that means, humility, and honor in word and deed. It has taught me that true martial arts is a way of life. It has also impacted my life by showing me that I love and enjoy teaching karate. I love being able to teach others what I have learned and be able to watch them learn, grow and succeed on their martial arts journey.

How has Grandmaster CYNTHIA ROTHROCK Influenced me?

I had the pleasure of meeting Cynthia Rothrock several years ago at the Legends Martial Arts Hall of Fame in Mt. Laurel, NJ. She is one of a handful of women who have paved the way for women in martial arts. She has set an excellent example for other women martial artists to follow through with hard work and perseverance. Even now, after all she has accomplished, Cynthia is one of the most down-to-earth and gracious women I have ever met. She has shown us women martial artists how to be the best martial artists and instructors we can be. I am thankful for her leadership in martial arts and for showing female martial artists that you can go as far in martial arts as you want.

Larry
CHASTEEN

"

The arts have helped me to learn how to push myself beyond my limits and understand that hard times are only temporary.

WHY THE Martial Arts?

I guess you could say that the original Karate Kid movie influenced me to begin my martial arts journey. After seeing it just once, I was hooked and begged my mom and dad to start taking karate classes. It took some convincing, but finally, my parents agreed. I wanted to be just like Johnny, the "bad boy." I wanted to be like his character so much that I recruited two neighbors and a friend from school to start classes with me. We even bought motorcycles. We decided that we were going to be the next Cobra Kai! Hard kicks, hard punches, "strike first strike hard – no mercy, sir" was all that rang through our heads. We wanted it badly. It was the hardest we had ever worked. But with the hard work came new ranks, and our journeys moved forward. As we grew, we started driving, girls came along, and we took a small break from being the "bad boys" of the neighborhood. The pretty girls were a slight distraction, but little did we know, the

TRAINING INFORMATION

- Martial Arts Styles & Rank: Chang Moo Kwan-4th Dan, Shorei Goju-Orange Belt, Brazilian Jiu-Jitsu-4 Stripe Purple Belt, IKI Krav Maga-1st Dan, SKMA-2nd Dan, Israeli Kickboxing-Brown Belt

- Instructors/Influencers: Carlos Catania, Jason Hamilton, Master Ricky Ellington

- Birthplace/Growing Up: Lafayette, GA / Rocky Face, GA

- Yrs. In the Martial Arts: 39 years

- Yrs. Instructing: 16 years

- School owner, Manger & Instructor at G1 Martial Arts, PKA Worldwide Member

PROFESSIONAL ORGANIZATIONS

- IKSA
- PKA

"Allies" of the world still liked the "Daniels and Johnnys" of the world. So, I regained my focus, began training and competing again, and it became my obsession. I knew then that I wanted to become a coach! I wanted to share the knowledge that I had received with others. I wanted to change their lives through martial arts. I started training in different styles so that my knowledge would grow. Finally, I could see things coming together. I started coaching my instructors. I loved it even more. I wanted to open my Academy. I was a bundle of nerves. Could I do it? Would it work? Did I know enough even to attempt it?

The late George Burns once said, "I'd rather be a failure at something I love than be a success at something that I hate." So, in 2009, I took a leap of faith and opened up G1 Martial Arts in my garage. I moved quickly to a local recreation center and an even larger facility. God was blessing me in each step of my journey. We started growing larger and larger every day. It was so amazing seeing my dreams begin to unfold. As a guy barely graduating high school, I was starting to see a successful business come into play. I had been so scared, but looking back, I am thankful for taking that first step. So, for those that have ever wanted to pursue their dreams but were anxious about doing so, remember this quote by Lucille Ball, "I'd rather regret the things I've done than the things I haven't done." So, thank you, Daniel Larusso and Johnny Lawrence, for the broken radios on the beach, the skeleton costumes on Halloween, and the famous "sweep the leg, and get him a body bag." I will forever be grateful for my martial arts journey, career, and legacy that I hope to leave behind.

PERSONAL ACHIEVEMENTS

- Father of four
- My Salvation in Jesus Christ
- Multiple Tournament Wins in Fighting
- Multiple Tournament Wins in Forms

MAJOR ACHIEVEMENTS

- I developed G1 Martial Arts Academy - starting in my garage, now serving approximately 150 students, where we teach several martial arts styles.
- Helped open and develop a business plan for a second business, The Annex.

How MARTIAL ARTS CHANGED My Life!

Studying martial arts has helped me to become a better person by allowing me to give back to the community. I love watching new students come into the Academy as an athlete knowing nothing of the arts or self-defense and watching them grow into strong and confident people. Helping them become a better person gives me a stronger desire to keep pushing forward. I understand that I am to be an example and a leader and the one to set the bar. This drives me every day to be a better martial artist and person. The arts have helped me to learn how to push myself beyond my limits and understand that hard times are only temporary. I have learned that my goals are never too far out of reach and that I can always attain them if I am persistent.

Whenever I started competing, I was a very timid young man that was not confident in my fighting ability even though I had been in several neighborhood scuffles. I learned quickly that I needed to apply what I had been taught, keep training, and trust the process. In my first tournament, I came in dead last. After my instructor scolded me for being so timid in the second tournament, I placed second in the state finals. The fights in the tournaments started becoming easier, the things in life started becoming easier, and the next thing I noticed was that I was applying martial arts to everything in life. My forms and weapons training helped me to focus more. I was becoming a person that I had always looked up to in life, a martial artist.

How has Grandmaster CYNTHIA ROTHROCK Influenced me?

I loved watching her movies as a child. She made the screen come alive. She was such a great competitor in weapons and forms and was an amazing fighter as well. She pushed the way for more women to start competing. Seeing her success has encouraged me to make sure that my gym is where women feel safe and encouraged to train. Our schedule boasts a women-only only Brazilian Jiu Jitsu class, and we regularly host a women's self-defense seminar for victims of domestic violence.

Joe CICCONE

> " It was the discipline of martial arts and having great teachers in each style he studied that influenced his life.

WHY THE *Martial Arts?*

Growing up, Joe attended a private school until the fifth grade, when he was transferred to a public school. That was an eye-opener. In private school, they were like a family, but when it came to public school, that's when the bullying started. He was chubby and dressed conservatively, wearing wingtip shoes, an insurance man's briefcase, with Vitalis in his hair. He was begging for a beat down, and he didn't even know it. One big kid didn't like his face because he was always talking about smashing it in. Every day after class, he would beat Joe down to the ground until finally, one day, his mother walked into his bedroom when he was changing and saw the bruises all over his body. He had to come clean about the bullying, and his mother put a stop to it. A teacher was fired over it because he allowed it to go on. Back in the early sixties, nobody ever did anything about bullying. They never thought it was a big deal. His father introduced him to working out,

TRAINING INFORMATION

- Martial Arts Styles & Ranks: Sil-lum Kung-Fu-3rd Degree Black Belt, Wing Chun, Choy Le Fut Advanced Student, Jiu jitsu, Taekwondo, Tang Soo Do-1st Dan, Hapkido Yee Chi Kwan-8th Degree
- Instructors/Influencers: Si gong Tai chueng sau, Master Duncan Leong, Master Soo Wong Lee, Master Jung Bai Lee, Master Harold Hankins, Master Gary Daniels
- Yrs. In the Martial Arts: 57 years
- Yrs. Instructing: 53 years
- Founder of Yee Chi Kwan, Yee chi Kwan Fighting Academy

PROFESSIONAL ORGANIZATIONS

- International Federation of Martial Arts
- EUSAIMAA
- International Martial Arts Association
- American Martial Arts Alliance Black Belt Membership
- PKA lifetime member
- International Congress of Grandmasters Member
- Sport Karate Museum Joe Lewis and History General Awards
- AMAA Author Award
- Black Dragons World Legion Award
- Spartan Hall of Warriors Certificate

wrestling, boxing, and martial arts. It was through martial arts that he learned confidence and self-esteem. Joe became very proficient at fighting and was able to protect himself and others. He would not tolerate bullying by anyone and was quick to come to others defense. As he continued through school, he had many opportunities to face his fears and to become an overcomer. It was the discipline of martial arts and having great teachers in each style he studied that influenced his life. As he would sit back and reminisce about his 57 years and realize how fortunate and blessed he's been, the wisdom he has attained through martial arts and his faith in God has changed the direction of his life for the better. He can only hope to continue on the path set before him, to give to others the knowledge and faith that he has learned.

He has done radio show interviews and has spoken at many venues about his book and faith as a Christian speaker. Joe has his own radio show, "Not Your Average Joe Show," which plays once a week. He's involved with the Christian speaker's network doing speaking engagements. Martial arts has had a significant impact on his life. When he was a child and was being bullied, it gave him confidence in himself. It has strengthened his body and mind and given him a purpose when he felt like he was defeated. Through the many styles he has learned, it was so interesting how different they were yet how intricately woven they could be. How accepting over the years, they have become and are more tolerant of other styles. In the early years, it was always a power struggle over which style was the best. When Joe competed, fighting was more primitive, short, and to the

PERSONAL ACHIEVEMENTS

- TRIS Tidewater Rape Information Services hired Joe to teach self-defense, and he was an advocate for women's self-defense and training.
- Joe Ciccone was the first person in the state of Virginia to teach and recognize nunchaku as a weapon and get it passed into law, as well as helping develop a side-handled baton modeled after the tonfa which eventually became the PR24 for the police department.
- He taught self-defense tactics and weapons training for the police department.
- Joe taught hand-to-hand and light weapons in Special Forces specialized training as well as government agencies specialized training.
- He was involved in making a martial arts movie in which he had a major role.

MAJOR ACHIEVEMENTS

- Founder and developer of his own style Yee Chi Kwan
- Joe competed in boxing while training in martial arts; he won the Golden Gloves
- Joe won the Full Contact Virginia State Championship in 1972
- He won the East Coast full contact championship in 1973
- He also won the USA National Championship full contact free style in 1974
- Competed in full contact free style and won the World Championship in 1975. When it was disbanded in 1978, He defended his title 3 times and was undefeated
- Joe was inducted into the Who's Who of the Martial Arts Elite in 1988
- He was inducted into the Who's Who of the Martial Arts in Karate International in 1992
- Inducted into the Who's Who in the Martial Arts of Masters and Pioneers in 2019
- Inducted into the Who's Who in the Martial Arts Legends and Pioneers as an Ambassador of the Year in 2020
- Inducted into the Who's Who in the Martial Arts Masters and Pioneers Lifetime Achievement Award in 2020
- Inducted into The World's Greatest Martial Artists in 2020

point compared to today's fighting, where it is flashy and all about showmanship. He would compete with taped hands and feet and bare-knuckled full-contact fighting. There were no weight divisions or rounds; you couldn't gouge the eyes, throat, or groin. The only way you could win was by knockout, concede or referee stopping the fight. His boxing background gave him the tools for great footwork, hands, head and shoulder movement, and coordination.

Joe's speed and precision led him to many victories. At a light bodyweight, he hit like a heavyweight. He would hit with combinations using his hands, elbows, feet, and head strikes. It was very difficult for his opponent to follow because you couldn't watch everything at once. By attacking several parts of the body simultaneously, it was very confusing. They couldn't grasp that it was the individual and not the training in the art they represented.

MAJOR ACHIEVEMENTS

- Inducted into the USA Martial Arts Hall of Fame in 2019 2020 and 2022.
- Inducted into the Martial Arts Extraordinaire Biography Book 50 years of Excellence in 2021.
- Inducted into the Action Martial Arts Hall of Honors History Book in 2021.
- Inducted into the Who's Who of America Publications Board as a Grandmaster 2019.
- Inducted into the North American International Martial Arts Hall of Fame 2019.
- Recipient of the United States of America International Rank Certification awarded 8th Dan.
- Inducted into the AFKA Hall of Fame in 2020.
- Joe was featured in the Deadly Art Of Survival magazine east coast legends in Dec. 2021.
- He was inducted into the Bill Wallace biography book in 2022.
- Joe has taught inner city children self-defense, boxing and life changing skills to better their chance of making it off the streets.
- He is an accomplished writer and author. His first book "Not Your Average Joe's Journey To Faith" has gained a lot of praise.
- He's working on other projects (books) and He's writing articles for Martial Arts Extraordinaire Magazine.
- Inducted into the Who's Who in the Martial Arts Cynthia Rothrock Tribute Book in 2023

Joe knew, through his studies, he learned to take whatever works from everything he has been taught and apply it to what is useful. When he teaches, he recognizes that not everyone's the same, so he can specialize in training that will work for each unique individual. Martial arts has taught him to be resilient in his approach to having a personal impact on his students. When he promotes, he uses different ways to stimulate his students' achievements, whether by rewarding them with belts, patches, sashes, or certificates.

As long as they feel a sense of accomplishment, they will strive to keep learning. He has learned this through many teachers and how their style differs from others. Over the years, he has attained wisdom and knowledge and a proper way of treating people like they need to be treated. If we put people first, we will teach more effectively because people know whether or not you care. If they know you care, it will inspire them to care about others, and they will be better students, teachers, and people in the martial arts and in life as a result. Studying martial arts has truly impacted Joe's life as well as his students and the people he has come into contact with. He hopes people's lives are changed and touched for the best by being a small part of a life that he has tried to live as an example.

Reggie COCHRAN

Dr. Reggie Cochran, PhD, DCH (Doctor of Clinical Hypnotherapy) is a consultant and business partner with GM Norris and his wife Gena. Reggie is an internationally known Consultant, Coach, Speaker, Best Selling Author & Cross Disciplined Champion Martial Artist.

Reg has co-authored books with Bill Gates, Donald Trump, Brian Tracy, Dr. Wayne Dyer, Deepak Chopra, to name a few. The latest book he coauthored "Think and Grow Rich Today hit #1 Best Seller status on Amazon the first day it was released. This earned him the coveted Quilly Award and induction into the National Academy of Best Selling Authors.

His personal clients read like an international who's who directory filled with actors, entertainers, pro wrestlers, MMA champs, Gold & Platinum recording artist / musicians, top 1% entrepreneurs and business professionals.

Dr. Reg is an Independent Strategic Intervention Coach. Reggie received his Strategic Intervention Coach training from the prestigious Robbins-Madanes Center, founded by Tony Robbins and Cloe Madanes. Reg is also an Independent Certified Coach, Teacher and Speaker with The John Maxwell Team.

His coaching, speaking. and writing has earned him 3 EXPY awards. This keeps him in high demand as a keynote speaker and trainer for audiences ranging from youth to corporate events.

Reggie found discipline and direction in the martial arts after his father passed away. He feels fortunate to have been able to train with some very talented instructors, to train with others that challenged him to become better, and to get to know many people around the world, that have become close family, friends, mentors and role models to him.

His martial arts career has many facets. As a martial arts competitor he has won many state, national, international and World Champion titles. He opened his first martial arts studio in 1978 and has been blessed to have helped thousands of students over the decades. Now most of his time in the martial arts world is spent serving his martial arts brothers and sisters through the various Board positions he has.

Due to his father's suicide, today he is working on a complete online training series geared to help people recover from various types of surgeries, injuries, and PTSD. He is very passionate on this as his dad took his life due to PTSD from a severe war injury.

He's a long-time member of the United Fighting Arts Federation and has earned a 9th Degree Black Belt from his instructor, GM Chuck Norris. Reggie has served in various UFAF leadership positions since 1986. He is currently on the UFAF Board of Directors UFAF BJJ and special projects.

Sensei Reg is also a 10th degree Black Belt awarded by GM Pat Burleson, GM Ted Gambordello and recognized by the Professional Karate Association Board of Directors lead by GM Joe Corley, GM Jeff Smith & GM Bill Wallace. Today Reg also serves on the Board of Directors for the PKA.

Professor Reg earned a 2nd Degree Black Belt in Brazilian Jiu Jitsu from Professors Richard Norton, David Dunn, Chuck Norris & Rickson Gracie.

Sifu Reg also holds Master Instructor ranks in Kung Fu, Tai Chi and Qui Gong and is a Director for the International Chinese Boxing Association.

He is also a cofounding member of the International Federation of Mixed Martial Artist with Big John McCarthy and David Dunn. The IFMMA was one of the first organizations to offer a structured training and ranking program in MMA.

He is a multi-time martial arts Hall Of Fame member, Chuck Norris Man of The Year, recipient of the first Howard Jackson Memorial Award, The Sport Karate Museum Chuck Norris Natural Fighter award, Joe Lewis Eternal Warrior award and the UFAF Wieland Norris award.

Although Dr. Reg is very humbled and proud of his various martial arts accomplishments, titles and ranks, he also understands that with those things, comes much greater responsibility of serving others, not being served. He does not like to be called Master, Grand Master etc. as he still considers himself a work in progress and a life-long student.

As an instructor, his goals have always been to help each student become much better and successful than he has been. Most importantly he trains his students to take the discipline and focus they learn in the studio and apply to the rest of their personal and business lives.

Reggie will be the first to tell you that most of his accomplishments as a speaker, author and coach are partially due to the skills he learned from his martial arts instructors GM Chuck Norris, GM Richard Norton, GM Al Francis, GM Ted Gambordello & Professor David Dunn.

He also credits his success to every person he fought in the ring and trained in seminars with over the decades. Each match and each seminar reinforced and layered his

determination, discipline and focus to be the best he can be in all areas of his life.

But first and foremost, he gives credit to God and his Lord and Savior Jesus Christ. Second to his wife Thresa Cochran who has stood by his side to support and encourage him. Thresa is also has Black Belts from GM Chuck Norris and GM Al Francis. And taught beside Reg over the years.

When asked what his highest titles are, his response is normally husband, father and grandpa. He continually strives to be a positive role model and influence to his family and friends. And to spread the good news of God's love, forgiveness and healing power through Jesus, with as many people as possible.

Become an
AMAA MEMBER!

Joe
CORLEY

" Martial Arts provided me with the opportunity to learn so many skills that apply to so many aspects of life.

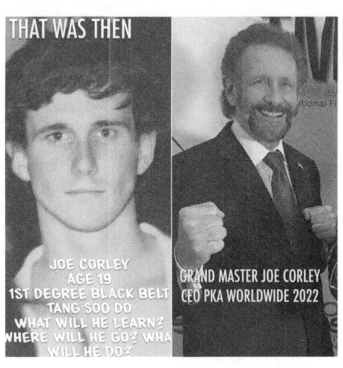

THAT WAS THEN

JOE CORLEY
AGE 19
1ST DEGREE BLACK BELT
TANG SOO DO
WHAT WILL HE LEARN?
WHERE WILL HE GO? WHA
WILL HE DO?

GRAND MASTER JOE CORLEY
CEO PKA WORLDWIDE 2022

WHY THE *Martial Arts?*

Atlanta's Joe Corley is still a black belt and sports entrepreneur with a mission, most recently honored for Lifetime Achievement in 2019 Who's Who in Martial Arts and on the cover of the 2017 LEGENDS edition of the AMAA Who's Who in the Martial Arts 2017 edition. Now a Grand Master instructor with more than five decades of experience in the martial arts and the producer of PKA KARATE & KICKBOXING for television, Corley's life-long purpose for being has been to share with everyone the positive feelings of confidence, courage, intensity, focus, personal discipline and integrity engendered by good martial arts training and competition. He has done that by promoting martial arts in his Atlanta chain of studios, his Battle of Atlanta World Karate Championship, and on television worldwide.

Corley began his karate classes at age 16, earned his black belt at 19, opened his first studio at 19,

HUMILITY OF A GRANDMASTER 10th DEGREE CERTIFICATE

One who has achieved the rank of GRAND MASTER in MARTIAL ARTS, in fact,

DOES NOT FEEL WORTHY…

Having BATTLED through the WARRIOR BLACK BELT RANKS OF 1ST, 2ND and 3RD DEGREE

And Having PROUDLY ADMINISTERED the TEACHER / INSTRUCTOR RANKS OF 4TH and 5th DEGREE

And Having SKILLFULLY & MASTERFULLY

EDUCATED THE INSTRUCTORS as a PROFESSOR 6th and 7th DEGREE and

Having CONSISTENTLY and DUTIFULLY GIVEN BACK TO THE MARTIAL ARTS COMMUNITY as 8TH and 9th DEGREE

The GRANDMASTER knows what he does not know; he knows how much there is left to learn.

At the same time, he embodies the sentiments in Master Educator Stephen R. Covey's 7 HABITS and his expression of HUMILITY: "Humility is the mother of all virtues. Courage is the father. Integrity the Child. Wisdom the Grandchild."

Having honorably carried out the BLACK BELT RESPONSIBILITIES above and having demonstrated exceptionally the virtues of

WISDOM, INTEGRITY, COURAGE and HUMILITY

THE PROFESSIONAL KARATE COMMISSION

DOES HEREBY BESTOW UPON

JOE CORLEY

THE GRAND MASTER RANK OF

10th DEGREE BLACK BELT

won three US titles in the next three years, founded the Battle of Atlanta at age 23, and has spread the word ever since. Joe has sought to share the most practical physical karate movements available and combine those real-life defensive techniques with modern American positive philosophy.

There are only a handful of men in martial arts anywhere in the world who have accomplished so much to further the martial arts philosophy and physical applications. As a fighter, Joe Corley won three United States Championships in point karate and retired as the number one ranked Middle Weight contender globally. Now a 10th-degree Black Belt in American Karate, Mr. Corley and his Black Belts have taught more than 50,000 men, women, and children in his chain of Atlanta studios.

As a Black Belt in Tang Soo Do, he opened Atlanta's first full-time karate studio in 1967 while he was still competing and expanded the studios to become the most well-known martial arts chain in the Southeast at that time.

In 1970, Joe Corley founded the BATTLE OF ATLANTA, one of the most prestigious open karate tournaments in the world. The Battle of Atlanta recently completed its 54th Anniversary. The Battle, now owned and produced by Truth Entertainment, again hosted competitors from all over the world. In the early '70s, Art Heller joined Joe Corley, Sam Chapman, Bill McDoanald, Larry Reinhardt, and Jack Motley in a meeting with Chuck Norris to kick off the South East Karate Association (SEKA) from which so many great Southeast Champions emerged.

In 1975, Joe Corley challenged Bill "Superfoot" Wallace for his PKA World Middleweight Title in what became a historic fight before 12,000 fans in Atlanta's Omni. Wallace won the first-of-its-kind 9-round bout. Master Corley would later be hired by CBS to cover Superfoot's future bouts because of his ability to articulate the inner workings of the sport and the techniques and strategies of the fighters.

Because of the great ratings at CBS, Master Corley also became the voice for American Karate and PKA KICKBOXING on other networks. He actually produced the programming and did commentary with long-term friends like Chuck Norris and the late Pat Morita (Mr. Miyagi) on NBC, CBS, ESPN, SHOWTIME, USA NETWORK, TURNER SPORTS, SPORTS CHANNEL AMERICA, PRIME NETWORK, SPORTSOUTH, and on international television syndication. As an expert analyst and host for PKA KARATE World Championships on the network, cable, and pay-per-view, Mr. Corley became synonymous with the sport to the millions of fans who followed the 1,000+ hours of coverage on television.

With events originating from such diverse locales as Canada, France, Belgium, South Africa, South America, and the United Arab Emirates, plus 50 cities in the United States, Joe Corley has educated 4 generations of sports fans.

Master Corley has been named Official Karate Magazine's Man of the Decade, was inducted into the prestigious Black Belt Magazine Hall of Fame and the International Tae Kwon Do Hall of Fame, and has received more awards than anyone can count.

But the thing that continues to drive Joe Corley is the knowledge that he and his accomplished associates can use all their experiences to share with everyone around the world on television the great feelings of confidence, courage, discipline, honor, and integrity that come from presenting the martial arts properly. His PKA WORLDWIDE KICKBOXING projects are the perfect vehicles to spread the messages of positive martial arts on a global scale.

"The unequaled success of the UFC, built on our previous successes, has set the stage for PKA Fighters to achieve the 'fame and fortune' the athletes of the UFC are now enjoying," he said. Joe is in regular meetings with astute sports entrepreneurs in order to kick off the new project for 2023 and beyond. "We have the UFC's own research to indicate the timing is perfect for us now," he said. At the same time, he is building the grassroots for PKA WORLDWIDE Associated Schools and Members with Don Willis—PKA Director of Membership--bringing together the best martial artists from around the globe.

Mr. Corley's bride--Christina-- is his right arm and chief administrator in PKA WORLDWIDE. Mr. Corley's daughter, Christiana, 25, continues to be his lustrous link in this new millennium and his compelling force to make the martial arts world an even better place.

Master Corley's closest friends point to the PKA (& PKC) 10th Degree Grand Master certificate, saying the language of the certificate reflects the philosophy and humility they know to be the real Joe Corley (See above).

Master Corley is consulting with several martial artists to share his experience and wisdom and has been recruited to consult on other projects outside of martial arts. One such project is the introduction of a generation system destined to change the worlds of Solar, Wind Generation, and later stage Electric Vehicles.

"Martial arts provided me with the opportunity to learn so many skills that apply to so many aspects of life," he said. "I look forward to this 'next half' of my time on the planet applying the skills learned. I also fiercely love being a student and look forward to learning as much as possible in this last half. Learning brings me joy", he smiled.

"After 19 years as a 9th Degree Black Belt, I was so proud to earn my 10th Degree from the PKC and Grand Master Glenn Keeney in 2016. I was honored to have GM Pat Johnson, GM Allen Steen, and GM Pat Burleson approve the PKC promotion. It was doubly sweet because lifelong friend Jeff Smith earned his that same day. These 5 men have greatly influenced my martial arts career in so many ways, and it was so special to share the experience with all of them!"

Joe Corley has been named as Chief Executive Officer at PKA WORLDWIDE. Here he is working alongside PKA Vice Chairman Robert Gutkowski (former President of Madison Square Garden and Vice President of Programming at ESPN), PKA President Jeff Smith, PKA International Ambassador Bill Wallace, and PKA Global Director of Fighter Development Rick Roufus in the PKA HUNT FOR THE GREATEST STRIKERS ON THE PLANET IN 2023 and beyond.

Grand Masters Jeff Smith & Joe Corley receive their PKC 10th Degree Black Belts at Battle of Atlanta 2016

At this printing, Joe and PKA WORLDWIDE had just completed their first 5 trials in New York, 2 in Texas, and in California and Washington state, where they identified 45 New Age Strikers to compete later in 2023 in the Semifinals heading to the new PKA World Titles.

In a recent interview, Joe said, "The Combat Sports World, built on the shoulders of the PKA Movement dating back to 1974, is now ready for our 2023 series ON THE HUNT FOR THE GREATEST STRIKERS ON THE PLANET!"

How has Grandmaster CYNTHIA ROTHROCK Influenced me?

The "Cynthia Rothrock Effect": More Than Just A Pretty Face

By Joe Corley, CEO Of PKA Worldwide

Cynthia first came to my attention as a great forms and weapons champion at the Battle of Atlanta. I still see an image in my mind's eye in a soft-style uniform from the Georgia Tech Coliseum, where she "oo'd" and "ah'd" everybody in the audience.

Fast forward to her achieving great film success, and I brought her action and "look" to the attention of the executive producer at Showtime, Jay Larkin (RIP). He said, "How would you feel about having her join the Broadcast team in our Showtime PKA KARATEMANIA Series?" I said,

"That's why you're a genius, Jay, and I believe it would be great for us!"

Zoom now to Ringside as Cynthia joins the Broadcast team and gives a wonderful set of insights into the fighting techniques, strategies, and mindsets of these great champions like Jean Yves Theriault, Rick Roufus, and more.

Thank you, Cynthia, for setting such a great example in the Competition Arena, on film, and in a Grand Analysis of the "state of the art"!

Please…keep on kickin', and I know you'll keep LOOKING GOOD doing what you do!

Paul
FULLER

"

Martial Arts have given me self-control in stressful situations and allowed me to de-escalate potentially violent encounters verbally.

WHY THE *Martial Arts?*

I began Martial Arts in 1981 after being constantly bullied in middle school. My first art was Mu Duk Kwan Tang Soo Do at the local YMC. I trained in Tang Soo Do for a year and a half before switching to a Taekwondo dojang where a friend trained. My Taekwondo training gave me the confidence and the skill set to stand up to bullies.

TRAINING INFORMATION

- Martial Arts Styles & Ranks: 4th Degree Black Belt Taekwondo, 4th Degree Black Belt American Kenpo
- Instructors/Influencers: Grandmaster James Bailey, Grandmaster Joe Corley, Master Bill Wendel, Kyoshi Fred DePalma
- Birthplace/Growing Up: Tuscaloosa, AL
- Yrs. In the Martial Arts: 33 years
- Yrs. Instructing: 25 years
- School Owner, Manager, Instructor at Zanshin American Karate and Kenpo, PKA Worldwide Member

PROFESSIONAL ORGANIZATIONS

- PKA Worldwide

How MARTIAL ARTS CHANGED My Life!

Martial Arts have given me the self-discipline to succeed in life. They have given me the confidence to deal with bullies in middle and high school. Martial Arts has also given me the discipline to complete my degree while working full time. The ability to set goals, focus, and prioritize has been instrumental in helping me to achieve success in my own Martial Arts School. Martial Arts have also given me self-control in stressful situations and allowed me to de-escalate potentially violent encounters verbally.

PERSONAL ACHIEVEMENTS

- I have trained in many styles, including Taekwondo, Yoseikan Budo, Shinkendo, Wing Tchun, Combat Hapkido, and American Kenpo
- I competed extensively in the 90s and won many championships in forms and sparring on the USTA/ITA circuit
- I have taught in Alabama, Georgia, North Carolina, Colorado, and Arizona

MAJOR ACHIEVEMENTS

- Bachelor of Arts Degree, University of Alabama in History with a minor in Anthropology
- Level1 STX Double Stick Instructor Filipino Martial Arts
- Battle of Atlanta Officials Hall of Fame 2009

John GRAHAM

"

He knows what works in a fight and what doesn't.

-Todd Doyle, Friend & Student

WHY THE *Martial Arts?*

John Graham was born in Gulfport, Mississippi, in 1953. In 1970, he enlisted in the Marine Corps. In 1971, he was a Marine stationed in Rota, Spain. It was there, on base, that he came across a martial arts class and fell in love with the discipline. He began studying Shotokan Karate at the USO. His training was interrupted when he was transferred on a ship to Charleston, South Carolina, where he continued his training in various martial arts on base. Having the opportunity to re-enlist in the Marine Corps, he put in for the job of personal security for the Commanding Officer of Naval Forces Europe, stationed in London, England. He knew the chief instructors of Europe would be located in London and Paris, which were the main strongholds of martial arts in the late 60s and early 70s.

Upon arriving in London, Graham sought out the best of the best: Iron Man of Karate, Steve Morris, at the famous Earlham Street Gym;

TRAINING INFORMATION

- Martial Arts Styles & Ranks: Superfoot System-8th Dan, Joe Lewis Fighting System -8th Dan, Chee Kim Thong-8th Dan

- Birthplace/Growing Up: Mobile, AL

- Yrs. In the Martial Arts: 55 years

- Yrs. Instructing: 50 years

- School Owner at Grand Master Grahams Martial Arts, PKA Worldwide Member private lessons with Tatsuo Suzuki, Chief European Instructor of Wadu Ryu; and KS Han, European Chief Instructor of Wuzuquan. Graham would laughingly say that he trained eight days a week. He continued to train with them until he transferred to Okinawa, where he found Masanobu Shinjo of Goju Ryu, considered a national treasure in the Okinawa arts. Graham has trained in different realms of the same art.

Wuzuquan is the grandfather of Okinawa Goju, which is the grandfather of Japanese Goju. Graham knew that once he saw Wuzuquan, the unlocking of the art of Goju was embedded into the catchings and set sparrings and the methodology of Wuzuquan. This was proven years later by researcher George Alexander and many others. Grandmaster Chee saw Graham's enthusiasm, zeal, and commitment to Wuzuquan, saw his skill in interpretation and dedication to teaching the art, accepted him as a disciple, and in 1990 promoted him to Chief Instructor of the USA. From 1973 until his death in 2001, Master Graham maintained a strong relationship with Grandmaster Chee. They each traveled across the world to see each other several times and performed in demos and TV interviews, and public events.

In 1989 Graham began training under Grandmaster Bill "Superfoot" Wallace. On an interesting side note, in 1974, while Graham was stationed in England, Wallace was representing the US and fighting in the World Kickboxing Championships in Europe. While Graham and his fellow Marines watched them, Graham said, "I'm going to be a student of his." All the Marines laughed and said, "You're from Mobile, he's from California, you guys will never meet."

WHY THE MARTIAL ARTS (CONTINUED)

Not true. Graham ensured that they met in 1989, and their relationship has been going on ever since. Graham met Joe Lewis through Bill Wallace, the Father of Kickboxing and a fellow Marine. Graham and Lewis shared an instant connection because of the Marine Corps and their love of martial arts. His school in Mobile, Alabama, was the first Superfoot School and the first to have Superfoot Instructor training. He was on the Board of Directors for both the Superfoot System and the Joe Lewis Fighting System. He has received an 8th Dan from the Joe Lewis Organization and an 8th Dan from Superfoot.

Graham also has an 8th Dan from the Chee Kim Thong Organization. He has close ties to Grandmaster Chee Chin Wei, the Nine Dragons Shaolin Temple Headmaster in Quanzhou, China. Master Xiao Feng, the Inspector General of the Quanzhou Wuzuquan Association, has trained with Graham, been to his school in America, and trained with his students. Graham has had his students train with Xiao Feng in his school in China. He shares a close friendship with Graham. Graham has trained privately with Grandmaster Alexander Co of the Beng Kiam Wuzuquan in the Philippines and with Grandmaster Bonaficio Lim. He also has a 9th Dan in Kong Han from Grandmaster Henry Lo of the Kong Han Wuzuquan Organization in the Philippines. He has regularly trained with him annually in the Philippines for the past 20 years and has brought students to train with Grandmaster Lo.

He has served as the 11th President of the Nan Shaolin Wuzuquan Association, which also awarded him a 10th Dan. He is a Delegate of the International Wuzuquan Association. He is a noted Grandmaster in two Martial Arts History books written by the Chinese Government. His fascination with the discipline has caused him to go to countries like Malaysia, the Philippines, and Thailand to study and learn.

Graham taught over 2000 police officers while an officer, and he was instrumental in inventing the minimal standards for corrections officers in the state of Alabama. He has taught at every level of state law enforcement, from City Police to Sheriff's department to State Troopers. He has received letters of bravery from the Mobile Police Department. His mettle was tested as a Marine and law enforcement officer on the streets. John Graham has trained in four different methods of Wuzuquan Kong Han, Beng Kiam, Quanzhou, and Chee Kim Thong. He presents a unique perspective on Wuzuquan that nobody else can offer after being in martial arts for over 50 years. From a personal perspective, I have seen the scars on his hands and arms from his fight with a man with a broken bottle, so I know that his techniques work, and he knows what works in a fight and what doesn't.

Written by Todd Doyle, a Friend and Student of Master Graham.

Become an
AMAA
MEMBER!

Matthew
JEANSONNE

"

The martial arts have changed my life in so many ways: the confidence that comes with knowing what your art is capable of.

Matthew Jeansonne

WHY THE *Martial Arts?*

I started martial arts because I did boxing and wrestling and wanted to try something different and be more rounded, which brought me to TKD and Karate, which helped with the kicking technique and power. Then it just kind of stuck. I enjoyed learning and continue to enjoy the techniques and incorporating the kicks from TKD and Karate with boxing. The benefits of mental clarity and physical health, flexibility, and self-defense are just a few reasons I keep training.

TRAINING INFORMATION

- Martial Arts Styles & Ranks: Oh Do Kwan Taekwondo-2nd Dan, Mo Duk Kwan Taekwondo-1st Dan, Kenpo Karate Shodan Superfoot System-1st Dan

- Instructors/Influencers: Pat Malone, Bill Wallace, Jerome Littrel, Daniel Reis, Josh Copson, Robert Shook, Chris Natzke

- Birthplace/Growing Up: TX / LA

- Yrs. In the Martial Arts: 10 years

- Yrs. Instructing: 4 years

- Instructor, PKA Worldwide Member

PROFESSIONAL ORGANIZATIONS

- PKA
- IMAF
- UMAA

How MARTIAL ARTS CHANGED *My Life!*

The martial arts have changed my life in so many ways. The confidence that comes with knowing what your art is capable of. The peace that comes with that is priceless. The mental clarity and the respect taught and learned through suffering and pain are some of the best teachers, and the relationships built there are on a different level.

PERSONAL ACHIEVEMENTS

- Won, competed in numerous tournaments and excelled in block breaking with a personal best of 11.
- I got to train with the legend Bill Wallace, made a personal goal to get my black belt under him, and succeeded in 2021.
- I competed internationally in world competitions and also placed very well in those.

MAJOR ACHIEVEMENTS

- Competitor of the Year 2020
- President Award of Excellence 2021
- Competitor of the Year Forms 2022
- 5-0 amateur kickboxing martial arts record

Become an
AMAA MEMBER!

Damian
LUTKA

"

Martial arts taught me: to improve the self, gave me physical strength, mental strength, humility, perseverance, and connecting the mind, body, and spirit.

WHY THE *Martial Arts?*

I started martial arts for a few reasons: It was suggested by my family, but most of all, I wanted to be able to protect myself in class and outside the classroom. My number one reason was actor and martial artist Steven Seagal. Watching him do all he did seemed magical to me, and I wanted to be as great as him, if not better. I never thought I'd take this journey. It still amazes me to walk into the Aikido studio, wear my uniform, and say, "This is my life, and martial arts are now an integral part of my life."

TRAINING INFORMATION

- Martial Arts Styles & Ranks: 7th Dan Black Belt in Aikido, Black Belt in Karate, Black Belt in Kung fu, Black Belt in Kendo, Black Belt in Taekwondo, Black Belt in Judo, Black Belt in Jiu-Jitsu

- Instructors/Influencers: Hiroyuki Namba, Shihan Hombu, Yoshimitsu Yamada Sensei, Andrzej Drewniak, GM Jerzy Konarski, Master Lim Won Sup, Hiromi Tomita, Waldemar Sikorski, Yuetao Wu, Jessica Ye

- Birthplace/Growing Up: Poland

- Yrs. In the Martial Arts: 23 years

- Yrs. Instructing: 4 years

- Instructor, PKA Worldwide Member, Instructor in the Army

PROFESSIONAL ORGANIZATIONS

- International Taekwon-do Federation
- PKA Worldwide
- International Judo Federation
- The Aikido Aikikai Polska Center
- United States Aikido Federation - USAF

How MARTIAL ARTS CHANGED My Life!

I have had many years to understand martial arts as a martial artist. I know how it has benefited me and what I use it for. Martial arts serve various purposes and appeal to many different types of people. Martial arts taught me: to improve the self, gave me physical strength, mental strength, humility, perseverance, and connecting the mind, body, and spirit.

PERSONAL ACHIEVEMENTS

- Being able to serve this country for 20+ years and retiring as Lt. Col. US Army Special Forces Green Beret Soldier.

MAJOR ACHIEVEMENTS

- Black Belts in 7 different styles

How has Grandmaster CYNTHIA ROTHROCK Influenced me?

Throughout my life, I met hundreds of people who have somehow influenced me physically or emotionally. However, only one person had a lasting and substantial impact on my inner world and changed my life dramatically, and her name is GM Cynthia Rothrock. I can call Cynthia my close personal friend; she is such a sweetheart. Regarding her achievements, there is nobody better especially being a woman. She is a true fighter filled with so many positive vibes, an incredibly tough actress who keeps going and going, and she is a huge inspiration to me, and I am glad and happy to call her my friend.

Become an
AMAA
MEMBER!

Carlos SILVA

> " Martial arts is part of my life. There is no me without martial arts. My whole life is dedicated to it.

WHY THE *Martial Arts?*

Grandmaster Carlos Roberto Silva (João Pessoa, December 4, 1961) is a Brazilian kickboxer. At the present time, he holds the Brazilian Confederation of Traditional Kickboxing Presidency.

At age 12, he began his studies in martial arts, practicing Judo and Shotokan karate. Later, he was introduced to Muay Thai by Professor Carlos Nunes. After that, he met Shihan Pericles Daiski Veiga and started in the Shorei Ryu style of then Master Moritoshi Nakaema and at the same time went on to promote events and the development of kickboxing.

After receiving a black belt in kickboxing from Master Alfredo Apicella of the World Association of Kickboxing Organizations (WAKO), he assumed the Chairmanship of the Hammerhilt Kickboxing Association of Paraíba and later, with advanced graduation and a

TRAINING INFORMATION

- Martial Arts Styles & Ranks: Kickboxing-10th Degree Black Belt, Shorei Ryu Karate-9th Degree Black Belt, Hapkido-5th Degree Black Belt, Taekwondo WTF-3rd Degree Black Belt, Ninjutsu Togakure Ryu-1st Degree Black Belt, Kru Muaythai

- Instructors/Influencers: Bill Wallace, Joe Corley, Morotoshi Nakaema, Yoshizo Machida, Yasuiuki Sasaki, John Pelegrini, Jack Stearn Papasan

- Birthplace/Growing Up: Joao Pessoa + Paraiba State, Brazil

- Yrs. In the Martial Arts: 43 years

- Yrs. Instructing: 38 years

- School Owner, Manager, Instructor at

PROFESSIONAL ORGANIZATIONS

- AMAA
- PKA

- ISKA
- IHC
- CBKBT
- WUKO
- WAKO
- WTKA
- USMA
- USKF
- NKKF
- DKI
- COME ON IN

PERSONAL & MAJOR ACHIEVEMENTS

- AMAA Hall Of Fame
- ISKA Man Of The Year
- Hall Of Honors Hall Of Fame
- USMAA Hall Of Fame

WHY MARTIAL ARTS (CONTINUED)

member of the Brazilian Kickboxing Confederation. Master Silva created the Federation of Kickboxing of the State of Paraíba, making this federation one of the first of the sport in the country, that later changed its name to Federation of Kickboxing Full Contact of the State of Paraíba.

In 1990 he founded the Brazilian Confederation of Traditional Kickboxing (CBKBT). Since then, CBKBT's mission has been to teach American kickboxing, known as "traditional," because it diverges from these chains that do not follow the line adopted in the United States of America to teach this modality.

Grandmaster Carlos Silva holds the title of 10th Dan in Kickboxing, 9th Dan in Karate Shorei Ryu, Kru in Muaythai, 1st Dan in Taekwondo Kukiwon, 5th Dan in Hapkido, 1st Dan in Shotokan Karate, and has also dedicated time to the study of Ninjutsu. Silva has been a cover of Fight Magazine in Brazil, and Kumite Magazine, Greece, has also published his work.

In 2019 Grandmaster Silva introduced PKA WORLDWIDE to South America. PKA is the organization that created professional martial arts for television in the United States in 1974, naming the first World Champions of Bill "Superfoot" Wallace, Jeff Smith, Joe Lewis (RIP), and Isaias Duenas. Grandmasters Bill Wallace and Joe Corley joined Grandmaster Silva in Brazil in 2019 for a series of PKA Seminars and Certifications.

How MARTIAL ARTS CHANGED My Life!

Martial arts is part of my life. There is no me without martial arts. I have been practicing martial arts for 43 years. My whole life is dedicated to it. I am an Ambassador of Martial Arts for the world.

Become an
AMAA MEMBER!

Jeff SMITH

WORLD CHAMPION

PKA KICKBOXING ASSOCIATION WORLD CHAMPION

FIRST PKA LIGHT HEAVYWEIGHT WORLD CHAMPION

BLACK BELT HALL OF FAME MEMBER

UNITED STATES KARATE CHAMPION

THE LIVING LEGEND
JEFF SMITH

"
Jeff Smith is one of the, if not THE MOST, multi-talented martial artists of all time!

WHY THE Martial Arts?

Jeff Smith is one of the, if not THE MOST, multi-talented martial artists of all time. Champion, Innovator, Manager, Teacher, Coach, Mentor, Leader...and...and...and...

On June 17, 2016, Jeff Smith was awarded the rank of Grandmaster by the Professional Karate Commission with his 10th Degree Black Belt by Grand Masters Glenn Keeney and Allen Steen with the additional signatures and approval of Pat Johnson and J Pat Burleson.

One of the most popular and highly respected martial artists in the world, Grandmaster Jeff Smith has influenced millions of Martial Artists around the world, both directly and indirectly.

Voted by his Top Ten peers as the Number One Point Fighter in the Nation in 1974 by Professional Karate Magazine, Jeff went on immediately to win the very first PKA World Light Heavyweight Kickboxing Championship title on ABC's Wide World of Entertainment.

All the while, he was training the next generation of International Champions, coaching

THE CURRICULUM VITAE OF GRAND MASTER JEFF SMITH

- 1964- Jeff enrolled in a Tae Kwon Do class at Texas A&I University in Kingsville, TX

- 1966–Jeff competes in his 1st Karate Tournament in Houston, Texas.

- 1966-Jeff receives his 1st Degree Black Belt from GM Jhoon Rhee in Kingsville, Texas.

- 1970-Jeff moves to Washington DC to Teach at the Jhoon Rhee Institute for Grand Master Rhee and enlists his top protégés to join him in DC, building the basis

- 1970-1985 Served as Senior VP for GM Jhoon Rhee's Institute of TAE KWON Do, training and managing all of the Managers and Instructors for his 12 locations.

- 1969-74 Jeff won many of the Top National Point Tournaments including Joe Corely's Battle of Atlanta, Ed Parker's International Karate , Allen Steen's US Championships, Mike Anderson's Top 10 Nationals Bob Maxwell's Ocean City United States Pro-Am, Jim Miller's Mardi Gras Nationals George Minshew's Houston Karate Olympics, The Pan Am Championships in Baltimore, Md. and the North American Tae Kwon Do Championships in Toronto, Canada to name a few.

- 1973-74 Jeff was ranked the number 1-point fighter in the USA in by Professional Karate Magazine.

- 1973-2016 Jeff has been on the cover of every major martial arts publication and was selected by Washingtonian Magazine as one of Washington's top athletes.

them to World Titles, as he managed and taught the instructional staff of the Jhoon Rhee Institute schools in Washington DC. As articulate as he is dangerous, Grandmaster Smith has appeared before the camera as a multi-talented point fighter and PKA World Champion Kickboxer and as an expert analyst for the next generations.

THE CURRICULUM VITAE

- 1974- Jeff is the first recipient of the Bruce Lee Award (selected by Mrs. Bruce Lee and Professional Karate Magazine) and listed is listed in the first Who's Who of Martial Arts.

- 1974-80-Jeff is recognized worldwide as the seven-time PKA "World Light Heavy Weight Karate Champion."

- 1975- 50 million worldwide viewers observed Jeff's title defense against Don King's heavy weight fighter Kareem Allah as the co-main event of the Ali vs. Frazier III World Boxing Title Fight, known as the "Thrilla in Manila."

- 1980-90 Jeff was coach of the WAKO World Champion United States Karate Team winning consecutive World Titles in all those 10 years.

- 1989-1993-Jeff performed at the White House for President Bush in the "Kick Drugs Out of Your Life" campaign and again with his students in California for President Bush in his "Drug Abuse is Life Abuse" program. Jeff conducted seminars in public schools all over the USA for the "Just Say No to Drugs" campaign.

- Jeff Smith has been named as Co-President of Sports and Operations at PKA WORLDWIDE. Here is working alongside PKA CEO Joe Corley and Co-Presidents Rich Rose and Howard Dolgon In the PKA HUNT FOR THE GREATEST STRIKERS ON THE PLANET IN 2022.

- At this printing Jeff and PKA WORLDWIDE had just completed their first trials in New York, where they identified 5 new Strikers to compete later in 2022 in Las Vegas in the Semifinals heading to the new World Titles.

- 1974-1985 Jeff appears on ABC's "Wide World of Entertainment," "The Champions" TV series, and does Expert Commentary on Showtime, ESPN and Pay-Per-View events

- 1990-92 Jeff performed for Arnold Schwarzenegger on the White House lawn with his students for the "Great American Workout" for the President's Council on Physical Fitness.

THE CURRICULUM VITAE

- 2000-2016 Jeff is inducted into the Tae Kwon Do Hall of Fame, Black Belt Magazine Hall of Fame, NASKA Hall of Fame, Action Magazine's Martial Arts Hall of Fame, The Battle of Atlanta's Centurion Hall of Fame Award, and with Chuck Norris, is the first recipient of the of the Joe Lewis Eternal Warrior Award.

- 2005-Present Jeff is the National Director of Mile High Karate Franchises and Martial Arts Wealth Mastery Consultant with GM Stephen Oliver. Jeff owns and operates his own Mile High Karate School in Sterling, VA.

- He also travels globally, officiating at National and International tournaments. He conducts both Business and Training seminars for Martial Arts schools all over the world.

Daryl
STEWART

"

GM Stewart has met many interesting people throughout his life. The Martial Arts has been the key.

WHY THE Martial Arts?

Professor Daryl Stewart was introduced to karate by his friend Buddy Raines. They were out surfing, and that day the surf was going off with waves crashing onto the beach. Buddy said to Daryl, "Come go with me." Professor Stewart said, "Buddy, look at the surf. It's really good." Buddy replied, "Hey, you will like it. It's about fighting." So off they went. His love of golfing also. Later, Professor Stewart was introduced to a gentleman named David Yeaman. He was introduced to karate in 1962 in Amarillo, Texas, but only there for a few weeks. So other than that, GM Stewart doesn't count that in his inventory of martial arts. He says his journey in the arts started in Galveston, Texas. It turned out that he would continue to be his instructor for most of his career. He is still doing it today and has been for over 60 plus years.

Daryl was very young when he started studying Judo and Karate. He believes that the martial arts played a major role in his life. The martial

TRAINING INFORMATION

- Martial Arts Styles & Ranks: Modern Arnis-10th Degree Black Belt, Tang-So-Do, Isshinryu, Japanese styles, Korean Tae-Kwon-Do, Kung-Fu

- Instructors/Influencers: Master David Yeaman

- Birthplace/Growing Up: Nixon, TX

- Yrs. In the Martial Arts: 60 years

- Yrs. Instructing: 58 years

- School Owner, Manager & Instructor, Promoter, Entrepreneur, Inventor (Patent Pending Status)

PROFESSIONAL ORGANIZATIONS

- Professional Karate Association "Lifetime Member 2020"

- Universal Martial Arts Hall of Fame "Vice President"

- Masters Hall of Fame Alumni

- Ambassador and History General for the Museum of Sport Karate for over 25 Years

arts gave him a solid framework of discipline and self-confidence growing up. He associated with like-minded people that had direction and helped him to stay out of trouble. While surfing and studying martial arts, he had a framework to stay in excellent shape. At this time, he was surfing in contests for major surfing companies and traveling all over to surf in competitions in the surfing community. At the same time, he entered Karate Tournaments. He was going to school. He got married at a young age and was raising his own child and working, training, and enjoying a kid's life. Not knowing then, he was setting the path that his life would be headed down into the future. He attended trade school for five years to become an International Brotherhood of Electrical Workers licensed electrician. Then went off to join the United States Navy Seabees for the Vietnam War for three years. He taught troops classes on base and overseas and had a Fighting Team for the United States Navy Seabees out of Gulfport, Mississippi.

The martial arts gave Professor Stewart confidence that he could take care of himself and his mother. He and his mother lived in Galveston, Texas, at the time. With his mother working long hours to support them and being single, he wanted a way to help watch over his mother. At this point, he struggled with his schoolwork and trying to make ends meet. With his dear mother's guidance and Martial Arts instructor, Mr. David Yeaman, he moved up through the ranks in karate and judo. He was always a natural in sports, so he took to karate naturally.

PROFESSIONAL ORGANIZATIONS

- Arbitrator for the "Texas National Tour Circuit" 1997
- Arbitrator and Judge for the National Black Belt league for the last 27 years for "The Great State of Texas"
- Judge- Amateur Organization of Karate
- Judge- Texas Karate Organization
- Judge- The United States Karate Association
- Remy Presas (IMAF) International Modern Arnis Federation
- Texas Martial Arts Hall of Fame
- Texas Karate Association for Ranking Requirements

PERSONAL ACHIEVEMENTS

Studying martial arts has given Professor Stewart confidence and the ability to focus on oneself and others. To spread the knowledge he has received throughout his career from other great people and the martial arts, helping him give back to our kids, adults, and future generations. To help them prepare for their lives and help prepare others in their pursuit of life. He always says martial arts is good for the Mind, Body, and Soul. To show them the way through martial arts knowledge and help keep them off the streets and out of trouble. To give them guidance and positive influences in their pursuit of happiness to keep their minds and body in shape, and to give off a positive attitude. To always be helpful to others in the martial arts and the community. He still travels across the United States and Canada, attending tournaments to help run them and giving seminars.

MAJOR ACHIEVEMENTS

- Coach and fighter for the United States Navy Seabees Fighting Team 1972-1975
- Induction into "The Universal Martial Arts Hall of Fame" in 2000 Houston, Texas
- Induction into "United State Hall of Fame" 2001 Oklahoma City, Oklahoma
- Induction into the "Action Martial Arts Magazine Hall of Fame" in 2001-2002 Atlantic City, New Jersey
- Induction into the "World Christian Martial Arts Hall of Fame" 2001 Newark, New Jersey
- Became Vice President of "Universal Martial Arts Hall of Fame" 2002
- Induction into the "International Black Belt Honor Hall of Fame" 2003

How MARTIAL ARTS CHANGED My Life!

Being introduced to Martial Arts was probably one of the best things that ever happened to Professor Stewart or possibly to anyone else. Through the training and discipline of Martial Arts, he has always tried his best to be kind and friendly to everyone he meets. To show kindness and help to anyone who may require his help or need some guidance. To be supportive of everyone and encourage others to do the same. He does his best to help the younger generation with their lives and encourage them to strive to be a better person, to reach out in life and embrace it with zest to reach their goals. In life, if you can envision it, you can reach it if you believe in yourself. And to teach them some life skills in Martial Arts to work on themselves to go through the belt system to prepare their minds, body, and soul and achieve their goals as they go through the ranks.

Martial Arts gave him a path to help him reach the goals he has wanted to achieve throughout his life. He has met many interesting people throughout his life. Martial Arts has been the key. He has been around the world several times in the military and has seen and done things many people may never have the opportunity to do. He thanks God for taking care of him along the way in his travels. He always strives to be a better person every day.

MAJOR ACHIEVEMENTS

- Induction into the "Keeper of the Torch Hall of Fame" 2004 Florida
- Induction into the "Master Hall of Fame" in Costa Mesa, California 2012
- "International Black Belt Hall of Fame" 2016
- Semi-Pro Surfer Featured in a recent movie "Broken Waves" a documentary of Surfing Culture on Gulf Coast by Lauryn Le Clere's productions. Galveston, Texas 2017
- "Professional Karate Association" 2019 now a lifetime member as 2020
- Remy Presas International Modern Arnis Federation
- Texas Martial Arts Hall of Fame
- Master Samurai Award from Grand Master Ralph Jasche
- To be featured in a Book with Grand Master Chuck Morris
- Giving back for a lifetime.
- Sport Karate Museum History Book
- To be featured in a Book Changing Lives Book with World Champion Superfoot Bill Wallace
- Presented: The President's Lifetime Achievement Award from The President of the United States 2023, Signed by: Joe Biden

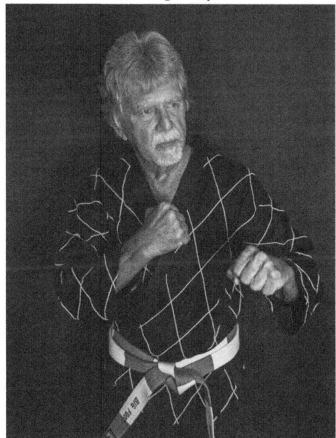

Craig TERRY

> " Being a member of the Martial Arts family has given me a wealth of dear friends and associates...

WHY THE *Martial Arts?*

As an 11-year-old delivering newspapers on my bicycle, I would stop and watch this karate class through the window - a group of kids about my age were wearing these cool-looking uniforms while doing some riveting kicks and punches. I became so enthralled with what I saw because I thought karate was just taught to adults. Now that I saw kids learning self-defense, never seeing it firsthand before - just reading and hearing about it; I had to join. I was so enthralled with the idea of doing all that punching, kicking, spinning, grabbing, and throwing people, that I ended up forging my parents' signature because they wouldn't have allowed it, since Karate in the '60s had a bad reputation according to a lot of people. I enjoyed my training for the next few months until I had to give it up because I quit my paper route, leaving me with no income. Months before discovering this karate school, this classmate of mine would push me down during recess and

TRAINING INFORMATION

- Martial Arts Styles & Ranks: Goju Ryu-5th Dan, Danny Lane Fighting System-2nd Dan, Kempo Goju-3rd Dan, Shotokan-Brown Belt
- Instructors/Influencers: GM Danny Lane, GM Paul Hickey, GM Israel Velez lll, Master Dane Emmel
- Birthplace/Growing Up: Caldwell, ID / Provo & Salt Lake City, UT
- Yrs. In the Martial Arts: 53 years
- Yrs. Instructing: 42 years
- School Owner & Instructor at AMarysvale Goju Ryu, PKA Worldwide Member

PROFESSIONAL ORGANIZATIONS
- Superfoot International Martial Arts Federation
- PKA WORLDWIDE
- USKA
- AAU

take whatever I was playing with. Time after time Carl P. would push me down and sometimes sit on me while laughing his head off. I decided that night at home that it would be the last time that he knocked me down. Two days later was a game-changer for the both of us, when I closed my eyes and punched him in the eye as he grabbed me. He ran off crying like a little baby - that ended my saga of being bullied. After I started my karate lessons, I often wondered what kind of awestruck technique that I would have done - rather than a hap hazard punch that miraculously landed. My few months of early training gave me a good insight on how effective karate can be. I was really excited about the many physical changes going on with me - I had more coordination, strength and agility which carried over for the next few years in other school sports. These few years passed by quickly before I was ready and able to start back up with karate - which I so badly missed. I was determined to become a black belt because I wasn't the most goal-oriented person. I wanted perhaps for the first time in my life to accomplish something that was recognized as most difficult to achieve, both physically and mentally.

I bumped into Master Dane Emmel who was teaching karate to a YMCA group. Several years later I earned my black belt in Goju Ryu from him. I was so ecstatic in accomplishing this feat, because I knew that it would provide a solid foundation in pursuing a better me for decades to come. I want others to experience some of the benefits of martial arts, so today, I'm giving back by volunteering self-defense classes to senior citizens - It's never too late to get started.

PERSONAL ACHIEVEMENTS

- Co-Established an accredited Physical Education Course at the Salt Lake City Community College
- Goju Ryu Instructor at the SLC Community College
- Self Defense Instructor(contractor) with the Salt Lake City Police Cadet Academy
- USKA (United States Karate Assoc) Certified Referee / Judge for *Fighting, Forms & Weapons

MAJOR ACHIEVEMENTS

- 2022 Masters of The Martial Arts Hall of Fame
- 2022 Spartan Warrior Hall of Fame / Italy
- 2021 International Hall of Fame / Brazil
- 2021 International Hall of Fame / India
- 2021 Board Breaking Champion / Martial Arts Got Talent
- 2021 Board Breaking Champion / International Breaking Federation
- 2020 Hall of Honors (Esteem Martial Artist) / Action Martial Arts Magazine
- 2020 Hall of Fame (Instructor of The Year - Goju Ryu) / Legends of The Martial Arts
- 2019 World's Greatest Martial Artists Book inclusion (Volume 2) / GM Ted Gambordella
- 2019 Martial Arts Masters & Pioneers Book inclusion (Who's Really Who) / AMAA
- 2019 Masters of the Martial Arts Hall of Fame.
- 2018 Hall of Fame (Who's Who Legends Award) / American Martial Arts Alliance
- 2018 Hall of Honors (Goodwill Ambassador) / Action Martial Arts Magazine
- 2018 Masters of the Martial Arts Hall of Fame
- 2017 Hall of Honors (Outstanding Achievements) / Action Martial Arts Magazine

How MARTIAL ARTS CHANGED My Life!

I would say that after 50 years of studying / practicing martial arts - it has had a significant influence on my life; learning to be more patient, understanding myself better, more focused on tasks, becoming more goal-oriented, acquiring more tenacity, and most of all, showing respect to everyone - regardless of race, gender, age, martial arts style, and ability. All this might seem cliche - but this lifestyle, these virtues / characteristics have carried over from the Dojo to my everyday endeavors. From the standpoint of Karate being a sport, it has provided years of exciting competitions while overcoming fears and building confidence in the process for me. Performing over the years as a certified referee / judge, has become a great teacher to me that emphasizes integrity and fairness - which in today's world, is essential in becoming a good person.

It goes without saying that practicing martial arts has benefited me in better physical / mental health, while acquiring a skill set of self-defense. Being a member of the Martial Arts family has given me a wealth of dear friends and associates with common interests and pursuits. Sharing ideas and talents with others requires respect for each and every one in order to keep the Bushido meaningful. Teaching martial arts has given me the greatest of rewards-seeing students excel in techniques while developing one's self-mastery.

How has Grandmaster CYNTHIA ROTHROCK Influenced me?

GM Cynthia Rothrock always amazes me with her high-voltage energy and charm. I've had countless conversations with her over the years at various Hall of Fame/Hall of Honors and texting. I'm always intrigued by listening to her worldwide adventures while being awestruck by her seminars. I give her credit for my improved stretching abilities and balance. Cynthia (Lady Dragon) Rothrock is truly the "Queen of Martial Arts" as a World Champion and on the Big Screen.

Bill "Superfoot" WALLACE

The entire world knows him as SUPERFOOT! He was featured on the Cover of Who's Who Legends 2017 with his brother in arms original world light heavyweight champion Jeff Smith and friends Joe Corley and Bill Clark. Five + decades after he started martial arts, Bill Wallace is a Grand Master Instructor and one of the global martial arts world's most influential personalities.

Grand Master Wallace was born in Portland, Indiana, and trained in wrestling during his high school years. He began his study of Judo in 1966 and was forced to discontinue his Judo related activities because of an injury he suffered to his right knee during practice. He then began to study Shorin-ryu Karate under Michael Gneck in February 1967, while serving in the U.S. Air Force.

Wallace was a prolific point fighter, and he won tournaments all over North America and fought on the US teams competing internationally. An injury to his right knee forced him to abandon kicking with that leg and he perfected kicking with the left leg. Clocked at nearly 60 miles an hour, he was perennially ranked as the premiere kicker in the country and among the top 10 fighters by all ratings services.

In September, 1974 the Professional Karate Association (PKA) emerged and held the world's first Full Contact Karate Championship in the LA Sports Arena. Bill Wallace was chosen to represent the Untied States and emerged as the world's first Full Contact Middleweight Champion on ABC's Wide World of Entertainment.

Honing in on his incredible speed and accuracy, he was nicknamed Superfoot, a moniker that became synonymous with Bill Wallace the world over. Superfoot's first title defense was against Atlanta's Joe Corley at the 1975 Battle of Atlanta, where he captured his first defense win in 9 rounds. As a result of his incredible reputation, CBS signed Wallace for quarterly live title defenses, and in 1977 they also signed Joe Corley to be the expert commentator for the Superfoot bouts. Superfoot would continue winning and would retire live on CBS in 1980, one of the few fighters who stayed retired and remained undefeated at 23-0.

The PKA promoted the sport of full-contact karate on NBC, CBS and ESPN. PKA Full-contact karate differed from Muay Thai style kickboxing in that leg kicks were allowed in kickboxing and forbidden in full-contact karate. Wallace, the epitome of high kicking, joined Joe Corley on ESPN for the Defense and Fitness Tips of the Week, where Wallace showed world-class athletes from golf, basketball, baseball, football and track the proper ways to use the sponsor's Power Stretch machine to improve their athletic performance and prevent injuries. Wallace and Corley together inspired thousands of viewers to join karate schools through their series.

In 1990 Bill Wallace (166 lbs) fought one last exhibition kickboxing/karate match with friend Joe Lewis (198 lbs) on pay per view. Both   Wallace and Lewis were refused a boxing license because of their age. The exhibition ended with one judge in favor for Wallace, another in favor for Lewis, and the third judge scored the bout a tie, ending the exhibition in a draw.

Wallace has taught karate, judo, wrestling and weight lifting at Memphis State University. The author of a college textbook about karate and kinesiology, he continues to teach seminars across the United States and abroad.

He was the arch nemesis of long-time friend Chuck Norris in A Force of One. His other film credits include Kill Point, with Cameron Mitchell, Continental Divide and Neighbors, with John Belushi; The Protector, with Jackie Chan; Los Bravos with Hector Echavarria; A Prayer for the Dying, with Mickey Rourke; Ninja Turf; and Sword of Heaven.

Wallace was the play-by-play commentator for the inaugural Ultimate Fighting Championship pay-per-view event in 1993 alongside fellow kickboxer Kathy Long and NFL Hall of Famer Jim Brown.

Wallace administers an organization of karate schools under his "Superfoot" system, all members of the PKA WORLDWIDE Associated Schools.

He was elected to Black Belt Magazine's Hall of Fame in 1973 as "Tournament Karate Fighter of the Year" and again in 1978 as "Man of the Year", has appeared on magazine covers the world over and still today is one of the most sought after instructors in the world.

SUPERFOOT: a Martial Arts Legacy for All Time!

Johnny WARREN

> " Martial arts not only gave me a chance to fight and become a world champion, but it is the biggest part of who I am...

WHY THE *Martial Arts?*

Johnny Warren began his martial arts journey at the age of three in Vietnam. He was always looked at as "the odd kid" because his father had been an American soldier fighting in Vietnam. Even when he was very young, Johnny never backed down from a fight, always looking for ways to release his aggression and anger. A Vietnamese uncle eventually began training Johnny so that he could learn how to protect himself, and for a long time, that was all that Martial Arts meant to the boy; it wasn't until much later, after many years of training and fighting, that Johnny understood how Martial Arts is so much more than just combat.

After moving to the United States, Johnny continued his training using a variety of instructors and systems. He was always trying to better himself as a fighter, so, on his uncle's advice, he enrolled in a boxing gym, hoping to

TRAINING INFORMATION

- Martial Arts Styles & Rank: WarKwanDo (8th Dan/Hachidan), KiDoKwan (8th Dan/Hachidan), Vovinam (2nd Dan/Nidan), Kongo-Do (1st Dan/Shodan), Kyokushin (1stDan/Shodan), Okinawan Shorin-ryu (1stDan/Shodan)

- Instructors/Influencers: Nguyen Van Tuoi, Akira Hachirou, Harold Diamond, Chuck Daily, Larry Shepard, Conrado P. Alvarado,

- Birthplace/Growing Up: Saigon, Vietnam / Panama City Beach, FL / San Francisco, CA

- Yrs. In the Martial Arts: 54 years

- Yrs. Instructing: 32 years

- School Owner, Manager & Instructor at WarKwanDo, PKA Worldwide Member

improve his hand technique and to continue his martial arts training. At the age of 14, at a point tournament, Johnny met Larry Shepard who noticed that Johnny was fighting — and winning — in the adult divisions. Larry encouraged the boy to get into kickboxing and began to train him; after three short months, Johnny had his first amateur fight and was hooked.

Johnny continued fighting after he moved to Florida, leaving PKA and moving to ISKA. After taking a few fights in Colorado, he turned pro under the ISKA banner, winning local and minor titles and championships. He eventually moved on to other organizations because of the lack of ISKA matches, but during his time with ISKA, he fought and beat such fighters as Felipe Garcia (former world ISKA, PKA champion), Rick and Randy Ford, James Chavez, Francisco Landin, Delfino Perez, Byron Robinson, Mario Liano, and many others.

Johnny is known for his fast, flashy, powerful kicks, and is considered by many of his peers — Steve Shepard, Curtis Bush, Harold Diamond, Chuck Daly, and others — to be one of the greatest kickers. Of the 30 KOs in his pro record, a significant number of them, 19, were by kicks. 38(W)-4(L)-1(D)-30 KO's.

PROFESSIONAL ORGANIZATIONS

- WarKwanDo
- KiDoKwan
- Kongo-Do
- PKA World Wide
- American Martial Arts Alliance
- Sports Karate Museum History General
- USA Martial Arts Hall of Fame

PERSONAL ACHIEVEMENTS

- Director/President of KiDoKwan System and promoted to 8th Dan/Hachidan before the passing of his first instructor- Nguyen Van Tuoi
- Owner/Director/President of the WarKwando system, which continues to grow, with his students taking it to another level on both the sports aspect and the Martial Arts community
- Raising two boys as a single parent and passing the Martial Arts to them

MAJOR ACHIEVEMENTS

- IKBO World Jr. Lightweight Champion
- IKBA World Lightweight Champion
- WCKB World Bantamweight Champion
- ISKA US Regional Featherweight Champ
- ISKA USA Bantamweight Champion
- ISKA Colorado State Bantamweight Champion
- IKBF North American Bantamweight Champion
- Colorado State Point/Kata Grand Champion

Become an
AMAA MEMBER!

How has Grandmaster CYNTHIA ROTHROCK Influenced me?

She has always been a great influencer and role model. Her kata and movies demonstrated to me what was needed when I was competing in kata at tournaments. Her strong, fluid, realistic moves are eye-openers for all to notice.

How MARTIAL ARTS CHANGED My Life!

Martial arts not only gave me a chance to fight and become a world champion, but it is the biggest part of who I am and what I have become — a leader and a teacher. So it will always be in my life.

Timothy
WHITE

"

My life as a martial artist has evolved through communications, learning and caring for those that think like you.

WHY THE *Martial Arts?*

I started martial arts while I was in the Army stationed in Darmstadt, Germany. I began this journey to enhance my self-defense skills and physical fitness levels. I met Mr. Wes Ruiz who was teaching in the racquetball court at the post gym. It was sort of funny since most of the class was Puerto Rican and I was the only white guy in the class. They accepted me as one of them. I continued studying with this group and the origin of Kiru-Do Karate. I felt like I was growing spiritually, and physically and it motivated me to continue studying in the martial arts. After two years of studying with Mr. Ruiz, Mr. Ruiz transferred back to the United States and I started studying Tae Kwon Do with Mr. Jay Park. I made it to 3 Kup in TKD. I then transferred back to the USA, and I got involved in police and security work. I started studying Kung Fu systems with GM Tak Cheung Wong (Deceased). GM Wong became my greatest mentor in the martial arts.

TRAINING INFORMATION

- Martial Arts Styles & Rank: Molum Pai Kung Fu-Grand Master, System Inheritor, Kiru-Do Karate-8th Dan, Okkuy-Ryu Jujutsu-7th Dan
- Instructors/Influencers: GM Tak Cheung (Felix) Wong), GM Wes Ruiz, GM Dan Onan
- Birthdate: August 22, 1954
- Birthplace/Growing Up: Milwaukee, WI / Indianapolis, IN
- Yrs. In the Martial Arts: 51 years
- Yrs. Instructing: 48 years
- School Owner & Instructor at PSI/Molum Combat Arts , PKA Worldwide Member

PROFESSIONAL ORGANIZATIONS

- Fraternal Order of Police
- Professional Karate Association
- Professional Karate Commission
- American Martial Arts Alliance
- Tournament Karate Association
- Military Police Regimental Association
- Health Safety Institute
- United States Martial Arts Association
- Eastern USA Karate Association

I started working for the Indiana State Capitol Police in 1977 and I met GM Dan Onan. I started training police tactics with him, since he was a lead instructor for the state department of corrections. This kept my interest in police tactics. After several years of teaching officers from different agencies, I realized there was something missing from the training, and that was a true martial arts concept. Martial arts led me to Active/Passive Countermeasures, PPCT, the Risk Management System and others. I then became an ASP and OC instructor, and then I became an Indiana Law Enforcement Training Board Certified Instructor, so that I could teach officers in the state of Indiana. I have continued that mission as of today. Martial arts let me be more than I had intended it to. Since I have been in the Martial arts, I have achieved many things, and it keeps me motivated to continue training.

How MARTIAL ARTS CHANGED My Life!

When I first started in the martial arts, I didn't really know where it was going to take me. I was seventeen years old and in the US Army. However, over the years, I have made strides to keep the martial arts close to my heart and soul. It has helped me in my law enforcement career, as a Defensive Tactic and Physical Force Instructor. It has brought me in contact with many well-known trainers, and opened my eyes to many different aspects of what martial arts is all about. I have been able to meet and train with some of the best in the business. This in itself has enabled me to survive during the pandemic of Covid-19. My life as a martial artist has evolved

PERSONAL ACHIEVEMENTS

- Keeping my martial arts studio open during Covid-19
- Winning TKA State Titles for Weapons and Forms
- Being inducted into the Sport Karate Museum
- Being inducted into the Warrior Society Hall of Fame
- Retiring from the US Army 1995
- Top Ten Competitor in the PKC 2002 to 2010

MAJOR ACHIEVEMENTS

- Co-authored Cell Extractions for Prisons and Jails
- Being inducted in the Who's Who books 2017 to 2022
- Being appointed an Ambassador for AMAA
- Being honored by Action Martial Arts Magazine 2015 to 2019
- Surviving Covid 19

through communications, learning and caring for those that think like you. Martial arts has taught me that I can compete on any level and still enjoy the competition and the winning.

In 2021, I was able to win 2 State Titles in Weapons and Forms in the Tournament Karate Associations tournament season. This had a great impact on how I may grow in the future.

At one point I thought I might have to close my club, and my black belts came in and helped teach, make donations to the club, rent, etc. They made sure they had a place to train and learn. I am honored to have such students in my martial arts club.

How has Grandmaster CYNTHIA ROTHROCK Influenced me?

Over the years, I have known GM Rothrock, and she has impressed me with her ever-loving attitude toward others. She inspires through her seminars and her ability to influence others. I met GM Rothrock several times when she was competing on the tournament circuit. Her ability to perform at the highest competition levels and several other competitors has inspired me to continue competing in my late 60s. I love the ability to be inspired by others, especially GM Rothrock. Her persona is amazing, and she projects it well. I have seen all her movies, and she has amazing skills. What an inspiration to others. I can't wait for her new movie to hit the market. She is the Best of the Best.

Don
WILLIS

"

The Martial Arts have made it possible to achieve a great many good things in my life, and to overcome many obstacles.

WHY THE *Martial Arts?*

I was a smaller person when I was young and that made me an easy target for bullies. I was picked on quite a bit, and I did not have a lot of self-esteem. I joined the military in 1960 when I was just 17 and I loved the hand-to-hand combat. I worked out with anyone I could for my three years in the service. When I was discharged in 1963 it was impossible to find a school, but was able to find a few guys that knew "a little." I finally joined a school in 1965 under the direction of I J Kim.

The Martial Arts have made it possible to achieve a great many good things in my life, and to overcome many obstacles. I have the idea that is due to the never quit mindset that is prevalent in the martial arts. As to myself, I have emphysema and I attribute my training in breath control and my never quit attitude to be able to keep going.

TRAINING INFORMATION

- Martial Arts Styles & Rank: 9th Dan-American Karate, 9th Dan-World Kobudo Federation
- Instructors/Influencers: I.J. Kim, Curtis Herrington, Andy Horne, Glenn Keeney, Joe Corley, Bill Wallace, Jeff Smith
- Birthplace/Growing Up: Canton, OH
- Yrs. In the Martial Arts: 62 years
- Yrs. Instructing: 40+ years
- School Owner, Manager, Instructor & Co-founder of PKA Worldwide, PKA Worldwide Director of Associated School and Members and Chairman, PKA Worldwide Rank Committee

PROFESSIONAL ORGANIZATIONS

- PKA Worldwide
- PKC Professional Karate Commission

PERSONAL ACHIEVEMENTS

- Police Training Sergeant - Canal Fulton, OH
- Nominated for Ohio Governor's Cup - National Competitor all divisions
  Presidential Sports Award from Richard Nixon
- Founder of the Don Willis American Karate System
- Opened the first Martial Arts school in Ft. Lauderdale, FL 1970
- Operated Martial Arts schools in Florida and Ohio
- Founded Don Willis International

MAJOR ACHIEVEMENTS

- Member, the Professional Karate Association Executive Committee
- As Chairman of the Professional Karate Association's Reps and Officials Committee, I have personally trained well over 1000 PKA Officials worldwide.
- In 1983, I was the only person ever to be awarded both Professional Karate Association Man of the Year and Professional Karate Association Official of the Year.
- On behalf of the PKA, I've traveled as far from home as Nice, France and Anchorage, Alaska, and I've represented the association in almost all of our CONUS states.
- I am the original United States Director of Operations for the Professional Karate Commission and I have work alongside GM Glenn Keeney in building that organization's recognition in the Martial Arts.
- Being presented with a Joe Lewis Eternal Warrior Award has been the highlight of my martial arts career.
- Most importantly, I have now teamed with GM Joe Corley to grow PKA WORLDWIDE. I consider my long-time friendships with GM Glenn Keeney and GM Joe Corley as a major achievement. These two have done more than I can say to build the Martial Arts.

Become an
AMAA
MEMBER!

Robert T. YARBOROUGH

"

The physical fitness gained through martial arts has provided me with an unassailable foundation...

WHY THE *Martial Arts?*

Robert T. Yarborough started his martial arts journey with a short-lived stint in Judo at the age of 10 in Hartsville, SC, and at 14, began formal study of Kempo under Dave dela Santos in Brevard, NC, earning his Shodan in 1979 at 19. Robert also earned his Army Aviator Wings at 19, having entered the Army's Warrant Officer Rotary Wing Aviation Course at Ft Rucker, AL, at age 18.

Robert spent the next 4-years stationed in Germany, where he continued his martial arts studies in Shotokan and Shorinryu, including another short-lived 6-month attempt at Judo. On his return to the United States, he was awarded Nidan in 1984 and opened his first dojo in Etowah, NC. While teaching, Robert continued Kempo training under Chester Israel. He also completed his last year of college, earning a bachelor's in Aeronautics. He returned to military service with the Air Force and relocated to Columbus, MS, where he opened his second

TRAINING INFORMATION

- Martial Arts Styles & Rank: Taekwondo Jidokwan-8th Dan, Kempo-7th Dan, Tangsoodo-5th Dan, Combat Hapkido-4th Dan, Hapkido Moohakkwan-2nd Dan, Jujutsu-1st Dan

- Instructors/Influencers: David Delos Santos, Chester Israel, David Andersen, Myong Sok Namkung Mayes, Hee Il Cho, Sung Soo Lee, John Pellegrini, Bram Frank, Ken Gee

- Birthplace/Growing Up: Cheraw, SC / Hartsville, SC / New Ellington, SC / Brevard, NC

- Yrs. In the Martial Arts: 49 years

- Yrs. Instructing: 30+ years

- School Owner & Instructor, PKA Worldwide Member

PROFESSIONAL ORGANIZATIONS

- Professional Karate Association (PKA) Life Member

- Martial Arts Masters Association (MAMA) Life Member

dojo. During the next 20 years, the Air Force took Robert to the far reaches of the globe (47 countries), where he had the opportunity to train in various arts, including Modern Arnis, Hapkido, Tangsoodo, Aikido, Taijutsu, and Jujutsu.

During his Air Force career, Robert taught on numerous military bases in Germany, Texas, Colorado, and Alabama. During his second tour of duty in Germany, he served as the first country director for the International Combat Hapkido Federation (ICHF) and Germany Director for the International Taekwondo Jidokwan Federation (ITJF) from 1994 to 1996. He continued to serve the ITFJ as Texas State Director from 1997-2000. From 2000 to 2004, he served as Vice President and member of the Board of Directors for the ICHF and as the Alabama State Director. He also served on the Master's Council of the Independent Taekwondo Association (ITA) from 2000 to 2006. In 1997, Robert was inducted into the World Head of Family Sokeship Council Hall of Fame as Instructor of the Year, and in 2001 received the Silver Life Achievement Award from the United States Martial Artist Association.

During his military career, Robert was a Special Operations pilot flying missions in Central and South America. He also flew Vice-Presidential Support Missions and Space Shuttle support for the Hubble Space Telescope launch and the Micro Gravity Laboratory. Robert logged over 5,000 flight hours as a military pilot and is a combat veteran with 62 combat missions and combat support missions in Operation DESERT STORM and 10 combat missions in Operation PROVIDE PROMISE (Bosnia and Herzegovina).

PROFESSIONAL ORGANIZATIONS

- International Karate Connection Association (IKCA) Life Member
- International Kenpo Karate Academies (IKKC) Life Member
- Independent Taekwondo Association (ITA) Life Member
- All Japan Budo Association (AJBA)
- Budoshin Jujitsu Yudanshakai
- Common Sense Self-Defense / Street Combat (CSSD/SC)
- American Institute of Aeronautics and Astronautics
- Professional Airline Pilots Association

PERSONAL ACHIEVEMENTS

- Masters of Fine Arts, Creative Writing, Full Sail University (Salutatorian)
- Master of Arts, Computer Resources & Information Management, Webster University
- Bachelor of Professional Aeronautics, Embry Riddle Aeronautical University
- Air Command and Staff College - USAF Air University
- Combat Aircrew Tactics School (CATS)/ Mobility Weapons School
- USAF Safety Center: Aircraft Mishap Investigation Course
- USAF Advanced Instrument School
- Program & Portfolio Management Certification (PPMC)
- Business Administration - Executive Certificate, University of Notre Dame
- Civilian Contract Management - Master Certificate, Villanova University
- Government Contract Management - Master Certificate, Villanova University
- Aviation Safety Award: Distinguished Achievement, Mar 84
- Company Grade Officer of the Quarter, 37th Airlift Squadron Jan-Mar 96
- Company Grade Officer of the Quarter, 86th Ops Group Jan-Mar 96
- Lance P. Sijan Leadership Award, 86th Operations Group Jun 95- Jun 96
- Instructor Pilot of the Quarter, 3rd Flying Training Squadron Jan -Mar 97

He also participated in Operations ABLE SENTRY in Croatia and Macedonia and again in Bosnia and Herzegovina during Operation JOINT ENDEAVOR.

In 2006, Robert retired from the Air Force as a Lieutenant Colonel with 27 years of service and over 50 military awards and decorations. After retirement, he continued his flying career as a government contractor Site Director, running training programs for foreign military pilots, and as an airline pilot for United Express. In addition to his work in the martial arts and the military, Robert is an award-winning photographer, reiki master, best-selling author, master herbalist, scuba diver, and holds two graduate degrees.

PERSONAL ACHIEVEMENTS

- Instructor Pilot of the Year, 3 Flying Training Squadron 97
- Professional Performer of the Quarter, 3 Flying Training Sq Jul - Sep 97
- Honor Graduate, AETC Quality Assurance Evaluator Course Feb 97
- Professional Performer of the Quarter, 3 FTS Jan – Mar 00
- USAF Advanced Instrument School Outstanding Graduate 2000
- Meritorious Service Medal (4 awards)
- Air Medal
- Aerial Achievement Medal (3 awards)
- Air Force Commendation Medal
- Air Force Achievement Medal
- Humanitarian Service Medal
- Southwest Asia Service Medal (3 awards)
- Kuwait Liberation Medal (Awarded by the Kingdom of Kuwait)
- Kuwait Liberation Medal (Awarded by the Kingdom of Saudi Arabia)
- Joint Meritorious Service Medal
- NATO Medal Military Outstanding Volunteer Medal
- Combat Readiness Medal (3 awards)
- Armed Forces Service Medal
- Armed Forces Expeditionary Medal
- National Defense Service Medal
- Air Force Organizational Excellence Award
- Air Force Outstanding Unit Citation with "V" device for Valor
- Air Force Outstanding Unit Citation (8 awards)

How MARTIAL ARTS CHANGED My Life!

Martial arts training was instrumental in shaping me for my military career and as a pilot. It forged within me the virtues of self-discipline, unwavering focus, unyielding mental strength, emotional well-being, impeccable physical fitness, relentless pursuit of knowledge, acute attention to detail, and unwavering precision. The demanding rigors of martial arts have instilled in me the discipline and dedication needed to thrive in the military environment, where adherence to rules and routines is paramount. Through rigorous training, I have developed the mental fortitude to maintain composure under intense pressure and make sound decisions in high-stress situations.

The physical fitness gained through martial arts has provided me with an unassailable foundation, enabling me to withstand the grueling demands of piloting, from enduring lengthy flights to overcoming the physical strains of G-forces. Moreover, martial arts have instilled an unquenchable thirst for continuous learning—a vital trait in the aviation industry, where staying abreast of cutting-edge technologies and refining one's skills is imperative. The precision and attention to detail ingrained in every martial arts movement have seamlessly translated into my flight maneuvers and adherence to operational protocols. Ultimately, martial arts have irrevocably transformed my life, empowering me with the indomitable qualities and honed skills needed to excel in the face of the formidable challenges and profound responsibilities that await both military and commercial pilots.

MAJOR ACHIEVEMENTS

- International Combat Hapkido Federation (ICHF) – Director for Germany 1994 to 1996
- International Taekwondo Jidokwan Federation (ITJF) – Director for Germany 1994 to 1996.
- World Head of Family Sokeship Council – Hall of Fame Inductee, Instructor of the Year 1997
- International Taekwondo Jidokwan Federation (ITJF) – Texas State Director 1997-2000.
- United States Martial Artist Association – Silver Life Achievement Award 2001
- International Combat Hapkido Federation (ICHF) – Vice President 2000 to 2004
- International Combat Hapkido Federation (ICHF) – Alabama State Director 2000 to 2003
- Independent Taekwondo Association (ITA) – Alabama State Director 2000 to 2001
- Independent Taekwondo Association (ITA) – Master's Council 2000 to 2006
- Bestselling Author: Amazon Bestseller and Barnes & Noble Bestseller
- Reiki Master in Usui Reiki Ryoho, Siechim Reiki, and Karuna Reiki.
- Certified Master Herbalist and Traditional Naturopath.
- Award Winning Photographer

Become an
AMAA MEMBER!

How has Grandmaster CYNTHIA ROTHROCK Influenced me?

Although I have not personally trained under Grandmaster Cynthia Rothrock, I greatly admire her accomplishments, skills, and contributions to the martial arts world. Rothrock's success as a female martial artist in a predominantly male-dominated field has been groundbreaking; she has shattered gender stereotypes and demonstrated that women could excel in martial arts, motivating me to create an inclusive and empowering environment for female practitioners in my classes. Rothrock's proficiency in multiple martial arts disciplines, including Tang Soo Do, Taekwondo, and Chinese Wushu, has showcased the importance of continuous learning and versatility. Her mastery of techniques, precision, and fluidity in her movements have served as a guide for me in refining my skills as an instructor and practitioner.

Join the American Martial Arts Alliance Foundation

"Empowering Martial Artists To Inspire The World"

BLACKBELT MEMBERSHIP INCLUDES:

- eFramable AMAA Black Belt Member Certificate
- AMAA Membership Patch
- Press Release Template
- FREE Elite Listing on the International Who's Who eDirectory
- Monthly Newsletter
- Online Blog
- Eligible for AMAA Grants & Scholarships
- 2 months FREE Host Your Online Class Platform from Click 4 Course

Join Today!

www.whoswhointhemartialarts.com/become-a-member

All black belt membership applicants must be 18 years of age.

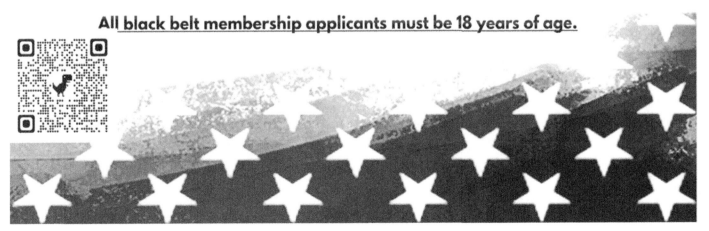

AMAAF ALUMNUS & INDUCTEES
In the Martial Arts

Dana
ABBOTT

> "
> The path of the sword has taught me the importance of dedication, focus, and continuous self-improvement.

WHY THE *Martial Arts?*

I began my studies in the Fall of 1978 in the southwestern town of Prescott, Arizona. It was in this quaint setting that my journey into martial arts began, specifically Korean karate, which I learned through the Police Athletic League (PAL) at the armory next to the courthouse. The very same courthouse that had gained fame as the filming location for the iconic martial arts movie of the 1970s, "Billy Jack," where Billy Jack's unforgettable kick to the guy's head took place. During this time, I worked as a surveyor for Yavapai County, Arizona, immersing myself in the study of martial arts while embracing my professional career.

As I delved deeper into my martial arts journey, I relocated to Tokyo, Japan, and found myself greatly influenced over the next 15 years by the teachings of several esteemed sword masters. These masters were seasoned combat veterans who had served in the Japanese Imperial Army

TRAINING INFORMATION

- Martial Arts Rank: Toyama-Ryu Iai-Batto do - 7th Degree Black Belt
- Instructors/Influencers: Abe Shinobu, Shizawa Kunio, Tanabe Tetsundo, Nakamura Taizaburo, Tabuchi Mitsunobu, and the great samurai movie actor, Mifune Toshiro
- Yrs. In the Martial Arts: 45 years
- Yrs. Instructing: 25 years
- School owner at Samurai Sports

during World War II. With their guidance, I began to grasp the essence of swordsmanship, training in various disciplines such as kendo, kenjutsu, iaido, and tameshigiri. My masters, including Abe Shinobu, Shizawa Kunio, Tanabe Tetsundo, Tabuchi Mitsunobu, and Nakamura Taizaburo, who was knighted by the Emperor of Japan, imparted their wisdom, shaping my understanding of the way of the sword. As a 7th Dan in Japanese swordsmanship, specializing in Kenjutsu and Toyama-Ryu Iai Batto-do, my expertise is highly respected in both Japan and the United States, where I currently reside. My extensive training and certification were obtained through Japan's esteemed Martial Arts University, Nihon Taiiku Daigaku, under the Japanese Department of Education and Recreation. Throughout my career, I have had the privilege of crossing swords with formattable opponents, who made me a stronger martial artist.

Reflecting on my journey, I am often asked about my experiences learning kenjutsu from the great sword masters in Japan. Many seek my guidance on mastering techniques and understanding the mental aspects of swordsmanship. In response, I paint a vivid picture, sharing the mental images that offer insights into the mindset of a Japanese swordsmanship student. My dedication to traditional practice and an unwavering pursuit of perfection set me apart. While some martial artists lean towards a less physically demanding approach, I remain committed to the age-old adage that practice makes perfect.

I firmly believe that one's dreams and desires, combined with motivation and determination,

"Find your Samurai Warrior within You"
Shihan Abbott's samurai sword seminar will help you efficiently execute kenjutsu cutting technique with a wooden bokken, after that you will advance onto the steel sword shinken section to experience the "Fear of the Blade" while safely drawing, cutting and sheathing.

LearnTheSword.com
Shihan Abbott's AI generated doppelganger

hold the key to achieving proficiency and mastery. My lifelong devotion to Japanese swordsmanship has propelled me to the forefront of my field, leaving an indelible mark on the martial arts community and igniting a passion for the ancient traditions I hold dear. I am grateful for the opportunities to share my knowledge and experiences, and I hope to continue inspiring others on their own martial arts journeys.

How MARTIAL ARTS CHANGED My Life!

Martial arts have left an indelible imprint on my life. Over 45 years of learning, practicing, and contemplating the art of the sword, I have been profoundly influenced by the traditions passed down by my sword masters. Each movement, technique, and transition has shaped my adult life, fostering discipline, perseverance, and a relentless pursuit of perfection. I envision myself as a protector, dedicated to maintaining consistency and good health well into my centenary years. The lessons and values instilled in me by martial arts guide my everyday actions and decisions. They have become an integral part of who I am, influencing my physical abilities, mindset, and character.

The path of the sword has taught me the importance of dedication, focus, and continuous self-improvement. It has given me the tools to overcome challenges and embrace a balanced and harmonious way of life. With each passing year, I strive to embody the principles of martial arts more fully, always seeking to deepen my understanding and refine my skills.

HOW MY LIFE IS CHANGED (CONTINUED)

As I progress along this lifelong journey, I am grateful for the profound impact the martial arts have had on me. They have shaped my perspective, my values, and my aspirations. I carry the spirit of the sword with me, embracing its teachings and using them to guide me on the path of personal growth and enlightenment.

Become an
AMAA MEMBER!

My martial arts career boasts numerous accomplishments and accolades. Notably, in 2004, I was honored to be inducted into Black Belt Magazine's prestigious Hall of Fame, a testament to my expertise and contributions to the martial arts industry. Yet, my proudest achievement lies in the present, as I have reached the same age as my masters before me, embodying their teachings and becoming a reflection of their wisdom. Through years of sword fighting and relentless practice, I have attained a sense of calm and peacefulness, cultivating a mindset that I believe will carry me well into old age. My dedication and skill have earned me recognition as a leader in the martial arts world. I have been fortunate to receive numerous honors and awards, including the Black Belt Magazine Hall of Fame, the Golden Shuto Award, the Elite Black Belt Hall of Fame, and the Martial Arts History Museum recognition, among many others. I have been commended for my dedication to preserving the spirit of Budo, and my achievements have been acknowledged with Lifetime Achievement Awards and the AMAA Who's Who in the Martial Arts, to name a few. It is a humbling experience to be recognized for my contributions and to know that my passion for martial arts has made an impact. I will continue to strive for excellence and share my knowledge and love for martial arts with others, carrying on the legacy of my master's and inspiring future generations.

Timothy
ALBRECHT

"

Martial Arts has made me humble to look upon myself and others and help in sports and their lives even after my retirement.

WHY THE *Martial Arts?*

I started my journey in Judo in 1981. Growing up with ADHD was a great focus set. I loved all types of martial arts. Chuck Norris and Bruce Lee were my greatest influence. I started Taekwondo under the Ata. in 1982. I learned the background of my Grandmaster instructor and his knowledge. It was the best thing at a young age in my life. It gave me life and physical goals. My main goal was to be a student first, then an instructor. Plus, competing with my fellow practitioners. I've still made some lifelong friends.

TRAINING INFORMATION

- Martial Arts Styles & Rank: Taekwondo; 6th Degree Black Belt, Judo; Yellow Belt
- Instructors/Influencers: Grandmaster Hu Lee, Grandmaster Mike Clark
- Birthplace/Growing Up: Rogers, AR
- Yrs. In the Martial Arts: 42 years
- Yrs. Instructing: 40 years
- Retired

PROFESSIONAL ORGANIZATIONS

- USTA
- USTF
- WTF
- ATA

How MARTIAL ARTS CHANGED *My Life!*

Martial Arts has made me humble to look upon myself and others and help in sports and their lives even after my retirement. Growing up with ADHD was different. To learn to focus set. Be it an everyday struggle or being companionate. Even today, I look back at how Taekwondo has changed. How hard my instructors were on us. The old way of learning pain and mental health. Also, growing up with martial art abilities helped me in my ten-year law enforcement career. It helped with more ways of looking at difficult situations. Understanding students and their goals in life was my main drive for years. I was trying to help them gain more knowledge all around. I taught TKD for many years free, because I love it so much. Even at a loss of money because I know somehow it makes a difference in just one person.

PERSONAL ACHIEVEMENTS

- Being a certified Taekwondo instructor
- Top in the nation for my rank in sparring and forms
- Having still the greatest Taekwondo Grandmaster friends

MAJOR ACHIEVEMENTS

- Being awarded my Lifetime Merit Martial Arts Qward from Grandmaster Jason Wadley

Chris
ANDERSON

"

The dojo is the only place where I can go to shut out everything wrong in my life and focus only on my karate.

WHY THE *Martial Arts?*

I had been interested in studying martial arts from an early age. My interest in martial arts grew stronger after seeing the original Karate Kid film in the theater in 1984. I also enjoyed watching television shows and movies with such martial artists as Chuck Norris, Bruce Lee, Steven Seagal, and Jean-Claude Van Damme. I used to "play karate/play fight," emulating my onscreen heroes with my friends, although we never actually hurt each other. I began studying martial arts in 1997 to be able to defend myself, my family, friends, and loved ones.

While attending Middle Tennessee State University in Murfreesboro, Tennessee, I enrolled in self-defense, beginner karate, and advanced karate over the following three semesters. After completing advanced karate, I enrolled in a local Taekwondo studio and studied Taekwondo for the next two years earning a 2nd Degree Red Belt (2nd Gup).

TRAINING INFORMATION

- Martial Arts Styles & Rank: Taekwondo - 2nd Degree Red Belt, Wado Ryu - 5th Degree Black Belt (Go Dan)
- Instructors/Influencers: Bill Taylor, Steve Holt, William Herzer, Newton Harris, Ronald Tucker, Paul Caruthers, Thomas Bain, Ned Coleman, and Lane Wommack
- Birthplace/Growing Up: Nashville, TN / Smyrna TN
- Yrs. In the Martial Arts: 26 years
- Yrs. Instructing: 5 years

PROFESSIONAL ORGANIZATIONS

- United States Eastern Wado Ryu Karate Do Federation
- Black Belt Club Member
- SWAT (Assistant Instructor)
- Lifetime Black Belt Member of the American Martial Arts Alliance

I then changed styles in 1999 to my current style of Wado-Ryu Karate at Bill Taylor's Bushido School of Karate in Murfreesboro, Tennessee. I've been studying Wado-Ryu Karate at Bill Taylor's Bushido School of Karate for 24 years and counting. I taught classes as an assistant instructor (SWAT) for three years while training to become a black belt, and then I taught for two additional years after earning my first-degree black belt. I received my first-degree black belt (Sho Dan) in December 2003 and my 5th Degree Black Belt (Go Dan) in April 2021.

I still attend class twice weekly to hone and sharpen my skills, and I'm working toward earning my 6th Degree Black Belt (Roku Dan). I hope to continue training in the martial arts as long as I live. For me, martial arts is not just a hobby. It has become an essential part of my life.

How MARTIAL ARTS CHANGED My Life!

Studying martial arts has played an incredibly positive role in my life. Studying martial arts has transformed me into a disciplined, self-confident, respectful, humble, patient, and tenacious individual. It has made me mentally and physically tough and kept me physically fit. Studying martial arts has helped me in college, graduate school, career, and personal life. Before studying martial arts, I sometimes gave up easily on certain tasks or obstacles for fear of failure. Learning new techniques, memorizing sometimes lengthy and difficult patterns/katas, sparring against bigger and stronger opponents, and passing difficult belt exams gave me the confidence I needed never to give up and

PERSONAL & MAJOR ACHIEVEMENTS

- Earned my 5th Degree Black Belt (Go Dan) and became an official Sensei.
- Awarded an Excellence in Teaching Award when I helped teach classes at my dojo as an assistant instructor.
- Trained numerous times with Wado-Ryu Grand Master Sensei Kazutaka Otsuka
- Attended multiple seminars and training with World Kickboxing Champion Bill "Superfoot" Wallace and training with Heavyweight Kickboxing Champion Joe Lewis.
- I had the honor of publishing my martial arts biography in the AMAAF Special Tribute to Bill "Superfoot" Wallace edition of the Changing Lives Series Biography Book, Volume 7, in 2022.
- Featured in the Martial Arts Extraordinaire Magazine, Issue 6, in 2023 for being named a new black belt member of the American Martial Arts Alliance, LLC.

continuously pursue my goals and aspirations.

Studying martial arts has also kept me focused and mentally strong during challenging seasons of life, such as the deaths of my parents, grandparents, and pets, in addition to romantic relationships and friendships ending. The dojo is the only place where I can shut out all the negatives in my life and focus only on my karate. In addition to this, the longer I study martial arts, the more I find myself becoming increasingly humble, calm, respectful, and patient with others as well as myself.

Studying martial arts has given me confidence and a sense of peace, knowing I can defend myself and my loved ones if the situation should arise in this unpredictable world. Lastly, studying martial arts has brought many friends and amazing individuals into my life, including classmates and instructors. If I had to change anything about my study of martial arts, I would have started studying much earlier in life.

Become an
AMAA
MEMBER!

Todd ANGEL

"
Martial Arts has given me a generous and indomitable spirit.

WHY THE *Martial Arts?*

As a teenager, I got into many fights and encountered bullies in my neighborhood. The frequent altercations, coupled with being drawn to martial arts through books and movies- Chuck Norris, Bruce Lee, Cynthia Rothrock, Sho Kosugi, to name a few. I talked my parents into letting me try Taekwondo. From the first moment, it was like I had found my space, which I truly loved. I grew up wrestling and playing Soccer and Basketball, but Martial arts has been my lifelong passion.

TRAINING INFORMATION

- Martial Arts Styles & Rank: Taekwondo -7th Dan, World Taekwondo Changmookwan -6th Dan, Zenkei Ryu Karate-5th Dan, Brazilian Jiu Jitsu- Brown Belt 2 stripe
- Instructors/Influencers: Grand Master Hong Kong Kim, Grand Master Bobby Clayton, Grand Master Rafael Medina, Grand Master Michael Bennett, Kyoshi William Frizzell
- Birthplace/Growing Up: Hamilton, OH / Fairfield, OH
- Yrs. In the Martial Arts: 38 years
- Yrs. Instructing: 20 years
- School owner & Instructor at ParaBellum Martial Arts and Strength

PROFESSIONAL ORGANIZATIONS

- US Armed Forces
- World Taekwondo Changmookwan
- Puerto Rico Changmookwan
- Power Athlete Methodology Block One Coach
- US Military Taekwondo Foundation
- Amateur Athletic Union
- Mason

How MARTIAL ARTS CHANGED My Life!

Martial Arts has given me a generous and indomitable spirit. I read a quote from a Korean Martial Arts Master who was taken as a prisoner of war during the Viet Nam war; he said something to the effect of "They could try to take everything from me; my food, sleep, and my clothing, but they could never take Taekwondo from me." As a young martial artist, this impacted me greatly.

I have served in combat; there were situations where I could have been taken as a prisoner of war-thankfully, I wasn't, but that sentiment weighed heavily on my mind.

As I grew in martial arts, I realized it was just a description of embodying an "Indomitable Spirit." This is so powerful that I decided to dedicate my life to sharing this with others. I carry this Indomitable Spirit with me in everything I do; I was diagnosed with HPV-related throat cancer at age 47. This was only six months after my wife had finished treatment for Breast cancer- it could have been easy to be beaten down and defeated. There is nothing harder than watching the love of your life fight cancer! Her fight, along with mine, while still running a full-time martial arts academy, gave me the opportunity to channel and develop my own indomitable spirit. I don't say this because it is something miraculous; many people battle through much worse, but I say that to say that I am grateful to the Lord above for allowing me to share this gift of martial arts and to allow me to have met and meet the great people that I have

PERSONAL ACHIEVEMENTS

- Retired from the US Army after 21.5 years of faithful service
- Married to Holly Angel for 27 years and father of 2 grown children (Payton (daughter); Todd James (Son)
- Owner and head coach of Parabellum Martial Arts and Strength for six years (7 years in September).
- While serving in the Army, I started martial arts clubs at each of the installations that did not have one established (Fort Leonard Wood, Belgium, and Joint Base Langley-Eustis).

MAJOR ACHIEVEMENTS

- Achieved Master Instructor Rank in Taekwondo and Karate.
- US Open National Taekwondo medalist
- World Open Karate medalist
- Member of All Army Taekwondo Team
- Coached and developed World and Pan Am Brazilian Jiu-Jitsu medalists
- Coached Nationally ranked Professional and Amateur Mixed Martial Arts Champions
- Coached Taekwondo National Champions
- Weightlifting and Powerlifting National and World medalists (drug tested)

been exposed to. I apologize if this is too long. That is the impact that martial arts has had on my life.

How has Grandmaster CYNTHIA ROTHROCK Influenced me?

I began my martial study in the 80s. At that time, I was trying to ingest anything I could find regarding martial arts. I was constantly checking out books from the library, watching movies, and reading martial arts publications. Watching GM Rothrock compete and perform in her movies gave us all an example to aspire to. She continues to be an example of perseverance and indomitable spirit with her longevity in the martial arts.

Become an AMAA MEMBER!

Holly
ARNOLD

"

Each one of my students has a special place in my heart...

WHY THE *Martial Arts?*

In 1996 Holly Arnold was attacked at a local grocery store, where she had to fend off multiple attackers. After this incident, she knew she needed help with self-defense and didn't want anything like this to happen to her or her family in the future. She enrolled herself and two young kids, ages 4 and 6, into American Taekwondo under the tutelage of Grand Master Bramer, Billy Smith, and Steve Parks.

Karate has been Holly's passion throughout the years. She volunteers as a women's and children's self-defense instructor to help them defend themselves from domestic violence, bullying, and trafficking. She enjoys teaching karate and assisting kids to find confidence, self-discipline, respect, and courage.

Holly is now a 5th degree Black Belt who teaches under Grand Master Billy Smith in Burleson, Texas. She is a community pillar and a North Texas Karate Association (NTKA) tournament board member. She was presented in the United States Martial Arts Hall of Fame in 2022 for her dedication and passion for her students.

TRAINING INFORMATION

- Martial Arts Styles & Rank: American Karate-5th Dan
- Instructors/Influencers: Grand Master Bramer, Grand Master Billy Smith, Grand Master Steve Parks
- Birthplace/Growing Up: Columbus, OH / Fort Worth, TX
- Yrs. In the Martial Arts: 27 years
- Yrs. Instructing: 5 years
- School owner & Instructor at BSAK

PROFESSIONAL ORGANIZATIONS

- North Texas Karate Alliance
- Billy Smith American Karate
- United States Martial Arts Hall of Fame

How MARTIAL ARTS CHANGED *My Life!*

"Each one of my students has a special place in my heart. I have seen them grow confident, face trials, and excel over hardships. They continue to strive, and I continue to teach. I will always be there to cheer them on, praise their confidence and support their futures."

Micah ASHBY

> " Martial Arts has taught me patience. Everything takes its own time in the universe, and I must accept that and not rush the process.

WHY THE *Martial Arts?*

As a child, I had watched and was intimidated by movie characters such as the Power Rangers, Walker Texas Ranger, Buffy, and China O'Brien.

However, I truly started in martial arts as a teenager due to being bullied in school as a child. I lacked confidence and was bullied for my big afro hair and skinny physique.

I wanted to be able to feel confident enough to hold my head up to people and the ability to defend myself if needed.

I began training in Brazilian Jiu-Jitsu as a gym was close to my house. After a few years of training, I eventually put the GI down and went to professional wrestling with no success due to being too 'slim' for the wrestling standards.

Shortly after, I returned to BJJ and also began training in MMA. My career would catapult during my early adulthood, with my sole focus being to become better and stronger than before by setting a goal to become a champion.

TRAINING INFORMATION

- Martial Arts Styles & Rank: Brazilian Jiu-Jitsu-Black Belt, MMA
- Instructors/Influencers: Charles Ontiveros, Andrew Bourgeois
- Birthplace/Growing Up: Dallas, TX / Dublin, Ireland
- Yrs. In the Martial Arts: 18 years
- Yrs. Instructing: 6 years
- Instructor

PROFESSIONAL ORGANIZATIONS

- Hard Head Hitters
- Magic Kingdom Academy

How MARTIAL ARTS CHANGED My Life!

My life has been impacted by martial arts by discipline. Martial Arts has taught me nothing will be handed to you. Dedication, hard work, and determination can obtain everything you dream of.

Martial Arts has taught me patience. Everything takes its own time in the universe, and I must accept that and not rush the process. As a Martial Artist, we set high standards for ourselves and never settle. Sometimes we feel the goal is not coming fast enough, but we see through focus that it is on the horizon.

How has Grandmaster CYNTHIA ROTHROCK Influenced me?

Grandmaster Rothrock was a cornerstone of my childhood with her movie "China O'Brien." I used to watch the VHS on repeat to the point I ended up burning out the VHS tape.

Her martial arts skills showed me the strength of a woman and how I wanted to raise my future daughter to be like.

PERSONAL ACHIEVEMENTS

- Remaining undefeated in MMA
- Fighting in multiple weight classes
- Winning the Texas Grappling Tournament

MAJOR ACHIEVEMENTS

- US Open MMA Lightweight Champion
- NAGA World Jiu-Jitsu Champion
- Professional Wrestling Tag Team Champion
- 2013 Fighter of the Year
- 2019 Grappler of the Year
- 2022 US Martial Arts Hall of Fame
- 2023 International Martial Arts Hall of Fame

Michael
BENNETT

"

Learning and studying martial arts impacted my life in many ways by starting off meeting great people to look up to.

WHY THE *Martial Arts?*

I started my martial arts training because my mom was worried about me defending myself because my brothers were in college. So she enrolled me in a Kung Fu class which started my martial arts career. I was able to learn how not to be afraid of achieving my status as a great martial artist.

Become an
AMAA
MEMBER!

TRAINING INFORMATION

- Martial Arts Styles & Rank: Grandmaster in CMK and KKW-7th Dan Black Belts, Master in Ju Bushi Do-5th Dan Black Belts, Black Belt in Aikido-1st Dan, Black Slash in Kung Fu
- Instructors/Influencers: GM Rafael Medina, GM Bobby Clayton, GM Carroll Baker, GM Robert Scott, Sensei David Ruffin, Sinfu Lee
- Birthplace/Growing Up: Shreveport, LA
- Yrs. In the Martial Arts: 52 years
- Yrs. Instructing: 40 years
- Instructor, Coach

PROFESSIONAL ORGANIZATIONS

- United States Army (retired)
- Federal Police Officer (retired)
- United States Military Taekwondo Foundation
- Masonry

How MARTIAL ARTS CHANGED My Life!

Learning and studying martial arts impacted my life in many ways by starting off meeting great people to look up to. It has given me the confidence to achieve anything I desire. My parents were my role models, but learning and meeting martial artists helped to build my character into what I am today. Martial arts have helped me impact the youth of America by teaching them how to be good citizens and stewards in their neighborhoods and how to be great parents.

PERSONAL ACHIEVEMENTS

- Graduated in Computer Programming with a Bachelor of Science from Southern University A&M College in Baton Rouge, Louisiana
- Graduated in Criminal Justice with an Associate Degree of Science from Houston Community College in Houston, Texas
- Finishing my Bachelor's Degree in Criminal Justice at Texas Southern University in Houston, Texas

MAJOR ACHIEVEMENTS

- Joining the All Army Taekwondo
- U.S. National Taekwondo Medalist
- U.S. Open Taekwondo Medalist
- U.S. Taekwondo Team Try-Out for the Olympics
- Serving 24 years in the U. S. Army: deployed to Iraq five times; Afghanistan; Panama; and other deployments
- Becoming a Police Officer and becoming a Federal Police Officer
- Becoming the National Junior Warden PHO Masonic Compacts of the United States in America

How has Grandmaster CYNTHIA ROTHROCK Influenced me?

As I was growing up, looking at these great martial artists, Cynthia Rothrock was one of the people who could show you a better way of life or experience in becoming a great person. Looking at her action-packed movies, she helped me understand not to limit myself in achieving my goals in life. There are so many things to say about Cynthia Rothrock, but this is what I will say, she is "Super Great"!

Kimberly BLAKE

"

I am blessed to continue my studies as a student, a Sensei, and a Professor on and off the mats.

WHY THE *Martial Arts?*

I began training in martial arts at 42 (currently 60). My interest in martial arts started at 13 when an after-school martial arts class was offered at my Jr. High School. Unfortunately, my father wouldn't consent because he said: "girls did not participate in combative sports." This was very hard for me to accept, but I still had my love for Bruce Lee and martial arts films.

It wasn't until I was 41 that I was posed with the question by my friend and mentor, Dr. Brenda Lloyd-Jones, "What is stopping you from achieving this dream now?" So, with the realization of having nothing to stop me, I enrolled in Karate class at Apollo's Martial Arts right after my 42nd birthday.

TRAINING INFORMATION

- Martial Arts Styles & Rank: 5th Degree Black Belt in Karate, Kickboxing and Japanese Jiu Jitsu, 2nd Degree Black Belt in Ketsugo, 1st Degree Black Belt in BJJ
- Instructors/Influencers: BJJ: Master Carlos Machado, Karate: Dale Cook, Randy M. Blake, Jr., Ketsugo: Dr. Patrick Sharp, Robert Hale
- Birthplace/Growing Up: Cleveland, OH
- Yrs. In the Martial Arts: 18.5 years
- Yrs. Instructing: 11 years
- Instructor

PROFESSIONAL ORGANIZATIONS

- Carlos Machado Affiliate Member
- IBJJF Athlete
- USA Martial Arts Hall of Fame
- Universal Martial Arts Hall of Fame
- Oklahoma Karate Association
- Sponsored by "The Athletes Sports Bag"
- Sponsored by " Elite Sports Company
- American Martial Arts Alliance Foundation

How MARTIAL ARTS CHANGED My Life!

Beginning my martial arts journey at 42 and still active after 18 years has taken me across many like-minded journeys and crossed paths with many amazing people. Seeding my journey into the lives of girls and women across the globe is very rewarding and enjoyable. I am blessed to continue my studies as a student, a Sensei, and a Professor on and off the mats. I have competed locally, regionally, nationally, and internationally. There is much to obtain and pass on to others I meet. This is my purpose.

PERSONAL ACHIEVEMENTS

- Girls in Gis Ambassador
- Grappling Getaways Brand Ambassador
- Sponsored by "The Athletes Sports Bag"
- Sponsored by " Elite Sports Company
- Retired from BP Pipelines NA 12/31/20
- Became a grandmother for the first time on 2/3/21

MAJOR ACHIEVEMENTS

- First Female BJJ Blackbelt in the State of Oklahoma
- First African American Female BJJ Black Belt under Carlos Machado Affiliation
- Tulsa, Oklahoma Impact Woman of Color of the Year
- 2x World Champion BJJ Master
- Ranked #3 Internationally for BJJ Female Black Belt Master 6
- 22 State Championships
- Multiple National Championships
- 40+ Karate Grand Championships
- Lifetime Achievement Award by the Whirlwind Classic Tournament
- 2nd Degree Black Belt Ketsugo under Harold Brosius
- 5th Degree Black Belt in Karate under Dale Cook
- 2017 USA Martial Arts Hall of Fame Inductee
- 2021 AAMA Inductee
- 2021 Universal Martial Arts Hall of Fame Inductee
- 2021 Sport Karate Museum Honoree
- 2021 Girls in Gis Black Belt Co-Instructor
- 2023 International Best-Selling Co-Author in the Elite Martial Artists in America Compilation Book

How has Grandmaster CYNTHIA ROTHROCK Influenced me?

Grandmaster Rothrock has devoted her life to Martial Arts. Pursuing black belts in multiple disciplines; is very impressive and inspiring. I started my journey late and was moments away from meeting her in 2014 at an Expo. I had met several male legends and was overly excited to meet a female Legend, but our paths did not cross that day. I will be honored to meet her finally. She is a strong pillar that I look up to in strong female Martial Artists.

Become an
AMAA MEMBER!

Randy
BLAKE, JR.

"

I've had a chance to travel worldwide as far as Japan. All of this came from a kid with no confidence who was bullied. I am forever grateful.

WHY THE *Martial Arts?*

I was bullied hard and bullied often early at the age of six. Every day after school, the same kid would come to me and punch me a few times. Shortly after, it always seemed to have ended in a headlock. I would let this kid have his way because I figured he would leave me alone. After a few weeks of these incidents, my aunt picked me up from school one day and recognized a big blob of spit in my hair, and she freaked out. Little did I know that headlock resulted from being spit on, which happened daily to me. Around this same time, I watched the movie "Blood Sports "by Jean Claude Van Dame almost daily. This movie inspired me to practice the moves I'd watch this man do because I thought he was pretty awesome, and I'd even do full splits like him. Once my mother (Kim Blake) found out about the bullying, she purchased me a hard canvassed Everlast bag and enrolled me in karate shortly after.

TRAINING INFORMATION

- Martial Arts Styles & Rank: Karate-5th Degree,Taekwondo, Aikijutsu, Goshin jujitsu, Kickboxing, Boxing
- Instructors/Influencers: Sylvester Meola, Jimmy Meola, David Vogtman, Peppe Johnson, Mike Eagen, Dale Cook
- Birthplace/Growing Up: East Cleveland, OH
- Yrs. In the Martial Arts: 30 years
- Yrs. Instructing: 17 years
- Instructor, 5-time World Champion

PROFESSIONAL ORGANIZATIONS

- ISKA - International Sport Kickboxing and Karate Association
- USA Martial Arts Hall of Fame
- AMAA- American Martial Arts Alliance

How MARTIAL ARTS CHANGED My Life!

After a few karate classes, I thought I was just as "bad to the bone" as I felt Jean Claude Van Dame was. I had been bullied weeks and months prior, and I thought I had what it truly took to get this bully to leave me alone finally. Once confronted again, I swung punches and kicks (in my head, I looked just like Jean Claude Van Dame) so hard that the bully seriously ran off and never bothered me again. That was the moment I knew martial arts was for me. I instantly gained confidence, improved my grades, and excelled in karate.

By the time I graduated high school, I had headed to college. I tried basketball and could walk on the team, but things didn't feel right. I dropped out of college and moved back home with my parents. I relived the dream back in martial arts, and things felt normal again. An instructor invited me to join the fighter's class because he thought I would be good at it based on my performance in karate class. I kindly turned down the offer but accepted it months later and gave it a shot. I soon fought for Chuck Norris' World Combat League (WCL), K-1, and Glory. I captured World Titles in Kickboxing and Muay Thai. I've had a chance to travel worldwide, as far as Japan. All of this came from a kid with no confidence who was bullied. I am forever grateful.

PERSONAL ACHIEVEMENTS

- Father
- Best-Selling Author
- Motivational Speaker
- Certified Life Coach
- Martial Artist of 30 years
- 16 years competing in kickboxing
- 52 wins, 7 losses, 35 KO's

MAJOR ACHIEVEMENTS

- 5-Time ISKA World Heavyweight Champion
- 2017 USA Martial Arts Hall of Fame Inductee
- 2012 - ISKA World Champion (Muay Thai)
- 2015 - ISKA World Champion (Kickboxing)
- 2016 - ISKA World Champion (Kickboxing)
- 2018 - ISKA World Champion (Muay Thai)
- 2019 - ISKA World Champion (Kickboxing)
- Chuck Norris' World Combat League (WCL) Veteran
- K-1 veteran
- Glory veteran

Snake
BLOCKER

"

Martial Arts has given me the courage to stand up for those scared, unwilling, or unable to help themselves.

WHY THE *Martial Arts?*

My influence to start martial arts came from watching Kung Fu Theatre, Bruce Lee movies, and the Kung Fu series. As a weak child and young boy growing up and one of the shortest boys in my class, I was picked on and bullied. Martial arts gave me the confidence and courage to stand up for myself and others.

How MARTIAL ARTS CHANGED *My Life!*

Martial Arts has allowed me to help many others become better protectors of the innocent. Society needs brave boys and girls and brave ladies and gentlemen. Evil is all around. It is in the small towns and the big cities. Evil never rests, and it lives in every corner of the world. Therefore, we need more people with the courage to step up. Sometimes, it is as simple as a few words, and sometimes it requires a warrior to step up and be willing to be the

TRAINING INFORMATION

- Martial Arts Styles & Rank: Master Instructor-Jeet Kune Do, 15th Khan-Muay Thai, 8th Dan-Balisong Knife Fighting, Silver Glove-Savate, 6th Dan-Scientific Fighting Congress Knife-Counter, 4th Dan-Kenpo, 4th Dan-Filipino Arnis, 4th Dan-Moo Duk Kwan Tae Kwon Do, 1st Dan-Kajukenbo, Brown II-Kodenkan Jiu-Jitsu, Instructor & Brown Belt -Shoot-Fighting/Wrestling, Purple Belt-II Jiu-Jitsu Global Federation Brazilian Jiu-Jitsu

- Instructors/Influencers: Dan Inosanto, Taky Kimura, Andy Kimura, Chris Kent, Tim Tackett, Gary Dill, Paul Vunak, James Demiles, Rick Mullinax, Ron Robes, Daniel Sulivan, Dennis Eli, Kai Li, Rod Kei, Clint Heyliger, Ric "Lek Suer" Sniffen, Frediun 'Iceman' Younossi, Carlos Silva. Steve Rodarte, Lorenzo Rodriques, John McCurry, Jean-Pierre Julemont, Nicolas Saignac, Rod Kei, Guy Chase. Ezequias Gonçalves Dos Santo, Salem Assli, W. Hock Hochheim, Joong K. Nam, Donald Cummins, Patrick Campbell, Daniel Saragosa, Bart Vale, Sam Muratore, Joe Moreira, Wander Braga

- Birthplace/Growing Up: Los Angeles, CA

- Yrs. In the Martial Arts: 45 years

- Yrs. Instructing: 28 years

- School owner & Instructor at Blocker Academy of Martial Arts

PROFESSIONAL ORGANIZATIONS

- Jiu-Jitsu Global Federation (JJGF) - Affiliate School, Practitioner & Educational Unit Member #5258

- Joe Moreira Brazilian Jiu-Jitsu - Affiliate School

- Wander Braga Brazilian Jiu-Jitsu - Affiliate School

strength for the weak. Martial Arts has given me the courage to stand up for those scared, unwilling, or unable to help themselves. Martial Arts have helped me in my law enforcement career. It has helped me during my 20 years in the Navy, and it has helped me be a mentor to many others. I love all martial arts and am always willing to wear my white belt all over again to learn a new art. Martial Arts have helped me with my Native community. I am a member of the Apache Nation, Lipan Apache Tribe of Texas, Sun Otter Band, and Herron Warrior Clan. I encourage all my tribal relatives to take up martial arts, as we have a great history of warriors. Keep up the traditions!

PROFESSIONAL ORGANIZATIONS

- American Jiu-Jitsu Institute - Charter School #4411
- USA Savate Federation
- Scientific Fighting Congress
- Saksithaawk Pontawee Camp International
- United States Muay Thai Association
- Progressive Fighting System Contemporary Jeet Kune Do
- Gary Dill's Jeet Kune Do Association
- Jun Fan Gung Fu Institute, Seattle Affiliate
- Jeet Kune Do Street Fighting System
- Jun Fan Jeet Kune Do Fellowship
- International Kenpo Karate Academies

PERSONAL ACHIEVEMENTS

- United States Muay Thai Association Honor Award
- Appointed National & International Director of the Native American League Muay Thai Association
- Appointed Vice-President of the Universal Balisong Society
- Confederacao Brasileira De Kickboxing Tradicional Brazil Master's Council: Designated Muay Thai Kru Suuan (Master Instructor) Diploma (#CBKBT-852-USA/BRAZIL).The Honor of Merit Diploma - Muay Thai/Thai Boxing BS Hall Da Fama Brasileiro (Brazilian Martial Arts Hall of Fame)
- Saksithaawk Pontawee Camp International: Designated Muay Kru Yai (Fully Licensed Instructor) - License #090620162220-USA
- World University: Grandes Metres Das Artes Marciais (Martial Arts Grand Master (GM)).
- Karate & Kung Fu Expo: Masters of Martial Arts Award - Pioneer in Martial Arts Masters of the Martial Arts Hall of Fame
- Philadelphia Martial Arts Society (PHMAS) Hall of Fame
- VITA SAANA/BITMA Martial Arts Hall of Fame
- Action Martial Arts Magazine Hall of Honor (AMAM Medal of Honor): Ambassador of Goodwill to the Martial Arts; Outstanding Achievements in the Martial Arts; Esteemed Modern Warrior
- In Hoc Signo Vinces Hall of Fame: Outstanding Contribution to the Martial Arts.
- RAVEN Tactical Hall of Fame: Tactical Military Combatives Instructor of the Year

How has Grandmaster CYNTHIA ROTHROCK Influenced me?

Grandmaster Cynthia Rothrock has influenced me many times. I have followed her career for years. She is an inspiration to many of us, especially those of us that started years ago in the kickboxing community. I love her energy and style. She is a legend; she has accomplished so much thus far and never stops. May God continue to bless her and her loved ones. I never give up, and I surround myself with many grandmasters and masters that have overcome great obstacles. It drives me to continue my journey in the martial arts.

MAJOR ACHIEVEMENTS

- Colorado Technical University: Bachelor of Science Degree in Management (Magna Cum Laude); Master of Science Degree in Project Management.

- US Navy Retired Veteran - Tours: Kuwait, Iraq, Afghanistan, USNS Mercy (Los Angeles)

- Requested by name to be featured for a permanent life-size 100-year Navy Reserve display celebrating the Centennial of the USA Navy Reserve (Display at Pentagon, Washington DC)

- Featured on the cover with other sailors for The Navy Reserve (TNR) Almanac 2017 magazine

- Navy First Class Petty Officer Association (FCPOA), Denver - President

- Navy Operational Support Center (NOSC) Sailor of the Year (SOY): NOSC Denver SAILOR OF THE YEAR 2012.

- Shriner's Medal of Honor Medal & Certificate for 6th Annual Uniform Service Recognition

- Chamber of Commerce Aurora, Colorado

- Chamber of Commerce Military Person of the Year (MPOY) 2012

Become an
AMAA
MEMBER!

Jessie BOWEN

> "
> Self-discipline is a critical life skill that enables you to succeed in anything you choose to do.

WHY THE *Martial Arts?*

In 2015, Grand Master Jessie Bowen started on a path to write the history of his generation in the martial arts and the pioneers who helped them move forward. Now, Jessie Bowen is taking an entirely new step in the Martial Artists Who's Who in the Martial Arts and Changing Lives Series Biography Book Series.

"This year, we're writing about the stars of today and tomorrow and letting everyone in our industry know about them, from newcomers to industry leaders. Then, we help these stars of today and tomorrow use the tools they have to tell students everywhere about the benefits of martial arts," Grand Master Bowen says. "These methods are meant to build from the ground up to meet the great achievements of the Lifetime Achievers and Pioneers who paved the way for today's martial artists."

TRAINING INFORMATION

- Belt Ranks & Martial Arts Styles: 10th Degree Black Belt
- Instructors/Influencers: Jan Wellendorf, Joe Lewis, Bill Wallace, Dan McFarland
- Birthdate: September 6, 1953
- Birthplace/Growing Up: Washington, NC
- Yrs. In the Martial Arts: 46 years
- Yrs. Instructing: 45 years
- School Owner (Karate International of Durham, Inc), Instructor, Manager, Author

PROFESSIONAL ORGANIZATIONS

- American Martial Arts Alliance
- Professional Karate Association

GRAND MASTER JESSIE BOWEN—4.8 DECADES OF FOCUS:

Jessie Bowen started his study in the Martial Arts in 1975 under the direction of Grandmaster Jan Wellendorf, co-founder of Karate International of North Carolina. As with most individuals that begin to study the martial arts, he was intrigued. There wasn't a mystical impetus for Jessie Bowen, rather he was motivated by a "nobody better mess with me" desire for becoming a great martial artist. His initial reason for joining the martial arts school then was out of desperation, and at the age of 21 he made the conscious decision that he would no longer be picked on.

Through elementary, middle, and high school, he was picked on and almost lost his life several times. As he looks back on it now, it was never because he couldn't defend himself, it was because of the lack of courage. One of Hanshi Bowen's coworkers had threatened to beat him up, and Jessie then learned his threat came from a black belt in Taekwondo. Jessie had never heard of Taekwondo, but he had recently seen Enter the Dragon and saw what Bruce Lee did to his opponents. Jessie's initial thought was "I need to learn some form of self-defense NOW." That is the moment that changed his life and for decades now he has been committed to empowering others physically, mentally and spiritually.

Hanshi Jessie Bowen spent the first three years of his martial arts study as a student, instructor, and competitor. He began teaching the martial arts full time as an instructor for O'Sensei Wellendorf and built a reputation of his own in Sport Karate.

ACCOMPLISHMENTS & ACHIEVEMENTS

- Action Martial Arts Magazine Hall of Fame as the 2014 Ambassador of Goodwill to the Martial Arts Member Solution Financial Services Top Achiever Award
- NRC Business Man of the Year
- American Martial Arts Association Hall of Fame Leadership Award
- Established Mastermind-Sports Performance Virtual Coaching Service
- American Martial Arts Alliance Sport Karate Tournament Promoter of the Year
- Action Martial Arts Magazine Martial Arts Instructor of the Year
- Certified Sports Hypnotist
- Certified Silva Method Lecture Developer Trainer
- Certified Silva Method Lecturer
- American Martial Arts Freestyle Golden Lifetime Achievement Award
- American Martial Arts Association Hall of Fame Man of the Year Award
- National Business Advisory Business Man of the Year Recipient of Super Star Black Belt Hall of Fame Living Legend Award 2003
- 2002 World Cup, Karate World Champion
- Black Belt Super Star Hall of Fame, WHO'S WHO in the Martial Arts Award
- Universal Martial Arts Hall of Fame Inductee as Outstanding Grand Master of the Year
- United States Karate Hall of Fame inductee as Most Distinguished Grand Master of the Year
- United States Karate Hall of Fame Inductee as Most Distinguished Grand Master of the Year
- World Karate Union Hall of Fame Inductee as Grand Master of the Year

Hanshi Jessie Bowen became known throughout the Southeast for his martial arts skills in Form, Weapons, and Fighting. He then took his first career step. The American Martial Arts Association was the first martial arts organization to offer a business degree in Martial Arts Management. Hanshi Bowen was one of its first graduates. The program was mandatory for anyone wanting to own a Karate International Franchise.

His school, Karate International of Durham, was founded in 1980, by Hanshi Jessie Bowen, as a Karate International franchise school under the Karate International brand.

Since opening, Hanshi Bowen has promoted more than 400 students to black belt. He has been recognized by organizations throughout the country for his contribution to the martial arts. He was one of the first martial arts instructors to integrate martial arts into sports. He started with Coach Dick Crum, Football Coach at the University of North Carolina at Chapel Hill in the mid 80's. He was also a Martial Arts Performance Coach for four seasons under Coach Mack Brown, former UNC Football Coach. He was also a Personal Trainer for Duke University Basketball star, Carlos Boozer and others.

After winning more than 2000 trophies and awards in martial arts competitions, Hanshi Bowen believed the next evolution in martial arts performance was in the mind. He is a certified Life Coach, Sports Hypnosis Coach, NLP Coach, Silva Life System Seminar Facilitator, and Mindfulness Coach.

ACCOMPLISHMENTS & ACHIEVEMENTS

- United States Karate Hall of Fame Inductee as Grand Master of the Year
- Sport Karate Tournament Promoter of the Year
- Sports Coordinator for the US Olympic Committee and North Carolina Amateur Sports for the US Olympic Festival, Tae Kwon Do competition in 1987
- Sports Coordinator for North Carolina Amateur Sports in Karate and Bowling
- Professional Bowler - PBA Tour Member
- USBC Bowling Coach
- Bowling Instructor Duke University
- Director of the nationally ranked Durham Karate Open tournament since 1981
- Action Martial Arts Magazine Award- Organization of the Year
- Action Martial Arts Magazine award- Excellence in Radio & Media Coverage
- Masters of the Martial Arts Award
- Action Martial Arts Magazine Award- Contribution in Publishing in the Martial Arts
- AFKA Award-Excellence in Martial Arts Journalism
- 2021 - Presidential Lifetime Achievement Award
- 2021 - Grandmasters Hall of Fame
- 2023 - Action Martial Arts Magazine Excellence in Publishing in the Martial Arts
- 2023 - World Head of Family/Sokeship Council Leadership Award
- 2023 - London International Hall of Fame Media Publication of the Year Award

Hanshi Bowen learned to apply the principles of martial arts and sports mind game coaching into Bowling, winning over 40 amateur titles before becoming a PBA Member (Professional Bowlers Association) in 2002. He became the Bowling Instructor for Duke University and Performance Coach for NCCU Women's Bowling Team, winning NCCU's first CIAA title.

O'Sensei Jan Wellendorf sanctioned the advancement of Hanshi Jessie Bowen to 10th Degree Black Belt and assigned him the task of creating his own system of Martial Arts Aiki-Shinkai Karate. Aiki means to fit, join or combine energy. Aiki is a Japanese martial arts principle or tactic in which the defender blends (without crashing) with the attacker, then goes on to dominate the assailant through the strength of their application of internal dynamics or Ki energy to effect techniques. Shinkai means the opening of uncultivated land, new frontiers.

Become an
AMAA MEMBER!

THE WHO'S WHO IN THE MARTIAL ARTS, MASTERS & PIONEERS AND THE CHANGING LIVES BOOK SERIES REPRESENTS NEW FRONTIERS, JOINING HIS PREVIOUS SUCCESSFUL EXPLORATIONS:

- Hanshi Bowen has written 18 books on Mind-Body Personal Development Training including Zen Bowling the Psychology of Better Bowling; The New You Self Discovery System; and Zen Mind-Body Mindfulness Meditation Training.

- In 2017 he was the recipient of the Action Martial Arts Hall of Honors award for the Who's Who in the Martial Arts Book and the 2017 AFKA Hall of Fame Martial Arts Journalism Award,

- In 2019 Action Martial Arts Magazine Hall of Honors presented another Award for his Online Media Blogtalk Radio,

- In 2018 & 2019 Jessie Bowen also received the Action Martial Arts Magazine Hall of Honors Martial Arts Organization of the Year awards.

How has Grandmaster CYNTHIA ROTHROCK Influenced me?

Cynthia Rothrock has been an icon for martial artists in sport karate and movies and as a mentor for martial artists worldwide. Competing against Cynthia in my early career was exhilarating and challenging all at the same time. She could mesmerize you with her technique and skills and become the person you sought to possess those same attributes of technique and performance. And later in her movie career, she set forth the place for women in martial arts today. She is still doing the same things of laying the groundwork for the future of women in martial arts.

Guy BRACALI-GAMBINO

> **"**
> Martial Arts helped my confidence to communicate and teach people to help break through barriers.

WHY THE *Martial Arts?*

I was eleven years of age in 1976; I would read magazines about martial arts superstars. I did not think I would be trained by some of them, let alone be on their teams someday, daydreaming about being like them. Martial arts world champions such as 12X World Champion Tony Satch Williams, multiple-time World Champion Woody Sims on Bay Area's Best, and World Champion Tami Whelan on Team Full Contact.

During the Bruce Lee era, we grew up in a neighborhood called Santa Venetia/San Rafael, CA, and my best friend's older brother, Staff Sergeant Fred Montero, a known neighborhood martial artist, took me by the hand to my first class. My first instructor was a former Green Beret and Sensei, Gus Johnson. In my late teens, I studied Muay Thai and Kickboxing. In 1983 I moved to Oroville, California, and started work as a bouncer. During that time, I met my Chinese Kenpo instructor, 3rd Degree Black Belt

TRAINING INFORMATION

- Martial Arts Styles & Rank: Chinese Kenpo-5th Degree, Shorin-Ryu 5th Degree, Kosho Shorei Ryu Kempo-1st Degree, Tong Soo Do, Kickboxing, Muay Thai, Arnis, Tae Kwon Do

- Instructors/Influencers: Grandmaster Bruce Juchnik, Master Lim Sison, Gus Johnson, Tony "Satch" Williams, Master Ron Cox

- Birthplace/Growing Up: Bay Area, Marin County, CA

- Yrs. In the Martial Arts: 47 years

- Yrs. Instructing: 37 years

- Former school owner & Master Instructor at Bracali's Martial Arts Academy

PERSONAL ACHIEVEMENTS

- My five children

- Several wards from IMACF

- Best instructor of the year two years in a row IMACF

- Best Competitor of the Year IMACF

- Best Official of the Year for 2 years IMACF

- 2021 Best Choreography for Eryx and the Void IMDb

Ron Cox. I trained with his Grand Master, Bruce Juchnik. Bruce became my Grandmaster in Chinese Kenpo and Kosho Shorei - Ryu Kempo. In 1989 I began training in Taekwondo NCTA, then on to WTF. In the late 80s, I was ranked in the PKL Professional Karate League and competed in the IMACF from 1984-1995. I won several awards as an instructor as well as a competitor. From 1993-1995 I competed professionally in the National Blackbelt League NBL.

My good friend/brother Paul Mendoza tried to form me as a point fighter from kickboxing which was hilarious. I was known to punch and kick guys through scoreboards and get disqualified in the first round. I got lucky if I advanced to the second fight. My coaching was great for my students, but I had too much full contact in my background. Paul significantly impacted my life as a fighter by understanding the full-contact point fighting as I describe today. A full-contact point fighter is like being a sniper with your hands and feet. You don't get a second chance against the wrong opponent. So, by becoming a better point fighter, I became more precise in my techniques and took control of the fight. Paul made the bay area's best national karate team in 1993. I followed shortly thereafter and made the team as the Number 2 super heavyweight; Woody Sims was number one, and I was their brick breaker. I began training with Tony Satch Williams, and we became a very close family. He lived with me during the summers. I then made Team Full Contact in 1994, Zane Fraiser (former Boston Celtics) was the #1 Super Heavyweight on the team, and I was the #2 Super Heavyweight and

MAJOR ACHIEVEMENTS

- Master Combative Instructor
- Department of Defense Contractor
- Bail Enforcement Agent
- IMDb Martial Arts Military Choreography
- Brick Breaking World Records 109 two-inch concrete blocks in 9.1 seconds; the previous record holder was 100 blocks in 19 seconds
- The first man to do a free dive 12 feet and break a two-inch block underwater
- I am preparing for the Navy Seal Legacy Foundation with my good friend, former Navy Seal Reuben (Red) Lowing as open water 30 meters deep, 6 inches of concrete with bull sharks, hammerheads, and tiger sharks in the Gulf of Texas to raise money for our fallen / Navy Seals this summer 2023

WHY MARTIAL ARTS (CONTINUED)

their brick-breaker. Then in 1995, I made Team USA Australia Goodwill Games, Olympic Center. I received an endorsement from US Congressman Wally Herger.

Several years later, I got into bail enforcement and training in the US Military as a master combative instructor and DOD Government Security Contractor. It was the best time in my life other than fathering my children, hanging out, training with, and competing on the same team with men and women I read about in Black Belt Magazine. I wanted to hit harder than Tony Satch Williams. One day he and I were sparring, and he got mad because he thought I hit him hard. He said, "Don't hit me like that again." I told him, "I barely hit you!"

Besides that, I trained my students who had nothing in a town where nothing existed. I kept them out of gangs and gained the respect of several gang members. I took them camping and boating and competed all over California and Nevada. We were a big family, and our

National Demo Team was 4X National Champions.

My first NBL World Title was in 1993. I called my father from New Orleans to Tiburon, California, at the Caprice Restaurant to give him the good news. I called and said, "Dad, I got World Champion!" He said, "Of what?" I replied, "Martial arts." He said, "Call me when you get home." He was proudly waiting for me at the airport.

In 1987 my rival in the super heavyweight division, Master Rocky Ryan, and I fought bare-knuckle on military bases. In 1995 after making Team USA, I became very good friends with the coach and became like family to him. Master Lim Sison ranked me Godan 5th Degree blackbelt in Shorin-Ryu in 2012. In my life, I've had the privilege to meet several phenomenal people who were legendary martial artists: some pretty tough and solid individuals, special operations, Navy, Marine, and Army. A lot of people I met were from events.

One of whom is my close friend, my brother Reuben (Red) Lowing, who has significantly impacted my life. I trust him with my life. He is a phenomenal boxer. He trained with Roy Jones, Sr., and Jr. and was Roy's sparring partner. Reuben boxed all Navy and spent ten years in the SEAL Teams. We became friends from the fight world and through other mutual friends throughout the teams and other special operation circles. Reuben has helped me out with PTSD and in my spiritual walk. I love him like my brother. One of the things I lacked in my martial arts career besides mercy was humbleness. And someone who has come to

WHY THE MARTIAL ARTS (CONTINUED)

every one of my tournaments, every event. Every time I was doing some event, I owed all my success and growth to. And I believe they worked through Kirby DeLaunay to make this happen for me today. I had never thanked them once in my career nor given them recognition when they believed in me more than anybody.

On my knees, I humbly thank my Heavenly Father, His only begotten Son Jesus, and the entire heavenly family for what He has done and is doing in my life. And to my parents, Roger and Jacqueline Bracali, my sisters Patricia and Marlene and their families, my lovely ex-wives, my son, and my 4 daughters. Thank you, God Jesus, I love you.

How has Grandmaster CYNTHIA ROTHROCK Influenced me?

I watched her movies growing up and had a major crush on her. Who didn't?

How MARTIAL ARTS CHANGED My Life!

It helped my confidence to communicate and teach people to help break through barriers. It helped me identify people's weaknesses and strengths in the development stages of martial arts or the combative world. I was able to pass on teaching and leadership to my daughters One of my daughters serves as an E6 in the United States Navy and is now an instructor. When she was not confident as a little girl, I am proud to say she has become the tip of the spear. Cora Rago Bracali Gambino.

Jason
BROOKS

> **"**
> Every aspect of my life is directly affected by my martial arts philosophies and training.

WHY THE *Martial Arts?*

Grandmaster Jason Brooks has been training in martial arts since 1977 as an understudy of Grandmaster John Natividad. Jason currently has three different black belt styles; Tang Soo Do, Karate-Do, and Krav Haganah. In 2021, Jason was awarded Bushinkai Ninjutsu Ni-dai Soki.

Jason's rich martial arts background lead him to join the United States Marine Corps, where he would come to serve as the lead instructor in the Marine Corps Martial Arts Program for his unit, 2D Marine Force Recon Battalion. Jason trained over 3500 active-duty Marines and Sailors and reserve forces in all aspects of NBC warfare.

As a Marine, Jason was deployed in Operation Iraqi/ Enduring Freedom as NCOIC of the Reconnaissance Operation Center in support combat operations. Staff Sergeant Brooks, along with his unit, received the Presidential Unit Citation for over 30 days of sustained Combat

TRAINING INFORMATION

- Martial Arts Styles & Rank: Tang Soo Do, Karate Do, Krav Haganah Master Instructor, Bushinka Ninjatsu - Ni-dai Soki
- Instructors/Influencers: Grandmaster John Natividad, Grandmaster Rob Mancini, Rev. David LeBleu
- Birthplace/Growing Up: Las Vegas, NV
- Yrs. In the Martial Arts: 46 years
- Yrs. Instructing: 34 years
- Traveling Instructor

PROFESSIONAL ORGANIZATIONS

- Member - Veterans of Foreign Wars
- Member - Marine Corps Association
- Member - First Reconnaissance Battalion Association
- Member - Armed Forces Benefit Association
- Member - Jewish War Veterans Association
- Member - American Legion
- Member -Wounded Warrior Program Alumni
- Member -Iraqi and Afghanistan Veterans of America
- AMAA Foundation Member
- Traditional World Karate Association
- Sport Karate History General and Ambassador
- International Association of Law Enforcement Firearms Instructors

while in Iraq. In 2005, Staff Sergeant Brooks was medically retired from the Marine Corps due to the injuries he sustained during combat operations in Iraq.

In 2017, Jason started working at CRI Counter Terrorism Training School as a lead instructor, veteran outreach coordinator, and recruiter. Additionally, Jason is an adjunct instructor for the National Association of Chief of Police and trains police officers in advance officer survival. Jason was also on the UFC executive protection security team and has been on numerous motorcade details for the President and First Lady of the United States when they visited Las Vegas.

Currently, Jason Brooks is co-owner and lead instructor of Assault Counter Tactics. This personal protection company trains in all levels in the use of force for private and professional security.

Jason is certified to teach escaping captivity (SERE) survive /evade/ resist/ escape; tactical medicine; protective security formations; VIP protective techniques; tactical driving; convoy operations; tactical shooting (rifle, pistol, shotgun); counter-ambush techniques; counter-kidnapping; VIP rescue recovery; radio procedures; weapons retention; defense against edge weapons and knives; throwing knives; weapon disarmament; defense against grabs/holds; counter strangulation; ground defense; takedowns; strikes; punches; blocks; and kicks.

Jason has been nominated into two martial arts Halls of Fame in 2021; the Universal Martial arts Hall of Fame and the United States Martial Arts Hall of Fame.

PERSONAL ACHIEVEMENTS

- Certified Peer Group Facilitator – Wounded Warrior Project
- Certified Peer Mentor – Wounded Warrior Project
- Peer Mentor – Veterans Court Treatment Program
- Certified Nevada Veterans Advocate
- Veteran Jobs Advocate
- Honor Award for Public Service by the American Police Hall of Fame

MAJOR ACHIEVEMENTS

- Combat Action Ribbon
- Navy Commendation Medal
- National Defense Medal
- Global War on Terrorism Service Medal
- Sea Service Deployment Ribbon
- Global War on Terrorism Expeditionary Medal
- Navy and Marine Corps Achievement Medal (3)
- Presidential Unit Citation
- Good Conduct Medal

How MARTIAL ARTS CHANGED My Life!

Martial Arts has impacted my life by guiding my personal growth and mental development. Preparing me physically as well as mentally for Marine Corps Bootcamp is just one example. My career in the Marines, including my conduct in battle, directly reflects the discipline and physical skills attributed to my martial arts training. My life after the Marines is another example, as I am a Counter Terrorism Instructor, tactical shooting instructor, and master firearms instructor. Every aspect of my life is directly affected by my martial arts philosophies and training. My personal and business relationships are another area where my core martial arts beliefs of honor, integrity, and faith take hold and drive me forward. I can definitely say that I am a better person because of my martial arts lifestyle.

How has Grandmaster CYNTHIA ROTHROCK Influenced me?

The first time I saw Grandmaster Rothrock was in a movie called "No Retreat, No Surrender 2," which came out when I was 14 years old. I had already been studying martial arts for ten years, but seeing her in that action-packed movie with Loren Avedon ignited a fire in my soul. Her talent, skills, and flexibility were awe-inspiring and motivated me to improve my kicking ability. Her Scorpion kick caused me much pain as I tried to mimic her signature move.

Watching her continue her movie-making career through the years and advancing martial arts in all that she does is a testament to her greatness. I am grateful for all her contributions to the martial arts world.

Become an
AMAA MEMBER!

Tariq
BROWN

"

Martial Arts has been integral to my life, shaping how I view and react to situations.

WHY THE *Martial Arts?*

As a Grand Master with several decades of experience, Tariq Brown has excelled in every facet of Martial Arts. An accomplished actor, a world champion competitor, an acclaimed instructor, a Hall of Fame Member, and an adept tournament promoter, his dedication to his craft is unparalleled. Highly revered as an innovator and a pioneer in the extreme segment of Martial Arts competition, Grand Master Brown played a pivotal role in popularizing tricking and bringing it to the forefront of current Martial Arts Tournaments.

A Tae Kwon Do practitioner with the legendary Jhoon Rhee System pedigree, Brown was fortunate to be personally taught and mentored By World Champions Jeff Smith and John Chung. Some would be daunted by the pressure to follow in the footsteps of these iconic martial artists. Still, Grand Master Brown's tenacity would propel him to regional, national, and eventually International Championships and

TRAINING INFORMATION

- Martial Arts Styles & Rank: Tae Kwon Do
- Instructors/Influencers: Jeff Smith, John Chung, Fazal Khan
- Birthplace/Growing Up: New York, NY / Falls Church, VA
- Yrs. In the Martial Arts: 36 years
- Yrs. Instructing: 31 years
- School Owner, Manager & Instructor at Brown's TKD Institute

PROFESSIONAL ORGANIZATIONS

- International Academy Of Martial Arts

Worldwide recognition. Although competitive accolades were a great accomplishment, he was also adorned with inductions into the Martial Arts Hall of Fame for these achievements, which made those victories even more exceptional.

Widely sought after for his teaching ability, Tariq Brown oversees the daily operations of Brown's TKD Institute - www.BrownsTKD.com, a martial arts studio based in Central Florida, geared to the advancement of youth, teens, adolescents, and adults in their Martial Arts endeavors. In his instructional capacity, Grand Master Brown has trained multiple World Champion Competitors, World Class Instructors, and highly skilled athletes. His instruction goes beyond students within his own facility; he also instructs Martial Arts teachers through his leadership academy, The International Academy of Martial Arts - www.IAOMA.com. This organization's primary mission is to teach advanced martial arts techniques and concepts to those impacting others. This gives them the tools, knowledge, skills, and resources necessary to affect their student body in the most impactful ways. Teaching is a passion, a calling, and an immense challenge, to which Grand Master Brown has transcendently risen.

How MARTIAL ARTS CHANGED My Life!

Martial Arts has been an instrumental part of my life. It gave me not just a vocation but a mission. It has taught me how to set goals, achieve them, and overcome obstacles. Martial Arts has been integral to my life, shaping how I view and react to situations.

PERSONAL ACHIEVEMENTS

- Advisory Board Member for Janna Educational Media, A Charitable Giving Organization

MAJOR ACHIEVEMENTS

- IAKSA - World Champion
- NBL - World Champion
- WSKF - World Champion
- Martial Arts Hall of Fame Member
- NBL - World Champion

How has Grandmaster CYNTHIA ROTHROCK Influenced me?

Cynthia Rothrock has been a pioneer of females in the martial arts. Her individuality pushed female athletics to new heights allowing diverse and inventive abilities to be displayed. Laying a foundation for female notoriety in martial arts through her proficiency gave others like me a platform to showcase new and previously unthought-of skills and techniques.

TARIQ BROWN
WORLD CHAMPION

Max
CARDOZA

"

I learned to be confident but not arrogant. I learned something from every class I took and later every class I taught.

WHY THE *Martial Arts?*

When I started, I was a shy and standoffish person. I learned to speak in public, which I was terrified to do. I learned a tremendous amount of confidence. I also learned that a small man, being me at the time, 5'4" and about 120 lbs., could overcome and beat larger people. I was blessed with blazing speed, which enabled me to outmaneuver most large opponents.

I, along with my son, teach for GM Billy Smith. We instruct for no compensation. The greatest part of giving back is to see the young students progress. It's just that much fun now.

TRAINING INFORMATION

- Martial Arts Styles & Rank: Shotokan Japanese Karate-1st Dan, American Karate 1st-10th Dan
- Instructors/Influencers: Shotokan Master Don Shaw, American GM J. Pat Burleson, American GM Billy Bramer
- Birthplace/Growing Up: Bronx, NY / Ville Platte, LA / Fort Worth, TX
- Yrs. In the Martial Arts: 55 years
- Yrs. Instructing: 53 years
- Instructor

PROFESSIONAL ORGANIZATIONS

- MKHAF
- USAHOF
- UNKHOF

How MARTIAL ARTS CHANGED My Life!

I found myself surrounded by some of the greatest martial arts practitioners ever. I fought in the late 60s & 70s. In Texas, it was known as the blood & guts era. A mouthpiece, cup, gi was all we had; no protective gear. As I mentioned earlier, I learned to be confident but not arrogant. I learned something from every class I took and later every class I taught.

PERSONAL ACHIEVEMENTS

- Started a Design Business in 1969. Today my firm employs nine full-time salesmen.

MAJOR ACHIEVEMENTS

- 2014 Master Karate Hall of Fame
- 2014 USA Karate Hall of Fame
- 2018 Universal Karate Hall of Fame

Become an **AMAA MEMBER!**

Paul
CASEY

"

Be the inspiration for others to accomplish their dream. Make today a perfect moment!

WHY THE *Martial Arts?*

I was inspired by the martial arts movies, television shows, and the excitement of watching the great men and women who are incredible athletes. e.g., Bruce Lee, Jackie Chan, Steven Segal, Eric Lee, Benny Urquidez, Frank Trejo, Cynthia Rothrock, and Karen Shepherd. When I met Ed Parker, founder of American Kenpo, I knew I would pursue a journey with his teachings. He influenced so many of the greatest martial artists. I am very honored and proud to be an Ed Parker Black Belt.

How MARTIAL ARTS CHANGED *My Life!*

Many have asked me about my life, four college degrees, and one doctorate. Historical events have raised tens of millions for the Las Vegas community, businesses, and charities for the past twenty years. Six brass plaques downtown recognizing iconic entertainers, Over five hundred VIPs attending Las Vegas Cars Stars.

TRAINING INFORMATION

- Martial Arts Styles & Rank: Ed Parker American Kenpo Karate 9th Degree Master of the Arts Black Belt
- Instructors/Influencers: Ed Parker Sr., Frank Trejo and Dennis Conatser Sr.
- Birthplace/Growing Up: Los Angeles, CA
- Yrs. In the Martial Arts: 45 years
- Yrs. Instructing: 43 years
- School owner & Instructor at Paul Casey Kenpo Karate, Founder of Kenpo Karate Hall of Fame

PROFESSIONAL ORGANIZATIONS

- Screen Actors Guide
- American Federation of Television and Radio
- Sigma Alpha Epsilon
- Delta Theta Phi Law Fraternity International

Sin City Halloween and AbbeyRoadLV. My efforts have resulted in recognition for Presidential Lifetime Service Award, Twice Entertainer of the Year, Atlantic/Valley Vue recording artist songs for TV and movie soundtracks, and written iconic song 'Only Las Vegas' for the LVCVA, City of Las Vegas. 9th Degree American Kenpo Black Belt and founder of Kenpo Karate Hall of Fame Clark County School District Educator working with autistic children. And my greatest accomplishment is being a proud parent of two beautiful children. "In the beginning, everything is difficult...then it becomes easier." I'm just beginning. More to do for our community. Thank you for your support and friendship. "Be the inspiration for others to accomplish their dream. Make today a perfect moment!"

PERSONAL ACHIEVEMENTS

- Two-time Entertainer of the Year
- Ambassador for Las Vegas
- Frank Trejo Inspiration Award
- Presidential Lifetime Achievement Award
- Twelve Time International Word Champion
- Twice Ed Parker's International Karate Championships
- Twenty-Three Proclamations from City, County, and State for humanitarian contributions

MAJOR ACHIEVEMENTS

- Paul Casey Kenpo Paul Casey Kenpo Karate continues the Ed Parker American Kenpo Karate System as taught by Grand Master Frank Trejo. Mr. Casey received his training/promotion at the original Pasadena school from 1978-1990. 1981 Black Belt Ed Parker, Frank Trejo testing with a panel of twelve senior belts. SMA Frank Trejo's first black belt. Parker - Trejo - Casey lineage. Paul Casey is a 9th Degree Black Belt recognized by Joe Dimmick, Bob White, Chuck Sullivan, Dave Hebler, Gil Hibben, Dennis Conatser, and fourteen Grand Master and !0th Degree signatures. Paul Casey is a licensed Frank Trejo Karate Association member. Paul Casey is a member of Lifetime Member WBBB under Master Kang Rhee, Kang Rhee Institute. Paul Casey is the creator and founder of the Kenpo Karate Hall of Fame—a Celebration of Greatness. The KKHOF recognizes American Kenpo, Tracy Kenpo, Kajekenbo, Lima Lama, Hawaiian Kenpo, Shaolin, Chinese, and Quan Fa systems. Honored to know, grateful to learn, and forever humbled by friendship. Salute Paul Casey, Master of Arts.

How has Grandmaster CYNTHIA ROTHROCK Influenced me?

Ms. Rothrock is an inspiration. Her talents and hard work have guided many young martial artists and helped your girls and women be their best. I admire her efforts and salute her recognition for these accomplishments. Ms. Rothrock has inspired me to be the very best and never quit. Thank you, Cynthia.

David CASTRO

> " Training sharpens my mind and reactionary skills. All of it is very much self-satisfying and useful.

WHY THE *Martial Arts?*

Grandmaster David J. Castro; is a 56-year experienced martial arts practitioner, a 46-year jujutsu instructor, a retired U.S. Army Combat Veteran, Chief Warrant Officer, and a retired government employee. He became interested in Martial Arts when he was ten but could not start official training until he was 12 years old. He lived in the Bronx, New York, on Vyse Avenue. The community lacked martial arts schools. His training started in Manhattan. What caught his interest was when three men were bullying his neighbors across the street. He observed the whole thing while looking out his window on the third floor. The three guys became violent, and one of his neighbors started defending the rest. He chopped, punched, and kicked. Well, he had never seen that before. As he knocked out one guy with a kick, the other two ran behind a car. He just jumped over the car, kicking one in the face and the other in the stomach.

TRAINING INFORMATION

- Martial Arts Styles & Rank: 8th Degree – U.S. Martial Arts Association (USMAA) Jujutsu (Certified Examiner), 7th Degree – Matsudaira-ryu Nihon Jujutsu & Kyokushin-Karate (Okinawan), 6th Degree – Judo, 5th Degree – Ninjitsu Tiger Claw, 4th Degree – Okinawan Goju, 2nd Degree - Taekwondo. Studied: U.S. Army Combatives, Praying Mantis, Pakua, Dim Mak, Tai Chi, Batto Sword, Budo Tai Jitsu, Jeet Kune Do, Krav Maga and Black Dragon Fighting Society techniques

- Instructors/Influencers: GM Cho Lin Lo, GM Mitsuyo Maeda, Sifu Lin Chow, NYPD Commissioner Michael J. Codd, GM Robert Dickey, GM Ronald Hansen, O'Sensei Philip Porter, GM Wilfredo "Wildcat" Molina, GM Joseph Valentine, GM Gogen Yamaguchi, GM Sonny Mahai, GM Un Yong Kim

- Birthplace/Growing Up: Manhattan, NY

- Yrs. In the Martial Arts: 56 years

- Yrs. Instructing: 46 years

- School Owner & Manager at Japanese Ancient Jukado & Tiger Arts LLC , System: Matsudaira-ryu Nihon Jujutsu & Kyokushin-Karate (Okinawan)

In a few moments, all three guys were knocked out. Police arrived shortly after and arrested the three guys. He was amazed and anxious to learn. As he ventured into martial arts from 1976 to 2005, he lacked a social media presence; he slightly improved in 2018. It was necessary to refrain from social media to protect his military status as a United States Army Counterintelligence, Counterespionage, and Counterterrorism Special Agent and Intelligence Officer. Exposure was controlled and limited to prevent complications. In 2005, the Honbu relocated from Tokyo, Japan, to Oahu-Hawaii.

PROFESSIONAL ORGANIZATIONS

- 1974-1976 – Black Dragon Fighting Society (BDS) (Renewal Pending)
- 1978 – U.S. Combat Martial Arts Association (Life Member)
- 1985 – International Black Belt Unity Program (IBBUP) (Life Member)
- 1985-1992 – Fort Bragg Green Team; Black Belt Team
- 1990-1993 – Professional Karate Commission (PKC)
- 1990-1996 – Amateur Athletic Union (AAU)
- 1991-1995 – Fort Bragg, North Carolina, U.S. Olympic Representative
- 1992-1995 – Fort Bragg Taekwondo & Karate Team; Head Coach
- 1993-1995 – National Youth Sports Coaches Association (NYSCA)
- 1997 – International Federation of Jujitsuans (IFOJJ) (Renewal Pending)
- 1997 – Federation of United Martial Artists (FUMA) (Life Member)
- 2000 – U.S. Martial Arts Association (USMAA) (Life Member)
- 2000 – U.S. Judo Association (Life Member)
- 2007 – President's Challenge Demonstration Center Examiner; Advocacy Expires 2024
- 2021 – U.S. Martial Arts Federation (USMAF) (Life Member) & National Technical Committee
- 2021 – U.S. Traditional Kodokan Judo (USA-TKJ) (Life Member)
- 2021 – U.S. Ju-Jitsu Federation (USJJF) (Life Member) & Senior Masters Caucus; National Technical Committee
- 2021 – American Martial Arts Alliance Foundation (AMAA) (Life Member)

PERSONAL ACHIEVEMENTS

- Aug 2003 – USMAA Hall of Fame; Law Enforcement Instructor of the Year
- Aug 2002 – USMAA Hall of Fame; Master Instructor of the Year
- Feb 1998 – Letter of Congratulations (Jiujitsu); from PCPFS Co-Chairperson Griffith Joyner
- Feb 1998, Oct 1997, May 1997, Nov 1996, June 1996 & Sep1993 – Presidential Sports Award (Jiujitsu); from POTUS Bill Clinton

How MARTIAL ARTS CHANGED My Life!

GM Castro commented: "I've encountered so many different martial arts styles. They all have very interesting and valuable techniques to offer. I perfected a few techniques, but it would take another lifetime or two to perfect or master them all. So, I practice what I can, the best I can, and consider all techniques useful in a self-defense situation. I do know there is no guarantee that what I practice will work when I use it because success depends on my opponent's skills, whether a weapon is involved, the surrounding environment, and my physical condition at that moment. I can only respond, expecting the worst and hoping for the best. Traditional and non-traditional techniques are all important. Training sharpens my mind and reactionary skills. All of it is very much self-satisfying and useful. Martial arts feed into my everyday life, growth, and development."

MAJOR ACHIEVEMENTS

Teaching and promoting martial arts for all styles and systems July 1977-Present; received multiple Presidential and military service awards associated with teaching martial arts to federal agents, law enforcement, servicemen, and women; 1977-1998 tenure in military service provided opportunities to train Military Police, members of the Special Forces, Counterintelligence/Counterterrorism Agents, Law Enforcement Officers, Federal Officials, military Soldiers and Officers, and self-defense to dependent civilians; 1974-1976 was the Rice High School, New York, Martial Arts Club President & VP.

PERSONAL ACHIEVEMENTS

- Apr 1995 – DCA Sports Manager; Special Recognition; Head Coach Post Karate Team
- Mar 1994 – Letter of Congratulations (Jiujitsu); from PCPFS Co-Chairperson Griffith Joyner
- Mar 1994 – Letter of Congratulations (Jiujitsu); from PCPFS Chairman Arnold Schwarzenegger
- Feb 1993 – Presidential Sports Award (Jiujitsu); from President George Bush
- Aug 1989 – Presidential Sports Award (Jiujitsu); from President George Bush
- Apr 1989, Jan 1989, Oct 1988, July 1988, May 1988 & Mar 1988 – Presidential Sports Award (Jiujitsu); from President George Bush
- Mar 1988 – Letter of Congratulations (Jiujitsu); from PCPFS Chairman Richard Kazmaier
- Jun 1987 – Presidential Sports Award (Jiujitsu); from President Ronald Reagan
- May 1989 – Letter of Congratulations (Jiujitsu); from PCPFS Chairman Richard Kazmaier
- July 2015, Aug 2013 & May 2012 – Presidential Champion – Silver Award (Jiujitsu); from POTUS Barack Obama
- May 2015, July 2013 & Mar 2012 – Presidential Champion – Bronze Award (Jiujitsu); from POTUS Barack Obama
- Apr 2015 & June 2013 – Presidential Champion – Platinum Award (Jiujitsu); from POTUS Barack Obama
- Aug 2011, June 2011, May 2011, Jan 2011, Oct 2010, Jun 2010 & Mar 2010 – National Physical Fitness Award (Jiujitsu); from POTUS Barack Obama
- Aug 2011, June 2011, Mar 2011, Jan 2011, Oct 2010, Aug 2010, Jun 2010 & Mar 2010 – Presidential Active Lifestyle Award (Jiujitsu); from POTUS Barack Obama
- Jun 2011, Mar 2011, Jan 2011, Oct 2010, Aug 2010, Jun 2010 & Mar 2010 – Presidential Physical Fitness Award (Jiujitsu); from POTUS Barack Obama
- May 2021 – AMAA Hall of Honors award & addition to the Ron Van Clief historical book for being an over 50-year martial arts practitioner.
- Jul 2022 - Al Dacoscas and Ron Van Clief Warriors Hall of Fame
- Jul 2023 - Al Dacoscas and Ron Van Clief Warriors Hall of Fame
- Jul 2023 - President's Volunteer Service Award

Jeanette
CHANCEY

"

My journey as a KLIMA martial artist taught me that every human being has a natural way of defending himself or herself.

WHY THE *Martial Arts?*

A native of the land of the majestic Mt. Mayon, in Legazpi City, Philippines, Kyudai Jeanette "Jing" Chancey was born to parents Jose and Dolores Casitas. She was the fourth child of four siblings. The youngest among the girls, she is very active, sociable, and constantly doing things, whether indoors or outdoor activities. Born a natural athlete, she participated in almost every sport in her elementary and secondary school years. She also became a member of her school's track and field team. Aside from her love of sports, she is very creative--she even represented her school in poster making contest and won several times. She is the only female participant at that time. Every summer, she would watch Kung-fu movies with her childhood friends. They would pretend to fight each other, copying the moves of martial arts celebrities such as Jet Li, Sammo Hung, Jackie Chan, Cynthia Luster, and Cyndi Rothrock. When she reached college, she continued to

TRAINING INFORMATION

- Martial Arts Styles & Rank: KLIMA International Martial Arts, 6th Degree Red-White-Blue Belt
- Instructors/Influencers: Senior Master Ariel B. Delgado, Grandmaster Neil C. Ablong, Dodong Capistrano, Grandmaster Alicia Kossmann, Grandmaster Bill Kossman, Grandmaster Lhod Villaluna
- Birthplace/Growing Up: Legazpi City, Albay, Philippines
- Yrs. In the Martial Arts: 33 years
- Yrs. Instructing: 15 years
- Instructor

PROFESSIONAL ORGANIZATIONS

- KLIMA International Martial Arts

show her love of sports. Her team in soccer won several times against their rivals at the university. In 1990, before her graduation, she had learned about the most popular martial arts in Legazpi: "Kuntaw ng Pilipinas (KNP), the ancient art of Filipino hand and foot fighting." What grabbed her attention and triggered her burning desire to practice Kuntaw was the discipline, dedication, and respect among the instructors and students of Kuntaw. Kuntaw is so popular that she can frequently hear over the local radio stations announcing the tournaments to be held not only in Legazpi City but also in the other cities or provinces of the Bicol region. She told herself, "One day, I will be one of those Kuntaw martial artists. I will be a blackbelt." She began to search for the Kuntaw martial arts school. After several months of searching, she finally found the Kuntaw gym! She immediately registered so that she could start right away. Since then, she has trained so hard, not missing a class. She has never forgotten her instructors: Senior Master Ariel Delgado, Grandmaster Nilo "Neil" Ablong, Kyud Leogildo "Dodong" Capistrano, and Kyud Joseph Abellano. She even remembered the instructors who often visited the gym: Eduardo Lancauon, the pioneer of Kuntaw martial arts in Albay province, Kyud Angel Torregoza, and Lito Mejillano, of whom they became her sparring partners/trainers. Because of her enthusiasm and determination to learn the art, she dragged her younger brother Jonathan to go with her to the gym. In 1990, she and her brother Jonathan officially joined Kuntaw ng Pilipinas, International Kuntaw Federation (KNP-IKF), Legazpi City Chapter. This made her train tirelessly, despite her busy

PERSONAL ACHIEVEMENTS

- Graduated with a Master of Arts in Criminal Justice (2013) from Keiser University, Tallahassee, Florida
- Graduated with a Bachelor of Secondary Education in General Science (1991), University of Sto. Thomas, Legazpi City, Albay, Philippines
- First Female Kuntaw Assistant Chief Training Instructor, Legazpi City, Albay, Philippines
- 1992 First Place Full Contact Women's Blackbelt Division, Iriga City, Camarines Sur, Philippines
- 2020 Hall of Fame Inductee, KLIMA International Martial Arts, Main Headquarters, North Carolina
- Appointed as State Director, KLIMA International Martial Arts, Tallahassee, Florida (2020)
- Leadership Awardee, KLIMA International Martial Arts, Main Headquarters, North Carolina (2021)
- Silver Pickle Awardee, Florida Department of Revenue, Tallahassee, Florida (2022)

MAJOR ACHIEVEMENTS

- Board Passer, Licensure Examination for Teachers (1992), Professional Regulations Commission, Philippines
- Distinguished Team of the Year Nominee (2018), Florida Department of Law Enforcement (Criminal Justice Information Services or CJIS, Seal & Expunge)

WHY THE MARTIAL ARTS (CONTINUED)

schedule as a working student at the Aquinas University of Legazpi, now known as the University of Sto. Tomas-Legazpi. Her weekly routine was to train indefatigably with her instructors and fellow students. She embraced Kuntaw as a way of life and practiced the ancient Filipino martial arts wholeheartedly. In 1991, along with her brother, both of them received their hard-earned blackbelt. She said, "This is a big deal; this is what I hoped, dreamed, and longed for." Subsequently, Master Ariel Delgado employed her as his assistant chief training instructor.

Master Jing continued teaching for almost three years. While training and teaching Kuntaw, she took it as a great learning experience. "It taught me to be humbler, to have more self-control or self-discipline, helped raise my self-esteem, and more respectful to other martial arts practitioners." She added, "It was a great honor to share the knowledge I learned from my senior black belts and instructors. It was an indescribable feeling to pass along all the techniques, be a guide in molding future 'Kyuds' (brothers) and 'Kyudais' (sisters), be an instrument to develop younger martial arts practitioners with their skills and hone their potential." In 1995, she temporarily suspended her Kuntaw training and teaching to teach Sciences at Pag-Asa National High School, now known as Legazpi City National High School (LCNHS). But her passion for Kuntaw never ceased. In October 1996, Janne Pearl, her only daughter, was born. Her daughter became a Kuntaw martial artist later on when she reached high school. Her daughter is currently a Registered Nurse and works at the University of Sto. Tomas Hospital, Legazpi City, Philippines. Master Jing also taught Kuntaw in the summers of 2001 and 2002 at MABA Laboratory School, Legazpi City, Philippines. Master Jing also taught Kuntaw in the summers of 2001 and 2002 at MABA Laboratory School, Legazpi City, Philippines. Master Jing became a self-defense instructor to some private citizens. The knowledge, skills, principle, and values of a Kuntaw instructor remained in her heart, mind, and spirit. She applied Kuntaw in her everyday life and at work. In 2009, Master Jing moved to Tallahassee, Florida. She married Donald

WHY THE MARTIAL ARTS (CONTINUED)

Chancey, her fiancé of five years. She began to work as a receptionist at Dr. Pat and Associates. Shortly after six months, she worked as Other Personal Services (OPS) employee at the Florida Department of Law Enforcement (FDLE). She worked at FDLE for nine years. In 2019, she moved to the Florida Office of the Attorney General as a paralegal. After more than two years, she moved to a different position as a Medicaid fraud analyst. In 2022, she moved to a different agency, the Department of Revenue, as a resource management specialist. She works with the Physical Security unit to provide security oversight, maintain situational awareness and enforce Department's Security and Access Control Policy and Procedures to provide for the security of state employees, contractors, and customers in the Department's facilities. Her busy schedule did not hinder her desire to continue teaching KLIMA. Master Jing is teaching KLIMA martial arts at Lake Talquin Baptist Church. When she first started her class there, she only had a few students. In a matter of three months, the number of students increased. A potential blackbelt is expected to graduate in November of this year. Master Jing is so grateful to her instructors; without them, she would never reach her dream of being one of them. Among the other things she is thankful for is the knowledge she acquired from her instructors; this contributed to her successful career in law enforcement and to what she is today. Master Jing stated, "Aside from God, I am also thankful to Grandmasters Alice Lanada Kossmann and Bill Kossmann for their leadership in Kuntaw Legacy (now known as KLIMA). Ultimately, to all the future KLIMA martial artists: always remember, there is no such thing as perfect martial arts; practice makes perfect."

~~How~~ MARTIAL ARTS CHANGED *My Life!*

I have always been an avid martial arts enthusiast. At a very young age, my curiosity began when I watched a movie and saw this short, tiny lady take down a man twice her size. I thought she was so impressive. So, I dreamed about being like her, a martial arts expert and a blackbelt. I tried to copy some of her moves but failed miserably. Several years passed, but I still had that burning desire to learn whatever martial arts she had. At that time, I, a young woman, who knew nothing about martial arts, how could I possibly be like that lady that I saw in the movie a long time ago? I told myself, there must be a way to do that! Then the search for scientific studying of martial arts started. I was born with a pinch of inferiority complex—that's the first personal issue that I need to tackle. Secondly, I have no one to go with. I am so embarrassed to go alone by myself! Thirdly, where can I find that martial arts school? Fourthly, I am too old to start training (I was around seventeen then). I struggled with those issues. I have no idea how I ended up at Master Ariel Delgado's gym. I recalled it was because of Kyud Dodong Capistrano, and I did not know then that he would be one of my instructors. I talked to him about karate and the like; then he quietly invited me to visit the gym where he practices. When I got there, I was astonished!

HOW MY LIFE IS CHANGED (CONTINUED)
Kyud Dodong is the training instructor of Kuntaw martial arts in that gym! He is humble and kind, and you can never tell he has a degree in blackbelt. So do Master Ariel Delgado, I thought he was only the owner, that he was there for his weightlifting or fitness/health club. These men appeared to be ordinary people, but I found out later on that they knew how to defend themselves and that they are martial arts instructors. In that gym, I met Grandmaster Nilo Ablong, Ed Lancawon, and some of the best instructors in the province of Albay. I learned a lot from them. I can still vividly remember what they said, "Never underestimate or overestimate your opponent, and respect others no matter what their age is." My journey as a KLIMA martial artist taught me that every human being has a natural way of defending himself or herself. What martial arts does is teach humans to react or respond without thinking, like an instinct. Thinking is dangerous when it comes to a sudden attack from a perpetrator. One of my long-time instructors said, "The key to avoiding an attack is quick thinking--like a fraction of a fraction of a second." We live in a very dangerous world, especially for a woman like me, I need to be prepared. I have to be.

How has Grandmaster CYNTHIA ROTHROCK Influenced me?

Grandmaster Cynthia Rothrock is one of the best female martial artists I have admired. I have not met her in person, but her talent, work, and entirety as a human being are inspiring. She opened my eyes so that somehow, I can be like her, live with a purpose, and share what I have learned as a martial artist. Grandmaster Cynthia Rothrock rocks! I hope that one day, I will see her personally and shake her hand. Pugay!

Become an AMAA MEMBER!

James
CLARK

"

As an instructor of the arts, it's a way to give back and help give people with self-confidence.

WHY THE *Martial Arts?*

When I was a young man, around 12 years old, watching TV, I saw this man defeat two men. A lady who witnessed the fight asked, "Where did you learn to fight like that?" He said, "I learned Judo in Japan." From that day, I said I would learn Judo if I ever visited Japan.

I ordered books on how to learn Judo. My cousin and I would practice from the book and practice throwing and taking each other down. When I joined the Army, I trained in hand-to-hand combat.

Then came the Bruce Lee movies, I was hooked and wanted to learn martial arts. In 1974 I was stationed In South Korea, I started training with Mr. Lee. and went on to get my black belt and won the 2nd Infantry Division Championship. I started teaching martial arts in 1975. I still teach today for the Jones County Sheriff's Office in Gray, GA. I also teach women self-defense classes for the Sheriff's Office.

TRAINING INFORMATION

- Martial Arts Styles & Rank: 1st Dan Black Belt in Tae Kwon Do, 2nd/3rd Degree in Chinese Goju
- Instructors/Influencers: Mr. Lee, Sensei James E. McCall
- Birthplace/Growing Up: Fayetteville, NC / Parkton, NC
- Yrs. In the Martial Arts: 50+ years
- Yrs. Instructing: 48 years
- Founder and Chief Instructor of the Fort Benning Tae Kwon Do Club

PROFESSIONAL ORGANIZATIONS

- Jones County Sheriff's Office Instructor

A drill campaign hat tilted low on the forehead. Pistol belt cinched tight around the waist. Perfectly pressed fatigues with all kinds of badges and the ever-present whistle on a cord. Underneath it all was a demon, a little bit of hell in the shape of a man whose ONLY pleasure was making life miserable for hundreds of trainees. That's my generation's impression of Drill Sergeants and of the Army in general. But I did not believe it... or maybe I did, and I just believed in myself a little bit more.

In any case, here I am with my campaign hat and pistol belt, and I have found out the Drill Sergeant's job may be the most physically demanding and mentally stimulating in the Army. He has to be tough but also has to be fair. He sometimes has to rant and rave, but he must also be understanding. He has to be demanding, but he also has to be compassionate. Throughout my life, I have been very fortunate. I was born and raised in Parkton, NC, right outside of Fayetteville and Fort Bragg, on January 22, 1948—the older of two children of Mr. and Mrs. Albert W. Clark. I attended elementary school in Partition and Lumber Bridge, NC, where I graduated from Oak Ridge High School. After being captain of the basketball team and selected all-conference honors in 1966, the summers and weekends were spent bagging groceries and working on my uncle's farm.

In September of 1966, I found myself with a basketball scholarship, but I had little desire to spend four years in college, so I signed up for Airborne Infantry training. If I was going, "I wanted to go all the way," I took basic training at Fort Bragg and was selected to attend the Leadership Training Course at Fort Gordon,

PERSONAL ACHIEVEMENTS

- 2nd Infantry Division Champion
- Fort Benning Heavyweight Champion
- Fort Benning Grand Champion
- Participated in 30-plus tournaments, placing 1st, 2nd or 3rd

MAJOR ACHIEVEMENTS

- Teaching self-defense to women for 40-plus years so they can survive an attack. I do this because a friend was raped and murdered, and I don't charge to teach these classes. I teach these classes now and will teach as long as possible. I also give lectures on SAFETY for Jones County at churches and senior citizens groups.

WHY THE MARTIAL ARTS (CONTINUED)

where I also had Infantry Advanced Individual Training. I then transferred to Fort Benning, GA, for Jump School. All of the schools were good for me and good to me. The Army's drill sergeant image I grew up with might have been a little more accurate then than now, but all that gruffness and barely restrained fury even then concealed an individual deeply concerned for his troops' welfare. They will hate one side of you and still realize that you are on their side. You belong to your troops, and they begin to take pride in you. And, incidentally, in themselves.

I consider that the main function of today's entry-level training program is to take civilians with various levels of education and degrees of motivation and turn them into technically proficient, highly self-confident soldiers, men with pride in themselves, in their profession, and in their country. Nearly all of the trainee standards are higher now than they were 14 years ago. Physical training, rifle marksmanship, and skill proficiency testing requirements are stringent, giving the troops valuable skills and, more importantly, self-confidence.

The pride my drill Sergeants gave me was more than a valuable luxury; it was a necessity. B co, B 1ST BN, 504Th Abn INF at Fort Bragg, and the 101ST ABN Division at Fort Campbell provided a training program before going to Vietnam. I also obtained leadership experience while stationed with B CO, 2nd BN, 501st Abn INF, as a Specialist Four Squad Leader, I arrived in Vietnam in December 1967, was promoted to E-5 in January 1968, and was hospitalized for wounds received in the 68 Tet Offensive in February. I was released from the hospital in March 1968, lucky to have a good leg again and with a Purple Heart. I returned to Fort Benning, GA, for Jumpmaster training, Pathfinder School, and the Instructor Training Course. I had a tour at Fort Wainwright, Alaska, and attended NCO Academy as an E-6, then I shipped out for another overseas tour. Camp Caser, Korea, isn't a bad place to be. I was NCOIC of the 2nd Replacement Detachment and served a 45-day tour as First Sergeant. I was both student and later an instructor in the Art of Tae Kwon Do. I attended Instructor Course for Tae Kwon Do during my tour, and that instruction paid off. I captured the 2nd Infantry Division Middleweight Championship and was awarded the 2nd Infantry Division Sweater. I count it as one of my most valued possessions.

I was transferred from Korea to Fort Benning, GA, as an Airborne Instructor for two years. This was the period of 1976-1978, with time out for the ANCOES Course as an E-7. My Next assignment was with Echo Co, 1st Battalion, 1st

WHY THE MARTIAL ARTS (CONTINUED)

Infantry Training Brigade at Fort Benning, where I attended Drill Sergeant School. I was assigned to E-1-1 as a Senior Drill Sergeant, where I was awarded twice the Distinguished Drill Sergeant Award and Honor Drill Sergeant Award, and the Fort Benning, GA, Drill Sergeant of the Year. I have also been fortunate to have been awarded the National Defense Ribbon, ARCOM, Good Conduct Ribbon (4th Award), and the Combat Infantry Badge.

I've developed interests in bowling, horseback riding, table tennis, pool, jogging, basketball, and coin collecting. I've never lost my love for martial arts, and I teach whenever possible. I also started teaching women self-defense classes because during my time in the military, a young female soldier was raped and murdered at Fort Benning, GA. I still teach advanced self-defense classes for women, so they will be able to defend themselves against a much stronger opponent/attacker and survive.

I think I've earned my campaign hat, and now I wear it tilted low with a pistol belt cinched tight around my waist, and I rant and rave sometimes, but the soldier has a challenge that has to be met on a one-to-one basis. All recruits are different now; I see a drill sergeant from the inside. I see and must be treated as such. A man has to have pride in himself, but a soldier must be proficient and disciplined. The challenge lies in making a soldier out of a man while ensuring that he remains a man. The Drill Sergeant must care, and his men must know he does. Without the desire and ability to fulfill these requirements, the Drill does not measure up to the standards expressed by the motto, "This we'll defend."

I am currently married to Tanisha Farley-Clark. My children are Kimberly Ann Whitehead, whom I trained in martial arts; SSG James A. Clark II, whom I trained in martial arts and boxing, where he had a 1st round knockout; Mr. Brandon M. Clark, whom I trained in Basic Self Defense; and my stepchildren Arnez and Ashunti Pitts.

I retired from the U.S. Army after 21 years as a First Sergeant. I am in the current position as Captain and Certification Manager at the Jones County Sheriff's Office and will retire after 22 years in August 2023.

How MARTIAL ARTS CHANGED My Life!

As an instructor of the arts, it's a way to give back and help give people with self-confidence. As an instructor, teaching young people and senior citizens is my way of helping others into a brotherhood like no other. Martial arts help everyone on the job and in school. It helps them to think fast, which makes them better students. People who learn the arts can teach others in the future. They will pass down the teachings from past and future masters, and some will become masters.

Per my reading, the oldest known art is Tae Kwon Do from 2300 BC. Other arts may be older but not in the history books. Overall it's the best way to help keep martial arts stay alive forever!

How has Grandmaster CYNTHIA ROTHROCK Influenced me?

Grandmaster Cynthia is doing good for all people. She is an inspiration to men and women so that they can protect themselves and their loved ones!

Any good instructor will impress you, but anyone that works hard to become a Grandmaster is someone you will always look up to with respect and admiration. You strive to walk in their footsteps and become a Grandmaster; you look at them as if they could walk on water!

John
CONNELLY

"

Martial arts have helped me overcome many hurdles and brought my spirit, mind, and body balance into my daily life.

WHY THE Martial Arts?

I got started in martial arts as a young boy because I loved the art, as I could see the benefits that training could bring to my life. Living in the countryside, it was hard to join a club. However, that changed when my brother's best friend's father noticed I was getting bullied at school and contacted my parents about it.

I was ashamed of being unable to control and deal with the situation. When I was seriously hurt, it opened the door to regular training and support from the martial arts community. For that, I am grateful.

When I started this journey, it was about the I - mastering the body and mind. It was never a natural process, as I had to work continuously on my journey. Part of the reason I was picked on and nicknamed "Jelly Legs" is the kids in the community loved to trip me up. This was because I developed an illness that caused my throat and ears to have emergency surgery. The

TRAINING INFORMATION

- Martial Arts Styles & Rank: Tang Soo Do - 6th Dan, Taekwondo 5th Dan, Hapkido
- Instructors/Influencers: Master Alan Leadbeater, GM Trevor Stone, GM Don Oi Choi, GM Yong Woon Kim, GM Brad Hope (Deceased), GM David White (Deceased), Master Robert McAlpine, Master Dang Nguyen, Mentors & clubs assisted in: Moo Duk Kwan, Moo Rim Kwan, Just Kicks Taekwondo, Total Taekwondo, United Taekwondo Centre
- Birthplace/Growing Up: South Australia
- Yrs. In the Martial Arts: 36 years
- Yrs. Instructing: 26 years
- Local government community coach

PROFESSIONAL ORGANIZATIONS

- Cynthia Rothrock Association
- World Hapkido Martial Arts Association
- Martial Arts Australia Association
- Australia Taekwondo Association
- Sports Taekwondo Australia Association
- Kukkiwon
- Kukkiwon Australia Association
- Moo Rim Kwan

ear operation caused me to lose my balance, coordination, and a significant amount of hearing in both ears.

Martial arts have helped me overcome many hurdles and brought my spirit, mind, and body balance into my daily life, which I am truly blessed and thankful for.

How MARTIAL ARTS CHANGED My Life!

The journey has allowed me to grow into the community coach and leader I am now, to which I have dedicated my last 27 years helping the community via face-to-face coaching, volunteering at competitions - or National Television appearance promoting martial arts and most recently by Radio.

The best part of this journey is I now have an International early learning children's book available in many countries to continue promoting martial arts and help other martial arts instructors to obtain more students to the art we all love.

This ensures the current and future generations beyond experience the love, joy, and family that martial arts provide us in our lives.

How has Grandmaster CYNTHIA ROTHROCK Influenced me?

Grandmaster Cynthia has enabled me to continue on my martial arts journey by allowing me to join her organization and recognize my achievements so I can continue to travel and promote my love for martial arts in Australia and worldwide.

PERSONAL ACHIEVEMENTS

- I have been able to overcome my shortcomings from being sick as a young boy and grow and become the person the divine and the universe intended me to be via the practice of martial arts.

MAJOR ACHIEVEMENTS

- Internationally recognized Author, Mentor, and Coach.
- Master Functional Trainer
- 2019 Seniors Martial Arts Playford City community award
- Coach of the Year 2011 Total Taekwondo
- Represented Australia in Korea in 2016 at the Kukkiwon headquarters
- 2016 International Masters - Medalist
- 2017 US Open Bronze Medalist
- 2018 International Master's Gold Medalist
- Author 2017 Award

Chucky
CURRIE

"

Martial arts have taught me to aspire to inspire before I expire, with the drive, discipline, and desire...

WHY THE Martial Arts?

I lived in Chicago's Chinatown with my Grandfather, who introduced me to a friend. The rest is history.

How MARTIAL ARTS CHANGED My Life!

Martial arts have taught me to aspire to inspire before I expire, with the drive, discipline, and desire to overcome obstacles and reach my goals.

I've met many truly inspiring martial artists, including Bruce Lee, Chuck Norris, Bob Wall, Danny Inosanto, Wally Jay, Howard Jackson, Benny Urquidez, Bill Wallace, Jeff Smith, Jhoon Rhee, Simon Rhee, Phillip Rhee, Ernie Reyes Sr. Ernie Reyes Jr. Jackie Chan, Steven Segal, Linda Lee Caldwell, Shannon Lee, Brandon Lee, Curtis Wong, Tom Wong, Julius Baker Jr. and many more!

TRAINING INFORMATION

- Martial Arts Styles & Rank: Tai Chi Chuan, Chinese Gung Fu, Karate, Hapkido, Judo, Kung Fu, Tae Kwon Do, Jeet Kune Do, Escrima, Kali, Wu Shu Kung Fu, Capoeira, Chuckido Mixed Martial Arts, 10th Degree Grand Master

- Instructors/Influencers: Grand Master Jemal Sally, Grand Master Julius Baker Jr. Grand Master Greg McKinney, Grand Master Luther Secrease, Grand Master Tom Wong, Sifu Anthony Chan

- Birthplace/Growing Up: Manhattan, NY

- Yrs. In the Martial Arts: 56 years

- Yrs. Instructing: 30 years

- School owner at Quick Kicks MMA, Private instructor and VIP Bodyguard

PROFESSIONAL ORGANIZATIONS

- United Martial Arts Federation

- World Black Belt Federation

- West Coast World Martial Arts

- Jun Fan Jeet Kune Do Association

I've traveled as the opening act with the Black Belt Hall of Fame West Coast Demonstration Team. I've worked in major Hollywood Motion Pictures, including Rush Hour 2, Oceans 11, The Hulk, XxX State of the Union, Twisted, and Succa Free City, as well as star, directed, and produced my award-winning International Action On Film movie Enter The Tiger which also won the San Diego Black Film Festival. It was featured on The Angry Baby Monkey Show hosted by Lionsgate and Time Warner Cable TV. in New York, New York. I've met and worked with many of my favorite celebrities, including Michael Jackson, Prince, Halle Berry, Danny Glover, Brad Pitt, Andy Garcia, Julia Roberts, George Clooney, Matt Damon, Denzel Washington, Sugar Ray Leonard, Janet Jackson, to name a few! God has been so amazing in my life! I can't thank him enough!

How has Grandmaster CYNTHIA ROTHROCK Influenced me?

Grand Master Cynthia Rothrock and I have been friends for decades! We performed with the Black Belt Hall of Fame West Coast Demonstration Team and competed in Major Martial Arts Tournaments. She inspires me to do my best and make my path to success in movies and television. I'm very happy that we are great friends! She's a real goal-go-getter! I congratulate her for all of her continued success! It's an Honor to be featured in this book with her on the cover! She's a great trailblazer!

PERSONAL ACHIEVEMENTS

- SAG/AFTRA Professional Actor
- Director, Producer
- Award-Winning International Action On Film Festival
- Best Short Film
- Black Film Festival San Diego Winner
- Black Belt Masters Hall of Fame
- Master's Hall of Fame
- World Black Belt Masters Hall of Fame
- Elite Black Belt Masters Hall of Fame

MAJOR ACHIEVEMENTS

- World Martial Arts Champion - Fighting Forms and Weapons
- Featured in the world's leading martial arts magazines, including Black Belt, Inside Kung Fu, Fighting Stars, Karate Illustrated, Professional Karate, Martial Arts Illustrated, and Masters Martial Arts Magazine.
- Named the New Bruce Lee by Chuck Norris
- Noted as the Fastest Kicker in the USA
- The Number One Martial Arts Performer in the USA, 1980.
- Worked in major motion pictures, Rush Hour 2, Oceans 11, The Hulk, XxX State of the Union, Jo Jo Dancer, Twisted, and star of Enter The Tiger

Louis
DAVIS

"

Martial arts accepted me without judgment nor prejudice and opened the doorway to the world...

WHY THE *Martial Arts?*

Louis Edward Davis was born in Chicago, Illinois on October 11th, 1970. In August of 1977, his family migrated to Minneapolis, Minnesota. By late 1985 he began training in martial arts at the age of 15, and by the summer of 1986, he began competing in local point Karate tournaments, some of which were hosted by Pat Worley. During the 1993 USTU National Championships held in St Paul, Minnesota, Louis came into contact with the All-Army Taekwondo team. After searching the venue, he learned that a team existed representing each branch of the US Armed Forces. After vowing (to himself) to become a member of one of these teams, he enlisted the following year. In 1995 while at his first duty station Fort Hood Texas, he was approached by Sergeant Michael Bennett, who was a member of the All-Army Taekwondo team competing in the heavyweight division. Under Sergeant Bennett and Sergeant Todd Angel's guidance, Louis went from an awkward

TRAINING INFORMATION

- Martial Arts Styles & Rank: 2nd Degree Black Belt Olympic Freestyle Taekwondo Intermediate level, 6 Combinations Southern Praying Mantis Kung Fu

- Instructors/Influencers: GM Michael R. Bennett, GM Todd Angel, GM Rafael Medina, GM Bobby Clayton, GM Bongseok Kim, Sifu Gary D. Eshelman

- Birthplace/Growing Up: Chicago, IL, Minneapolis, MN

- Yrs. In the Martial Arts: 38 years

- Yrs. Instructing: 10 years

- Instructor

PROFESSIONAL ORGANIZATIONS

- USA Masters Taekwondo Team

novice to one of three Fort Hood Taekwondo team captains. In late April 1997, Louis, along with fellow Fort Hood Taekwondo teammates John Swan, Nicolau Andrade, Ryan Lundy, Howard Clayton, and of course, Sergeant Bennett and Sergeant Angel, attended 1997 All Army and Armed Forces Taekwondo trial and selection camp held at Fort Indiantown Pennsylvania. On April 27th Louis took the silver medal in the welterweight division during the Armed Forces Championships, securing a place on the 1997 Army team. In December 1997, Louis relocated from Fort Hood, Texas, to Harvey Barracks in Kitzingen, Germany. By October 1998, Louis began to establish himself as a competitor throughout the Bavarian (Bayern) area, winning the Bavarian championships later that same year, holding said title until 2000. During this time, Louis received guidance by phone from coach Rafael Medina on how to maximize his training and improve his skill set. One of these many phone conversations led him to Georg Streif, the head coach of the German Armed Forces and German national team. Georg had invited him to attend one of his training camps, which greatly improved Louis' growing abilities. In 1999, Louis returned to Fort Indiantown Gap. He secured a place on the team after defeating Daryll Woods in the finals and defeating London Arevalo of the Air Force Taekwondo team during the Armed Forces Championships. In 2000 Louis began visiting Pickens, South Carolina, and entered a mentorship with former All-Army and national champion Reginald Perry. It was here that Louis began to research the history of the All-Army team. The following year Louis returned to

PERSONAL ACHIEVEMENTS

- Retired Army (20 years) Associate Degree
- Computer Support & Network Administration
- Associate Degree in Computer Forensics

MAJOR ACHIEVEMENTS

- 1996 – 1997 Fort Hood Taekwondo Team, one of three team captains
- 1996 Fort Hood Championships – Bronze
- 1997 Armed Forces Championships – Silver
- 1997 Fort Hood Championships – Gold
- 1998 Bavarian Regional Championships – Gold
- 1998 Bavarian Championships – Gold
- 1998 Italian Open – Gold
- 1999 All Army Championships – Gold
- 1999 Bavarian Regional Championships – Gold
- 1999 Bavarian Championships – Gold
- 2000 Bavarian Regional Championships – silver
- 2000 Bavarian Championships – Gold
- 2001 All Army Championships – Silver
- 2002 South Carolina State Championships – Gold
- 2003 South Carolina State Championships – Gold
- 2003 Commander's Cup Korea – Gold
- 2003 Area 1 Championships Korea – Gold
- 2003 8th Army Championships Korea – Gold
- 2003 Mid Atlantic Championships – Gold / Grand Champion
- 2003 World Taekwondo Hwarang Festival, Jincheon Gun – Bronze
- 2004 Jeju Island Invitational – Bronze
- 2004 Area 1 Championships Korea – Gold
- 2004 8th Army Championships Korea – Gold
- 2005 Commander's Cup Korea – Gold
- 2005 Area 1 Championships Korea – Gold
- 2005 8th Army Championships Korea – Gold
- 2005 USA Taekwondo National Championships – Gold
- 2007 USA Taekwondo National Qualifier – Silver 2009
- USA Taekwondo National Qualifier – Bronze 2009

"The Gap," securing a position as one of two middleweights on the Army team and by January of 2003, relocated from Germany to South Korea, joining All-Army teammates Kevin Williams and Johnny Birch as a member of the 2nd Infantry Division's taekwondo team. During this four-year tenure in Korea as a member of the 2nd Infantry Division's taekwondo team, Louis quickly established himself as a talented competitor, winning any competition held by Camp Casey or Camp Hovey, respectively, winning both the 2003 and 2005 Friendship Cup (AKA the Commander's Cup) The 2003-2005 Area 1 Championship, and the 8th Army championship. In 2005 Louis took Gold in the USA Taekwondo National Championships in San Jose, California, and his second National Medal (Silver) in Austin, Texas, in 2009. In early to mid-2007, Louis was asked by Rafael Medina to attend the inaugural Taekwondo Hall of Fame banquet in Teaneck, New Jersey as a representative of the US Armed Forces, later becoming a technical advisor. Louis himself received recognition from the Hall Of Fame for his efforts as a competitor. Louis continued to work as a technical advisor representing the US Armed Forces until 2015. After retiring from both the Army and Taekwondo competition, Louis returned to Minneapolis, Minnesota, where he volunteered his knowledge and experience as a coach in support of a collective of Taekwondo School owners within the twin cities metro area, his former All Army coaches and former teammates who operate Taekwondo schools themselves and is currently a D-Level referee, D level coach under USA Taekwondo and a Coach under the Amateur Athletic Union.

MAJOR ACHIEVEMENTS

- USA Taekwondo National Championships – Silver
- 2011 Armed Forces Championships – Bronze
- 2012 Armed Forces Championships – Gold
- 2013 Armed Forces Championships – Bronze
- 2021 US Masters Cup - Gold
- 2023 Asian Pacific Masters Games - Gold
- 2012 - 2015 Taekwondo Hall Of Fame Technical Advisor
- 2022 - Taekwondo Hall Of Fame Inductee

WHY THE MARTIAL ARTS (CONTINUED)

In addition to coaching, Louis is currently researching the History of the All Army and Armed Forces Taekwondo program by locating many of its pioneers, former champions, and team members.

How MARTIAL ARTS CHANGED My Life!

"When the pupil is ready, the master will appear" This best describes how my continued study of martial arts has impacted my life. What began as a quest for the tools to seek justice for the abuse I suffered in a group home became a journey that would enrich my life in ways that I could not fathom. It offered me more than a physical form of unarmed combat. It allowed me to dodge the pitfalls that befall the average young black men at that time. It accepted me without judgment nor prejudice and opened the doorway to the world, which led me to enlist in the Army in hopes of studying abroad in a country where one of these arts originated. Its discipline coincided with the discipline instilled in me by the Army. It offered me purpose, direction, and motivation. It became my constant friend and a secondary ally (God will ALWAYS be my primary ally). My thoughts and feelings about this go beyond words.

How has Grandmaster CYNTHIA ROTHROCK Influenced me?

Apparently, GM Rothrock first gained my attention via a little-known KFC commercial where she struck and broke the sidewalk. As time went on, I was reintroduced to her via Black Belt magazine, Inside Karate, and Inside Kung Fu magazines, respectively, and lastly, several distinct films of hers: Righting Wrongs aka Above The Law, Shanghai Express and the Tiger Claw series with Jalal Merhi, No Retreat No Surrender 2 with London Avedon. I enjoyed watching her display her abilities in some of the best fight choreography of that era.

Kenneth
DAY, SR.

"

To this day, Tae Kwon Do has been an important part of my life and has made me who I am today.

WHY THE *Martial Arts?*

I come from a family of twelve children living in a two-bedroom house. My mother died when I was just fourteen years old.

In 1974, I took my first Tae Kwon Do class under Grand Master Myuang Hak Kang, located in Arlington, VA, and the Grand Master is still teaching classes today. I studied Tae Kwon Do in 1976 with Grand Master Jhoon Rhee and trained with Jangs Tae Kwon Do from 1976 until 1981.

My training continued in Maryland with Grand Master Dongju Lee at the Lee Karate Studio and Grand Master Apollo Ladra at Apollo's East Coast Tae Kwon Do School.

I was diagnosed with cancer in 1990. I endured radiation and chemotherapy, including two cancer recurrences in 1992 and 1998.

To this day, Tae Kwon Do has been an important part of my life and has made me who

TRAINING INFORMATION

- Martial Arts Styles & Rank: Tae Kwon Do (3rd Degree Black Belt)
- Instructors/Influencers: Grand Master Myuang Hak Kang, Grand Master Jhoon Rhee, Master Cleanzo Vollin, Master Instructor Andre Yamakawa (deceased), Grand Master John Chung, Grand Master Dongju Lee, Master Apollo Ladra Grand Master Michael Coles
- Birthplace/Growing Up: Washington, DC / Arlington, VA
- Yrs. In the Martial Arts: 49 years
- Yrs. Instructing: 16 years
- Instructor

PROFESSIONAL ORGANIZATIONS

- The World Cup Martial Arts Organization

I am today. I strive to be fair, compassionate, and loyal in everything I do; that is how I live my life. I have mentored other cancer patients and young martial arts students, instilling them with determination and the spirit never to give up, whether in athletics or health-related situations.

How MARTIAL ARTS CHANGED My Life!

Martial arts have had a significant impact on my life over the years. It keeps my body in shape, and it also keeps me busy. I've learned discipline, which motivates me to share the knowledge and techniques I've learned over the years. When I was young, I watched Bruce Lee movies and practiced the moves he used to do. I am honored to have been taught by one of Bruce Lee's good friends, Grand Master Jhoon Rhee.

PERSONAL ACHIEVEMENTS

- I am a 31-year cancer survivor.
- I retired from Giant Food after 32 years of working.
- I am currently the Roving Chief for Anne Arundel County Public Schools for 20 years.

MAJOR ACHIEVEMENTS

- In August 2017 and June 2019, I received the "Who's Who Legend" Award.
- In 2020, I received the "Ambassador Of The Year" Award from AMAA and the "Golden Years" Award from the World Cup Martial Arts Organization.

James
DEBROW III

"

Martial arts have added value to my life and given me the following skills: discipline; respect; motivation...

WHY THE Martial Arts?

My father and two uncles were professional boxers and black belts, so I began boxing and martial arts at four (1959). My father and uncles gave me my first four black belts. I also studied martial arts in the United States Army in the Republic of Korea (ROK), Okinawa, and Tokyo, Japan. I was promoted by Dr. Al Francis, 10th Dan black belt, Al Francis Karate Organization, 5th Dan to 10 Dan black belt in San Antonio, Texas (1985-2020).

- Shinjimasu International Martial Arts Association, Black Belt Advancement Certificate 9th Dan Black Belt Shaolin Goju ID#Nbq 10137 on July 18, 1993, by Soke Charles Dixon, 10th Dan, Chairman of the Counsel and the Shinjimasu Board of Directors, Temple, Texas

TRAINING INFORMATION

- Martial Arts Styles & Rank: Tae Kwon Do-8th, 9th & 10th Dan, Goju-6th to 10th Dan, Hapkido -6th Dan, Police and Military Combat Instructor: Physical Fitness & Defensive Tactics Instructor/Coordinator-Texas Department of Public Safety (State Trooper) agency-wide

- Instructors/Influencers: James Debrow, Jr., Herbert Debrow, Johnny Davis, Al Francis, Dr. Abel Villareal, Professor Charles Dixon, Grand Master Richard Dixon, Grand Master Mike Fillmore, Dr. Dan Roberts

- Birthplace/Growing Up: San Antonio, TX

- Yrs. In the Martial Arts: 63 years

- Yrs. Instructing: 55 years

- School owner, Manager & Instructor at James Debrow Fighting Tiger School, LLC

- Shinjimasu International Martial Arts Association, United Federation of International Grand Masters, Letter of Recognition and Inauguration, Recognized as a 10th Dan Black Belt, Professor of Martial Arts, Lifetime Member on June 22, 2019, by Soke Charles Dixon, 10th Dan, Chairman of the Counsel and the Shinjimasu Board of Directors, Temple, Texas

- International Police Tactical Training Academy, Appointed International Director of Training of the International Police Tactical Training Unit on June 26, 2020, by the President, Grand Master Robert J. Fabrey, 10th Dan Black Belt and President, United States Karate Federation, National Headquarters, St. Portia, Florida

- Since 1997, he has been promoted and a registered member of the United States Karate Federation

- Philadelphia Historic Martial Arts Society, Martial Arts Hall of Fame Inductee Class of 2020

- United States Martial Arts, Martial Arts Hall of Fame Inductee Class of 2020 and Membership. International Martial Arts Council of America. Hot Springs, Arkansas

- The Universal Martial Arts Hall of Fame Inductee Class of 2020 and Membership

PROFESSIONAL ORGANIZATIONS

- Al Francis Karate Organization
- Shinjimasu International Martial Arts Association
- Global Tae Kwon Do Association
- Tae Kwon Do, Yong Moo Kwan Federation, and the World Moo Duk Kwan Alliance-United States Branch of Tae Kwon Do Association, etc.

PERSONAL ACHIEVEMENTS

- Shinjimasu International Martial Arts Association, Temple, Texas: Golden Life Achievement, Karate Achievement, and Black Belt Advancement Certificate (Grand Master Levels)

MAJOR ACHIEVEMENTS

- Physical Fitness and Defensive Tactics Coordinator for the Texas Department of Public Safety-State Trooper Training Academy agency-wide 1994-2003, developed and implemented the physical fitness and wellness program and the defensive tactics program for recruiting school cadets and agency incumbents, Use-of-Force Expert/policy developer, Court-certified Use-of-Force, assigned to develop, implement and instruct in the new Texas Concealed Handgun Program at the Texas Department of Public Safety as approved by the Texas Legislatures.

- Philadelphia Historic Martial Arts Society, Martial Arts Hall of Fame inductee Class of 2020; United States Martial Arts, Martial Arts Hall of Fame Inductee Class of 2020; and The Universal Martial Arts Hall of Fame Inductee Class of 2020; Texas Amateur Martial Arts Association-Executive Committee Chair; The World Moo Duk Kwan Do Alliance appointed as Central Director of the National Hapkido Association; and International Police Tactical Training Academy of the International Police Tactical Training Unit

Become an AMAA MEMBER!

How MARTIAL ARTS CHANGED My Life!

Martial arts have added value to my life and given me the following skills: discipline; respect; motivation; trust; leadership; communication; teamwork; teaching; followers; emotional control; physical fitness; mental fitness, resiliency; character; spirituality; attention span growth; calmness; loyalty; commitment; veracity; tenacity; competitiveness; goal orientation; cognition; and motor performance.

Martial arts help me to meet all races, both male and female, domestic and international. I worked with elementary, junior high school, and high school at-risk students and helped many of them stay in school and graduate. Karate was also a source of income.

Martial arts helped me be promoted to sergeant at the Texas Department of Public Safety-State Trooper Training Academy. I served for over eight years in the state police training bureau. Karate has been my life and still is today. I am working on a program to help children with memory, attention span, and concentration skills.

Martial Arts has been the best thing that has ever happened to me!

Deedra DeCOSTER, Ph.D.

"
My long-time slogan has been, 'Hard Work is Dedication, and Dedication is Hard Work.'

WHY THE *Martial Arts?*

My martial arts journey began humbly at 15 in 1981, in a private American Kenpo after-school youth program in Apple Valley, California. I signed up seeking an activity that I found interesting. What I discovered was far more than interesting; Kenpo became a catalyst for me to join Asian and American martial arts alike. Eventually, my training inspired me to join the United States Navy to see the world, and I was fortunate to train in Hong Kong and Japan while stationed abroad. In the following summers, I would spend time at the BKF schools watching fighters sparring with each other, thinking I wanted to do that, too. I began taking BKF formal classes to prepare myself for the military. Little did I know that Kenpo and Taekwondo would turn out to become my life-long career. While in the United States Navy, I was extremely fortunate to work with the Seabees, through which I met Navy Seal Chief GM Jackie Cotton, founder of the SAFE Shinjimasu

TRAINING INFORMATION

- Martial Arts Styles & Rank: BKF-Great Grand Master 10th Degree

- Instructors/Influencers: Josi Saabir Q. Muhammad, GM Pablo Rodarte, Sijo James Culpepper, Sr. GM Clarence McGee, GM Jackie Cotton, GM Jerry Smith, Pat Salantri, Master Joel Colbert, Ph.D., Sr. GM Carl Ray Scott, GM Eddie "Flash" Newman, GM Roy Leavenworth, Master Mike Galuski, Sijo Harold Credle, Sr. Masters' Paul and Elizabeth Leitzke

- Birthplace/Growing Up: Honolulu, HI / Aiela & Hilo, HI / Victorville, Apple Valley, Carson, CA

- Yrs. In the Martial Arts: 42 years

- Yrs. Instructing: 33 years

- School owner, Instructor & Headmaster at IKKON Martial Arts, LLC and DeCoster Kenpo Academy

PROFESSIONAL ORGANIZATIONS

- BKF Alpha Warrior Society (1st Class 2019)

- Black Karate Federation

- Sigma Gamma Rho Sorority, Inc. Undergrad-Omicron Rho (Charter Member-CSUDH SP99) and Graduate-Theta Epsilon Sigma

- American Karate Taekwondo Association (AKTA)

organization. Under his tutelage, I continued my training up until 2012.

I am truly blessed that he has known me, worked with me, and has been my mentor for most of my martial arts career. Looking back on the early years of my career, I was on a continual quest to immerse myself in Asian and Ohana philosophies for my search for the warrior within me. As Native Hawaiian, my family history is entrenched in Ohana and Asian culture. In 2013, I became the Executive Vice President of Edmund Kealoha Parker Jr's Paxtial Arts International, Inc. This allowed me to gain incredible knowledge of the Martial Arts business and deep Kenpo knowledge through private insights taught to him by his father, Sr. GM Edmund Parker Sr., the founder of the American Kenpo Association and father of American Kenpo. I listened intently and learned the value of loyalty to one's art, family, and inner circle and the importance of commitment to excellence in the day-to-day representation and promotion of Kenpo by communication within global martial arts organizations. Through recollections, sayings, readings, teachings, photos, and stories from the old days, I have a deeper, more profound appreciation of Kenpo. My experiences with the Ed Parker family have given me humility, and the opportunity was a blessing.

To this day, I am still humbled and honored to be an inductee in the first Inaugural call of the Ancient Alpha Warrior,1st Black Karate Hall of Fame, along with the elevation to the rank of Great Grand Master 10th degree Black Belt on April 26, 2019, from Josi Steve (Sanders) Muhammad.

PROFESSIONAL ORGANIZATIONS

- Alpha Gamma Sigma, Honor Society
- California Workforce Connection (CWC)
- AMVETS Lifetime Membership
- DAV-Disabled Veterans of America Lifetime Member
- World Elite Black Belt Society (WEBBS)
- Laguna Seca Volunteer Association (LSVA) Monterey, CA
- Sport Karate Museum Ambassador
- Grandmaster Hall of Honors
- Christian Karate Association
- World Elite Black Belt Society 05/31/2021 Teaching Diploma-International Instructor
- Board of Directors for Faith Anointing Christian Bible College since 2023
- Professional Speaker for Anti-Bullying prevention, Workplace Violence, Situation Awareness and Senior Self Defense, and Executive Career Services Workforce topics.

PERSONAL ACHIEVEMENTS

- 6-time Hall of Famer
- Ancient Alpha Warrior,1st Black Karate Hall of Fame, along with the elevation to the rank of Great Grand Master 10th degree Black Belt on April 26, 2019, from Josi Steve (Sanders) Muhammad.
- Masters of the Martial Arts Hall of Fame 2022
- Grandmasters Hall of Honors 2016 and 2021
- Action Martial Arts Hall of Fame
- Blacks in Martial Arts Historical Legacy (BITMA) President and Founder Nom: Mwanzo Mwalimu Umeme JC(RIP) 2013
- Masters of Martial Arts Hall of Fame Awards-Kungfu& Karate Expo Showcase 2021
- Sport Karate Museum Ambassador since 2021Sport Karate Museum Military Award 2021
- Soke Council Member for Hapkido Since 2012
- State of California-SEIU Union Steward 2011-2018
- State of California-SEIU Veterans Committee Member 2022-2024
- AMVETS Lifetime Member, Department of California, Commander Post 48 Long Beach, CA, and District 2 Commander 2023-2024

How MARTIAL ARTS CHANGED My Life!

As a United States Navy veteran, dedicating myself to martial arts has been a lifelong quest to find harmony by joining my mind, body, and spirit. My long-time slogan has been, "Hard Work is Dedication, and Dedication is Hard Work."

My love and passion for Kenpo, Taekwondo, Hapkido, Shinjimasu/Shinjimatzu (Goju-Ryu), and Bushido have propelled me to become a Professional Martial Artist, Motivational Speaker, and Martial Arts Growth Coach. It has been my pleasure to have served as a martial arts leader with several high accolades, notably as a well-versed curriculum writer, fight technician, and applied Martial Science Grandmaster.

With profound reverence, I look back on my 40+ year journey as a practitioner and realize this; to grow in martial arts, you must continue to learn and push past your comfort zone to reach peak performance in all areas of your life.

MAJOR ACHIEVEMENTS

- 6-time Hall of Famer
- Presidential Lifetime Achievement for Leadership and Community Service 5,699 hrs. 2021
- Ph.D. in Humanities Faith Anointing Christin Bible Institute (FACBI) Reston, VA 04/28/2023
- Board of Directors for Faith Anointing Christian Bible College since 2023
- Masters in Christian Communication and Counseling, Marriage Therapy (FACBI) Reston, VA 11/08/2022
- Bachelors in Sociology, Minor in Psychology California State University, Dominguez Hills, Carson, CA 2003
- Associate in arts- Liberal Arts Transfer Psychology, Minor in Sociology
- United States National GrandMasters Hall of Fame, Hall of Honors 2016 Inductee
- International Kenpo Lifetime Achievement Award City of Los Angeles, Original Warrior Association 2018
- Action Martial Arts Magazine's, Hall of Honors 2018 Inductee
- World Elite Black Belt Society Teaching Diploma-International Instructor 05/2021
- Books: Featured: pages 178-179, 182-182 "BKF Kenpo, History and Advanced Strategic Principles" by Muhammad and Williams 2002

How has Grandmaster CYNTHIA ROTHROCK Influenced me?

Grandmaster Rothrock has inspired me through her countless appearances and tireless devotion to including women in the martial arts world. Over the years, I have had the distinct pleasure of attending events, attending her training, and having a few meaningful minutes of conversations. She continues to lead by example, celebrating the women in martial arts and creating pathways for women to participate in the sport and the art of Karate in entertainment, awards events, and imparting martial arts wisdom wherever present.

Kirby DELAUNAY

"

The Martial Arts study has given me self-confidence, courage, the utmost respect and the correct understanding of how things work...

WHY THE Martial Arts?

I started martial arts when I was three years old. My mother wanted my brother and me to learn how to defend ourselves at any point. That time was needed - especially after her time was done here on earth. I grew up in Grass Valley, CA. My schooling was successful, and I graduated two years early. My junior year, I was the only one picked out of the school Nevada Union for Who's Who Among Students for having the highest GPA of 4.0 and higher. I have had my bumps through the years.

I have studied Kempo Karate, Shotokan, aikido, BJJ, boxing, kickboxing and Tang Soo Do under Jake Dabis, GM Ed Parker Sr., GM Gary Garrett and Kioshi Rocknew Ryan. I am now studying under Soke Jody Perry and Master Jay Perry. I was determined I would just not give up. On top of that, I am a severe asthmatic, which made things much harder for me to accomplish; but I did it - I got mad and stayed with it no matter

TRAINING INFORMATION

- Belt Ranks & Martial Arts Styles: 4th Dan
- Instructors/Influencers: Soke Jody Perry & Master Jay Perry
- Currently Resides: North San Juan, CA
- Yrs. In the Martial Arts: 45 years
- Yrs. Instructing: 30 years

PROFESSIONAL ORGANIZATIONS

- Masters Hall of Fame, Hall of Honors

PERSONAL ACHIEVEMENTS

- Two-time belt holder for International Martial Arts Confederation for sparring, kata, as well as a point leader, seven-time belt holder for Golden State Karate Association for sparring, kata, point leader, Undefeated brick break champion. Two-time record holder in brick breaking for GSKA. I was the first within 19 years to break a record of 69 bricks in 2013. In 2014, I went back and beat my own record, breaking 100 bricks. I made history with these two breaks. 2016 Broke for Guinness book of World Records 150 bricks in 1 min and 33 seconds. I am hoping to break this record this year with 300 bricks.

what. Now I use my martial arts knowledge to share with our youth how never to give up, and how they too, can become a true martial artist if they just pick the right path to humbleness and stay drug free. I had many obstacles to overcome, but determination, heart and support helped me to stay focused. I have had many goals, I have achieved almost all of them, and then some. The martial arts study has given me self-confidence, courage, the utmost respect and the correct understanding of how things work growing up not only to myself, but also to many others. I never thought this all would've happened, but again here I am succeeding because of those who believed in me. So, a big thank you to those who have been with me on this wild journey.

My utmost respect, love and support goes to my mother and dad. I started teaching at the age of 17. I have many idols, Bruce Lee, Cynthia Rothrock, The Dragon, Steven Seagal, Billy Blanks, Tony Satch Williams, Bill Wallace, Eric Lee and Larry Lamb were just a few that inspired me. I think the most awesome feeling was growing up and now being able to communicate and saying "thank you" to these exceptional martial artists. But my number one was my mom she was a green belt under me. Besides the martial arts world, I played basketball, did speed skating, played softball and when I was young, I started playing music. I am a drummer and a piano player, and I have messed around with a guitar. Music was also second nature. I always was very active.

I was asked in 1999 by Big John McCarthy and Doug Guns Ekman to come train with them and prepare for the UFC. My mother started tearing

MAJOR ACHIEVEMENTS

- 2015 - Featured in my first role in "Jackson Bolt" as a hospital hit woman, starring my mentor, Ambassador GM Robert Parham.
- 2016 - Inducted into the Masters Hall of Fame by GM Robert Parham.
- 2017 - Inducted into the Hall of Honors as an Ambassador for outstanding achievements in the
  martial arts. I also starred in a short film called "What If You Had to Choose," by Glenn Spillman.
- 2017 - Starred in my first lead role in "Soul Cage" as Sloane.
- 2018 - Inducted into the Hall of Honors for Goodwill Ambassador to the Martial Arts.
- 2019 - Contributing writer for the Martial Arts World News Magazine.
- Broke a new World Record for breaking bricks. 2x6x24 280 on the clock time of 2 minutes and 41 seconds 301total
- Appeared in the movie "Snow Black" directed by GM Robert Parham
- Best female Action Star for 2021 & 2022
- Attempting a new world record in 2024.
- Received Best Female Action Star for Soul Cage for 2023-2024 for a new role in "Mama's Don't Mess" as a psychotic agent that protects kids.
- Inducted in Hall of Honors in Sept 2023 for Rising Action Star

WHY THE MARTIAL ARTS (CONTINUED)

up and asked not to take it that far. I just couldn't do it knowing she was that worried. So, I decided to do everything but that. I started breaking boards when I was 16, when I was told I couldn't break bricks because I was a girl, I took that as a challenge. That's when I started the brick breaking with my head. I got up to 10 with my head. I am a Two-time record holder in brick breaking for GSKA.

Rayot
DIFATE

"

I encourage my older karate comrades to put themselves out there and continue to participate when possible!

WHY THE *Martial Arts?*

Hachidan Rayot Difate was born in 1941 in Yonkers, New York. He entered the army in 1960 and volunteered for the 101st Airborne Division. Upon being sent to Korea for a period of 3 years, he began the study of Judo. Upon being honorably discharged in 1963, he returned to White Plains, New York to continue his studies in Kyokushin Karate. In 1965, he joined the Yonkers Police Department while continuing his martial arts training. After a one year of intense training program, under Sensei Shigeru Oyama, Rayot became the 1st Black Belt student to be promoted in the US, in 1967, in the style of Kyokushin Karate Do.

In 1976, during an undercover operation with the Yonkers Police Department, Rayot sustained life-threatening injuries, forcing his retirement from the Police Department, due to permanent disabilities followed by years of multiple surgeries. As part of his personal physical and mental rehabilitation, he returned to the dojo

TRAINING INFORMATION

- Belt Ranks & Martial Arts Styles: World Oyama Karate, 8th Dan
- Instructors/Influencers: Shigeru Oyama (Deceased)
- Birthplace/Growing Up: Yonkers, NY/West Harrison, NY
- Yrs. In the Martial Arts: 62 years
- Yrs. Instructing: 57 years

PROFESSIONAL ORGANIZATIONS

- Yonkers Police Department (Retired 1978)
- Veterans of Foreign War, Post 4037
- American Federation of Martial Arts
- New Breed Life Martial Arts Association
- Eastern USA International Martial Arts Association
- Bushiken Karate

with a modified training program. In 1998, he was promoted to the rank of Shihan.

From 1998 to present, Rayot has taught at the White Plains Dojo, under the direction of Shoshu Oyama. Shihan has spent the past 58 years in both the study and instruction of martial arts. On September 10, 2014, after 55 years of training with World Oyama Karate, Shihan Rayot was awarded promotion to 8th Degree Black Belt. He has also been inducted into the American Federation of Martial Arts Hall of Fame, as Diamond Lifetime Achievements in 2013, Ambassador of Goodwill to the Martial Arts in 2014, International Instructor of the Year in 2014, and The New Breed Life Arts Education Association in Harlem, in 2015.

Hachidan has participated and given seminars in the US, Canada, Panama, Haiti, and the Dominican Republic. Upon turning the age of 70, Hachidan decided that his "Bucket List" would consist of competing in 100 tournaments, over the next 5 years. In July of 2017, upon turning 76 years old, he completed this goal. He continues to participate in tournaments in the Tri-State area, displaying his form and techniques in Kata, Weapons, and Self-Defense. He takes great pride in his trophies and medals surrounding his family room. He enjoys membership with the Harrison, New York Veterans of Foreign War.

He continues to be a source of inspiration to other martial artists, wherever he goes, as the oldest competitor, doing what he truly finds both motivating and rewarding. In 2008, at the invitation of Shihan John Turnball, he was accepted into the American Federation of he was

PERSONAL ACHIEVEMENTS

- As of the age of 70 years old: Started and completed 100 tournaments through age 75 years old, in both national and international competitions.

- Continues to be one, if not, the oldest Tri-state competitor in New York, New Jersey, and Connecticut. Continues to both train and compete on a regular basis.

MAJOR ACHIEVEMENTS

- Completion of 100 tournaments between the age of 70 and 75, in both national and international Karate tournaments

- Membership in the Harrison, New York, Veterans of Foreign War, Post 4037

- Honorary discharge from the US Army in 1963

- Honorary Retirement from the Yonkers Police Department in 1978

- One, if not the oldest, competitor in the Tri-State Martial Arts Tournaments

- Achievement of 10th Dan in Martial Arts

- 9th Dan presented by Adolfo Ennever, Hanshi/ Soke of the American Federation of martial arts on December 3, 2018.

- 9th Dan, by Eastern USA International Arts Association, under Grandmaster John Kanzler, Soke, on November 10, 2018.

- 10th Dan, presented by Grandmaster Lamar Thornton, under New Breed Life Association, October 10, 2015.

conferred the rank of Black Belt 7th Dan. Also, in 2014, he was awarded the rank of 8th Dan by both Shugeru Oyama and the American Federation of Martial Arts. In 2015, he was conferred with the rank of 10th Dan by Grand Master Lamarr Thornton of NBLA. In 2017, he was inducted into the Eastern USA International Martial Arts Association. Presently, Hachidan is a member of Bushiken Karate.

On June 30th 2019, Grandmaster Rayot Difate competed in Hue, Vietnam in a 3-day martial arts tournament sponsored by NGHIA Dung Karate-Do Mo Rong.

This was the first time in 60 years that this Asian tournament was open to Americans. Grandmaster traveled with a party of five, to be only one of two Americans competing.

Grandmaster took third place in Kata and 5th place in weapons. There were 800 competitors over the entire three-day event. He competed in the 50-year and older Masters division, in which he had the honor of being the oldest competitor at the age of 78. Besides representing the USA, were other Asian countries with Australia and Canada. He continues to teach, train, and compete. He encourages his older karate comrades to put themselves out there and continue to participate when possible.

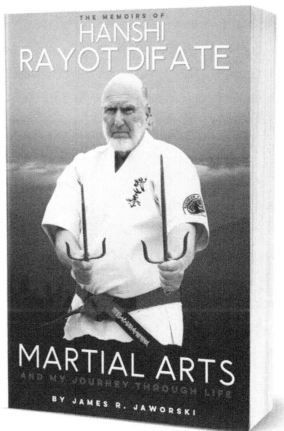

THE MEMOIRS OF
HANSHI
RAYOT DIFATE

MARTIAL ARTS
AND MY JOURNEY THROUGH LIFE
BY JAMES R. JAWORSKI

TO PURCHASE YOUR COPY, VISIT WWW.HANSHIDIFATE.COM

AL FARRIS

"

My philosophy is to Touch Lives, Change Lives, and Save Lives!

WHY THE Martial Arts?

Growing up, GM Farris lived in a low-income and high-crime community. The area he lived in constantly had violence, drugs, assaults, and people just trying to get by in life. He watched the police and criminals exchange gunfire at times, thinking this was normal. He was jumped and attacked growing up. He was bullied all through school. He had an extraordinarily strong motivation to learn martial arts.

After searching for a martial arts system, GM Farris found a Shaolin Kung Fu school to begin his training. He realized his training would be a lifelong journey. He also realized that one system might not be enough for every situation that could be encountered in life. Hence, he realized that mixed martial arts was the path for him to follow.

Forty-three years later, GM Farris is beyond thankful for the instruction, teaching, and systems he has been blessed to learn.

TRAINING INFORMATION

- Martial Arts Styles & Rank: Shaolin Kung Fu,10th Degree Black Belt, Grandmaster; Modern Warrior System 360, Mixed Martial Arts, Grandmaster-Soke; International Taekwondo Confederation, 9th Dan; Gracie Jiu-Jitsu, Law Enforcement Instructor, Edged Weapons, Law Enforcement Instructor, Jeet Kune Do, Mixed Martial Arts, Wing Chun, Boxing, Judo, Aikido, Taekwondo, Karate, Silat

- Instructors/Influencers: Grandmaster Paul Newton, Grandmaster Henry Cook, Rokudan Earl Cheatham, various Instructors, Masters and Grandmasters over the last 43 years

- Birthplace/Growing Up: USA

- Yrs. In the Martial Arts: 43 years

- Yrs. Instructing: 41 years

- School Owner at The Modern Warrior System 360, designed for first responders

PROFESSIONAL ORGANIZATIONS

- World Taekwondo Order (WTO)

- International Taekwondo Confederation (ITC)

- Director of the ITC Law Enforcement Board

How MARTIAL ARTS CHANGED My Life!

Studying martial arts made such a positive impact early on in GM Farris's life. Once he began a career in law enforcement, he could see a tremendous need for various forms of martial arts training. As an officer, he would run into criminals who refused arrest and seemed to feel no pain. The bad guys do not always comply with law enforcement officer requests. GM Farris realized that an officer must be well-rounded in this career. Our adversary may see us as a hurdle or roadblock to freedom. So, with all respect, it is quite clear that law enforcement officers will need a complete, well-rounded martial arts system or defensive tactics system! Martial arts have saved his life on numerous occasions. Once he began to see how much of an impact it had had on him and others, GM Farris developed a unique system for emergency first responders. He devoted decades to studying, analyzing, and developing a system that has worked very well. He incorporated the techniques utilized in self-defense to contain, restrain, control, and submit violent individuals. They would then be taken into custody without injury to the officer or threat most of the time - a unique system for a warrior of today. Hence, the Modern Warrior System 360 came about and has saved many lives in law enforcement and the community. The training he has provided during the civil unrest, protests, and riots over the last three years has saved the lives of officers and those in the community. Many are referring to him as the Law Enforcement Officer of the Decade.

PROFESSIONAL ORGANIZATIONS

- Co-Director of the ITC Advisory Board
- Co-Director of the Tactical Technology Board.
- Martial Arts Hall of Fame
- Martial Arts Hall of Fame, Alliance
- United States Martial Arts Hall of Fame
- International Council of Grandmasters
- International Congress of Grandmasters
- Action Martial Arts Hall of Honors
- Master's and Pioneer, the American Martial Arts Foundation
- American Freestyle Karate Association (AFKA)
- International Martial Arts Head Founders Grandmasters Council, International Martial Arts Council of America
- American Martial Arts Alliance Foundation
- American Martial Arts Alliance Foundation, Board of Advisors

PERSONAL ACHIEVEMENTS

- Achieved a Black Belt in Shaolin Kung Fu
- Been in the Martial Arts for 43 Years
- Serving in Law Enforcement for 38 Years with Dignity, Honor and Pride
- Top Gun Award
- Bachelor's in Business and Marketing
- Master's in Philosophy
- Ph.D., in Philosophy

He has assisted in developing a program to stop active shooters in our country that have gone national. Grandmaster Farris believes in helping people. His philosophy is clear and straightforward, "Touch Lives, Change Lives, and Save Lives!"

MAJOR ACHIEVEMENTS

- Shaolin Kung Fu, 10th Degree Black Belt, Grandmaster
- The Modern Warrior System 360, 10th Degree Black Belt, Grandmaster - Soke
- International Taekwondo Confederation, 9th Dan - Grandmaster
- Inducted into the Martial Arts Hall of Fame
- Inducted into the Hall of Heroes
- Inducted into the United States Martial Arts Hall of Fame
- Inducted into the Action Martial Arts Hall of Honors, Modern Warrior Award
- Master's and Pioneers, the American Martial Arts Foundation.
- Grandmaster of the Year Award
- International Grandmaster of the Year Award
- Law Enforcement Defensive Tactics Instructor of the Year Award
- American Freestyle Karate Association (AFKA), Modern Warrior Award
- Law Enforcement Officer of the Year
- Grandmaster of the Year - Law Enforcement
- Officer of the Year Award - Law Enforcement
- AMAA Changing Lives Award
- Law Enforcement Superior Leadership Award
- Officer of the Year
- American Freestyle Karate Association (AFKA), Law Enforcement Officer of the Decade
- Grandmaster of the Year Award Hall of Honors
- Honorable Elite Modern Warrior Award Hall of Honors
- World Taekwondo Organization, Hall of Honor, Leaders of Martial Arts Award
- The American Martial Arts Association Who's Who in the Martial Arts Metaverse Museum

MAJOR ACHIEVEMENTS

- The International Taekwondo Confederation (ITC) promoted him to 9th Dan and Grandmaster. The ITC has appointed him as the Director of the Law Enforcement Board, Co-Director of the Advisory Board, and Co-Director of the Tactical Technology Board.
- Grandmaster Farris has been appointed to serve with the United States Martial Arts Hall of Fame on the International Martial Arts Head Grandmasters Council.
- Grandmaster Farris has been selected to serve on the American Martial Arts Alliance Foundation Board of Advisors. These are all honors of a Lifetime.

LAW ENFORCEMENT AWARDS

- The Medal of Honor – Law Enforcement
- The Veteran of Foreign Wars Award – Law Enforcement
- The Millennium Maker Award – Law Enforcement
- The Medal of Honor – Law Enforcement
- Deputy of the Year Award
- Exemplary Performance
- He has been certified to instruct in over seventy specific areas of law enforcement and martial arts applications. Additionally, Grandmaster Farris has had the opportunity to train with and train agents - from the ATF, FBI, DEA, United States Secret Service, United States Marshals Service, local, state, federal law enforcement agencies, swat teams, dignitary protection teams, training divisions, and various agencies throughout the United States of America during his tenure.
- The training he provides is based upon real-life, real-world, street-proven experience.
- He has been recognized as a Use of Force Subject Matter Expert and speaks on various topics upon request.
- His students and peers refer to him as The Gold Standard in the World of Martial Arts Applications.
- Many refer to him as the Law Enforcement Officer of the Decade and he has received such awards.
- Grandmaster Farris is currently one of the highest-ranking martial artists in the world, actively serving as a law enforcement officer.

How has Grandmaster CYNTHIA ROTHROCK Influenced me?

Grandmaster Cynthia Rothrock first influenced his life as a martial artist. She was very inspirational to him early on in his martial arts journey. Her commitment and dedication to the martial arts touched his life in several ways. He realized from her movies playing the role of a law enforcement officer that he could truly protect himself and others by being proficient in various martial art styles. GM Farris is thankful to have had Grandmaster Rothrock as a mentor and now a dear friend in life. He always says she is genuine and down-to-earth whenever they talk. Thank you so much for everything and for being an incredible martial arts leader of our time.

GRANDMASTER FARRIS WAS NOMINATED FOR THE FOLLOWING PUBLICATIONS

- Nominated for the inclusion and honor of being in the Masters and Pioneers Book, American Martial Arts Foundation, a Special Tribute to Grandmaster Chuck Norris, being featured in the book and on the front cover. This book is by Grandmaster Jessie Bowen.

- Nominated for the inclusion and honor of being in the American Martial Arts Alliance Foundation, the Changing Lives Series. A Special Tribute to Grandmaster Ernie Reyes and being featured in the book and on the front cover. This book is by Grandmaster Jessie Bowen.

- Nominated for the inclusion and honor of being in the American Martial Arts Alliance Foundation, a Special Tribute of Who's Who in the Martial Arts Hall of Honors is featured in the book and on the front cover. This book is by Grandmaster Jessie Bowen and Sifu Alan Goldberg.

- Nominated for the inclusion and honor of being in the American Martial Arts Alliance Foundation, the Changing Lives Series. A Special Tribute to Grandmaster Bill "Superfoot" Wallace and being featured in the book and on the front cover. This book is by Grandmaster Jessie Bowen.

- Nominated for the inclusion and honor of being in the American Martial Arts Alliance Foundation, a Special Tribute for Elite Martial Artists in America Compilation Book, and on the front cover. This book is by Grandmaster Jessie Bowen.

- Nominated for the inclusion and honor of being in the American Martial Arts Alliance Foundation, Special Tribute of Who's Who in the Martial Arts Hall of Honors is featured in the book and on the front cover. This book is by Grandmaster Jessie Bowen and Sifu Alan Goldberg.

- Nominated for the inclusion and honor of being in the American Martial Arts Alliance Foundation, the Changing Lives Series, and Special Tribute to Grandmaster Cynthia Rothrock, featured in the book and on the front cover. This book is by Grandmaster Jessie Bowen.

Professor DYRUS GALOM

"
Martial Arts has given me a platform to pour into people of all ages positivity and self-esteem.

WHY THE *Martial Arts?*

I have always loved martial arts films. As a child, I would watch them and teach myself moves. One day my cousin took me to several karate schools where I did free lessons because we couldn't afford to pay for the classes. I went to the schools until I met Grand Master Walter E. Justice. He took me under his wing and taught me his systems of Tang Ken Ru Ju-Jutsi-Kenpo. This helped me develop self-esteem, self-control, patience, and a winning attitude. I knew that was something I wanted to teach others. Especially kids that were bullied, abused, or just felt alone in the world; like I once did. I wanted them to have the self-confidence to know they have a place in this world and a purpose. So don't give anyone the power to take that away. I learned this through martial arts and wanted them to know the same.

TRAINING INFORMATION

- Martial Arts Styles & Rank: Tang Ken Ryu Ju-Jutsi-Kenpo-6th Dan, Chinese Tai Kenpo Karate -3rd Dan, Combat Kenpo-2nd Dan
- Instructors/Influencers: Grand Master Walter E. Justice, Senior Prof. Bernard Strickland
- Birthplace/Growing Up: Elk City, OK / OK, TN, MO, Seattle, MS
- Yrs. In the Martial Arts: 30 years
- Yrs. Instructing: 25 years
- Professor at T.I.G.E.R. KENPO-JIUJITSU RYU

PROFESSIONAL ORGANIZATIONS

- TKKO Lifetime Member

PERSONAL ACHIEVEMENTS

- President Pin Kirby Award
- Gold Digger Ring Kirby Award
- Masters of Martial Arts Hall of Fame Trophy
- Masters of Martial Arts Hall of Fame Ring

MAJOR ACHIEVEMENTS

- Masters of Martial Arts Hall of Fame Member - June 10th, 2023

Martial arts gave me the self-confidence to endure things I could and could not control in life. The determination to make a difference in this world. That's what martial arts has always done for me. It made me a leader and someone who inspires others.

How MARTIAL ARTS CHANGED My Life!

In my studying martial arts, I have learned to stay calm. Meditation will help you think through all situations, and through self-control, I can resolve disagreements without going straight to fighting. I am slow to anger, and I listen more. Martial arts have helped to speak up and not be used and abused. It allows me to stand in my truth and not let the traumas I went through as a child and adult define me. I can release stress and all the negative energy through my daily practice. But most of all, it has given me a platform to pour into people of all ages positivity and self-esteem.

How has Grandmaster CYNTHIA ROTHROCK Influenced me?

Through Grandmaster Rothrock's movies, I learned right from wrong, self-confidence, and to help those who sometimes can't help themselves.

Garry
GASCOYNE

"

My journey hasn't ended. It is still evolving...

WHY THE *Martial Arts?*

I became interested at the age of 10 by reading the fundamentals of jiu-jitsu and applying the techniques on my siblings. In the sixties, karate schools were not available as they are today. To get any information, you needed to travel to a big city, Boston being the closest, and coming from a family of 9 with one vehicle, that was not financially possible. The Plymouth public library in the jiu-jitsu section (no karate section as yet) became my dojo.

1976: Graduated high school and enlisted in the Air Force a few months later, became a Security Specialist earning a Presidential recognition for exceptional duty. I was trained in hand-to-hand combat skills and various weapons during that time. I also trained in the art of boxing to improve my skills.

1981: I continued my studies in martial arts trying several styles over many years, Taekwondo, Uechiryu, etc. I realized choosing a discipline was like choosing the right suit; it needs to choose you.

TRAINING INFORMATION

- Martial Arts Styles & Rank: U.S.A. Gojudo-9th Dan
- Instructors/Influencers: The late: GM Walter Parks, GM Peter Urban
- Birthplace/Growing Up: Plymouth, MA
- Yrs. In the Martial Arts: 33 years
- Yrs. Instructing: 25 years
- School owner & Instructor at White Horse Urban Gojudo

PROFESSIONAL ORGANIZATIONS
- The Moose American Door Assoc.

1987: I began Gascoyne Garage Door and Motor company and built a thriving family business, still in operation today.

1995: I was introduced to the USA. Goju by my then instructor Sensei Walter Parks and mentored by GM Peter G. Urban, reaching the rank of 7th Dan until their passing.

1999: I own and operate the White Horse Urban Gojudo Karate School, which is still thriving. My students had taken many first-place awards in years of tournament play. Awarded GM Urban's coveted "E" flag and the Urban Cup.

2019: Promoted to 9th Dan by Grand Master Sekwii Sha of the Shanando system.

I have been honored to be recognized for my years in the arts by some very notable organizations, such as: A.M.A Hall of Honors - Sifu Alan Goldberg, W.H.O.F. S. C.- Grand Master Frank Sanchez, Florida Hall of Fame and Publisher of "The Karate Voice" Grand Master Katsaitas, Kung fu/karate Hall of Fame Sifu Cliff Kupper.

I have and will continue to improve my martial arts skills and pass on my knowledge and experience to my students and those my life touches.

How has Grandmaster CYNTHIA ROTHROCK Influenced me?

I've met Cynthia several times throughout the years. She was always open and welcoming to me. She showed a genuine interest in engaging in conversation. She is an absolute example of you work hard; you reap the benefits.

PERSONAL ACHIEVEMENTS

- Husband, Father, Grandfather, Great Grandfather, Business Owner, and Dojo Owner

MAJOR ACHIEVEMENTS

- Vietnam-era Veteran Dept. of Defense retired Federal Officer

How MARTIAL ARTS CHANGED My Life!

The martial arts training has built my self-confidence in business and home life. I come from a large family where the probability of going down the wrong road was real. My life would be very different if it had not been for my time in the military and my found martial arts. Martial arts brought out the best in me. I can't fully explain my gratitude for the Senseis that influenced me in the past, present, and future. My journey hasn't ended. It is still evolving.

Alan
GOLDBERG

One must wonder what Master Goldberg, publisher and promoter of the event is thinking looking out in this vast sea of martial artists. How did it all start? Over fifty years ago Alan Goldberg set forth on a path in Martial Arts that some of us could only dream of. Master Goldberg's early training was in the art of Shotokan Karate and he studied with Masters Manard Miner and George Cofield. He would later learn the traditional and non-traditional arts of Five Animal Kung Fu.

As the 1970s entered, Master Goldberg met a young Master who took him on the path to where he is at today. That young Master was Jason Lau.

As the 1970s entered, Master Goldberg met a young Master who took him on the path to where he is at today. That young Master was Jason Lau.

Sifu Lau is the disciple of famed Shaw Brothers stable, Master Jiu Wan. Sifu Lau and Master Goldberg would form a student and Master bond that has lasted over thirty years. Their friendship so close that they even spent five years living in a Shaolin Wing Chun temple with three other disciples, and Master Lau now holds the title of #1 Disciple of the Family. Master Goldberg jokes of those days saying, "Sifu Lau would wake up at 2:00 in the morning, telling his disciples it was time to train." For Master Goldberg, it was like a dream. But sometimes woke up the next morning wondering was it or wasn't it. "I would have lived there longer with Sifu Lau, but I was due to get married soon and my wife did not agree with

my continued plan of living in a temple." (And he wonders why not...)

When Sifu Lau left New York City in the early 80s, he suggested Master Goldberg train with the late Sifu Moy Yat of the Yip Man family. This would give Master Goldberg the opportunity to study Wing Chun under different Sifus and allow him the chance to have a well-rounded education in the art. Known for his longevity in the art, Master Goldberg is a pioneer of Wing Chun in the United States.

Master Goldberg now teaches Wing Chun Kung Fu in the heart of Brooklyn to a small but dedicated group of students. The temple has been active for over 25 years and there have been opportunities to expand it as a business. "I have had opportunities to expand, but I am really not interested in having a large school because it loses some of the tradition and close family ties that I have built with my students," Master Goldberg tells us. The tradition continues as three of his oldest disciples teach in different areas of the United Stated. Master Goldberg's other notable students include actor Joe Piscopo of Saturday Night Live, Heavy-weight World Champion Dimitrius "Oak tree" Edwards who is notoriously known as the man who broke Mike Tyson's ribs in a sparring match, and world renown orthopedic surgeon Dr. Richard Pearl. Others associated with his kung fu family include Phil Morris from Seinfeld, and Joe Venerrie from the oldies group the Tokens.

Master Goldberg is the holder of Black Belt Magazine's "Kung Fu Instructor of the Year – 2004" award, and has been inducted into 70 other Halls of Fame. He holds a position on boards in major martial arts federations. He is a founding member of Martial Arts Grand Master International Council (MAGIC), a founding member of World Black Belt along with Chuck Norris and Bob Wall and he is a board member of the International Sports Hall of Fame with Dr. Bob Goldman and Arnold Schwarzenegger.

Become an
AMAA MEMBER!

Publisher of Action Martial Arts Magazine, the largest free magazine in the United States today, he created one of the nation's hottest martial arts fads, Action Martial Arts Magazine Collector Cards. Master Goldberg created Law Enforcement Survival System (LESS), the only self-defense course taught to the NYC Emergency Service Unit of the New York Police Department. He starred in Great Karate Inspirations was the only person performing Kung Fu. He has an instructional video on Wing Chun produced by Yamazato Productions, and appears in Rising Suns' production Martial Arts Masters. He has also taken a position as Vice-President of Shaolin Brand Products, is a board member of the Martial Arts History Museum, the Martial Arts of China Historical Society, and Black Belt Magazine's Festival of Martial Arts, and is Co-President of Sidekick Publications.

He was also one of the promoters and Vice-President of 21st Century Warriors, which showcased some of the legendary martial artists of our time. This event saw the return of Don "The Dragon" Wilson, Royler Gracie, Orlando "The Warrior" Rivera, Dan "The Beast" Severn and others battling it out on Pay-Per View.

His proudest moment is yet to come at the Atlantic City Tropicana Casino and Resort, when he will again produce his MEGA Martial Arts weekend showcasing the Action Martial Arts Magazine Hall of Fame Banquet, and the world's largest martial arts trade show and expo.

Dr. Robert GOLDMAN

Dr. Goldman is a 6th-degree Black Belt in Karate, a Chinese weapons expert, and a world champion athlete with over 20 world strength records and has been listed in the Guinness Book of World Records. Some of his past performance records include 13,500 consecutive straight leg situps and 321 consecutive handstand pushups. Dr. Goldman was an All-College athlete in four sports, a three-time winner of the John F. Kennedy (JFK) Physical Fitness Award, was voted Athlete of the Year, was the recipient of the Champions Award, and was inducted into the World Hall of Fame of Physical Fitness, as well as induction into numerous Martial Arts Hall of Fames in North America, Europe, South America, and Asia. He founded the International Sports Hall of Fame, recognizing the world's greatest sports legends, with ceremonies held annually at the Arnold Schwarzenegger Sports Festival-the largest sports festival in the world, with over 200,000 participants, 70+ sports represented, and over 20,000 competing athletes, making it double the size of the Olympic Games.

Dr. Goldman holds two Physician & Surgeon Medical Degrees and two Medical Doctorates and has served as a Senior Fellow at the Lincoln Filene Center, Tufts University, and as an Affiliate at the Philosophy of Education Research Center, Graduate School of Education, Harvard University. He also holds Visiting Professorships at numerous medical universities around the world. He co-founded and served as Chairman of the

Board of Life Science Holdings and Organ Inc, biomedical research & development companies with over 150 medical patents under development in the areas of brain resuscitation, trauma and emergency medicine, organ transplant, and blood preservation technologies. These led to the formation of Organ Recovery Systems Inc. and then LifeLine Scientific Inc, a Public Company which became a world leader in organ preservation and transport. He has overseen cooperative research agreement development programs in conjunction with the American National Red Cross, NASA, the Department of Defense, and the FDA's Center for Devices & Radiological Health.

Dr. Goldman received the 'Gold Medal for Science, the Grand Prize for Medicine, the Humanitarian Award, and the Business Development Award. Dr. Goldman has also been honored by Ministers of Sports and Health officials of numerous nations. The President of the International Olympic Committee awarded Dr. Goldman the International Olympic Committee Tribute Diploma for contributions to the development of Sport & Olympism. Dr. Goldman was also awarded the 2012 Life Time Achievement Award in Medicine & Science. He was among the few recipients of the Healthy America Fitness Leader Award, presented by the United States Chamber of Commerce and President's Council.

Dr. Goldman served as Chairman of the International Medical Commission for over 30 years, overseeing Sports Medicine Committees in over 194 nations, and Chairman of the IFBB and NPC Medical Commissions. Dr. Goldman also served as Chairman of the AAU/USA Sports Medicine Council, which oversaw several million amateur athletes. He founded NASM (National Academy of Sports Medicine), the premier fitness certification organization, coined the term CPT (Certified Personal Trainer), and wrote the first certification exam ever done for that profession.

He has served as a Special Advisor to the President's Council on Physical Fitness & Sports and is the founder and international President Emeritus of the National Academy of Sports Medicine (NASM) and Board Member Emeritus for the US Sports Academy and Chairman of their Board of Visitors. The US Sports Academy is the #1 sports academy worldwide. Dr. Goldman is also the Co-Founder and Chairman of the American Academy of Anti-Aging Medicine (A4M), with outreach to over 120 nations. A4M is the world's largest preventative medicine and medical conference/exposition organization that has trained over 150,000 medical specialists since 1992. Dr. Goldman Co-Developed the American Board of Anti-Aging & Regenerative Medicine (ABAARM) and American Board of Anti-Aging Health Practitioners (ABAAHP) Board Certifications, as well as the American College of Sports Medicine Professionals (ACASP) certificate exams and such, has overseen Post Doctoral Medical Education programs the last 30 years. He is a co-founder and Chairman of the World Anti-Aging Academy of Medicine and a Co-Founder of the Tarsus Medical Group, which comprises a family of medical conferences and exposition divisions.

Dr. Robert Goldman was promoted to the level of KNIGHT COMMANDER by His Royal Highness Prince Gharios in 2020, following his 2019 Knight Hospitaller of the Equestrian Order of Michael Archangel under the Royal House of Ghassan appointment.

He has also received Dynastic adoption, which has never been done outside the Royal family's bloodline in 1,800 years, as now a full member of the Imperial and Royal Family.

Dr. Goldman's official Royal Titles from Sovereign Imperial and Royal House of Ghassan: Knight Hospitaller of the Equestrian Order of Michael Archangel, KNIGHT COMMANDER, Duke of

Tartous, Sheikh of Margat, Representative of the Royal House to the United Nations, and Medical Director of the Sovereign Royal House.

The Royal House of Ghassan is accredited by the United Nations and is one of the oldest Christian Royal Houses in the world, dating 400 years before the First Crusade. Sir Dr. Robert Goldman is also a member of the International Board of the Royal House of Ghassan, the Heath Director, and also a member of the inner Special Counsel to the Sovereign Prince, and the Main Representative of the Royal House of Ghassan to the United Nations.

Dr. Goldman donates 80% of his time to charitable pursuits worldwide, supporting sports, fitness, and medical education for the sports and medical communities worldwide, visiting dozens of nations focusing on youth mentorship.

How has Grandmaster CYNTHIA ROTHROCK Influenced me?

Grand Master Cynthia Rothrock has inspired many worldwide, including me, with her remarkable athletic achievements, focus, discipline, and maintaining a modest, kind attitude toward all students. She is one of the most personable teachers in the field of martial arts

Scott GRAHAM

> " Studying martial arts has given me an amazing sense of belonging and self-worth. The impact it had upon my life is nothing short of incredible.

WHY THE *Martial Arts?*

As a young man, I had a troubled past. I had an abusive and neglectful upbringing. I discovered martial arts at 15. My instructor became my father figure and role model, and my training partners became my family. The spirit of togetherness gave me a feeling of acceptance. It also encouraged me to grow as a person. With this came a feeling of newfound confidence and faith in myself. I then became an instructor myself and have mentored over 5000 adults and children to help them build confidence in themselves and help realize their full potential.

TRAINING INFORMATION

- Martial Arts Styles & Rank: Honorary 1st Dan-Shotokan Karate, Kukkiwon 4th Dan-Taekwondo, Honorary 1st Dan-Hapkimudo, Blue Belt-Kickboxing (working towards Black Belt)

- Instructors/Influencers: Paul Powers, Andy Hill, Nick Maskrev

- Birthplace/Growing Up: United Kingdom

- Yrs. In the Martial Arts: 33 years

- Yrs. Instructing: 27 years

- School owner, Manager, Instructor at Steel City Martial Arts

PROFESSIONAL ORGANIZATIONS

- Word Taekwondo Federation

- British Taekwondo©

- British Taekwondo Council

How MARTIAL ARTS CHANGED My Life!

Studying martial arts has given me an amazing sense of belonging and self-worth. The impact it had upon my life is nothing short of incredible. If I hadn't discovered martial arts, my life would have turned out very definitely for the worse. The discipline and respect that martial arts have given me have made my life successful. I have an amazing family and a loving wife who has trained and taught alongside me since 2000. My daughter has helped me coach since achieving her 2nd Dan at age 12, and I also have a son who helps with our online marketing in martial arts. To summarize, martial arts has united me and my family as a close unit. It enables us to help other people in martial arts.

How has Grandmaster CYNTHIA ROTHROCK Influenced me?

We invited the amazing Cynthia Rothrock to our martial arts school in Sheffield in May 2023, where she gave us an amazing seminar and inspired us all.

Grandmaster Cynthia Rothrock inspired our female students and crowd. Having a female influence like Cynthia is crucial in a male-dominated sport. It has inspired our female students to train more and start doing things they would be scared of or wouldn't have enjoyed, like sparring. It's amazing to see the courage it has given our female students, thanks to Grand master Cynthia Rothrock

PERSONAL & MAJOR ACHIEVEMENTS

- Former British Champion Taekwondo 1996
- European Bronze Medalist Taekwondo 2000
- Numerous Regional 1st place Medals
- UK Martial Arts Hall of Fame 2022 and 2023
- Kaizen Outstanding Contribution Award 2023

Become an AMAA MEMBER!

Rick GREENE

> **"**
> The martial arts gave me a safe path to become a better person and father than I had growing up.

WHY THE *Martial Arts?*

I got started in martial arts in 1978, in my mid-twenties. I was looking for something to help me get into shape. My wife and I had a newborn son. I was working in a factory and needed something to do. Each night after work, I would go for a run. I would run about 5 miles each night. I would run past this martial arts school, it was hot outside, and they would keep the front door open. As I went by, I could hear them screaming. I told myself that someday I would stop and check it out. When I returned home, I told my wife about Yorktown, the Martial Arts Center. I told her I might be a little late returning home from my run tomorrow.

So, the next night, as always, I started my run. I would run past the school and to the Police Station and turn around to return to where I had come. Here I am, this twenty-something man telling myself I'm too old to start the martial arts, but I went inside and sat down. It just so happened that the Jujutsu class was on the mat

TRAINING INFORMATION

- Martial Arts Styles & Rank: Combat Jujutsu Shodan, Yoshin Ryu Jujutsu Shodan, Shiho Karano Ryu Jujutsu Godan, Shiho Karano Kenpo Jujutsu Godan, Founded the Art of Midori Kazoku Bushi Jujutsu, 1986

- Instructors/Influencers: Joan Gilbert, Dr. Clement Riedner

- Birthplace/Growing Up: Muncie, IN

- Yrs. In the Martial Arts: 44 years

- Yrs. Instructing: 42 years

- School owner & Instructor at Bushi-Kan Dojo

PROFESSIONAL ORGANIZATIONS

- World Warrior Org

this night. As I sat there, a small woman approached me and asked, "Are you interested in Jujutsu?" I said, "I'm not sure I was just checking it out." I sat there for about an hour, and the class was over.

The same woman said, why don't you come back and try a free class? I told her I would think about it. So the week I went to try the thing called Jujutsu, I walked in, and she smiled at me, showed me where to stand in line, and began class. After the class warmed up, she asked me to take the center, and not knowing what was to come, she would call out a number, and the student with that number would step inside the circle and grab me. The next thing I knew, I was on the mat looking up. This went on for close to an hour. I must admit I was worn out and glad that hour was over. At the end of my first class, she approached me and said, I hope you come back and join our class. Oh, and welcome to Jujutsu. That was in 1978, and I have never stopped.

All the ups and downs, the good and the bad have been worth every minute. I would not change a thing! I received Yudansha in 1980 and, at the same time, inherited the school from my Sensei. I moved my school/dojo to my residence a year later and built the Bushi-Kan Dojo.

I don't advertise for students. With that said, I have a waiting list for new students in their 40+ years. I have promoted 13 Black Belts to Yudansha; most have over twenty-plus years of training! My sons both trained with me as well as my late wife. She passed away in 2012 from cancer. My oldest son Chris followed in my

PERSONAL ACHIEVEMENTS

- I'm a retired Police Officer
- I'm the proud father of two sons

MAJOR ACHIEVEMENTS

- 2010 Inducted into the Shinto Martial Arts Association Martial Arts Legend
- 2013 Inducted into the Shinja Martial Arts University Jujutsu Instructor of the Year
- 2019 Inducted into the American Martial Arts Alliance Who's Who Legend Award

WHY THE MARTIAL ARTS (CONTINUED)

footsteps, went into law enforcement, and is with the Yorktown Police Dept. He has reached the grade of Menkyo Kaiden. My style is Midori Kasoku Bushi Jujutsu. 2006 I received Shodai Soke from Dr. Clement Riedner from his Gathering of the Clans Sokeship. I trained under his guidance from 1985 till his passing in 2021. In 2013 in Sarasota, Florida, from the Shinja Martial Arts University, I received the grade of Judan from John Enger.

How MARTIAL ARTS CHANGED My Life!

I came from a rough neighborhood where crime was happening, with gangs from both sides. I had four brothers. One went to prison, two died of drug overdoses, and my parents were alcoholics. I was the only one in my family that graduated from High School. My two sons have never seen me smoke or take a drink of alcohol. The martial arts gave me a safe path to becoming a better person and father than I had. Our neighborhood was called Shedtown because of the run-down homes in that low-income area. Martial arts guided me. I looked up to the Black Belts in the school and did not want to let my instructor down. Growing up, I was a small kid under a hundred pounds—the smallest kid in our High School. I learned really quick I had to fight if I was going to survive. The martial arts gave me the confidence I was looking for. I'm 69 years young now. I look forward to teaching and helping others that may need someone to look up to! I enjoy watching my students grow and become strong in body and spirit. My school has the motto, "Seven times down, eight times up." My late wife would say this to herself after each chemo treatment. She was a true "Warrior!" I build martial artists, not Black Belts. Yudansha's are a dime a dozen. Anyone can claim rank in a time and day where everyone wants to be a tenth degree. In my eyes, most don't make the grade. The martial arts have taught nothing worth having comes easy.

How has Grandmaster CYNTHIA ROTHROCK Influenced me?

I love that she's a woman in Martial Arts with her success and her movies!

Become an AMAA MEMBER!

Rita Hundley
HARRIS

"

Martial arts helped me cope with skills to effectively respond to agonizing, unbearable, or unjust situations.

WHY THE *Martial Arts?*

At the age of three, my parents placed my twin and me in the Dutchess Community College Laboratory Nursery School, where they studied twins. Interestingly, their observations of me were, "Rita is compassionate and observant of other children with special needs, and her muscular coordination is exceptionally good. This is evidenced by the ease with which she uses her body". In our second year of twinship studies, it was stated that "Rita enjoys being outdoors where she has more space and freedom to move. She uses her body easily and gracefully when she climbs, jumps, runs, or pumps herself in the swing.

My parents were licensed social workers who raised four children in Washington, D.C. They had a simple goal for their four children: to obtain our education, participate in structured community programs and serve others. Like most children, we were exposed to our recreation centers, and we were enrolled in

TRAINING INFORMATION

- Martial Arts Styles & Rank: Tae Kwon Do - 7th Degree
- Instructors/Influencers: Sensei Robert Morton, Sensei Ralph Hundley, Sensei Charlie Neal, Grand Master Johnny D. Houston (Current)
- Birthplace/Growing Up: Queens, NY / Washington, DC
- Yrs. In the Martial Arts: 51 years
- Yrs. Instructing: 35+ years
- Instructor

PROFESSIONAL ORGANIZATIONS

- American Psychological Association (APA) Member
- Psi-Chi National Psychology Honors Society (Member)
- National Association of Housing and Redevelopment Officials (NAHRO)
- National Association of Housing Counselors and Agencies, Inc. (NAHCA)
- The Order of the Eastern Star - Past Grand Matron
- Union Wesley AME Zion Church – Vice-Chair of UW Housing Development

Howard University's summer gymnastic and swimming programs. My father believed his children should be able to protect themselves as we traveled throughout the D.C. area. So, my martial arts training started at eight years old. Many commercial Dojangs in Washington, D.C., had established names and wore fancy uniforms; however, my parents had a strict budget and only allocated $3 monthly for martial arts training. I learned early that I could be an instructor and have my fees waived. Learning and practicing martial arts at Banneker Recreation Center taught me that it was not the fancy martial arts school with the most students, but the martial arts instructors and their life lessons were the most important.

At twelve years old, my twin brother and I earned our black belt in Tae Kwon Do under the tutelage of Sensei Robert Morton at Banneker Recreation in Washington, D.C., adjacent to Howard University. As soon as I began training seriously in martial arts, I realized I was different from my siblings. The difference was that my physical and mental attributes inclined me towards martial arts and sports. Some of my physical characteristics were that I could hit hard, kick high, run fast, jump high, and climb almost any tree. Mentally, I had the heart and mindset of a champion before I knew what that meant.

"Champions do not become champions when they win the event, but in the hours, weeks, months and years they spend preparing for it. The victorious performance itself is merely the demonstration of their championship character."
~ Alan Armstrong

PERSONAL ACHIEVEMENTS

- Wife to Don Harris since January 28, 1992
- Mother to DeVyn Walter and Daelyn Edward Harris
- Obtained a double major in Biology and Psychology
- Mary Baldwin College Athletic Hall of Fame for Martial Arts
- Obtained a Master's Degree in Clinical Psychology
- An active member of Union Wesley AME Zion Church for 52 years
- 37 years in the Affordable Housing Industry profession
- Community Advocate for Seniors, Veterans, Homeless, and the Disabled since 1986

MAJOR ACHIEVEMENTS

- 1982 Most Athletic - The Academy of Notre Dame
- 1982 Mid-Atlantic Practitioner Outstanding Black Belt Kata Award
- U.S. Capital Classics First Women's Sparring Grand Champion 1982-1983
- National Regional PKL Rating, ranked #1 in Forms and Fighting
- Defending Champion - Everhart's Tri-Area Karate and Kung Fu Championship
- 1986 Athlete of the Year, Mary Baldwin College
- 1985 & 1986 Krane New England Open Black Belt Superstar Finalist
- Fighting Strategy Seminars
- Self-Defense Seminars
- 1997 3rd Annual Living Legend Awards – Sensei Robert Everhart, Kenpo Karate Washington, D.C.
- 2010 Mary Baldwin College – Hall of Fame
- 2011 U.S. Capital Classic – Hall of Fame
- 2012-Present Union Wesley AME Zion Board of Trustees
- 2017 Leadership Tomorrow Inductee
- 2017 Who's Who In The Martial Arts-Legends Edition
- 2019 Montgomery County Lead for Impact Inductee
- 2022 Montgomery County Illuminate Your Leadership Inductee

I began my competitive martial arts training at age 12, and soon I could compete at the age of 16 in the women's division. I won numerous local, state, and national U.S. martial arts tournaments. I attended Notre Dame Academy, a private girls' school in Washington, D.C. I competed in Track and Field events and participated on the Pom-Pom Team, in swimming, and in Karate. In my senior year, I won "Athlete of the Year." In the same year, I was recognized by the Mid-Atlantic Martial Arts Practitioner for Outstanding Black Belt Kata Award Winner. Over and over, I repeatedly won in my chosen sports and proved that being a woman has no bearing on excellence.

In the 80s and 90s, getting martial arts recognized in most academic circles did not align with typical sports such as basketball, track and field, volleyball, etc. Therefore, getting martial arts recognized in high school and college was challenging; however, I soon earned respect and could couple education with martial arts. While at Mary Baldwin College in Staunton, Virginia, where my skills continued to shine, I represented the college at competitions locally and nationally. In my senior year, I was not only selected and chosen by my classmates for Who's Who of Colleges and Universities, but the College's Athletic Department and the student body chose me as "Athlete of the Year" in 1986.

Upon graduating from college, I continued participating in tournaments and ranking tests. Since I started in martial arts, the wins kept coming, but the losses taught me my greatest lessons. Martial arts taught me not to be

MAJOR ACHIEVEMENTS

- 2022 USHOFMAA 2022 International Hall of Honor Inductee
- 2023 Co-Author of Best Seller-Elite Martial Artist Secrets to Life, Leadership & Business by GM Jessie Bowen
- 2023 Women's Hall of Honors
- 2023 AmeriCorps and the Office of the Presidents Lifetime Achievement   Award for volunteer service

WHY THE MARTIAL ARTS (CONTINUED)

obsessed, mad, or overthink my decisions when I lose. The most important takeaway from starting in martial arts through today is that failure begins the learning process. My experience in martial arts taught me mental and physical conditioning. The lessons in martial arts taught me to align my priorities, exercise self-control even when the going gets tough, develop a stick-to-itiveness attitude, and always finish whatever I start.

How MARTIAL ARTS CHANGED My Life!

The impact of martial arts was not just for discipline, confidence building, or protecting myself from bullies. Martial arts helped me cope with skills to effectively respond to agonizing, unbearable, or unjust situations. Unfortunately, we encounter bullies in childhood and adulthood at work or in the community. I always wanted to use martial arts for the skill of self-preservation. Awareness that I would know what to do in difficult situations without overthinking is one of the most impactful lessons I learned.

A second way that martial arts has impacted my life is with focusing, memory retention and developing what is now referred to mindfulness. Learning the offensive and defensive patterns that are required in performing Kata's helped me in school and in life to buckle down and keep my head in the game especially through adversity. In life, building not only your physical but mental strength is important. Martial Arts improves your overall memory. Through repetition of most sports techniques you will improve your muscle memory. In life there will be many things that distract you and Martial Arts develops your focus and helps you to perfect task until they are second nature to you. Finally, Martial Arts teaches you calmness and peace of mind through meditation, intentional breathing techniques and practicing patience. Anchoring in to your spiritual power makes all of the above only that much greater. As for me, my soul is anchored in the Lord.

HOW MY LIFE IS CHANGED (CONTINUED)

The third impact of martial arts in my life was to be of volunteer service and always be concerned for others. I dedicated my life to volunteering to serve the homeless community, persons with disabilities, veterans, seniors, and many other populations in need.

Finally, the impact of martial arts in my life is to continue staying active in the Tae Kwon Do community by conducting self-defense seminars and volunteering as a referee for local and national martial arts tournaments. I am especially grateful to impart any wisdom on to those who are practicing or participating in the Youth only tournaments.

How has Grandmaster CYNTHIA ROTHROCK Influenced me?

In Kata, Grand Master Cynthia Rothrock inspired me because we were fellow competitors in the DMV area. I would win Women's Hard Forms, and GM Cynthia Rothrock would win Women's Soft Forms. Whenever I see Cynthia out and about, I am reminded of her dedication and commitment to Martial Arts. As a fellow Weapons and Kata Champion, I admired how GM Rothrock got her edge and beat the rest of us out in the competition. Internally, it drove me to work harder and find truth in the statement "iron sharpens iron". As a reflection, today, I can say that Grand Master Rothrock was and is the catalyst for change in how our beloved Martial Arts is viewed today in the area of media, film, and production. I am so proud of how far she has come and wish her only continued blessings.

James HOGWOOD

"

Tai Chi has helped me heal my body, keep my mind focused, and restore my spirit.

WHY THE *Martial Arts?*

In 1973, my older brother Joel started me off in Wing Chun when I was five. From then on, every Military Base my Father was stationed at had some Martial Arts. I learned Shotokan, Aikido, Kendo & Judo in Hawaii while continuing my Shaolin Training. In Virginia, I studied Greco-Roman Wrestling & Tang So Do. In Alabama, I studied Shotokan, Taekwondo & Ninjitsu. In Pennsylvania, I studied Taekwondo, Baquazhang Tai Chi & Police Defensive Tactics, which I later found was developed from Hapkido.

In 1988 I was promoted to black belt and developed my own system of the Martial Arts Long Tai "Dragon Kick." Over the next 25 years, I devoted my life to developing defensive tactics in Law Enforcement. I began Kali and Hubud training to sharpen my skills.

I progressed over the years to Grand Master in several art forms and a Master in others. I became the International Senior Master

TRAINING INFORMATION

- Martial Arts Styles & Rank: Shotokan Karate-1st Dan, Baquazhang Master-5th Dan, Tai Chi Master-5th Dan, Kyuk Kum Sool-Grand Master 7th Dan, Taekwondo-Grand Master 8th Dan, Hapkido-Grand Master 9th Dan, Long Tai-Founder & Soke, Movement & Control-Founder & Soke

- Instructors/Influencers: Brain Bradford, Leonard Hall, Joel Blevins, Timothy Warfield, Ed McIntyre, Francisco Conde, Tony Grano, Charles Parker

- Birthplace/Growing Up: San Diego, CA / Military Kid

- Yrs. In the Martial Arts: 50 years

- Yrs. Instructing: 37 years

- School Owner, Manager & Instructor at The Academy of Self Defense

PROFESSIONAL ORGANIZATIONS

- Korean Martial Arts Instructors
- Korean Hapkido Federation
- USA Hapkido Chairman

Instructor for Hand to Hand, Baton, Knife Defense, and Small Unit "Operators" Tactics for all US Military and Law Enforcement Branches. My Highest Current Rank is my 9th Degree in Hapkido.

How MARTIAL ARTS CHANGED My Life!

As a Law Enforcement Officer, I was involved in over 2,000 altercations. As a result, I have had over 50 surgeries on my body. Right Shoulder 5 cables, Left Shoulder 3 cables, Left Bicep bitten in half, metal mesh from a Bilateral hernia, Right Hip 3 Cables, Bilateral Tibia Ostectomy, Bilateral Knee Replacement, Brain Damage, and Cardiomyopathy. Through all this, Tai Chi has helped me heal my body, keep my mind focused, and restore my spirit.

PERSONAL ACHIEVEMENTS

- Master's Degree in Government Business
- Graduate School Human Resources and Law
- Medical Program Director Over Health Sciences

MAJOR ACHIEVEMENTS

- Founder & Master Instructor of the National Self-Defense Agency, Inc. 501c3 for the empowerment of victims of Domestic Violence & Sexual Assault

How has Grandmaster CYNTHIA ROTHROCK Influenced me?

She was the first Female Action Star and inspired others to pursue their dreams.

Kevin
HOOKER

"

Without martial arts, I know I'd not have accomplished many life-changing opportunities.

WHY THE Martial Arts?

I originally started Martial Arts while in college. Shotokan Karate was my first experience. After graduating and moving to my new hometown of Omaha, Nebraska - I found Kenpo. But I didn't find it right away. From being a collegiate athlete and loving sports all my life - I wanted to maintain the physicality and hard workouts of being active. After college, I was missing that concept and the trials of being an avid sports enthusiast. So, I began training in Kenpo Karate to fill that void. In the beginning, it was exciting and invigorating. The euphoric feeling of being back in action was almost intoxicating. Actually, it was intoxicating. My training took over much of my life and I was in the dojo every chance I could get. The school I attended shifted directions several times - but my instructor stayed humbled and maintained a course of true character - finding deeper roots to the kenpo lineage. It was extremely challenging mentally and over time that thrilling feeling dulled a little. As the school settled into a more

TRAINING INFORMATION

- Martial Arts Styles & Rank: Kenpo Karate - 5th Degree Black Belt, Brazilian Jiu Jitsu - Black Belt
- Instructors/Influencers: Professor Nick Chamberlain, Master Greg James, Sensei Tom Scott. Trained with: Hanshi Tadashi Yamashita, Shihan Fumio Demura, Choki Motobu Sensei, Shifu Bill Chun, Jr.
- Birthplace/Growing Up: Grand Island, NE
- Yrs. In the Martial Arts: 30 years
- Yrs. Instructing: 15 years
- School Owner, Manager & Instructor at Elite Academy of Martial Arts

PROFESSIONAL ORGANIZATIONS

- Member USKF
- Member Kenpo Arts Alliance

organized atmosphere, I found peace and tranquility in my training. I think it's important to note that I never felt burdened by the training. I truly enjoyed it and still do (now more than ever). However, life did get very busy with three kids and a business that was taking off. As time progressed my teacher retired. I bought his school and took on the role of ownership in a karate business (alongside my current business that was now highly successful). That changed my perspective completely. My "why" about becoming a martial artist became about giving back. I settled into an already accomplished school with instructors and students. Time passed and many chapters in my journey left me with fun stories to tell. As karate business sometimes do - change happened again and I had to start over, very recently. This reinvigorated me once again - even after 25 years in my art - I found a deeper love once again in creating something that I can, not only give back to my community, but challenge my "older" body even further. My "why" now is not just about me learning new skills, honing my art, maybe adding a form or technique to my repertoire and it's even deeper than just giving back. Teaching life lessons like discipline, honor, humility, character, integrity and confidence, just to name a few - through my passion has become something I found along the way. I didn't intend for it. I didn't plan for it. But God has a way of putting incredible opportunities in front of you if you only step up to it. Now – I'm focused on sharing my experience with others, creating relationships, and building a better community one student at a time.

PERSONAL ACHIEVEMENTS

- Competed at our state games for several years earning gold & silver medals each year
- Competed in BJJ Tournament, earning the silver medal
- 2017 Awarded Master Rank and title of Shihan (Godan)

MAJOR ACHIEVEMENTS

- 2023 USKF Black Belt Hall of Fame Excellence Awards Outstanding Small School
- 2022 Co-Author Karate Book "Men in the Martial Arts Secrets to Life, Leadership & Business"
- 2019 Keepers of the Flame Instructor
- 2018 Keepers of the Flame Instructor

How MARTIAL ARTS CHANGED My Life!

After my first one retired, I was extremely fortunate to find a new teacher. Without martial arts, I know I'd not have accomplished many life-changing opportunities. I've visited both coasts several times for seminars and testing and south through Texas. I continue to gain and maintain confidence in my skills as a martial artist and my professional and business leadership skills. I've learned how to de-escalate confrontations, and I've also learned how to control my emotional responses to outside influences. Martial arts have given me confidence in my physical ability to handle many situations and my mental ability to think through scenarios and find proper outcomes. My journey has been wrought with challenges with interesting twists and turns. Suffice it to say – that overcoming each obstacle has been rewarding and inspiring. I have had the blessing of teaching my wife and son, which has been an amazing experience that we will always cherish. As my passion takes up many hours away from my family, it also allows us to follow our dreams and gives us time for self-reflection and growth. The relationships I've built over the past 25 years have truly and pleasantly shaped me. I look forward to many more and creating new ones moving forward. I also know that those that come and go within this journey are always welcome with friendship and respect. Another area that truly has been amazing is the ability to teach and share my vision and knowledge with so many others across the United States and, at the same time – learn from them as well. There are so many

HOW MY LIFE IS CHANGED (CONTINUED)
incredibly talented people from all over this astounding country. Working with people, training them, and giving them positive life lessons of growth has been extremely fulfilling.

Become an AMAA MEMBER!

Michael
HORNSBY

"

The impact of martial arts in my life has reached beyond my personal life and has impacted my professional life.

WHY THE *Martial Arts?*

Dreaming of being Bruce Lee after my father took me to a Bruce Lee movie, I took an interest in martial arts as a very small child. He then took me to a karate demonstration, and I was hooked. My father casually enrolled me into a martial arts school around the corner of our house, thinking I would not stick with it. Getting more serious about martial arts and martial arts training in my preteens, I began my life-long journey in the Martial Arts resulting in over 40 years of training in the martial arts with Black Belts in Tae Kwon Do, Tang Soo Do, Soo Bak Kee including formalized training in Ju Jitsu and Filipino Martial Arts. Nothing that I have accomplished in the arts could have been achieved without having amazing Instructors like Grandmaster Mike Fillmore, Grandmaster Able Villarreal, Grandmaster Rodney Kauffman, Grandmaster Johnny Thompson, and Grandmaster Dan Roberts, along with many more martial artists and Instructors who have had a direct influence in my martial arts life.

TRAINING INFORMATION

- Martial Arts Styles & Rank: Tae Kwon Do - 8th Degree, Tang Soo Do - 7th Degree, Soo Bak Kee - 8th Degree
- Instructors/Influencers: Grandmaster Mike Fillmore, Grandmaster Abel Villerrreal, Grandmaster Rodney Kauffman, Grandmaster Johnny Thompson, Grandmaster Dan Roberts
- Birthplace/Growing Up: Alaska
- Yrs. In the Martial Arts: 40+ years
- Yrs. Instructing: 25 years
- School owner & Instructor at True Force Tae Kwon Do

PROFESSIONAL ORGANIZATIONS

- Founder/President of True Force International Martial Arts Alliance
- Vice President of the World Moo Duk Kwan Tae Kwon Do Alliance
- World Moo Duk Kwan Alliance Grandmaster Council
- Vice President of the Federation of International Martial Arts

With many rank promotions, like my 4th Dan in 2002, 5th Dan in 2009, 6th Dan in 2010, and 7th Dan in 2017. I was promoted to 8th Dan Grandmaster in 2018. Being promoted to the rank of Grandmaster was a true blessing by the Lord. I am humbled and thankful for the belief in me of many fellow martial artists.

How MARTIAL ARTS CHANGED My Life!

Studying Martial Arts has not only impacted my life but has also ultimately shaped my life. Martial Arts aligned with the same ideals and values that my parents instilled in me. Being a forever martial arts student has taught me how to be a productive citizen, caring father, loving husband, and servant leader. There is nothing like being able to serve others.

Studying martial arts has allowed me to formulate and build the foundation for my students. The foundation of Courtesy, Integrity, Perseverance, Self-Control, and Indomitable Spirit will enable those students to reach and achieve their dreams and become the great men and women they are destined to be.

If not for my studying martial arts, I would not have been placed in front of the right men and women in the arts. It was not so much these men and women were the best kickers, punchers, or world title holders, but the men and women with the right character, values, and belief system.

PROFESSIONAL ORGANIZATIONS

- NE-DU-U-KON -Tae Karate Kung Fu Federation
- Tang Soo Do Karate Association
- Black Knight Karate Association
- Texas Tae Kwon Do Association
- International Martial Council of America

PERSONAL ACHIEVEMENTS

- International Champion
- World Champion
- National Champion
- State Champion
- Promoter of the True Force Global Internationals Martial Arts Championship

MAJOR ACHIEVEMENTS

- 2021 Universal Martial Arts Hall of Fame: Distinguished Grandmaster of the Year
- 2021 United States Martial Arts Hall of Fame: Executive Competitor of the Year
- 2020 The United Kingdom Blackbelt Hall of Fame: Devoted Award
- 2020 International Martial Arts Hall of Fame: Platinum Life Award
- 2018 United States Martial Arts Hall of Fame Inductee: Outstanding Grandmaster
- 2017 United States Martial Arts Hall of Fame Inductee: Silver Life Award
- 2016 United States Martial Arts Hall of Fame Inductee: Distinguished Master
- 2010 NE- DU-U-KON TAE Karate Kung Fu Federation Hall of Fame Award: Outstanding Contributions to the Martial Arts
- 2009 World Organization of Martial Arts Athletes Hall of Fame Inductee: USA Coach of the Year
- 2009 USA International Black Belt Hall of Fame Inductee: Master Black Belt of the Year
- 2006 USA International Black Belt Hall of Fame Inductee: School of the Year Award
- 2004 World Karate Union Hall of Fame Inductee: Master Instructor of the Year
- 2004 World Wide Martial Arts Hall of Fame Inductee: Outstanding Contributions to the Martial Arts
- 2003 USA International Black Belt Hall of Fame Inductee: Pinnacle of Success Award

The impact of martial arts in my life has reached beyond my personal life and has impacted my professional life. It has given me the skill sets to not only own and run a school but also the skill sets to work in the managerial arena in different career fields.

How has Grandmaster CYNTHIA ROTHROCK Influenced me?

Grandmaster Cynthia Rothrock has influenced my life and many others in a way that she laid out the blueprint for how to be a martial artist. Though Cynthia Rothrock is the queen of martial arts, she has always stayed true to herself and her Ideals. With many championship

MAJOR ACHIEVEMENTS

- 2002 North American Black Belt Hall of Fame Inductee: Master Instructor of the Year

- 2002 US Team/Alliance Hall of Fame Inductee: Competitor of the Year

- 2002 USA International Black Belt Hall of Fame Inductee: Master Instructor of the Year

- 2002 United States Martial Arts Hall of Fame Inductee: Outstanding Martial Artist of the Year

- 2002 Universal Martial Arts Hall of Fame Inductee: Black Belt of the Year – Tae Kwon Do

- 2002 World Wide Martial Arts Hall of Fame Inductee: Male Competitor of the Year - Tae Kwon Do

Donald JETT

"
Martial Arts gave the external and internal foundation of life and sharing culture to make a difference.

WHY THE *Martial Arts?*

It was in 1968 that I discovered Chinese Martial Arts. Playful as I was and seeing Kung- Fu movies, my father put me in the care of a Taiwanese Soldier, which gave me my first introduction. As a precocious child, as recalled by older siblings, people saw me as shy and self-preserved but energetic. Any disturbance, I would seem to disappear into a room and listen to Asian music. Being the youngest, if I was being picked on, my older brother told me that he would beat me and the other person if I were beaten up. That fear alone turned me into a fighter.

First, at hand, I would like to give honor and respect to Grandmaster Bill "Superfoot" Wallace, who has set a path and platform for other martial artists to follow. He has given me great inspiration in my years of practice. He has a phenomenal story that surpasses many during his era and now. I remember watching his many films and as a strong male figure as a child.

TRAINING INFORMATION

- Martial Arts Styles & Rank: Kenpo Karate, Shotokan Karate, Long Xing Pai (Long Hsing Dragon), Pai Lum (White Dragon), Yong Chun (Wing Chun), and Ca Li Fu (Choy Li Fut), Kung Fu

- Instructors/Influencers: Grandmaster Anthony Goh, Grandmaster Wang Jurong, Grandmaster Johnny Lee, Master Charles Dixon, Grandmaster Alex, Tat Mau Wong, and Grandmaster Shawn Liu

- Birthplace/Growing Up: El Paso, TX / Worldwide

- Yrs. In the Martial Arts: 53 years

- Yrs. Instructing: 40 years

- School Owner, Manager, Instructor, Department of Justice Instructor

PROFESSIONAL ORGANIZATIONS

- A.C.E. Certificate

- National Organization Black Law Enforcement Executive Justice By Action

- Kung Fu Federation

He persevered in his struggle and overcame the many obstacles that came his way. You were among the best among the other pioneers I looked upon! Thank you, Bill "Superfoot" Wallace, for contributing to all martial artists.

How MARTIAL ARTS CHANGED My Life!

Martial Arts gave the external and internal foundation of life and sharing culture to make a difference.

How has Grandmaster CYNTHIA ROTHROCK Influenced me?

The Lady Dragon has a devastating Scorpion kick. She has been a significant contributor to the Martial arts and the industry. A Champion of Forms with the beauty and most incredible heart that is compassionate toward others. Thanks for all your contributions. She has led by example!

PERSONAL ACHIEVEMENTS

We are all loved first. To be positive is to know yourself and the creator. A good leader is acquired when you know yourself no matter what you do in life. If you don't know yourself, you will never appreciate anything in life.

Today's work of a great human being is to know yourself and assist others. I have discovered this self-help through personal experience and dedicated learning. It's the greatest help to a given task. It seems there is no end to this ongoing process. Remember to stay positive is to enjoy yourself, plan, and accomplish with gratitude. Staying positive is the greatest personal

MAJOR ACHIEVEMENTS

A martial artist is a human being first. Just as nationalities have nothing to do with one's humanity, they have nothing to do with martial arts. Life is a constant process of relating. So this formed some major achievements in my life. In America, many students are taught to defend themselves from school bullies or feel more confident while out at night. Others belong to karate or dojo clubs and follow the tournament circuit collecting as many trophies as their talents can win.

I wanted to learn the seemingly complex philosophical concepts or constraints with ethical notoriety from past warrior societies. The martial way taught me technical proficiency and the external reward of athletic success. It opened the door to a rich heritage of ethical principles, training approaches, and esoteric capabilities that enriched my martial arts experience. It sharpened my ability to defend myself or succeed in competition, but most importantly, it is a way of living. It's a holistic discipline aimed at pursuing excellence in the training hall and life. I strived to apply the way in every vocation to achieve every field of my endeavor. This set a foundation for major achievements like working with the Department of Justice, Big Brothers Mentoring Program, Eastern Band of Cherokee Youth programs, and many martial art awards. I owned and operated a health and wellness center and a fitness center. I organized the Art of War and China Comes to Atlanta (China Cultural Arts Festival and Expo 2003), bringing various cultures and masters from around the Globe. I've officiated many tournaments for many years, including the Battle of Atlanta and the International Chinese Martial Arts Championships. I thought a career in corporate law was my answer, but I became an Instructor with D.O.J., which opened doors to give back to society and bring cultures together; it was an outstanding achievement.

John L.
JOHNSON

"

Martial arts have taught me to keep going and never to give up on goals that I have set for myself.

WHY THE *Martial Arts?*

After meeting Sensei James Clark while being assigned to an Airborne Training Unit at Fort Benning, GA, I was messing around and ran into a block and punch that got my attention, so I contacted him later to find out he was an instructor in arts of Tae Kwon Do. After talking with him, I was accepted as one of his students, one of the best decisions I've made. He not only taught me form and fighting techniques, but he also taught me more discipline, self-control, and much more. So I love the arts, and we went to many tournaments and were always placed in the top three in forms and fighting. The patience he instilled helps me even to this day as well as serving in the military.

I'm a native of Shellman, Georgia, and the Son of the Late John L. Brown and Lillie B. Johnson. I have five siblings. In 1968 I graduated from Shellman Vocational High School in Shellman, Georgia.

I joined the Army in September 1969 and attended basic training at Fort Benning, Georgia,

TRAINING INFORMATION

- Martial Arts Styles & Rank: 2nd Dan Black Belt
- Instructors/Influencers: Sensei James Clark
- Birthplace/Growing Up: Shellman, GA
- Yrs. In the Martial Arts: 40 years
- Yrs. Instructing: 5-10 years
- Instructor

PROFESSIONAL ORGANIZATIONS

- Military

and Advance Infantry Training at Fort Polk, Louisiana. Once I graduated and received my jump wing, I was sent to Vietnam, where I was wounded. After being cared for in Camp Japan, I was sent to Fort Benning for continued recovery. Once I was released and was able to, I was sent to duty as a paratrooper, assigned to an airborne combat unit. As I rose in rank, I was sent to Germany for two years as a Squad Leader.

I was sent to Drill Sargant School at Fort Jackson, South Carolina, where I was assigned to basic training as a Drill Instructor for two years. During that time, I became Senior Drill Sargant and won Best Drill Sargant Platoon and Best Drill Instructor several times. I was reassigned to Fort Benning as Airborne Instructor after going through Jump Master School; I was then assigned to the Ground Branch, then Jump Branch; I was there for several years and was selected to go to Equal Opportunity School in Florida. After completion, I returned to Fort Bragg as Equal Opportunity Advisor/Counselor. I was promoted to 2nd Dan Black Belt Tae Keon Do.

I went back to Germany as a Mechanize Infantry Platoon Sargent for two years, returning back to Fort Bragg as an Airborne Infantry Platoon Sargent. The unit I was assigned to was deployed to Saudi Arabia for the Deserts Storm War. After my return, I was assigned to Brigade Headquarters until retirement.

At Fort Benning, I met Sensei James Clark. After meeting, I joined his Tae Kwon Do Class. The training wasn't easy; however, it paid off. We went to about 15 or more tournaments placing in the top three in kata and fighting. I continued to

PERSONAL ACHIEVEMENTS

- Associate degree in General Education
- Associate degree in Criminal Justice
- Associate degree in Pastoral Ministry

MAJOR ACHIEVEMENTS

- Two daughters, six grands, and three great-grands
- Honorably Retired from the Military
- Associate Pastor
- Received or attained 2nd Dan Black Belt under the instructor I started with

train, and when Sensei saw I was prepared, I was tested and earned My 1st Dan Black Belt in 1985 under Sensei James A. Clark, I started training in 1981.

The different phases of training I have received in the military, in which my primary mission was to be able to be ready to defend the Constitution of the United States and the one I help train. I was able to carry out the mission.

Training with Sensi Clark has helped me with self-control, patience, and focus on different training techniques. I was trusted by Sensei Clark to teach classes in his absence when duty had him committed to task.

This sport can make you better focused, teach you discipline and respect, make you stronger, more flexible, and much more. I help the young people in my community and church with discipline, self-control, and self-defense.

I have achieved several Associate Degrees in college, from General Education, Criminal Justice, and Pastoral Ministry; all school and training have helped me to move forward. I have attended many courses to help me be proficient in the position I held in the Military, martial arts, and now ministry, where I teach and preach, along with counseling. In the Military, I received National Defense Service Medal, Air Medal, Good Conduct, Army Accommodation, MSM, Bronz Sta, Purple Heart, Master Parachutes Jump Wing, and others.

I'm married to Cynthia G. Johnson, the Author of her first book, An Inspirational Book of Powerful Testimonies. We have two children, six grands, and three great-grands, I am one proud Papa/Great Grand Papa.

How MARTIAL ARTS CHANGED My Life!

After coming in contact with Sensei Clark, I have grown mentally and physically by staying active, even with a hip replacement. Martial arts have taught me to keep going and never to give up on goals that I have set for myself. I have more patience and the ability to be positive in most situations by taking necessary action to deactivate, when possible, rather than confrontation.

James
KELLER

"

Studying the martial arts has made me a better person, husband, and friend.

WHY THE Martial Arts?

Growing up in Brooklyn and later working in Manhattan, I met Grandmaster Richard Lenchus who was head and founder of Legend Shotokan Karate Association. I started learning karate under him for over 35 years. I have studied with Guru Greg Alland Arnis and Pencak Silat, Grandmaster Joe Onopa Kwon Bop Do to rank of 9th Degree Black Belt, and Guru Billy Bryant Cadena De Mano, eskrima to the rank of instructor. I also have a Grandmaster rank under GM Rudy Jones in Eagle Star Self Defense System who studied under Moses Powell and Prof Vee. Now I'm studying with Soke Najee Hassan and his wife in Sirat as Sayf. I am also studying Tai chi yang style under Sifu Allan Fung and Master Lee.

In 2011, I inherited the Legend Martial Arts Association from GM Lenchus. I was a coach on the USA Martial Arts team from 1996-2000.

I've been inducted into the following Martial Arts Hall of Fames: World Christian Martial

TRAINING INFORMATION

- Martial Arts Styles & Rank: Legend Martial Arts-10th Degree Black Belt, Kwon Bop Do-9th Degree Black Belt, Arnis and Pencak Silat Eagle Star Self Defense-10th Degree Black Belt, Cadena de Mano, Kuntao, Silat, Eskrima-Instructor, Sirat as Sayf- Level 4 Green Belt, Tai Chi

- Instructors/Influencers: GM Richard Lenchus, GM Joe Onopa, GM Billy Bryant, Guru Greg Alland, Soke Najee Hassan, GM Rudy Jones, Sifu Allan Foung, Master Lee

- Birthplace/Growing Up: Queens, NY / Brooklyn, NY

- Yrs. In the Martial Arts: 45+ years

- Yrs. Instructing: 30+ years

- Instructor

PROFESSIONAL ORGANIZATIONS

- International Grandmasters of the Roundtable

- Legend Martial Arts System

- Kwon Bop Do Federation

- Sirat as Sayf

Arts and Pastoral United International Kung Fu Federation, World Karate Union HOF, Action Martial Arts Magazine HOF, World Head of Family Soke Council HOF, Masters of Martial Arts Awards HOF

I have taught kids, adults and women self-defense classes in several centers and schools in Brooklyn and Queens.

I am committed to teaching and sharing my knowledge to children and adults hoping to make a positive impact in their lives.

Become an
AMAA MEMBER!

PERSONAL ACHIEVEMENTS

- Being married to the same beautiful woman for 50 years.
- Still being in the martial arts for 49 years and still have the thirst to still wanting to learn more.

MAJOR ACHIEVEMENTS

- To still be able to teach students and have a positive impact on their lives.

How MARTIAL ARTS CHANGED My Life!

Studying the martial arts has given me the chance to travel nationally and internationally to judge and referee at tournaments events. During these travels, I have met many great people, teachers, and friends.

Studying the martial arts has made me a better person, husband, and friend. Also, the martial arts has given me the chance to work with disadvantaged youth in NYC as well as teaching self-defense classes for women. During my travels, I was given the opportunity to do demos and seminars.

I had the chance to study several different martial arts cultures. I have studied Shotokan Karate, Kwon Bop Do, FMA (Arnis, Escrima, Kali, dirty boxing), and Tai Chi.

Dexter V. KENNEDY

"

I am dedicated to martial arts and deeply passionate about helping others improve their lives.

WHY THE *Martial Arts?*

Like many, I became committed and determined after seeing "Fists of Fury." Immediately I started mimicking the moves I had seen. My first martial arts classes came by signing up for a six-week Taekwondo class taught by one of Eddie Gaston's black belts, a well-known martial artist in the Columbia area.

During the first week of classes, I became frustrated with the instructor's teaching methods and the limitations of the art, challenged the instructor, and beat him just from what I had learned from watching the movie. So, of course, I left that school and later found Genova Karate School. This is where I was tested and truly challenged. All the milestones and achievements of my career are a culmination of dedication and focus, which were enhanced through my training. This is especially impressive, considering I started my first karate school in 1986, shortly after receiving my black belt from Mike Genova, Bruce Brutschy, and Keith Vitali. These teachers were foundational to my approach to martial arts and beyond.

TRAINING INFORMATION

- Martial Arts Styles & Rank: American Karate (Ishinnryu)-5th Degree (Godan) Black Belt
- Instructors/Influencers: Mike Genova, Bruce Brutchy, Keith Vitali
- Birthplace/Growing Up: Columbus, GA / MD, NJ, OK and Europe
- Yrs. In the Martial Arts: 49 years
- Yrs. Instructing: 30+ years
- Past School Owner, Help StandUp Against Violence Everyone (S.A.V.E) Columbia, Author, Inventor

PROFESSIONAL ORGANIZATIONS

- United States Hall of Fame
- Sport Karate Museum
- AMAA

How MARTIAL ARTS CHANGED My Life!

I am extremely proud of my career accomplishments thus far. In particular, I am grateful that I had the opportunity to pass my knowledge on, inspiring people with my skills and passion for keeping the fire of martial arts alive and burning. Obviously, I am dedicated to martial arts and deeply passionate about helping others improve their lives.

I invented and have an approved patent for the Self-Defense Belt Weapon System (#10,076,146). The patented Self-Defense Belt Weapon System is an innovative belt that features five blades. It's essential for self-defense, and what makes it stand out is that it can be worn with any outfit without looking conspicuous. It's made of stainless steel, leather, rubber, and elastic and can be used to strike, cut, or spear an attacker.

In addition to this, my books on martial arts are available on Amazon. They include: "Taking on the NFL with ProTeams Kumite Sport," "Pro Teams KumiteSport - Martial Arts," "Taking on the NFL: The National Martial Arts League," "Team Point Fighting: In a Professional Martial Arts League," and "Team Point Fighting Investors Game Plan: In a Professional Martial Arts League."

I'm currently working on my much-anticipated audiobook, "The Blood 120." This book delves into my research on how blood is the life source for healthy living. Foods one person eats may act as medicine for one and poison another solely because of blood type. It is impressive that I am not only a leader in martial arts but also a talented published author with many books under my belt.

PERSONAL ACHIEVEMENTS

- Certified Emergency Medical Sciences - City Colleges Chicago - 1981
- Retired United States Army Chief Warrant Officer Two - 1994
- Retired University of South Carolina - IT Project Manager - 2020

MAJOR ACHIEVEMENTS

- Patent for the Self-Defense Belt Weapon System (#10,076,146)
- Authored several books, which include: An Amazon best seller, "Taking on the NFL with ProTeams Kumite Sport," "Pro Teams KumiteSport - Martial Arts," "Taking on the NFL: The National Martial Arts League," "Team Point Fighting: In a Professional Martial Arts League," and "Team Point Fighting Investors Game Plan: In a Professional Martial Arts League."
- Hall of Fame Induction into the United States Martial Arts Hall of Fame

Chris KESTERSON

"
My life, base, and core values are heavily influenced and shaped by my 40-plus years in martial arts.

WHY THE *Martial Arts?*

My father got my brother, and I started at an early age. I was fortunate to grow up in an era of popular martial arts movies. I watched as many youths at the time as actors/artists like Bruce Lee and Chuck Norris perform amazing performances on the screen. I was in awe!

I began my journey as many did with the available arts at the time in my location. Isshinryu was my first discipline, followed several years later by Taekwondo. I enjoyed the athletic qualities of both arts. As I aged, I could travel more, and other arts became available. I was hungry to try each I encountered, and over the past 40-plus years, it has been an amazing journey.

TRAINING INFORMATION

- Martial Arts Styles & Rank: Kestese 8th Dan, Karate 2nd Dan, TKD, Judo, BJJ, Ketsugo, Krav Maga, Boxing
- Instructors/Influencers: Howard Pittenger
- Birthplace/Growing Up: Knoxville, TN
- Yrs. In the Martial Arts: 46 years
- Yrs. Instructing: 32 years
- Instructor

PROFESSIONAL ORGANIZATIONS

- AMAFF (Who's Who Inductee & Ambassador)
- USMA
- USMAA
- WBBB
- MAMWF
- IBJJF
- CAC Leadership
- Shekinah Masonic Lodge
- Moose Lodge
- Tennessee Sheriff's Asso.
- ICMAF
- SKKA
- American Legion
- AZA
- POI
- Kentucky Colonels

How MARTIAL ARTS CHANGED My Life!

I have learned that no matter how many years you dedicate to your art, the degrees you earn, and how many disciplines you study to improve your craft and art, we should all hunger for more knowledge. We should be that anxious, eager, and hungry white belt we began as. Knowledge is the true power in martial arts, and the ability to constantly learn is crucial. My life, base, and core values are heavily influenced and shaped by my 40-plus years in martial arts.

How has Grandmaster CYNTHIA ROTHROCK Influenced me?

I recall watching Cynthia on film and was always amazed at her athletic ability. She is one of the martial artists that made me want to pursue an acting career. Every time I have been fortunate to meet and talk with Cynthia, I am amazed at how nice and knowledgeable she is. She is an inspiration to many other martial artists throughout the world and me.

PERSONAL ACHIEVEMENTS

- IMDB listed actor
- Tennessee Firearms and Defense Instructor
- HOF entries for martial arts
- Ambassador for AMAA
- SPF world record holder.

MAJOR ACHIEVEMENTS

- I am recognized for my contributions to Martial Arts through several organizations.

Marvin KING

"
Martial Arts have become who I am. Everything is based on the philosophy of martial arts.

WHY THE Martial Arts?

My martial arts journey started as an adolescent in the 60s when martial arts schools were traditional, tough, and gritty. As a new student in my first Karate class, I was paired with a bigger student who choked me out by applying too much neck pressure during a basic choke escape drill. That first experience was painful and nearly caused me to quit. But I didn't. During those early days in the dojo, I quickly learned that you need discipline, patience, and courage to earn a black belt. I remember falling a lot, picking myself up, and pushing my physical limits as my Sensei drilled us in the art of kicking, punching, sparring, and self-defense. I eventually earned a green belt in Tae Kwon Do with discipline and hard work, but because the school was far from home and expensive, I stopped training there. Being removed from the dojo was disappointing, but unbeknownst to me then, that transition would be what ignited my great love, commitment, and journey in martial arts. It also reminded me of what my parents

TRAINING INFORMATION

- Martial Arts Styles & Rank: Tae Kwon Do, Traditional Shuai-Chiao, Ch'ang style T'ai-chi-ch'uan and Hsing Jing (Ch'ang's "essence of Hsing-I"), Shaolin Do Kung Fu, Hung Fut Southern Shaolin Kung Fu, Krav Maga, Target Focus Training (TFT), Korean Sulsa, Ju-Jitsu, Sun Style Tai Chi Chuan

- Instructors/Influencers: Grandmaster Ch'ang Tung-Sheng, Grandmaster Chi-Hsiu Daniel Weng, Ph.D, Grandmaster Sin Kwan The 8th Generation, Grandmaster Tai Yim, Grandmaster Bryant Fong, Master Tim Larkin, Pavel Tsatsouline

- Birthplace/Growing Up: Cleveland, OH

- Yrs. In the Martial Arts: 50 years

- Yrs. Instructing: 40 years

- School owner & Instructor at Bowie Kettlebell Health and Wellness Center

PROFESSIONAL ORGANIZATIONS

- Project Management Institute (PMI): Project Management Professional (PMP)- 2012 to present.

- Project Management Institute (PMI): Agile Certified Practitioner (PMI-ACP)

- Duke Certified Lean and Agile Practitioner (DCLAP) Project Manager taught me about not settling for the status quo and to keep moving forward.

My turning point was when I realized that being a martial artist was not about a school or a system but about practice, discipline, consistency, perseverance, and patience!

Curious to know more, I researched books and literature and accumulated and absorbed everything on the subject. I learned about strength training, kinesiology, bodybuilding, philosophy, meditation, and diet. Bruce Lee movies also inspired me. I appreciated the variety in martial art systems and was humbled to know that each system offered abundant knowledge, tradition, and history.

By age 12, I transformed my body by consuming healthier foods and adding weight training and meditation to my martial arts practice. During the '70s, I took Karate classes in gyms and auditoriums and trained with accomplished Tae Kwon Do Black Belts. 1980, I joined the International Shuai-Chiao Academy in Cleveland, Ohio, with Master Chi-Hsiu Daniel Weng Ph.D. Master Weng would often host his teacher Grandmaster Ch'ang Tung-Sheng (aka The Flying Butterfly), when he visited from Taiwan. I was humbled after witnessing the power, balance, and grace of these Masters and was excited to finally learn Chinese Kung Fu. Shuai-Chiao training included the Ch'ang style T'ai-chi-ch'uan and Hsing Jing (Ch'ang's "essence of Hsing-Yi"). I stayed with Shuai-Chiao, practiced hard every day, and was honored to earn my first Black Belt from the late Grandmaster in 1982. I successfully competed in many Shuai-Chiao and Karate tournaments in

PERSONAL ACHIEVEMENTS

- 2 Time Marine Corp Marathon Finisher
- 1 Time Philadelphia Marathon Finisher

MAJOR ACHIEVEMENTS

- CEO / Owner of the Bowie Kettlebell Health and Wellness Center, teaching Kettlebells, Joint Mobility, Strength Stretching, Qigong, and Martial Arts Science.
- 2023, Who's Who International Hall of Honors Legends Awards
- 2022, Martial Arts Author of the Year Award for; "The Art of Being Well, Healthy Strategies for Daily Living."
- Certified Wellness Coach
- 2021, President Joe Biden Ameri corps Lifetime Achievement Award
- 2021, "Outstanding Martial Arts Instructor" award from the American Freestyle Karate Association (AFKA)
- 2021, American Martial Arts Alliance Board of Advisors
- 2021, Inducted into the Argentina International Martial Arts Hall of Fame.
- 2020, Represented the United States Instructors in the first "World Martial Arts Live" International event in which over 40 countries were presented.
- 2020, "Lifetime Martial Arts Achievement Award" from the American Freestyle Karate Association (AFKA)
- 2019 Inductee into the American Martial Arts Alliance (AMAA) Who's Who Legends Hall of Honors.
- Featured in the 2019 Martial Arts Masters and Pioneers Autobiography Book.
- 2020 Action Martial Arts Hall of Honors Inductee and received the (40-Year Martial Arts Golden Lifetime Contributions Award

in the years following my training and was appreciative when tournament rules were changed to accommodate more fighting styles.

Today, I'm focused on the "Wellness Lifestyle" and the minimalist approach to Reality-Based Self Protection, Qigong, Tai Chi, and the development of functional strength best achieved from Hardstyle Kettlebell exercises. Under the guidance of Kettlebell and strength expert Pavel Tsatsouline, I earned the Level 1 and Level 2 Russian Kettlebell Challenge (RKC) Certifications. I was fascinated and awestruck with how quickly the Kettlebell 1-Arm Swing and Turkish Get Up (TGU) improved the martial artist's fighting endurance and power. I immediately implemented the RKC strong man philosophy and minimalist training methods in my martial arts practice with immediate positive results. Hard Style Kettlebell Swings teach the Martial artist how to generate explosive hip power while relaxing the arms and anchoring the feet. Like the Yin / Yang, the TGU (Yin) develops the elusive soft elements of strength while the Kettlebell Swing (Yang) accentuates the martial artist's ability to generate explosive power.

MAJOR ACHIEVEMENTS

- Featured in the 2020 Action Martial Arts Hall of Honors World History Book
- Black Sash in Hung- Fut Kung fu with 8th Generation Grandmaster Tai Yim
- 1995, World Kung Fu Federation (WKF) National Forms and Weapons Grand Championship
- 1982, Black Belt in Shuai-Chiao from Grandmaster Ch'ang Tung-Sheng and Master Chi-Hsiu Daniel Weng Ph.D.
- Member of the first-generation USA Shuai-Chiao Black Belts
- Brown Belt in Shaolin Do, where I learned the Qigong breathing meditations under Grandmaster Sin Kwan The National Council of Strength and Fitness (NCSF) Certified Professional Trainer (CPT) 1999 to present
- Russian Kettlebell Challenge (RKC) Level 1 Certification
- 2006 to present with Kettlebell and strength expert Pavel Tsatsouline.
- Russian Kettlebell Challenge (RKC) Level 2 Certification – 2009.

WHY THE MARTIAL ARTS (CONTINUED)

In 2014, I created the Bowie Kettlebell Club (BKC), a strength and holistic wellness-based school that teaches and trains students to be functionally fit at any age using Joint Mobility, Kettlebells, Qigong, and Martial Arts. In 2020, during the COVID-19 pandemic, the business went virtual and officially changed its name to the "Bowie Kettlebell Club Health and Wellness Center." The program expanded internationally to represent and show others that the goal of a really good fitness program is to teach the "Art of Being Well." We call this approach to wellness "Forever-Young-Forever," which has become the philosophy behind the training method. Like the martial arts progression from beginner to advanced, the student learns that the art of being well is more about the little things you do every day to remain functionally youthful for a lifetime. Self-protection classes at the BKC focus on understanding actual violence and the simple tools anyone can use to protect themselves. No previous training or martial arts prerequisites are required for this class. The BKC "Loaded Yoga" and "Forever-Young-Forever" Programs are a creative blend of Kettlebells, Joint Mobility, Strength Stretching, Qigong, and Martial Art exercises that, when done regularly, will improve each person's ability to maintain a state of athletic readiness. The programs can also be adapted to complement any training method.

I'm humbled by this opportunity to serve others and live by a simple philosophy, "You don't have to please anyone! You only have to be the best you that you can be!" So, "Find a path, stay humble, and always march forward courageously!"

How MARTIAL ARTS CHANGED My Life!

Martial Arts have become who I am. Everything is based on the philosophy of martial arts. The ability to incorporate my skills learned in martial arts into everyday living has inspired me to write my first book entitled "The Art of Being Well, Healthy Strategies for Daily Living." Martial arts have inspired me so much that I cannot remember when I haven't practiced martial arts in some capacity each day. I look forward to fellowshipping with my martial arts like-minded friends for years to come.

How has Grandmaster CYNTHIA ROTHROCK Influenced me?

I first saw Cynthia perform in the 1980s at a martial arts event in a central hotel in downtown Cleveland, Ohio. I didn't know much about her then, but I immediately saw an extremely good ability in her martial arts form performance. She was by far the best performer and won all her events. From that point forward, everything she has received to date has been well deserved and earned 100 times over. Now that I am a Master Martial Artist Hall of Famer, I see her often and can appreciate how she, as a celebrity, has remained humble and true to the martial artist warrior code. Grandmaster Cynthia Rothrock exemplifies the true essence of being a Martial Arts Grandmaster, and I'm proud to know her as an alumnus of the American Martial Arts Alliance.

John
KRAFT

"

Martial Arts is my home. It's simply a lifestyle, and everywhere I go.

WHY THE *Martial Arts?*

In 1971, a friend invited me to join him in Tae Kwon Do. We were both Juniors in High School. It was fun. In 1978 I began in Ralph Castro's Shaolin Kenpo on a more serious level; I needed self-defense and had my life threatened, being told I would be killed. I was raising a family in those years, and family came 1st, so training was hit and miss. In the late '80s, I began to teach children, then adults, and compete in local tournaments, doing well in fighting. In 1993 I opened a school with my family and long-time training partner Sue Messenger and her family. Our school: Pacific Shaolin Kenpo in Aberdeen, WA was a thriving and successful school. A series of bad things happened at the end of the 90s, and I had to quit teaching and training, returning from retirement in 2014. After being received with open arms in the Martial Arts community, I began to notice my peers were struggling, having stayed day after day, year after year. I've been trying to unite Martial Arts and help Grandmasters in their retirement years.

TRAINING INFORMATION

- Martial Arts Styles & Rank: Ralph Castro's Shaolin Kenpo-4th Degree Black Belt (2016-Kajukenbo, Intermediate)
- Instructors/Influencers: GGM Ralph Castro, GGM Rob Castro, Master Sonny Pabuaya
- Birthplace/Growing Up: Aberdeen, WA / Central TX, Washington State, Upstate NY
- Yrs. In the Martial Arts: 50+ years
- Yrs. Instructing: 20 years
- School Owner, Manager & Instructor at Pacific Shaolin Kenpo

PROFESSIONAL ORGANIZATIONS

- Northwest Shaolin Kenpo Association

Now, I teach self-defense as a community service. I'm very grateful to be recognized as an instructor on a National level for my past accomplishments in the ring, notably competing at a World Championship Level when I retired, and for the many students who were instrumental in my success as an Instructor.

How MARTIAL ARTS CHANGED My Life!

Martial Arts is my home. It's simply a lifestyle, and everywhere I go. I know I can walk into a school and find those who are family. Kids or adults often test and try Martial Arts to see if they like it. We have joined a very large family for those who stay with it. Moms, Dads, and kids will often stay and keep going back because of the love we feel. For example, no one wants to leave the home they love, their family, or those closest to them. Some special places such as Martial Arts, become so large a part of who we are that it will be the only home that will ever fill the hole and void when we are absent from it and those we love.

PERSONAL ACHIEVEMENTS

- 1970-71 11th grade, began Tae-Kwon do, Bryan, Texas
- 1978 Began in Ralph Castro's Kenpo Karate, Aberdeen, WA
- 1993 Awarded 1st Degree Black Belt Kenpo Karate by Maria Warwick
- 1993 Co-founded Pacific Shaolin Kenpo with partner Sue Messenger
- 1994 Accepted as a student of Professor Ralph Castro
- 1994 Pacific Shaolin Kenpo Accepted into the International Shaolin Kenpo Association
- 1994 Promoted to 3rd Degree Black Belt
- 1990 thru 1998 Sports Competition Year
- 1995 Presidential Sports Award
- Became 'NBL' Center Referee
- 1995 and 1996 Earned invitations to the Super Grands, Nationals, and World Championships
- 1996 Tied 2 Current World Champions in regular time, Lost in overtime.
- 1996 1997, Ranked #4 by Sport Karate International' SKI' in the Pacific Northwest Region.
- 2015 Awarded Northwest Representative to The International Shaolin Kenpo Association,' ISKA,' by Great Grandmaster Ralph Castro
- 2015 16, 17, 18, Attended Masters Training Seminars in San Francisco
- 2016 Awarded a 4th Degree Black Belt
- 2018 Attended GGM Ralph and Pat Castro's 65th Wedding Anniversary
- 2019 Memorial for Ralph Castro. 1 of 3 families invited to the Castro family private Memorial
- 2021 Founded The 'Northwest Shaolin Kenpo Association' as a legally registered non-profit in Washington State.
- 2021 Northwest Shaolin Kenpo Association, or 'NWSKA.' Moved forward with new strategies to reach local, National, and international communities to bring healthy and positive change.
- 2022 With "Unity" as a goal and the help of our International Partners, we have achieved some success bringing Branches of Chinese, Japanese, Hawaiian, and American Arts towards a new beginning and with connections under One Tree. Rebuilding our Tree and finding our roots from the past has led to a new awareness that we are all family.

How has Grandmaster CYNTHIA ROTHROCK Influenced me?

GM Cynthia Rothrock has been an influencer ever since I first saw her on the silver screen, punching and kicking those bad guys into the future. In the '80s and '90s, Cynthia was a huge influencer that inspired me, my family, friends, and students to try, work, and learn to improve. For those in competition, her movies were like the Gospel of "how to's" for many of us. Today, in my life, she is still an influencer with her adventurous lifestyle, a lifestyle many of us can't do or are afraid to try. Yet, she is still encouraging us to try harder and do better. She is the ideal of the perfect role model for the generations.

PERSONAL ACHIEVEMENTS

- 2023 VIP Instructor and Award recipient at Cervizzi's Martial Arts Extravaganza in Boston, Mass. Assistant Instructor to GGM Rob Castro and a Guest Instructor at SGM Samuel Lee Ellis's UGMAA 2023.

- 2023 I am personally and directly responsible for helping put together a Team under the direction of the Head of the International Shaolin Kenpo Association, my instructor, Great Grandmaster Rob Castro, his family, my good friend and Kajukenbo Instructor Master Sonny Pabuaya, and Black Belt School owner in Austin, Texas: Cat Gurinsky. Because of the efforts of this team, the Shaolin Kenpo Family tree is currently being updated, bringing many broken branches into focus as one Tree. Those without a home can now find one. Under the guidance and direction of GGM Rob Castro and a hard-working group of Professionals, a fresh breath is now with the Shaolin Kenpo Family. The Old is meeting the New. How exciting as we rebuild together for a bright new future in 2023/2024.

MAJOR ACHIEVEMENTS

- Learning what it takes to understand the needs of those who are bullied and don't know what to do, and take them from that moment and reach them, gaining their trust to teach children, women, and men how to stay safe.

Become an **AMAA MEMBER!**

Thomas LEBRUN

"

Martial arts have impacted my training, and helping others is an everyday event, not a part-time endeavor.

WHY THE *Martial Arts?*

My "why" in the martial arts was many. I was intrigued by how martial artists moved and were influenced by Bruce Lee in the early 70s, the show Kung Fu with David Carradine, and heavyweight boxing champ Joe Frazier.

I was a big muscular young man feeling my oats and did a fair amount of boxing at the time and thought I could handle myself. So, I wandered into a local Judo class where I was thrown twice by someone a lot smaller than me. I liked this gentle art. I signed up for a class with Sensei Bob Jones (RIP). After a few years, the Sensei moved on, and I liked the art but did not achieve rank. I found a local Tae Kwon Do school and stayed with Master Kim. He, as well, moved on. I continued boxing and sparring with many practitioners of the arts and experienced boxers and kickboxers alike. I began studying under Sensei Porter in Okinawan Kenpo a few years later. I achieved Shodan rank in 1985. I also trained briefly with Sensei Brett Mayfield and

TRAINING INFORMATION

- Martial Arts Styles & Rank: Judo, Tae Kwon do, Boxing, Aikido, Defensive tactics, Escrima, Pressure Point Application, Okinawian Kenpo-Shodan, Ju Jitsu Shodan-Sandan, Black Dragon, GM Ernie Reynolds 6th Dan, American Combatives-8th and 9th Dan

- Instructors/Influencers: Robert Jones, Master Kim, Peter Porter, Mike Donnely, Brett Mayfield, Michael Depasquale Sr., and Jr., Course work in Pressure Point Application; Russell Studley and Steven Burton, Various coaches in Boxing and Defensive Arts

- Birthdate: December 20, 1954

- Birthplace/Growing Up: New Hampshire

- Yrs. In the Martial Arts: 49 years

- Yrs. Instructing: 34 years

- Instructor and Founder of LeBrun's American Combatives 2017

PROFESSIONAL ORGANIZATIONS

- American Society of Industrial Security (ASIS)

- American Martial Arts Alliance

- Intellenet; Global Security and Investigative Org

- Board member of the Business of Executive Protection Professionals (BEPP)

Sensei Mike Donnelly, who taught Aikido. In the early 90s, I achieved Shodan and Sandan levels in Yoshitsune Ju-Jitsu under Michael Depasquale, Sr., and Jr.

My vision started to change towards actual street self-defense application vs. traditional as I worked the doors in nearby establishments. In 1988, I started my own security company, Nighthawk Security and Training Systems. My training continued in various disciplines, as did my rank with proficiency. My company would specialize in the close personal protection of individuals and protect persons from harm in all forms. I received Executive Protection Specialist of the Year in 1999 and 2005 and Black Belt Hall of Fame awards in Success, Leadership, Humanitarian efforts, and Advanced Martial Arts studies. I received my 6th dan and 8th dan ranking later in the decade from Grand Master Ernie Reynolds and Soke John Kanzler, respectively. In 2009 LeBrun's American Combatives was first recognized.

Fast forward; In early February 2017, I was home, and my phone rang. It was Shidoshi Glenn Perry. He indicated that my self-defense system was being considered for recognition as a certified 21st-century martial arts system for self-defense worldwide. With the endorsement of my martial arts system for self-defense, the bar was now set at an extremely high level, as were future expectations from those who had now entrusted me with their confidence and blessings. I needed to take my training, as well as my teaching, to a whole new level. Thus, a more unique, refined system based on real-world experiences continued. My rank Hanshi,

PERSONAL ACHIEVEMENTS

- 1984 Runner-up Strongest Man in New England. Lost by 1 point
- 1988 Created Nighthawk Security and Training Systems
- 1991 J Edgar Hoover Distinguished public service award
- 1991 N.H. State Director / Executive of the U.S. Police Defensive Tactics Association
- 2009 LeBrun's American Combatives
- 2012 Sports Injury Specialist (NASM) National Academy of Sports Medicine
- 2017 MMA Conditioning Coach (NESTA) National Exercise and Sports Trainers Association and NASM
- 2022 Grand Master of the Year Award, International Hall of Fame

MAJOR ACHIEVEMENTS

- Executive Protection Specialist of the Year Award 1999 and 2005 Tactical Hall of Fame
- 2005 College of Advanced Education and Martial Arts Studies- Degree in Philosophy EUSAIMAA
- 2012 Advanced Close Protection Course 12 Month course. Passed with Distinction - Dr. Mark Yates
- 2013 Certified Level 3 Maritime security as it has to do with Anti-Piracy issues
- 2015 Certified Master Anti-Terrorism Specialist (CMAS) ATAB
- 2017 Headmasters Certificate Registered founder of LeBrun's American Combatives
- Hanshi level achieved

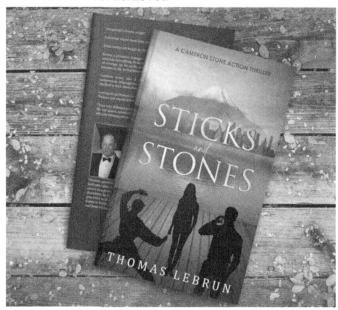

or 9th Dan, was presented at a ceremony in Rutland, Vt April 2017 by Hanshi Stephen Douglas, Sr.

My unique system is a living hybrid structure made up of various concepts to help all practitioners (originally for close protection operators) learn real-world applications of techniques derived from a number of Martial Arts disciplines. The goal is to bridge the gap between pre-arranged movements and possible real-world scenarios and encounters. I have emphasized that street combat differs significantly from merely practicing simulated attacks in a more controlled environment such as the dojo. I strongly feel, however, that the practice mentioned above is a necessary element. Equally important is how the student deals with fear/emotion and adrenaline management during a confrontation. To do this, I teach students various fighting styles and synchronicity of offensive and defensive movements. Then I redirect the pupil to experience combative applications through unchoreographed interactions found in randori or free sparring. In February 2022, I was promoted to 10th dan by Grandmaster Ron Van Clief within my system, aptly named Hogoshin-do "The Way of the Protector."

MAJOR ACHIEVEMENTS

- 2019 Grandmaster Hall of Honor award Inducted into the IFOJJ Tribute to the Pioneers Hall of Honor
- 2021 Published Author " Hiding in Plain Sight" My Life and Adventures Protecting Celebrities, Book of the year 2021 (Amazon ISBN # ISBN-13: 978-1098358358 Print ASIN: B08YNX6KC5 eBook)
- 2022 #1 International Best-Selling Author "Sticks and Stones" A Cameron Stone Action Thriller
- Inducted in the Ultimate Warriors class of 2022 Hall of Fame
- 2022 Awarded Security Expert of the Year by The Israeli Martial Arts Federation
- 2022 Promoted to 10th dan by GM Ron Van Clief
- 2023 #1 International Best Seller Book Elite Martial Artists of America- Co-Author Capacity to Lead

How MARTIAL ARTS CHANGED My Life!

Martial arts have impacted my training, and helping others is an everyday event, not a part-time endeavor. The discipline in the arts of climbing the next mountain or obstacle has given me my drive to strive forward, and my accomplishments create self-pride and confidence that can be handed down to others. It's a great feeling when you can mentor and watch individuals accomplish what they may have thought of as not possible. As a teacher, I have found that each student brings their own complex life and lifestyle, of which strengths and weaknesses will be at the forefront; I am sensitive to that. I understand that their ambitions (big or small) and the psychological and emotional maturity they, the students, will be challenged over time because of the rigorous nature of training. It's also great to get my practitioners in the state of "Mushin," no mind, no clutter, and focus on the now.

Even in my late 60s, I continue to train six days per week, at times twice per day alone or with students, to continually improve and refine my abilities and techniques in the martial arts and my tradecraft.

I have found that the following resonates with me on a deeper personal and training level.

Promoted to Shidoshi (Shidoshi -Teacher-/ Leader/ /Enlightened Gentleman Warrior.

A personal thought - A positive role model for others should exist on any level.

How has Grandmaster CYNTHIA ROTHROCK Influenced me?

The timeless consummate professional in all that she does. Highly respected as a person and as a martial artist. Traits that all martial artists should seek.

Professor Gary LEE

TRAINING INFORMATION

- Belt Ranks & Martial Arts Styles: 9th Degree Black Belt, Okinawa Karate
- Birthplace/Growing Up: Honolulu, HI

MAJOR ACHIEVEMENTS

- Gran, Hawaiian Kosho Ryu Kenpo Jiu-Jitsu
- International Black Belt Hall of Fame
- Top Weapons in Texas, 1980
- Top Ten Fighters in Texas, 1979-1999
- Rated by Karate Illustrated Magazine, rated National
- Who's Who in Karate, 1982
- 3rd Degree Black Belt Test, 1982, Lama Nationals, Chicago IL
- Creator Six Flags Amusement Park Shows, Gary Lee's Texas Karate All-Stars,
- 1984-1994, {5,000 shows}
- Texas State B.A.S.S Federation Champion, 1987
- Filmed SIDEKICKS the movie, 1990
- Gold Medalist USAKF Nationals, Dallas, Texas, 1992
- Won five {5} National NBL TITLES, Atlantic City, NJ, 1992
- Sabaki Ryu Challenge 3rd Place Kumite, Honolulu, Hawaii, 1992
- National Black Belt League World Champion, Breaking, New Orleans, USA, 1993
- Man, of the Year, Bushshiban 1993
- BIG BASS TOURNAMENT, Sam Rayburn, Jasper, Texas, 2nd Place, 3,200.00 winnings, earned a 3rd round seed into the Classic Championship 1993, Yeah Baby!!!!
- Texas NBL Arbitrator
- Star of Hollywood Stunt Show, Astroworld, Six Flags, Houston, Texas, USA, 1993
- Creator 'KIDS EXPO" Astrodome, Houston Texas.1993-1996

MAJOR ACHIEVEMENTS

- Golden Greek Top Texas Overall Winner, AOK RATINGS, 1997, 1998
- Nominated Black Belt Magazine "Player of the Year", 1997
- Texas Sport Karate Player, MVP
- Opened World Championship Karate Studios, 1998
- Created the Living Legends Celebrity Roast; 1999 - present.
- To date Professor Lee has celebrated 15 American Pioneers in Sport Karate.
- Staff Writer for WORLD BLACKBELT, 1999
- Created Tales OF the Old Sensei for World Black Belt, monthly column
- Master of Ceremonies, Martial Art History Museum, Las Vegas, Nevada, 1999
- Director Michael Matsuda says 'Gary Lee is the voice of Karate, Black Belt Magazine
- Director of Junior World Black Belt Kids Club
- Produced and Directed Living Legends, 'the Tim Kirby Celebrity Roast, Houston, Texas, USA, 2000
- Kumite International Black Belt Hall of Fame Award and Scholarship given in Professor Gary Lee's name for $1,000.00, Pittsburg, Pa, 2000
- Creator of BLACK BELT TV, A online network for Martial Artist and Martial arts Exclusive personal interviews with the stars of martial arts.

Wesley LEE

"

Sometimes we fail to do the right thing, but if we practice and persevere, we can overcome anything and succeed.

WHY THE *Martial Arts?*

I grew up in the Midwest in a small town with no martial art schools. I took wrestling from elementary through high school but never took striking or traditional martial arts. It was not until I was in my late 20s that a coworker invited me to try a class at a school he had opened. At first, I thought it would be a waste of time. Hearing the class was Taekwon-Do did not interest me at first. I only considered what I had seen at 'McDojos,' but I tried a class to be respectful.

I was instantly hooked on the style Taekwon-Do Master Payne taught. It was a traditional Korean combat style, not flashy, but effective. It was the style taught to the Korean ROK soldiers. Everything that Master Payne taught had a purpose and not just "because that is how we do it."

At first, I saw it as a great way to complement my grappling by adding a solid striking game.

TRAINING INFORMATION

- Martial Arts Styles & Rank: Taekwon-Do 6th Dan
- Instructors/Influencers: Grand Master Harry Payne
- Birthplace/Growing Up: Fox River Grove, IL
- Yrs. In the Martial Arts: 20 years
- Yrs. Instructing: 18 years
- School owner, Manager and Instructor

PROFESSIONAL ORGANIZATIONS

- IJTF (Treasurer)
- JTF-USA (National Director)
- KMATA (Founder and President)

I started doing tournaments only four months into training. In the beginning, tournaments drove me to get in shape, improve my technique, and train every chance I got.

This quickly changed from wanting to learn how to punch and kick to how to improve myself: physically, mentally, emotionally, and spiritually. Finally, I went from being a student to an instructor, now a school owner and active in running the IJTF. Taekwon-Do went from just a striking art to who I am.

How MARTIAL ARTS CHANGED My Life!

Taekwon-Do started as a desire to learn how to strike, which became a way of life. I learned that I could overcome adversity with practice and perseverance. I learned that you will be beaten sometimes, but it is in those times that you can learn the most. You need to open your eyes, ears, and heart to see what defeat can give you.

That applies to tournaments and life in general. The skills I learned to overcome losing a match apply to my work and family life. Sometimes we fail to do the right thing, but if we practice and persevere, we can overcome anything and succeed.

PERSONAL ACHIEVEMENTS

- Competed and won many tournaments, both purely Taekwon-Do and open styles
- Helping to bring about a tournament community in Tucson, AZ, by getting location schools of different styles to start competing together

MAJOR ACHIEVEMENTS

- Opened Vail Taekwon-Do Academy in 2014
- Appointed to Regional Director of IJTF in 2015
- Appointed to IJTF Administration as IT Director in 2016
- Appointed to Umpire and Tournament Director of the JTF-USA in 2017
- Appointed to IJTF Treasurer in 2017
- Appointed to JTF-USA National Directory in 2017
- Inducted into the US Kido Federation Black Belt Hall of Fame 2017 for Outstanding Instructor of the Year
- Inducted into AMAA Martial Arts Masters & Pioneers in the Black Belt section in 2019
- Founded the Korean Martial Arts Tournament Association in 2020
- Inducted into the US Kido Federation Black Belt Hall of Fame 2023 for Master Instructor of the Year

John
LOMBARDO

"

Martial Arts has provided me with the skills and mindset to achieve the goals set for me by others and myself.

WHY THE *Martial Arts?*

My journey in martial arts began in 1978 when I attended my first class at the urging of my closest childhood friends. We were excited to be the next martial arts superstars.

At that time, I had no idea what I was getting myself into by stepping on the mat. I spent four years at that dojo studying Isshinryu karate under Master Dennis Bootle. After a brief break in training, I began training in the art of Shotokan karate under various instructors while serving in the United States Air Force as an Information Systems Specialist. After my military service, I continued to practice my martial arts skills and searched for a new home. I began training at NY Budo in the mid-1990s under Shidoshi Jean-Pierre Seibel. NY Budo was part of the Bujinkan Dojo of Soke Masaaki Hatsumi under the oversight of An-Shu Stephen K. Hayes. As part of that organization, I had the honor and privilege of training with An-Shu

TRAINING INFORMATION

- Martial Arts Styles & Rank: Bushi Ban International 5th Dan Master, Isshinryu Karate - Brown Belt, Shotokan Karate - Brown Belt, Ninpo Taijitsu - Brown Belt, Yammani Ryu Kobudo - Green Belt, United States, Chanbarra Association – Instructor, American Judo System - Instructor

- Instructors/Influencers: Grand Master Zulfi Ahmed, Senior Master Hassan Saiyid, Hanshi Kiyoshi Nishime, Shihan Dan Abbott, Grand Master Dr. Maung Gyi, Grand Master Masayuki Ward, Sensei Jimmy Pedro, Anshu Stephen K. Hayes, Shidoshi Jean-Pierre Seibel, Master Dennis Bootle

- Birthplace/Growing Up: Bayside, NY

- Yrs. In the Martial Arts: 45 years

- Yrs. Instructing: 16 years

- School owner, Manager, Instructor & Student

PROFESSIONAL ORGANIZATIONS

- Bushi Ban International
- United States Chanbarra Association
- Yammani Ryu Kobudo
- American Judo System

Stephen K. Hayes on several occasions. My career and family caused me to take a break from formal training for a few years, but I continued to hone my skills and live by the warrior codes and martial principles taught to me over the years.

In April 2004, while seeking out an instructor for my son Vincent, I met then Sensei, now Senior Master Hassan Saiyid of Bushi Ban, Connecticut. I was immediately taken in by his openness and warmth; needless to say, I enrolled both of us in Bushi Ban that very day, and just like that day in 1978, I had no idea what I was getting myself into. As part of the Bushi Ban family, I have had the privilege of meeting and training not only with Senior Master Hassan but with so many amazing martial artists, most notably Great Grand Master Dr. Maung Gyi, Great Grand Master Masayuki Ward, and Grand Master Zulfi Ahmed (Founder, Bushi Ban International).

I was awarded my Bushi Ban Black belt on March 24, 2006, and honored with the award of my 5th Dan and Master title on October 23, 2022.

Through the generosity of GM Zulfi and SM Hassan, I have trained in numerous systems and achieved ranking and certifications from Shihan Kiyoshi Nishime, Shihan Dana Abbott, and Master Jimmy Pedro. My weapons of choice are the Katana and Tanto. In addition to those, I enjoy the Bo, Sai, Tonfa, and Kali Stick. In October 2010, I became the Director of Bushi Ban Southbury. With the guidance of Senior Master Hassan and the assistance of Sensei Joe Guarente, we began to broaden the influence of the Bushi Ban System on the East Coast.

PROFESSIONAL ORGANIZATIONS

- American Martial Arts Alliance - AMAA
- Masters Hall of Fame
- Black Horse for Heroes

PERSONAL ACHIEVEMENTS

- 5th Dan, Master- Bushi Ban International
- Regional Director - Bushi Ban International
- Director, Information Technology - UBS AG
- Senior Airman (E-4) - United States Air Force

MAJOR ACHIEVEMENTS

- Black Belt of the Year - Bushi Ban International - 2012
- Masters Hall of Fame - Outstanding Contribution - 2012
- American Martial Arts Alliance - Legends Award - 2019
- American Martial Arts Alliance - Ambassador Award - 2020
- American Martial Arts Alliance - Alumni Award - 2021
- American Martial Arts Alliance - Alumni Award - 2022
- Martial Arts Extraordinaire Magazine - Featured Bio - April 2022

the Bushi Ban System on the East Coast.

In January 2018, after the relocation of SM Hassan to Texas the year before, I assumed the reins of Bushi Ban Seymour. I assumed the role of Director of Bushi Ban CT which covered both the Southbury and Seymour locations.

These past 19 years as part of the Bushi Ban Family have taken me to places I had never thought of going and opened my eyes to all that there is yet to achieve.

…and the journey continues.

How MARTIAL ARTS CHANGED My Life!

Studying martial arts has taught me to believe in the greater good and that we all must positively impact the world. Furthermore, it has provided me with the skills and mindset to achieve the goals set for me by others and myself.

Become an
AMAA MEMBER!

Donald
MATHEWS

"

Martial Arts have been a transformative experience, shaping me into who I am today.

WHY THE *Martial Arts?*

Donald P Mathews was born in Columbus, Ohio, on May 22, 1956. From grade school thru high school, he played baseball and basketball and was a track team member. His pursuit of excellence and curiosity in martial arts began in 1983 when a few of his co-workers were attending classes at a local dojo and asked him to watch a demonstration they were doing. He watched them perform open-hand katas, weapons katas, and self-defense techniques. He was mesmerized by everything that they were doing. It took him only a short time to sign up as soon as possible. And it did not take long for him to realize that it turned his curiosity into a passion to learn everything. He immersed himself in not just the katas, the weapon katas, the physical aspects of training, and the self-defense movements. Still, he delved into the fundamental physiological characteristics of martial arts. After training in a few different martial arts styles, he finally settled into the kind

TRAINING INFORMATION

- Martial Arts Styles & Rank: 9th Degree Black Belt - Unified Kempo Karate Systems, 4th Degree Black Belt - Japan Karate Do Ryobu-Kai

- Instructors/Influencers: Fumio Demura, Kiyoshi Yamazaki, Bill "Superfoot" Wallace, Don "the Dragon" Wilson, Cynthia Rothrock, Joe Lewis, Hideharu Igaki, Greer Golden, Remy Presas, Phil Maldonado, Angelito Barongan

- Birthplace/Growing Up: Columbus, OH

- Yrs. In the Martial Arts: 40 years

- Yrs. Instructing: 37 years

- School owner & Instructor at Warrior Spirit Karate, LLC, PKA Worldwide Member

PROFESSIONAL ORGANIZATIONS

- Unified Kempo Karate Systems

- U.S. Association of Martial Arts

- USA-NKF

- AAU

of Shito-Ryu. He has also trained in Shotokan, Gojo-Ryu, and Barongan Kempo.

His introduction to the competition was eye-opening when he was disqualified for knocking out his opponent in the Kumite event. He was not letting this setback deter him. He went back into the dojo and trained harder than ever before. He entered the Ohio State Martial Arts Championship and walked away with three trophies that day, including first place in open-hand kata. From there began a string of tournament wins that continued into his 60s. His favorite competition is open-hand kata because he believes this is the martial arts essence. Over the years, he was able to compete nationally and internationally and has been a judge in the USA Karate, AAU, Ko Sutemi Seiei Kan, MVTA, and many other associations.

In October of 2011, he opened his dojo, Warrior Spirit Karate, with a handful of students and the vision to become the essence of what martial arts were historical. After nearly 35 years of experience competing and teaching, he is still passionate about passing on that extensive knowledge and expertise to his students. His eye is on maintaining the true traditional history and education; He immerses his students in the technical teachings and the rich history and philosophy that will enrich their personal growth. He is focused on youth development, fusing traditional martial arts values with cutting-edge child development and parenting skills. His statement, "The balance of old and new thinking creates a dynamic learning environment that helps each child be their best." With values such as focus, discipline, confidence, teamwork, respect, and family,

PERSONAL ACHIEVEMENTS

- Opened dojo in 2011
- Promoted to 9th Dan in 2022
- Published two books: "A Comprehensive Guide To Finding The Right Martial Arts School For Beginners" and a children's book, "Jake and Mia: A Journey of Martial Arts Mastery"

MAJOR ACHIEVEMENTS

- International Competitor.
- Competitor in AAU, USA-NKF, MVTA, Alliance, and Ko Sutemi Seiei Kan organizations.
- Won numerous Medals and Trophies in competitions
- Taught numerous National and International seminars
- Referee for local, regional, and national events.
- 2022 Esteemed Martial Artist of the Year - Action Martial Arts Hall of Honors
- 2021 Esteemed Martial Artist of the Year - Action Martial Arts Hall of Honors
- 2020 Cleveland Martial Arts Hall of Fame
- 2020 Whos Who In The Martial Arts Legends Award - American Martial Arts Association
- 2019 Esteemed Martial Artist of the Year- Action Martial Arts Hall of Honors
- 2018 Esteemed Martial Artist of the Year - Action Martial Arts Hall of Honors
- 2016 Diamond Award - Miami Valley Tournament Association
- 2012 Karate Lifetime Achievement Award - International Karate and Kickboxing Hall of Fame

every student learns the life skills necessary to become our leaders of the future.

Throughout the years, he was fortunate to train with some of the world's most accomplished and recognized instructors today. Fumio Demura, Kiyoshi Yamazaki, Bill "Superfoot" Wallace, Don "the Dragon" Wilson, Cynthia Rothrock, Joe Lewis, Hideharu Igaki, Greer Golden, Remy Presas, Phil Maldonado, and Angelito Barongan are on the list.

His dedication to pursuing excellence has brought him many awards and honors, including being recognized and inducted into several martial arts Hall of Fame associations. In 2020, he was recognized by the American Martial Arts Association and placed in the "Who's Who in the Martial Arts" directory.

His passion for learning is still as great as ever, even after all these years. He is constantly reminded that even though he is an instructor, he is still a student and always will be. He is still curious to seek out the best instructors and learn everything he can from them. Martial Arts has been his life and will continue to be his life until the day he passes onto the next world.

He has also published two books, "A Comprehensive Guide To Finding The Right Martial Arts School For Beginners" and a children's book, "Jake and Mia: A Journey of Martial Arts Mastery."

Don has been practicing martial arts for 40 years and is ranked 9th degree Black Belt with the UKKS and a 4th degree Black Belt in the Japanese Karate Ryobuki organization.

WHY MARTIAL ARTS (CONTINUED)

He lives in Grove City, Ohio, with his fiancé Janet and their dog Grace.

Besides martial arts, he enjoys reading, golf, and practicing his gunmanship. He is available to teach seminars and loves passing on his knowledge to all generations.

How MARTIAL ARTS CHANGED My Life!

For the past 40 years, I have been practicing martial arts, and I can confidently say that it has changed my life in more ways than one. Learning self-defense has become a lifelong passion that has taught me invaluable lessons about discipline, respect, and perseverance.

One of the most significant ways martial arts has impacted my life is by instilling discipline. Through rigorous training and strict routines, I learned how to set goals for myself and work towards them tirelessly. I also learned the importance of consistency and commitment, which are skills that have helped me in all areas of my life.

Another way that martial arts has transformed my life is by teaching me about respect. In martial arts, concern is fundamental and earned through hard work, dedication, and humility. I have learned to respect my instructors, training partners, and myself. This respect has spilled over into other areas of my life, such as my relationships with family, friends, and colleagues.

Finally, martial arts have taught me about perseverance. Through countless hours of practice, injuries, and setbacks, I have learned that success is not about being perfect but pushing through when things get tough. This skill has helped me personally and professionally, as I have learned to persevere through challenges and emerge stronger on the other side.

In addition to these personal benefits, martial arts have brought me many accolades and awards. I have won numerous competitions and championships, and these achievements have brought me a great sense of pride and accomplishment.

HOW MY LIFE IS CHANGED (CONTINUED)

In conclusion, martial arts have been a transformative experience, shaping me into who I am today. Through discipline, respect, and perseverance, I have achieved success both on and off the mat. I am grateful for the lessons that martial arts have taught me and look forward to continuing my practice for years.

Become an
AMAA MEMBER!

Dawn
MCLAUGHLIN

"

Martial arts is who we are and is truly a part of our soul and something that will always continue with our family.

WHY THE *Martial Arts?*

I started martial arts after seeing my daughter work towards her black belt. Once she had earned hers, I knew that it was time for me to go for mine. I knew I was starting a bit later in life than most, and it would be a bit harder, but I was not going to let that stop me. There were times that it was truly a struggle as my body did not want to let me do certain things, but I had decided that this was something I wanted and would not let age get in my way.

I was blessed to have my family's encouragement, which helped keep me going. I earned my first-degree black belt in 2013 and then my second degree in 2016. Within the school I take classes, I am the oldest student that has earned a second degree, and I am proud of holding that title. When I trained and tested for my second degree, the other three students were 10 and 20 years younger than me. It was truly a proud moment for me to be able to earn that rank alongside them.

TRAINING INFORMATION

- Martial Arts Styles & Rank: 2nd Degree Black Belt in Tae Kwon Do
- Instructors/Influencers: Master Mike McLaughlin
- Birthplace/Growing Up: Phoenix, AZ / Ontario, CA
- Yrs. In the Martial Arts: 17 years
- Yrs. Instructing: 10 years
- Instructor

PROFESSIONAL ORGANIZATIONS

- ActivStars Athletics

How MARTIAL ARTS CHANGED My Life!

Martial arts have greatly impacted my life. I met my husband through martial arts; it has become a huge part of our family. I have had the privilege to train with many different martial artists. We enjoy taking seminars every chance we get, and even on vacations try to get a seminar in no matter where we are. Martial arts is who we are and is truly a part of our soul and something that will always continue with our family.

How has Grandmaster CYNTHIA ROTHROCK Influenced me?

Cynthia was instrumental in showing women they could compete in martial arts. She paved the way for all females following in her path. Hearing her story of how she pushed through is truly inspiring. My husband and I were blessed to have brought her out for a seminar in 2017 and had the chance to get to know her. She is one of the sweetest people you would ever want to meet. Her spirit is infectious, and the hardest part of being her friend is keeping up with her. I am proud to call her one of my best friends.

PERSONAL ACHIEVEMENTS

- Mom
- Nana
- Associates Degree in Public Administration
- Foster for the AZ Humane Society

MAJOR ACHIEVEMENTS

- Combat Medic
- United States Army Humanitarian Ribbon
- Desert Storm Ribbon
- 2nd Degree Black Belt

Become an
AMAA MEMBER!

Mike
MCLAUGHLIN

"

The martial arts have not only had a major impact on my life, the martial arts are part of who I am.

WHY THE *Martial Arts?*

Mike McLaughlin got started in the martial arts because of a desire to learn self-defense techniques and a love for The Karate Kid and Bruce Lee movies. He has been training in the martial arts for nearly 40 years. During that time, he earned a 4th Degree Black Belt in Arnis and a 3rd Degree Black Belt in Tae Kwon Do. Mike is also a Sifu in the Ip Man lineage of Wing Chun. In addition, Sigung Richard Bustillo certified Mike as an instructor in Jeet Kune Do. Mike has also trained in Aiki Jujutsu, Judo, Muay Thai, and Goju Ryu. Mike began his martial arts journey in Maine and also began instructing there. He has been teaching martial arts for more than 30 years. In 1997, Mike moved to Arizona and began teaching martial arts for the Young Olympians organization, which later became Activstars Athletics. Mike is a Hanshi with Activstars Athletics. He has taught more than ten thousand students in the Phoenix area, and 165 of his students have earned their Black

TRAINING INFORMATION

- Martial Arts Styles & Rank: Wing Chun-Sifu, Arnis-4th Degree Black Belt, Tae Kwon Do-3rd Degree Black Belt
- Instructors/Influencers: Paul Noto, Richard Oakes, Ronda Stone, Tim Byers, Frank Williams, Logan Williams, Andrew Grim, Richard Bustillo, Dan Inosanto, Ron Balicki
- Birthplace/Growing Up: Corinth, ME
- Yrs. In the Martial Arts: 39 years
- Yrs. Instructing: 30 years
- Instructor

PROFESSIONAL ORGANIZATIONS

- Activstars Athletics
- National Academy of Sports Medicine
- United States Martial Arts Hall of Fame
- Masters Hall of Fame

Belts. He has also assisted with training Phoenix, Houston, and Dallas instructors. In 2002, Mike led a group of students, parents, and instructors to China to visit the Shaolin Temple and train with monks from the temple. Mike is also proud to be the coach of the 8-time champion demo team "Focused Intensity." In addition to teaching martial arts, Mike promotes fitness among his students. He is a certified personal trainer with the National Academy of Sports Medicine. He is also a certified Performance Enhancement Specialist, MMA Conditioning Specialist, Youth Exercise Specialist, Behavior Change Specialist, and Weight Loss Specialist with NASM. Mike is also a certified JrFit Youth Fitness Specialist with the American Academy of Health and Fitness. Mike also holds a bachelor's degree in journalism and has written extensively about martial arts for newspapers and websites. He also earned an associate's degree in motion picture/television production and has made many short martial arts films. Mike is an associate producer on Cynthia Rothrock's upcoming film "Black Creek." Mike was inducted into the United States Martial Arts Hall of Fame in 2014, 2015, 2017, and 2018. He was appointed Regional Director in the Southwest for the Hall of Fame in 2017. He has also taught at the Hall of Fame International Training Camp. In 2019, Mike was inducted into the Master's Hall of Fame in Costa Mesa, California.

PERSONAL ACHIEVEMENTS

- Bachelor of Arts Degree in Journalism
- Associate in Applied Science Degree in Motion Picture/Television Production
- Steve Grady News Writing Award
- Almost Famous Film Festival Top 20
- Personal Trainer - National Academy of Sports Medicine
- JrFit Youth Fitness Specialist - American Academy of Health and Fitness

MAJOR ACHIEVEMENTS

- Instructor of the Year - United States Martial Arts Hall of Fame
- Excellence in Martial Arts Leadership - United States Martial Arts Hall of Fame
- JKD Honor Award - United States Martial Arts Hall of Fame
- Distinguished Master - United States Martial Arts Hall of Fame
- Masters Hall of Fame Inductee

How MARTIAL ARTS CHANGED My Life!

The martial arts have had a tremendous impact on my life. I have been inspired by many of my instructors to become a better person and to reach my full potential. For more than 30 years, I have strived to be the best instructor I can be. My goal is to teach the same values that I learned to as many students as possible. I have had the honor of teaching these values to thousands of students. I have also made many lifelong friends through the martial arts. I even met my wife because of the martial arts, which is a huge part of our family's life. I have had the opportunity to travel across the country and worldwide to pursue more knowledge. I have also had the opportunity to learn from many legendary martial artists, including Dan Inosanto,

Richard Bustillo, Bill Wallace, Benny Urquidez, and Cynthia Rothrock. The martial arts have not only had a major impact on my life, the martial arts are part of who I am. I cannot imagine my life without the martial arts. I am so grateful to my parents for taking me to my first karate class nearly 40 years ago. That decision changed the trajectory of my life and, as a result, the lives of thousands of others.

How has Grandmaster CYNTHIA ROTHROCK Influenced me?

I remember watching Cynthia Rothrock movies and seeing her in martial arts magazines as a kid. I was always impressed with her skills. In my twenties, I was excited that I had the chance to meet her briefly at a martial arts event. Little did I know then that I would eventually become good friends with Cynthia. My wife and I brought Cynthia to Arizona for a seminar in 2017. We had the opportunity to hang out with her and get to know her. Her stories about martial arts and her enthusiasm for adventure inspired us. Over the past six years, we have attended many martial events with Cynthia and gone on many adventures with her. Her energy is infectious, and sometimes the biggest challenge is trying to keep up with her.

Become an
AMAA
MEMBER!

Rafael Antonio MEDINA-CASTRO

"
Learn and teach the values of others. Respect life because it is only one; being humble cost nothing.

WHY THE *Martial Arts?*

I was born in Humacao, Puerto Rico, in 1955, and I spent the first 16 years of my life in El Barrio Candelero Arriba. For the most part, I had a good childhood. There were some dark factors looming. My brothers and I lived with my grandparents, who took care of us most of the time. The neighborhood I grew up in was not very welcoming to us.

My inspiration for martial arts was watching the episodes of Green Hornet. I was smaller than my peers and an easy mark for the bullies in my tough rural Puerto Rican neighborhood. To shift the balance, I had to learn some kind of self-defense. I was tired of being the loser or feeling the agony of defeat. I wanted something different in my life. As a teenager, I was beaten almost every month after school and by my friends sometimes. At that time, fighting outside the school was not the school's concern.

TRAINING INFORMATION

- Martial Arts Styles & Rank: 9th Dan Chang Moo Kwon, 9th Dan Chang Hon Kwan, 9th Dan World Taekwon-Choodo Federation, 9th Dan Sport Taekwondo Center Associates, 7th Dan Kukkiwon, 7th Dan United States National (USA-TKD), 7th Dan ITF-America International TKD Federation Black Belt, 1st Dan Kyokushinkai-kan, 1st Dan Kuk Sool Won

- Instructors/Influencers: Master Luis Díaz, Master Juan Ruiz (RIP), Sensei Michael, Sensei Miguel Acevedo, Sensei Fernando Caraballo, GrandMaster Giovanni Rosario (RIP), Master Pedro Laboy, GrandMaster Bobby Clayton

- Birthplace/Growing Up: Humacao, Puerto Rico

- Yrs. In the Martial Arts: 54 years

- Yrs. Instructing: 30 years

- School owner, Manager & Instructor at Sport Taekwondo ChangMooKwan Center, Coach, WT International Referee, USAT & AUU National Referee

PROFESSIONAL ORGANIZATIONS

- United States Armed Forces
- United States Military Taekwondo Foundation
- Federación de Taekwondo de Puerto Rico
- World Taekwondo Federation
- Kukkiwon
- United States America Taekwondo (USAT)
- Amateur Athletic Union (AAU)
- Taekwondo Hall of Fame
- World Taekwondo Chang Moo Kwan
- The World TaekwonMoodo Federation

By the time I was 7, my first day in elementary school, I was on my way home and got my first taste of bullying. There was a strong disconnection between me and most of the kids in my school, and the taller kids tended to go after me. It started with the typically teasing and mean words but eventually escalated to stabbing me with leaves with thorns, and from time to time, I would get into fights that I never started and run away in fear most of the time.

Luis Diaz was the head instructor. At the time, he was 16, a green belt in Okinawa-Te Karate, and had experience in self-defense (something I didn't have). Nothing came easy, but I loved fighting with him. I would always instigate sparring and play fighting with him whenever I had the chance. I would be bruised and thrown around, but I never wanted to quit. I had heart, which made him take me to the next level.

My first years' of learning karate were difficult because my father didn't want me to learn this new way of life. He didn't believe in violence. I did train in secret from my father. Over the years, I inched my way through the beginning ranks and into the advanced ones. Rank is a good showing of success and growth. The belts or certificates don't make you; you make them.

Soon the bullying was less manageable as I was able to confront myself with some of my friends and schoolmates, specifically the ones closer to my age. I don't condone kids getting in fights, and when asked about it, I always encourage kids to listen to their parents and school teachers. "The best way to win a fight is not to fight." On the same note, I don't think anyone should put up with abuse, and we all have a

PERSONAL ACHIEVEMENTS

- Twenty-two years of Military Service
- International Master Instructor License with Kukkiwon
- Chang Moo Kwan International Instructor License
- Cable Technician/Installer certified
- A happy husband, father, and grandfather
- Ambassador of the 1st - 4er Armed Forces Taekwondo Reunion
- Selected as the best referee in 4 different taekwondo events
- Established the motto "One team, one fight." Unifying the sport of Taekwondo for all the armed forces.
- First president of the United States Military Taekwondo Foundation

MAJOR ACHIEVEMENTS

- 1996-2000: All Army and Armed Forces Coach
- 1995-1998: Fort Stewart Head Coach
- 1987-1994: All Army Taekwondo Bantam weight medalist
- 1987–1998: Armed Forces Taekwondo Bantam weight medalist
- 1987: World CISM Military International Bantamweight medalist
- 1987 First Latino and Puerto Rican representing the United States armed forces in a (CISM) International Military Sports Council of Taekwondo event.
- Taekwondo Hall of Fame's Technical Advisor.
- In May 2019, I was recognized as a Grandmaster of Taekwondo by the government of Puerto Rico and certified by The House of Representatives of PR. GM William Sanchez Cardona did this.
- In September 2019, the International Military Sports Council (CISM) selected me as the first military and the only person in the United States to represent the nation in the World Military Taekwondo Championship as an athlete, coach, and International Referee.
- Nominated by the Taekwondo Hall of Fame for the Outstanding Pioneering Player Award for the US Armed Forces.
- First president of Chang Moo Kwan in Puerto Rico.
- First president of the US Armed Forces, Chang Moo Kwan.

right to protect ourselves. Martial arts gave me more confidence, endurance, and agility.

I am thankful for the people I have had in my life to support me and keep me strong. I hope to have many blessings in the eyes of God and continue to do the best I can for my family and friends.

How MARTIAL ARTS CHANGED *My Life!*

My first training was hard, and I even cried. At that moment, I learned the best lesson of my life. Nothing is easy; we have to fight for what we want to achieve our goals. Discipline and humility go hand in hand. Learn and teach the values of others. Respect life because it is only one; being humble cost nothing.

Twenty-two years in the military, I learned to value it and thank God for each day.

Because of having an agitated, fearful, mistrustful, and disoriented youth life, we should never lose our self-confidence. Loneliness must be avoided.

Martial discipline (military or martial art) leads to physical, mental, and emotional benefits that can improve the quality of your life in different ways. Obstacles will always be in our paths, but our quality of life must improve. Don't judge yourself by society; seek help. We are not alone. Prepare for a better future and that of the family. A friend helps us when we need it most.

How has Grandmaster CYNTHIA ROTHROCK *Influenced me?*

Cynthia Ann Christine Rothrock is an American martial artist and actress in martial arts films. She has always been a fighter in and out of the ring. She is a real example for all young women. Hopes are in your future.

Maggie Cole
MESSINA

> **"**
> The Martial Arts woke up a fire and gave me the Platform for being the change the World needed....

WHY THE *Martial Arts?*

One day, Maggie was in a park with her sister-in-law, Awilda; she started to teach Maggie some basic kicks and punches. Maggie caught on quickly and loved the way it made her feel. She fell in love with the feelings of freedom matched with control—taking her outside of herself into a more peaceful place.

Maggie Messina started training with one of Grandmaster Sir Henry Cho's black belts privately in her late teens. She made her way to green belt with GM Cho. Maggie loved the arts and wanted to train with other martial artists. So, she sought out her first "real" martial arts school.

This was hard for her. It was in the mid-'80s, and not many women were trained. Her search continued for a long time, but she kept hearing about a school known for its hardcore, no-nonsense training in Brooklyn. As it turned out, it was just what she was looking for. But, when

TRAINING INFORMATION

- Martial Arts Styles & Rank: TaeKwon Do-8th Dan, Shotokan-Black Belt
- Instructors/Influencers: GM Cho, GGM Suh Chong Kang, GM Tae Sun Kang
- Birthplace/Growing Up: Nyack, NY
- Yrs. In the Martial Arts: 37 years
- Yrs. Instructing: 35 years
- School owner, Manager & Instructor at Taecole Tae Kwon Do and Fitness Inc., Entrepreneur, Author

PROFESSIONAL ORGANIZATIONS

- International TAEKWONDO Black Belt Association (ITBA)
- International TaeKwonDo Federation (ITF)
- Kuk Mu Kwan (KMK)
- All American Black Belt Association (ABBA)
- World Kickboxing Commission (WKC)
- North America Sport Karate Association (NASKA)
- National Association Education of Young Youth (NAEYC)
- Marquis Who's Who Publication
- Action Martial Arts Organization (AMAO)

she went to check it out, she couldn't work up the courage to walk up the long, dimly lit stairs. It took her three months to climb those steps finally.

Once inside, she loved the smell of sweat and the sound of training. While the black belts standing in the back did intimidate her a bit, she continued to train. This environment was different from the basement she'd been training in previously.

Maggie states, "Since earning the rank of brown belt, her vision of having her school was born. I knew there were many hurdles to overcome." Those early days were tough but made me who I am today. To this day, I stay true to my core values and remember why I am here. I fell in love with how Tae Kwon Do helps develop people, and it helped me develop into the woman I am today.

"I had started teaching at the Brooklyn school," said Maggie, "That is when, as a student, I began to understand and know the material. You cannot be a good instructor unless you truly know the material." Upon leaving the school, Maggie began teaching at various community centers and upscale high rises in New York City, but owning her own school was her true vision.

She did a lot of research, finally deciding upon a location in Albertson, New York, feeling that the neighborhood was a strong community with family values. She signed the lease for her school at the same time as the 9/11 attacks, creating a need for intense perseverance as she battled the emotional conflict of the nearby terrorist attacks along with building a school from the ground up.

PERSONAL ACHIEVEMENTS

- Published her (memoir) book, making Maggie "Little Miss Tri-County"
- Earned CDA National Credentials
- Earned Preschool Licensing (New York State)
- Awarded 6th Dan Black Belt by the ITF (A-6-95)
- BBB A+ Accredited since 2006-Present
- Taecole earns ITF Certified
- Volunteer for Girls, Inc.
- Volunteer for Isaacs Park/Recreation
- Master Instructor of the Herricks Junior / High Schools Community Center Martial Arts Program
- Best Adult Black Belt of the Year 2001-2003 (WCMAO)
- 2001 Master Instructor of the JCC/Searingtown After School TaeKwonDo Program
- World Champion Korean Traditional Forms / Fighting / Breaking (2000*2004) 2010
- Hall of Fame Golden Warrior Lifetime Achievement Award Teach Self Defense / Fitness Awareness to several NYC Youth Organizations
- 15 Years Medical Experience with Sloan Kettering Cancer Hospital

MAJOR ACHIEVEMENTS

- 2023 New York State Congressional PTA Community Service Award for her dedication to the youth and children in NYS (Helen Hoffman, President 2023).
- 2023 Promoted to 8th Dan Black Belt (ITBBA)
- 2023 Silver Lifetime Award for dedicating more than thirty-five years to Martial Arts (American Martial Arts Alliance).
- 2023 Inducted into the Women's Hall of Honors (AMAAF)
- 2023 Lifetime Presidents Award from President Joe Biden
- 2022 Martial Artist Legacy Award (AMAA)
- 2022 Inducted into the Ocean State International Martial Arts Hall of Fame
- 2021 Inducted into the Amerikick International Martial Arts Hall of Fame
- 2019 Awarded the Most Powerful Woman in Business for NYS (Schneps Media).

She outgrew the building by 2005 and needed to find a new location. Luckily, right across the street was the perfect spot for a new state-of-the-art facility. TaeCole Tae Kwon Do & Fitness prospered at the new location and several community programs that Maggie instructed at local schools and centers.

As Maggie says, "We turn no one away; keeping children safe and aware is our number one priority." She goes on to say, "My students come first. I use TKD as a tool to help others be all they can be. Planting the seed of confidence in a child that they can be all they dream of is the key. TKD has allowed me to make the difference I want to see in the world by reaching out to others. People trust us; it is important that we do not abuse our position to hurt others. We are all just people at the end of the day. The question is, did we make a POSITIVE impact on the day of another."

MAJOR ACHIEVEMENTS

- 2019 Presented Special Congressional Recognition for her outstanding and Invaluable service to her community and everywhere she makes her mark.

- 2019 New York Assembly Certificate of Merit for Female Fighters Matter Too (Founder and President) mission to bring equality to young girls and women worldwide.

- Recognized by NYS Senator Joseph P. Adabbo, Jr. for her selflessness and tireless commitment to the State of New York and for her Loyalty and Dedication to the betterment of the State of New York.

- 2019 Marquis Who's Who Woman of Integrity, Excellence/ Entrepreneur Award

- 2017 Awarded Women of high honors distinction award 2019 Cover of Tae Kwon Do Life Magazine (First woman to make the cover edition).

- 2018 #FFM2 (#Femalefigtersmattertoo) Worldwide Campaign, Bringing attention to equality for Female Athletes Worldwide.

- 2014 Twin Towers Hall of Fame

- 2014 ISKA Forms Champion

- 2014 NASKA World Champion Women's Forms

- 2014 LIWO is the Northeast Regional Championship for the World Class Martial Arts Organization

- 2012 Earned her 7th Dan under GGM S.C. Kang (Kuk Mu Kwan Kang System)

- 2012 Hosted her first tournament LIWO (Long Island Martial Arts Winter Open)

- 2012 Inducted into the Martial Arts Hall of Fame

- TKD Times School of the Month (March 2010)

- 2007 New York / New Jersey U-ITF Regional Director

- Certified International (#A-17-Class A) Instructor

- Founder/President at TaeCole Tae Kwon Do & Fitness, Albertson, New York

- Director of TaeCole Tae Kwon Do & Fitness House Call Network

- Member USA 2018 USA Martial Arts Team (WKC) USA GOLD MEDALIST.

- 2018/19 Voted Best Martial Arts School Long Island NY

- NASKA World Champion Women's lightweight BB fighting

Staying true to your heart is a success because, at the end of the day, this is all you have. The richest person is the one richest in the heart. It is very easy to live against your values and gain popularity. One can be comfortable or have a million-dollar home or a fancy car, but I believe that I don't have anything to prove to anyone.

How MARTIAL ARTS CHANGED My Life!

Martial Arts gave me an inner strength I thought only existed in others. Although there were setbacks every now and again, I always got back up and kept pushing forward. Being a woman and being treated differently than men never sat well with me. This only heightened my fighting spirit. The martial arts woke up a fire and gave me the platform for being the change the world needed.

We are who we choose to be. The harder the task, the bigger the victory. It started with kicking, punching, and blocking. Here we are 35 years later, changing the world, one task at a time.

How has Grandmaster CYNTHIA ROTHROCK Influenced me?

My generation owes a debt of gratitude to Cynthia Rothrock, a pioneering woman who cleared the path for us. Her tireless efforts have lightened the load of our journeys, and we are forever thankful for her contributions.

MAJOR ACHIEVEMENTS

- NASKA World Champion in BB Tradition and Creative
- Forms
- WKC USA Team (Ranked #1 Traditional Forms)
- Team USA GOLD Medalist (Traditional Forms)
- WKC USA Team (Ranked #1 Traditional Forms)
- NYS 2009 Champion in Woman's Black Belt Fighting
- Woman's Grand World Champion in Fighting (WCMAO)

Dana MILLER

"

The arts have given me meaning and a mission. Through these years, I have learned many lessons...

WHY THE *Martial Arts?*

My friend's semi-pro boxer dad taught us basic boxing fundamentals. Also, a relative of mine who had some experience with techniques and training of the British Commandos of WWII, told stories, sharing their exploits and techniques that they were taught. When JFK started the Green Beret Program, I decided that was what I wanted to do with my life. At the time in the 1960s, there weren't any Martial Arts schools in my area, but there were a couple of clubs where people could get together and share training methods. I soon added Judo to my practice. A neighbor at the time was practicing Karate, so we worked out together too. In high school, I was a gymnast. The flexibility and strength gained helped with the high kicking needed for that art. And the practice of Katas was similar to the sets or routines in gymnastics, which appealed to me.

TRAINING INFORMATION

- Martial Arts Styles & Rank: 10th Level Red Sash-Zu Wei Shu Gong Fu, 9th Level Black Belt -American Combat Karate, 6th Level Black Sash -Chuan Lu Kenpo, 3rd Level Black Belt-Tang Soo Do, Honorary Ranks: 3rd Dan-Tae Kwon Do, 1st Dan-Shotokan Karate, 1st Dan-Goju Kai Karate, 1st Dan-Judo

- Instructors/Influencers: Raymond McCardie, George Fibbson, Nathaniel R. Wilson, Paul S. Landon, Don B. Jones, Joe Pereira, Grand Master Chen, Jim Cravens, John Allen, Rick Faye, Larry Seiberlich, Fu Wei Zhong, Master Chunvi Lin, George Hu, Liang Sho Yu

- Birthplace/Growing Up: St. Paul, MN

- Yrs. In the Martial Arts: 63 years

- Yrs. Instructing: 55 years

- School owner, Manager & Instructor at U S Chuan Fa Martial Arts Center

PROFESSIONAL ORGANIZATIONS

- United States Chuan Fa Association AAU Judo President, U.S. Chuan Fa World Martial Arts Hall of Fame 1994

- World Head of Family Sokeship Counsel Member, National QiGong Assn. USA, 1997 Member QiGong Empowerment Assn. 1995 NDEITA, Personal Trainer member

How MARTIAL ARTS CHANGED My Life!

Martial Arts has been my life's major focus and purpose from an early age. The arts have given me meaning and a mission. Through these years, I have learned many lessons from my martial practices, integrity, honesty, commitment, personal responsibility, discipline, self-knowledge, and passing on that knowledge. Through teaching and sharing with others since the age of twenty, I have learned how much growth is possible for students. Through the years, I've helped change the lives, I hope, for the good of hundreds of students from all over the country. I will always be grateful for the opportunity I have had to help develop young people, leading them to become respectful and successful adults who will positively contribute to society. It has been my greatest personal achievement to watch my students; Bob Berube, Peter Rudh, Steve Kubic, Mike Kaiser, Levi Wilson, Billie Brown, Gail Behr, Heide Hindsman, Kenny Patterson, Brian Bailey, Bryan Lewis, Tom Shipp, Paul Methven, Rudy Bormann become masters.

Become an
AMAA
MEMBER!

PERSONAL ACHIEVEMENTS

- President of 3M Corporation Chinese Boxing Club 1975-1994 6th Dan Master level Chuan Lo Chinese Boxing Association, 1979 Republic of Taiwan Koushu Mission instructor certificate 1983 Head of Family, U.S. Chuan Fa Assn. 1992 -present Grand Master of the Year, World Martial Arts Hall of Fame, WMAHF, 1995 Member world head of Family Sokeship Council, 1994 Awarded Professor of Martial Arts degree, WMAHF, 1998 Graduate, Three Rivers Crossing Center for Qigong Traditional Chinese Healing,1996 Certified Medical QiGong Instructor, 1998 Presidential Sports Award in Karate, 1993, (G.W. Bush)

MAJOR ACHIEVEMENTS

- Elected lifetime president of U.S. Chuan Fa Association 1981
- Inducted into the World Martial Arts Hall of Fame 1994
- Inducted into World Head of Family SokeShip Council 1995 Inheritor of Combat Karate System from Paul Steve Landon 2016
- Developed and Founded Zu Wei Shu System Martial Arts1980
- 6th-degree promotion in Chuan Lu 1979
- Professorship from the World Head of Family 1998

Toby
MILROY

"

Master Toby Milroy has been studying the martial arts for more than 40 years and has helped thousands of martial arts school owners find success in the martial arts business.

WHY THE *Martial Arts?*

My fascination with the Martial Arts started when I was very young.

The media in the late 70's was my original inspiration for studying martial arts. I first saw a snippet of Enter the Dragon in 1978. I still remember being in awe of the Super Hero like speed and skill I saw in those few stolen minutes of the film. Then I became a somewhat ravenous seeker and consumer of all things martial arts. "Kung Fu" re-runs on television, Black Belt and Karate Illustrated Magazine, and even some early Chuck Norris movies solidified my passion and resolve to study the martial arts.

I was fortunate enough that a family friend was a part time martial arts instructor at a local collage, and he agreed to work with me once a week. After a few months, my enthusiasm for training had only grown, and I was finally able to convince my Mother to enroll me in the local

TRAINING INFORMATION

- Belt Ranks & Martial Arts Styles: TaeKwonDo (5th Dan), TangSooDo (5th Dan)

- Instructors/Influencers: Master David Schmidt, Master Jason Farnsworth, Grandmaster Jeff Smith, Grandmaster H.U. Lee, Grandmaster Stephen Oliver

- Birthplace/Growing Up: Dubuque, IA

- Yrs. In the Martial Arts: 42 years

- Yrs. Instructing: 26 years

- Executive Vice President - AMS, President and Editor in Chief - Martial Arts World News Magazine

PROFESSIONAL ORGANIZATIONS

- Successful Multi School Operator

- Author – Coaching Children to Succeed in Life

- Author – The Path to Leadership

- 2007 - Chief Operating Officer - NAPMA (National Association of Professional Martial Artists

- 2007 -Chief Operating Officer – Martial Arts Professional Magazine

"real" full time Karate School.

At that time, it was NOT standard practice to accept student as young as I was, but the school made an exception and allowed me to attend classes. The 'full time' structured training at the Dubuque Karate Club, under Master David Schmidt was a LIFE changer for me.

I was already passionate about martial arts, but this experience lit a fire in me that has helped me create a level of success in the martial arts, in the martial arts business, and in my life that I never would have thought possible.

The Martial Arts has given me a "core" set of skills that has created an amazing life and career for me. It has imbued me with the sense of self-confidence and focus of will that has allowed me to accomplish goals that most people think are impossible to reach.

When I first opened a Martial Arts school, I was a good Martial Artist, and I wanted to pass on the arts that I loved so much, but I was clueless about running a successful school. I was missing a LOT of martial arts business fundamentals.

I pretty quickly realized that running successful martial arts schools requires a COMPLETELY new set of skills that I'd never really learned as a martial arts student, BUT I also realized that IF you apply the same PRINCIPLES you master while studying the martial arts, you can easily acquire the new skills you need, and implement them to create amazing businesses and make a substantial positive impact on your students and your community.

The discipline, focus and "indomitable spirit" you develop in your martial arts training are an

PERSONAL ACHIEVEMENTS

- 2015 - Executive Vice President - AMS (Amerinational Management Services)
- 2015 - President and Editor in Chief - Martial Arts World News Magazine
- Helped Thousands of Martial Arts School Owners Create More Successful Schools

WHY THE MARTIAL ARTS (CONTINUED)

amazingly powerful force when you apply them to ANY aspect of your life. Not only do these principles empower you to be successful in a martial arts school, but in ANY career path, profession or avocation you might want to pursue.

It's been the greatest honor of my life to help so many martial arts students and school owners reach their goals and impact more of the world with the positive values of the martial arts.

Jack MORALES

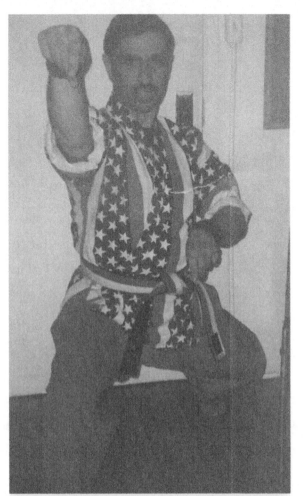

Shihan Jack Morales a native New Yorker with over 50 Years in the martial arts. He started training at the age of four by six family members. Shihan Morales is a 7th Dan Black Belt (Shichidan) in Goju-Ryu, under GGM Aaron Banks; Green Belt (Rokkyu) in Judo, under Master Paul Kamiesky; and Brown Belt (Ichkyu) in Kyokushin, under Shuseki Shihan William Oliver.

Shihan Morales is a 3x former World Champion, 9x Hall of Famer, named "Man of the Year" in 2009 & 2016, has competed nationally and internationally, and won numerous championships in breaking and fighting.

He was awarded New York, Connecticut, Rhode Island, and Pennsylvania State Division Championships, as well as in Muay Thai.

In 1998,1999 and 2007, Shihan Morales was a top official for the Professional Kickboxing Federation and the United States Muay Thai Association. Shihan Morales was also awarded Archangel of the Year (2016), Brick of the Year (2022), Outstanding Leadership Award (2022), and Guardian Angel of the Year (2023) with the NYC Guardian Angels Safety Patrol.

He has achieved and experienced so much in his martial arts career and is extremely grateful for the support in love of his family, friends, and instructors.

Phil
MOULTON

"

Dedicating 53 years of my life has made me the successful person I am, which has helped many others.

WHY THE Martial Arts?

We all have a dream in life to achieve something. Following a footpath is often not easy. We have obstacles and barriers which we sometimes put in our way. My journey started 53 years ago, in 1970, in North Manchester, UK. Like many, I came from a modest background with very little money to support my goal in life. In my book, Phil Moulton, the Bodyguard: Overcoming the Bullies, I outline my battle to make it. You must hold a passion in your heart, which gives you that drive. It's not about overcoming failure but wanting to win. Throughout my Karate journey, I have competed at every level. I lost a few and won a few, but I took away the pride of achieving that goal and lesson. I trained seven days a week, sometimes twice in one day, practiced at every opportunity, and competed at every competition I could attend. My mindset was to become a first Dan (black belt), which I attained in 1982. It took longer than it should have done as I had been

TRAINING INFORMATION

- Martial Arts Styles & Rank: Traditional Shukokai Karate-9th Dan

- Instructors/Influencers: Jeff Parker, Maggie Chan, Jeff Corbishley, Dennis Cassey, Neil Fagen, Terry Pottage, Danny Connors, Charles Gidley

- Birthplace/Growing Up: Middleton, Manchester UK

- Yrs. In the Martial Arts: 53 years

- Yrs. Instructing: 43 years

- School owner & Instructor at Bushido Karate Club, Trainer in Self-Defense since 1990

PROFESSIONAL ORGANIZATIONS

- City and Guilds 7307 teaching qualification in adult learning

- Award Education teaching City and Guilds 3 (12 units)

- Level 3 Award first aid at work (Valid FAAW QCF trainer)

- Level 3 physical intervention

more focused on Kumite (fighting) and Kata (form) than taking grades, but becoming a black belt was the start of the real journey. Phil Moulton is a man who started life with a mission to be a success. Raised on a tough council estate in Manchester, he thrived in adversity, took on the bullies that marred his youth, had no money from his parents, and had to scrub the dojo floors (my choice) to get his lessons. Despite the challenges thrown at him, he fought his way to the very top of his sport and profession. The former World Open Karate Champion combined the skills and techniques honed in the dojo with the knowledge and training he developed to make him one of the UK's most respected personal security and close protection specialists. For over twenty-seven years, the karate 9th Dan black belt has protected stars from the world of sport and entertainment, safeguarding members of international organizations and advising and training government agencies, corporations, and the military. The Bodyguard is the true story of one man's determination to succeed. It's an example to all that anything is possible if you work hard enough and have the desire and commitment.

As a bodyguard, I have protected many of the world's elite from stage and screen. Not being ex -force, it was a challenge but with my dedication and experience, many trusted me with their lives as a protection operator.

Here in the UK, we are not allowed to carry any weapons, so it is all about planning and research. Did my karate skills help me? 100% yes; it gave me a strict understanding of the discipline. Being a World Champion also gave me some status, but as a humble person, it did

PROFESSIONAL ORGANIZATIONS

- BTEC level 3 Instructor in Conflict Management
- BTEC level 3 National close protection course license (active)
- BTEC Levels 3 instructor in Close Protection SIA accredited
- Trainer in personal safety and awareness (author of training program MANCAT)
- Trainer/operator in surveillance and counter-surveillance
- Attended and assisted numerous training courses under former British SAS
- CPD Trainer and author of edge weapons awareness program
- Training courses tabletop operations for Hostile surveillance by the British Special Branch
- GSAT general security awareness training (Aviation Security 2016)
- Certificate in dealing with infectious deceases (COVID-19)
- Certificate ACT (Action Counter Terrorism 2022 May)
- Certificate ACT (Action Counter Terrorism 2022 eLearning June 2022)
- Certificate ACT) Action Counter Terrorism 2022 eLearning security awareness 2022)
- 2017 completed NXCT National Xray competence training
- Level 2 Aviation Security leaders' qualification
- DBS registered and Counter terrorist check completed via MAG /SIA and 2022 Commonwealth Games

PERSONAL ACHIEVEMENTS

- My achievements have spanned over 5 decades as a karateka and a successful professional bodyguard, trainer, and operator for the last 28 years.
- Protection for VIPs, including a few too many to mention: 2023 Cynthia Rothrock (Martial arts hall of Fame), Ms. Whitney Houston, Football Legend Pele/Eric Cantona/David Beckham, HRH Prince William (FA duty), HRH Prince Edward 2008/ 2022
- Head of security for the following England National football team England U21 England Squad Security Manager 4 English premier football clubs

MAJOR ACHIEVEMENTS

- Awarded my 9th Dan black belt in 2021.
- 53 years of constant training gradings and courses in between
- Gaining my 1st dan blackbelt 1982

AUTHOR & COURSE WRITER

- 2020 Gained Worldwide accreditation for the advanced close protection course.
- 2018 CPD National standards office gained accreditation for the personal safety and weapons awareness course.
- 2012- present Gained National center status to deliver OFQUAL security and other qualifications Industry Qualifications/SFJ Awards
- Edxcel 2005 till 2013 Gained National Center status to deliver BTEC Close protection and other courses.
- GMOCN 2001 until 2005 gained center status to deliver close protection and personal safety awards.
- 1999 until 2005, author of 5 courses that were accredited by GMOCN (close protection 1-2 surveillance and counter surveillance- personal safety- hostile environment-event stewarding (MANCAT)

CHAMPIONSHIPS OVER 50 YEARS

- 1996 World Open all styles karate champion 1996
- European Karate champion 1998/99
- Ranked 4th in the World Championships USA 2002
- British Nationals runner-up 2013
- Shukokai Karate Union National champion runner up 81/82/83 (Belle-Vue)
- Quest for Champions 1981 (New Century Hall) kata kumite
- SKU National championships 1981/82 Kata/kumite
- Many interclub championships kumite/kata
- SKU England squad 1980/84 kumite
- TBSKA England squad 1998-2003 kata kumite
- Lancashire Opens Kumite/team 1982
- Refereed many national championships

work against me. Find the balance between being boastful or just letting people know your achievements in life.

PERSONAL ACHIEVEMENTS

- Responsible for the safety of several five and 4-star hotels.
- The British Prime Minister Boris Johnson under (RaSP)
- The French Government Minister.1998
- Former Thai Prime Minister
- England football Managers from 2004-2012
- Set up the 1st witness protection program dealing with gangs in the inner city of Manchester for 11 years.
- Tasked to look after a notable person under severe threat.

How MARTIAL ARTS CHANGED My Life!

As a young lad, I was bullied like many. I trained myself firstly by the book and then finding a local dojo. It has given me a sense of purpose and direction over time, helping others achieve their black belts and winning many tournaments. My career as a professional bodyguard has enabled me to support others who were bullied and lost confidence. Dedicating 53 years of my life has made me the successful person I am, which has helped many others. I teach in the karate arena and as a close protection (bodyguard). I have instructed nearly 3000 students who have taken their careers to many levels as protection officers. Competing at every level, from regional, National, and World competitions, gives you a sense of achievement by being a part of a team. Being graded as one of the highest in the UK is very humbling, and we know we have a sense of duty to promote karate -do fellowship. From being a scruffy kid in Manchester, with holes in my shoes, wearing cast-off clothes and a tatty GI with no confidence and no standing in life to becoming someone who may have relied on for so much.

LIFETIME ACHIEVEMENTS

- The author of my book The Bodyguard: Overcoming the Bullies. It received #1 on Amazon in 2018.
- My Documentary the Bodyguard: Saving the Stars (YouTube)
- 2020 - Positive Role Model award for inspiring others
- 2022 Martial Arts Hall of Fame (traditional karate)
- 2023 Martial Arts Hall of Fame (Karate legend)

How has Grandmaster CYNTHIA ROTHROCK Influenced me?

I have known of Cynthia's work in films and Martial arts for many years, and my first instructor (Maggie Chan) was a lady karateka. It is a good synergy; seeing anyone achieve what she has done in her life is fantastic by any stretch of the imagination. Meeting Cynthia at the UKMAS in Doncaster and then being asked to act as her (bodyguard for the evening) has taken pride on my list, knowing of her skills. Thank you for that opportunity.

Become an AMAA MEMBER!

Jae MUN

"

Martial Arts has allowed me to meet many excellent martial artists while also giving me the confidence to know that I can defend myself.

WHY THE *Martial Arts?*

I was fascinated with the jump-spinning hook kick performed by my childhood friend Jong Woo only to discover it was Tae Kwon Do. South Korea was very poor at the time during the '60s. I had many hobbies; fishing at Han River, hunting with a slingshot, and ice skating in the field during winter. I joined the baseball team at my elementary school- Gang Nam but took Tae Kwon Do lessons outside of school at the neighborhood's Do Jang (Tae Kwon Do School).

The self-defense aspect appealed to me since there were fights at school and neighborhood gangs. I studied during the '70s in Baltimore. Practicing self-defense was exciting. A dozen kids surrounded me with axes at a golf course and by gangs outside a memorial baseball stadium. It helped me make new friends and build my reputation at school as a karate kid. I had a smooth school life, unlike other Asian kids

TRAINING INFORMATION

- Martial Arts Styles & Rank: IJTF - International Jung Tong Tae Kwon Do 9th Dan; Black Belt World-6th Dan-WTF; World Combat Arts Federation 6th Degree Black Belt; World Black Belt Bureau 5th Dan; Kukkiwon, ITF International Tae Kwon Do Federation 1st Dan

- Instructors/Influencers: South Korea Moo Duck Kwan Masters, Kong Young II, Kong Young Bo, Al Pigeon, Sang Ki Eun

- Birthplace/Growing Up: Seoul, Korea

- Yrs. In the Martial Arts: 54 years

- Yrs. Instructing: 20 years

- General Manager

PROFESSIONAL ORGANIZATIONS

- Alumni Westminster Theological Seminary

- Korean Pastors

- Kentucky Colonel

- Ordained Minister of the Gospel through Kosin Presbyterian Denomination (2003)

PERSONAL ACHIEVEMENTS

- Master of Divinity from Westminster Theological Seminary in PA
- Youth pastor for 20 years at numerous Korean churches (AK, WA, DC, MD, and PA)
- I prepared and led short-term missions to Mexico and Peru
- I helped organize the 1980 Worldwide Evangelization Crusade in South Korea-International affairs
- Interpreter and guide to Dr. Bill Bright, Founder of Campus Crusade for Christ
- Seminar speaker for SFC
- Four-year Senator Scholarship-MD
- BS for Philosophy & Religious Studies at Towson State University

MAJOR ACHIEVEMENTS

- Master of Divinity from Westminster Theological Seminary (2001)
- Ordained Minister of Gospel (2002)
- Promoted 9th Dan by IJTF (2018)
- Hall of Fame- Grandmaster of the year and best school owner of the year by the United States Kido Federation 2-time award recipient for the spreading and contribution of Tae Kwon Do by Jun Lee, President of Black Belt World (2018 and 2019)
- Hall of Fame - Evangelist/Instructor of AFKA-American Freestyle Karate Association
- Head instructor-New Life Black Belt Academy
- Inclusion into the Martial Arts Extraordinaire Biography Book: 50 Years of Martial Arts Excellence (2021).

who got bullied at school. I did Junior and Senior High demonstrations, so everyone knew I did Tae Kwon Do. At the time, kids knew it as Karate and gave me respect or were at least wise enough not to pick a fight.

I liked competing in tournaments. It gave me purpose, took my mind off my worries, and I wanted to make my dad proud. I also continued because I liked my instructor, Al Pigeon, who led me to Christ and socializing with members after class by attending Friendly's Ice Cream. I chose Tae Kwon Do, even though I made a Varsity Soccer Team in High School. I thought I would have a better chance of getting a job during my college years as an instructor. My investment in training in Tae Kwon Do paid off as a General Manager for four years in Maryland, only to heed my calling as a minister of the Gospel, pursuing a Master's of Divinity at Westminster Theological Seminary in Pennsylvania. I worked full-time as a program director for many Tae Kwon Do Schools, helping them succeed in member enrollment and eventually becoming President of All American Tae Kwon Do Academy. I enjoy Tae Kwon Do; I use it to minister and help develop future leaders in America.

How MARTIAL ARTS CHANGED My Life!

Martial arts have helped me maintain my physical health. It has helped me obtain a job now that I hold the title of a founder of the All-American Tae Kwon Do Federation position. It has allowed me to meet many excellent martial artists while also giving me the confidence to know that I can defend myself.

Chris
NATZKE

> " As martial arts masters and leaders, we are at our best when we are taking what we have learned and using it to help others.

WHY THE *Martial Arts?*

I began my martial arts training in September of 1973. I was a short little chubby kid enamored with the popular T.V. show at that time called "Kung Fu." In the series, Shaolin monk Kwai Chang Caine was wandering the American desert, avoiding the authorities. He would then come into a small town, be confronted by a group of bad guys, and take care of them using his Kung Fu. As a 10-year-old, it was the coolest thing I had ever seen, and I literally begged my mom to let me go to my first class. She finally relented, and when I went to the class and watched the students demonstrating their precise and powerful movements, I felt like I was at home. That was almost 50 years ago as of this writing, and I still have a deep and profound love for martial arts, and what it has done for me and the thousands of students I have been blessed to teach and impact throughout the years.

TRAINING INFORMATION

- Martial Arts Styles & Rank: Superfoot System (Bill "Superfoot" Wallace)-8th Dan, United States Chang Moo Kwan Tae Kwon Do-7th Dan, Kuk Ki Won-6th Dan, International Combat Hapkido Federation-2nd Dan

- Instructors/Influencers: Grandmaster Bill "Superfoot" Wallace, Grandmaster Jae Kyu Lee

- Birthplace/Growing Up: Oconomowoc, WI

- Yrs. In the Martial Arts: 50 years

- Yrs. Instructing: 47 years

- Vice President of Business Development/Black Belt Testing Coordinator for Superfoot Systems, President/Master Instructor at Colorado Alliance of Martial Arts

PROFESSIONAL ORGANIZATIONS

- Superfoot System
- United Stated Chang Moo Kwan
- Kuk Ki Won
- National Speakers Association
- Master Networks

How MARTIAL ARTS CHANGED My Life!

Martial arts have been the guiding force of my life for almost 5 decades.

When I first entered the dojang (training hall), it was all about the physical nature of the arts, kicking, punching, sparring, forms, and board breaking. However, over time, I truly have come to realize what my original instructor, Grandmaster Jae Kyu Lee, would often speak about – martial arts was and is about becoming a "Life Champion".

It is about having a Purposeful Vision for our lives that inspires us and helps us to grow and expand. It is about living with a Conscious Persistence that assists us in overcoming life's obstacles when they occur. And finally, it is about living a life of Compassionate Service and being dedicated to positively impacting others through the wisdom and experience we have gained from practicing martial arts.

While I have achieved much personal success in my martial arts career, what I am most humbled by and proud of are the numerous people I have been able to help in their lives either through directly training them in martial arts or through my martial arts-inspired work now as a life-leadership coach, keynote speaker, seminar leader, and author.

As martial arts masters and leaders, we are at our best when we are taking what we have learned and using it to help others. It is through the giving and the serving that we truly receive.

I believe Author, William Arthur Ward, said it best when he stated,

PERSONAL ACHIEVEMENTS

- Master's Degree Spiritual Psychology from the University of Santa Monica (August 2013)
- Author of two books: Black Belt Leadership: 7 Keys to Creating a Life of Purpose by Discovering Your Inner Champion (2013), Breaking Through: 3 Winning Strategies to Create Breakthrough Results in Your Life, Business and Relationships (2021) - AMAZON #1 BEST-SELLER
- Completed walk of Camino de Santiago - 500-mile walked across northern Spain (2014)
- Father of two grown sons
- Delivered over 300 talks/trainings of as a professional speaker

MAJOR ACHIEVEMENTS

- 8th Dan Superfoot System - July 2019
- 7th Dan United States Chang Moo Kwan Taekwondo - May 2008
- 1999 United States Taekwondo Union (USTU) National Heavyweight Gold Medalist - Black Belt Division - Ages 33-40
- Regional Director - National Association of Professional Martial Artists - (2000 - 2004)
- Graduate of Ultimate Black Belt Class (UBBT) Team 1 (2005) - Tom Callos
- Cover of "Martial Arts Professional Magazine" (1996)
- Martial Arts School Owner of Family Martial Art Center of Aurora, CO (1995 - 2013)
- President of the Colorado Alliance of Martial Arts (1996 - 2013)
- Promoted 1,500 students to Black Belt
- Generated over 250,000 Random Acts of Kindness through the CAMA Black Belt Candidacy Program (2005 to present)

"We must be silent before we can listen. We must listen before we can learn. We must learn before we can prepare. We must prepare before we can serve. And we must serve before we can lead."

It is through martial arts that I learned this most profound life lesson and that is why I am continually inspired to do the work that I do.

Become an
AMAA
MEMBER!

Maurice NOVOA

"

Pursuing martial arts mastery is an ongoing journey, and it has instilled in me a lifelong learning and growth mindset.

WHY THE *Martial Arts?*

Maurice is a well-known name in the world of martial arts. Born in Uruguay of Basque heritage in the year of the tiger, Maurice moved to Australia at four and discovered his passion for martial arts as a young boy. He began his martial arts journey by practicing Judo at eight, followed by Karate. During his Karate training, Maurice's interest in martial arts deepened as he became more interested in the philosophy and principles behind the movements rather than just the physical techniques themselves.

At seventeen, Maurice became a full-time student of Wing Chun in Flinders St, Melbourne. He was captivated by the elegance and simplicity of the Wing Chun style and soon began training twelve lessons per week for two years. This intense dedication and commitment allowed Maurice to achieve his level 3 certification, which permitted him to train in the senior classes. However, his passion for Wing

TRAINING INFORMATION

- Martial Arts Styles & Rank: Honorary Blackbelt in Arnett Sport Kung Fu, Level 10 Gold Sash in Wing Chun Kung Fu, Instructor Level in Wing Chun
- Instructors/Influencers: Grandmaster Anthony Arnett, Grandmaster Felix Leong
- Birthplace/Growing Up: Montevideo, Uruguay / Melbourne, Australia
- Yrs. In the Martial Arts: 32 years
- Yrs. Instructing: 12 years
- School owner & Instructor at Melbourne Sport and Street Wing Chun Kung Fu

PROFESSIONAL ORGANIZATIONS

- Arnett Sort Kung Fu Association

Chun didn't stop there. Maurice had a burning desire to become a Wing Chun instructor in Melbourne and worked tirelessly to achieve this goal. He continued to train and hone his skills, immersing himself in the philosophy and principles of Wing Chun.

Over time, Maurice became a master of the Wing Chun style, achieving his gold sash and becoming affiliated with some of the world's most respected Wing Chun academies. He achieved his dream of becoming a Wing Chun instructor in Melbourne and has since taught countless students the art of Wing Chun. Today, Maurice continues to share his love and knowledge of Wing Chun with others. He is a respected figure in the martial arts community, and his journey inspires others who are passionate about martial arts and the pursuit of mastery.

Maurice's training in Wing Chun began in 1991, and he worked hard to achieve level 5 by 1997. He subsequently trained with different instructors before finally competing and testing to reach level 10 gold sash under Grandmaster Anthony Arnett's tutelage. Maurice won 1st and 3rd place in two tournaments in the USA due to Arnett's teachings and full-time coaching. In 2012, he started his own Wing Chun school and eventually became affiliated with Grandmaster Arnett's Academy. The following year, he developed an affinity with Grandmaster Terry Lim's Loong Fu Pai Academy, which annually holds martial arts tournaments. Maurice and his students, known as the "Fighting Tigers," have consistently participated in Loong Fu Pai's MATA tournaments for almost a decade.

PERSONAL ACHIEVEMENTS

- Won 1st place in the Sensis Yellow Pages Fast Forward Award
- Ranked as the Number 1 account manager in Australia at Sensis
- Inducted into the Commander Australia Hall of Fame for achievements in Sales
- Taught Wing Chun Kung Fu in Melbourne for over ten years

MAJOR ACHIEVEMENTS

- Founder and head instructor of the Melbourne Wing Chun Kung Fu Academy
- Obtained a Level 10 Wing Chun Black Belt, the highest level possible in the International Wing Chun Academy system
- A dedicated philanthropist who has contributed to various charitable causes, including disaster relief efforts and supporting community leaders
- Maurice and his students, also known as the "Fighting Tigers," have actively participated in Loong Fu Pai's MATA tournaments for nearly a decade. What's impressive is that they have always managed to secure either 1st, 2nd, or 3rd place in every competition they've participated in.

How MARTIAL ARTS CHANGED My Life!

Martial arts have profoundly impacted Maurice Novoa's life, transforming him physically and mentally. From the early age of eight, when he first started practicing Judo, to his journey through various disciplines such as Karate and Wing Chun, Maurice's life has been shaped by the principles and teachings of martial arts.

Physically, martial arts have provided Maurice with a level of fitness and strength that has carried over into all aspects of his life. The rigorous training and constant practice have improved his physical abilities and instilled discipline and perseverance. Through martial arts, Maurice has developed extraordinary control over his body, honing his reflexes, coordination, and overall agility.

However, the impact of martial arts extends far beyond the physical realm. It has become a way of life for Maurice, guiding his actions and shaping his character. The philosophy and principles underlying martial arts have taught him invaluable life lessons, such as respect, humility, and self-discipline. These qualities have become ingrained in Maurice's character and have influenced his interactions with others, both within and outside the martial arts community.

Martial arts have also provided Maurice with a sense of purpose and direction. His passion for Wing Chun grew as he delved deeper into his training, driving him to become a certified instructor and share his knowledge with others. This pursuit of mastery and the desire to pass on the teachings of Wing Chun has given Maurice a sense of fulfillment and accomplishment.

Moreover, martial arts has served as a source of inspiration and motivation for Maurice. It has given him a constant challenge, pushing him to push his limits and strive for continuous improvement. Pursuing martial arts mastery is an ongoing journey, and it has instilled in Maurice a lifelong learning and growth mindset.

How has Grandmaster CYNTHIA ROTHROCK Influenced me?

Cynthia Rothrock, a legendary figure in the world of martial arts, has left an indelible impact on the life of Maurice. Known for her unparalleled skills and achievements in the field, Rothrock has been a constant source of inspiration and motivation for Maurice's martial arts journey.

Maurice Novoa admired Rothrock's prowess and dedication to martial arts from an early age. As he watched her perform incredible feats on the screen and read about her numerous championships and accolades, he became captivated by her extraordinary abilities. Rothrock's remarkable skill set and unwavering commitment to her craft fueled Maurice's passion for martial arts and ignited a desire to follow in her footsteps.

Beyond her impressive physical abilities, Rothrock's influence on Novoa extends to her determination and perseverance. She faced numerous challenges and barriers throughout her career, but she never allowed them to deter her. Rothrock's resilience and unwavering spirit taught Novoa the importance of pushing through obstacles and never giving up on his dreams.

Moreover, Rothrock's success as a female martial artist was a powerful example for Novoa. In a predominantly male-dominated field, she shattered gender stereotypes and proved that dedication and skill know no boundaries.

CYNTHIA ROTHROCK (CONTINUED)

Her achievements paved the way for aspiring martial artists like Novoa to pursue their passion without limitations or societal expectations.

As Maurice embarked on his martial arts journey, he carried Rothrock's teachings and principles. Her emphasis on discipline, respect, and continuous self-improvement became guiding principles in Maurice's training. He embraced her dedication to mastering the techniques and honing his skills, striving to embody the same excellence that Rothrock demonstrated.

In summary, Cynthia Rothrock has played a pivotal role in shaping the life of Maurice Novoa. Her unparalleled skills, unwavering determination, and trailblazing spirit have inspired Novoa to pursue his passion for martial arts with dedication and fervor. Rothrock's influence is a constant reminder that with hard work, perseverance, and a strong mindset, one can overcome any obstacle and achieve greatness in martial arts.

Become an AMAA MEMBER!

Daisy
ORTINO

"

The dojo is our happy home. As we always say, the family that trains together stays together.

WHY THE *Martial Arts?*

I was only 29 years old when I lost my first husband. He left me with three beautiful daughters. I wanted my daughters to grow up knowing how to defend themselves. My priority goal was for my daughters to grow up strong and not be bullied at school. I was bullied when I first came to Hawaii from the Philippines when I was 14 years old. I couldn't really speak English then. I saw this Thailander girl being bullied at school and she did a spinning hook kick on this bully. I was so impressed. No one bullied her again. When I met Paul Ortino, he became our Sensei in 1996. We loved karate, weapons and all the friends we were making. The other martial arts students became family to us. The dojo became our home. We trained with Sensei Paul (now my husband) for over 12 years. We had karate in the brain. All my girls became black belts and also graduated in college with honors.

TRAINING INFORMATION

- Belt Ranks & Martial Arts Styles: Sandan in Okinawa Kenpo Karate and RHKKA
- Instructors/Influencers: Hanshi Paul Ortino Jr.
- Birthplace/Growing Up: Philippines and Hawaii
- Yrs. In the Martial Arts: 26 years
- Yrs. Instructing: 13 years
- Instructor

PROFESSIONAL ORGANIZATIONS

- Okinawa Kenpo Karate Dharma-Ryu Dojo
- Ryukyu Hon Kenpo Kobujutsu Association
- Hawaii Karate Congress

The Martial Arts has impacted my life in so many ways. Since I began training in 1996, my health has improved. I used to have severe asthma when I was growing up and heart palpitations.

Working out and training made my body stronger. My girls and I were happier and healthier. Cheryl, Sherry Anne and Shanelle were more focused in school and more confident. They always did homework first and then trained with us. All three of my daughters as well as myself became black belts and assisted teaching Sensei Paul in all of his dojos. Sensei Paul and I got married in May 1998. We had the best time of our lives while training. We developed a stronger bond together. The dojo was our happy home. As we always say, the family that trains together stays together.

PERSONAL ACHIEVEMENTS

- Achieved 3rd Degree Black Belt in Okinawa Kenpo Karate as taught by Grandmaster Seikichi Odo
- Assistant Commissioner to the Aloha State Games in Hawaii 1990 until 2003
- Assistant Instructor to the Okinawa Kenpo Karate Dojos in Hawaii 1999 until 2006
- Assistant Instructor to the Okinawa Kenpo Karate dojo in Naples FL 2006

MAJOR ACHIEVEMENTS

- A top competitor in Hawaii Karate Congress tournaments and rated in Kumite, Kata and Kobudo for many years
- Helped to run all the Aloha State Games Karate tournaments as well as all the annual tournaments put on by the Okinawa Kenpo Karate Dharma-Ryu Dojos in Hawaii
- Taught Karate for the military and their dependents in Hawaii from 1999 until 2006
- Asked to become the female representative for the Strike Back Training System

Paul ORTINO

"

The martial arts has been a blessing to me and I want to share the traditions with all who want to learn.

WHY THE *Martial Arts?*

I began my Martial Arts study when I was 13 in Judo because I wasn't that big and was getting into fights a lot with what we now call bullies. Wanting to be able to defend myself, I pleaded with my parents to let me take martial arts. I then started taking karate in Reading, PA and never stopped.

Everywhere I moved I signed up for Karate, Taekwondo or Kung Fu. The funny thing was that the better I got the less fights I was getting into. Having Senseis such as Robert Dunn (Taekwondo), Al Smith (Red Dragon), Charlie Lewchalermwong (Shotokan) and finally Richard Gonzalez and Seikichi Odo (Okinawa Kenpo) I was taught the principles of Karate as well. I realized that it was better to walk away from a fight not because I was afraid of getting hurt but because I really didn't want to hurt someone else. The Martial Arts taught me to be humble, respectful and to refrain from violent behavior.

TRAINING INFORMATION

- Belt Ranks & Martial Arts Styles: Hanshi,9th Degree Black Belt Okinawa Kenpo Karate Karate (GM Seikichi Odo,GM Richard Gonzalez), 9th degree black belt (GM Robert Dunn Taekwondo), 6th Dan Hawaii Karate Kodanshakai(GM Bobby Lowe,GM James Miyaji), 3rd Degree Black Belt Red Dragon Karate (GM Al Smith), 3rd Degree Black Belt Shotokan Karate, 3rd Degree Black Belt Chi lin Chuan Fa

- Instructors/Influencers: GM Seikichi Odo Okinawa Kenpo Karate (10th Dan), GM Robert Dunn Taekwondo (9th Dan), GM Al Smith Red Dragon Karate (10th Dan)

- Birthplace/Growing Up: Philadelphia PA / HI, FL, NC / Las Vegas, NV

- Yrs. In the Martial Arts: 54 years

- Yrs. Instructing: 48 years

- President and Chief Instructor (Okinawa Kenpo Karate Dharma-Ryu Dojo)

In the beginning I just wanted to protect myself but after I started training, I realized there was so much more to karate than meets the eye. It became a way of life. I no longer wanted to fight other people and was able to walk away feeling confident about myself. From the moment I entered the dojo of GM George Dillman back in the late 60's I wanted to become a Black Belt. Even before I became a Black Belt, I was an assistant instructor.

How MARTIAL ARTS CHANGED My Life!

I wanted to help others get their self-confidence back and be able to protect themselves. I believed that every man, woman and child should learn to protect themselves and my wife Daisy, my daughters Cheryl, Sherry Anne and Shanelle all became Black Belts and helped me teach in Hawaii. My son Angelo is working his way to being a Black Belt one day. The family that trains together stays together.

Become an
AMAA MEMBER!

PROFESSIONAL ORGANIZATIONS

- Ryu Kyu Hon Kenpo Kobujutsu Association (BOD)
- American Martial Arts Alliance
- Hawaii Karate Kondanshakai (original member)
- Hawaii Karate Congress (former President)
- Seishinkai Karate Union (former Shibucho to Hawaii- GM Robert Burgermeister, Kaicho)
- Pennsylvania Black Belt Society
- Florida Black Belt Association

PERSONAL ACHIEVEMENTS

- Won Triple Crown -1st place kata, weapons, kumite (GM James Miyaji tournament/ Waipahu HI)
- Rated in the top 10 kata, weapons and kumite in the Hawaii Karate Congress annual ratings
- Represented USA at GM Ken Funakoshi's Annual tournament San Jose CA Kumite division
- Made 4 DVDs of the Okinawa Kenpo System as taught by GM Seikichi Odo
- Martial Arts Representative for the "Strike Back Training System"
- Co-founded Florida Academy of Judo-Karate with Master Don Rosenthal 1978

MAJOR ACHIEVEMENTS

- Former President of the Hawaii Karate Congress
- Karate Commissioner for the Aloha State Games (1990-2003)
- Taught all branches of the US Military in Hawaii for 26 years
- Promoted to 9th Degree Black Belt, Hanshi June 10th 2010
- Co-founded the UNC-Greensboro Karate Club under the direction of Master Charlie Lewchalermwong 1972
- 2019- awarded " The History General Award" by Professor Gary Lee and the Sport Karate Museum

John PELLEGRINI

"

I have been able to turn my passion for the arts into a successful and rewarding professional career.

WHY THE *Martial Arts?*

My first exposure to martial arts was when I was a teenager in Italy in the early 1960s. There were a few gyms, not commercial schools, but community centers or sports centers, where local Instructors offered some classes in Judo, Karate, and Kung Fu. I had a few friends enrolled, and I went with them occasionally, but not consistently or seriously. That changed when I went into the Army in 1968. I became very interested in learning and began to appreciate the physical, mental, and spiritual value of training in the arts.

Because I was serving in the most elite unit of the Army, the Paratroopers Brigade (Folgore), I received considerable training in Hand-to-Hand Combat; the Lt. teaching the course told us that it was based and derived from Japanese Jiu-Jitsu. In addition to acquiring technical skills, the course was instrumental in developing and forging the "Warrior Spirit" that has remained

TRAINING INFORMATION

- Martial Arts Styles & Rank: Combat Hapkido-Founder / 10th Dan, Traditional Hapkido-9th Dan, Taekwondo-9th Dan, Aikido-1st Dan, JKD-Instructor
- Instructors/Influencers: Grandmaster Michael Wollmershauser, Grandmaster Kwang Sik Myung, Grandmaster In Sun Seo, Grandmaster Y.J. Song, Grandmaster Jung Soo, Fumio Toyoda Sensei, Sifu Paul Vunak
- Birthplace/Growing Up: Florence, Italy
- Yrs. In the Martial Arts: 50 years
- Yrs. Instructing: 38 years
- Founder, The International Combat Hapkido Federation, The Independent Taekwondo Association, The World Martial Arts Alliance

PROFESSIONAL ORGANIZATIONS

- The World Ki-Do Federation

with me throughout my life. By the time I left the Army, I was "hooked." Shortly after I moved to the USA in 1970, I began formal martial arts training. Over the years, I was forced to experience a few interruptions in my training due to several career changes and geographical relocations, but never major or permanently disruptive.

Another reason why I chose martial arts early on instead of other sports or disciplines is because I was never athletically gifted, or physically strong. Being of fairly small build, I soon recognized the necessity to learn survival skills and techniques not dependent on size or muscles to defend myself. During my Law-Enforcement career, the ability to control and neutralize violent attackers proved to be literally life-saving.

PERSONAL ACHIEVEMENTS

- My greatest personal achievements are being a wonderful husband and father

MAJOR ACHIEVEMENTS

- Inducted in over 25 Martial Arts Hall of Fames.

- Featured on the cover of over 20 magazines, including Black Belt (2 times), TaeKwonDo Times (5 times), and Budo International (3 times).

- 2004 Black Belt Hall of Fame "Instructor of the Year"

- Author of 4 books and over 30 training DVDs.

- Conducted training courses for many Police Departments, including Costa Rica Swat Team and Royal New Zealand Police.

- Conducted training tours in Afghanistan, Iraq, Germany, Columbia, and Italy.

How MARTIAL ARTS CHANGED My Life!

Starting with my first experience in the Army, the study of Martial Disciplines has gifted me with the internal development of the "Warrior Spirit" and, on a cognitive level, the acquiring of the "Warrior Mindset." And more than just an "impact" on my life, martial arts have literally saved my life on several occasions. But, besides the practical benefits, I cannot adequately explain how the study of the arts has enriched my life beyond measure. It has allowed me to meet and train with some of the greatest Teachers, Founders, and Masters of the arts in the world. Many, sadly, have passed on, but their teachings and their memories will remain with me forever.

I have had the honor and privilege to become friends with many martial arts celebrities, champions, pioneers, action stars, authors, and industry leaders. I have been able to turn my passion for the arts into a successful and rewarding professional career spanning almost four decades, a career that has allowed me to travel internationally to 25 countries teaching my system; and that, in turn, has provided me with the opportunity to touch the lives of tens of thousands of students and instructors around the world.

So, yes, the study of martial arts has impacted and enriched my life in many positive ways. But, on a very personal level, the most life-changing impact that stands out above all others is that I, through martial arts, met my wife, and because she shared my passion, she became first my student and then my business partner. Today, Master Trina is well-known and respected in the martial arts community and has contributed immensely to the success of our organizations. And our martial arts journey continues to impact our lives in many special ways.

Become an
AMAA MEMBER!

Trina
PELLEGRINI

> 66
> Martial arts introduced me to my husband, and that's a huge impact!!

WHY THE Martial Arts?

I started martial arts when I was 17. My little brother, Devin, loved martial arts movies, Bloodsport in particular, so my mother signed him up for TaeKwonDo classes at a local school. He would always ask me to come and watch him in class, so after several months, I took him to his class. The Master Instructor came out of his office to talk to me, asking me why I wasn't taking classes. I said I was just there to watch my brother, but after talking with him, I signed up for classes too! First, I started taking TaeKwonDo, but the Master Instructor said I was old enough to take the other class he offered called "Hapkido." So, I started taking that class as well. After about a month and a half, I was at work (I worked at a gas station), and I was attacked. I got away with a few bumps and bruises by doing a sidekick to his knee. That started my love of martial arts. I did get my 1st Dan in TaeKwonDo, but then I switched and concentrated on Combat Hapkido.

TRAINING INFORMATION

- Martial Arts Styles & Rank: TaeKwonDo-1st Dan, Combat Hapkido-6th Dan
- Instructors/Influencers: Grandmasters Mark Gridley, David Rivas, John Pellegrini
- Birthplace/Growing Up: Missouri
- Yrs. In the Martial Arts: 32 years
- Yrs. Instructing: 11 years

PROFESSIONAL ORGANIZATIONS

- HanMinJok Hapkido Association
- World Ki-Do Federation
- ICHF

How MARTIAL ARTS CHANGED My Life!

Remember that cute Instructor? I married him, and we've been married for over 30 years. Martial arts introduced me to my husband, and that's a huge impact!! We also started the International Combat Hapkido Federation (ICHF) and the Independent TaeKwonDo Association, which is also my business. I started "Unafraid Women," an organization dedicated to helping women learn valuable Self Defense skills.

How has Grandmaster CYNTHIA ROTHROCK Influenced me?

First, she has influenced my life by paving the way for female martial artists worldwide to practice and be taken seriously within our chosen art. She has shown the world that female martial artists can be fierce, strong, feminine, and beautiful all at the same time, and that is something that would be enough for me. But I also have the honor of being one of her best friends. We have known each other for over 20 years, traveled together, had some amazing adventures, and are still going strong! We have laughed and cried, been silly and sad, and it is a friendship, a sisterhood that I will always cherish. Cynthia, thank you for doing everything that you have done and are continuing to do daily to help girls take that first step into a martial arts class and for inspiring women of all ages to get out there and learn an art. You truly are an inspiration to us all!! I love you!!

MAJOR ACHIEVEMENTS

- 2010 Inducted in the Action Martial Arts Magazine Hall of Fame - "Outstanding Contribution"
- Author of the book "Legacy - Journey of a Martial Arts Pioneer" (2013)
- September 2015 Feature article in Budo International magazine
- 2016 Appointed to the Board of Directors of the "Budo Masters Council"
- March 2015 feature article in TaeKwonDo Times magazine
- January 2017 Cover feature Budo International magazine
- 2017 WHFSC - Hall of Fame "International Woman of the Year" Award
- 2019 - 200 hour Yoga Instructor Certification
- 2020 - Inducted in the Action Martial Arts Magazine Hall of Fame - "Woman of the Year"
- 2021 - Inducted in the U.S.A. Martial Arts Hall of Fame "Female Hapkido Master of the Year"
- 2021 - Inducted in the U.S.A. Martial Arts Hall of Fame "Self-Defense Woman of the Year"
- 2022 - Inducted in the WHFSC - Martial Arts Excellence Award

Terry
POINTER

"

Martial arts helped me to focus on my personal goals, learn the importance of discipline, and helping others in need.

WHY THE *Martial Arts?*

I started martial arts because of the violence in Chicago. 1970s Chicago was nothing but a war zone. You don't know how to defend yourself, you wouldn't make it in the streets of Chicago. I used to get bullied a lot. I can recall one day I went to the movies to go see *Enter the Dragon* and that was the moment in my life I wanted to learn martial arts.

*****

Forty years of teaching Karate has led to a strong traditional approach with an open mind for new ideas and concepts for growth. Teaching Karate for more than technique, Grandmaster Pointer attempts to help people find themselves, discover their creativity and their capacity for overall growth through the study of martial arts. He believes that each person has much growth and sees his purpose as nourishing the seed so that his student's potential may be reached. His understanding of Karate-do is to preserve the

TRAINING INFORMATION

- Martial Arts Styles & Rank: 10th Dan-Founder of AM Self-Defense System, 9th Dan-Kempo Ryu Kan Kay Bugei, 8th Dan-Shorin Ryu, 8th Dan-Lethal Strike Combat Karate, 7th Dan-Shuri – Ryu, 3rd Dan-Soul Karate Unlimited, 1st Dan-Tae Kwon Do (Moo Duk Kwan), 1st Dan-Shotokan, Fundisha (instructor)-African Federation Shugunda

- Instructors/Influencers: Grandmaster Jessie Brown, Mr. Pak, GM Edward Brown, Sifu Roger Miller, GM Gaudiosa Ruby, GM James Newton, GM Alvin Linzy

- Birthplace/Growing Up: Chicago

- Yrs. In the Martial Arts: 48 years

- Yrs. Instructing: 43 years

- Instructor

true essence of the art by maintaining a committed spirit to preserve human decency with honesty, trustworthiness, humility, understanding, compassion, bravery, fairness, discipline, and commitment.

Master Pointer began his martial arts journey when he was 15 years old; he was sick of being picked on by the neighborhood gangs. His father gave him two choices, learn how to fight and protect himself or deal with him... he did not want any part of his father, so he decided to check out the local YMCA, where he was introduced to a whole new world. At the time, the art he was so amazed by was Kung-fu, but he had no idea what it was all about, but he was amazed by what he saw, and he liked it. Just so happened that 5 Fingers of Death and Enter the Dragon was playing at the movie; at that point, he knew what he wanted to do.

While stationed in Germany during his enlistment in the U.S. Army in 1976, Master Pointer had the opportunity to study under SC Johnson from 76 to 78.

Master Pointer returned to the States in 1979. While stationed in Florida, he continued his martial arts training. He earned his black belt training 5 hours a day for a year. In 1980 Master Pointer was confronted by 4 attackers, 2 had weapons, one had a gun, and the other had a knife. He knew this would not be a pretty outcome for him, but he could protect and defend himself with his martial arts training. At this point in his life, he took martial arts and self-defense very seriously.

Grandmaster Pointer has lived and trained in several countries and states during his time in

PROFESSIONAL ORGANIZATIONS

- International Combat Martial Arts Union Association
- U.S.A. Warlord Martial Arts Magazine
- World Kumite Organization
- The International Bujutsu Society
- Kokusai Bujutsu Kesha World Masters Council
- Member of Board of Directors/World Masters Council-Illinois Representative
- Organization Ronin Ryu Ecuador Life member
- Organization Ronin Ryu Official Representative of Chicago
- Kempo Jujutsu Bugei
- Professional Karate Commission
- United States Karate Alliance
- Modern Warrior Arts Union
- U.S. Association of Martial Arts
- U.S. Italian Martial Arts Alliance
- YUDANSILA BELA DIRI CLOSE QUARTERS DEFENSE ACADEMY
- Tactical-Combat-Association International
- United States Taiho Jutsu Federation
- International Martial Arts Union
- Molum Combat Arts Association
- Lethal Strike Combat Karate
- Life Time member International Taiho Juts Federation
- Martial Arts Masters Association
- World Organizer of Martial Arts
- SKU School of Self-Defense
- Kuro Bushi International Illinois State Representative
- Kuro Bushi Council of Elders Member
- WOMA Group International Broad of Directions 2019
- Master Mind Jiu-Jitsu System Council of Advisors 2022

the armed forces. He attributes his success to his faith in God and the leadership of his teacher Mr. Pak. While stationed in Korea in 1981, he had the opportunity to meet and train with Grandmaster Pak, who taught him the art of Moo Duk Kwan. Mr. Pak became a father to him, as well as a friend. His teacher once told him his job as a martial artist is to help preserve and help others to rebuild the martial arts when needed. The path of a warrior is sometimes lonely; the road as a practitioner is long and hard. Few choose it, and even fewer reach its end.

In 1982 his study of Shuri Ryu Okinawan karate began with his teacher Master Jessie Watkins. Karate-do has helped impact his life. Later making his military career, he had the honor to train under GM Edward Brown, GM Jessie Watkins, Grandmaster James Newton, Sifu Roger Miller, and Grandmaster Gaudiosa Ruby. After he got out of the army, he had the opportunity to train with Grandmaster Azziz Anthony Muhammad, Soke Lil' John Davis, Grandmaster Anton Muhammad in yearly seminars, and Grandmaster Alvin Linzy in Shotokan Karate.

Grandmaster Pointer has been training and teaching martial arts for 50 years. A true martial artist will always be a student and have an open mind to learn new things.

PERSONAL ACHIEVEMENTS

- College Degree
- Became an Officer in the military
- Achieved high rank in the martial arts

MAJOR ACHIEVEMENTS

- 20 Year Veteran
- 2010 Action Martial Arts Hall of Fame Recipient
- 2011 Action Martial Arts Hall of Fame Inductee
- 2011 American Federation of Martial Arts Hall of Fame Recipient
- 2011 Masters Hall of Fame Recipient
- 2012 Action Martial Arts Hall of Fame Recipient
- 2012 Hall of Heroes Recipient
- 2012 Masters Hall of Fame Inductee
- 2012 World Head of Family Sokeship Council Inductee Silver Life Achievement
- 2014 World Head of Family Sokeship Council Inductee
- 2015 The Universal Martial Arts Hall of Fame Inductee
- 2022 World Black Belt Club Council Recipient
- Founder of AVM Self-Defense System

How MARTIAL ARTS CHANGED *My Life!*

Martial arts helped me to focus on my personal goals, learn the importance of discipline, and helping others in need.

How *has Grandmaster* CYNTHIA ROTHROCK *Influenced me?*

Grandmaster Cynthia Rothrock inspired me by showing that anything is possible.

Become an
AMAA MEMBER!

Lourdes
RADELAT

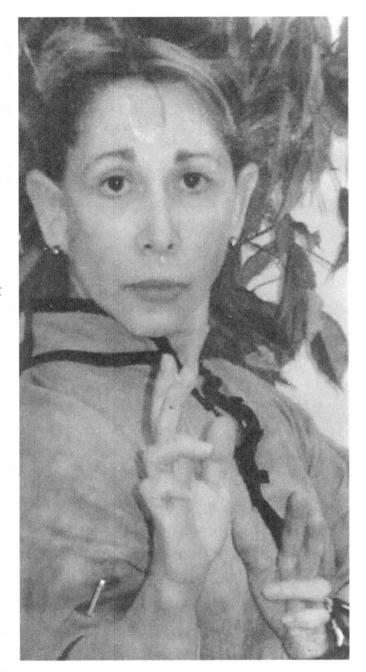

"
Martial arts made me who I am today. It has become a way of life for me to the present day.

WHY THE Martial Arts?

I began my martial arts training in 1976, which was a dream which I had since I was 3-4 years old. But I could not begin my training due to being a girl with an extremely strict father who did not believe girls should fight. After leaving home, I began my training. I had no idea about the different styles. Nor the fact that the Japanese taught Karate. And the Chinese taught Kunfu. Although I was determined to learn. And the first school I checked out was an Okinawan Goju Ryu Karate school under Sensei Jay Trombley. I was fortunate enough to have the opportunity to be accepted (not everyone was accepted to train there), and I immediately began my training.

My Sensei was a United States Marine who had trained while stationed in Okinawa. In those days, it was uncommon for an American soldier to be accepted into a Japanese Karate School in Japan. Fortunately, he was accepted by his Japanese teacher. The Japanese were not

TRAINING INFORMATION

- Martial Arts Styles & Rank: Karate-8th Dan, Kung Fu-8th Level
- Instructors/Influencers: Jay Trombley, Hank Huegly, Jim Thompson, Kenpo Sijo Gray
- Birthplace/Growing Up: Havana, Cuba / Texas
- Yrs. In the Martial Arts: 47 years
- Yrs. Instructing: 45 years
- Instructor

PROFESSIONAL ORGANIZATIONS

- Cancer Warrior Martial Arts Warrior

accustomed to accepting and teaching white American men in those days. It was quite rare. But he was accepted. Sensei Trombley had finished his military training as a United States Marine in Okinawa. But he wasn't personally ready to leave he's training in Okinawan Goju Ryu. So he had to make a formal request to be able to stay in Okinawa to be able to continue more training in the Okinawan Karate School. The United States Marines approved and extended his remain in Okinawa. When he left the United States Marines and returned to the USA, he opened a school in Fort Worth, Texas. And I was fortunate enough to be a female and allowed to begin my martial arts training with him. He was a very militant instructor. And the manner of his training was similar to how he had trained in Okinawa. He had a very select handful of students. Because his manner of teaching was very hardcore, the average American could not last one week under his exercise and brutal training style commands. And it didn't matter to him if a student would not make it through his militant teaching and training in his classes. We were being trained as if we were U.S. Marines. That's how he was taught and wasn't teaching us any different. We had it in us, or we didn't. It didn't matter to him. So, needless to say, the training was excruciating, to put it mildly.

I was the only female with all men; it was extremely difficult and brutal. I didn't receive any special softer treatment that differed from what the men had to do. But I was addicted and determined never to quit! I actually didn't know any different. For my first three years, I felt like I had been hit by a Matt Truck! And after all, it

PERSONAL ACHIEVEMENTS

- Outstanding Competitor Award from Jay Trombley's Okinawan School Of Goju Ryu Karate (1976-1980)
- Lion Team MMA & MSSRKF
- Vale Tudo-MMA Muniz Team Seminario Internacional Federation For Fighting and Defense Systems
- Award of Honor Kyoshi 8th. Dan/International Ambassador Award Sport Karate Museum 8th. Dan Awarded by Professor Gary Lee Sport Karate Museum
- Professor Gary Lee Kata Award Sport Karate Museum The History General Award

MAJOR ACHIEVEMENTS

- Hall Of Fame Award
- Silver and Double Gold Medalist World Champion Fighter
- Kung Fu Broke World Record
- In my World Title Fight in Kung Fu
- 19 Point Combo World Record Holder
- 19 counted Combinations kicks and Punches Connected in 30 Seconds
- Sanchou Fighter Gold Medalist Continuos Fighter Gold Medalist Kata Competitor 1st Place
- I am a Cancer Warrior Martial Arts Ambassador Awarded by GM Kennyg Rebstock.

WHY THE MARTIAL ARTS (CONTINUED)

had been my childhood dream to learn Karate. So it didn't matter how difficult it was to hold up against all odds. I was NOT quitting, no matter what I was put up against! I LOVED it! And never even considered quitting. And I just thought that this was 100% normal. And I thought all my pain had become a part of my life. And that was never going to change. So it was wonderful when I felt no more pain after three years! I was committed and devoted to him.

Later, I had to move, found another Karate School, and studied Isshinryu from Sensei

Hank Huegly in Nashville, TN. I received my 7th Dan under Sensei Huegly. I then decided that I had been an external practitioner for years and wanted to train in the Internal arts. So I began training in Chinese Kung Fu and other internal arts. Wow, it was different than the external art. So soft yet so powerful and so beautiful! I fell madly in LOVE with it also! Although it was challenging in the beginning to go from so many years in the external brutal and HARD Karate styles. To begin lightning and softening up everything, I had begun learning to go in an opposite form and manner of training! It wasn't easy for me because I had become such a brutally hard style in my training style of Karate in my original time in martial arts. I never imagined it would be such a drastic change for me. But none of that mattered. And again, I knew that this was for me. I knew it would also become another amazing and beautiful sweet treasure to insert into my soul. I was born to be a martial artist. It became a way of life for me. In all aspects, it is my passion! It is what I was born to be. I had trained and dreamed of becoming this all my life. My dream became my life. I love being a martial artist more than anything else in my life. It has given me many opportunities throughout my life and in my career. I thank God it allowed me to become what I love more than anything else. It hasn't been easy, but I treasure that so much.

Martial arts made me who I am today. It allowed me to be different than others. It provides me with a different and full perspective of life as a martial artist, and everything I do daily became so different, and comparatively speaking was so different than other individuals in my life.

WHY THE MARTIAL ARTS (CONTINUED)

It allowed me to be an individual with different ways of doing and living in my world. We, as martial artists, live differently than everyone else. Only another martial artist can understand what I am talking about. If you try to explain it to anyone else, they don't have the same knowledge that has carried me through life. I love who I am and must always nurture my body differently than what I would have done without knowing the difference.

How has Grandmaster CYNTHIA ROTHROCK Influenced me?

Grandmaster Cynthia Rothrock influenced me in all aspects of Karate and Kung Fu. She is exceptional in Katas and Weapons and an amazingly physical and outstanding fighter. She is absolutely beautiful and a very stunningly gorgeous and classy woman. I admire her and love what she has done for all of us women in the martial arts world. I send her my deepest Bow and most genuine and sincerest Salute with all my Honor and Respect. Oss

How MARTIAL ARTS CHANGED My Life!

Being a martial artist in karate has been my dream since I was around four years old. I had to wait until I left home after graduating from High School because my father did not believe that a young girl should be training and fighting with men in the early 1970s. I was extremely shy and barely 5' tall, weighing 110 pounds. I had to put on 15 extra pounds to help fight against male fighters. Martial arts gave me a voice, and I lost my shyness. It taught me to be more disciplined and attain much more Honor and Respect. I became very successful in the martial arts and my professional career. It made me who I am today. It has become a way of life for me to the present day. Oss

Become an AMAA MEMBER!

Carlos
RIVERA

"

Martial Arts has impacted me significantly with my job as a police officer in NYC homeless shelter.

WHY THE Martial Arts?

Greetings, my name is Carlos Rivera. I was born and raised in the Bronx. I was motivated by martial arts as I watched martial arts movies and other action movies. I was a big Mortal Combat and street fighter fan. My brother came to NYC. For the first time in the late 90s, he got to move up so that he would say kata he was practicing. I truly fell in love, but he left. Not until 2000, when I saw my brother again for a visit to Puerto Rico, did I see him compete in a tournament I wanted to learn. In 2003 he moved to NYC, where he would teach me some self-defense moves to help me at my Jon.

In 2007, I officially put on my 1st Gi. It was all the help from my mentor, Dr. Smith, from Monroe, who told me about this Goju class. I was hooked. I worked during the day, took college courses in my free time, and hit the community center until 2009. They stopped the program. I was a green belt.

TRAINING INFORMATION

- Martial Arts Styles & Rank: Master instructor W.EB.B.S, 6th Degree Sash U.K.M.A.S, Blue Belt Brazilian Jiu-jitsu, 5th Segree Anthony Worldwide Martial Arts Karate-do, Godan GM Hahle, 4th Degree Krav Maga Junior Master, 3rd Degree American Sento Ryu Bujutsu, 3rd Degree black Goju, 1st Degree in Mushin Kai Senpai, 1st Degree American Seto Ryu Bujutsu, 1st Degree APLEA RANGERS, Krav Maga Black Belt Okinawan Kempo, Kickboxing instructor, Krav Maga instructor

- Instructors/Influencers: Dr. Tony Ruiz, Grand Master Smith, Sijo Jay, Sifu Rick Villaibus, Sifu Mark, Coach Jorge

- Birthplace/Growing Up: Bronx, NYC

- Yrs. In the Martial Arts: 16 years

- Yrs. Instructing: 4 years

- Instructor

My brother told me about a school he was friends with in NYC, and I went over there and started my training under a new system, Japanese karate. I had to start all over again. I was there until around 2011 when my brother visited my dad in NYC from Puerto Rico, told me about his karate tournament, and helped me get a Kyoshi to prepare me to compete. One-on-one personal training helped so much because I have a learning disability, and this was much better. I left Japanese karate school because Kyoshi Tommissini helped me and told me I could keep my rank. He was training in Goju, which was my 1st style. I was so happy to be back in a system I was comfortable with. Ultimately, I had the opportunity to study Krav Maga with Sifu Mark. It helps with my law enforcement and kickboxing as well. Martial arts is my medication to deal with the stress of work. I was blessed to find Kyoshi Shihan, Sifu, and Grandmaster to help me. One major lesson I learned from Zen in my martial arts journey is to have an Emptiness and always be open to learning. As the 12 principles of karate state, your training should be like boiling water never let it get cold. I want to thank GM Anthony for my continued growth in martial arts. Keep training, Gung-ho.

PROFESSIONAL ORGANIZATIONS

- Martial Arts Organization
- World Elite Black Belt Society
- Martial Arts Association Eastern USA
- International Martial Arts Association
- Federation Israel Martial Arts
- World Black Belt Club Society
- Peaceful Warrior's FOP

PERSONAL ACHIEVEMENTS

- Started my martial arts program, Kaizen-Do Bujutsu Lion's DEN CQC (2019)
- Blue belt Brazilian Jujutsu
- NYPD Letter of Commendation for Word Trade Center
- Response Award of Merit Excellence on Duty - Bronx Borough
- President Community Service Award
- Local 237 President Award for Excellence
- 2x Triple Crown winner
- Krane 2x Prime League World Championship
- Zen Combat Martial Arts Association Soke Tittle

MAJOR ACHIEVEMENTS

- The World's Greatest Martial Arts Volume 46
- 2x Action Magazine Hall of Honor
- 2x USA Martial Arts Hall of Fame Martial Arts of the Year - Martial Arts Spirit
- Martial Arts Legacy Awards
- Ambassador Master of Hall Fame Eastern USA
- International Martial Arts dedication
- Martial Arts Sports Association Hall of Fame
- Martial Arts Hall of Fame
- Authority of India 15 years - Master of the Year
- World Black Belt Hall Honor
- International Hall of Honor
- B.S. in Criminal Justice Monroe College, A's in Criminal Justice
- Monroe College Dean's List Winter Semester 2010
- John J. College Peace Officer completion 2009

How MARTIAL ARTS CHANGED My Life!

It has impacted me significantly with my job as a police officer in NYC homeless shelter. I have worked in law enforcement as volunteer police since 2001 to the present day. In my job training, we attend a health and wellness class. In this class, they state that as officers, we have to find ways to calm ourselves and deal with the daily stress of work. For me, martial arts, as I stated, is my medication. When I am in the dojo or sometimes called the lab for jujutsu, I feel the stress leaving my body, plus I also learn how to survive a major incident. I deal with mental health in my shelter. Often my martial arts training comes in handy. The muscle memory of martial arts comes to play. Usually, I have a plan in my head and a basic flow. I have a daughter, and I train her to defend herself. I enjoy spreading my instructor's knowledge, Grandmaster Sifu, to other new students and training in self-defense and dealing with today's world. Martial arts saved my life at work. I almost got stabbed at work with a knife. I couldn't get to the tools on my belt. My hands and feet were my weapon.

How has Grandmaster CYNTHIA ROTHROCK Influenced me?

I met Grandmaster Cynthia Rothrock several times in the Tri-State area in the Hall of Fame and Honors. She has done some great self-defense seminars expressing her martial arts resume and history. She showed me how to stretch. She is a pioneer and legend in martial arts showing women that all things are possible as long they put their minds to it. I was so happy to finally get a copy of the Black Magazine with her on the front and get it signed.

Randy ROBINSON

> Every morning when I leave for the dojo, I focus on one goal – making a positive difference in at least one person's life that day...

WHY THE *Martial Arts?*

As a young adult serving in the U. S. Navy in Hawaii, I was drawn to Chinese Kempo because I liked the fact that the ability to succeed was my responsibility. After many months of training, I began to understand the real reason for studying martial arts. My instructor, Professor Martin Buell, told me, "This is not about kicking and punching. This is about making people's lives better - physically, morally, and spiritually!" That changed my life forever.

I realize that I can't make sweeping changes like creating world peace or eradicating hunger, but if I can have a small impact on just one life each day, maybe there will be a little less hate, prejudice, and divisiveness in the world, and perhaps a bit more love, kindness, and empathy. My dad told me two things that have stuck with me throughout my life. The first was that "having a calling" did not mean that a loud voice from Heaven told you that you should follow a

TRAINING INFORMATION

- Martial Arts Styles & Rank: Grand Master in Sakura Ryu Karate (10th Dan), Kyoshi in Goju - Shorin Karate (7th Dan)

- Instructors/Influencers: Grand Master Ernest Dukes, Soke Michael DePasquale Jr., Dr. James Dozia, Grand Master Bill McDonald, Professor Martin Buell

- Birthplace/Growing Up: Asheville, NC / Old Fort, NC

- Yrs. In the Martial Arts: 51 years

- Yrs. Instructing: 49 years

- School Owner, Manager & Instructor at Robinson Martial Arts, Editor of The Martial Arts Extraordinaire Magazine

PROFESSIONAL ORGANIZATIONS

- American Martial Arts Alliance

- Kuro Bushi Martial Arts Organization

- Dojo Organization

- American Independent Karate Instructors Association

a specific path. Rather a calling was seeing a need that caused you to burn with a desire to fill that need – to make a positive difference. The second thing he said was that failure was not the act of falling down but rather the refusal to get back up and try again. I've held on to those precepts throughout my life.

I feel strongly that those of us who get up every day and go back into our dojos dedicated to making a difference; those who run organizations like the American Martial Arts Alliance; those groups help us grow our schools so we can reach more potential students; and the masters who write to give us advice and inspire us have all answered the call to make this world a better place. And, as we search for our place in that arena and run into obstacles to reaching success, we're going to get up, dust ourselves off, and try again because we're martial artists, and failure is not an option.

How MARTIAL ARTS CHANGED My Life!

The past 51 years seem to have gone by so quickly. But, Albert Einstein said that time passes more rapidly when you are doing something you enjoy. So maybe that's the reason. I've looked forward to every workout. Competition became a positive drug. And, sharing this passion with my wife, son, and grandchildren has given me the greatest joys of my life. My personal life has been enhanced because I've gained the things that martial arts offer to everyone who will work for them: discipline, integrity, and respect for others. But, probably most important, my life has been better

PERSONAL ACHIEVEMENTS

- Battle of Atlanta Division Winner
- AAU State Champion
- AAU Tri-State Champion
- American Martial Arts Alliance Board of Advisors
- Kidz Action Martial Arts Choice Awards Board of Advisors
- Pediatric Cancer Treatment Foundation Board of Directors
- Hardee's NASCAR Board of Directors
- BA Degree in Literature
- Professional Writer (Commercial, Non-Fiction, Fiction)
- Founder of Sakura Ryu style of Karate

MAJOR ACHIEVEMENTS

- American Martial Arts Alliance Legends Hall of Fame
- U.S. Martial Arts Hall of Fame
- Masters of the Martial Arts Hall of Fame- Kuro Bushi Hall of Honor
- Action Martial Arts Magazine Hall of Honor

Become an
AMAA MEMBER!

because I've been given the opportunity to help improve other people's lives by passing on the principles of martial arts. I believe that our reason for existence is to help others live happier, more productive, safer, and healthier lives. Many people do this through volunteer activities. Some physicians and school teachers, for example, do this through their jobs. I have been unbelievably fortunate to have that opportunity by teaching martial arts full time. Every morning when I leave for the dojo, I focus on one goal – making a positive difference in at least one person's life that day. Hopefully, I have been able to do that by creating a safe environment to learn and cultivate martial arts and life skills – and by setting an example through my own behavior.

Darrell
SULLINS, SR.

"

Studying martial arts has given me the confidence to overcome self-imposed limitations and inspire others to do the same.

WHY THE *Martial Arts?*

In the early 70s, ABC had a show called The Wide World of Sports, hosted by Jim McKay. "Spanning the global, to bring you the constant variety of sports. The thrill of victory and the agony of defeat (as a ski jumper begins to slip and fall off the slopes), the human drama of athletic competition" is how the show began. One Saturday, they featured Aaron Banks' Oriental World of Self-Defense. Held at Madison Square Garden, great martial artists such as Ron Duncan, Joe Lewis, Jeff Smith, Bill Wallace, Ron Van Clief, and many others did martial arts demonstrations and performed some amazing feats. This inspired me to go to the library to find any book on Karate.

I later enrolled in free classes at the Cory Recreation Center in Cleveland, Ohio. Then later enrolled in classes at the John F. Kennedy Recreation Center, where I met the Sensei that changed my life. Grand Master Ken Ferguson.

TRAINING INFORMATION

- Martial Arts Styles & Rank: 6th Degree Black Belt in Isshinryu Karate & Kenpo Karate
- Instructors/Influencers: Grand Master Ken Ferguson
- Birthplace/Growing Up: Cleveland, OH
- Yrs. In the Martial Arts: 51 years
- Yrs. Instructing: 45 years
- Instructor

PROFESSIONAL ORGANIZATIONS

- AAU Coach
- USA Karate Federation Coach
- International Association of Professional Recovery Coach

It was his example, motivation, and inspiration I earned a spot on the United States World Karate Team and the United States Pan-American Karate Team, winning a gold medal in the 1981 Pan-American Games.

How MARTIAL ARTS CHANGED My Life!

Studying martial arts has given me the confidence to overcome self-imposed limitations and inspire others to do the same.

How has Grandmaster CYNTHIA ROTHROCK Influenced me?

I believe I first saw her in the movie Super Cops. I asked, " Who in the heck is this person with these explosive poetic movements?" She, like some others, inspired me to want to act in an action movie. In 2020 I had a scene in an action-comedy movie called "Rumble TV" Thank you for the inspiration!

PERSONAL ACHIEVEMENTS

- 2021: Ministry Team, Counselor, Elder-Providence Baptist Church
- 2019: Certified Professional Life Coach-Akron University
- 2019: International Professional Recovery Coach-Net Institute, California
- 2016: Business Administration-Indiana Wesleyan University
- 2012: Personal Trainer Certification-Hondros College
- 2009: Dominion Energy Volunteer of the Year
- 1993: East Ohio Gas Samaritan Award
- 1983-87: United States Marine Corps

MAJOR ACHIEVEMENTS

- 2023: Ferguson Karate Hall of Fame
- 2023: Action Martial Arts Magazine Hall of Honor
- 2022: Martial Arts Masters Hall of Fame
- 2021: Cleveland Martial Arts Karate Hall of Fame
- 2015: USA Karate Federation Hall of Fame
- 1988: USA vs. Canada World's Greatest Martial Arts Team Champion
- 1984: Island Wide Karate Grand Champion (Okinawa, Japan)
- 1983: Okinawa Karate Referee's Association Fighter of the Year (Okinawa, Japan)
- 1982: AAU National Champion
- 1982: United States World Karate Team Member
- 1981: United States Pan-American Karate Team Member
- 1981: United States Pan-American Karate Games (Gold Medal)
- 1980: AAU National Team Champion
- 1978: Most Valuable Competitor
- 1978: United States Karate Association Grand National Champion
- 1977: Penn State Champion
- 1976: Penn State Champion
- 1976: Ohio State Champion

Hiram
TEELER

"

Martial Arts are everyday life for me. It has made me a better person. I have made the best of friends in Martial Arts.

WHY THE Martial Arts?

It started in 1968. My mom, an insurance lady, could not afford daycare for me and my four brothers, so she made a deal with a Karate school next door to her office. The instructor Chuck Loven would teach us boys Karate and be our babysitter, and my mom would take care of all his insurance needs. My dad was a boxer and started teaching us boys at an early age how to box.

TRAINING INFORMATION

- Martial Arts Styles & Rank: 5th Degree Master Black Belt-Tae-Kwon-Do, 5th Degree Master Black Belt-American Karate, 5th Degree Master Black Belt-Shizen Na Karate

- Instructors/Influencers: GM Chuck Loven, GM Pat Burleson, GM Richard Morris, GM Curt Brannan, GM Thaine McVean, Terri Norman, Donnie Norman, and many others

- Birthplace/Growing Up: Fort Worth, TX

- Yrs. In the Martial Arts: 55 years

- Yrs. Instructing: 27 years

- School owner & Instructor at Hiram Teeler American Karate, Life-long student

PROFESSIONAL ORGANIZATIONS

- National Black Belt Club

- National Association of Professional Martial Artists

- World Martial Arts Ranking Association

- American Karate Black Belt Association

- NRA

- COP Citizens on Patrol

How MARTIAL ARTS CHANGED *My Life!*

Martial Arts are everyday life for me. It has made me a better person. It has helped me in my jobs and school. I have made the best of friends in Martial Arts. It has helped me raise my son. He started Karate at four years old and is now a 31-year-old 3rd Dan. We just celebrated our first grandchild. I had her punching and kicking on a BOB at two months. The first thing my son said when she (Olive) was born was that I had to teach her Karate. Like that was an option, haha. I have had the privilege of owning one of the largest Martial Arts Schools in Fort Worth American Academy of Arts (AAMA). I sold it to one of my instructors and started Hiram Teeler American Karate. I have been blessed to have the instructors that I do.

PERSONAL ACHIEVEMENTS

- I have been happily married for 41 years

MAJOR ACHIEVEMENTS

- Being nominated for Who's Who in the Martial Arts Biography Book & Award

Become an
AMAA MEMBER!

Earl
TULLIS

"

Martial Arts gave me a path to help me reach the goals I wanted to accomplish throughout my life.

WHY THE *Martial Arts?*

Grandmaster Tullis was introduced to the Martial Arts in 1970 by the U. S. Army. Like all soldiers back in the day were told, we are going to teach you hand-to-hand combat, but do not use this downtown because it will get your butt kicked. So as a young teenager, I said, "Why are you teaching us something that does not work?" "Private, shut up, and just do what you are told. After eight years in the Army and trying many different Martial Arts schools, I came here to Baytown and found an old Karate Master in town who was old school (Matt Long). All we did was fight, Kata, and physical exercise. After three years of this, Matt died. I had nowhere to train. After a few years of looking for another school to train at, I heard of this man in Dickinson, Texas. His name was Al Garza. I visited his school, and Al Garza Primer Martials has been my home for 35 years. Thanks to Grandmaster Al Garza, I met and trained with many great martial arts. But four of them taught

TRAINING INFORMATION

- Martial Arts Styles & Rank: 7th Degree Black Belt-Modern Arnis, 5th Degree Black Belt-Small Circle Jujitsu, 5th Degree Black Belt-Combat Jujitsu
- Instructors/Influencers: Grand Master Garza
- Birthplace/Growing Up: Dickinson, TX / Baytown, TX
- Yrs. In the Martial Arts: 53 years
- Yrs. Instructing: 48 years
- Instructor and a promotor

PROFESSIONAL ORGANIZATIONS

- Universal Martial Arts Hall of Fame
- Remy Presas (IMAF) International Modern Arnis Federation
- Professor Jay's Small Circle Jujitsu

and showed me the true martial way, and they are GM Remy Presas (Modern Arnis), GM Willy Jay (Small Circle Jujitsu), GM Ron Van Browning (Self Defiance), and GM Al Garza, my instructor now for 35 years.

How MARTIAL ARTS CHANGED My Life!

Being introduced to Martial Arts was one of the best things ever happening to GM Tullis or anyone else. Through the training and discipline of Martial Arts, he has always tried his best to be kind and friendly to everyone he meets. To show kindness and help to anyone who may require his help or need some guidance. To be supportive of everyone and encourage others to do the same. He does his best to help the younger generation with their lives and encourage them to strive to be a better person, to reach out in life and embrace it with zest to reach their goals. In life, if you can envision it, you can reach it if you believe in yourself. And to teach them some life skills in Martial Arts to work on themselves to go through the belt system to prepare their minds, body, and soul and achieve their goals as they go through the ranks. Martial Arts gave him a path to help him reach the goals he wanted to accomplish throughout his life. He has met many interesting people throughout his life. Martial Arts has been the key. He has been around the world several times in the military and has seen and done things with many people in his travels. He always strives to be a better person every day.

PERSONAL ACHIEVEMENTS

- Studying martial arts has given GM Tullis confidence and the ability to focus on oneself and others.

- To spread the knowledge that he has received throughout his career from other great people in the martial arts.

- Help them give back to our kids, adults, and future generations. To help them prepare for their lives and help prepare others in their pursuit of life. He always says martial arts are good for the Mind, Body, and Soul. To show them the way through martial arts knowledge and help keep them off the streets and out of trouble. To give them guidance and positive influence in their pursuit of happiness, keep the mind and body in shape, and give off a positive attitude.

- To always be helpful to others in the martial arts and the community.

- He still teaches four weekly classes and travels across the United States, France, England, and Ecuador to give seminars.

MAJOR ACHIEVEMENTS

- Induction into "The Universal Martial Arts Hall of Fame" 2013

- CEO of the Modern Arnis Federation 2020

- Grandmaster Level in Modern Arnis 2021

- To be featured in the Book Changing Lives with Grandmaster Cynthia Rothrock

Jason VELEZ

> **"** Martial arts enabled me to become physically fit, mentally strong, and spiritually balanced.

WHY THE *Martial Arts?*

GM Jason Velez got involved with martial arts from watching Bruce Lee on the Green Hornet TV series in 1966 and from his uncles, who were in the military and knew martial arts. This led him to seek out martial arts training, boxing, and wrestling, and eventually join the military to study martial arts worldwide.

GM Velez founded the 9 Dragons Martial Arts Academy in Las Vegas, NV, 2005 - present. GM Velez is considered one of the leaders in Close Quarters Combat and offers his unique military, law enforcement, and extensive martial arts expertise to all seeking this knowledge.

A world-renowned martial arts master, GM Velez trained in Asia, Europe, and South America and across the USA under many grandmasters & founders of the martial arts while serving as a Vietnam-era US Raider-Recon Marine and later in the Middle East as a US Army XVIII Airborne Corps/10th Mountain Infantry commando. Specializing in authentic

TRAINING INFORMATION

- Martial Arts Styles & Rank: Sokeship 10th Dan-Ultimate Kenpo System, 9th Dahn-DoJu Nim/ Fdr. SF Hapkido & Sulsa-Do, Master Instructor-Universal Jeet Kune Do, Board Member, Inst. of Combat Technology Ldrs. Pukulan Pencak Silat Tempur, 8th Dan-Combat Kenpo Jujitsu, Shihan 5th Dan-Okinawa Te, Self-Defense-Expert Krav Maga, Si Gung (Master)-Tai Ji Quan

- Instructors/Influencers: Master Airr Phanthip, Meijin Bill Solano, Hanshi Jim Rivera, Si Gung John Lopez, JoSi James Robinson, GM Tiger Chin P. Kim, GM William Hayes, Kru Ralph Janus, GM Roberto Bonefont, My Father

- Birthplace/Growing Up: Dickinson, TX / Baytown, TX

- Yrs. In the Martial Arts: 62 years

- Yrs. Instructing: 57 years

- School owner & Instructor at 9 Dragons Martial Arts

PROFESSIONAL ORGANIZATIONS

- Universal Martial Arts Hall of Fame

- Remy Presas (IMAF) International Modern Arnis Federation

- Professor Jay's Small Circle Jujitsu

traditional battlefield martial arts and modern military combatives. GM Velez also holds master certifications in the holistic arts of Reiki, Tai Chi, and Qi Gong.

He's a professional soldier in USMC and the U.S. Army XVIII Airborne Corps. An award-winning "All Army" Trainer/Cadre, training elite units like the 10th Mountain Div. (Commandos). A Hand2Hand combatives and weapons expert with numerous military awards and qualifications.

He was honorably discharged after 20-plus years of service in 2003. These real-world police actions and combat service make Ret.US Army Combat Veteran SFC Jason Velez one of the world's most qualified martial artists/Close Quarters Combat instructors. Clients include Law Enforcement and Military, including Army Special Forces & Rangers, Navy SEALS, Marine FORCE RECON, civilian sector Security Officers, VIPs, Actors, and private citizens.

GM Velez is the founder of Special Forces Martial Arts, a fusion of the best of 9 Korean martial arts:

1. Teuk Gong Mu Sul (Special Forces Combatives)

2. Tae Kwon Do (Korean Karate & Olympic sport)

3. Kuk Sool Won (National martial arts of Korea)

4. Hap Ki Do (Comprehensive Self-defense MA)

5. Kyuk Too Ki (Korean-style Kickboxing)

6. Ship Pal Ki ("18 Skills" Shaolin Kung Fu)

7. Hwa Rang Do (Hwa Rang "Korean Samurai")

PROFESSIONAL ORGANIZATIONS

- Martial Arts Society International (MASI Founder)
- Special Forces Hapkido "Teuk Kong Mu Sul HKD" (MASI)
- The Akribis Group/Henly-Putnam University (Member) The Harvard of Combatives
- Institute of Combat Technology Leaders – Pukulan Pencak Silat Tempur
- US Army Museum (Founding Member)
- Life member – Raven Tactical
- Martial Arts Museum – Burbank, CA (Member)
- Universal Black Belt Society (UBBS) Life member
- Member - Black Kobra Striking Systems/Black Kobra MMA/Team Relentless
- L1FE Wellness Org. – Director of Martial Arts & Sciences programs
- Okinawan Society Karate Federation – Life member
- Owaza Ryu Ju Jitsu-Judo Institute – Soke Dai
- Mountain River Budo Kai – Life member
- International Kenpo Kaikan – Life member
- Cintron's Tang Soo Jitsu Combat Systems
- Jukido Kai Ryu Modern Vee Jitsu
- Universal Grappling Arts – UGA (Founder Jason Uga)
- Barela Martial Arts Academies (Fdr. Christopher Barela)
- Sr. VP - Survival Solutions Jeet Kune Do Association
- Bushido Martial Arts Foundation
- International Martial Arts Combat Union Association
- USJJF - United States Jiu Jitsu Federation (Life Member)
- USMAF - United States Martial Arts Federation (Life member)
- USMC-MAA - US Marine Corps Martial Arts Association
- AKMAA (All Korean Martial Arts Assoc.) NV Rep
- Int'l Krav Maga Alliance - NV Rep
- U.S. Shorin Ryu Assoc. (Okinawan Karate)
- Running Fist Kung Fu Assoc. (Sifu rank in Running Fist)

8. Su Bahk Do (Original Korean MA a.k.a. tangsoodo)

9. Sulsa Do (Korean Ninjitsu system)

* Plus Japanese, Chinese, Indonesian, Filipino martial arts, Western Boxing, Wrestling, Israeli Krav Maga, MMA, and Bruce Lee's Jeet Kune Do Concepts! GM Velez has learned the best of everything throughout his lifelong studies, taught by a traditional Korean martial arts foundation.

Note: 9th Degree blackbelt is the highest achievable rank in Korean martial arts, equivalent to a 10th Degree Red Belt in other styles like karate, jujitsu, kung fu, etc.

Jason Marcos Velez
Stunt Actor *CBT VET Martial Arts Master
JasonMarcosVelez@gmail.com   702-292-8203

PROFESSIONAL ORGANIZATIONS

- World Warrior Camp Alumni
- World Warrior Alliance (Founding member)
- World Combat Muay Thai Alliance
- Radical Thai Boxing Society
- Rebellion Team Int'l
- Radical Martial Arts Holding Group
- Military Police & Security Systems World Society
- Combat Hawaiian Martial Arts Society
- Int'l Combat Martial Arts Union
- American Kenpo Karate Academies
- World Gung Fu Pai Society
- Kobushinkan Bujutsu Kai
- Kobushin Kan Karate Jutsu Kai
- Combat Korean Martial Arts Society
- Shinja Buke University
- Vale Academy of Martial Arts
- Shorin Ryu Kempo Kai
- Wu Dang Nei Jia Quan Do Assoc.
- Green Dragon Society
- Tang Soo Do Korean Karate Assoc.
- Int'l Karate Do Shobukai
- Member - International MMA Association

PERSONAL ACHIEVEMENTS

- GM Velez is an ambassador to many martial arts organizations. Inducted into the Action Martial Arts Magazine Hall of Honors Platinum Award (2011) and Goodwill Ambassador Award 2014 & 2015. (Academy Awards of martial arts)
- Award of Excellence in Krav Maga-Salon De Gala (Host GM Sergio Barrriga/Cynthia Rothrock) Tampa, FL (2015)
- Awarded Soke Dai of Owaza Ryu Ju Jitsu-Judo under the founder Soke Hanshi Jim Rivera, 10th Dan. (2019)
- GM Velez is the National Training Instr. for the All Korean Martial Arts Assoc. (AKMAA) under GM Sam Albright

How MARTIAL ARTS CHANGED My Life!

Martial arts have given GM Velez the tools, knowledge, and skill sets to become a modern-day warrior scholar and the best version of himself: self-discipline, self-confidence, self-defense, increased flexibility & energy. Martial arts enabled him to become physically fit, mentally strong, and spiritually balanced. It allowed him to help people from all walks of life reach their full potential and enjoy life to the fullest. In the military, it gave him an edge over his peers physically and mentally, like a secret weapon. He's constantly told that he doesn't look his age. He gives all the credit to living life as a martial artist by learning not only the physical side of the arts but also the internal holistic side of the arts.

How has Grandmaster CYNTHIA ROTHROCK Influenced me?

As a lifelong fan of martial arts/action movies, GM Velez became a fan and friend of GM Cynthia Rothrock. GM Rothrock paved the way for many Westerners to enter the Asian martial arts film industry. GM Cynthia Rothrock leads by example and continues to raise the bar as a living legend, global ambassador of martial arts, movie star, and incredible human being. She truly is the Queen of Martial Arts!

GM Cynthia Rothrock has influenced GM Velez to pursue his bucket list wish of becoming an Action Actor in the film industry. In 2021, he,

MAJOR ACHIEVEMENTS

- GM Velez is the Martial Arts Program Director for 1 Life Wellness (L1FE) Organization under Navy Veteran/Motown recording artist B. Taylor, the Armed Forces Global Ambassador of Entertainment. L1FE offers holistic alternative therapies to those dealing with PTSD and is sanctioned by the U.S. Pentagon, Wash., DC.

- GM Velez is on the advisory board of the Henley-Putnam University School of Strategic Security (center for counter-terrorism and intelligence studies) and the Akribis Group under Dr. Nirmalya Bhowmick, Ph.D.

- Becoming a stunt actor & stunt coordinator in several films, including Bridge of the Doomed, Arena Wars, Bermuda Island, Desert Fiends, Transmorphers, The Wrecker, and Boneyard, to name a few. As well as starting the Vegas Empire Stunts Academy!

- Desert Storm Gulf War Veteran - Liberation of Kuwait with the 10th Mountain Div Light Infantry Commandos (1990-91)

CYNTHIA ROTHROCK (CONTINUED)

along with GM Airr Phanthip and SiFu Xueli Zhang, opened the Vegas Empire Stunts Academy, training actors and the public in movie stunts and martial arts. GM Velez is an actor, stuntman, stunt coordinator, fight choreographer, writer, director, and producer in the film industry. They have joined forces with The Film Post (A full-service production company) under the guidance of Producer, Director, Writer, and Actor Asif Akbar in Las Vegas, NV.

Charles
VITULLO

"

I am glad to have found that martial arts has had an amazing impact on both me and my family.

WHY THE *Martial Arts?*

I was going to accept my nomination a couple of years back. Master Joe Corley called me and walked me through and explained what I needed to do, and after we talked, I realized how I could not go through with this at the time as I still had not come to terms with who I am or even sure where I wanted to go. It still seems sad to be that old in life without direction, yet here I was.

I had a chance years ago, in 1983, to take up boxing and squandered an opportunity with instructors whom I didn't appreciate as I was not an honorable student and much too young mentally to commit to the challenge - during a three year off and on yet not a fully realized dream as I was far too immature to appreciate the opportunity laid out before me then.

Fast forward through years of searching, partying, and finally bottoming out, as I tried to bury myself in many different ways, I met my then-future wife, Linda, who would no longer

TRAINING INFORMATION

- Belt Ranks & Martial Arts Styles: Boxing, Hapkido, 3rd Dan-Taekwondo
- Instructors/Influencers: KJN Dan Allebach, Master Joseph Mertz
- Birthplace/Growing Up: Egg Harbor Township, NJ
- Yrs. In the Martial Arts: 12 years
- Yrs. Instructing: 4 years
- Instructor

PROFESSIONAL ORGANIZATIONS

- Cherry Hill Martial Arts and Fitness

let me drown or wallow in self-pity. She gave me her background, which was as rocky as mine, yet it amazed me that she kept going forward. I asked her where she found that resolve. And through her testimony, I would finally find peace in turning my life over to Jesus Christ. With that moment of clarity, I am thankful because not only did I grow and come back to life, but I also began a family, and as I raised my daughter, Jessica, I have finally grown into a man I could live with.

Jessie became my world. When she asked me to join the martial arts, I agreed, and through a proud moment of her doing her first tournament, I told her she could have anything she wanted. Her request was for me to do the martial arts with her. We found Cherry Hill Martial Arts and met Grandmaster Dan Allebach, and my journey was underway. The challenge to do martial arts at 41 was an incredible experience. I was not conditioned and undoubtedly not ready mentally for the change that was about to happen. My daughter means the world to me, so I tried to absorb as much as I could as I found this was not only a great way to get in shape yet also a way to show her through example what it means to start something and see it through.

I see the power of building someone up from within through the arts. I have seen kids and some adults, as well as myself, come out of the shadows of self-doubt and fear of trying something new and pushing their boundaries to a place they never knew they could reach. Life in the arts is the embodiment of the world around us, for it helps you to learn to tread and try the unknown, be willing to fail, and yet, at the same

PERSONAL ACHIEVEMENTS

- 2018 Goodwill Ambassador by Action Martial Arts Magazine's Hall of Honors Esteemed Martial Artist
- 2019 by Action Martial Arts Magazine's Hall of Honors Esteemed Martial Artist 2020 by Action Martial Arts Magazine's Hall of Honors Male Black Belt of the Year
- 2019 USA Martial Arts Hall of Heroes Universal Song Do Kwan 1st Dan Certification Universal Song Do Kwan 2nd Dan Certification

MAJOR ACHIEVEMENTS

- Became an instructor at Cherry Hill Martial Arts - to me, this moment and earning my black belt are my personal Superbowl victories in life outside of faith and my family

WHY MARTIAL ARTS (CONTINUED)

time, dust yourself off and get to your goal. It is okay to fail, just not okay to quit. It sounds like rhetoric, but it is a lesson everyone needs to learn to succeed at whatever they set out to do in life. To me, this is what the martial arts is all about.

Since earning my black belt and continuing my martial arts journey, I have taken on the instructor role. Believing that I should not only set a good example as someone at the front of the room, a man of Christ and a father - I had to come to terms with myself as a person. The Lord blessed me with many people who kept and still help keep me from sliding backward and continue pushing me forward. Combined with teaching younger people to be true to themselves and those around them, I have finally come to do the same. Peace and God bless.

How MARTIAL ARTS CHANGED My Life!

I am glad to have found that martial arts has had an amazing impact on both me and my family. The martial arts are more than just techniques and patterns. It is a great way to get in shape while providing a way to learn self-defense. It has helped me calm down and released me from a bad day at work.

I love how it has helped bring my family together and brought us a fair amount of fun competition. As we have grown in the martial arts, I have found I get a lot more out of passing it on to new students and helping others improve their techniques. The best part of martial arts is that you never stop learning like the drums and the guitar I have been playing all these years.

How has Grandmaster CYNTHIA ROTHROCK Influenced me?

Grandmaster Cynthia Rothrock has impacted my life in a lot of different ways. I have had the pleasure of knowing her through our school and our relationship with her through the Hall of Honors that bears her name over the years. She has inspired my family with both words of guidance and encouragement and positive inspiration for my daughter, who thinks she rocks and never misses a chance when she's in town to attend her seminars. With that all being said, I feel it is an honor to be a part of the book that reflects her influence in the martial arts.

Lonnie
WALKER

> **"**
> For me, it is not about rank; it is the knowledge gained.

WHY THE *Martial Arts?*

The main reason I started the study of Martial Arts was to help with my anger and depression issues. When I got out of the Army and Vietnam, I was suffering from PTSD and didn't know it. My weight was out of control, and I was angry. I began studying Tae Kwon Do to get exercise. I had prayed for a way to get my life in control. God answered my prayers with the Martial Arts. Martial Arts became a way of life for me.

TRAINING INFORMATION

- Belt Ranks & Martial Arts Styles: 9th Degree Black Belt Tae Kwon Do, Tang Soo Do American Kenpo, Tai Chi
- Instructors/Influencers: Master Jun S Kim (RIP), Master Benny Scott (RIP), Master Steve Amaro, Master Steve Cooper, Sifu Tyson Kern
- Birthplace/Growing Up: Las Vegas, NV
- Yrs. In the Martial Arts: 51 years
- Yrs. Instructing: 45 years
- Instructor

PROFESSIONAL ORGANIZATIONS

- AMAA
- DAV
- VIETNAM VETERANS OF AMERICA
- THE ORDER OF THE PURPLE HEART

How MARTIAL ARTS CHANGED My Life!

Martial Arts changed my life for the better. I went from bitter and angry to healthy and wise. Like I said before the Martial Arts is a way of life, not a fad. For me, it is not about rank; it is the knowledge gained. Martial Arts is much like life, a long journey with lots to learn along the way.

How has Grandmaster CYNTHIA ROTHROCK Influenced me?

I enjoyed watching GM Cynthia Rothrock competing in Tournament Days. I also enjoy watching the many movies she has starred in. She is a great Ambassador for Martial Arts.

PERSONAL ACHIEVEMENTS

- I have been competing in Martial Arts tournaments since 1974. I have competed in major tournaments and minor tournaments. I never saw a match I wouldn't go to. I have competed in the NASKA, NBL, AKO, TPA, USKA, and IMAC and a lot other I have forgotten. I haven't always won first place, but I know I have the most 2nd and 3rd places in the USA.

MAJOR ACHIEVEMENTS

- The biggest and most significant thing I have ever done was accepting Jesus Christ as my Lord and Savior.

- I was inducted in the Who's Really Who Legends and Pioneers, the Master's Hall of Fame, and the Rocky DiRico's International Black Belt Hall of Fame.

Chris WETHERINGTON

"

Martial arts has impacted me so humbly that I've decided to serve others with the highest level of integrity.

WHY THE *Martial Arts?*

I got started in martial arts to help others to break the cycle of abuse and suffering. I became a victim's advocate to help and serve others, knowing one can grow up without access to support and, worst of all, hope. Through numerous top martial arts mentors guiding me through my martial arts journey, I have taken the approach to serve the martial arts community and help others with all that I do. I believe life is precious, and everyone needs special love and attention. It's my honor to be a champion for hope and bless all with the best quality of life I can provide through martial arts.

TRAINING INFORMATION

- Martial Arts Styles & Rank: Tang Soo Do Karate -2nd Degree Black Belt
- Instructors/Influencers: Louis D, Casamassa, Chris Casamassa, Professor John Terry, Mentor: Grandmaster Michael Hornsby
- Birthplace/Growing Up: Paducah, KY / Carlinville, IL
- Yrs. In the Martial Arts: 25 years
- Yrs. Instructing: 12 years
- School owner, Manager & Instructor at Balanced Warrior MMA & Karate, LLC.

PROFESSIONAL ORGANIZATIONS

- AKKF-American Karate Kung-Fu Federation,
- AKA-American Karate Association
- USAWKF-United States Wushu Kung-fu Federation

How MARTIAL ARTS CHANGED My Life!

I, Sensei Chris Wetherington, President and Chief Instructor of Balanced Warrior MMA & Karate LLC, have taken the approach to be the champion for Victim's Advocacy and Anti-bullying. Martial arts has impacted me so humbly that I've decided to serve others with the highest level of integrity.

How has Grandmaster CYNTHIA ROTHROCK Influenced me?

Grandmaster Cynthia Rothrock has inspired me to be a champion for integrity in the martial arts.

PERSONAL ACHIEVEMENTS

- Advocate for victims of Anti-bullying

MAJOR ACHIEVEMENTS

- 2018 United States Martial Arts Hall of Fame-Instructor of the Year
- 2019 United States Martial Arts Hall of Fame-Anti-bullying Advocate Award
- 2021 Universal Martial Arts Hall of Fame-Outstanding Achievement Award
- 2022 USA Martial Arts Hall Of Fame-Unsung Hero Award
- 2022 International Martial Arts Hall of Fame/Martial Arts Authority of India-Instructor of the Year Award
- 2023 International Martial Arts Hall of Fame/Martial Arts Authority of India-Black Belt of the Year Award
- 2023 Universal Martial Arts Hall of Fame-Humanitarian of the Year Award
- 2023 USA Martial Arts Hall of Fame–Black Belt of the Year Award
- 2023 Soke Little John Davis Black Belt Hall of Fame-True Mastery of the Martial Arts Award
- 2024 International Martial Arts Hall of Fame-Netherlands, TBD AWARD
- 2024 Action Magazine Martial Arts Hall of Award Fame–Elite Modern Warrior Award

Become an AMAA MEMBER!

Dr. John
WILLIAMS

"

The impact that studying the art has had upon my life is that it has made me learn more about myself and my abilities...

WHY THE *Martial Arts?*

I got started in the martial arts because my brother, GM Jesse Mack Williams, was my hero growing up; he was a champion kickboxer. I soon found myself using him as a shield, and never knowing how to defend myself, he would train us as children every chance that he got. I must say that until I started taking martial arts, I never fought back. One day, I got tired of getting beaten down and took classes at the Roy Walker Gym in Clovis, New Mexico, where my instructor was Master Westly Scott. After a few fights under my belt and winning being easier and easier, I defended myself and those around me. I remember I only had one fight in high school, and it ended with me kicking a boy through a window, then dragging him out, and mounting him for the finish before the teachers pulled me off of him. I must say that martial arts have taught me much-needed discipline. I learned to use it as a very last resort!

TRAINING INFORMATION

- Belt Ranks & Martial Arts Styles: Tae Kwon Do- 4th Degree Black Belt in both American and Korean Style, Modified System of Shoto-Kan- 5th Degree Black Belt, Combative Aikido- Brown Belt

- Instructors/Influencers: Mrs. Brandi Johnson, Mr. Edward Gunderson

- Birthplace/Growing Up: Blytheville, AR

- Yrs. In the Martial Arts: 39 years

- Yrs. Instructing: 9 years

- School owner, Manager & Instructor at Williams Elite Martial Arts School, Tiger Rock Martial Arts Colorado, MMASC (Midwest Martial Arts Southern Conference) Grand Master Anthony's Martial Arts School, Fighting Tiger Karate School, Williams Elite Martial Arts School

How MARTIAL ARTS CHANGED My Life!

I've had the honor of meeting some of the most incredible people over my relatively short career as a martial artist. I have traveled and competed with some of the best of the best. The impact that studying the art has had upon my life is that it has made me learn more about myself, my abilities, and it has taught me to always push beyond what you think is your stopping point. To take a child who has never had the privilege to step into a dojo, then to have them progress from white belt to black belt, then to fight for a championship is what I, as a leader, look forward to each time I train a new student.

The greatest influence on my life has been having parents believe in me and what I'm doing, inspiring them to express that they want their children to be like me... Priceless!

PROFESSIONAL ORGANIZATIONS

- AMAA Lifetime Member
- Ambassador MMASC (Midwest Martial Arts Southern Conference)
- US Martial Arts Fame Of Fame Inductee 2022
- USA Martial Art Hall Of Fame Inductee 2022
- Universal Hall Of Fame Inductee 2022
- Kappa Alpha Psi. Fraternity
- Extraordinary People Award- Awards Director
- Today's International World Pageants- Manbassador/ Board Member
- Today's International Men's Mr. International
- Come On In, Inc. CEO/FOUNDER
- C.O.IN Community Academy Founder/ President

PERSONAL ACHIEVEMENTS

- Lifetime Achievement Presidential Award 2019 and 2021
- Presidential Volunteer Award (Gold) 2018 and 2021
- MMASC 1st Place Super Senior Division Black Belt Forms
- MMASC 1st Place Light Heavyweight Sparring
- MMASC 2nd Place Senior Black Belt Sparring
- MMASC Co- King of The Midwest 2020
- MMASC Triple Crown Winner 2017, 2018, 2020
- MMASC Men's Black Belt Competitor of the year 2017,2019, 2020
- Team Council & Coach Combative Martial Arts Team USA 2019
- MMASC National Hall Of Fame 2020
- Ozzie Crew Hall Of Fame 2019
- Iron Fist 424 Black Belt Fighting Club 2016
- Founder Of Come On In, Inc.
- Founder Of C.O.I.N Community Acdy.
- Founder Williams Elite Martial Arts School
- Director Of Presidential Volunteer Awards
- Executive Director Of Who's Who Black Globe Awards

How has Grandmaster CYNTHIA ROTHROCK Influenced me?

Grandmaster Cynthia Rothrock is an influential person not only to women but to men as well. During the years, she's exemplified champion qualities in movies and inside and outside martial arts. She sets an example for many to follow in a very positive way. For that, we say thank you.

MAJOR ACHIEVEMENTS

- MMASC National Hall Of Fame 2020
- Ozzie Crew Hall Of Fame 2019
- Iron Fist 424 Black Belt Fighting Club 2016
- Lifetime Achievement Presidential Award 2019 and 2021
- Presidential Volunteer Award (Gold) 2018 and 2021
- MMASC Triple Crown Winner 2017, 2018, 2020
- MMASC Men's Black Belt Competitor of the year 2017, 2019, 2020
- 23x Grand Champion
- 27x Grand Champion Runner- Up
- Tiger Rock Martial Arts 7xNational Champion
- Tiger Rock Martial Arts 3x World Champion Board Breaking Champion
- Tiger Rock Martial Arts 7x District Champion

Become an AMAA MEMBER!

Kevin
WILLIAMS

"

One of the most significant impacts that studying martial arts has had on my life is the development of discipline.

WHY THE Martial Arts?

As a child, my fascination with martial artists defending themselves and their loved ones in movies sparked my interest in martial arts. However, it was the influence of my family members that truly inspired me to pursue this passion. Each of them trained in different styles, with my dad in Karate, my stepdad in Taekwondo, and my eldest brother in Kung Fu. Little did I know that embarking on this journey would have such a profound impact on my life. Destiny seemed to guide me toward martial arts, and I could never have anticipated the transformative power it would hold.

TRAINING INFORMATION

- Belt Ranks & Martial Arts Styles: Taekwondo-5th Dan, Kung Fu-8th Degree Brown Belt, Tai Chi, Judo, Kickboxing
- Instructors/Influencers: Master Hwang Lee, Master Bobby Clayton, Master Rafael Medina, Master Michael Bennett
- Yrs. In the Martial Arts: 41 years
- Yrs. Instructing: 20 years (coaching)
- School Owner & Instructor at Uplift Taekwondo & Fitness Academy

PROFESSIONAL ORGANIZATIONS

- US Army
- Omega Psi Phi Fraternity, Inc.

PERSONAL ACHIEVEMENTS

- I am incredibly proud of my personal achievement as a member of the All-Army Tae Kwon Do Team and the All-Armed Forces Tae Kwon Do Team. Being part of these elite teams required significant dedication, hard work, and perseverance. Through this experience, I had the opportunity to compete at the highest level of military sports and represent my country in

How MARTIAL ARTS CHANGED My Life!

One of the most significant impacts that studying martial arts has had on my life is the development of discipline. Martial arts require consistent practice and dedication to improving oneself. This discipline has translated into other areas of my life, such as my career and personal relationships. I can better prioritize my time and focus on the things that are important to me.

Studying martial arts has also taught me the value of perseverance. In martial arts, progress is made through hard work and dedication over time. This lesson has helped me to stay motivated and persistent in achieving my goals, even when faced with challenges or setbacks.

In addition to these personal benefits, studying martial arts has also connected me with a community of like-minded individuals who share similar values and goals. This sense of camaraderie and support has been invaluable to me in both my personal and professional life.

Overall, studying martial arts has had a profound impact on my life. It has taught me important values such as discipline, perseverance, and community, which have helped me to become a better leader, professional, and coach. I am grateful for the lessons and experiences that martial arts have provided me, and I look forward to continuing to learn and grow through my practice.

PERSONAL ACHIEVEMENTS (CONTINUED)

international competitions. Additionally, I was selected to be a member of the Army's World Class Athletes Program, allowing me to train full-time and focus on improving my Tae Kwon Do athlete skills. This dedication paid off as I was also chosen to participate in the Tae Kwon Do Resident Program at the Olympic Training Center, which provided me with world-class training facilities, expert coaching, and to attend several Olympic trials. These experiences have helped me grow as an athlete and a person, and I am grateful for the opportunities I have had to represent my country and pursue my passion for Tae Kwon Do.

MAJOR ACHIEVEMENTS

- My major achievements in my life are truly unreal to me, even to this day. First and foremost, becoming a father of 5 wonderful children is an incredible accomplishment and one I am truly proud of. Not only that, but it's an amazing feeling to be trusted by others to be a father figure and mentor to other kids and athletes, which is a testament to my motto, "Blood Bonds, Love Unites Families." Additionally, serving 24 years in the military, retiring after such a long and distinguished career, and following in the steps of my family

How has Grandmaster CYNTHIA ROTHROCK Influenced me?

Grandmaster Cynthia Rothrock has influenced my life in so many ways. I would like to acknowledge and appreciate her contributions to the martial arts world and her role in inspiring others of all ages and genders to pursue their passions. Rothrock's dedication to her craft and ability to break barriers as a female martial artist has undoubtedly paved the way for many others to follow in her footsteps. Her commitment to teaching and sharing her knowledge with others is also commendable and serves as a reminder of the importance of mentorship and passing on skills and knowledge to the next generation.

Kevin
WILSON

"

I have felt incredibly fortunate to have martial arts as a medium of self-development, both physically and mentally...

WHY THE *Martial Arts?*

As a young boy, I was always fascinated with martial arts. While formal training never crossed my path as a child, at the age of 19, I was able to locate a formal training curriculum. I wanted to make up for lost time, so I devoted much of my time to studying and training.

My initial training was an introduction to Okinawan Shorinryu karate. As I advanced, I later joined Shoshin Nagamine's (the founder and Grandmaster) organization W.M.K.A. World Mastsubayashi Karate-Do Association. My introduction into a larger world increased my skills in karate. Also, it opened doors to judo and jiu-jitsu, and eventual training with Dillman Karate International, which introduced pressure points, small circle jiu-jitsu, and modern arnis. I have also trained for many years in tai-chi.

TRAINING INFORMATION

- Belt Ranks & Martial Arts Styles: Okinawan Shorinryu-Dillman Karate International-7th Degree, Judo - 3rd Kyu, Jiu Jitsu, Arnis, Tai Chi

- Instructors/Influencers: Ruben West, George Dillman, Takayoshi Nagamine, Katsumasa Nohara, Ron Vowell, John Vansickel, Ronnie Moore

- Birthplace/Growing Up: Topeka, KS

- Yrs. In the Martial Arts: 30 years

- Yrs. Instructing: 25 years

- School Owner & Instructor at Professional Martial Arts

PROFESSIONAL ORGANIZATIONS

- Dillman Karate International

While my martial arts have served me well physically and mentally, the larger lessons have sustained my training and teaching over many years. I have applied these lessons through my discipline to many aspects of my life, including starting, maintaining, and selling successful companies.

PERSONAL ACHIEVEMENTS

- Co-founder/Owner/Instructor of Professional Martial Arts, est. 1997
- 7th Degree Black Belt Okinawan Karate/ Dillman Karate International
- 1st Degree Black Belt, World Matsubayashi Karate Do Association
- Author - "Woman Talk! The Encrypted Language Women Never Wanted Men to Know"
- Co-Author - "Change One Thing: Take Your First Steps Towards Massive Success"
- Co-Author - "Difficulty Demon"
- Founder - "Difficulty Demon YOUniversity - What They Forgot To Teach YOU in School"
- Self-Made Millionaire
- Public Speaker
- Co-founder/Owner - Professional Medical Associates, Inc.
- Co-founder/Member - Elite School of Surgical First Assisting, LLC
- Co-founder/Member - ESSFA Acquisitions Company, LLC
- Co-founder/Member - Your Extra Hands Surgical Services, LLC

MAJOR ACHIEVEMENTS

- Bachelor of Business Administration - Washburn University, Topeka, KS
- U.S. Martial Arts Hall of Fame Inductee 2006 - Instructor of the Year
- U.S. Martial Arts Hall of Fame Inductee 2014 - Shorinryu Master of the Year
- Multiple placements in local and national martial arts tournaments
- Three silver medals State Games of America 2015
- Stunt training certification with Michael Depasquale Jr. and Action Film Academy
- Tactics training with Fred Mastison and Force Options international
- I Change Nations Award 2017
- World's Greatest Martial Artist recognition 2022
- Bill Wallace "Living Legacy Award" recipient 2022

How MARTIAL ARTS CHANGED My Life!

To say that martial arts have impacted my life is a huge understatement. I have felt incredibly fortunate to have martial arts as a medium of self-development, both physically and mentally, for many years. In turn, it is an honor and a privilege to absorb knowledge from teachers and pass it down to students. I am myself a forever student.

Self-defense and self-awareness have become a way of life since training in martial arts. On the mat and in the dojo is a perfect place to hone one's skills, but the overlap of application in day-to-day life is the training goal. Public awareness, driving, parenting, and teaching are where the true lessons of martial arts training can have the greatest impact.

Being a firm believer in growth and development, martial arts continues not to disappoint. I believe it was in Shoshin Nagamine's book "The Essence of Okinawan Karate-Do," where he discusses the aspects of character and training in the dojo and challenges our dojo in the world. This, to me, seems to be the ultimate goal.

Become an
AMAA MEMBER!

Brendan
WILSON

"

Martial arts have helped me focus on becoming a better leader, filmmaker, novelist, and diplomat.

WHY THE *Martial Arts?*

In 1974, I got cut from the high school varsity baseball team. That day I went to Roberts Karate in Alexandria, Virginia, and began training in Tae Kwon Do. Later, while at university, I trained at Tong's Studio of Tae Kwon Do in Harrisonburg, Virginia, where I received my first Dan in 1980. Upon graduation, I entered the Army as a 2nd Lieutenant and qualified as a US Army Ranger, during which I also trained in combative military techniques. While in the Army, I continued my training, including a year in the Republic of Korea. I was the coach and team captain for two military martial arts teams: one from the 101st Airborne Division and one from XVIII Airborne Corps. Additionally, while overseas, I trained the NATO commander's close protection team in weapons-disarming techniques. Finally, while serving in Iraq as a diplomat, I trained personnel at one of the Allied embassies.

TRAINING INFORMATION

- Belt Ranks & Martial Arts Styles: Taekwondo-8th Dan
- Instructors/Influencers: Stan Alexander, Gary Harvey, GM Sugman Park, GM Jackie Kwon, Larry Wilk, GM George Petrotta, GM Song
- Birthplace/Growing Up: Hampton, VA / Miliary family (moved many times)
- Yrs. In the Martial Arts: 49 years
- Yrs. Instructing: 42 years
- School owner, Manager & Instructor at Aristos Martial Arts, LLC.

PROFESSIONAL ORGANIZATIONS

- Superfoot System Affiliate
- International Sungjado Association
- Kukkiwon
- Jung Do Kwan Association
- International Chang Hon Taekwondo Federation

I won the Silver medal at the US Open held in Las Vegas in my age group in 2009. In 2010, I was selected to be an international judge for the US Open. I have competed in numerous tournaments over my career, and in 1996, I was the AAU Louisiana state champion for sparring, forms, and musical forms. In the mid-1990s, I was ranked in competition by the National Black Belt League and Sport Karate International Magazine. In 2022, I was inducted into the Bill Wallace AMAA Hall of Honors, received the Changing Lives award and the international Impact Award. **Contribution:** I am the founder of the martial arts style of Aristos, a style based upon Korean hard-style techniques and the philosophy of classical Greece. I have trained students from 13 countries.

How MARTIAL ARTS CHANGED My Life!

Martial arts have helped me focus on becoming a better leader, filmmaker, novelist, and diplomat.

Studying martial arts has been a wonderful journey for me, and that journey continues. The feeling I have in the most significant measure is gratitude. I am grateful for the discipline that helped me through some of the toughest military training in the world. Six years of Tae Kwon Do training helped me get through the US Army Ranger School. My martial arts instructor in college would say during a grueling session when students dropped out from exhaustion that "if you can't go on, make sure it is your body that has failed you, not your spirit."

PERSONAL ACHIEVEMENTS

- Martial Arts Awards: Inducted into the Hall of Honor, AMAA, 2022, Changing Lives Legacy Award, AMAA, 2022, International Impact Award, AMAA, 2022, Silver Medal, US Open, United States of America Taekwondo (USAT), Las Vegas, NV, 2009, Gold Medal, AAU Louisiana State Championship, Forms, Sparring, Musical Forms, 1995, Ranked 4th, Dixie Region, National Blackbelt League, and Sport Karate International, 1993

- Certifications: International Referee, Pan American Taekwondo Union (PATU), Served as International Referee for the US Open competition in 2010, Las Vegas, NV

- Martial Arts Leadership: Team Coach and Captain for two military competition teams, taught NATO Commander's close protection team in weapons disarming techniques, founded the NATO Military Taekwondo Association, founded Aristos Martial Arts, LLC.

- Martial Arts Publications: The Achilles Battle Fleet, Literate Ape Publications, 2021; WTF Poomsae: Time for a Course Correction; Totally Tae Kwon Do, May 2010, Paradise Lost: Tae Kwon Do and the Art of Simplicity; Totally Tae Kwon Do; June 2009, Co-author

- State of the Art in Tae Kwon Do: ITF versus WTF, Totally Tae Kwon Do; May 2009

- The Principles of War and the Martial Arts, Inside Martial Arts, Summer 1995

- Tournament Blues, Martial Arts Masters, May 1995

- Perseverance: A Day at Ranger School, Inside Karate, December 1994

- The Essence of What is Real, Masters Series, September 1994

- Martial Arts Films: Aristos Documentary, Athens, Greece, Equal Productions Greece, producer, writer, actor, 2014; Aristos Training Video, Athens, Greece, El Oso Diablo Productions, LLC, producer, writer, actor, 2014.

In Ranger School, we were driven 22 hours a day and given so little food that many dropped 30 pounds in nine weeks. In the year I attended, five students died from exhaustion and exposure. It was a modern Shaolin Temple. When I felt I couldn't go on, I remembered my instructor telling me that the spirit decides.

Forty years later, I found myself in Iraq at an Embassy about to be overrun by armed rioters. I had written an article about the Korean ROK Marines at the Battle of Tra Binh in Vietnam in 1967. In that battle, the ROK Marines, trained in Tae Kwon Do, fought in hand-to-hand combat and overcame a much larger force that had attacked their firebase. In Iraq, I reached for the calm that came from the tradition of my art and those who had come before me. I knew that whatever came next, I would do what was right and justified.

I am also grateful for the great people I met and trained with over the years: soldiers, martial artists, and competitors from many countries. There is a bond that forms with sweat, effort, and the occasional tears.

MAJOR ACHIEVEMENTS

- Publication of Martial Arts novel, The Achilles Battle Fleet, Book one of the Mei Ling Lee Series, Literate Ape Press, 2021
- Wrote and produced two award-winning films: Doug's Christmas, 2014, and A Child Lies Here, 2011. El Oso Diablo Productions
- Volume Two of the Mei Ling Series is scheduled for release in December 2023
- Military Service: Retired as Lt. Col. with 25 years of service, US Army Ranger, Paratrooper, Air Assault Qualified, Commanded a Firebase in the Republic of Korea, Served in 101st Airborne Division and 18th Airborne Corps
- Diplomatic Service: NATO Defense Planner for 15 Years, Served in Iraq, Bosnia, Libya, Ukraine, Belarus, Russia, Korea, and Turkey
- Education: Juris Doctor (JD), Northwestern California University School of Law, 2022, Doctor of Philosophy (Ph.D.), International Relations, Berne University, 1999, Masters of Business Administration (MBA), Oklahoma City University, 1988, Bachelor of Science in Economics (BS), James Madison University, 1981

How has Grandmaster CYNTHIA ROTHROCK Influenced me?

When I have been interviewed about my first novel, The Achilles Battle Fleet: Book One of the Mei Ling Lee Series, I am often asked why I chose a woman as the main martial arts character. Throughout my career as a soldier, martial artist, diplomat, and writer, I have been blessed by the examples of an inspirational women who have taken on adversity and had the courage to push through to success. Cynthia Rothrock is one of those people. Few professionals of her level of success maintain her sense of dignity, modesty, and charitable demeanor.

Bruce Lee
WYNN

"

...I was named after Bruce Lee and was born in 1973, the year he passed away. A bit of his spirit came upon me.

WHY THE *Martial Arts?*

I started organized, structured martial arts training in 1991 under Mr. Philip Plumber, MSM, at Windsor Village Church. He has recognized me to this day and now holds a 7th degree black belt under his system at Phil's Karate School. After I received my 1st Degree Black Belt in December 1995, I started my system in 1996. It's called WYN-GYM-KATA Martial Arts System.

TRAINING INFORMATION

- Belt Ranks & Martial Arts Styles: Tae Kwon Do - 7th degree, trained in Jun Fan Jeet Kune Do, Filipino Martial Arts, Grappling, Thai Boxing, Wing Chun, Tai Chi, French Savate, Arnis Stick Fighting, Kenpo Karate

- Instructors/Influencers: Philip Plumber, James Smith, Joseph A McDaniel III, Glen O'Mary

- Birthplace/Growing Up: Chicago, IL / Houston, TX

- Yrs. In the Martial Arts: 35 years

- Yrs. Instructing: 27 years

- School Owner at WYN-GYM-KATA Martial Arts System

PROFESSIONAL ORGANIZATIONS

- M.W. St Joseph Grand Lodge Scottish Rite of Texas

- Sixth Ward Lodge #1290, Houston, TX

- Canaan Lodge of Perfection #12, Houston, TX

- Consistory #10, Houston, TX

- Malta Temple #95, Houston, TX

- A&A Supreme Council of the USA.

- A.A.O.N.M.S Grand Council of Texas

- Imperial Supreme Council of A.A.O.N.M.S

- DAV

- American Legion

How MARTIAL ARTS CHANGED My Life!

Martial arts enabled me to keep on and never quit, even when I wanted to stop. There is always something about it that draws me back to martial arts. It is a part of my life, what I am known for, and what I was born to do. I was named after Bruce Lee and was born in 1973 when he died. A bit of his spirit came upon me.

How has Grandmaster CYNTHIA ROTHROCK Influenced me?

Grandmaster Cynthia Rothrock influenced me to do action films. My Movie "Thug Life" is an ubran action film choreographed by me; Bruce Lee Wynn. Growing up watching her films motivated me to want to make martial arts film.

PERSONAL ACHIEVEMENTS

- Motion Picture credit: Thug Life - Fight Choreographer
- Diamonds from the Bantus
- McHammer Story
- America's Most Wanted Episode
- Deadly Words(z)

MAJOR ACHIEVEMENTS

- B.S Degree in Criminal Justice - CTU Online
- Masters of System Management- CTU Online
- U.S Army Retired - SFC/E7 Disable Veteran

Bruce Lee Wynn
3rd Degree Black Belt

NBL World Champion - 1997
INT State Champion - 1997

Chuck
YOUNG

"

...My confidence and my physical strength increased, and I gained a wealth of common sense and life lessons...

WHY THE *Martial Arts?*

Growing up in a boxing family, I thought it was normal to have a father take you to the gym and teach you how to box, fight and protect yourself. I would sit in awe, watching my father train and witness his almost superhero-like feats. Having a superhero Dad in the house and growing up in the 70s, it seemed like Bruce Lee was always there. I don't remember discovering Bruce Lee. I remember coming out of the theaters after seeing The Big Boss and Fist of Fury and then sometime later Enter the Dragon in the mid-70s, and from that moment on, I was the "Little Dragon."

TRAINING INFORMATION

- Belt Ranks & Martial Arts Styles: Boxing, Tae Kwon Do-Black Belt, Kickboxing, Muay Thai Kickboxing, Hep Ki Do-Brown Belt, Hiep-Tinh-Mon-Grandmaster

- Instructors/Influencers: SFC Charles M. Young, Adrian Davis, Choi Ji Jun, Lou Chung, Sensei Randy Wozin, Grandmaster Tai Yim, Supreme Grandmaster Quoc Dung Pham

- Birthplace/Growing Up: Washington, DC

- Yrs. In the Martial Arts: 47 years

- Yrs. Instructing: 34 years

- Instructor, Former co-owner of Best Martial Arts Styles

PROFESSIONAL ORGANIZATIONS

- Black Magic Filmworks, Incorporated

- Ciyoung Productions LLC

- BloodRose ind. Productions

How MARTIAL ARTS CHANGED My Life!

The type of person I am has made it easy to study the arts. With my attention to detail and love of knowledge, I find it fun, fascinating, and challenging at the same time. The results from years of dedicated training were well worth it. As I grew into adulthood, my cognitive skills and situational awareness were sharpened, my confidence and my physical strength increased, and I gained a wealth of common sense and life lessons, not to forget all of the different types of people I've had the pleasure to meet and interact with.

How has Grandmaster CYNTHIA ROTHROCK Influenced me?

Early in my film career, my path crossed with GM Cynthia occasionally. She has always been warm and welcoming. I've watched her prepare for events, and her work ethic was something to behold.

Become an
AMAA MEMBER!

PERSONAL ACHIEVEMENTS

- Teaching Martial Arts, "I love empowering people with the ability to defend themselves and others."
- Becoming a stuntman in the independent film industry
- Inducted in the 2008 USA Martial Arts Hall of Fame
- Inducted into the 2013 & 2019 Legends of Martial Arts Hall of Fame

MAJOR ACHIEVEMENTS

- Raising an awesome son who has started his own company and doing very well for himself.
- Being a single dad, I am very proud of both of my kids, and I'm proud to say that I have raised two great kids on the same values my parents raised their children on.
- Starting a film company and producing four short films

Danny ZANELOTTI

"
In my line of work, I experience fear a lot, but martial arts have been the driving force to make me continue.

WHY THE *Martial Arts?*

When I was young, I lived in a bad neighborhood in Buffalo, NY, and would get jumped daily by the same three kids. A friend's father started training me with his son so I could defend myself. I continued training when I moved to Louisiana, then formal training in Oklahoma, NY, Hawaii, Korea, and El Paso, TX.

TRAINING INFORMATION

- Belt Ranks & Martial Arts Styles: Shu Ri Ryu Karate (1st Dan), Okinowan Kenpo Karate (3rd Dan), Tae Kwon Do (1st Dan)

- Instructors/Influencers: Elvis Presley, Shihan Paul Ortino, Sabonim Kim

- Birthplace/Growing Up: Buffalo, NY

- Yrs. In the Martial Arts: 37 years

- Yrs. Instructing: 25 years

- Instructor

PROFESSIONAL ORGANIZATIONS

- Red Dragon School of Karate

- Okinowan Kenpo Karate Daharuma Dojo

- 2nd Infantry Division Tae Kwon Do team

- US Army

- Shreveport Airport Police Department

How MARTIAL ARTS CHANGED My Life!

Martial Arts has taught me to have courage when I am afraid. To be patient, to have self-discipline, respect, and self-restraint, to help others, and most of all, to try to be a good person.

Growing up in South Buffalo, NY, was a neighborhood you always had to prove yourself every day. Not the place for a pacifist. I had the same three kids jump me every day after school, so my friend's father started training me with his son. I not only learned to defend myself but learned the honor, discipline, and some of the culture of the Asian world.

I left NY when I Was 13 and trained everywhere I could. I moved around with my job and relocated to Oklahoma City, where I started training toward my black belt and kickboxing with World Class Championship Kickboxing Association. Soon after, I joined the US Army and was stationed all over, and I continued to find schools of different arts along the way, from Aikido to Karate, and Tae Kwon Do, to Tai Chi. I trained in everything I could that was available to me.

While stationed in Hawaii, I found a Karate Dojo taught by Shihan Paul Ortino. I found my home for the next two years, helping teach Okinowan Kenpo Karate and immersing myself in the history of Okinowan Karate and weapons. Later, when stationed in Korea, I was chosen to be the unit Tae Kwon Do instructor, which entailed attending a 3-day course. On the first day of the course, the Sabonim (Master) saw me stand out

PERSONAL ACHIEVEMENTS

- Earning my Black Belt
- Graduating as Honor Graduate from Shreveport Police Academy
- Writing and Acting in my films

MAJOR ACHIEVEMENTS

- Working as a Bodyguard for President Hamid Karazai (former President of Afghanistan), as well as Bill Gates and Steve Ballmer of Microsoft
- Becoming a Bodyguard Instructor
- Graduating from US Army Infantry School

in a class of 100 and recruited me to be on his Tae Kwon Do team for the 2nd Infantry Division. I was one of the team's first members and spent the next 14 months traveling all over South Korea, putting on demonstrations, teaching, and testing US Army soldiers in the art of Tae Kwon Do. Before I left Korea, I had the honor of testing for my black belt at World Tae Kwon Do Federation Headquarters in Seoul, Korea.

While stationed in El Paso, I attended the US Army Combatives Instructor Course, which is a 2-week long course, learning grappling techniques, and achieved the rank of Level 2 (of 4 Levels). I continued teaching US Army soldiers until my discharge in Aug. 2004. Since I left the army, I have continued to train in arts that I can use as a bodyguard, and Police Officer, which involves moves I can do while wearing 40 pounds of equipment.

Martial Arts has impacted my everyday life. It has taught me to have courage when I am scared. In my line of work, I experience fear a lot, but martial arts have been the driving force to make me continue. It also has taught me discipline, maintaining focus in highly stressful situations, staying calm, and not panicking. Every morning I work out and practice on a heavy bag as part of my workout, using different styles and techniques or trying new ones.

Learning to stay humble, try to be a good person, and help others is the most martial arts taught me.

Become an
**AMAA
MEMBER!**

Printed in Great Britain
by Amazon

26009066R00176

BENEATH THE SEVEN SEAS

Edited by George F. Bass

BENEATH THE SEVEN SEAS

Adventures with the Institute of Nautical Archaeology

With 433 illustrations, 410 in colour

Half-title: *A Canaanite gold pectoral from the Uluburun shipwreck, Turkey.*

Title-page: *Anchor from the probable wreck of the* Glamis, *built in Dundee, Scotland, in 1876 and lost on Grand Cayman's East End in 1913.*

Contents pages: *Canaanite gold jewelry, including a fertility goddess, from the Uluburun shipwreck; replicas of iron javelin heads from the Kyrenia ship, Cyprus; Byzantine gold coins from the 7th-century Yassıada shipwreck, Turkey; bronze lion from the Shinan wreck, Korea; gold earring from the Pepper Wreck, Portugal; Chinese porcelain from the Sadana Island wreck in Egypt; door handle from* Cleopatra's Barge, *Hawaii; pewter tableware from Port Royal, Jamaica.*

First published in the United Kingdom in 2005 by Thames & Hudson Ltd,
181A High Holborn, London WC1V 7QX

www.thamesandhudson.com

British Library Cataloguing-in-Publication Data
A catalogue record for this book is available from the British Library

ISBN-13: 978-0-500-05136-8
ISBN-10: 0-500-05136-4

Printed and bound by Tien Wah Press Pte Ltd, Singapore

Above **A treacherous reef running out from Yassıada, literally "Flat Island" in Turkish, has sunk nearly a dozen ships from Roman times until 1993, when a modern freighter went down. Excavating remains of these ships, some lying just below the wooden diving barge, the author spent seven summers in a camp established on the barren rock. The 20-m (66-ft) trawler *Kardeşler*, also anchored off shore, served INA's initial 1973 survey.**

New Tools for Undersea Archaeology

During our next excavation, in 1967 and 1969, a wreck from the late 4th or early 5th century AD at Yassıada, Fred and I were obsessed with improving seabed efficiency. Our greatest enemy was time. To understand why, one must understand decompression sickness, or the bends.

When a diver descends, the weight, or pressure, of the water on his or her body would soon crush the diver's lungs, ears, sinuses, or other air-filled cavity unless the diver is breathing air at a pressure equal to that of the surrounding water. Diving equipment provides such pressurized air, whether through a hose to an air compressor on the surface or through a regulator attached to a tank of compressed air on the diver's back. There is, however, a limit beyond which divers cannot descend while breathing compressed air. Nitrogen, which comprises 80 percent of air, produces an increasingly narcotic effect as pressure increases when the diver goes deeper. A rule of thumb is that every additional 15 m (50 ft) of depth is like drinking another gin martini, a major reason sport divers should not try to imitate the deep work mentioned above. In addition, oxygen, the other 20 percent of air, becomes increasingly toxic under pressure. Nevertheless, although slightly tipsy from narcosis, we regularly work between 30 m (99 ft) and 40 m (132 ft) deep.

While working at depth, our bodies absorb the compressed air we breathe. At reasonable depths, this does not present a problem – as long as we remain at depth, under pressure. If one ascends too rapidly at the end of a dive, however, the gas in the diver's body can come out of solution and form bubbles, just as the sudden release of pressure on champagne causes it to bubble. Nitrogen bubbles in one's blood can block its flow, leading to paralysis or death.

To avoid this diver's illness, called the bends, the diver must ascend in stages, pausing to breathe off the pressurized air. This is called decompressing. According to tables designed by diving physiologists, the deeper the dive, and the longer the dive, the longer must be the decompression. In the 1960s, we sometimes worked for 40 minutes at a depth of 40 m (132 ft), requiring extremely long, twice daily decompression stops. To avoid the cold and boredom (although we soon learned that paperback books can last for weeks under water without disintegrating), I designed a submersible decompression chamber into which the divers could swim and let themselves up 3 m (10 ft) at a time, while sitting in dry comfort. (Today, on the advice of specialists in hyperbaric medicine, we never work at depth for more than 20 minutes, decompressing with tables designed by Richard Vann of Duke University,

which call for us to switch from air to pure oxygen during decompression to flush the nitrogen out of our bodies more quickly.)

To provide a safety refuge in case of equipment failure and a place from which to speak to the surface by telephone, Michael Katzev and Susan Womer, by now Mr and Mrs Katzev, designed what we call an "underwater telephone booth," an air-filled Plexiglas dome into which divers can swim and stand, dry above their shoulders, in case of equipment failure.

At this time we also experimented with methods of finding wrecks deeper than we could dive. The catalyst for building *Asherah* was a sponge-dragger's netting, in 1963, of the bronze statue of a tunic-clad African youth at a depth of 85 m (280 ft), beyond the limits of compressed-air diving. Limited visibility through our submersible's small ports, however, made her unsuitable for open water searches. Thus, although we knew the general area where the statue had been caught, we wanted to pinpoint the wreck before sending *Asherah* down. Volunteer engineer Donald Rosencrantz, who had helped design *Asherah* and who had perfected a method of accurately mapping the seabed from the sub by stereo-photography, organized a search with side-scan sonar, although no ancient shipwreck had been found by sonar. In just one morning a team from the Scripps Institution of Oceanography spotted a wreck in the area with its sonar, a target verified by *Asherah*.

During those early days we also used a towed, one-person submersible called a Towvane, shaped like an early Mercury space capsule. The pilot, by depressing or raising the leading edges of wings on the capsule's sides, could make it descend or ascend. After one of our team found himself being bounced upside down over the seabed at a depth of around 90 m (300 ft), we decided this was not the safest method for finding wrecks!

Another device tested in our research in Turkey in the 1960s was a magnetometer – an instrument capable of detecting iron – brought to us by Englishman Jeremy Green, who describes some of his own research in these pages.

Above right **The single occupant of the Towvane, seen being lowered over the side of a Turkish trawler, planed downward by angling the vanes or wings while being towed.**

Right **INA's underwater telephone booths, air-filled acrylic hemispheres, allow divers to remove their mouth pieces and, dry from their chests up, talk to one another or, via cable, to the surface, or to change their scuba in case of equipment failure.**

Left **Maurice McGehee of the Scripps Institute of Oceanography, examines the paper print-out of a sonar that in a single morning revealed the position of an ancient shipwreck, positively identified from the submersible *Asherah*, in the center of the area being searched for the wreck that yielded the African youth and two other statues.**

copper ingots stacked as originally stowed in the hull of a ship. I focused my gaze and saw more ingots jutting out from seemingly sterile sandy patches. Everywhere I looked there were ingots; we counted 84 during our week-long survey of the site, but never guessed that beneath the sand and marine encrustation were a staggering 354 four-handled ingots, several times more than all the ingots of their type found until then in the entire Mediterranean region!

I saw two-handled pottery jars with the pointed bases typical of Canaanite containers. Higher and lower on the steeply sloping seabed lay huge storage jars, several at around 50–55 m (165–182 ft) deep. Hand-fanning sand from a rectangular stone slab, I uncovered a rectangular hole that revealed it to be a stone anchor weighing about 200 kg (440 lb). Overwhelmed with the excitement of discovery, I found it difficult to leave these new treasures when the time came to surface; my 20-minute dive seemed like seconds. But I was to return to excavate the wreck from 1984 to 1994, living for months at a time in a small "village" we built on the steep cliff above. George directed the first campaign, and then turned the project over to me.

Two large stone anchors at the site's deeper end suggested the ship's bow, with its stern at the highest extremity. Based on the cargo, it appeared that the ship was sailing

Painstaking recording of the positions of thousands of artifacts over many years resulted in this plan of the wreck site.

Legend:
- Copper oxhide ingots
- Copper bun ingots
- Tin ingots
- Stone anchors
- Ceramics
- Ebony logs

from the coast of Syria-Palestine or Cyprus and was headed in a northwesterly direction when it failed to clear craggy Uluburun. Perhaps the ship was dashed against the rocky promontory by a fierce south wind that unexpectedly rose in summer, when the prevailing wind blows from the northwest.

Early finds on the wreck suggested that the Uluburun ship plied the Mediterranean towards the end of the 14th century BC, one of the most active and colorful periods of the ancient world. During this century Late Bronze Age Greeks were constructing the great palace at Mycenae from which they received their name: Mycenaeans. They established trading outposts and colonized the islands and shores of the Aegean and Ionian Seas from Asia Minor to southern Italy. To the east lived the seafaring Canaanites, a term used to denote generally the Semitic peoples along the Syro-Palestinian coast during the second millennium BC. They traded extensively with Egypt, Cyprus, Crete, and lands beyond, and their ports served as hubs for overland trade routes connecting Egypt, Mesopotamia, and the Hittite Empire. In this century Egypt was ruled by the heretic pharaoh Akhenaten, whose queen was the beautiful Nefertiti. During Akhenaten's reign Egypt's foreign influence waned, but it was in his city on the Nile, known today as el-Amarna, that 382 clay tablets inscribed in cuneiform were found. Some 350 of them, known as the Amarna letters, offer a vivid portrait of Egypt's diplomatic relations with Cypriot, Hittite, Kassite, Assyrian, and other rulers, as well as with vassals in Syria and Palestine. While the exact nature of international trade during this period is not fully understood, and the presence of private enterprise is suggested by textual evidence, the Amarna tablets show that much of the trade at palace level was conducted as exchanges of "royal gifts."

"…this ship [is] the king's"

The minister of Alashiya (Cyprus) to the minister of Egypt, from a clay tablet found at el-Amarna, Egypt

The Uluburun ship's cargo seems to represent a royal dispatch of enormously valuable raw materials and manufactured goods, matching many of the royal gifts listed in the Amarna letters.

"I will bring to thee as a present two hundred talents of copper"

The king of Alashiya (Cyprus) to an Egyptian pharaoh, from a clay tablet found at el- Amarna, one of several mentioning shipments of copper ingots

The Uluburun ship's cargo consisted mostly of raw materials – trade items that before the excavation were known primarily, and in some places solely, from ancient texts or Egyptian tomb paintings. The major cargo was 10 tons of Cypriot copper in the form of flat, four-handled ingots and similar, but previously unknown, two-handled ingots, weighing on average about 25 kg (55 lb), approximately an ancient talent. In addition there were more than 120 smaller plano-convex discoid, or "bun," ingots of copper.

"…tribute to [Tutankhamun] offered by Syria"

Inscription beneath a painting in the tomb of Huy, Egyptian viceroy to Nubia, showing a Syrian bearing a four-handled copper ingot

Syrian merchants and tribute-bearers carrying four-handled ingots are depicted in Egyptian tomb paintings. Similar ingots are found throughout the eastern and

Below George Bass carefully fans sediment from a storage pot, keeping the surrounding water clear by use of a small airlift, a kind of underwater vacuum cleaner. The pot trapped and preserved much organic material such as components of well-crafted boxwood boxes, bits of rope, and great quantities of seed, all of which would otherwise have perished.

central Mediterranean, from southern Germany and France to Mesopotamia, and from Egypt to the Black Sea. Those of the 15th century BC, with less prominent handles, are from unknown sources, but all of those from the 14th and 13th centuries BC are apparently from Cyprus, as shown by lead-isotope analyses by Noël Gale and Sophie Stos at Oxford University's Isotrace Laboratory.

Originally stowed in four transverse rows across the Uluburun ship's hold, the ingots in each row overlapped one another like roof shingles, the direction of overlap alternating from layer to layer to prevent slippage during transit.

In addition to the copper, the ship yielded the earliest well-dated tin ingots. Most occur in the four-handled form, often cut into quarters, each quarter retaining one handle. Others are rectangular slabs, or sections cut from ingots of indiscernible shape. One, however, is shaped like a stone anchor with a large hole at one end, reminding us of bearers in Egyptian tomb paintings carrying similar metal ingots previously identified as silver or lead. Because in some cases the tin has assumed the consistency of toothpaste, which we carefully scooped from the seabed with teaspoons, it is not possible to know the exact amount of tin carried on the ship, but we recovered a ton. When alloyed with the copper, this would have made 11 tons of bronze in the standard 10 to 1 ratio of copper to tin.

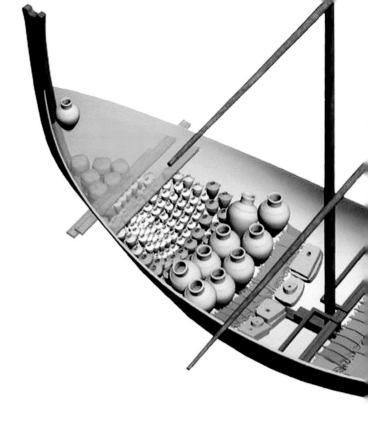

Remarkable finds were made on the seabed. The ceramic flask is Near Eastern in origin and the two-handled cup is Mycenaean Greek, but the origin of the bi-conical gold chalice remains undetermined.

The source of our tin has not yet been determined. Preliminary results of Noël Gale's lead-isotope analyses indicate that it was not derived from known sources in eastern Europe, Spain or Cornwall – but ancient texts from western Asia hint at tin sources somewhere to the east, perhaps in Iran, or even Afghanistan or central Asia, from which it was transported overland to the Mediterranean by donkey caravans. This lends weight to the supposition that the ingots' shape was designed for ease of handling and for transportation by pack animals.

The Uluburun ship also carried about 150 Canaanite jars, vessels widely distributed over Syria-Palestine, Egypt, Cyprus, and Greece, which served as containers for shipping all sorts of liquids and solid commodities. The shipwrecked jars fall into three general sizes, with three quarters of them representing the smallest size, having an average capacity of 6.7 liters, the medium size about twice that volume, and the largest about four times the smallest value.

One jar was filled with glass beads, and several with olives, but about half of them contained a yellowish material chemically identified as terebinth resin from the *Pistacia* tree group, which grows around much of the Mediterranean. This resin cargo, which originally weighed about half a ton, revealed for the first time another raw material that was part of the complex eastern Mediterranean trade of the Late Bronze Age.

We carefully decanted each jar we raised of its sand and silt, which we searched for tiny finds before passing it through a series of fine-mesh sieves to recover every seed, some smaller than a pin's head such as figs and black cumin, and other minuscule bits missed during the visual sorting. During these processes, I spotted small land snails in the resin. Francisco Welter-Schultes, a malacologist at the Zoologisches Institut in

A computer-generated version of the ship, by Shih-Han Samuel Lin, allows archaeologists to move cargo, some of which had slid down the steep slope of the seabed, into positions that would have provided the best ballast.

Berlin, identified one as a species with an extremely limited geographical distribution, which has changed little during the last 10,000 years. These snails, entrapped in the resin as it oozed out of the cuts made in trees, suggest that our resin was gathered from regions to the west-northwest of the Dead Sea in Israel, a suggestion strengthened by analysis of the plant pollen extracted from the resin.

Jars labeled *sntr* in Egyptian hieroglyphs are depicted in an Egyptian tomb painting of royal storerooms displaying Canaanite tributes. Decades ago a French Egyptologist translated *sntr* as terebinth resin, which he said was recorded as brought to Egypt from the Near East, primarily for use as incense. Over a five-year period in the annals of pharaoh Thutmose III, the volume of *sntr* received averaged 9,250 liters per year, approximately twenty times the amount carried aboard the Uluburun ship.

"Payment to the palace, 1,320 liters of ki-ta-no; *still owed, 240 + liters"*

> *Record of payment to royal stores, written in Mycenaean Greek on a clay tablet found in the palace at Knossos, Crete*

Terebinth resin may also correspond to Mycenaean *ki-ta-no*, which had been interpreted as meaning nuts related to the modern pistachio. Palace inventories on Crete record enormous quantities of it, more than 10,000 liters in one case. No large quantities of *Pistacia* nuts have been found at Bronze Age sites, however, and since the word *ki-ta-no* was written with a symbol suggesting that it was an aromatic or a condiment, it may be that resin, rather than nuts, was inventoried. Was terebinth resin used as incense in the Aegean as in Egypt? Or was it used in the manufacture of scented oils, as today in parts of the Near East?

"The king, my lord, has written to me about the mekku-*stone that is in my possession, but I have already given one weighing one hundred [units] to the king, my lord"*

> *Prince Abi-milki of Tyre to Egyptian pharaoh Akhenaten, from a clay tablet found at el-Amarna*

A well-preserved cobalt-blue glass ingot, cast to imitate rare lapis lazuli mined in Afghanistan. Such ingots would have been melted down and formed into a variety of objects or vessels.

Some 170 cup-cake shaped glass ingots approximately 15 cm (6 in) in diameter and 6.5 cm (2.5 in) thick were found on the wreck. They are among the earliest intact glass ingots known. Cobalt blue, turquoise, lavender, and amber, they are quite likely the *mekku* and *ehlipakku* mentioned in Amarna letters sent from Tyre, Akko, and Ashkelon, among others, to Egypt, and listed in other Near Eastern tablets as exports from the region. Their colors must have been favored for their likeness to the highly sought semi-precious stones and material of their day: lapis lazuli, turquoise, amethyst, and amber. When cakes of lapis lazuli and turquoise are shown as tribute in Egyptian art, they are sometimes called "genuine" in Egyptian hieroglyphs; our discovery has led Egyptologists to believe that glass imitations of those precious stones are depicted if the word "genuine" does not appear. Robert Brill of the Corning Museum of Glass reports that our ingots of cobalt blue are chemically identical to contemporary blue Egyptian vessels and blue Mycenaean relief beads, suggesting a common source – perhaps Near Eastern glassmakers who kept secret the formulas for the "simulated" stones they exported.

"One hundred pieces of ebony I have dispatched"

Amenhotep III to King Tarkhundaradu of Arzawa, from a tablet found at el-Amarna

Small dark logs of what the Egyptians called ebony, known today as African blackwood (*Dalbergia melanoxylon*), were another unique find. Egyptian tomb paintings show such logs being brought as tribute to the pharaoh from Nubia, south of Egypt, and furniture in King Tutankhamun's famous tomb is made of ebony. The skilled craftsmen needed to shape this hard material would only have been in the employ of palaces. Ebony was exclusively for elite consumption, then, and along with ivory comprised some of the prestige goods carried aboard the Uluburun ship.

"Now, as a present for thee…one elephant's tusk…I have sent"

The minister of Alashiya (Cyprus) to the minister of Egypt, from a tablet found at el-Amarna

Other raw materials include a 20-cm (8-in) length of neatly sawn elephant tusk. More than a dozen hippopotamus teeth, both canines and incisors, were also recovered.

Below left **Faith Hentschel holds one of the logs of African blackwood, which the ancient Egyptians called "ebony," but which differs from the wood called ebony today.**

Below right **INA archaeologist Sheila Matthews measures a section of elephant tusk as Faith Hentschel looks on. Raw ivory on board also included hippopotamus teeth.**

The large number of hippopotamus teeth surprised us, for archaeologists had assumed that most Late Bronze Age ivory came from African and Asian elephants. After we published our findings, several contemporaneous ivory collections in museums were restudied with the unexpected discovery that hippopotamus ivory had been used more frequently than elephant ivory, especially for smaller pieces, in one collection accounting for 75 percent.

Other raw materials of animal origin included thousands of tiny opercula, the button-like plates attached to the feet of marine mollusks that serve as protective doors when the animals retract into their shells. They seldom survive in the archaeological record. Ours were from murex snails, but they were found in clusters without the corresponding numbers of dead murex shells nearby, some in recognizable patterns suggesting that they had been stored in bags that had long since disintegrated. We later learned that opercula were another ingredient of incense. Ours were almost certainly by-products of the Canaanite industry that extracted the legendary purple dye from murex glands.

We also found fragments of seven tortoise carapaces that had been modified into sounding-boxes for stringed musical instruments, probably lutes, and three ostrich eggshells that were probably modified into ornate vases by the addition of glass or metal bases and necks, now lost.

There were also manufactured goods on board. At least three of nine large storage jars contained Cypriot export pottery. Four faience drinking cups were crafted as the heads of rams and, in one case, the head of a woman. Copper and/or bronze vessels of several types, although poorly preserved, also appear to have been in the cargo, some found nestled one inside another.

"...fourteen seals of beautiful hulalu [stone], overlaid with gold"

> Gifts listed on a tablet from King Tushratta of Mitanni to Pharaoh Akhenaten, found at el-Amarna

An astonishingly rich collection of both usable and scrap gold Canaanite jewelry (a few of Egyptian origin) surfaced during the excavation: pectorals, medallions, pendants, beads, a small ring ingot, and an assortment of cut and deformed fragments. One pendant bears the repoussé figure of a nude female holding a gazelle in each hand, almost certainly a Canaanite fertility goddess. Among four gold medallions is the largest known Canaanite gold medallion. A gold pectoral, in the shape of a falcon with a hooded cobra clutched in each claw, is worked in repoussé and granulation. A goblet, the single largest gold object from the ship, is of uncertain origin.

Nine cylinder seals – of hematite, quartz, stone, and faience – probably belonged to those on the ship. Their geographically widespread places of manufacture need not indicate a crew of diverse origins, however, for such items could have been obtained from different regions while others were passed down from one generation to another. For example, the oldest seal, of hematite (a black iron ore), is of Babylonian origin. Dominique Collon of the British Museum noted that it was made in the 18th century BC, originally depicting a king facing a goddess with the

The best preserved of four faience drinking cups shaped like ram's heads. Such vessels were used for ceremonial purposes.

The Uluburun wreck yielded the largest collection of Canaanite jewelry of any excavated site. The larger pendant depicts a fertility goddess with gazelles in her hands, and the smaller carries a typical Canaanite star-and-ray design of the type depicted at the necks of Canaanites in Egyptian tomb paintings.

small figure of a priest between them; she further noted that probably in the 14th century, in Assyria, a new scene incorporating a winged griffin-demon and a warrior with a sickle sword was engraved over a cuneiform inscription alongside the old, by now worn, scene. Two cylinder seals of quartz show the Kassites, foreign invaders who ruled Babylonia around the time the Uluburun ship sank.

"The Beautiful one has come"

Literal translation of the name Nefertiti

Egyptian objects of gold, electrum, silver, and steatite were also found. The most significant is a unique gold scarab inscribed with the name of Nefertiti, wife of the pharaoh Akhenaten. It is considered to be one of the most important Egyptian discoveries ever made in the eastern Mediterranean outside Egypt. Other scarabs, mostly older than the wreck, refer to Thutmose I or have either unreadable combinations of signs or good-luck and prophylactic signs.

Additional finds include two duck-shaped ivory cosmetic boxes, the ivory figurine of a female acrobat with her feet on her head, and more tin vessels than had previously been found throughout the entire Bronze Age Near East and Aegean. Beads of glass, agate, carnelian, quartz, gold, bone, Baltic amber, seashell, ostrich eggshell, and faience were raised by the thousands. A bronze female figurine, with hands extended forward, and with the head, neck, hands, and feet covered with gold foil also appeared. Probably representing a deity, she may have served to protect the ship from peril.

Above This 17-cm (6.7-in) tall bronze statuette of a goddess, partly clad in gold foil, may have been the ship's protective deity. The position of her hands indicates a gesture of blessing.

Left One of two duck-shaped ivory containers that were found on the Uluburun wreck. Each has pivoting wings that served as a lid for its body cavity, which contained cosmetics.

Weapons on board included arrows, spears, maces, daggers, an axe, a single armor scale of Near Eastern type, and swords. The bronze swords are of interest as they represent three unrelated types. Two are typical 14th-century Aegean products. The best preserved is a heavy Canaanite weapon with ivory and ebony inlay in its hilt; three daggers similar to it resemble a dagger from a 14th-century tomb in Israel. The last and most poorly preserved sword is similar to swords found in southern Italy and Sicily.

A large number of tools, which included sickles, awls, drill bits, a saw, a pair of tongs, chisels, axes, double axes, a plowshare, whetstones, and adzes, came mostly from the aft section of the ship. Virtually all are either of Near Eastern types or are shapes ubiquitous in the Eastern Mediterranean, but a few point to an Aegean connection.

Most of the Uluburun ship's cargo could have been taken on at a port in Syria-Palestine or Cyprus, but the origin of the cargo does not necessarily reveal the homeport of the ship that carried it. The latter is best revealed by the 24 stone anchors carried on the ship, which are of a type virtually unknown in the Aegean, but are often found in the sea or built into temples on land in Syria-Palestine and on Cyprus. Moreover, the ship itself was built of Lebanese cedar, a tree indigenous to the mountains of Lebanon, southern Turkey, and central Cyprus. Cultic and ritualistic objects aboard the ship, such as the probable bronze female deity, an ivory trumpet carved from a hippopotamus tooth in the likeness of a ram's horn, and a pair of bronze finger cymbals are probably also of Canaanite origin. Canaanite, too, are the oil lamps

Above **The thick-bladed bronze sword with flanged hilt inlaid with ivory and Egyptian ebony (right), is Canaanite, as is the dagger with hilt plates of an unidentified wood; the dagger's missing pommel was discovered later and attached to it. The lighter sword on the left, with fine midrib and grooves, is Mycenaean.**

Right **An archaeologist excavates delicate finds trapped between copper ingots (in the foreground) and two stone anchors in the general area of the ship's mast.**

used on board, revealing the crew's preference for this lamp type over the more abundant Cypriot variety carried in pristine condition as cargo inside one of the large storage jars that was used, like a modern china barrel, to transport new Cypriot pottery.

Approximately 150 weights from Uluburun comprise the most complete groups of contemporaneous Late Bronze Age weights from a single site. As such, all standards and sets necessary for a merchant venture should be present. Most of the weights are of hematite or stone carved into known geometric shapes of the period, but the assemblage includes the largest set of Bronze Age zoomorphic weights, cast in bronze and sometimes filled with lead; these include a sphinx, bulls, cows, a calf, ducks, frogs, lions, a fly, and even the figure of a cow herder kneeling before three of his calves. While the bronze weights have suffered damage from corrosion, the other weights are generally well preserved and mostly correspond to a weight system based on a unit mass of 9.3 g, the standard commonly used along the Syro-Palestinian coast, on Cyprus and in Egypt. The numbers of sets suggest that there were at least three or possibly four merchants on the ship. Three sets of copper or bronze pans for balances, one pair nested and encased in its wooden sleeve, strengthen this view. The weights may be taken as nearly conclusive evidence of Canaanite or Near Eastern merchants on the ship. With one exception, no weights conform to the Aegean mass standard.

Foodstuffs, whether as cargo or for shipboard use, include almonds, pine nuts, figs, olives, grapes (or raisins or wine), black cumin, sumac, coriander, and whole pomegranates, along with a few grains of wheat and barley. Lead net sinkers, netting needles, fishhooks, a barbed spear and a trident of bronze indicate that the crew fished.

Estimated to have been about 15 m (49 ft) long and built of cedar, the Uluburun ship was constructed in the "shell-first" method with pegged mortise-and-tenon joints holding its planks together and to the keel. Used in Greco-Roman ships, this edge-joined planking technique contrasts with the more familiar "skeleton-first" construction method, whereby the planking is formed around and fastened to a pre-erected frame. In spite of our detailed examination of the hull remains, no evidence for any framing has emerged. Perhaps the preserved hull section is not large enough to include frames (ribs) or bulkheads, or evidence for securing such elements to the planking. The keel of the ship, which is wider than it is high, originally protruded into the hull rather that outward, as in later construction. This timber would have served as the ship's spine, as well as protecting the planks and supporting the ship when beached or hauled ashore. Unlike keels of later sailing ships, however, it would have done little to help the ship hold course or point nearer the wind under sail – in other words, it appears rudimentary in design rather than a keel in the traditional sense.

"Then he fenced in the whole from stem to stern with willow withies to be a defense against the waves, and strewed much brush thereon"

Odyssey, Book 5.256–7

Remains of a wicker fence call to mind the weather fencing on Syrian ships depicted in nearly contemporary Egyptian tomb paintings, and of the wicker fence

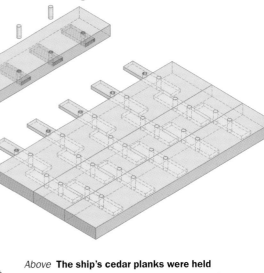

Above **The ship's cedar planks were held together by oak tenons inserted into mortises and then locked in place with oak pegs.**

Right **"Then he fenced in the whole from stem to stern with willow withies," *Odyssey*, Book 5.256–7. The Uluburun ship's wicker fence was still preserved on the seabed.**

Below **A diver illuminates some of the ship's mortise-and-tenon joined hull planks as they were found on the seabed. The keel protruded farther inboard than outboard. No evidence for framing was found.**

Below **The expedition's home for three months was a narrow strip of beach about an hour's sail from the wreck site. Seen here on a calm day, it was abandoned when the first south wind of autumn sent waves crashing over it.**

Below right **Excavation director George Bass (left) and Peter Throckmorton puzzle over bits of wood and corroded bronze implements in the camp's simple "conservation laboratory."**

I had married Ann Singletary shortly before sailing to Turkey. She joined me after completing her master's degree in music, carrying two suitcases, one of clothes and one of music – expecting to find a piano?

French diver Claude Duthuit had the only pup tent.

"Take it, George," he gallantly offered. "It's your honeymoon."

Claude remains my closest friend!

The Excavation

Daily we sailed to the site, where we had permanently moored metal oil drums to which we tied our boats. We dived 40 minutes in the morning and 28 minutes in the afternoon, working hard on the seabed, with only a few minutes of decompression after each dive. Without a physician, or recompression chamber, or even medicinal oxygen, we must have had a guardian angel, for we suffered no cases of the bends.

When our little high-pressure compressor broke down and had to be sent to the nearest machine shop, an overnight sail away, we could no longer fill scuba tanks. Peter and I attached a hose to the sponge-boat's originally hand-cranked compressor, having made gaskets from old leather shoes, and continued to dive, although we were in what our pilot book said was the strongest current in the Mediterranean. We held on for dear life descending and ascending a rope running to the bottom, our bodies flapping like laundry on a windy day, and took turns bracing ourselves between rocks to hold our partner's hose so that he or she could let go and work with freed hands.

Chief diver Frédéric Dumas, on loan from Jacques-Yves Cousteau, was regarded as the world's greatest diver. He told Peter and me we were crazy, and refused to dive with our jury-rigged gear. Normally, however, we dived with scuba.

Cargo from the Age of Bronze: Cape Gelidonya, Turkey **49**

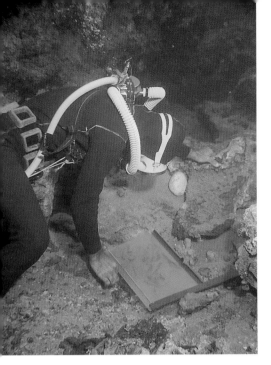

Laboriously we mapped the site by measuring with meter tapes from spikes we drove into the rock around the mostly metal cargo. This cargo was embedded in rock-hard seabed concretion that had built up in thickness over the years. Dumas suggested that we bring the cargo to the surface still encased in this concretion, so that we could extract it more carefully back at camp. From that time we hammered and chiseled to free massive lumps of concretion that we raised with air-filled lifting balloons, and then fitted back together on the beach.

The depth of sand was not sufficient to have covered and protected from shipworms and other marine borers the ship's wooden hull, although we found a few scraps of wood and, under some of the metal cargo, layers of twigs with the bark still preserved. This explained the brushwood Odysseus spread out in a ship he built, which had puzzled classicists. The twigs formed dunnage, a cushion for the cargo.

We removed sand with airlifts, nearly vertical metal pipes to whose lower ends we pumped air from the surface through hoses; as the air entered the pipes, it formed bubbles which rushed upward, creating a suction that pulled in both water and whatever sand we swept into the pipes' lower ends.

We had all but completed the excavation before the first south wind of autumn sent waves crashing completely across our narrow beach in mid-September, driving us from the Cape.

Above **With an ordinary pencil Claude Duthuit draws on a sheet of frosted plastic the positions of artifacts lying in a rocky gully.**

Below **The cargo was brought to the surface still embedded in large chunks of concretion that were put back together at the camp like pieces of a giant jigsaw puzzle. Ann Bass removes concretion, revealing copper ingots.**

Fatal Final Voyage

We had excavated a ton of metal. Thirty-four flat, four-handled ingots of almost pure Cypriot copper, weighing on average 25 kg (55 lb), were still stacked as they had been in the ship 3,200 years before. A material like white toothpaste was later shown, by chemical analysis, to be the remains of tin, probably tin ingots. Mixed with the ingots

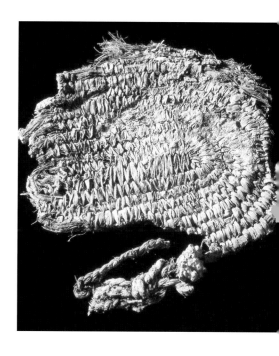

Below **A bronze swage, 10 cm (3.9 in) long, was used like a small anvil for shaping metal. Sockets for tools were hammered out at one end.** *Above center* **Stone hammers 6 and 8 cm (2.4 and 3.1 in) in diameter, displayed with modern wooden hafts, resemble more recent hammers used for working metals.** *Below center* **Pan-balance weights of stone were based on Near Eastern weight standards.** *Above right* **The remarkably preserved bottom of a woven basket that held scrap bronze in the cargo.** *Center right* **Scarabs were Syro-Palestinian imitations of Egyptian scarabs.** *Below right* **A stone seal about the diameter of a pencil is like those once worn at the wrists of Near Eastern merchants. It is shown with modern string and modern clay onto which it has been rolled.**

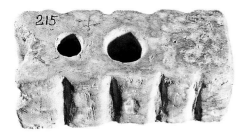

were broken bronze tools made on the island of Cyprus and carried in baskets, one of which we found remarkably preserved. The copper and tin, ingredients for making new bronze, and the scrap bronze, were all intended to be melted down and cast in molds to form new bronze objects.

The discovery of a grooved and pierced bronze swage (a kind of small anvil), two stone hammerheads of types sometimes used in metalworking, a whetstone, numerous stone polishers, and a large, close-grained stone with flat top that could have served as an anvil suggested that a traveling smith, or tinker, may have been on the ship's last voyage.

At one end of the site, which we believe to have been the living quarters of the ship, probably at the stern, we found the personal possessions of those on board – along with olive pits that had been spat into the bilge. About 60 small stone objects, some shaped like domed marshmallows and others like pointed American footballs flattened on one side so they would not roll, were merchants' weights for pan balances. The ship's saucer-like lamp, its rim pinched to form a spout to hold in place a wick that once floated on oil inside, was intact, but most of the pottery was broken. Each of two stone mortars was carved with a spout and three stubby legs.

From here, too, came unbroken metal objects such as a bronze razor and a small chisel once used for cutting mortises, four scarabs and a scarab-shaped plaque, and a cylindrical stone seal of the kind rolled out on clay documents as a kind of signature by Near Eastern merchants. An astragalus, or knucklebone, of a sheep or goat, reminded us of the game of knucklebones still played, like dice, in Europe. In antiquity, knucklebones were also used in divination, to receive a sign from the gods, and I wonder if it was by tossing a knucklebone that "fair-haired Menelaus" received such a sign when he debated which route to sail in the *Odyssey* (Book 3.173).

Anyone reading this can date a photograph to the early 20th century or to the late 20th century from the style of clothes, hairdos, or automobiles in it. Archaeologists similarly date artifacts, for styles have always changed. Thus, we knew early on that the ship sank around 1200 BC, probably just before, a date later verified by the radiocarbon dating of some of the twigs.

Above **Like tribute bearers in ancient Egyptian tomb paintings, Turkish sponge-divers carry copper ingots from the wreck to the waiting hands of Captain Kemal Aras, discoverer of the site, for transport to storage and eventual display in Bodrum.**

Rewriting History

At the time of the excavation, virtually all Classical archaeologists and ancient historians held that Late Bronze Age Greeks, today called Mycenaeans after Agamemnon's great citadel at Mycenae, monopolized maritime commerce in the eastern Mediterranean in the 14th and 13th centuries BC. They further believed that Semitic traders and seafarers, best represented by Phoenicians, did not begin their famed seafaring activities until the Iron Age, after 1000 BC, and more especially after 800 BC. Indeed, the main reason most scholars have dated Homer's composition or compilation of the *Odyssey* to the Iron Age, long after the Bronze Age events described in his epic poems, is his frequent mention of Phoenician seafarers, merchants, and metal smiths.

Small wonder that throughout the excavation, my colleagues and I assumed we were excavating a Mycenaean ship.

It was not until I began to study the stone weights that I had my first stirrings of doubt. Before hand-held calculators, I sometimes sat up through the night doing long division, trying to learn the standards of the weights. Just as today, where some nations use pounds and others use kilograms, there were various weight standards in antiquity. When I realized that the Cape Gelidonya weights were often multiples of 9.32 g, an Egyptian *qedet* used throughout the Near East and Cyprus, or 10.3 g, a Syrian *nesef*, I wondered why a Mycenaean merchant carried Near Eastern weights; anthropological studies show that merchants traditionally carry their own, familiar weights, even when they travel abroad.

From library research I learned that our terracotta lamp was probably Canaanite, and that the stone mortars had been manufactured on the Syro-Palestinian coast where the Canaanites lived. An Egyptologist determined that our scarabs were not Egyptian, but were Syro-Palestinian imitations of Egyptian scarabs, the hieroglyphs on them only meaningless decorations. Lastly, two scholars recognized the cylinder seal as having been carved in north Syria, although it seemed to be centuries older than the wreck, probably an heirloom passed from father to son. The bronze razor was another personal possession of Near Eastern origin.

With surprise I concluded, from these personal possessions, that our ship was Canaanite or proto-Phoenician or Syrian – in other words, of Near Eastern origin. A single ship, of course, is not a fleet, nor can it rewrite history. Our shipwreck was only the catalyst that led me to question prevailing views of scholars around the world.

Below **The ship's sole source of light after dark was a terracotta Canaanite bowl with pinched rim to hold a wick floating on olive oil inside.**

I re-examined virtually all published Egyptian tomb paintings and found that in the 14th and 13th centuries BC, four-handled copper ingots brought as tribute to the pharaoh are identified as Syrian, in one case even shown being borne from a Syrian ship. Another painting depicts a Syrian merchant fleet newly arrived in Egypt. Nowhere do we see Greeks. I turned to hundreds of 14th-century BC cuneiform documents excavated at el-Amarna in Egypt. They describe gift cargoes from various Near Eastern lands, without mention of Greece. I later learned that in Bronze Age Greek, written in what scholars call Linear B script, there is not even a word for merchant.

What had been the evidence before 1960 for the presumed Mycenaean monopoly on maritime commerce? The frequent finds of Mycenaean pottery throughout the Near East, including Egypt and Cyprus. Because there were not similar finds of Near Eastern goods in Greece, it was assumed that Mycenaean ships carried all this pottery.

To me there was a flaw in this reasoning. That Mycenaean pottery reached the Near East was unquestioned, but nothing proved it was carried there in Mycenaean ships. Further, I doubted that Mycenaean sailors were sailing around the eastern Mediterranean giving out free samples of their pottery. Something of equal value had to be coming back to Greece in return. Yet that something had to be invisible to the archaeologist. My published doctoral dissertation suggested that the invisible cargoes must have been raw materials – copper, tin, ivory, gold, cloth, and spices – things that left no trace in the archaeological record because soon after reaching port they were quickly consumed or manufactured into objects of the land or culture that imported them.

My publication received universally unfavorable reviews by Classical archaeologists. Luckily, I lived long enough to begin the excavation of another Late Bronze Age ship, one that sank about a century earlier, off the very next cape to the west, at Uluburun. Cemal Pulak, who directed most of its excavation and is responsible for its interpretation and publication, describes it elsewhere in this book. Its 20 tons of raw materials – copper, tin, ivory, ebony, glass, resins, shell, and spices and other foodstuffs – carried on a ship of almost undoubted Near Eastern origin,

On a return visit to the wreck nearly three decades after its excavation, the Institute of Nautical Archaeology's research vessel *Virazon* is anchored directly over the site, which lies between two of five small islands that extend out from the cape, seen in the distance.

convinced most scholars of an appreciable Semitic presence in the Bronze Age Aegean. Because of underwater archaeology, Homer's Phoenicians are no longer anachronistic.

Return to the Cape

By the 1980s, the Institute of Nautical Archaeology (INA) had its own research vessel, *Virazon*, fully outfitted with diving and underwater excavation equipment, including a double-lock recompression chamber. In 1987, while we were excavating the Uluburun site, Claude Duthuit, by now an INA director, suggested:

"Why don't we run over to Gelidonya with *Virazon*, just for nostalgia."

Cemal Pulak, to whom I had by now entrusted the excavation at Uluburun, came with us – and immediately found a sword, the first weapon from the site, which we had

somehow overlooked nearly two decades earlier. With a better metal detector than we had in 1960, INA's Tufan Turanlı found additional metal finds, some trailing toward a pinnacle of rock that reached nearly to the surface and almost certainly tore open the bottom of the Bronze Age ship. Motorized underwater scooters now allowed INA divers to search far from the original cargo during almost annual visits to the Cape.

Discoveries were also being made in College Station. In 1990, Peter Throckmorton died quietly in his sleep, leaving his library, notes, and photographs to INA. Cemal Pulak soon recognized in photographs of scanty wood remains evidence that the Cape Gelidonya hull was constructed like his earlier Uluburun hull, in the same technique as that used to build the much later Kyrenia ship, also described in this book.

In 1994, Don Frey and Murat Tilev, using scooters, located the Cape Gelidonya ship's large stone anchor. It is of a type found throughout the Near East and Cyprus, both under water and on land, but in the Aegean only at a Bronze Age site on Crete that seems to have served as a harbor for Near Eastern traders. If we had found the anchor in 1960, perhaps my assigning a Near Eastern origin to the Cape Gelidonya wreck would not have been so controversial.

Above **On visits to Cape Gelidonya in the 1980s and 1990s, divers with motorized underwater scooters were able to explore far beyond the original excavation site, allowing them to discover the ship's stone anchor.**

Right **Although the cargo found at Cape Gelidonya weighed only a tenth of that at Uluburun, the Cape Gelidonya ship's anchor, being weighed on *Virazon* by Cemal Pulak, was heavier than any found on the earlier wreck.**

Cargo from the Age of Bronze: Cape Gelidonya, Turkey

ANCIENT GREEK WRECKS

Ancient Greece depended on the ships that brought essential grain to her ports from the Black Sea, transported and supplied her colonists throughout much of the Mediterranean, and defeated her enemies in naval engagements. Without ships, Athens could not have become the definitive icon of Greek splendor. The Institute of Nautical Archaeology remains at the forefront of writing a detailed history of ancient Greek ships.

Excavations of 6th-century BC vessels found in Italian and French waters revealed construction methods unlike those associated with Classical shipbuilding of the 5th century BC and later. Their planks, instead of being fastened together by mortise-and-tenon joints, were laced together through pre-cut holes along the edges of the planks. Some scholars hypothesized that this was a peculiar Western Mediterranean tradition, perhaps representing and/or reflecting an Etruscan tradition, and that mortise-and-tenon joints continued in the Eastern Mediterranean from the Bronze Age (as we have seen in the Uluburun and Cape Gelidonya hulls) through the 4th century BC (as we shall see in the Kyrenia hull).

As described here by Elizabeth Greene, INA excavated for the first time in the Aegean a 6th-century BC shipwreck, at Pabuç Burnu on the Turkish coast. Almost certainly Greek, the hull was laced. We can now say with some confidence, therefore, that Greek ships of the Archaic Period (7th and 6th centuries BC) that preceded the glorious Classical Period (5th and 4th centuries BC) were all or mostly laced. And we may now assume that the 6th-century ships excavated in the Western Mediterranean were also Greek.

While Texas A&M University graduate student Sam Mark was working in the field with INA, he published two controversial articles proposing that the ships described by Homer were laced. Is it possible, then, that laced Greek hulls were the norm in the Bronze Age, the time of the Trojan War, and that Greeks borrowed mortise-and-tenon construction from Near Eastern Phoenicians in later Classical times? We need to find a Mycenaean hull, but when we do, I suspect that it will be laced, from a time when Near Eastern ships were already mortise-and-tenon joined.

INA has conducted the first complete seabed excavation of a Greek wreck from the 5th century BC, the century of the Parthenon, of philosopher Socrates, of political leader Pericles, and of dramatists Sophocles and Euripides. Deborah Carlson describes the Tektaş Burnu wreck and its excavation here.

The Kyrenia ship, built in the 4th century BC, has become the hallmark of nautical archaeology in the Mediterranean. It not only was the first shipwreck of its period fully excavated, but it was the first ancient hull ever raised from the Mediterranean

Archaeology student Deniz Soyarslan raises a large shallow bowl from the Pabuç Burnu shipwreck site. Items such as this, intended for shipboard use, are frequently found in the galley area of a wreck, usually located toward the stern of the vessel.

Above **Three rows of millstones from Nisyros lie centered over the Kyrenia ship's keel, serving for trade and ballast. Rhodian amphoras are stacked above them.**

Below **Places mentioned in this section, with the featured wrecks in bold.**

and reassembled on land. Further, two full-scale replicas have been built to show the public, from Greece and Cyprus to the United States and Japan, the exact appearance of the ships on which the ancient Greeks were so dependent. Even more, one of these replicas sailed from Greece to Cyprus and back, demonstrating its seaworthiness when going through a gale. Susan Womer Katzev, a driving force in the ship's excavation and conservation along with her late husband Michael, has taken time from completing the definitive scholarly publication of the site to share some of the highlights of the project here.

Although it sank about a quarter century later, it seems that the Kyrenia ship was built before the death of Alexander the Great in 323 BC. Thus we consider it a Classical Greek ship. After Alexander's death, three of his generals divided his empire among themselves, starting the two-century age known today as the Hellenistic Period.

INA has partly excavated two Hellenistic wrecks, one in Italy, at La Secca di Capistello, described here by Donald Frey, and the other at Serçe Limanı, Turkey, described by Cemal Pulak. Because of extreme conditions – the depth of the former and the fact that the latter was found to be partly covered by a rockslide of huge boulders – neither of these excavations has yet been completed.

As these lines are being written, INA archaeologists off the coast of Turkey are examining other 6th- and 5th-century BC wrecks to see if any are worthy of full-scale excavation. Annual surveys have revealed the locations of over 150 ancient wrecks on just a small part of that coast, but we believe that a wreck should not be touched unless it offers much new information about the past.

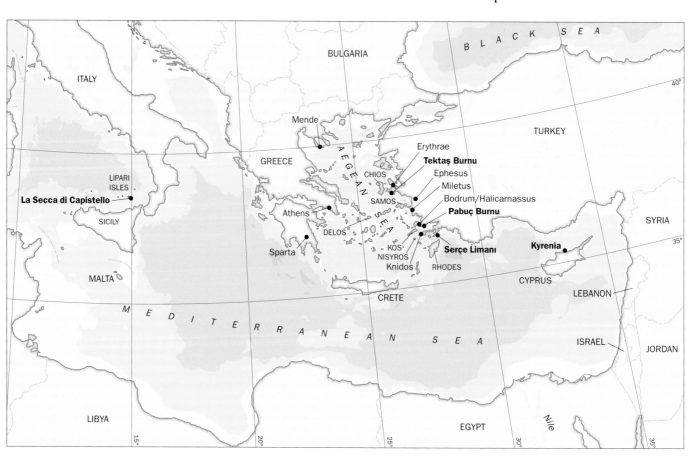

An Archaic Ship Finally Reaches Port: Pabuç Burnu, Turkey

ELIZABETH GREENE

Pabuç Burnu

Date   6th century BC
Depth   42–45 m (139–149 ft)
Found by   Selim Dincer
Excavation   2002–2003
Number of hours on wreck   921.4
Amphoras onboard ship   c 200
Hull   c 20 m (65 ft) long

From INA's submersible *Carolyn*, Feyyaz Subay and George Bass (right) watch Mutlu Gunay uncovering an amphora from the Pabuç Burnu site during the 2001 survey.

"Is it really a shipwreck?" photographer Don Frey wondered aloud. Don had just surfaced from an exploratory dive to investigate a scatter of ceramics reported by Turkish diver Selim Dincer. Intact and broken amphoras, or two-handled storage jars, dotted the sloping surface of the seabed 40 m (132 ft) underwater off the coast of Pabuç Burnu. "Shoe Point," shaped like a curved sandal, lies about 35 km (21 miles) from Bodrum, the site of ancient Halicarnassus, where the tomb built by King Mausolus became one of the seven wonders of the ancient world.

George Bass, director of the 2001 survey, felt sure it was a wreck when, from the submersible *Carolyn*, he watched Mutlu Gunay lift an amphora from the sand, revealing a nearly intact wine pitcher beneath. These must mark more than the cargo jettisoned from a ship in distress. The team's spirits rose higher after Mark Lawall, an amphora expert at the University of Manitoba, dated an emailed photograph of one of the jars to the mid-6th century BC. No shipwreck from the Archaic Period, which laid the foundation for the glory of Classical Greece, had ever been excavated in the Eastern Mediterranean!

As George and I wrote proposals for the project, we wondered, "What picture can we draw of Archaic trade?" From land excavations and literature, scholars construct images of the Greek tyrants who acquired exotic items through gift-exchange, much like the aristocrats of Homer's *Iliad* and *Odyssey*. We imagined the treasures we might find: the richly painted wine cups of lyric poets who composed songs for drinking parties, or the bronzes dedicated in great sanctuaries like Hera's temple on the island of Samos. But the fact that we conducted two seasons of excavation without discovering any commodity that could be labeled as luxurious forced us to consider what other goods moved throughout the Mediterranean.

The Cargo

Instead of painted pottery or the precious metals valued by an elite aristocracy, the majority of artifacts found on the Pabuç Burnu shipwreck are intact and broken amphoras, crafted perhaps at the nearby sites of Knidos, Ephesus, or Miletus. Ancient documents give a sense of the goods transported by the traders of the Greek East: Miletus was famed for its wool, Chios for its wine, Rhodes for sponges, Knidos for herbs, and Kos for raisins. Indeed, the sieved contents of our amphoras yielded grape seeds and olive pits – hints to stores of wine and oil, capped by tree bark stoppers. On the seabed, loose seeds suggest another cargo of foodstuffs, loaded on the ship in sacks along with other now-lost organic goods.

Day after day of excavation yielded thousands of amphora sherds, their scattered

distribution perhaps caused by the trawling nets of modern fishermen. In a discrete area of the site, lying on the upper slope of the seabed, a number of rough pitchers, cooking bowls, and cups mark the ship's galley, or kitchen area, in the stern of the vessel. These locally produced wares were likely used by members of the ship's crew for cooking, dining, and shipboard sacrifice, rather than destined for trade. A lone stone anchor stock, located in the center of the site, suggests a moderate-sized vessel, slightly smaller than the 22 m (73 ft) spread of ceramic remains. All of these remains were placed on a three-dimensional site plan made from digital photography and computer modeling.

Above **These large shallow bowls or *mortaria*, discovered in what was probably the ship's galley area, may have been used on board by the ship's crew for preparing food.**

Left **Over 200 intact and broken transport amphoras once carried the ship's primary cargo of wine or olive oil. From their size, shape, and diagnostic features, amphora specialist Mark Lawall suggests an origin in nearby Knidos, Ephesus, Miletus, or even Halicarnassus.**

Right **Discovered in the center of the wreck site, this large stone anchor stock weighs about 115 kg (250 lb). It would have helped the anchor's wooden flukes, now consumed by marine organisms, grab the sea floor.**

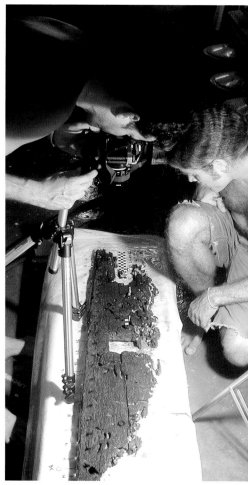

Above **INA Conservator Asaf Oron aids Assistant Excavation Director Mark Polzer (right) in his recording of the hull remains. On the edge of the plank, the lacing holes indicative of the ship's construction are clearly visible.**

Left **Archaeologist Robin Piercy excavates one of six fragmentary planks from the ship's hull. This one measures over 2 m (6.6 ft) in length and preserves evidence of the lacing techniques used to hold the vessel together.**

Construction

Don's initial doubts about the site were fully resolved by the middle of the first excavation campaign, when he sent up a note from the decompression stop. "Today *is* the day! I've found the hull." With excitement, Robin Piercy and I began work in the area on our next dive. As we moved sand with airlifts, Robin bubbled at me enthusiastically through his regulator, then made sewing motions with his free hand. Through our masks, we saw triangular holes on the edges of the plank that marked its construction; the ship's pine planks had been laced together like a sneaker, an appropriate find off the coast of Shoe Point.

Echoes of Homeric poetry ran through my mind as I looked at the plank. Before his departure from the island of Calypso, the hero Odysseus builds a boat for his journey:

He felled twenty trees in all, and shaped them with his bronze axe,
and smoothed them expertly, and trued them straight to a chalkline.
Meanwhile Calypso, the shining goddess, brought him an auger
and he bored through them all and fitted them to each other
with dowels, and then with cords he lashed his boat together
(*Odyssey*, Book 5.244–48)

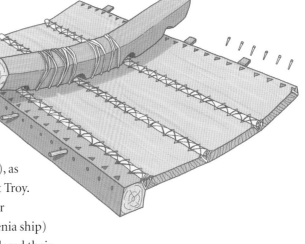

Below **Mark Polzer's study of the hull remains suggests this reconstruction. Dowels and tenons formed the preliminary method of joinery before the hull planks were laced together. Lashed frames were then inserted to reinforce the vessel.**

As Assistant Excavation Director Mark Polzer has determined through careful research on the hull remains, construction features of the Pabuç Burnu wreck call such details to mind: widely spaced dowels join the planks in preparation for the laces that held them together. It may be cords and rotting hull planks like these that King Agamemnon laments in the second book of the *Iliad* (2.135), as he describes the damage wrought to the ships by nine long years of disuse at Troy. Before the East Greek tyrants such as Polycrates of Samos adopted sturdier "modern" building techniques (or mortise-and-tenon joints, as on the Kyrenia ship) in the late 6th century BC for their multi-level triremes, they appear to have laced their vessels together.

What boats did the Greeks imagine the heroes of Homeric poetry sailed? What vessels carried wandering sages like Thales and Pythagoras? And what cargoes did ships bear other than wisdom or the spoils of war? Ventures must have included the occasional jaunts of local farmers, like those to whom the Archaic poet Hesiod offers advice. Recommending journeys in late summer, after the harvest and before the autumn rains, Hesiod cautions (*Works and Days* 689–91), "Do not put all your goods in hollow ships; leave the greater part behind and put the smaller part on board; for it is a bad business to face disaster among the sea's waves." With its cargo of wine, olive oil, grapes, and organics stored in locally crafted amphoras, the wreck at Pabuç Burnu may represent just such a voyage: of a moderate-sized merchant vessel, carrying goods from a collective of farmers, that met ruin on the wine-dark seas.

Left **On this 6th-century BC Attic black-figure cup in the British Museum, a pirate galley powered by sail and oars chases down a tubby merchant vessel that may resemble the Pabuç Burnu ship.**

A Wreck from the Golden Age of Greece: Tektaş Burnu, Turkey

DEBORAH CARLSON

Tektaş Burnu

Date   440–425 BC
Depth   38–45 m (125–149 ft)
Found by   INA survey, 1996
Excavation   1999–2001
Number of dives   5,046
Amphoras   213

I will never forget the first time I saw the cliffs at Tektaş Burnu. It was June of 1999 and three of us – Murat Tilev, William Murray, and myself – had been sent ahead as a scouting party to assess the site's livability. What greeted us was a towering wall of razor-sharp, jagged spires of rock separated by deep, dark crevices. Weeks earlier, Murat, with several workmen, had driven pieces of angle iron into the rock and welded them together as a steel framework that, he hoped, would serve as the foundation for a dive platform. Within weeks, however, waves had utterly destroyed this experimental platform, pitching the arc welder into the sea, and leaving behind

Below **The *Artemis*, a wooden-hulled US Navy minesweeper-turned-passenger ship that housed the 1999 team, anchored in the lee of Tektaş Burnu, the "Cape of the Lone Rock." In the distance is the lone island that gives the cape its name.**

Above **The so-called Siren Vase of *c* 480 BC shows Odysseus tied to the mast of his ship while the singing Sirens attempt to divert him and his shipmates. The bow is outfitted with eyes similar to those found at Tektaş Burnu.**

Below right **Once on the sea bed, divers often removed their fins in order to negotiate the amphora mound without damaging artifacts or compromising visibility.**

only gnarled bits of steel that looked to me like tiny, twisted pipe cleaners.

What had brought us to Tektaş Burnu – Turkish for "Cape of the Lone Rock" – were the remains of a Greek shipwreck from the 5th century BC, what archaeologists call the Classical Period. This was the century in which the Greeks decisively defeated the invading Persian army, and Athens built a vast maritime empire funded in large part by tribute exacted from all Greek cities allied against the Persians. But the Athenians' domineering tactics earned them the resentment of the Spartans, and by the last quarter of the 5th century the two Greek superpowers had dissolved into civil war – the Peloponnesian War.

Shipping of both commercial and strategic goods played a vital role in the history of Classical Greece, yet no 5th-century shipwreck had been excavated in its entirety in the Aegean Sea.

The Tektaş Burnu wreck had been found in 1996, during one of INA's annual surveys of the Turkish coast, this one directed by Tufan Turanlı. As with most ancient shipwrecks, all that was visible of the ship was a portion of its cargo – a small mound of about 60 amphoras heaped on a sloping ledge between 38 and 45 m (125 and 149 ft) deep. The amphora mound was so small that on my first dive to the wreck in 1999 I swam right past it! Divers on the 1996 survey raised two amphoras from the site:

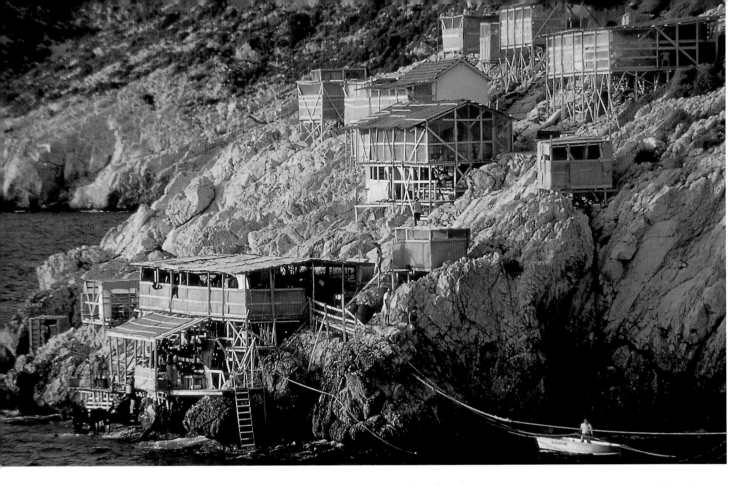

one could not be identified with certainty, but the other had been produced in the northern Greek city of Mende some time between 450 and 425 BC. The team was surprised to find that the Mendean amphora was filled with dark, gooey pine tar, still viscous and odorous after nearly 2,500 years on the seabed!

As the field director, it was my job to report our impressions of that unforgettable visit in 1999 to the overall director of the project, George Bass. It was clear to all who had visited the site that the construction of any facilities on the rocks above the wreck would require a substantial investment of time and labor. George decided that we could simultaneously initiate both excavation of the wreck and construction of a camp if we could find a ship large enough to house our team of more than 30 students, professionals and INA staff. The challenge was to find such a vessel.

Preparations

After weeks of searching, we found the *Artemis*, a decrepit, 45 m (150 ft) long, wooden-hulled former US Navy minesweeper, which had been converted into a passenger ship that could accommodate upwards of 50 people in 28 berths.

Unfortunately, the challenge of finding the *Artemis* proved to be nothing compared with the daily stress of living aboard. Electrical failures were routine, and the pumps never worked properly, so that fresh water seldom reached the galley or bathrooms, and bilge water had to be pumped out manually, leaving the cabins on the lower deck in a chronic state of unbearable sogginess. Project historian William Murray, inspecting the *Artemis* during the ship's first days at Tektaş Burnu, observed: "There is a shark's bite out of the ship's stern, and the patch looks like someone nailed

Above **The 2000 camp at Tektaş Burnu became a permanent summer home for almost 30 people. The structures nearest the sea are the artifact conservation facility and dive platform, while the higher buildings include dormitories and a galley for meals and meetings.**

half of a ping-pong table to the transom and then stuffed Styrofoam around the edges on the starboard quarter." In addition to a smattering of other, smaller holes in the hull, the bowlines were badly frayed, and the rusty anchor chain terminated in an anchor of unknown size and dubious quality. The anchor was put to the test, however, during an extremely windy morning in August, when I emerged from my cabin and saw that the camp was unusually far away. A quick check revealed that both bowlines had parted and the ship was drifting frighteningly close to the rocky coast. It seems the *Artemis* might well have become the second ship wrecked at Tektaş Burnu, if the rusty anchor chain had not held long enough for us to secure new lines to shore.

The unpredictable and increasingly unpleasant living conditions aboard the *Artemis* hastened camp construction on the rocks, guided by the creative genius of INA's Robin Piercy. Unfortunately, the pace of progress on the seabed was conspicuously slower, due to a delay that year in the issuance of our excavation permit. As if sensing our frustration, however, the Turkish Ministry of Culture granted us permission to prepare the site for excavation, which meant that our team was able to dive on the wreck to set up safety equipment and install datum stakes and towers in preparation for mapping the site.

When our excavation permit arrived toward the middle of August, the majority of the team was set to return to their respective universities, leaving a small group to carry out the excavation. We moved ashore and watched *Artemis* steam away – forever, as it turned out, since she later ran aground, a total loss.

Initial Excavation

Though few in number, initial finds provided an unexpectedly accurate snapshot of the ship's cargo: large transport amphoras, smaller flat-bottomed jugs called table amphoras, oil lamps, shallow one-handled bowls, and black glazed drinking cups. Each amphora, once raised, was carefully emptied and its contents sieved in search of botanical remains such as grape seeds and pollen grains. In the case of one

Above **Archaeologist Elizabeth Greene produces one of more than a dozen table amphoras excavated from the wreck. Most were lined with pitch, suggesting that they were intended for transporting and serving wine.**

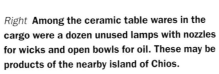

Left **Travis Mason and Mutlu Gunay examine the contents of an amphora after sieving for macrobotanical remains. On occasion archaeologists recovered small nails, tacks, and pottery fragments that had been pulled inside amphoras by resident octopuses – one amphora even produced an intact oil lamp.**

Right **Among the ceramic table wares in the cargo were a dozen unused lamps with nozzles for wicks and open bowls for oil. These may be products of the nearby island of Chios.**

A Wreck from the Golden Age of Greece: Tektaş Burnu, Turkey　　**67**

Mendean amphora, sieving proved impossible because the jar was chock-full of butchered cattle bones, mostly ribs and tail bones – presumably the remains of salted beef, an uncommon commodity in the ancient world, and a powerful reminder that transport amphoras were used to ship far more than just wine and olive oil (and pine tar!).

A fascinating artifact appeared during the 1999 excavation campaign in the loose sand at the shallow end of the wreck: a white marble disk about the size of a saucer, incised with concentric lines and pierced through the middle by a large lead spike. Many of us were initially quite puzzled by the find, and various interpretations were advanced: was it an axle, part of a child's toy, or an obscure calendrical device? Perhaps it was the lid of an elaborate box or part of an ancient sculpture? Team members Troy Nowak and Jeremy Green simultaneously but independently identified the mysterious object as one of the ship's two eyes, or *ophthalmoi,* which would have adorned the bow of the vessel on either side of the stem. This contradicted the view that eyes in antiquity were simply painted on ships, as they are in the Mediterranean today. The second *ophthalmos* was discovered the following year, just meters away from where the first had surfaced.

Trials of Camp Life

Life on the rocks at Tektaş Burnu had its own set of challenges, which included biting flies, grasshoppers the size of a human fist, seasonal moth swarms, and the occasional rat, snake and scorpion. The winds that had snapped the bowlines of the *Artemis* were the *meltem,* which typically arrived after lunch and could agitate the sea sufficiently to make afternoon diving a harrowing experience. The "Cape of the Lone Rock" lay virtually totally exposed to the northwest – the source of the *meltem,* which could reach gale force overnight and was consequently responsible for many sleepless nights in camp. But these occasional hardships were offset by evenings of staggering sunsets and nights under a breathtaking canopy of stars.

Despite our initial success in taming the raw wilderness of Tektaş Burnu – which George deemed the most inhospitable place he has ever worked – we did receive an occasional reminder that Poseidon was ultimately the one in charge. As the 1999 season drew to a close, we opted to leave most of the camp structures standing, knowing that we would return to Tektaş Burnu the following summer. In an effort to protect the two enormous one-ton generators that had been hoisted onto shore in order to power the camp, we hauled them up and far away from the water, covering them with plastic sheets and huge metal cases. Still, to our dismay, rough seas brought by winter storms plucked one of these two massive machines from the rocks and hurled it into the sea more than 40 m (132 ft) down.

Productive Dives

We salvaged the lost generator, along with the welder that had earlier suffered the same fate, and returned to Tektaş Burnu in June of 2000 for what was to be our most productive summer. In just 12 weeks, our team of more than two dozen archaeologists excavated the bulk of the amphora mound and much of the surrounding area, systematically uncovering, mapping and raising an impressive array of artifacts that included cooking pots, drinking cups, and a large decorated

Above **Archaeologist Ken Trethewey uncovers the second of the ship's two marble eyes, or** *ophthalmoi.* **Ancient Greek mariners gave eyes to a ship to help it see its way through treacherous seas, a phenomenon that is still common in parts of the Mediterranean.**

Right In camp, team members spent hours mapping and digitally modeling artifacts to produce an accurate final site plan of the wreck, shown overleaf.

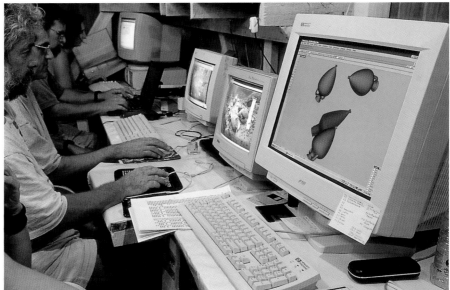

Above This Greek *alabastron*, an alabaster container for perfumed oil, came from the ship's stern area.

Below Each of the Tektaş Burnu anchors was manufactured by pouring molten lead into a wooden stock. Earlier anchor stocks, like those from Pabuç Burnu, were of stone, while later anchors often had stocks made entirely of lead. Four lead cores are all that remain of the anchors after more than two millennia on the seabed (*below right*). Each of the two cores to the right has a cylindrical casting bolt protruding from its center, which indicates that the original wooden stock was about 4 cm (1.5 in) thick.

decanter called an *askos*. Other objects seemed to be of a more personal nature: a lone alabaster bottle for holding perfumed oil, small square tiles of animal bone (perhaps gaming pieces), and an unusual ceramic lamp, different from the others, with a thick, heavy base and deep oil well that made it ideal for use on board a ship at sea. Scattered about the wreck in sets of two or four we located 14 notched lead bars, the remnants of five wooden anchor stocks, which had been hollowed out and filled with molten lead to give the anchor weight.

Working dives at Tektaş Burnu typically lasted 20 minutes, and on an average day about 15 divers would visit the wreck in both the morning and afternoon, meaning that we spent a combined daily total of at least ten hours under water. But one team member, who made her debut at Tektaş Burnu in 2000, was unlike any of us inasmuch as she could stay on the bottom for hours on end. She was *Carolyn*, a two-person

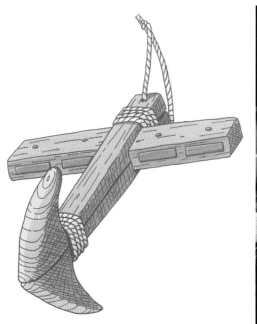

submersible that joined the INA fleet primarily as a survey tool, but which proved to be a useful addition to the excavation at Tektaş Burnu. The *Carolyn* made it possible for George or myself to study the progress of the excavation over a period of hours, instead of mere minutes, and make suggestions or alterations in order to improve our level of efficiency.

Working under water is really all about striking a balance between precision and speed, organizing your dive, your equipment, and your thoughts so as not to waste a second of time on the seabed. At Tektaş Burnu, one aspect of the excavation that was made markedly more efficient was the mapping of the site, which relied on a system of photogrammetry designed by Tufan Turanlı and fine-tuned by Jeremy Green and Sheila Matthews. In essence, Tufan or Jeremy recorded the provenience of each object using calibrated digital cameras, and then processed the digital images to create a three-dimensional map of coordinates. In a separate process, Sheila digitally modeled each artifact individually, and then inserted the image onto the pre-existing coordinates, creating a very realistic computer-generated site plan with centimeter accuracy.

We returned to Tektaş Burnu with a small team to complete the excavation in 2001. By this third season, our camp had become a kind of palatial summer retreat complete with a dishwasher and flushing toilets. Only the dive platform, which was nearest sea level, had to be rebuilt at the beginning of every summer. The 2001 season, however, brought with it some particularly inclement weather, and just days after the completion of our new dive platform, the enormous swells of a fast-approaching storm dismantled the platform in less than an hour. On the wreck, it seemed even the local marine life was ready for us to depart Tektaş Burnu. When on one dive I descended to excavate a small cluster of three amphoras, I arrived to find a 3-m (10-ft) long moray eel coiled like a cobra ready to strike. I might have found the courage to stand tall, had not Robin Piercy earlier been bitten on the foot by another moray!

EPY

George is fond of saying that the most exciting archaeological discoveries are made in the library, sometimes long after the excavation is finished. To be honest, this rubric had always struck me as something one says to conciliate those who have not experienced the thrill (and exhaustion) of three months in the field. But I will admit now that, for me, the most meaningful moment of the Tektaş Burnu shipwreck excavation occurred neither at Tektaş Burnu nor during the excavation, but in the Bodrum Museum of Underwater Archaeology, one year after the excavation was over.

It was the first study season, and three of us – Kristine Trego, Catharine Corder, and myself – were busy taking artifact photographs and gathering volumetric data on more than 100 intact transport amphoras. While measuring the capacity of one jar, Kristine noticed that it had been stamped on the neck with an unusual mark: a circle framing the Greek letters EPY – Epsilon, Rho, Upsilon. We immediately recognized this as the abbreviation of Erythrae, an ancient Greek city on the western coast of Turkey not far from Tektaş Burnu.

In antiquity, Erythrae and 11 neighboring cities and islands along the western coast of Turkey were part of a region called Ionia. It was the Ionian Greeks who, by revolting from the Persian Empire in 499 BC, precipitated the Persian invasion of

Above **A digital site plan – another INA first – shows how the vessel came to rest between two large rock outcrops in an area roughly 12 m (36 ft) long and 4 m (12 ft) wide. The rocks kept the hull exposed to marine organisms which devoured the wood.**

Above right **An artist's rendering of the ship sinking at Tektaş Burnu. The absence of any plainly personal items on the wreck suggests that the crew had sufficient time to escape with their possessions.**

Left **The only lettered amphora stamp from Tektaş Burnu carries the Greek letters Epsilon, Rho, Upsilon and represents Erythrae, one of the 12 cities of Ionia. Other amphora stamps from the wreck include simple circles and a leaf motif.**

mainland Greece and, ultimately, the Athenian defeat of the Persians 20 years later.

Erythrae's closest neighbor to the west was the island of Chios, visible from Tektaş Burnu on all but the haziest summer days. During the course of the excavation, trips to the Chios Archaeological Museum revealed that several pottery types from Tektaş Burnu had strong Chian parallels, while the presence of a lone Chian amphora enabled us to refine the date of the wreck to between 440 and 425 BC.

The discovery of the EPY amphora stamp not only permitted the identification of a previously unattributed amphora type, but also offered proof of what many of us had long suspected: that the Tektaş Burnu ship was a modest, local merchantman carrying a cargo of wine, pine tar, and East Greek pottery and following a coastal course, probably southward, when it was wrecked off the unforgiving rocky coast of Ionia.

During the second Tektaş Burnu study season, in 2003, Kristine and I were walking along a quay of the Bodrum harbor one evening when we spied a small boat, not more than 10 m (33 ft) long, dwarfed by the *gulets* and their colorful banners advertising exotic daily charters. On the stern of this modest vessel sat an old sailor on a makeshift stool, heating his dinner in a pot by the dim light of a small lamp. Kristine and I stopped, transfixed by the sight of what seemed to us to be a perfect modern rendering of the small-scale merchant venture that ended nearly 2,500 years ago at Tektaş Burnu.

Resurrecting an Ancient Greek Ship: Kyrenia, Cyprus

SUSAN WOMER KATZEV

"The bow plank that was a glowing golden color just last week…it's turning brown. Oxygen must be getting to the wood. We don't dare leave that hull on the bottom over another winter. But how are we going to raise her?" Laina Wylde Swiny, architect in charge of mapping the ancient ship, up from her morning dive, voiced our worst fears. Were we about to lose the precious treasure lying 27 m (90 ft) below…the most perfectly preserved ancient Greek ship ever found?

It all began in the autumn of 1965. Town councilman Andreas Cariolou, diving for sponges, chanced upon a mound of 80 graceful amphoras emerging from a carpet of eel grass on the flat seabed less than a mile from Kyrenia, his home on the north coast of Cyprus. For two years he kept his secret until meeting my husband Michael Katzev and me and guiding us over the wreck. In the most dramatic dive of our lives we were alone with the ancient jars, now homes for darting squirrelfish, untouched by man for 2,300 years.

Two summers of excavation peeled away layers of cargo, dining wares, tools, ship's rigging, and even four bone eyelets from a sailor's sandals. Cradling them like open hands was the still curving ship that had borne them from foreign ports and at last took them to the sea floor. Sixty percent of the ship and more than 75 percent of her representative timbers lay exposed. How could we raise the softened wood before the coming autumn storms?

The ship had sunk on an even keel, her cargo intact, striking the soft bottom and then rolling onto her port side. While currents slowly buried and preserved that side, the bow and stern broke away under the weight of an anchor, amphoras, millstones, and iron ingots. Then the exposed starboard side, easy prey to teredo worms, fell

Kyrenia

Built c 325–315 BC
Sunk c 295–285 BC
Depth 27–30 m (89–99 ft)
Found by Andreas Cariolou
Excavation 1968–1969
Conservation 1969–1974
Team 54 (international)
Total cost $300,000
Hull 14 m (47 ft) long, 4.2 m (14.5 ft) wide

Right **With plastic grid frames and one last amphora still in place, the preserved hull is ready for lifting. This bow view shows how the ship broke apart. To the right on the better preserved port side jagged lead sheathing projects beyond the ribs. A few years before sinking this last repair was meant to keep her watertight.**

Opposite above **The author's first dive over the mound of amphoras from Rhodes that was the tombstone for the Kyrenia Ship.**

outward, breaking off from the keel and leaving most of the cargo compressed in the better-preserved port side. Could we raise each side intact? We learned through the American Embassy that no helicopter in the Mediterranean was capable of hoisting 5 tons of our ship off the bottom. We would have to take the delicate hull apart piece by piece.

With rolls of Dymo tape, Laina labeled every scrap of wood. Using three different methods of mapping for insurance, our 54-member team recorded the hull with stereo photos, manual triangulation, and a new invention of movable vertical rods called "the cheesecutter".

As the first autumn storm strained the moorings of our diving barge, the last lifting trays of wood broke surface and reached the safety of a fresh-water holding pool inside a vaulted gallery of the massive Crusader castle that dominates Kyrenia harbor. Like first parents we scrubbed, bathed, and photographed each timber, then catalogued and made full-scale tracings of each side until thousands of pieces of the old ship were safely recorded. It took seven people five years. Our goal was to preserve and reassemble the original ship inside this gallery.

"We cannot settle for less than 100 percent saturation," said conservator Frances Talbot Vassiliades, fresh from studies at London University. "Look how this test piece twisted and shrank at lower concentrations…we cannot risk doing that just to save time. So let's start figuring on years, not months of treatment." The saturation would be with a water-soluble wax called polyethylene glycol, PEG for short. Visits to European labs had shown that PEG was our only hope. But no one had yet reached 100 percent saturation. So riddled was our ship's Aleppo pine with ancient teredo worms that the timbers easily soaked up the preservative in heated tanks. Almonds treated in seven months, but hull members demanded over a year for each tank load.

At the end, 6,000 separate pieces of the Hellenistic ship lay successfully preserved on shelves in the castle. But who could put Humpty-Dumpty back together again?

Just as Michael Katzev's first lecture in Cyprus had brought the tip leading to Andreas and this spectacular wreck, Michael's lecture in Lancaster, Pennsylvania, attracted the attention of electrical contractor J. Richard Steffy. Dick Steffy's basement models were already testing construction theories for the Yassıada Byzantine ship, but the chance to work on an actual hull sparked him to leave his comfortable business, move with his wife and two sons to Cyprus, and immerse himself in unraveling the secrets contained in the ship's timbers.

The Ship Speaks

Over four years, aided by Michael and apprentices Robin Piercy and Chip Vincent, Dick pieced the Kyrenia ship back together, pinning the brittle wax-treated timbers to each other using stainless steel rods. "The men who built the Kyrenia ship were real craftsmen," he says. "In fact they were sculptors. Today we are in a hurry and we penny-pinch to use the least materials. So we start a ship by building a skeleton of ribs, or "frames," bolted to the keel, and then we wrap sawn boards around the outside to plank the ship. Kyrenia's builders adzed those outer planks first. They carved away over 70 percent of the original wood to sculpt the entire outer shell, without an interior framework."

Like weaving a basket upwards, the shipwrights joined the first carved plank to the keel using mortise cuttings linked with oak tenons spaced every 12 cm (4.7 in). Pegs locked them together. It took nearly 4,000 mortise-and-tenon joints to attach all the

Far left **Unloading tanks of now waxy wood, team members Laina Wylde Swiny (left), David Steffy, author Susan Katzev and Netia Piercy sponge off excess wax, then bag the timbers to cool slowly.** *Left* **Pieces of the ship's flooring lie atop full-scale tracings on archival mylar. Found fragmented from the weight under water of the millstones and amphoras, these planks bear 22 carved Greek letters, their meaning a mystery.** *Right* **Masking tape alignments guide Dick Steffy as he drills a long stainless steel rod to join the wax-filled original timbers.** *Far right* **The late excavation director Michael Katzev (left) discusses the ship's original lines with Dick Steffy. Katzev's 30 years of research on the ship will be published in INA's Nautical Archaeology Series by a team of specialists.**

Above **The hull fully reconstructed, representing over four years' work by Dick Steffy and his apprentices.**

pre-carved planks edge to edge over the whole 14 m (47 ft) length of the ship, fitting them so tightly that no caulking was needed. Only after eight or nine of the 13 planking rows were securely linked did the Greeks shape the first ribs to fit inside the shell. Driving pure copper spikes from outside through the ribs and clenching them down like staples, the builders locked the ribs in place to stiffen the ship. But the shell of planks was the ship's true strength.

Life on Board

Launched close to the year Alexander died, 323 BC, our merchantman must have moved tons of cargo through the eastern Mediterranean in the turbulent years when Alexander's surviving generals were carving his empire into kingdoms of their own.

Rhodes, the most prosperous island in the region, whose merchants the orator Lycurgus said, "sail the entire civilized world for trade," used her navy and diplomacy to remain independent of the generals. I believe our merchant captain could have homeported in one of her thriving harbors and that his name began with the letters EUP, which he scratched into the base of a plate designed for dipping tidbits of fish into a spicy sauce. He needed to be literate to keep his books and deal with harbor documents. We found his inkwell and perhaps a personalized wine amphora marked EU. Much of the ship's black glazed pottery lay in two distinct areas – the far bow and stern. A short deck in the bow carried a wooden anchor, its stock filled with poured lead as on the Tektaş Burnu ship (see page 69). Clusters of small folded lead weights tell us that one of two fishing nets was on this deck. In foul weather, the crew slept in the open space below, among seven amphoras from Samos filled with over 10,000 almonds.

Above **Jill Scott Black holds the smallest of the ten types of amphoras. The different shapes identified the city or island producing them and can even reveal the approximate date.**

Below **The ship's pottery served a crew of four. Behind the ladle is a specialty plate designed for dipping tidbits of fish into sauce in the center depression, its base inscribed EUP. Above it, the captain's inkwell.**

How many men lived aboard this trader, 14 m (47 ft) long by 4.2 m (14.5 ft) wide? Four oil jugs, four identical drinking cups, four salt dishes, four wine pitchers and four wooden spoons tell the story of a captain and three sailors.

Aft of the foredeck rose the single mast carrying a broad square sail, which reefed upwards through lead brail rings like a Venetian blind. Beside the mast lay logs useful for making on board repairs and iron tools to shape them. Dick thinks a ton or two of cargo is missing from the bow, probably perishables such as food stuffs or cloth.

Loading Up

I picture our captain and crew at Rhodes loading for their last voyage. They already had the almond-filled Samian jars stowed bow and stern, along with the perishables mentioned above, and a leftover shipment of 29 heavy millstones fashioned on the nearby volcanic island of Nisyros. The odd number, and a lack of matching pairs, suggests that they were sold singly to replace bakers' broken stones, meanwhile serving as ballast in three rows centered over the keel.

Now they filled the open hold with Rhodian amphoras, their conical shape handy for wedging in across the wide-bellied ship. Some jars were stamped on their handles with names of potters, magistrates, or traders, and all had been swirled inside with hot, black pine pitch to make them watertight. The wine they carried – most likely the popular table wine Rhodes exported north to the Black Sea and south to Egypt – took on the resin flavor that survives as "retsina" in modern Greece.

Each full amphora weighs 41 kg (90 lb). We think a circular bronze strap and ring were the end of a hoist our crew used to lift each jar off the dock, swing it inside, and lower it into the neat stacking pattern we found. On Cyprus we made replica amphoras and practiced loading them with all 17 tons of cargo found on the original ship into a sailing replica named *Kyrenia Liberty. Liberty* is equipped with her own hoist, called a "mast derrick." Using pulleys and a hook just like one found in excavation, a crew of four could load a grain mill or offload a full amphora in just 20 seconds. At this rate the entire cargo could easily be loaded in a morning. All together over 380 amphoras in ten different shapes were aboard when the ship left harbor heading east to Cyprus. Just-harvested millet, grape seeds and almonds tell us the season was September or October, and coins and amphoras indicate the year was about 295 to 285 BC.

The helmsman on the aft deck steered with two oars called "quarter rudders." We found the blade of the starboard rudder lying outside the collapsed stern. Through the hatch near his feet, the captain could drop down into the only closed cabin. Here was a cargo of nearly pure iron ingots; a spare sail, its many lead rings sewn in rows; spare rope and tackle; and a bow drill and other ship's tools. All were preserved inside a large concretion that formed around the iron ingots. A tiny votive lamp, the captain's inkwell, an elegant bronze ladle ending in a duck's head, a fish hook, and many studded nails, possibly decorating a wooden box, were cemented in the mass. The captain's drinking cup and inscribed plate lay nearby.

Here, too, was a marble ceremonial basin resembling a modern birdbath. Such basins are found in sanctuaries and shipwrecks, reminding us of references to ceremonies asking and thanking Poseidon for safe passage. Perhaps our captain was prepared to give thanks for safe arrival in Kyrenia. Whether he ever entered the harbor we will never know.

Why Did She Sink?

"All those years of voyaging had taken their toll," Dick learned. "The Kyrenia ship was tired and weak." After many repairs, with a patched bow and years of teredo worm damage, she had been sheathed in lead as a last effort to keep her watertight. The golden plank Laina had seen was a recent repair. But under the millstones, years of bilge water had softened the old ship's backbone, and the lack of attachment between ribs and keel proved the ship's "Achilles heel."

Did the captain, knowing of the accumulated ravages from decades at sea, decide to give it all up and scuttle his ship to cover up some shady deal?

The riddle of her sinking, within sight of Kyrenia, remains unsolved. Violent storms drive down from the Taurus mountains of southern Turkey without warning, and Kyrenia's ancient harbor may have been dangerously exposed. Before the modern breakwater was built the locals always put to sea in the face of incoming storms. Perhaps our merchantman was attempting this maneuver when her old hull finally failed. With no natural hazards to wreck her, this seemed the best explanation until, years into studying the artifacts, we came upon unexpected finds.

"Spears! These are spearheads or maybe javelin tips, and there are eight of them. Look, four have lead sheathing, even scraps of wood attached, and one tip is bent. What were spears doing underneath the hull?" Michael had just sawn apart small lumps of iron concretion that had lain on our storeroom shelves since being found some years after the ship was raised. Then he cleaned iron dust from inside the molds and made rubber casts of the rusty

Above **Found beneath the hull, eight iron spearhead or javelin tips survived to be cast in these rubber replicas. Their presence hints at piracy to explain the ship's sinking.**

Below **A reconstruction of the ship as she may have looked, with cutaway areas to show the cargo and construction techniques used. Lead sheathing ensured that the hull remained watertight.**

RICHARD SCHLECHT

Left **Fitting outer planks together over close-spaced tenons, shipyard owner Manolis Psaros (below) and master shipwright Michaelis Oikonomou of Perama, Greece, recreate ancient shell-first construction.**

originals – light javelin heads. Had the ship sunk on the site of a previous naval battle? Unlikely. But what if these javelins had been imbedded in our hull during a pirate attack? In a Greek vase painting a pirate ship appears ready to ram a merchantman in her starboard bow. In this area of our ship no wood survived, but our worm-riddled bow would have offered little resistance. Possibly attackers drove javelins into the hull to pull their craft alongside for boarding. With the bow slowly taking water, there would have been time for pirates to snatch up valuables and take captive the four mariners, leaving the ship to sink. Slave markets prospered in Delos, Crete, Syria and the nearby south Turkish coast. But in a kinder scenario, captives could also be ransomed back to their families.

In Alexander's wake, his Macedonian general Antigonus, with his son Demetrius, were now at war with the Egyptian general Ptolemy I. Caught between were the islands of Cyprus and Rhodes. In 306 BC Demetrius captured Cyprus from Ptolemy, then turned his attention to independent Rhodes, sending ships to seize any merchants sailing to Egypt from Rhodes. When the Rhodians refused to yield, Demetrius besieged their island for a year, spreading the noose of his navy and pirates to intercept Rhodian shipping. With Ptolemy's aid the Rhodians broke the siege, preserving their sovereignty. But the seas of the eastern Mediterranean teemed with pirates for years to come.

Piracy would explain why certain things one might expect to find are missing from the wreck. Only seven bronze coins minted 306 to 294 BC were found. These were small change, not the high values needed for business. And how could a ship trade without several sizes of bronze balance scales and sets of weights? This most basic equipment found on other wrecks is absent in ours. What happened to the

Left **Inside a full-scale section of the hull made for the ship's museum, builder Robin Piercy adds the central flooring known as "limber boards."**

Below **Kyrenia II, sponsored by the Hellenic Institute for the Preservation of Nautical Tradition in Athens (president: Harry T. Tzalas), cuts through the Aegean on an experimental voyage from Cyprus to Athens. Spanning the open hold are two pairs of oars for use in harbor. All four crewmen are on the aft deck above the single cabin. Lead rings sewn to the outside sail guide the brail lines that raise and lower it. The eye, seen in Greek vase paintings, stares down evil and sees the course ahead. Two marble eyes were found in the bow of the 440–425 BC merchantman at Tektaş Burnu.**

personal possessions of our crew? Four sandal eyelets and two bronze beads were hardly the belongings of four men.

Another sinister surprise waited on the storeroom shelves. A folded lead sheet known as a "curse tablet" had been slipped inside a lead envelope and pierced with a copper spike. Its find spot suggests the spike was driven into the ship's main crossbeam, then clenched downward to hold the curse in place.

Similar tablets found throughout the Greek and Roman world were inscribed with morbid spells naming the curser's enemies and begging gods of the underworld to wreak miseries upon them and their families, dragging their tortured souls down into hell. Tablets found uninscribed, like ours, are thought to be the work of illiterates. Inside our tablet were two pieces of white string, perhaps to bind the accursed down. All materials for the tablet were on board…fish net string, lead sheathing, and the copper spike. Was a seaman disgruntled with the captain? Or had illiterate pirates incanted a spell to bind the sinking ship into the sea? If so, they succeeded…but only for 2,300 years. The old ship has risen to display again the masterful craftsmanship of her builders, and to honor the men who shared her life.

Saturation Diving for Archaeology: La Secca di Capistello, Italy

DONALD A. FREY

La Secca di Capistello

Date 3rd century BC
Depth 59–80 m (195–264 ft)
Excavation 1976–1977
Mixed gas dives 5.5 hours on site
Saturation dives 3 teams, 157 hours on site

I had second thoughts as I stood in my vertical steel coffin and heard the hatch bolted shut. The re-breathing mask strapped over my face only added to my claustrophobia in the cramped Robertina diving bell. Two days earlier I had helped lower the bell to 250 m (825 ft) and seen it come up dry inside. This time I would descend only 65 m (215 ft), where stresses would be considerably reduced. But what would happen if a porthole struck a rock on the slopes below?

As the bell descended I thought about my meetings with Giunio Santi, Director of Subsea Oil Services (SSOS) of Milan. He believed that the deep divers SSOS continually trained would be better motivated if they had something more interesting to occupy them than artificial tasks on the seabed. At the same time, these trainees could excavate deeper than INA divers. We decided to join forces.

Now, on a hot August day in 1976, I was descending into the cool, blue sea to monitor SSOS divers excavating a 3rd-century BC Hellenistic ship that had wrecked at La Secca di Capistello, a reef off Lipari in the Aeolian Sea north of Sicily. Through the bell's ports, I watched and photographed teams of SSOS trainees as they airlifted the sediment covering an intact layer of amphoras. I had chosen the wreck for excavation because it seemed less pillaged than other wrecks I had seen, with George Bass and Robin Piercy, on an INA/SSOS survey several months earlier.

The trainees were learning mixed-gas diving. When breathing compressed air SSOS divers do not work deeper than 50 m (165 ft). But with a nitrogen-free mixture of helium and oxygen, divers can descend hundreds of meters. The expense of mixed-gas diving, and the requisite technical support, had until now precluded archaeologists from excavating shipwrecks deeper than 50 m (165 ft); indeed, an attempt to excavate this wreck on air had ended with the deaths of two German archaeologists in a 1969 diving accident.

In 1977, I returned to La Secca di Capistello with a team being trained for saturation diving. During the previous year, trainees' bottom time was limited to 20 minutes by the need to decompress at the end of each dive, in order to release gradually the nitrogen in their blood that could otherwise form fatal bubbles. Saturation diving overcomes this. At every depth there is a limited amount of dissolved gas the blood will hold – a saturation point. Divers can take advantage of this by diving and living at the same pressure not for minutes, but for *weeks*, before resurfacing through a single, lengthy decompression. On the SSOS training ship *Corsair*, divers lived in a chamber filled with a mixture of helium and oxygen maintained at a pressure equal to that of 60 m (198 ft) of water. Daily they entered a personnel transfer capsule (PTC) locked onto the chamber with the same pressure

Above **Teams of four Italian divers lived for a week at a time inside a pressurized chamber on the training ship** *Corsair*, **and were lowered in this pressurized PTC (personnel transfer capsule) to the wreck, where they could work outside for hours without daily decompression.**

Left **Don Frey enters the Robertina diving bell to be lowered to the site for observation of work in progress.**

Below **Saturation diving allowed careful excavation of cargo and hull at greater depths than scuba divers can work.**

of gas inside. Sealed in the PTC and lowered to the seabed, divers then took turns working outside while breathing the gas mixture through umbilical hoses.

During 21 days, three different groups of four divers lived in the chamber. Each morning and afternoon a two-man team descended to the site to work for about four hours. Sometimes one of the INA archaeologists – Faith Hentschel, Donald Keith, and Michael Katzev – observed the work from the PTC, or from a maneuverable two-person submersible. At other times, we followed progress by closed-circuit television, giving instructions over the divers' umbilicals.

Using closed-circuit television we also obtained exceptionally clear videotapes. These, along with sharp, time-exposure photographs taken by the divers from portable photo towers, allowed us, on *Corsair*, to draw a site plan. As expected, the hull was built in the shell-first manner common to Greco-Roman vessels, its planks held together by mortise-and-tenon joints.

Many of the Greco-Italic amphoras, whose contents included olives, grapes, and pistachio nuts, still had cork stoppers. We could date the cargo to the first quarter of the 3rd century BC by the shapes and decorations of ceramic drinking cups, fish plates, lamps, and black-glazed Campanian wares.

Our La Secca di Capistello excavation was at its time the deepest ever conducted under archaeological controls, and the first use of saturation diving for archaeology. INA had opened a new door to underwater excavations.

Digging into an Avalanche: The Hellenistic Wreck at Serçe Limanı, Turkey

CEMAL PULAK

Serçe Limanı Hellenistic Wreck

Sunk   280–275 BC
Depth   35–37 m (115–121 ft)
Found by   Mehmet Aşkın
Survey   1973, 1977
Excavation   1979–1980
Amphoras onboard ship   c 1,000
Number of dives   c 1,800
Hull   c 18 m (60 ft) long

We were 36 m (118 ft) deep, on a nearly barren seabed. Large boulders lay landward of us. George Bass signaled that we were on the Hellenistic wreck. I strained to see what he had seen, but could make out only occasional amphora fragments, the bits of pottery found nearly everywhere along this coast. Seeing my puzzlement, George chose a spot and began to fan furiously by hand, lifting billowing plumes of milky silt, which quickly engulfed him. As the silt cloud moved slowly away, I could make out features through the haze. I caught George's eyes beaming through his mask. He pointed at the gaping hole he had dug in seconds. In it were the intact amphoras, one on top of the other, of a wreck.

A rocky promontory flattened by sledge hammers served as a dive platform with double-lock recompression chamber and air banks (right), and bins for diving equipment. The two hoses leading into the sea provided surface-delivered air to archaeologists working on the wreck.

We were in Serçe Limanı ("Sparrow Harbor"), a natural harbor on the southwestern coast of Turkey, to excavate the 11th-century medieval shipwreck described in this book. I had asked George to show me the Hellenistic wreck, about 150 m (500 ft) away. Sponge-diver Mehmet Aşkın had described it to him four years earlier, in 1973, when Mehmet also guided George to the medieval wreck. A single visible amphora then dated this site to 280–275 BC, but Mehmet said at least 200 other amphoras had been removed by looters.

We briefly explored the Hellenistic site in 1978, but full-scale excavation began in 1979, as an adjunct to work on the 11th-century wreck. That year our diving barge, a veteran of projects since 1961, had to be scrapped, so we dived from land. Precipitous cliffs with razor-sharp edges, however, discouraged us from building a dive platform close to the wreck, so with sledge-hammers we leveled a nearby area of rocky promontory to hold our air compressors and double-lock recompression chamber. Even divers using hookah (surface-delivered air) swam the 150 m (500 ft) to and from the wreck with scuba, leaving the long hookah hoses permanently in place on the site.

In the final season of excavation in 1980, conducted from INA's *Virazon* rather than from shore, we learned that the wreck runs under a rockslide of multi-ton boulders. Fearing that the removal of additional boulders might start a new slide, we discontinued the excavation.

Excavators struggle to remove a huge boulder from the site with lifting bags and air-filled 55-gallon steel drums. The excavation was discontinued from fear that removing boulders might start a new rock slide, endangering the wreck and the divers.

Cemal Pulak exposes one of 27 bulbous jars dispersed among the ship's ballast stones and wine jars from Knidos. The striated rectangular rock is the lower block of a two-part mill whose upper hopper block is obscured by the diver. Such finds suggest that this area corresponded to the ship's galley.

We had learned that the Hellenistic ship was a mid-sized merchantman carrying wine in amphoras made at Knidos on Turkey's southwestern coast; about half of the pitch-lined amphoras still preserved grape seeds.

As the site was not fully excavated, we can only approximate the ship's size and capacity by the amphoras. We recovered approximately 400 of them, in two sizes, of which roughly 120 large and 24 small amphoras were intact. Each large amphora held about 37 liters of wine and each empty amphora weighed about 14 kg (31 lb), totaling 51 kg (112 lb); each small amphora carried 10 liters and weighed about 5.4 kg (12 lb), totaling 15.4 kg (34 lb). Another 400 amphoras probably remain on the seabed, which, along with the 200 or so reputedly looted from the site, bring the total to some 1,000 amphoras. If we assume that the ratio of large to small amphoras is the same for the entire site, then the total cargo of full amphoras weighed about 44 tons.

Several large sections of crumpled lead sheets, only 1 to 1.5 mm thick, indicated that the wooden hull was sheathed in lead for water tightness and protection from marine borers. The lead was placed over an inner lining of pitch-impregnated fabric of wool or hemp, and secured with small copper tacks. Lead sheathing was used from the end of the 4th century BC until about the 2nd century AD, our wreck providing one of its earliest examples.

Above **A large marble trip-ring probably facilitated the freeing of snagged fishnets or the ship's anchor cable if it became fouled.**

Right **Ann Bass assembles Knidian wine amphoras from hundreds of sherds. The ship carried an estimated 1,000 amphoras of two sizes, the larger containing about 37 liters of wine, and the smaller about 10 liters.**

Below **Twenty-seven bulbous jars, without handles, may represent a secondary cargo of unguents.**

At one extremity of the site, we encountered hull wood 1.5 m (5 ft) below the surface. With it was a section of lead pipe 6 to 8 cm (2.4 to 3.1 in) in diameter, most probably for discharging bilge water raised to deck level by the ship's pump. If so, this is the earliest evidence for the use of a bilge pump. Neighboring finds included a marble trip-ring for freeing anchor cables and fishnets, the upper and lower blocks of a hopper-rubber mill, and a flat quern. Glazed and plain ceramic pitchers, bowls, jugs, and dishes also appeared. All these finds were probably in the ship's galley. Twenty-seven small globular jars also found here, however, are too numerous to have belonged to the crew, and may represent a secondary cargo of unguents on the ship.

We hope one day to overcome the logistical difficulties of the site so that work can be resumed on this unique and important shipwreck.

ROMAN AND BYZANTINE WRECKS

I once found wooden hulls somewhat boring, and left the interpretation of often small and unattractive bits of wood to my expert colleagues Fred van Doorninck, J. Richard (Dick) Steffy, and Cemal Pulak, while I studied and published the "more glamorous" cargoes and personal possessions found inside the hulls. Slowly I came to accept that the ship itself – the Greek *naus* – is often the most important and exciting artifact on any shipwreck site. In the following pages, you will see how INA archaeologists have for the first time traced the evolution from ancient to modern ships – although I hope you will also be dazzled by the "more glamorous" artifacts from shipwrecks such as the 11th-century Serçe Limanı "Glass Wreck."

Because of excellent excavations and publications by French, Italian, and Spanish archaeologists of Roman shipwrecks off their own coasts, the Institute of Nautical Archaeology has not undertaken the excavation of a Roman wreck. INA's only involvement with the Roman-period fishing boat excavated by Shelley Wachsmann, when he was still Underwater Inspector for the Israel Antiquities Authority, was the model of the boat he had built by INA's Bill Charlton, a veteran of the Uluburun, Bozburun, and Tektaş Burnu excavations. Because of biblical associations, the Sea of Galilee Boat is one of the best-known ancient craft discovered anywhere.

The hulls of most ancient shipwrecks are only partially preserved. Marine borers devoured all their exposed wood long ago. That is why I find so exciting the incredibly preserved Early Byzantine ships found by Robert Ballard in the anaerobic depths of the Black Sea, where such borers do not live. When these ships can be fully uncovered, they will provide unprecedented knowledge of Byzantine ships to specialists like his colleague Cheryl Ward.

Between the 4th century AD, when Constantine moved his capital from Rome to Byzantium (later named Constantinople and now Istanbul), and the fall of that city to the Turks in 1453, the Byzantine period is sometimes seen as a transitional period between the ancient and modern eras. It was, indeed, a transitional period for ship construction, for it saw hull design evolve slowly from ancient shell-first construction to modern frame-first construction.

A late 4th- or early 5th-century wreck at Yassıada, Turkey, excavated first by the University of Pennsylvania Museum and then INA, showed the beginnings of the evolution toward modern hull construction. The mortise-and-tenon joints that held its planks together were smaller and farther apart than in the hulls of ships from at least the Late Bronze Age through Classical Greek and Roman times. In other words, the strength of the Yassıada hull was more dependent on its internal framework, or skeleton, than before. This trend continued with a 7th-century wreck also excavated

Over 30 m (99 ft) below the surface of the Aegean Sea, excavation director Fred Hocker puzzles over a group of pitchers found in the stern of the Bozburun wreck, perhaps the remains of the captain's last meal before he abandoned his ship.

Above **Cemal Pulak holds a demijohn from the Serçe Limanı Glass Wreck. Perhaps the largest glass vessel surviving from antiquity, it was mended from pieces identified among perhaps a million glass shards.**

Right **Places mentioned in this section, with the featured wrecks in bold.**

at Yassıada by the University of Pennsylvania Museum and INA. The hull of this wreck, described by Fred van Doorninck, was truly transitional, built in the ancient manner below the waterline and in the modern manner above.

Exactly when the full transition from ancient to modern design was complete remains unknown. The 11th-century ship that sank in Serçe Limanı, Turkey, is the first fully excavated "modern ship," built in the same manner as the ships that took Columbus across the Atlantic and Magellan around the world. Shelley Wachsmann, however, has found a partial 5th- or 6th-century hull in Tantura Lagoon, Israel, that shows no evidence of mortise-and-tenon joinery.

The 9th-century shipwreck excavated by INA President Fred Hocker at Bozburun, Turkey, was thought to be an even earlier example of a modern ship than the 11th-century Serçe Limanı ship, until Fred van Doorninck, who studied and published the latter hull, as well as the two Yassıada hulls, intently examined the Bozburun planks while they were still soaking in fresh water, and discovered that they had been held edge to edge by wooden pegs similar to the tenons of earlier hulls.

Now Nergis Günsenin, with modest support from INA, is excavating a 13th-century Late Byzantine shipwreck at Çamaltı Burnu in Turkey's Sea of Marmara. Her hull specialist is Jay Rosloff, who studied nautical archaeology with us at Texas A&M University and later excavated the hull of a ship of around 400 BC in Israel.

By now the reader must wonder what these Turkish words *burnu* and *burun* mean (as in Taşlıkburun, Uluburun, Pabuç Burnu, Tektaş Burnu, Bozburun, Çamaltı Burnu). It's the same word, meaning "cape" or "promontory," which simply takes a different form if preceded by an adjective.

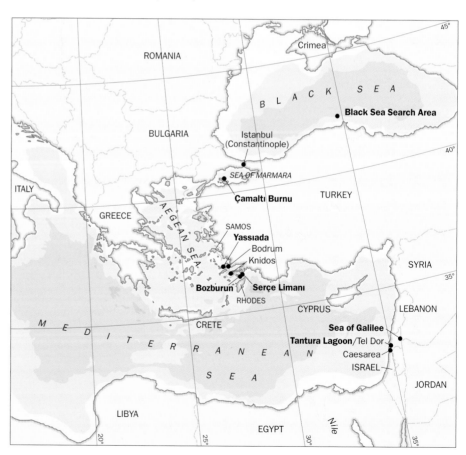

Left Diving off the wooden barge in 1961. One diver carries a bouquet of plastic tags with wire stems used to identify artifacts in grid photographs.

Below left The two-person submersible, *Asherah*, stereo-mapping the Byzantine wreck. Mounted toward either end of a long bracket are a camera and stroboscopic light; in the middle, a television camera monitors the photography.

Below right Fred van Doorninck, his fins removed to minimize wreck damage, measures the vertical distance of tagged artifacts beneath a 3-m (10-ft) square grid.

policy, which we have followed for four decades, of living as close to our diving sites as possible.

That year we also used an improved mapping system. We erected and leveled on pipe legs nine angle-iron frames, each measuring 6 m (20 ft) by 2 m (6.6 ft), like giant steps running up the 1:4 slope on which the wreck lay. We slid 4-m (13-ft) high photo towers over these steps, taking pictures down through the towers' square, wire-grid bases. Although still time-consuming, this system yielded a highly accurate three-dimensional wreck plan.

It was in that year that I volunteered to attempt a reconstruction of the quite fragmentary hull for my PhD dissertation. I was put in charge of all wreck plans as Assistant Excavation Director.

To reduce mapping time further, we developed a system of stereophotogrammetry during the last two summers of excavation. We floated a horizontal bar at a precise height over the wreck and suspended a camera from it on a gimbal. We then took vertical photographs at calibrated intervals along the bar, each two pictures forming a stereo pair. It was the first use of stereo-photography for three-dimensional mapping under water, leading to a US Navy grant that allowed us to refine the technique in order to map a neighboring 4th-century Byzantine wreck at Yassıada with a pair of cameras mounted on the two-person submersible, *Asherah*.

A Fast and Well Appointed Ship

When the 7th-century ship sank, it landed on a steep slope. Listing to port, with her bow pointing upslope, she slid down until her stern bottom dug into sand. The forward half of the hull remained on bedrock and did not survive, but much of the stern half did survive, some up to deck level, protected from marine borers by the sand.

Top **The counterweight of the ship's largest steelyard, a bust of Athena wearing her helmet and Medusa's head, is here shown with some gold coins from the wreck.**

Above **The inscription on the bar of the largest steelyard reveals that the ship's captain, Georgios, was also a priest.**

Opposite **A basket of amphoras from the 4th-century Byzantine wreck is made ready for lifting by balloon. In the foreground are globular amphoras from the 7th-century wreck.**

Below **One of the tiles from the roof of the ship's galley, here being mended by Ann Bass, had a round, collared hole through which smoke from the galley firebox escaped.**

Using the seabed evidence, along with detailed drawings made on land of all the significant hull remains, I reconstructed the hull's general shape aft of midships. My restoration of the missing bow, however, produced something less than seaworthy. This was remedied by a series of scale models built by volunteer consultant Dick Steffy; these confirmed most of my reconstruction and successfully projected the hull lines into the bow.

Although the ship, at just under 21 m (69 ft) long, could carry some 60 tons, her hull, with a slim 4:1 length-to-width ratio and a maximum breadth well aft of midships, was primarily designed for speed.

Economy took precedence over appearance in building the hull. Four pairs of heavier planks called wales and most timbers lining the ship's interior were little more than half logs. Construction methods were much more economical than in earlier Greco-Roman hull construction, where the outer shell of planking was built first by edge-joining the planks together with large mortise-and-tenon joints fixed in place by pegs. In this hull, the joints were much smaller, more widely spaced, unpegged, and used only up to the waterline, above which the planking was simply nailed to already erected frames (or ribs). The skeleton of keel and frames rather than the shell was now the principal source of hull strength, representing a transitional stage in the evolution from ancient to modern hull construction.

The ship had been well equipped. Despite her small size, she carried 11 iron anchors. Four bower anchors were ready for use, two on either bulwark just forward of midships. Stacked on deck between them was a set of spares and, at the bottom, three sheet anchors for use as a last resort in storms.

The distribution patterns of tiles, metal and ceramic vessels, and other items found at the stern revealed the dimensions and layout of an elaborate galley set low within the hull. A large tile firebox with adjustable iron grill occupied the port half of the galley floor. A superstructure rising above deck level to give access and interior light to the galley was roofed with tiles. Galley wares included at least 16 pantry jars and the ship's water jar, a mortar and pestle, 21 cooking pots, two cauldrons, a bake pan of copper, several copper or bronze pitchers, 18 ceramic pitchers and jugs, a half-dozen spouted jars, and four or five settings of fine tableware.

A storage locker in the galley's forward wall contained the ship's valuables: 16 gold and 50 copper coins, three steelyards and a set of balance-pan weights, a carpenter's chest containing all the tools needed for ship repairs, 16 unused lamps perhaps to be used as dedications in churches and shrines en route, and a bronze censer surmounted by a cross. The latest copper coin had been minted in the year 625/626. An inscription on the largest steelyard gives the name and title of its owner: Georgios, priest sea captain. A boatswain's locker, just aft of the galley, contained a grapnel for the ship's boat, tools for use in foraging for water and firewood on land, needles and lead weights for repairing fish nets, and lead weights and lures for deepwater line fishing.

The Last Voyage: A New Interpretation

The ship was carrying approximately 900 amphoras. Some 700 were globular jars stacked three deep in the hold; the rest were cylindrical jars placed horizontally between the necks of the top layer. We raised only 110 amphoras during the excavation. Their pitch-coated interiors suggested they had contained wine, and in

the excavation report, *Yassi Ada: A Seventh-Century Byzantine Shipwreck* (1982), we state that the ship probably had been a coastal trader involved in wine commerce.

A chance discovery in 1980 of graffiti on many of the raised amphoras, which had been mostly hidden by concretion, was to lead to a very different conclusion. The newly established presence of a permanent INA staff in Bodrum soon made possible the recovery of 570 of the amphoras still on the site and a new amphora study under my direction that entailed a thorough cleaning and cataloguing, including drawings of all distinct types and sizes, capacity measurements and the collecting of the organic contents of intact amphoras. Recording of graffiti was mostly done by my wife, Betty Jean. Peter van Alfen published a study of the cylindrical amphoras in 1996; he and I continue the study of the globular amphoras.

What we learned about the amphoras and their contents was unexpected and not easily explained. The recovery on average of just under a dozen grape seeds from the intact amphoras indicates that most, if not all, amphoras in the cargo were carrying low-grade wine. Differences in decoration, typology and fabric revealed 11 distinct types of cylindrical and some 40 distinct types of globular amphoras. Approximately 80 percent of the globular amphoras had been made shortly before the ship's sinking, but other globular types had been made at least several decades earlier. Graffiti indicate that many of the recently made amphoras had earlier carried olives, possibly preserved in sweet wine, and some of these jars contained, along with grape seeds, degraded bits of olive pits. Some older jars had once held lentils. Several dozen different marks of ownership occur on the globular amphoras, some jars having had more than one owner.

As we learned more about the unusual nature of the ship's cargo, we began to comprehend the unusual nature of the ship itself. In the early 1990s, at the urging of the Bodrum Museum Director, Oğuz Alpözen, INA, under the direction of Fred Hocker and Taras Pevny, constructed a full-scale replica of the ship's stern. Building the replica led to a better appreciation of the hull's highly streamlined design.

I now believe that the ship, with her priest-captain, belonged to the church and

Above **George Bass inspects globular amphoras from the 7th-century Byzantine wreck as they are lifted onto the deck of INA's research vessel, *Virazon*.**

Right The replica of the galley complex with its tile roof, tile firebox and storage facilities and the after part of the hold with its cargo of amphoras gives visitors to the museum a vivid impression of what shipboard life was like.

had been designed for speed and the feeding of passengers so that it might transport churchmen as well as cargo; the tile galley roof added a touch of suitable elegance. The ship sank near the end of a long war with Persia, a war so costly that the church had to lend major assistance in provisioning the army, partly through levies of produce from church-owned lands. Particularly in view of rather frequent allusions to the Christian faith among the amphora graffiti, it appears likely that the ship's cargo of low-grade wine in recycled amphoras had been a part of this effort.

Below A 1:10 scale replica of the ship showing the internal hull construction on the port side, the general structure of the stern galley complex (left), and the location of the bower anchors and pile of anchor spares on the deck just forward of midships.

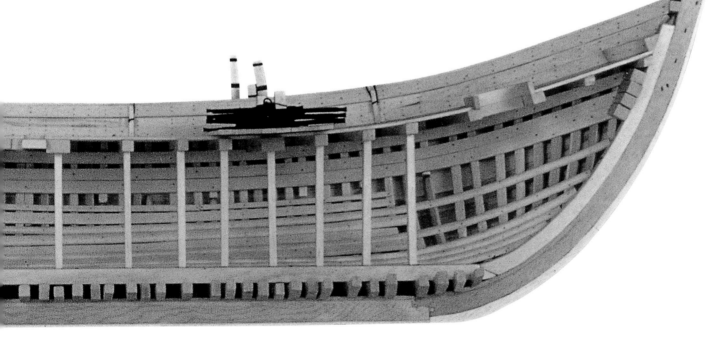

The Graveyard of Ships:
Tantura Lagoon, Israel

SHELLEY WACHSMANN

The flash came from above as I examined the planking of a newly discovered hull. My first thought was, who in the world is using our flash unit to take underwater photographs? Then I remembered that I had taken the unit to Tel Aviv for repair. By the time I saw the second flash, I was looking straight up and realized that I was witnessing lightning strikes as viewed from underwater. Moments later I was rushing the team out of the lagoon….

Tantura Lagoon is one of the few natural harbors along Israel's remarkably straight and shallow Mediterranean coastline. Its protected waters have served as an anchorage for Tel Dor, one of the largest ancient mounds in Israel, as well as for Dor's immediate environs. This region has been almost continuously inhabited for 4,000 years, and few other Mediterranean ports have the potential for hiding remains from such a breadth of history. Now, with a team of faculty, staff, and students – from INA, Texas A&M University, and Haifa University's Recanati Center for Maritime Studies (now, The Leon Recanati Institute for Maritime Studies) – I was coaxing some of that history from beneath the cove's shifting sands.

Remarkably, in an area only about the size of a basketball court, we uncovered remains of seven different hulls! To find them, we used a hydraulic probe, consisting of a pipe connected by a hose to a pump. This simple tool proved more effective than any electronic method available in locating waterlogged timbers under as much as 2 m (6.6 ft) of sand. Trenches sunk over the timbers revealed buried hulls. In two cases we located lead-filled wooden anchor stocks, in this area the archaeological equivalent of finding "needles in a haystack."

With but one exception, the wrecks date from the 4th to the 10th centuries AD. We studied two hulls in particular detail. The Tantura A wreck consists of about a quarter of the bottom of a small coaster, apparently of local origin, dating from the mid-5th to the mid-6th century AD. Originally, it was probably about 12 m (36 ft) long.

Number of shipwrecks 7
Dates of shipwrecks 4th–10th
centuries AD, 18th century AD
Excavation 1994–1996
Historical context ancient
harbor of Tel Dor
Dor first mentioned Ramesses II

Right **Tantura Lagoon has so filled up with sand over the centuries that at times the excavators had to dig holes in which to dive. This aerial photo shows the excavation of the Tantura B shipwreck in extremely shallow water. Among the finds was this intact jar (***left***), found lying next to the keelson.** *Below* **Team member Andrew Lacovera examines the wreck. The hull's narrow lines strongly suggest that it was a galley.**

Opposite below **The hull of the Tantura A shipwreck had come to rest on the 52-kg (115-lb) stone stock of a wooden anchor, which predates the vessel by about a millennium.**

We were surprised to find that the hull planking and keel contained no evidence of mortise-and-tenon joinery, which at the time of its discovery was considered a hallmark of contemporaneous ship construction. This led to some concern that the ship might be of later date than originally determined, but the subsequent discovery of Byzantine-period pottery stuck to the hull with resin, together with a series of radiocarbon dates, clearly confirmed the early date range. This makes the Tantura A wreck one of the oldest recorded hulls discovered in Mediterranean waters that had been built in the innovative methods that were to evolve more fully and eventually become the standard in the medieval period.

The Tantura B hull lies about 10 m (33 ft) west of Tantura A. It appears to be part of a large vessel dating to the first half of the 9th century AD. Its unusual combination of angles, breadths, and what appears to be a lack of longitudinal stiffening make it unlike any other known Mediterranean hull. This led noted hull reconstructor Dick Steffy to propose that we may have part of an oared galley, a particular rarity in the archaeological record. We speculate that Tantura B may have been one of the Andalusian Arab vessels used to raid Crete during the early 9th century, leading to the island's Arab conquest around AD 824.

As on land, we repeatedly found stratified artifacts in the lagoon. Indeed, in 1996, we learned that the Tantura B hull rested on an earlier vessel – known as Tantura C – which dates to the early 4th century AD.

The ships that we examined in Tantura Lagoon from 1994 to 1996 show evidence of traumatic ends. All appear to have sunk when forced against a lee shore during storms.

Perhaps each vessel had tried to make a desperate run for safety between the lagoon's islands and had been smashed on the rocks before being battered into the lagoon by the pounding waves. Once flushed into the lagoon, large sections of hull were quickly buried in the shifting sands, preserving them and their contents, through the centuries, in an anaerobic embrace.

Sampling a Byzantine Vintage: Bozburun, Turkey

FRED HOCKER

Bozburun

Built AD 874
Sunk c AD 880
Depth 30–35 m (99–115 ft)
Found by Mehmet Aşkın
Excavation 1995–1998
Number of dives 8,500
Cost (fieldwork) $400,000
Cargo c 1200–1500 amphoras
Hull c 15 m (49 ft) long,
c 5 m (16 ft) wide

The early summer wind had blown steadily out of the northwest, as it often did in the Aegean, but now, just as they were approaching the entrance to the harbor, the wind veered abruptly to the northeast. They would not make the harbor. The captain turned west to run before the squall for the shelter of Crescent Island, but he did not count on the sudden shift in wind jibing the sail and cracking the yard. Unable to sail and being blown onto a rocky lee shore, he had no option but to anchor and wait out the wind or make repairs. First one anchor was dropped, and then another, but the channel was deep with a sloping bottom, and the anchors would not bite. The ship's head did turn into the wind, but the stern now came closer to the limestone cliffs with each wave, until it was driven onto the rocks. Water began to flood through sprung seams. With the stern pounding on the shore, the crew tried to save the ship by lightening it, throwing cargo overboard, but the damage was too great. There was only enough time to gather up their valuables and scramble ashore. They huddled on a small spur bulging from the cliff face and waited for a local boat to rescue them, while they watched their broken ship disappear.

How can we know the details of a wreck that happened more than 1,000 years ago? The sailors are long gone, only the bottom of the ship survives, and the cargo, amphoras that once contained wine, seems uniform and unremarkable. Partly it is from our own experience of four summers on the same rocky spur, excavating the shipwreck. We are sailors too, and felt the prevailing northwesterly wind. But when it veers around toward the northeast, the cliffs on either side of narrow Hisarönü Bay divert it and keep it flowing into the bay from the west until it veers far enough to come through the passes to the northeast. Then it shifts suddenly and with little warning. This happens most often in late spring and early summer, before the wind settles into its stable summer pattern. It is still not inherently dangerous, as it is possible to run back down the channel and get into the safety of the lee of one of the islands. Something else had to have happened to the ship.

The wreck, itself, offers clues, although it is not *what* was on the bottom of the Aegean that is so enlightening, but *where* it was, and even more so, what was *not* there. Most of the amphoras were in a compact mound, the classic Mediterranean wreck, but many were spread out, some around the corner of the rocky spur, and a few even under the hull. The last had been thrown overboard and sank before the ship came down on top of them. The ship itself lay at the bottom of the cliff, with its stern pointed at the rocks. What was missing is the final key. There was only one anchor still on the ship, at the bow. Most medieval ships found in the Mediterranean have a large stack of spare anchors on deck, but this ship had already cast all but one, a clear sign of desperation. There were no coins, no objects of value, and almost no personal possessions, although such things are common on other wrecks – the crew had escaped, and had had time to collect the things important to them.

What the Finds Can Tell Us

But why excavate such a dull site? No gold, no jewelry, no exotic goods or artwork, just day after day of amphoras and amphora sherds. Some 960 amphoras and over 2 tons of sherds, to be exact. However, what *is* there on the bottom tells another story, about what happened before the ship ran into trouble. That story is part of one of the

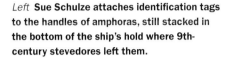

Left **Sue Schulze attaches identification tags to the handles of amphoras, still stacked in the bottom of the ship's hold where 9th-century stevedores left them.**

Right **One of three tiny glass goblets found in the stern, too fine for regular shipboard use but perfect for entertaining important guests or prospective buyers in port.**

Below **A selection of earthenware jugs from the galley, most for serving wine, but one (front row, left) was full of whole grapes, still plump and juicy after over 1,100 years.**

great political and economic conflicts of the Middle Ages, the life-or-death struggle between the Byzantine Empire and the Muslim Caliphates for dominance in the eastern Mediterranean. This little ship and its cargo of wine came along at one of the turning points in that struggle, when an exhausted Empire came back from the dead, re-established its long-distance economy, and began to re-conquer its lost territory. The Bozburun ship is one of the few pieces of evidence that might tell us how that happened.

George Bass was the first archaeologist to see the wreck, when Mehmet Aşkın, a local sponge diver, took him to it on INA's first shipwreck survey in 1973. It was the "next" wreck on INA's long-term plan for many years, but George and Don Frey kept finding ever more spectacular sites. By the time Cemal Pulak finished the excavation of the Bronze Age wreck at Uluburun in 1994, I was ready to look at this medieval wreck. In a way, it was a return to INA's roots, excavating a site very similar to the Byzantine wreck at Yassıada, but building on the knowledge that George, Fred van Doorninck and Dick Steffy had squeezed out of that site and others and then taught me when I was a student at Texas A&M University.

When we arrived in May of 1995, the area had only just become accessible by road. Local villagers still harvested wheat by hand from terraced fields, and tourist traffic was light. We established camp on one edge of the village of Selimiye and Robin Piercy built a three-story dive platform on the same rocky spur where those sailors had once huddled. We could dive from shore, only a short boat ride from camp, which greatly simplified logistics. We also had space for a large field conservation lab, where finds could be registered and initial cleaning could take place, reducing pressure on our Bodrum conservation lab in the winter.

The site itself was relatively simple to excavate. It was "only" 30–35 m (99–115 ft) deep, shallow for an INA project in Turkey, and the wreck lay on a clean, sandy slope. We dived for 30 to 40 minutes at a time, twice a day, sometimes breathing a special mixture of air called nitrox, with an unusually high ratio of oxygen, enabling us to dive longer without increasing our chances of suffering the bends. As we airlifted away the sand and exposed the cargo, we learned that the upper layers had been battered by fishing-boat anchors over the years, but the material below was in good condition. By the second season, we had cleared enough of the broken material to see that the amphoras had been at least two layers deep, that there was a galley in the stern, and that well-preserved hull remains lay underneath. By the third season, it was clear that the lower layer of cargo was still in its original position. I was busy that year excavating the stern, where part of the hull was appearing, but our divemaster, Bill Charlton, told me one day I should take a look at the middle of the site where he was working.

The next day, I went on the first dive, before the water became murky from airlifting, and did an overall site inspection before going to my little patch of wood. The overall shape of the wreck was clear when I was still 20 m (66 ft) above it. As I got closer, I could see the bottom layer of amphoras marching solemnly down the slope in orderly files, their handles aligned like soldiers on parade, just as the stevedores had stacked them 1,100 years ago. It was easy to imagine ropes running through the handles to keep them in place.

Opposite **Our three-story, split-level dive platform clinging to the same rocky spur that claimed the Bozburun ship. Robin Piercy, a Turkish stonemason, and a team of archaeology students used five weeks and over 8 tons of hand-mixed concrete to construct it.**

Below **A photomosaic of the Bozburun shipwreck as it looked soon after George Bass first surveyed it, a weed-covered mound of amphoras. The wreck slopes from the stern (top of picture), at 30 m (99 ft) depth, to the bow, at 35 m (115 ft).**

Bad Amphoras, Worse Wine

Over the years, we had become familiar with the uniformly bad quality of these jars. They were small, egg-shaped, made from poor clay, and unevenly fired. They tended to break if not kept wet and handled very carefully. What was remarkable was where they came from, what was inside them, and what was written on them.

The jars and the wine in them were not from any of the traditional Aegean vineyards, from Rhodes or Samos or Knidos. They had been made in kilns in the Crimea, at the northern end of the Black Sea, thousands of kilometers away. That area was a distant outpost of the Greek world, but clearly still connected to the main Aegean heart of the Empire. Long-distance trade had to have recovered significantly already for shipping of such a low-value bulk commodity to make economic sense.

We carefully sieved the contents of whole amphoras. This generally consisted of mud, and it was a sweaty, monotonous task to extract it and then wash it through the sieve. Indeed, it took about twice as long to process an amphora in the lab as it did to excavate it, map it for the site plan, and raise it to the surface. In addition to the occasional octopus's shell collection, the mud almost always contained organic remains, usually grape pips, sometimes by the hundreds. This wine would appeal to the sort of person who likes pulp in his orange juice. In addition to the pips, there were other seeds and plant remains, as well as fragments of fish bones. Dylan Gorham, who analyzed the contents, reported that we were looking at red wine flavored with spices and fish paste. This kind of wine is still drunk in the Black Sea region, including the northern coast of Turkey, but it is an acquired taste.

We found about 60 jars that still had their pine-bark stoppers in place, sealed with pitch. The mud had got past the seal on most of these, but 15 jars contained only liquid, usually seawater. In two instances, when we removed the stoppers, our noses were greeted by the unmistakable stench of decomposed organic material, and when we emptied the contents into the sieve, it was a dark red liquid. Yes, we tasted it (who could resist?) but AD 874 was not a very good year.

About a quarter of the amphoras had letters carved into them. Such graffiti have been common on amphoras since Classical times, and usually are owners' initials. In our ship, we have many different people represented, each with a few jars, but two owners had more than 30 jars each. AN (Anastasios?) owned most of the jars in the still-stacked lower layer, while GE (Georgeos) owned much of the upper layer, including the amphoras jettisoned to save the ship. Another owner signed his jars EPIS or EPISKO, short for *episkopos*, or bishop. The church was a major landowner, and so it is not surprising that a bishop was shipping wine. What is most interesting about the graffiti is how they were distributed. In each case, all of the jars belonging to one owner were together. This tells us that there were a large number of owners of this cargo, even though it all came from the same place, and that they were still involved. It suggests, further, that this particular shipment was a collective venture in private enterprise rather than state-organized requisitioning, providing a vital clue to how long-distance commerce might have resurrected itself after nearly two centuries of depression.

Above **The Bozburun project was a popular attraction for the media – hosting five TV crews, from the US, Turkey and Japan. Here excavation director Fred Hocker prepares to take a Turkish journalist on a guest dive.**

Below **While most of the amphoras were full of red wine, one, found in the galley, contained olives. These were probably provisions for the crew rather than cargo, but carried in the same kind of Crimean amphora.**

Below right **Pine bark was used both for amphora stoppers, which were sealed in place with pitch, and for fishing net floats (top).**

Below **Conservator Jane Pannell Haldane holds a mold-blown flask of glass as thin as a light bulb, found in the stern with three glass goblets.**

A Final Toast

The ship itself is no less intriguing. After three-and-a-half seasons of lifting clay jars, we were able to dismantle and raise the ship's timbers. The ship was probably about 15 m (50 ft) long, and most of the starboard side of the bottom survives, enough to show how the ship was built. Matthew Harpster's careful recording and analysis has shown that the oak planking and pine frames were assembled with a consistent unit of measurement and that some basic arithmetical proportions were used to lay out the main dimensions. These proportions are similar in concept to the more sophisticated method used to build the Serçe Limanı ship 150 years later, and take our knowledge of systematic methods in ship design back into the first millennium.

As a final surprise, we discovered that the crew did not vanish completely without a trace. In the stern, down between the frames, were three extraordinarily fine glass goblets and a fluted glass bottle, much too delicate for regular shipboard use. The captain or a merchant must have been carrying this drinking set for special occasions or as a gift, and it adds a welcome social note to an otherwise practical story of 9th-century commerce.

Solving a Million-Piece Jigsaw Puzzle: Serçe Limanı, Turkey

GEORGE F. BASS

Drop a light bulb. Try to put it back together again.

Drop three light bulbs. Stir the pieces. Then try to put them back together again.

Drop six light bulbs, four glass vases, and a dozen wine bottles, stir the pieces, and try to put them all back together, as if they were new.

That is like the problem I faced, starting in 1977 – except I was dealing with between 10,000 and 20,000 smashed glass vessels. But now, after more than two decades of year-round mending, my colleagues and I have assembled by far the largest collection of medieval Islamic glass in the world.

But I am getting ahead of myself.

The Discovery

During INA's initial 1973 survey along the Turkish coast, retired Bozburun sponge-diver Mehmet Aşkın told me that he had seen fellow divers bring handfuls of broken glass from the bottom of a nearby bay called Serçe Limanı ("Sparrow Harbor"), just opposite the Greek island of Rhodes. I was living with two other American and three Turkish divers on *Kardeşler*, a 20-m (66-ft) trawler, our recompression chamber, compressors, and air banks strapped to its sometimes wildly rolling deck. We sailed immediately for Serçe Limanı, where Yüksel Eğdemir, our commissioner from the Turkish Ministry of Culture, soon reported:

"There's glass everywhere! You can't fan the sand without cutting your fingers."

On a single, brief dive on the site, I decided that it would be a significant wreck for INA to excavate. But it was not the glass that interested me. It was the wreck's date.

During excavations described elsewhere in this book, at Kyrenia, Cyprus, and Yassıada, Turkey, my colleagues and I had been tracing for the first time the slow evolution of hull construction, from completely shell-first hulls in Bronze Age and Classical Greek times to Late Roman and Early Byzantine hulls in which frames, or ribs, that helped shape the hull were erected before the hull shell was completed. We wondered when the first "modern" hulls appeared in which frames were erected before construction of the hull shell was even begun. This wreck might provide the answer. An amphora I uncovered by sweeping sand away with my hand was from later in the Byzantine period than those at Yassıada. Amphora expert Virginia Grace soon dated it, from a photograph, to the 11th century AD.

The Excavation

Other projects delayed the onset of full-scale excavation at Serçe Limanı until 1977, when we built a camp of stone, concrete blocks, woven mats, and mosquito netting in

Serçe Limanı Glass Wreck

Date *c* 1025
Depth 33 m (110 ft)
Found by Mehmet Aşkın
Excavation 1977–1979
Cargo glass cullet, glazed bowls, wine
Glass vessels *c* 10,000–20,000
Hull 15.6 m (51.2 ft) long
Crew Bulgarian

which as many as 35 people would spend the next three summers.

Excavation was in most respects routine. We put down our underwater telephone booth for safety and covered the site with a metal grid to break it into squares 2 m (6.6 ft) on a side so that each diver, or pair of divers, could be responsible for the excavation of a specific area of the wreck. We mapped the wreck with underwater drawings, photographs, and measurements taken from fixed metal stakes driven into the rock around the site.

Every wreck, however, has its own peculiarities. Soon we were uncovering not only the expected ceramic and metal artifacts, but dozens, then hundreds, then thousands of shards of glass. I don't believe in wearing gloves during underwater excavation. So much depends on touch. But soon our bandaged hands looked like they were excavating razors.

At a depth of 33 m (110 ft) the color red is absorbed from daylight and does not appear. Probably every excavator lost valuable bottom time by squeezing a cut finger or palm in order to watch in fascination the bright emerald blood that spiraled up into the seawater.

Another distraction was Fred, the octopus that lived in an amphora in Fred van Doorninck's square and never tired of trying to pull his watch off, or pull the glittering glass from his hands. On one of my dives I felt a shudder in the metal grid

on which I rested my body, looked for the cause, and saw an octopus, presumably Fred's grandfather or grandmother, coming toward me with tentacles that reached from one side of a square to the other. I decided to end my dive early.

We had to abandon any thoughts of labeling every glass shard, but instead gathered shards from squares 50 cm (20 in) on a side, and placed them into labeled plastic bags.

One day Texas A&M graduate student Donald Keith asked in surprise, when he saw us washing the mud from an amphora: "What in the world are you doing?"

"Cleaning the mud out."

"What about the seeds?" Don asked.

Above **A metal grid placed over the wreck divided the site into squares that were assigned to pairs of divers for excavation. At this early stage, wood, amphoras, ballast stones, millstones, dark chunks of raw glass, and iron anchors had already come to light.**

Right **Much of the broken glass was embedded in rock-hard seabed concretion and had to be extracted with dental tools by Jay Rosloff and other expedition members.**

"There aren't any seeds in here, not after a thousand years."

"Don't be so sure," Don responded. "Let me show you."

We were pioneers. We made mistakes. For years we had casually hosed the sediment out of amphoras. Soon Don was sieving the mud, and followed that with flotation, the method of retrieving seeds and pollen from swirling water that has been used at archaeological sites on land for years. The results, as we shall see, were astonishing.

At the end of three summers, the real archaeology began. Finding, mapping, and raising things represent only the first step. Now we began a process that would last decades.

The Million-Piece Jigsaw Puzzle

Oğuz Alpözen, who had first dived with us at Yassıada in 1963 as an undergraduate archaeology student, was now Director of the Bodrum Museum. He assigned to us as workspace the entire English Tower of the Castle of the Knights of St John of Malta, in which the Museum is housed, and additional space in which to build a conservation laboratory. Fred van Doorninck and his family spent the academic year 1978–1979 organizing the tons of material we had retrieved from the wreck, and the following year Ann and I took our 12- and 9-year-old sons out of school so that we could continue the task.

My first job was to tackle the 3 tons of glass we had raised from the wreck, now separated by Fred into 2 tons of raw glass chunks and 1 ton of broken glass vessels. Much of the broken glass was encased in large lumps of rock-hard concretion, from which we removed the shards with dental picks.

We hoped to start mending the broken vessels. All of us still assumed that we were dealing with vessels that had been broken by the impact of the shipwreck. That meant that the fragments of individual vessels should have been found near one another on the site. So we built wooden tables around the entire bottom floor of the English Tower and, using the labels on the bags, laid out all of the shards from a single 1-m (3.3-ft) square, keeping the glass from each bag still separated from the glass from other bags by wooden strips that acted as dividers. After weeks, we had not found a

single join and gave up, defeated. We began to sketch and catalogue thousands of bases, rims, and handles, an incredibly boring job.

One day it suddenly struck me. How does one work a jigsaw puzzle? Usually by separating out pieces that might join together, putting into separate piles, say, the pieces with green grass or blue sky or red bricks. Might this work with the glass?

None of us was a glass expert, so we invented our own 18 categories of glass: plain glass, green glass, purple glass, dimpled glass, purple dimpled glass, green-threaded rims, purple dimpled glass with green-threaded rims, and so on. Then we were almost ready to begin.

But there was a problem. To put all of the purple glass together into one pile meant taking all of the purple shards out of their labeled bags, losing forever any record of where they had been found on the wreck. Artifact provenience is vital on archaeological excavations. So, we copied each of the four or six-character provenience codes with black ink onto each of between half a million and a million shards, covering each number with clear fingernail polish to prevent its being inadvertently rubbed away. We shanghaied passing tourists to help; one young man, on his way around the world, became so fascinated he stayed on the job for months. I even put my young sons to work, thankful that Charles Dickens was not around to write about it!

Once the shards were individually labeled, we could take all of one category and begin the task. I might sit before a pile of several thousand plain purple shards, dividing them into two piles: lighter purple and darker purple. I would then put one of the piles into storage and start again, dividing the remaining shards into darker and lighter shades, again putting one of the resultant piles into storage. After doing this long enough, I might have left before me on the work table only 18 or 19 shards, but all of exactly the same shade of purple. Then we would find the joins and stick the shards together temporarily with tape (often keeping their shapes in individually cut Styrofoam forms), until our conservators could mend them permanently with special glue.

It was only then, at the end of the first year, that we realized something startling about this part of the ship's cargo. We were dealing with a cargo of broken glass intended to be recycled! All of those millions of digits we had inked onto the shards were meaningless, except they provided the proof that the glass had been shoveled randomly into the ship's hold from some even larger pile of broken glass. In no case were all the pieces of any specific vessel on board, meaning either that all of the pieces of any one vessel had never made it onto the ship, or that some of the glass had already been sold during the ship's final voyage. For a long time we had trouble convincing even authorities on ancient glass that shipping broken glass was economically feasible, but some years later roughly contemporary documents were published that described the shipment of broken glass from the Near East to the glass factories of Venice.

Part of the hold had contained a cargo that left no trace, possibly plant ash used in making glass, a commodity known to have been shipped with broken glass from the Near East.

Some 80 intact glass vessels were not from the ship's hold, but from what we eventually proved were living quarters, at the ship's stern and bow; they were

probably carried in bundles by merchants who were prepared to sell them intact.

Glass mending continued year-round for more than two decades. We saw the local glass menders who joined us right out of school not only become expert, but marry and raise children. At the end, they had assembled by far the largest known collection of medieval Islamic glass.

Almost certainly the broken glass was factory waste from one specific source. Some deformed vessels were clearly factory rejects. Other pieces, such as 11,000 moiles (tops of vessels that are cut off and discarded), could only have been factory waste. Robert Brill, Chief Scientist at the Corning Museum of Glass, showed by chemical analysis of samples that almost all of the glass was chemically homogeneous, as if it came from one factory, or perhaps several closely associated glassworks. Lastly, Spanish archaeologist Berta Lledó, lining up one on top of another of Sema Pulak's incredibly accurate drawings on transparent Mylar, showed that even vessels of completely different shapes had started out in the same few molds, and then been crafted into varied forms by the glassblowers.

Dating the Wreck

It was glass, too, that provided the closest date for the wreck. On board were 16 glass disks that had served as weights for pan balances. Some bore the name of a caliph in Egypt and the year of his reign. Michael Bates of the American Numismatic Society, using casts and photographs, informed us that the latest dated to either AD 1024/25 or possibly 1021/22, dates not contradicted by those on three Islamic gold coins,

Above **Glass menders triumphantly raise examples of vessels they put together during two decades of year-round glass mending.**

Below **When small change was needed, bits of gold were simply cut from Islamic coins and carefully weighed.**

Above **Amphoras for wine and olive oil were scratched with their owners' initials, leading to the realization that merchants on board were Hellenized Bulgarians.**

ship's amphoras. First he noted that all the amphoras marked with "M" (probably "Michael") were found together, as were those marked with "Leon." Eventually Fred identified about a dozen owners. He further noted that many of the amphoras had been damaged but kept in use, sometimes with lips filed smooth after being chipped when a stopper had been pried out, and other times when a handle stump was smoothed down where a handle had been broken away. Unlike the amphoras of the Imperial Roman fleets, which were discarded at voyage's end, these amphoras belonged to individual merchants who prized and protected them, sometimes for many years.

So far, so good. But Fred noticed that one of the amphoras was marked MIR. He couldn't guess what Greek name that represented. His realization that it stood for a Slavic name such as Miroslav, however, led to his teaching himself to read Bulgarian, Rumanian, and Russian, so that he could easily read Slavic and Rumanian excavation reports. He determined that the crew of the ship that sank at Serçe Limanı were Hellenized Bulgarians who lived on the shore of the Sea of Marmara not far from Constantinople. His theory was borne out when Nergis Günsenin excavated some pottery kilns on the shore of the Sea of Marmara that had manufactured amphoras identical in all respects to those on our shipwreck. Nergis, who describes her own shipwreck excavation in this book, had been a non-diving volunteer during the excavation of the Glass Wreck when she was still only a high-school student.

Our ship, it seems, had sailed from near Constantinople to a port on the Syro-Palestinian coast, such as Caesarea, where gold jewelry, glazed bowls, glass jars, and copper buckets like those on the ship have been found. After taking on its Islamic cargo, the ship on its return voyage sought shelter at an anchorage used for millennia inside Serçe Limanı. But then what happened?

The Anchors

Again, Fred van Doorninck's careful detective work provided the answer. After making epoxy replicas of the ship's nine Y-shaped anchors, Fred determined that, as on the 7th-century Yassıada shipwreck, there were two bower anchors on one bulwark near the bow, ready for use, and another on the opposite bulwark. Spare anchors – in this case five – lay stacked on deck near by. But what of the missing bower anchor? It was found where it had been cast, some distance forward of the bow, its shank snapped, presumably from the force of a sudden gust of wind, freeing the ship to be dashed against the rocky shore.

Fred further calculated that the weights of the anchors were multiples of Byzantine pounds, pointing toward the conclusion that laws governing the weights of anchors on ships of various sizes were in force earlier than realized. The unusual Y shape allowed anchors to be of greater weight without being weakened by overly long shanks.

Decades after the diving ended at Serçe Limanı, a 550-page analysis of the ship and its passengers was published, a collaboration of over a dozen scholars on three continents. It is only the first of three volumes of equal size. The second volume will present the Islamic glass and ceramic cargoes. Diving to an underwater site is no more important than driving a jeep to a terrestrial site. It is not the fieldwork, but the years of research, analysis, and interpretation that make it true archaeology.

A 13th-Century Wine Carrier: Çamaltı Burnu, Turkey

NERGİS GÜNSENİN

Çamaltı Burnu

Date early 13th century
Depth 22–35 m (72–115 ft)
Excavation 1998–2004
Dives 4,295
Conservation 2004 onwards
Hull c 25 m (82 ft) long, c 5–6 m (16.5–20 ft) wide
Cargo c 800 amphoras and 37 scrap iron anchors

When I first saw the amphoras on the seabed at Çamaltı Burnu, in 1993, I knew that I had found my "fortune." To understand why, we must go back to the 1980s. I was then developing a typology of late Byzantine amphoras throughout Turkey's museums for my doctoral thesis, which resulted in my finding an important amphora production area at Gaziköy on the northwest coast of the Sea of Marmara. Gaziköy, known as Ganos in ancient and medieval times, was an important monastic center from the 10th century onward. Its monks, along with neighboring villagers, like those of many monasteries, had a virtual monopoly over the production and sale of wine in the area.

My survey of workshop areas at and around Gaziköy, followed by excavation of an amphora kiln, revealed a large amphora production, which indicated an equally large

Below **General view of the amphora cargo during the 2002 excavation campaign. Most of the amphoras, which show a wide range of dimensions and capacities, survived intact and yielded grape seeds.**

production of wine, most of which would have supplied the markets of nearby Constantinople (modern Istanbul). Each time I returned to the region I dreamt of those monasteries and their vineyards – and the thousands of amphoras waiting to be loaded with Ganos wine. Enthusiasm for nautical archaeology, inspired by my meeting George Bass during the summer of 1979, at last led me to search for the ships that sailed from Ganos with those amphoras. My quest began at Marmara Island in the summer of 1992, shortly after completing the excavation of the kiln at Gaziköy. I still search around it and other islands in the Sea of Marmara, and so far have found eight shipwrecks loaded with Ganos amphoras.

The surveys also located a tile wreck, a water-pipe wreck, and, importantly, a marble wreck. The very name of Marmara Island, the site of one of the biggest marble quarries of late antiquity, comes from the Turkish word for marble. Many architectural pieces of the temples, monasteries and churches in Constantinople, throughout Anatolia, and even in Ravenna in Italy came from those quarries, yet this is the only marble wreck ever discovered near the island.

Let's return to the day I first dived at Marmara Island's Çamaltı Burnu (Cape Under the Pine). I was not looking for just any ancient wreck. At that time, the major archaeological material related to Byzantine maritime activities came from three wrecks excavated by INA along the Anatolian coasts: at Yassıada (7th century), Bozburun (9th century), and Serçe Limanı (11th century), all of which are described

Below **Nergis Günsenin with two glazed bowls and a table amphora of recognizable Byzantine origin from the Çamaltı Burnu shipwreck off Marmara Island.**

A 13th-Century Wine Carrier: Çamaltı Burnu, Turkey **119**

in this book. Chemical analyses by Helen Hatcher of Oxford University on samples from the Serçe Limanı amphoras showed that most had been made in the region around Ganos, and so excavation of another 11th-century shipwreck would break little new ground. I was looking for a younger wreck. The amphoras on the seabed at Çamaltı Burnu were just that, of the 13th century – my "fortune."

These were the last major group of Byzantine ceramic containers used to transport wine in the sea trade, their place soon taken by wooden barrels. Further, little is known of the shipbuilding technology of this period, most of our knowledge being derived from written texts rather than archaeological remains. Thus the excavation of what I called the Çamaltı Burnu I Wreck might well contribute much new information about Byzantine maritime activities, particularly in the region of the Sea of Marmara, during or shortly after the brief period of Latin rule at Constantinople (1204–1261).

Even so, it took courage to decide to excavate the wreck. It would be the first Turkish underwater excavation. I had a very small team and budget. But I remembered George Bass's famous phrase in his book, *Archaeology Beneath The Sea*: "If you don't grab the bull by the horns when you have the chance, you will never get anywhere." So I grabbed the wreck! The day that I raised the first amphora, on 1 October 1998, two dolphins jumped over them. It was unbelievable. Was I liberating some spirit by showing sunlight to those ceramic jars after almost 800 years?

Wine Jars

The amphoras were distributed on a sloping sandy seabed in three principal pockets between 22 and 32 m (72 and 105 ft) deep. At least 30 anchors lay 17 m (56 ft) away from the amphoras, with a group of two-handled, flat-bottomed jars inbetween. We began the excavation by establishing a grid system to divide the site into 160 2-m (6.6-ft) squares and putting datum points around it. Each diver had his own square in which to map every object by taking at least three measurements with meter tapes from four datum points. Using the same computer software as that used by INA during its Bozburun excavation, we recorded extremely accurate three-dimensional locations of all the artifacts on the sea floor. My students had to measure carefully but quickly for at this depth each of us had only 28 minutes for the morning dive and 18 minutes in the afternoon.

Late Byzantine cargo amphoras are not like the Greek or Roman amphoras with which most people are familiar: although thin-walled, they are huge, with large bellies, their size reflecting a need for greater capacity. They represent the transition from clay to wood transport containers.

The amphoras show a wide range of dimensions (41–80 cm (16–31.5 in) high) and capacities (15.5–98.5 liters). The sieved contents of intact amphoras usually yielded grape seeds, which, along with the amphoras' watertight pine-pitch linings, point to a primary cargo of wine. A few amphoras, however, were filled with pine pitch. The large mouths of the flat-bottomed storage jars suggested that they contained some commodity that was not liquid. The ship was carrying around 800 amphoras in total, and we estimate that the weight of the entire cargo of ceramic jars was between 50 and 60 tons.

Amphoras at the excavation house after most had been cleaned of marine growth and desalinated (the process by which salt from seawater is removed from the fabric of artifacts) before being mended.

While the search for human habitation sites was ultimately unsuccessful, the ancient landscape was visible to us once more through images acquired by specially constructed remotely operated vehicles (ROVs) called *Argus* and *Little Hercules* (*L'il Herc* for short). *L'il Herc* looks like a bright yellow balloon on a black "string" attached to *Argus*, and moves more freely and easily because it is not directly towed by the support ship. The ROVs could send video images back to the ship along the thickly clustered wires in the umbilical cord that allowed pilots to maneuver precisely along the seabed and, we knew, within the archaeological sites there.

The tow-sled *Argus* acts as a platform for lights, a video camera, an electronic still camera, and a 35-mm color still camera. *L'il Herc* carries cameras capable of providing extremely high-quality images; it also has a variety of sensors for pressure, depth, and compass heading, and thrusters for movement both laterally and vertically. It carries obstacle avoidance sonar, which was vital to quickly locating the acoustic anomalies we wanted to investigate.

2000 season   CHERYL WARD

A little before midnight, on my first watch after boarding the ship, I came into the "van" where all the equipment is set up, to serve as nautical archaeologist for the watch. "Slowly, slowly, THERE!" said the ROV pilot as we approached our first target and saw *L'il Herc*'s lights suddenly illuminate a wall of amphoras standing about 2 m (6.6 ft) above the seabed. Shipwreck A, the season's first shipwreck, sank with a cargo of dark orange, carrot-shaped shipping jars typical of the Sinop region and probably dates between the 4th and 6th centuries AD.

We moved to another target location, with a quick stop along the way to check what turned out to be a large rock, and almost immediately to a third anomaly that, like the first on my midnight watch, turned out to be a shipwreck marked by a large pile of Sinopian shipping jars. A few jars with a more oval shape were scattered across the top of the site, and indicate a slightly later date of the 4th to early 7th century.

A third significant target became Shipwreck C after ROV inspection. Buried deeply in the sediments is another lost cargo of the early Byzantine period. In the

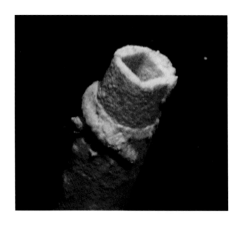

Above **A side-scan sonar survey pass over Shipwreck D showed an upright acoustic shadow more than 10 m (33 ft) long. The ship's mast, its tip illuminated here by *L'il Herc*, heralded the discovery of the best-preserved shipwreck from antiquity.**

Mediterranean, archaeologists have studied many amphora wrecks, but most are swathed beneath a bed of poseidon grass or other sea growth. The shipwrecks we found at depths of 85–100 m (280–330 ft) are all characterized by piles of amphoras in a mound above the seabed, but without the Mediterranean-style cloak of grass. And the wrecks differed in other ways as well: loose timbers scattered on the surface of the site were relatively well preserved, even if we weren't able to identify any of them as hull components.

The last find of the 2000 season was identified in water 320 m (1,050 ft) deep and was the last target to be visited. Its sonar signature – a long, slender, upright feature – transformed itself into the wooden mast of Shipwreck D, standing about 12–14 m (40–46 ft) above the seabed. The mast lacks any trace of erosion, and is beautifully preserved. Hints as to its rigging exist in a fragment of cordage wrapped around the head of the mast just below a squared cavity that might have supported a separate masthead for attaching rigging.

At deck level, the mast disappears into thick brown sediment topped with a fluffy, whitish organic substance biologists call "marine snow," the remains of tiny organisms that live in the water column. A number of spars, partially covered with drifted sediments, lay along the deck, some between two pairs of stanchions aft of the mast. Frame (rib) ends rise above the sediment, and let me generate a rough tracing of the ship's shape and dimensions that came into startling focus in 2003.

2003 season   ROBERT D. BALLARD

Below **The success of the 2000 Black Sea survey provided inspiration and impetus for the construction of *Hercules*, a larger ROV designed and built especially for exploration and testing of archaeological sites in the deep sea.**

During the years leading up to the Black Sea Project, it became increasingly clear that the modern tools of oceanographers could be used to find and document ancient shipwrecks lying in the deep sea in increasing number. Advanced ROVs could also conduct surface sampling of exposed artifacts should that be desired by the Project Archaeologist, but what was also clear was the fact that ROVs developed by the oceanographic community were not ready to conduct an archaeological excavation effort in the deep sea that met standards of excavation techniques for shallow water sites.

My early attempts using the Navy's research submarine NR-1 and the *Jason* ROV from the Woods Hole Oceanographic Institution to excavate a series of Roman trading ships on Skerki Bank proved that excavating a shipwreck buried in the fine-grain sediments of the deep sea was going to be a truly challenging task.

For that reason, we formed a design team consisting of archaeologists, oceanographers, and engineers that resulted in the *Hercules* ROV system, the first ROV ever built to carry out archaeological excavations in the deep sea. In 2003, *Hercules* joined our robotic team and helped us more thoroughly explore the remains of Shipwrecks B and C. But it was the fourth shipwreck that momentarily silenced the usual chatter in the control van as we watched *Hercules* approach it. In nearly three days of work at the site, *Hercules* excavated sediments, collected shipping jars and their contents, acquired acoustic data, and produced thousands of photographs and hours of tape that will let the archaeologists analyze it more carefully.

Our cruise to the Black Sea was the first field testing of the *Hercules* ROV. Using advanced imaging systems, a force-feed-back manipulator, precise closed-loop

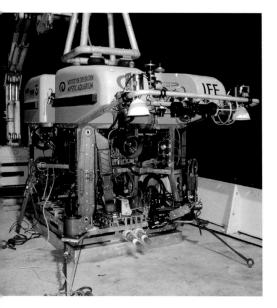

Right In a control room on the research vessel *Knorr*, navigators, ROV pilots, archaeologists, photographers, scientists, and graduate students watch views from over a dozen cameras as *Hercules*, far below in the toxic waters of the Black Sea, carries out around-the-clock commands of project staff.

Below The frames, beams, and parts of the superstructure of Shipwreck D were perfectly preserved despite their long years of exposure. The real test of *Hercules* and its tool set occurred during the delicate recovery of wine jars (below right and bottom right) and the cleaning of timbers adzed to shape in the early 5th century, including the futtock head with hole for a pin (bottom left and center); the beam at 90 degrees to it probably indicates midships as the mast is just behind it.

control, and a sophisticated jetting/pumping system, we easily removed the deep-sea muds surrounding Shipwreck D. The excavating system fulfilled its design specifications and maintained visual supervisory control at all times, proving itself fully capable of excavating an ancient shipwreck.

But this was just a test; further time is now needed to carry out a sustained investigation to determine if the full excavation of deep-water shipwrecks is feasible.

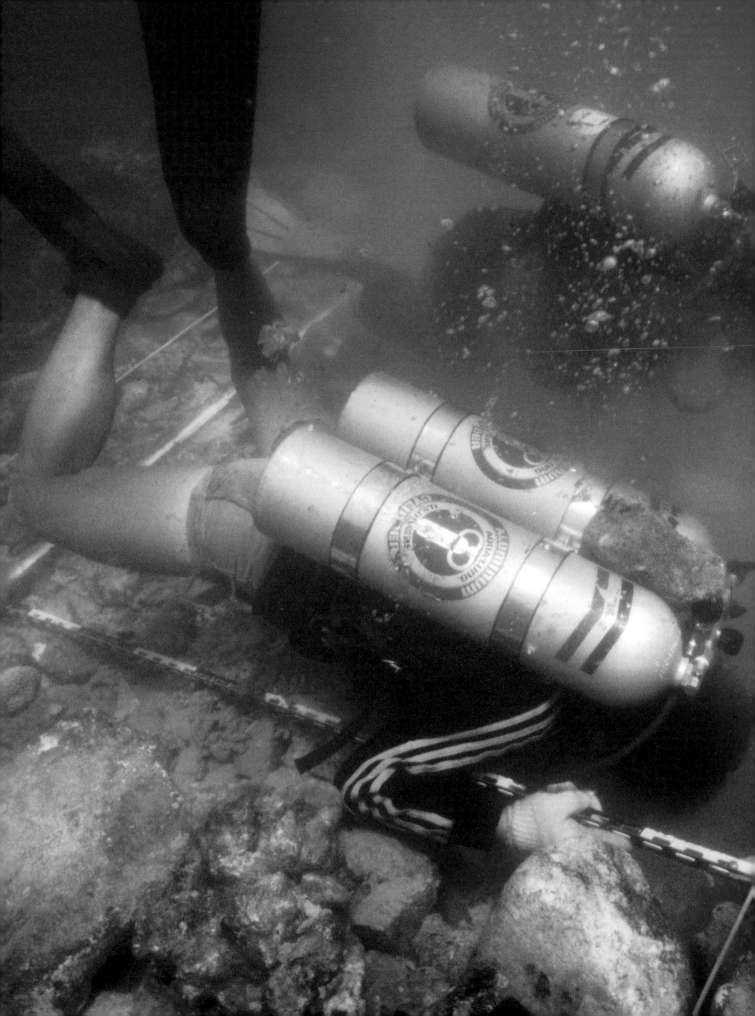

MEDIEVAL AND RENAISSANCE WRECKS

'm a Bronze Age scholar. I'm so ignorant of the medieval and Renaissance periods of Europe that when I was asked to speak on medieval and Renaissance shipwrecks at a national conference of historians, I asked my wife: "When was the medieval period? And when did the Renaissance start?"

"I think the medieval period was when everybody got the plague," she jokingly replied, "and the Renaissance is when they all got well."

These days I'm slightly better informed. The medieval period is also known as the Middle Ages and, more provocatively, the Dark Ages. So as not to confuse you, I will pass over quickly the fact that the Byzantine period we just left in the last section was also part of those Dark Middle Ages!

Although at the end it will return to Yassıada, Turkey, this section will finally take us out of the Mediterranean, with its long and well-recorded history of seafaring, and its long history of marine archaeology, to Southeast Asia and to the Far East – far from medieval Europe. It also takes us to a land excavation, for nautical archaeologists are interested in ships wherever they are found, including those intentionally buried in earlier times, whether by ancient Egyptians or by Vikings, Anglo-Saxons, or other northern Europeans.

The excavation of the 14th-century Shinan wreck was a purely Korean operation, but the Institute of Nautical Archaeology's Donald H. Keith was twice sent to the project by the National Geographic Society, both to offer advice and to recount the story of the excavation to English-speaking readers. More recently, INA Research Associate Jeremy Green visited the National Maritime Museum at Mokpo, which houses the vessel's hull, and talked to those who continue research on the wreck and its valuable cargo.

Although I have twice been to Korea, I have not yet seen the finds from Shinan in the museum at Mokpo. In 2004 in China, however, I was able to see the results of the excavation of a contemporaneous Chinese wreck, equally rich in beautiful, varied, and intact ceramics, excavated opposite the Korean Peninsula under the direction of Zhang Wei of the National Museum of Chinese History in Beijing. Because I knew Zhang Wei when he studied nautical archaeology at Texas A&M University in the spring of 1989, it gave me great pleasure also to visit, in the South China Sea, the diving barges from which he is now excavating an earlier, 12th-century wreck, raising thousands of pieces of intact, glazed ceramics, many of which I saw in the Yangjiang Museum. The publication of these wrecks should be truly extraordinary.

Fred Hocker next takes us to the Zuidersee of the Netherlands, where hundreds, or perhaps thousands of wrecks lie beneath the soil that has been reclaimed from

Two students excavate inside a 2-m (6.6-ft) grid frame on a shallow 16th-century wreck site at Ko Kradat, Thailand. The diver in the foreground, finding himself slightly buoyant, has supplemented his diving weights by placing a rock on his scuba tanks!

the sea. There are so many vessels there that Dutch archaeologists welcome help in recording them, which led to an arrangement whereby graduate students in the Nautical Archaeology Program at Texas A&M University had the opportunity for original research and publication. Fred describes his excavation of a cog, the primary merchant ship of Northern Europe from the 13th through to the 15th century.

Then Jeremy Green transports us to Thailand. The Western Australian Museum, where Jeremy heads the Department of Maritime Archaeology, is perhaps the only institute outside INA that conducts field operations globally, as seen in this book. We are pleased that Jeremy has also worked off and on with us, from the Mediterranean to the Indian Ocean, for nearly four decades. He describes here just one of a number of wrecks he studied during a nautical archaeology training program he conducted for Thai archaeologists.

Lastly, we are introduced to an Ottoman ship of the late 16th or early 17th century. I was personally involved in this one, for when I started tracing timbers going off at an angle from the late 4th- or early 5th-century Byzantine hull I was uncovering at Yassıada, Turkey, in the late 1960s, I thought it was part of the same ship. The Byzantine ship, I assumed, had broken into two pieces, and I was tracing the timbers of one of those pieces. Eventually we realized that this was a later, almost empty ship that had sunk directly onto the Byzantine ship. Cemal Pulak excavated this later ship, dated by a coin to the time of Philip II of Spain, or slightly later, and identified as Ottoman by its contents.

Above **Glazed bowls carried aboard an Ottoman ship that sank in the 16th or early 17th century off Yassıada, Turkey.**

Below **Places mentioned in this section, with the featured wrecks in bold.**

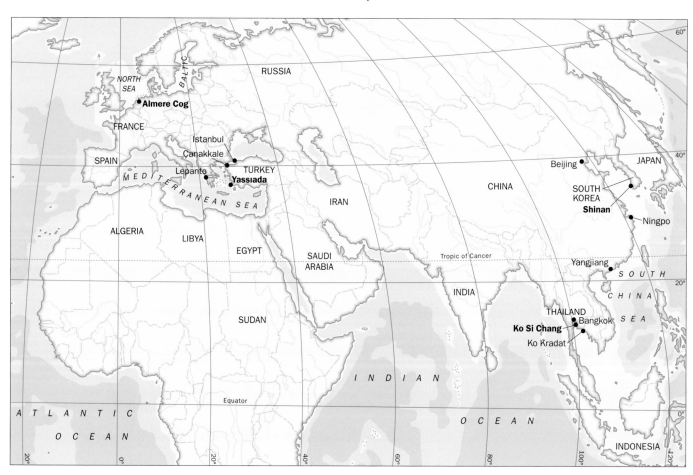

Shinan Wreck

Date c 1323
Depth 20 m (66 ft)
Found by Choi Hyung-gun
Celadons 12,359
Coins 7,000,000
Hull 28.4 m (93 ft) long,
6.6 m (21.5 ft) wide

A 14th-Century Chinese Wreck: Shinan, Korea

GEORGE F. BASS

The glazed statuette of the Buddhist deity Kuan-yin, 24 cm (9 in) tall, was found on the Shinan wreck with part of its head cleanly broken away.

The Institute of Nautical Archaeology's first foray into the Far East, like so many INA adventures, began with a phone call. The year was 1979.

"The Korean Navy is excavating a 14th-century Chinese junk. It's the first real underwater excavation in the Far East. Would you go over as an adviser – and write an article for our magazine?" It was the National Geographic Society.

My hands were already more than full in Turkey.

"I can't make it, but I have the perfect person for you."

I was thinking of Donald H. Keith, who had been with me at Şeytan Deresi and Serçe Limanı, and even on a Revolutionary War wreck in the York River, Virginia. Not only an innovative and brilliant student, Don was one of the finest diver/excavators I knew, uncannily skilled at making beautiful and accurate drawings on the seabed. Don would go on to excavate for INA what was then the oldest known shipwreck in the New World, at Molasses Reef in the Turks and Caicos Islands, where he later established a museum for the display of the finds.

Within days Don was descending a line down 20 m (66 ft) in zero visibility in the Yellow Sea, off the port city of Shinan in southwest Korea. A strong current tugged at him. On the bottom, his dive partner, Lieutenant In Seong-jin, guided Don's hands over what proved to be porcelain and wood protruding from the sediment. Don described what he learned during two trips to Korea in *National Geographic* and, later, *Archaeology* magazines.

The Discovery

The site was found in 1975 by fisherman Choi Hyung-gun, who netted pieces of pottery that were identified by experts as celadons – prized for their resemblance to jade – of the Yuan Dynasty (1260–1386). Choi and his younger brother were rewarded by the South Korean Cultural Properties Preservation Bureau for reporting the discovery, but before a proper excavation could be undertaken, other, less scrupulous fishermen were mining the site for celadons to sell to an antique dealer. Arrests were made, the celadons were recovered, and the Cultural Properties Preservation Bureau, assisted by a Korean Navy squadron commanded by Captain Choi In-sang, began full-scale excavation 2 km (1.2 miles) off shore, sometimes diving in the freezing cold of winter.

In 1982, INA Research Associate Jeremy Green, as part of a research project with Professor Zae Gun Kim of Seoul University, visited the Conservation Laboratory of the National Maritime Museum at Mokpo, and studied a one-fifth scale research model of the ship.

The Finds

By 1989, years after the visits by Don and Jeremy, the results of the excavation were astonishing. Seven million coins, weighing 26.8 tons, provided the earliest date the ship could have sunk; although the coins had been minted over six centuries, the latest was from 1310. An even more precise date for the sinking was provided by a wooden cargo tag with the year 1323 written on it. In addition, with thousands of pieces of porcelain, Korea had attained the largest collection of Yuan Dynasty celadons in the world, many found still cushioned by peppercorns in well-preserved wooden crates.

It seems that sailors of all nationalities have passed their time at sea playing games. On the 11th-century Serçe Limanı Glass Wreck, those on board had played both chess and backgammon, and on wrecks of all periods of antiquity in the Mediterranean,

Below **Among the thousands of objects recovered from the Shinan wreck were Chinese ceramics still packed in remarkably preserved wooden crates – that on the right still marked with the words "great luck." One crate was marked on its top with the grid pattern for the Chinese game of Go, presumably played by the mariners on board.**

Right **This late 18th-century painting of a Chinese ship by William Alexander is one of the earliest by a westerner. Korean and Chinese archaeological excavations are now adding greatly to our knowledge of still earlier Chinese ships.**

Below right **This small bronze lion, only 10 cm (4 in) high, was a censer or incense burner whose head could be removed and replaced.**

sailors seem to have played knucklebones. On top of one of the crates raised at Shinan someone had carved the board for the Chinese game of Go.

Although the lack of visibility prevented the excavators from making a site plan to the accuracy we are accustomed to in the Mediterranean, they placed a metal grid over the site, dividing it into squares 2 m (6.6 ft) on a side, and recalled just where every object in each square had been found during debriefing sessions immediately following each dive. The hull of this, the first seagoing Chinese vessel ever excavated by divers, was in many respects as expected: flat, with transom ends at bow and stern, its interior divided into eight compartments by seven bulkheads.

An inscription on a counterweight for a balance on board suggests the ship may have sailed from Ningpo in China. But what was her destination? Because the Koreans themselves made celadons in the 14th century, it is less likely that the ship was heading for Korea to unload its wares than that it was on its way to Japan, where Chinese celadons were prized imports. Probably driven onto rocks by a storm *en route*, the ship never reached her intended port.

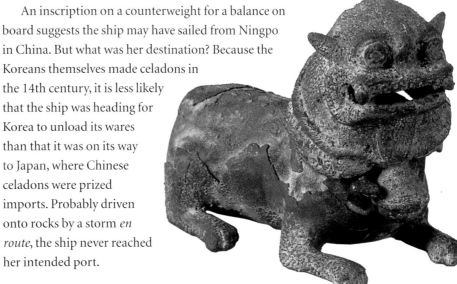

A 15th-Century Cog in the Zuidersee: Almere, Netherlands

FRED HOCKER

The landscape is eerie, disorienting. The ground is flat as far as the eye can see, interrupted only by drainage ditches at regular intervals. Trees are all exactly the same height, in even rows under a gray sky that gives no sense of direction or contrast to the land stretching away to the horizon. This is Flevoland, the land the Dutch reclaimed from the Zuidersee. It is an artificial landscape, the world's largest gardening project, and one of its richest repositories of shipwrecks. It was once a busy artery on the most important east-west sea route in northern Europe, and ships were lost here from the 13th century until draining began in the 1920s. Since 1944, Dutch archaeologists have investigated over 400 shipwrecks in this new land. Many are nearly complete, with contents wonderfully preserved by the bottom mud, including medieval clothing, Renaissance mandolins, and Baroque woodcuts.

Among those wrecks are almost a dozen cogs, the heavy ships that carried the commerce of the High Middle Ages and helped make the Hanseatic League the world's first successful, multinational corporation. One was recovered from the frozen ground in the new town of Almere in the spring of 1986, but there were no resources to document it. No cargo survived, only a few small finds, but these included a human skeleton and a curious wooden clapper. The clapper, in the form

Almere Cog

Sunk 1422–1433
Excavation 1986
Recording 1988
Hull 16.4 m (54 ft) long,
4.2 m (14 ft) wide
Cargo capacity c 30 tons
Cargo unknown

Left **The substantially complete remains of the cog lie flattened out in the mud where they were discovered in 1986, during construction of a new subdivision in the town of Almere.**

Right **A spade, axe and adze found on board the vessel. They were not worth retrieving when the cargo was salvaged, probably soon after the sinking.**

Right **Conservation of the only coin found on the wreck revealed it to be a silver 4-reale piece issued between 1566 and 1589 by Philip II of Spain.**

Below **An archaeologist photographs the oak ribs or frame timbers of the Ottoman shipwreck; the bow is at the bottom of the picture. The site is divided into 2-m (6.6-ft) square grids for mapping purposes and the timbers labeled with tags for easy identification.**

anticipation, INA exposed again the bow section to lift its shroud of mystery. Unfortunately, the campaign was brief, for the outbreak of hostilities between Turkey, Cyprus and Greece that year necessitated immediate evacuation of Yassıada. The waterlogged timbers were abandoned once more.

In 1982, when George Bass decided to re-initiate the excavation of this shipwreck for a Council of Europe field school that INA was hosting in Turkey with the Bodrum Museum of Underwater Archaeology, the coin had been thoroughly cleaned, and identified as a 4-reale piece issued between 1566 and 1589 by Philip II of Spain. My interests lay in 16th-century seafaring, but particularly in ships of the Ottoman Turks – and I suspected this was an Ottoman ship because of its date and location. No intact early Ottoman shipwreck had ever been found and excavated, which meant we knew far more about Classical Greek, Roman, and Byzantine ships than early Ottoman ships. Yet, in the 16th century, the Ottoman Empire had built one of the largest and most formidable navies in the Mediterranean. A major reason for this disparity is that perishable barrels and skins replaced easily detectable and virtually indestructible amphoras in maritime commerce after the 13th century.

At the conclusion of the 1982 campaign we had a fairly good idea about the size of the Ottoman ship and its construction details, but its precise date and function remained a mystery. In hopes of answering these two questions we began our final campaign the following summer. Unlike the previous campaign, conducted from a comfortable camp built on Yassıada for the field school, the 1983 excavation was to take place with only a handful of veteran INA archaeologists and field personnel operating exclusively from *Virazon*.

We again exposed the hull and recorded it on our site plan. The extant timbers suggested that the ship had been at least 20 m (66 ft) in length and about 6 m (20 ft) in beam, of moderate size for its time, but obviously not a rowed war galley of the type used extensively by the Ottoman fleet. With the exception of a few artifacts and a handful of pottery, the ship was empty. Nor was there any indication that it had been carrying perishable cargo, such as grain, that disappeared after the ship sank. This made it all the more puzzling, for how could a ship sink and stay down for three centuries without the weight of heavy cargo or ballast? With its frames and planking of oak, all fastened with iron nails, the ship would have been heavier than a comparable pine-built vessel, but still not sufficiently heavy to sink to the bottom on its own. The answer may be found in the fact the ship was empty, for no ship would sail without taking on some cargo or ballasting to increase its stability during sailing. This meant that after striking the reef, the wounded vessel remained suspended on it for a time before gradually sinking to its watery grave, as had been the fate of the Lebanese freighter that sank in 1993. Evidence for this is found in the ship's badly battered keel, which was broken at three different places. While the ship remained afloat on the reef, there must have been time to salvage everything of value. Nothing of worth, not a single anchor, nor tools or weapons in any quantity, was left on the ship. Even the cargo, whatever it was, had been removed, perhaps transferred to an escort ship or to some vessel that had come to the sinking ship's aid. What remained probably spilled on the reef from the gaping holes in the bottom of the hull. It is impossible to know how long our ship remained suspended on the reef, but it must have been long enough for its oak planking to become waterlogged and sufficiently heavy to sink rather than float off to be smashed apart by pounding waves on some rocky coast.

An Ottoman Naval Vessel?

We wondered if our ship could have played a role in the Battle of Lepanto, one of the greatest sea battles ever fought and the last major battle fought with oared ships. On 7 October 1571, off Lepanto in western Greece, the advancing Ottoman fleet met the most powerful fleet ever launched by Christendom, consisting of Venetian, Spanish, papal, Genoese, Savoy, and Maltese galleys, as well as six large Venetian galleasses. The Christian fleet won a decisive victory, marking the end of unchallenged Ottoman naval supremacy in the eastern Mediterranean. Was our ship a transport or supply vessel that carried marines or provisions at Lepanto? The 4-reale coin indicated that the ship could not have sunk before 1566, but it could have any time after that date. Had the nearly one hundred cannonballs we found spilled on top of the reef come from our ship? Could they and the two stone and one cast iron cannonballs of smaller gauge found aboard indicate that our ship had been a naval supply vessel?

We found two large and ten smaller glazed bowls on the wreck. Aside from differences in size and glazing, they are similar – deep bowls with slightly incurving rims and conical pedestal bases. They are decorated inside with the *sgraffito* technique, the design incised on the top layer of glaze. The bowls correspond in number to the number of crew for a medium-sized naval supply ship with two officers and ten sailors. Duplicate bowls come from excavations at Saraçhane in Istanbul, the Agora of Athens, and Bodrum Castle, all associated with Ottoman military presence (it is fitting that the last location now houses the Bodrum Museum of Underwater Archaeology where the Yassıada Ottoman shipwreck finds are kept). It is likely, therefore, that the bowls represent military consignments. This seems substantiated by the discovery of several bowl fragments of the same type from a pottery workshop on the Dardanelles at Çanakkale, which served as a base for one of the Ottoman fleets. Analysis by Sophie Stos revealed that the lead isotopes in the bowls' glazing is consistent with that mined in the region of Çanakkale, suggesting that all the bowls were made in a single area that produced pottery for Ottoman naval use. But even with an established connection between the Yassıada ship and the Ottoman Navy, what of the battle of Lepanto?

Tree-Ring Detective

We turned to Peter Kuniholm of the Wiener Dendrochronology Laboratory at Cornell University. Since radiocarbon dates were not sufficiently precise, I hoped he could help us accurately date the ship. Matching the growth rings of undated wood with those that have been assembled into a continuous sequence of rings, dendrochronologists are able to determine the date of any well-preserved wood precisely to the year and sometimes to the season during which a tree was felled, providing that the sample has sufficient number of rings present and its bark is preserved. I sent a 5-cm (2-in) thick slice from the ship's keel to Peter, who provided a tentative working date of 1572. However, since an indeterminable number of growth

Below **Illustrator Netia Piercy studies a large glazed bowl for illustration purposes. A total of 12 glazed bowls of three sizes were found on the wreck; examples of medium and small-sized bowls can be seen on the drafting table.**

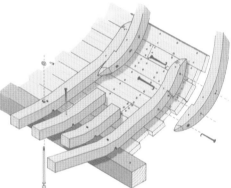

Below Sectional reconstruction of the ship. Each frame, consisting of a futtock fastened to either end of the floor timber with a hook joint and three double-clenched nails, is secured to the keel with a large spike or a forelock bolt. A smaller keel-like timber, called a keelson, that sat atop the frames had completely vanished.

rings had been shaved off during the fashioning of the keel, the tree from which it was made would have been felled well after that date, indicating that the ship was built after Lepanto, although probably not much later.

The Yassıada Ottoman shipwreck nevertheless remains the best-preserved and only completely excavated 16th- or early 17th-century Ottoman period shipwreck. With the exception of part of the ship's planking, all of the timbers have been raised and are in wet storage in the Bodrum Museum of Underwater Archaeology. Even though the full study of the timbers and preliminary reconstruction of the ship is yet to be completed, we have already learned much about a relatively recent but hitherto unknown period in the maritime history of the Mediterranean.

Upon sinking, the Ottoman ship's starboard side came to rest partly on the amphora cargo of a 4th-century merchantman near its bow (left). The ship listed to port, quickly burying that side under sand, preserving it, while the starboard side perished almost completely. The large timber at the right is the ship's sternpost.

SEVENTEENTH-CENTURY WRECKS

INA archaeologists need to keep their passports up to date. For the 17th-century sites they describe here, they excavated in both northern and southern Europe, on two Caribbean islands, and in East Africa, and then conserved an entire ship raised off the coast of Texas!

Robert Neyland, who would go on to salvage and conserve the famous Confederate submarine *Hunley* off Charleston, South Carolina, here describes an excavation he conducted in a hay field for the Netherlands Institute of Ship- and Underwater Archaeology (NISA) when he was still a doctoral candidate in the Nautical Archaeology Program at Texas A&M University. He takes us again to the Zuidersee, where Fred Hocker excavated the medieval Almere cog. Where else are nautical archaeologists photographed with windmills in the background?

In Portugal, as I stood high on Lisbon's São Julião da Barra fortress one day in 1998, I had goose bumps. Francisco Alvez, head of his country's outstanding program of nautical archaeology, was vividly recounting to a group of us the tragic events that had transpired below almost four centuries earlier. The *Nossa Senhora dos Mártires*, returning from India, tried again and again to enter the mouth of the Tagus River during a storm. Failing, the doomed ship was destroyed, with great loss of life, in full view of the families of those on board who were returning home after so many months away.

Filipe Castro, one of Francisco's assistants, whom I met the same day, soon enrolled at Texas A&M University, where he earned a doctorate, and then joined the faculty of the Nautical Archaeology Program. How pleased I was, then, when my new colleague, Filipe, completed the excavation and study of that terrible tragedy, which he describes here.

The role of Peter Throckmorton in the history of nautical archaeology should be clear by now to readers of this book. Not only had he initially involved me in diving on and excavating shipwrecks, but he did the same for Jerome Hall, who later served as president of the Institute of Nautical Archaeology. Jerome was earning a Master's degree in marine biology at Nova University in Florida when he met Peter, then on the university's faculty. It was Peter who directed Jerome to the Dominican Republic and the Monte Cristi wreck, the Pipe Wreck that Jerome describes in the following pages.

One rare wreck I can visit without a passport is that of famous French explorer La Salle's ship *La Belle*. In only 20 minutes I can drive to Texas A&M University's Conservation Research Laboratory, where I am repeatedly awed by the conservation of the ship's hull and contents, under the direction of INA's current president, Donny

A diver raises a decorative wooden cherub from the wreck of *Santo Antonio de Tanna* in Mombasa Harbor, Kenya. Carved wooden wings were found nearby.

Above **Donny Hamilton gingerly removes concretion from an Amerindian vulture-headed metate (corn grinder) found at Port Royal.** *Below* **Places mentioned in this section, with the featured wrecks in bold.**

Hamilton. Or I can step a few feet away from my office into the office of Barto Arnold, who joined INA shortly after discovering *La Belle* and overseeing construction of a cofferdam around it to enable its excavation in dry air.

Donny seems fated to deal with thousands of artifacts wherever he works. In 1692, the infamous pirate stronghold of Port Royal, Jamaica, at that time the richest English colony in the New World, became the submarine equivalent of Pompeii when it sank beneath the waves in a massive earthquake. In 1980 I was invited to Jamaica, where Prime Minister Edward Seaga asked if INA would undertake the archaeological excavation of the sunken city. Although this was not primarily a ship-wreck excavation – a ship was later found driven into the city by the earthquake's accompanying tsunami – I accepted on the spot, and then asked Donny Hamilton to direct the project, which he did in exemplary fashion for the following decade as a Texas A&M University field school.

INA's involvement in East Africa similarly began with an invitation, this one from Hamo Sassoon, Curator of the Fort Jesus Museum in Mombasa, Kenya. Hamo asked me if INA would examine a wreck located by local divers in Mombasa Harbor, thinking it might be one of the Portuguese ships that had come to the aid of Portuguese Fort Jesus when it was besieged by Omani Arabs at the end of the 17th century. I asked Don Frey and Robin Piercy to undertake the examination, which they did in 1975. Two years later Robin began full-scale excavation of the wreck of the Portuguese *Santo Antonio de Tanna*, which takes him regularly back to Mombasa to study the artifacts for his ultimate publication of the site.

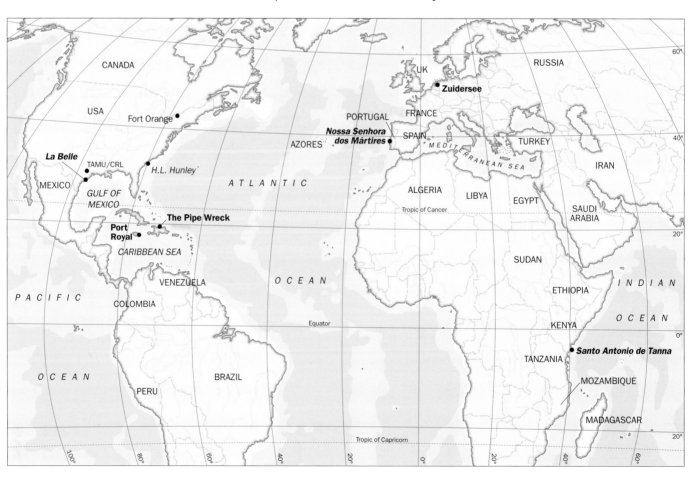

Zuidersee
OH 107 Wreck

Date Late 17th century
Found by NISA, 1962
Excavation 1989
Length 16.5 m (54 ft)
Cargo unknown

Ship Archaeology in a Hay Field: Zuidersee, Netherlands

ROBERT S. NEYLAND

Lucas van Dijk, NISA conservator, prepares a site plan of OH 107 by tracing the hull timbers with a mechanical device called a pantograph. The pantograph uses a series of cables and reduction gears to reduce the original shape of the hull timbers traced to a 1:20 scale.

The wind rippled through the expanse of grass growing over what was once the seabed of the Zuidersee. I imagined an unlucky day for the captain and crew of the newly unearthed boat as the winds began to fill her sails…the breeze starting to blow, building up the waves, and swamping the little freighter. In 1692, or a few years thereafter, these poor souls lost their boat and all their possessions.

OH 107

Our shipwreck lay in agricultural lot "H 107" in the Dutch Province of Flevoland. Named simply "OH 107" when discovered in 1962 by Dutch archaeologists of the Netherlands Institute of Ship- and Underwater Archaeology (NISA), its excavation would wait until I arrived in 1989 with a team of Dutch, German, and Texas A&M University archaeologists. In only three months we unearthed and recorded the 16.5-m (54-ft) long hull and its contents. A similar feat underwater would have taken several field seasons. "We ran an iron-man marathon in archaeology, with events in excavation, hull disassembly and recording, and conservation," commented an exhausted Birgit Schröder, who helped me direct and publish the excavation.

OH 107 is a typical Dutch find in the diked, drained, and reclaimed land called the "IJsselmeerpolder." The wreck was discovered when a machine cutting an agricultural drainage ditch in the newly reclaimed land chewed through ship's wood. Geology revealed to the Dutch NISA staff that the wrecking occurred after AD 1600, when a storm surge increased salinity of the water and deposited salt-laden clay and a thin but distinct layer of marine shells. OH 107 clearly broke through these layers as it sank into the soft seabed. Objects of the crew's everyday life – clay pots, glass bottles, tobacco pipes, and coins – confirmed that the vessel sank no earlier than 1692. Tree rings in the boat's timbers revealed that the trees were harvested between AD 1685 and 1693. An absence of scars from repairs in the unblemished hull suggested that it had only a short career before its owner lost it…and his livelihood.

Excavation

A few shovelfuls of mud made it clear that the bow was the center of life onboard – and the fragile state of the artifacts, which needed to be documented and rescued before being destroyed by the sun, demanded that excavation start there. In the bow was the cabin where the captain slept, managed finances, and took meals. The boat's hearth was a brick and glazed-tile fireplace with wood chimney. A few peat blocks, which provided fuel for the cooking fire, lay scattered among the fireplace bricks. An assortment of glazed ceramic pots, bowls, a pitcher, glass bottles, a cast-iron pot and a bronze skillet represented the galley. A single oil lamp provided enough light for the captain to keep his eye on the compass, found here, and to administer the boat's business, evidenced by a pencil and a pair of lead tokens that were carried as proof of payment for tolls on the canals. Clay tobacco pipes, a sewing kit, and even an ice skate were for more leisurely pastimes.

As our excavation moved away toward the middle of the boat, and the cargo hold, recovery of artifacts slowed. No cargo remained, but it was evident from the absence of protective ceiling planking, or flooring, over the frames (or ribs) that the boat was designed to carry a cargo unlikely to damage the hull, perhaps agricultural produce or peat, the indispensable fuel for the fires of both Dutch industry and homes. An amazing find was part of the mast and its supporting framework called a "tabernacle." The weight of a cannon fragment had prevented the mast from floating away, for clever Dutch boat-builders had recycled the fragment for use as a counterweight for the mast, fastening it on with heavy iron straps. This arrangement allowed a small crew to man the boat while frequently raising and lowering the mast as they passed beneath bridges along the rivers and canals of their route.

I anticipated another significant area of finds at the stern. Here would be another cabin, perhaps the mate's lodging or an area for storing the boat's equipment. The excavation quickly revealed that the stern was used differently than the bow. A small and unfurnished cabin was only a humble cuddy containing a caulking iron, clay pot with caulk, chamber pot, and iron scrap. A jumble of bricks proved to be a crude floor. The stern cuddy had the most menial of tools and was too crude to lodge a crewman. A hammer, apparently on the stern deck when the boat careened onto its port side, slid with such force across the deck that it was found still firmly lodged inside the port scupper. "The hammer…used with the caulking iron to drive caulk in the seams… tells the story of our helmsman's hurried struggle to plug a leaking hull," I speculated.

A Working Boat

The captain's possessions told the boat's story. They spoke of a freighter that worked the northern waters of the Netherlands, but also made trips south, plying a route between what are today the Netherlands and Belgium. Most of the artifacts were typical of the northern Dutch provinces, although a few clearly originated in the lower Rhine and show a Flemish connection. One unique find was a green glass bottle wrapped in woven straw, much like a modern Chianti bottle. This type, known as "Fransche Flessen," contained not wine but water from the famous source in Spa in the Southern Provinces. Another surprising discovery was the tureen that served soups prepared in the forward cabin. It was decorated with a stylized "IHS," a Jesuit symbol common in Catholic regions to the south, an exceptional find for the Protestant region where the boat was lost.

OH 107 was a working boat built to ply bulk cargo along the rivers, canals, and over the open waters of the Zuidersee. Built and lost in the last decades of the 17th century, she provides a window into the culture and technology of the time. Despite the boat being 300 years old, its construction shows strong affinities with Dutch boats from the 20th century, perhaps not surprising in a nation of ancient boat-building traditions. It was similar to those built in South Holland, as well as in the provinces of the north, again indicating Dutch and Flemish connections.

Above **A green glass bottle wrapped in woven straw of a type used between 1650 and 1750 for exporting water from the famous source in Spa. They are often referred to as "Fransche Flessen" or French bottles.**

Opposite **The port side and bottom hull planking of OH 107 lies exposed in the hay field. The view is from bow to stern. All of the artifacts, mast and mast step, and frames have been removed. The planking was then recorded and removed.**

Below **Soup was served to the crew in a tureen decorated with a slip glaze that depicts the stylized Jesuit symbol "IHS."**

The Pepper Wreck: Nossa Senhora dos Mártires, *Lisbon, Portugal*

FILIPE CASTRO

Above **The *naus da India* were among the largest ships of their time, designed and built for very long voyages.**

Right **Raising a garboard plank. These massive hull timbers, 11 cm (4.3 in) thick, ensured the sturdiness required to survive the harsh conditions of a six-month trip covering almost 12,000 nautical miles (22,200 km).**

Those on shore, awaiting the return of their loved ones, must have watched in horror at what they saw unfolding in the fury of the storm blowing from the south. The day before, although within sight of Lisbon, Captain Manuel Barreto Rolim had not risked sailing into the Tagus River, but had dropped anchor at Cascais Bay, 33 km (20 miles) to the north. Now, on 14 September 1606, he was willing to try the narrow entry. He almost made it through. But the wind must have fallen for a moment, allowing his ship to be dragged by violent tidal currents running in the channel. And there, at the entrance of the Tagus River mouth, in full view of wives and children, the Portuguese Indiaman *Nossa Senhora dos Mártires*, returning from India, struck a submerged rock and sank.

Witnesses said that within two hours there was such an enormous amount of debris floating around the shipwreck site that it looked more like the loss of an entire fleet than of a single ship. In the fierce storm many did not make it to land, in spite of the scarce 200 m (660 ft) that separated the sinking hull from the fortress of São Julião da Barra. On that very day more than 50 bodies washed ashore on the nearby beaches, and the body count rose to over 200 in the days that followed.

Left **Portuguese merchants as seen by Kano Domi, a Japanese artist in the last decade of the 16th century. Portuguese merchants first arrived in Japan in 1543.**

Pepper Wreck

Sunk **14 September 1606**
Depth **10 m (33 ft)**
Excavation **1996–2001**
Cargo **peppercorns, ceramics, luxury goods**
Hull **c 40 m (132 ft) long**
Crew and passengers **c 600**
Casualties **over 200**

The enormous amount of peppercorns stored in the holds of the *Nossa Senhora dos Mártires* floated to the surface, forming a black tide that drifted up and down the river for many days after the shipwreck. In spite of the dreadful weather the population made it to sea in small boats to salvage as much pepper as they could, and to recover all the boxes, bales, and barrels that washed ashore, as the soldiers patrolling the beaches were unable to stop them.

Arrangements were made in the fortress of São Julião da Barra to accommodate all the peppercorns that were recovered by the king's officers; the pepper was put out to dry, to be sold afterwards, although at a reduced price. The arduous bureaucratic process of identifying bodies and merchandise began immediately.

A Portuguese Indiaman

Indiamen were enormous by early 17th-century standards. Measuring more than 40 m (132 ft) from bow to stern, they sailed annually from Lisbon to Goa or Cochin, on the Indian subcontinent, and returned with heavy loads of rich merchandise from Asia: peppercorns, ginger, and white cotton cloth from India; cinnamon from Ceylon; cloves, nutmeg, and mace from the Moluccas in today's Indonesia; as well as many exotic goods such as precious woods, drugs, gold, diamonds, jewels, exotic animals, and pearls from the Red Sea; furniture, silks, many types of pottery, and stoneware jars from Pegu, in today's Burma; and highly prized Chinese porcelain.

Manned by crews of over 150 sailors and officers, these *naus da India*, as they were called, transported hundreds of soldiers and passengers, sometimes carrying as many as 800 people. It was said that, in spite of the small space, weeks went by after leaving port before first-day acquaintances encountered one another on the crowded decks.

When all went well, these trips lasted six months each way, but the *Nossa Senhora dos Mártires* arrived in Lisbon nine months after leaving Cochin, India, after a stop

Below **Peppercorns, one of the richest cargoes of the Portuguese Asian trade in the 16th century, were transported in the holds of the Indiamen in compartments sealed and caulked to resist the humid environment during the long voyage from India to Portugal.**

over in the Azores. Aires de Saldanha, a former Portuguese viceroy in India returning home on this ship, died during the voyage and the *Nossa Senhora dos Mártires* put up in the Azores to bury him.

We do not know more about the shipwreck or, for that matter, much about these ships and most of their voyages. In 1755 Lisbon was destroyed by an earthquake and its archives and libraries burned for weeks afterwards. A detailed account of this shipwreck was mentioned in an 18th-century inventory of books and documents of Portuguese libraries, but it must have been lost before the second half of the 19th century, since it was not mentioned in a later inventory of Portuguese literature dating from 1860.

A handful of names associated with the voyage survived in Portuguese and Spanish archives. Manuel Barreto Rolim, the captain of the ship, for example, had left Lisbon the previous year, seeking his fortune in the India trade after being disinherited by his father following an unapproved marriage.

Another name we know is that of Francisco Rodrigues, a Jesuit priest from the Japanese mission who was coming to Europe in the company of a young Japanese Catholic called Miguel. Father Rodrigues refused a place in the ship's boat and lost his life when the *Mártires* wrecked. Miguel survived and is known to have sailed back to Asia, dying in China years later, without ever returning to Japan.

A third name related to this voyage is that of cabin boy Cristóvão de Abreu, whose life illustrates well the lives of the adventurers who sailed on such ships as the *Mártires*. He survived another shipwreck a few miles from this one four years later, in 1610, on the way to India aboard the *Nossa Senhora da Oliveira*. Pursuing his career as an apprentice on the India Route he engaged in many other voyages, survived the shipwreck of the *Nossa Senhora de Belém* on the coast of South Africa in 1635, and the 800 km (480 mile) march that followed to the nearest Portuguese trade post in Mozambique. After surviving his fourth shipwreck, on the ship *S. Bento*, in 1642, Cristóvão de Abreu died at sea in 1645, returning from India as boatswain of the *nau S. Lourenço*.

In the summers that followed the shipwreck much of the artillery, anchors, cables, and rigging were salvaged by the king's officers. The shipwreck of the *Nossa Senhora dos Mártires* was forgotten soon afterwards and its remains covered by a layer of white sand. Large rocks found their way over the hull remains, possibly carried by the tidal waves that followed the earthquake of 1755, or by some other storm of which we have no record.

Archaeology of the Wreck

In 1994 the remains of the hull were found, during a survey conducted by a team from Lisbon's National Museum of Archaeology. Nobody had ever excavated a *nau da India*, and the "Pepper Wreck" presented itself as a great opportunity for both archaeologists and naval historians. Although we have several texts, descriptions, and images of these ships, based on the historical data alone it is very difficult to form a good idea of their actual size, how they performed on the sea, and most importantly to nautical archaeologists, how they were designed and built.

In 1996 Francisco Alves, director of the Centro Nacional de Arqueologia Náutica e Subaquática, and I began the archaeological excavation of the site, which we

Below **One of three astrolabes found on the Pepper Wreck, named São Julião da Barra III, bears a maker's mark "G" from the Lisbon Goes atelier, and the date of the departure of the nau *Nossa Senhora dos Mártires* from Lisbon to Goa: 1605.**

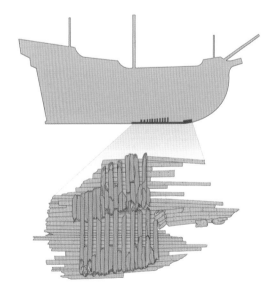

continued through 1998. Soon an impressive collection of artifacts was uncovered, including three astrolabes, nautical dividers, and sounding leads. Gaming pieces, pewter plates and personal jewels illustrated daily life aboard. Most impressive was the collection of artifacts related with trade, the main reason for these voyages. Exotic wood, red coral, a gold bead, and pots from Burma, China and Japan, gave an idea of the geographical span of commerce in which the Portuguese merchants were involved. Chinaware, a luxury possessed by only a few, was also found among an extensive layer of peppercorns that marked in the strata the historic moment in which the shipwreck occurred.

But the most interesting item in the artifact collection was the ship's hull, which I excavated between 1999 and 2001 for the Portuguese authorities and the Institute of Nautical Archaeology. We know so little about these large floating cities, described by their Asian trading partners as tall, black, smelly, and swarming with the activity of its pale, fierce, and long-nosed sailors, soldiers and passengers!

A small portion of the hull survived four centuries of currents and swells, resting between two rocky outcrops, under a layer of peppercorns that was often as much as 35 cm (about 1 ft) thick. It was solidly built of stone pine planks nailed to frames of cork oak with long iron spikes. Using some of its critical dimensions, and applying sets of proportions described in three Portuguese treatises on shipbuilding from the late 16th and early 17th centuries, we tentatively reconstructed the hull. Computer simulation techniques will allow us to test the performance of this hull model under sail, and for different conditions of weather and cargo loads, providing a better understanding of a largely unknown ship type's sailing abilities.

Our archaeological study provides a wonderful opportunity to learn firsthand about the size, strength, and performance of Portuguese Indiamen, and how they offered a living environment for an enormous crowd of sailors, soldiers, merchants, and adventurers – and even to speculate on the hopes and dreams of the inhabitants of "these dark wandering places," as Joseph Conrad describes large oceanic ships, as they saw for the first time the Indian Ocean and the exotic realms of Asia.

Below The hull remains of the Pepper Wreck preserved only a small portion of the ship, but the existence of carpenters' design marks yielded enough information to allow its reconstruction with a fair degree of certainty.

A Tobacconist's Dream:
The Pipe Wreck, Monte Cristi,
Dominican Republic

JEROME LYNN HALL

When Peter Throckmorton, pioneer of nautical archaeology, shared his excitement late one winter evening about a shipwreck on the north coast of Hispaniola, I sensed a new adventure was unfolding. "Pipes," he whispered as we sat in the Oceanographic Center library. "She's littered with thousands of clay tobacco smoking pipes."

The gleam in his eyes and the way that he nervously studied the people moving about the room befitted someone who had just stumbled upon a cache of gold, not clay pipes. Sensing that I had no idea why such a cargo was considered a prized find, he jumped again into his animated narrative. "They're important tools for dating archaeological sites. If analyzed properly, these pipes will be of great benefit to scholars studying the colonial history of the Americas."

The wreck – little more than a pile of timbers and scattered cargo – forms a small coral reef in the shallow bay of Monte Cristi in the Dominican Republic, only a few miles east of the Haitian border. "She was," he mused quietly, "likely English and contemporary with the *Mayflower*." That alone made it unique since, according to Peter, no English merchant hull from this period had ever been studied. Furthermore, a considerable portion of her timbers remained, making an excavation worthwhile.

Right **Peter Throckmorton, pioneer of nautical archaeology, whose vision and encouragement led to the Monte Cristi Shipwreck Project.**

Monte Cristi
Pipe Wreck

Date 1658–1665
Depth 4.4 m (14.4 ft)
Found by Johnny Bigleaguer
Excavation 1991–present
Cargo *c* 500,000 clay pipes
Nationality Dutch

Above **Isla Cabra, home to the Monte Cristi Shipwreck Project. Large salt pans dominate the central portion of the island. The "Pipe Wreck" lies in the shallow water between the shore and the mainland in the foreground.**

Opposite above ***Still Life*, by 17th-century Dutch artist Pieter Claesz, offers a tantalizing glimpse into the paraphernalia of smoking: a ceramic brazier holds embers from which fire is transferred to the pipe by "spills," or lighting sticks. Note, too, a Rhenish stoneware jug on its side, another artifact type found on the "Pipe Wreck."**

Opposite **Team member Yvonne Broeder works at the dredge screen as the site is uncovered.**

As his tale unfolded, it became clear that in spite of apparent damage from years of extensive looting, this "Pipe Wreck," as it was commonly known, was a remarkable site. What it deserved – and had never been given – was a proper archaeological study.

A few weeks later, Peter surprised me with an invitation to join his survey team. Faced with such an opportunity, everything else in my schedule seemed relatively meaningless. We departed Miami and landed in Santo Domingo, making our way by bus across the island to the barren northern hinterlands. Our summer itinerary dictated that in addition to the "Pipe Wreck," we would survey some of the numerous other shipwrecks to be found in the area. When the season finally ended, we had examined over 30 sunken vessels spanning the 16th to the 19th centuries, yet it was the "Pipe Wreck" that sent Peter home with visions of a full-scale excavation.

The following year, Peter busied himself with myriad other projects while simultaneously trying to raise the funds necessary to return to the Dominican Republic. I joined the INA excavation at Uluburun in Turkey and quickly became "immersed" in the Late Bronze Age. Our dream to return to the "Pipe Wreck" never lost its luster until one afternoon when, immediately after our morning dive on the Bronze Age wreck, a somber Don Frey – then Vice-President of INA – put his arm on my shoulder and told me he had received sad news: Peter had passed quietly in his sleep a few days earlier.

Why it was up to me to pick up the pieces of Peter's dream isn't certain, except, perhaps, that I too had fallen under the spell of the "Pipe Wreck." After days of quiet deliberation, I decided that this odd assortment of broken timbers, ceramic sherds, and clay tobacco pipes would finally get what it deserved: a proper archaeological excavation.

I returned to America and fell on the financial graces of friends, family, and several granting organizations. A new team was assembled and we soon embarked on what clearly would be a multi-year project. Our research was predicated on several important questions: what was a northern European vessel doing on the north coast of Hispaniola? Whence did it come? Where was it headed? When and why did it sink?

Above **Bearded faces decorate the necks of the Bartmannkrüge, Rhenish stoneware jugs excavated from the site.**

Below **Francis Soto Tejeda, Director of the shipwreck conservation laboratory in Santo Domingo, holds a silver ochos reales, one of 28 coins recovered from the site. Inset Six of these were from the Potosí mint in Peru and were manufactured sometime after 1649. Here, a devaluation counter stamp in the form of a circled crown lies sideways beneath the Jerusalem Cross.**

The Excavation

We arrived at Monte Cristi in the summer of 1991 and set up our base camp on Isla Cabra, a desert island – overrun with rats, scorpions, and a host of biting insects – some 150 m (492 ft) leeward of the site. With the help of Johnny Bigleaguer, the Monte Cristeño fisherman who found the wreck in the early 1960s, we placed our small wooden platform, the R.V. *Rummy Chum*, directly over the reef, 4.4 m (14.4 ft) below, and began working.

What emerged in the following months – and consistently throughout subsequent years – was a cornucopia of 17th-century commercial goods: sherds of blue-and-white glazed earthenware and Rhenish stoneware ceramics, thimbles, combs, straight pins, curtain rings, nested weights, glass beads, iron cooking cauldrons, and assorted brass lighting implements.

And, of course, clay tobacco smoking pipes. Fishermen, salvors, and government officials who worked on the wreck in the early 1960s estimated that they had raised at least several hundred thousand pipes before our team arrived. Some even approximated the total to be over 500,000! Peter's observation that pipes were useful for dating archaeological sites was accurate. Because 17th-century clay pipes were stylish and fragile, they were also popular and disposable. Their ephemeral composition meant that they were constantly broken and replaced, and that their form changed – as most fashions do – on a fairly regular basis. An artifact group that can be distinctly and easily assigned to a specific, but narrow, time frame is nothing short of an archaeologist's dream.

Our collection – meager by comparison – numbers close to 10,000 and yet comprises only two types: pipes with barrel-shaped bowls – accounting for roughly 93 percent of the assemblage – and those with bowls shaped like inverted cones, known as funnel pipes. All are of Dutch manufacture and date to the mid-17th century, but while the former were preferred by Europeans and European-American colonists, funnel pipes are clear imitations of Native American designs and were intended exclusively for the tribal trade.

We know from the silver coins minted in South America that our vessel met her demise sometime after 1651. Exactly why she sank hasn't yet been established, but a small cluster of approximately 800 glass beads may hold a tantalizing clue. Originally strung in hanks, these once spherical beads are now, according to Robert Brill of the Corning Museum of Glass, "slumped and fused" into each other, a phenomenon which occurs with intense heat that lasts for a short period of time. Divers have also uncovered many large "splatters" of melted brass and lead, as well as numerous pieces of charred wood. Interestingly, only 13.9 m (45.6 ft) of outer planking, ceiling, and framing from one side of the keel remained. Do these clues point to an explosion on board?

Interpreting the Evidence

Studies of the ship's timbers by the Dutch Dendrochronology Center in Amsterdam indicate that the hull was constructed from English oak sometime after 1649. Though English-built, our ship apparently flew the Dutch Tricolor, for its typically Dutch cargo compares well with archaeological collections from upstate New York and, specifically, the Dutch-American settlement at Fort Orange (modern-day Albany).

The archaeological record held other important secrets: beef, pork, salted fish, and conch were the foodstuffs that sustained the sailors on board. They weren't the only ones who enjoyed these stores, however, for along with three small rat femurs, many of the bones that we found bore numerous rodent incisor marks.

When applied to our research questions, these critical bits of information reveal a 17th-century merchant vessel that carried a cargo of European-manufactured trading goods, part of which was intended for Native American tribes of the eastern seaboard of North America. Sailing in the middle of a period of volatile competition between the English and Dutch for maritime, mercantile, and military supremacy in both Europe and the Americas, our vermin-infested ship passed along the northern coast of Hispaniola, where it came to rest in Monte Cristi Bay.

The historical record supports the notion that the vessel may have entered the area to engage in illicit trade with the many smugglers known to inhabit the northern coast. Or perhaps she sought a cargo of sea salt. Today, Isla Cabra – as well as the outskirts of the town of Monte Cristi – is home to large, shallow evaporating pans that are harvested regularly for their precious payload of salt. How far back this practice reaches is not known, although Christopher Columbus mentioned at the close of the 15th century that the region held great potential for salt production. Documents note that 17th-century European merchant ships frequently sailed into clandestine bays along the island's northern coast to offload finished goods in exchange for natural resources such as salt, leather, and tobacco, all of which were abundant in the area.

And so it seems that Peter's dream did unfold, after all, into an adventure. The "Pipe Wreck" continues to play a major role in the regional history of the Caribbean Basin. Her cargo – though not yet fully excavated – is still one of the largest and most diverse ever recovered from an inbound merchantman destined for the Americas. This remarkable shipwreck has demonstrated that not all disturbed archaeological sites should be viewed as worthless. They may, if managed properly, yield tremendous information.

Above **Pipes from the Monte Cristi "Pipe Wreck." The funnel pipe (left) was a form manufactured in the Netherlands and exported to the New World for trade with Native Americans. This type comprises 7 percent of the pipe cargo excavated from the site.**

Below **Fort Orange, on the Hudson River, in 1635. This outpost, vital to the expansion of the Dutch empire, was, perhaps, the destination of our ship some three decades later.**

La Salle's Ship Belle: Matagorda Bay, Texas

J. BARTO ARNOLD III AND DONNY L. HAMILTON

The Discovery   **J. BARTO ARNOLD III**

It was the first day of testing magnetic anomalies. I had begun this Texas Historical Commission survey a month earlier, my second large-scale effort to find *La Belle*, a small ship lost in 1686 by famed French explorer René Robert Cavelier, Sieur de La Salle. With four ships and 300 men, La Salle was attempting to colonize the lower Mississippi, but missed the great river's mouth by hundreds of miles and ended up in Matagorda Bay in what is now Texas. The loss of *La Belle* to a winter storm cut the expedition off from outside help, dooming the already troubled expedition. There were only a handful of survivors. La Salle himself was murdered by his own men.

In 1978 I'd directed a prior survey in search of this and other historical wrecks in the bay. We found several interesting historic wrecks with our magnetometer, but *La Belle* eluded us. Over the intervening years declining state funding limited our fieldwork, but study continued. Robert Weddle's archival research on La Salle provided more detail on the ship's location, reinforcing my earlier ideas of where, generally, to search. Then, in 1994 and 1995, I was given the time to raise the funds that led to our return to Matagorda Bay for another large-scale search.

That is how, on the morning of 5 July 1995, we relocated the most promising magnetic anomaly I had identified in miles and miles of survey data. It lay just outside the boundary of the 1978 search area and showed tantalizing characteristics of a wreck site. The first dive team located a few artifacts, but nothing of definitive nature. Any wreck up to as late as 1880 or so could have produced them. Then a bronze buckle was handed up to the deck of the dive boat. In form it whispered to me, "I date before 1800."

The second team finished their dive. Chuck Mead, a Florida State University graduate student, and Sara Keys from the University of Texas at Austin climbed on deck. Chuck said, "I think we have a cannon!"

I donned my gear and followed him down to the seabed, 3.4 m (11 ft) below the surface and with visibility at about 15 cm (6 in), retaining with difficulty a skeptical pose of scientific detachment. Chuck put my hand on what was indeed the lifting ring of a cannon. As I put my face mask closer, practically touching it, I saw that, even better, it was a bronze cannon. Not only bronze, but highly decorated. The lifting ring was cast in the form of a leaping dolphin. At that moment I knew that *La Belle* was no longer lost. After 17 years of seeking we had found her before lunch on the very first day of test excavation!

Limited test excavations continued for the rest of July to determine what

Below **Portrait of René-Robert Cavelier, Sieur de La Salle.**

remained of the ship and her contents. At the end of the month we successfully raised the cannon to great fanfare. Then began a year of planning and fund raising. The political leaders of Texas agreed that the wreck and her delicate waterlogged contents deserved the most careful treatment possible. *La Belle* is not just a Texas treasure. She is a nationally and even internationally important heritage icon. We designed and built a cofferdam to enclose the site and pumped out the water so that a Texas Historical Commission team could excavate carefully and effectively rather than blindly. In this way the maximum data was recorded and the delicate, fragile organic remains were preserved for posterity. At that time, I left my position with the State Historical Commission to join the Institute of Nautical Archaeology and my role in fieldwork on *La Belle* ended.

Below **The site was prepared for excavation by construction of a "donut" cofferdam formed by driving 18-m (60-ft) long steel sheet pilings into the seabed in two concentric circles around the wreck and filling the ring with sand. Water was then pumped from the interior to allow a dry, shaded excavation.**

The Conservation   DONNY L. HAMILTON

My involvement with *La Belle* began when the Texas Historical Commission contracted the Conservation Research Laboratory (CRL) at Texas A&M University to conserve the ship and her contents, a project that is set to last more than 20 years.

Surrounded by her artifacts, the hull of *La Belle* is to be the central display in the Bob Bullock Museum of Texas History in Austin, the state capital. Together they will tell the story of La Salle's ill-fated attempt to establish a French colony on the coast of the Gulf of Mexico. Although archaeologists spent more than nine months excavating and recovering material from the wreck site, the overall success of the project, as well as the other excavations described in this book, rests with the conservation laboratory and its conservators. Conservation is a continuation of any archaeological excavation, but especially so in nautical archaeology, and is much more than just stabilizing and preserving artifacts. During conservation, additional artifacts are found in encrusted material, and diagnostic features and other details appear that must be thoroughly documented, described, identified, analyzed, and conserved. After more than four decades of experience, Frederick van Doorninck estimates that proper conservation doubles the knowledge gleaned from any shipwreck site, and George Bass has estimated that in general INA spends two years on conservation for every month it dives.

As *La Belle* was excavated, her contents and component parts were shipped to CRL, one of the oldest and best-known laboratories in the United States and an integral part of the Nautical Archaeology Program at Texas A&M University. From the beginning we decided to use the most advanced processes available to treat the material, and to extract as much data as possible. We also decided to share the ongoing hull reassembly and conservation of artifacts with the public by installing cameras and maintaining a web site (http://nautarch.tamu.edu/napcrl.htm).

Above **Among more than 500 personal items from *La Belle* were pewter plates, and a sieve, dipper, and candlestick of brass.**

Opposite **The ship just prior to the final disassembly of the keelson, keel, frames, and outer planking for shipment to Texas A&M University for conservation.**

Below **During the early stages of excavation crosswalks supported archaeologists, under the direction of the Texas Historical Commission's James Bruseth, as they excavated the contents of the heavily laden hold of the ship. The wooden hull was covered with wet burlap bags to prevent its drying out.**

Polearm Conservation

On historic-period archaeological sites in the United States the most commonly found metal artifacts are made of iron, the metal most prone to corrode and the most difficult to conserve. Conservation problems are compounded when the iron is recovered from a marine environment, for the metal is covered with calcareous concretions which hide encapsulated artifacts, and contaminated with corrosive chloride.

Most people, on seeing vats of encrusted iron artifacts, are not impressed. The hafted polearms from *La Belle*, among the most interesting of the ship's iron objects, provide an example. In their encrusted state they were barely identifiable, yet their iron blades included distinctive shapes that eventually identified them as partisans, spontoons, and halberds. As today, when carried by the Pope's Swiss Guard, they served in 1686 more for ceremonial purposes than as weapons.

Before study or display, the polearms required extensive conservation. We photographed them, analyzed radiographs, and traced X-rays carefully, recording every detail. Next we strategically broke the encrustations to expose the voids left by the corroded iron, which we cleaned out before reattaching the fragments and filling the voids with epoxy. After the epoxy set, we removed the encrustation with pneumatic chisels, revealing epoxy casts of the polearm blades, perfect duplicates of the originals. If an epoxy cast contained areas of metal or corrosion products, however, we made a silicone rubber mold of the object and cast that with epoxy to create a permanent replica of the original object.

Electrolytic Cleaning of Iron

Large iron artifacts tend to be in better condition than smaller items like blades because of their mass. A swivel gun, a type of small, breech loading gun used from the 16th to the 18th century, was the only deck gun recovered of the six to eight originally on *La Belle*. When found it was loaded with a cannonball in the barrel, a breech block loaded with black gunpowder, and a breech wedge securing it in the breech chamber. We mechanically removed marine concretion from it with pneumatic chisels, cleaned the bore of the barrel, freed the cannonball, and loosened the breech block and wedge. The chloride corrosion products present in the iron, however, continued to attack it. We effectively removed the chloride compounds by putting the iron through electrolytic reduction over a period of months. This was followed by intensive rinsing in boiling de-ionized water. Then we treated the surface with tannic acid, which converted the surface iron to a black, corrosion-resistant film. Lastly we placed the gun in a vat of molten microcrystalline wax to seal it from atmospheric oxygen and moisture. With proper storage or display, the gun should be stable for years, but being made of iron, it will always remain prone to corrosion.

Right **Conservator John Hamilton uses a pneumatic chisel to remove thick encrustation from the swivel gun, loaded and ready to shoot at the time the ship sank – as revealed by its breech wedge, breech block, and cannonball, shown here above the fully conserved gun.**

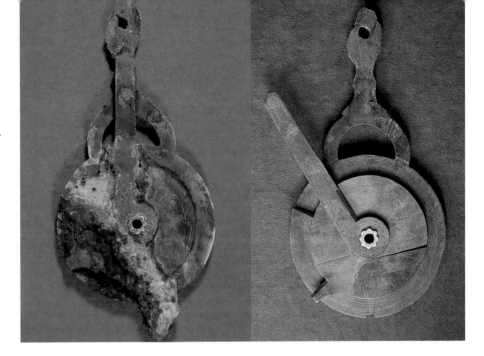

Conservation of a Boxwood Nocturnal

The most difficult artifacts to conserve are those made of wood, leather, rope, and fabric. During centuries in the sea their cellular structures become so degraded that only the water in the cells supports their original shapes. A unique wood device called a nocturnal, of English manufacture, required special treatment. Before clocks, nocturnals were used to determine time at night by the user sighting on the North Star through the center hole and aligning the two arms on two stars in the Little Dipper or the Big Dipper. The measured angle between the stars told the time. The *La Belle* nocturnal is made of four thin sheets of boxwood – a central dial with a front and back piece and a sighting arm on top – attached together with a brass grommet so the four sheets rotated on each other. Because of the thinness of the boxwood, the sheets were prone to warp. This tendency was compounded by the fact that the nocturnal was found in close contact with iron which deposited corrosion products along the top surface and between the top three sheets. The expansion of the iron corrosion products had separated the sheets and caused the center dial to split. Successful conservation required that there be no shrinkage or warping and that the sheets be freed so they might rotate on each other as originally designed. Additionally, the surfaces of the nocturnal have stamped and engraved markings.

Previous experimentation showed that a silicone oil treatment perfected at CRL had the best chance of achieving the conservation objectives. In this treatment, the waterlogged nocturnal was dehydrated through a graduated series of water/ethanol baths and then ethanol/acetone baths until it was in 100 percent acetone. The nocturnal was then placed in a vat of silicone oil mixed with a cross-linker. The vat was placed in a chamber under a low vacuum which allowed the oil to penetrate into the wood as the acetone was pulled out. The nocturnal was then removed and excess oil allowed to drain off over a period of days. It was then placed in a sealed plastic bag with a small amount of liquid catalyst. The fumes of the catalyst started the silicone oil cross-linking with itself, stabilizing the wood. The contrast between the nocturnal

before and after conservation is striking. All of its diagnostic features are preserved and it is once more in working condition, although inaccurate if used today because of the shift in the constellations that occurs over time.

Silicone oil treatments result in a dry, natural looking wood that undergoes less shrinkage than in all other treatments. Importantly, artifacts conserved by silicone oils remain as re-treatable as objects conserved by so-called reversible processes. We used variations of the treatment to conserve leather artifacts, rope, glass bottles, trade beads, and small wood artifacts, including blocks and pulleys. However, while extremely effective, its high cost limits its use to small artifacts.

Conservation of the Hull of La Belle

Approximately a third of *La Belle*'s hull survives, weighing just over 12 tons. We did not want it left submerged in a vat, out of sight and out of mind, during conservation. Thus, we sank into the ground a poured concrete wood-conservation vat 18.3 m (60 ft) long by 6.1 m (20 ft) wide by 3.65 m (12 ft) deep, with a platform built inside that can lift 35 tons by means of four winches. The vat, the largest in the world for conservation by immersion, holds 363,400 liters (96,000 gallons) of liquid.

In order to transport the hull to CRL, some 240 km (150 miles) from the Gulf Coast, it was disassembled in the field. At CRL, the wood was stored in a variety of vats as we began removing the original iron fasteners and wood treenails so the fastening holes could be used to reassemble the hull with threaded, reinforced fiberglass rods and stainless steel bolts. The hull was reassembled prior to conservation because if the individual components of the ship were conserved individually, each would undergo some dimensional changes, preventing the fastening holes from lining up.

During its reassembly, the hull has been supported on the platform by means of a preformed, laminated fiberglass and carbon-fiber shoe under the keel and a series of carbon-fiber sheets molded to the underside of each frame (or rib). The platform easily raises the entire hull out of the liquid when desirable for work or viewing.

It is planned that the hull will undergo treatment for eight years in polyethylene glycol, followed by a year of controlled drying. After conservation the ship will be

Above **Items of the ship's rigging, including wood blocks, pulleys, deadeyes, parrel trucks, and a mast fid, were conserved with silicone oil.**

Below ***La Belle*** **being reassembled in the wood conservation vat at the Conservation Research Laboratory, Texas A&M University. To prevent its drying, the hull can be raised from and lowered back into the water by four winches capable of lifting 35 tons.**

disassembled again and transported the 160 km (100 miles) to Austin, where it will be reassembled one last time. The same carbon-fiber system used during conservation will support the museum display.

Since only the lower third of the ship remains, Glenn Grieco, by combining data from the actual hull with data from historic records, other ships, and period paintings and drawings, built a scale model of *La Belle* as she appeared in 1686.

Putting a Face on History

During the excavation, a human skeleton was found lying on anchor rope in the bow of the ship. A physical anthropologist determined that it was that of a 28- to 35-year-old male of European descent who had suffered a broken nose, had lower back problems, and had severe dental problems. Astonishingly, brain tissue was preserved in the anaerobic environment of the sealed cranium, but unfortunately, results of DNA samples were inconclusive.

For a facial reconstruction of this crewman, we took the skull to the Scottish Rites Hospital for Children in Dallas, Texas, where a detailed CT scan was made of the skull. From the CT data a resin cast of the skull was made by CyberForm International in Arlington, Texas, using a process known as stereolithography: each CT image slice was projected sequentially via an ultra-violet laser into a vat of light-sensitive resin. When the resin hardened, the resultant cast duplicated every detail of the original skull. Then Professor Denis Lee at the University of Michigan positioned tissue depth markers on the resin cast and, guided by these, molded the facial features in clay. A silicone rubber mold of the clay model allowed a plaster cast to be made and painted for a more realistic effect. He probably would be recognized by his family, although he most likely had a beard and would have been considerably emaciated from the travails he suffered in the New World in the last year of his life.

The bones of the skeleton were thoroughly cleaned to facilitate analysis by the physical anthropologist, but were otherwise not treated since it was known that this crewman would be interred. In 2004 he was buried with due ceremony in the Texas State Cemetery in Austin, his grave becoming the oldest marked grave in the State.

Thousands of other artifacts from *La Belle* have been conserved over a seven-year period in a process that continues. Clearly the conservation phase of any marine archaeology project is as critical as the excavation phase, contributing as much data as the fieldwork – sometimes even more.

Above left **Glenn Grieco, master model builder at Texas A&M University, putting the finishing details on a scaled model of *La Belle*.**

Above **Details of the bow end of *La Belle* show the forecastle deck, windlass, main deck, hatch cover, cast iron cannon and carriage in gun port, and a wrought iron swivel gun mounted on the starboard railing.**

Below **Professor Denis Lee shows the facial reconstruction he made from the cast of a sailor's skull found on *La Belle*.**

Resurrecting "The Wickedest City in the World": Port Royal, Jamaica

DONNY L. HAMILTON

I was preparing to enter Kingston Harbor behind the old Naval Hospital in Port Royal, Jamaica. It was January, 1992. I adjusted my scuba gear, entered the water, and swam northwest down what had once been Lime Street, now carpeted with a layer of eel grass. Then 45 m (135 ft) out, in 2.7 m (9 ft) of water, I could see the low profile of a raised mortar foundation that once supported the walls of a wood frame house (known as Building 3) previously used to store various commodities. Following this foundation, I came upon the corner of what had been a two-story brick row building (Building 1) containing three business establishments. The herringbone pattern of the brick floors, although now covered with moss, was still obvious to the trained eye. I swam along the brick sidewalk of the building, past the entrance of a pipe shop; over 2,000 new pipes once lay on the floor of the first room. I continued on to the doorway of the tavern where numerous corked liquor bottles

Port Royal

Earthquake 11:43 a.m.,
7 June 1692
Destroyed 13 hectares of Port Royal
Population 7,000–8,000
Casualties c 5,000
Excavation 1981–1990
Depth 2.7 m (9 ft)

Above **Hypothesized reconstruction of Building 1 with its pipe shop, tavern, and cobbler shop.**

Left **Margaret Leshikar-Denton inspects the wood framing of a stairwell on the brick floor of Building 1.**

Right **The partly cleared circular brick walls of a cistern at the back yard corner of Buildings 5, 6, and 7.**

had stood. The occupant of the last premises conducted cobbling, butchering, and wood turning.

I passed over the other front corner of the building and the sand of the 1.2-m (4-ft) wide alley separating it from the corner of a brick foundation that supported another wood timber house (Building 2). Following the front wall, I paused at the plastered brick buttress. From there, I could see the plaster floor and the narrow extension of Queen Street that ran alongside the building.

I continued northwest to the paired, back-to-back hearths used by the occupants of the two halves of a single story, double-roomed building (Building 4). Beyond, I could make out the low brick walls of two hearths used by adjacent buildings (Buildings 5 and 7). I swam to the circular brick wall of a cistern that provided fresh water for three intersecting building lots (Buildings 5, 6, and 7). As I ventured up the brick wall separating the yard of the building from the room housing the large hearth, I could not help but remember the long-handled iron skillets that once rested on the hearth, and reflect on the skeleton of the child lying beneath a fallen wall on the brick floor in front of it. One front room had a plastered floor, while the smaller room had a herringbone brick floor with the wooden beams of a stairwell embedded in it. From the stairwell I could see the front doorway where another small child had lain just outside. Swimming on, I stopped in the hold of a large ship, believed to be the *Swan*, sitting on the brick floor of Building 4. When the city was inundated, it had plowed through the front of the building, shoving both walls and floor forward as it came to rest.

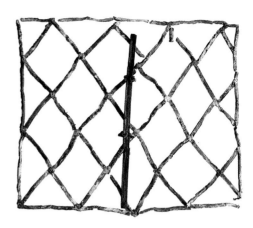

Above **Lead came framing with support rod of a window from Building 5. These grooved bars were used to fasten together small panes of glass.**

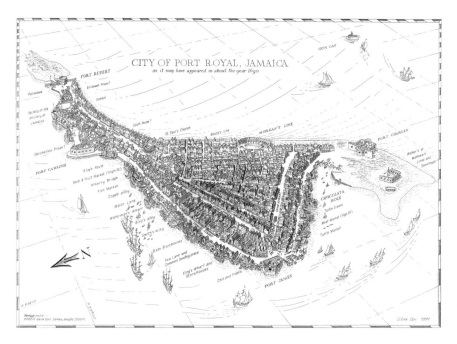

Above **A town plan drawn in 1992 by London architect Oliver Cox shows his version of how Port Royal might have appeared just prior to the 1692 earthquake.**

Above right **A modern view of Port Royal situated at the end of a 29-km (18-mile) long sand spit that separates the Caribbean Sea (right) from Kingston Harbor (left) showing the dotted extent of the sunken city. Kingston can be seen in the background across the harbor.**

Below **Field-school student Janet Mulholland admires an intact, corked bottle she has just excavated.**

The 1992 dive was a nostalgic return to Port Royal 16 months after I had concluded ten years of archaeological excavations (from 1981 to 1990) for INA, the Nautical Archaeology Program at Texas A&M University, and the Jamaican National Heritage Trust. Had it not been for the excavations, none of the features described would have been exposed. They, like the rest of the submerged city, would have been hidden, protected by a carpet of eel grass, underlying sediments, and a thick layer of dead coral. Port Royal's significance as the dominant force in Jamaican politics had ended abruptly when two thirds of the town sank into Kingston Harbor during a catastrophic earthquake; Port Royal became the Pompeii of the New World.

History

How did Jamaica, a Spanish possession, become an English island? And how did Port Royal become the largest, most affluent English town in the New World? In December 1654, Oliver Cromwell, Lord Protector of England, sent an invasion force under the commands of Admiral Penn and General Venables to capture Hispaniola for his Puritan merchant supporters. They wanted to establish trade contacts with the Spanish New World and needed a centrally located English port. However, the Spanish were forewarned of the attack and soundly defeated the English forces attempting to capture the city of Santo Domingo. Fearing Cromwell's wrath, Penn and Venables sailed south to Jamaica, and in May 1655 captured the poorly defended island with little resistance. In short, Jamaica became a consolation prize to appease Cromwell.

Although Port Royal was designed to serve as a defensive fortification, it assumed greater importance since ships could easily be serviced and loaded there within the well-protected harbor. Ships' captains, merchants, and craftsmen established themselves in Port Royal to take advantage of the trading, outfitting, and raiding opportunities, and as Jamaica's economy grew between 1655 and 1692, the town flourished and became the most economically important English port in the Americas.

Port Royal was the mercantile center of the Caribbean and was the principal provider of manufactured commodities and slaves to the Spanish colonies. From its trade contacts and pirating activities, Port Royal was more affluent than towns in other English colonies, and at the time of its destruction was the largest English town in the New World, with a population of 7,000–8,000 inhabitants. Its social milieu was quite different from that of New England, with its religiously ordered towns, or from the tobacco-driven economy of Maryland and Virginia. Port Royal had a tolerant, laissez-faire attitude that allowed for a diversity of religious expression and lifestyles. Mention is made of merchants and a citizenry consisting of Quakers, "Papists," Puritans, Presbyterians, Jews, and Anglicans, practicing their religion openly alongside the free-wheeling sailors and pirates who frequented the port, giving the town its reputation of being the "wickedest city in the world."

Port Royal's heyday came to a sudden and disastrous end shortly before noon on 7 June 1692: the massive earthquake sank 13 hectares of the "storehouse and treasury of the West Indies" into the harbor. A pocket watch made in about 1686 by Paul Blondel, a Frenchman living in the Netherlands, was recovered during underwater excavations; its hands, frozen at 11:43 a.m., serve as an eerie reminder of the catastrophe. It is also the first recorded instance of a stopped watch recording the time of a disaster. An estimated 2,000 persons were killed outright with an additional 3,000 citizens dying of injuries and disease in the following days. Salvage and looting began almost immediately and continued intermittently for years.

As one walks along the narrow streets of the fishing village of Port Royal today, it is hard to imagine that it was once the largest and most economically important English settlement in the Americas. It is now an isolated town at the end of a long sand spit with a population of 2,000 people who view themselves as "Port Royalists," rather than simply Jamaicans. Its unassuming presence belies the unique and unparalleled archaeological record that lies untouched beneath the surface of the adjacent harbor.

It is important to remember that Port Royal is different from most archaeological sites. It belongs to a small group of unique sites that includes Pompeii and Herculaneum in Italy, Akrotiri in the Aegean, Ozette in the State of Washington, and most shipwrecks. All can be termed "catastrophic" sites, for they were created by some disaster in a matter of minutes, preserving the associated material and the all-important archaeological context. In these sites, the archaeologist is not dealing with a situation where, over time, houses, shops, churches, and other buildings were constructed, expanded, neglected, abandoned, razed, and rebuilt. In these cases, archaeologists are mostly studying the refuse that has been left behind. At catastrophic sites, in contrast, the archaeologist is dealing with material left exactly in its place of use. Time is frozen, revealing a complete picture of life in the past as it once was.

Archaeological Excavations

In 1981, the three institutes named above began the ten-year underwater excavation of the submerged portion of the 17th-century town. Present evidence indicates that while areas of Port Royal lying along the edge of the harbor slid and jumbled as they sank, destroying most of the archaeological context, the area investigated by INA,

Above **A broadside (newspaper of the day), published in August 1692, reports the news of the Port Royal disaster to its London readership.**

Below **Remains of a 17th-century watch made in 1686 by the French watchmaker Paul Blondel, recovered by Edwin Link in 1960. An X-ray revealed that the watch hands stopped at 11:43 a.m. marking the time of the earthquake.**

located a short distance from the harbor, sank vertically, with minimal horizontal disturbance as a result of a process called liquefaction.

The investigation of Port Royal yielded a vast array of material from each excavated building. A large number of perishable, organic artifacts such as leather shoes, fish baskets, and even textiles were recovered. Together with complementary historical documents, the excavation allows us to reconstruct details of everyday life in this English colonial port city.

The Port Royal Project concentrated on the submerged, 17th-century buildings situated on Lime Street, near its intersection with Queen and High Streets in the commercial center of the town. Working from a support barge anchored over the excavation area, we investigated eight buildings. Our main excavation tool was a water dredge. The divers breathed air delivered from the surface via hoses so that each dive could last hours. This work contributed a more detailed body of data on the buildings and their *in situ* artifacts than any previous excavations at Port Royal. The recovered assemblage is incomparable. Large collections of 17th-century English tools, ceramics, pipes, candlesticks, and miscellaneous household goods were found. There is an impressive array of trade pottery including Chinese porcelain, German stoneware, and Spanish olive jars. Significantly, Port Royal has the largest collection of English pewter in the world from a single site. The pewter utensils are particularly significant for they are invaluable in identifying the occupants of the different buildings.

Above left **An array of pewter items (tankard, baluster, plates, chargers, spoons, syringes), brass candlesticks, and glass liquor bottles from the INA excavations at Port Royal.**

Above **Margaret Leshikar-Denton records a remarkably preserved wicker fish basket, still in situ.**

Opposite **An excavator uncovers a layer of clay smoking pipes, liquor bottle fragments, and a pewter baluster on the brick floor of Building 1.**

Below left **Items of Chinese export porcelain include blue-on-white medallion cups, Batavia and blanc de Chine tea cups, and a Fo dog.**

Below **English Delftware flower vase with the surface glaze flaked off.**

Documentary Evidence

Historical archaeology is an intimate marriage of the archaeological record and historic records and documents. At Port Royal we are fortunate to have an unparalleled archaeological record. But, equally important, Jamaica has the best-preserved archives and public records in the Caribbean. Using the archaeological and documentary record together it is possible to interpret accurately the excavated areas and learn a great deal about the occupants of the town.

The relevant historical documents for 17th-century Port Royal, housed in the Jamaica Public Archives and the Island Records Office in Spanish Town, were microfilmed for reference. The land patents, wills, and probate inventories from 1660 to 1720 allowed us to determine the owners of the site's building lots, and compare the contents of households and businesses at Port Royal, and throughout Jamaica. However, while the documentary record was an integral part of our research, it had little direct relevance to our investigation until we could tie the excavated buildings to specific individuals. Once this was done, we could focus our documentary research.

Simon Benning, Pewterer

One of the first challenges encountered was identifying an unknown maker's mark found on a pewter plate. The small oval mark consisted of a pineapple surrounded by a rope braid, with the initial "S" to the left of the pineapple and the initial "B" to the right. There were no parallels for the mark in the standard references on English pewterers, but we found a reference to a pewter maker by the name of Simon Benning who worked in Port Royal.

Whenever one searches for background on individuals it is always a gamble whether or not the documents recording their activities survived the centuries. Simon Benning turned out to have a well-documented life. Since he was identified as a pewterer, it was logical to assume that he was trained in England and that there would be records on him at the Worshipful Company of Pewterers in London. We

Above **An excavator holds one of 18 complete Chinese porcelain cups found around a window frame in a fallen wall.**

Below **The ownership mark "NCI" of Nathaniel Cook and his wife Jane over Simon Benning's maker's mark.**

Bottom **The ownerships mark "IC" of Jane Cook on a newer set of pewter plates following the death of her husband, Nathaniel, whose initial is now missing.**

found that he was apprenticed in London to John Silk in 1650 before emigrating to Barbados in 1657. There was a reference to a London will that we found in the Prerogative Court of Canterbury which handled the probates of all individuals with property, both in England and in the colonies. Simon's will, written on 19 February 1656, states that he was a pewterer about to embark on a voyage to Barbados.

In the 1660s, many Barbadians moved to the larger island of Jamaica, where there were more opportunities to prosper. A plot of land facing northward on High Street was granted to Benning in 1665 and there he built his pewter shop. Two adjacent lots were acquired in 1667 and in 1670. We next found Simon Benning and the occupants of his home and shop in a census taken at Port Royal in 1680. His Jamaican will was written in 1683 and was entered, soon after his death, into the Island Records Office in Jamaica in 1687. This will provides information on the property that he bequeathed to his wife and each of his children. Simon, the eldest son, inherited the house, shop and tools on High Street and carried on the pewtering trade. The last documentary record of Simon Benning, Jr tells us that he sold the last of his property in 1696. What happened to him remains unanswered, but there is evidence for his death: his married sister, Sarah, returned to Port Royal to settle property claims. Thus there were two Simon Bennings, pewterers, father and son, working in Jamaica in the years between 1663 and 1696.

Identifying the Occupants of Building 5

It was at this stage of research that we asked: "What do the ownership marks found on objects in Building 5 tell us?" The ownership mark "NCI," found on pewter plates, silver forks and silver spoons, and a silver nutmeg grinder, tells us that a family with a surname starting with "C" and a man with the first initial "N" and a wife with the initial "I" or "J" lived in the building (during the 17th century, the letter "I" was commonly used for "J"). But there were two sets of ownership marks on the Benning pewter plates. One set has the pineapple maker's mark and the ownership mark "NCI" on their backs. These plates have numerous knife-cut marks on their interior surfaces and appear very worn. The newer set has considerably fewer cut marks, and has the ownership mark "IC" on interior surfaces and the maker's mark on the backs. The two sets of maker's marks provided the necessary leads to identifying the owners of Building 5.

A search of all the documents (wills, inventories, land plots, and grantor records) found only one family fitting all the required conditions. This was Nathaniel Cook and his wife Jane. The "IC" marks appearing alone on one set of pewter plates indicate that her husband had probably died, after which she had more plates made, with only her initials on them. Later we found a record of Jane married to a different husband. The new "IC" plates were most likely made by Simon Benning, the son, while the older "NCI" plates were probably made by Simon Benning, the father.

This is only one of many stories that can be told by interpreting the archaeological data through documentary records. By the end of the century the buccaneers had left and most of the small planters were also gone. Jamaica, the largest English Caribbean island, which seemingly offered good prospects to ex-servants and small freeholders, had been taken over by the large planters who consolidated the arable land into huge plantations manned by armies of slaves.

The Tragedy of the Santo Antonio de Tanna: *Mombasa, Kenya*

ROBIN PIERCY

Santo Antonio de Tanna

Built 1681, Bassien near Goa, India
Sunk 20 October 1697
Depth 18 m (59 ft)
Found by Conway Plough
Excavation 1977–1980
Cargo relief supplies
Keel c 30 m (99 ft) long

The train moved slowly through the African night. I lay on my couchette savoring the strange tropical smells that came through the open carriage window. On the bunk below Don Frey leafed through a notebook checking off details of our progress so far.

Tomorrow we would be in Mombasa and work would begin in earnest. We had a fortnight in which to learn everything we could about a ship that was said to have sunk below a reef in the late 17th century. Before we had left our base in Turkey,

Right **Among many pieces of jet jewelry found on the wreck were earrings.**

Far right **Only four silver coins were recovered from the wreck, all minted in Goa in the decade preceding the wreck.**

and bolts, a wooden bucket, cannon quoins, and large quantities of rope, all of which suggested a boatswain's store, an idea strengthened the following year, 1978, by the discovery of a mass of sail and rope, caulking tools, and unused caulking. At that time we found Chinese porcelain and many lathe-turned hardwood spindles that were probably furniture fragments or elements of decorative woodwork. Two large concreted boxes adhering to several concreted rigging components were loosened by means of very small explosive charges. Elsewhere on the wreck excavators found wooden combs, shoe leather, many barrel staves, and shell lantern lights.

Excavations in the bow in 1979 produced a stoneware Martaban jar with stamped neck, more Portuguese faience ware, some unusual earthenware Indian flasks, and large quantities of iron shot. Among the small finds were musket shot, Chinese porcelain, brass buckles, and glassware. Once more, a large number of barrel fragments appeared among the ballast stones. At the end of the season, two test trenches down-slope of the wreck yielded many more objects.

A considerable quantity of collapsed hull structure uncovered in the stern area prompted the decision to focus efforts here in 1980, the last year of excavation. Thousands of artifacts came to light, including more pewter ware, a silver-plated candlestick, fine porcelain bowls and plates, jet pendants and earrings, a second bronze swivel gun (dated 1677), a wooden gun port lid, and a coat of arms and figurine of carved wood.

Finds of pottery from Mozambique were evidence of General de Mello Sampaio's voyage to and long stay at Mozambique aboard the *Santo Antonio de Tanna*. The ceramics, published by Hamo Sassoon in the journal *Azania*, constitute a significant comparative collection because they have been assigned a firm *terminus ante quem*, which has already allowed them to date two sites in Mozambique.

At the end, the excavation had yielded nearly 6,000 objects. To cope with this bonanza, the National Museums of Kenya funded the first conservation laboratory in Africa for waterlogged material, which over the decades since has stabilized all but a few pieces.

A representative selection of the artifacts is now included in a display in Fort Jesus that tells the story of its siege, and provides a clear picture of the underwater excavation. Artifacts alone are often of little interest to much of the viewing public, especially if they have no apparent monetary value, but when seen in context, as here, they evoke strong images of life in another time and place.

Below **National Museums of Kenya representative Sayid Mohamed and conservator John Olive clean newly raised objects in the Fort Jesus conservation laboratory.**

The Hull

Careful excavation over the years laid the hull bare. Jeremy Green of the Western Australian Maritime Museum measured sections across it and we recorded it in its entirety with pairs of stereo photographs.

Then we faced a difficult decision. Should we attempt to raise and preserve the hull? We had hoped that it could be the centerpiece for an eventual museum display. Sadly, the sheer size and volume of the 30 by 9.65 m (99 by 32 ft) remains excluded this on economic grounds. We reburied the hull with the mud and sand that had kept it so well preserved for 300 years, to await a future generation with the means to attempt such a huge undertaking. We contented ourselves with the careful records we had made of the finest details of the structure. It certainly deserved the care we gave it.

Despite the importance of the ships that once made Portugal the world's greatest maritime power, our knowledge of Portuguese ships and life aboard them was extremely limited. We did not know to any great extent how the ships were built, nor are we even now certain of the specifics of their terminology. For instance, *nao* and *fragata* as they are used in contemporary Portuguese literature are not clearly understood. Such differences are more distinct for Dutch and British vessels of the time, as known from both archaeological investigations and surviving records. The *Santo Antonio de Tanna* was referred to in contemporary records as a *fragata*, generally translated as a warship, but excavation has revealed a more lightly built hull than would be expected of a warship. An additional research objective was an examination of how her hull differed from those of contemporary Dutch and English vessels, which were more specifically designed for either warfare or trade.

Further, we wanted to determine if the variation between Lisbon-built and India-built vessels was due in any degree to the influence of local shipbuilding traditions. Contemporary Portuguese records show that the average ship built in the dockyards at Lisbon rarely had a life span of more than a decade, whereas ships built in India of Indian teak were expected to have a useful life of at least 20 years. At the time, as the

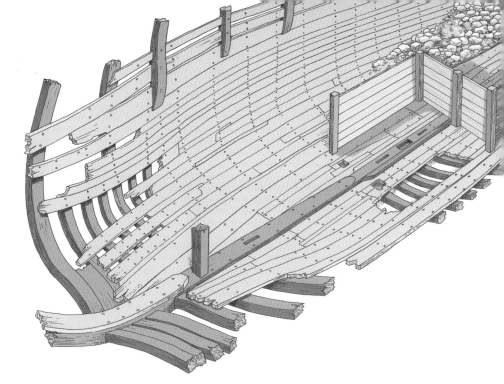

Right **This artist's impression of the excavated stern shows the ship's hull preserved up to the lower deck in addition to a substantial part of the pump well that surrounded the pumps and mast step.**

only Portuguese vessel built in India that had been excavated, the *Santo Antonio de Tanna* provided a unique opportunity to ascertain if the high quality of Indian timber was the sole reason for this disparity. A Portuguese student, Tiago Miguel Fraga, is now searching for answers to such questions as part of his Texas A&M University Master of Arts thesis.

Ordnance

Below **Outsize bomb shot dwarf grenades and hand-thrown earthenware incendiary devices.**

Similarly, an analysis of the armaments has yielded insights into the military, financial, and therefore political aspects of Portugal's situation in India, and thus in Portugal itself, at the time the *Santo Antonio de Tanna* was lost.

Examination of the ordnance revealed that the *Santo Antonio de Tanna* was carrying a very light complement for her size and mission. This, and a lack of standardization in the assemblage, appears to reflect the strained circumstances of the Portuguese at this time. That the Portuguese were in economic difficulties is corroborated by Jean-Yves Blot's archival research, which has shown that guns had to be taken from Murmugao Fortress in India to boost the *Santo Antonio de Tanna*'s fire power; apparently there were no other guns available in Goa at the time.

Postscript on the Siege

By cruel fate, almost all of the crew who made it into the safety of Fort Jesus soon died of disease, whilst the remainder chose to die at their posts during the final assault rather than surrender. After 33 months of fighting, the loss of many vessels, and countless lives – more than 3,000 on the Portuguese side alone – only two Indians survived to bring the news to Goa some two years later!

The Tragedy of the Santo Antonio de Tanna: *Mombasa, Kenya* **179**

EIGHTEENTH-CENTURY WRECKS

Having been an avid science-fiction fan in my youth, I was thrilled when I received a telephone call from famed author Arthur C. Clarke while I was still a graduate student at the University of Pennsylvania. He was visiting Philadelphia, and invited me to tea. At his hotel, he asked if I would be interested in studying a shipwreck recently found by a friend in Sri Lanka, where he lived. It lay at a place called the Great Basses Reef. As so often has been the case, my continuing work in Turkey prevented my taking on any additional research, and thus it was my mentor in underwater archaeology, Peter Throckmorton, who went to the reef in 1963 to excavate the wreck.

Exactly three decades later, INA Research Associate Jeremy Green was conducting a nautical archaeology training program for Sri Lankan archaeologists when the Sri Lankan Department of Archaeology asked him to undertake an inspection of the early 18th-century site, which he describes here.

Cheryl Ward then transports us from the Indian Ocean to the Red Sea, where she and Douglas Haldane, both former students in the Texas A&M University Nautical Archaeology Program and veterans of INA fieldwork, excavated what was probably a local merchantman that sank soon after 1765.

Any reader jealous of the nautical archaeologists whose photographs show them swimming in the crystal waters of the Red, Mediterranean, and Caribbean Seas, or camped on the bright sands of the Egyptian desert, as was Cheryl Ward, will be in for a surprise when they see the conditions under which Fred Hocker and his team excavated a small sloop lost in the last decades of the 18th century near Savannah, Georgia, in the southern United States. Since Fred has set the scene, we will remain outside clear water for the next two wrecks.

I'm proud that the Institute of Nautical Archaeology undertook the first scientific excavations of both colonial American and British ships of the American War of Independence. The first wreck was reported to me by Captain W. F. Searle, former head of US Navy diving and salvage and a Founding Director of INA. When his students tested a sonar unit during a joint Maine Maritime Academy and Massachusetts Institute of Technology summer training project in Penobscot Bay, Maine, they discovered the wreck, soon identified as that of the *Defence*, a colonial vessel scuttled in 1779. David Switzer, who excavated the site, describes how we were both introduced to it on a January dive, when ice formed on our regulators and we were wearing only neoprene wet suits. As I hit the water it was as if my cheeks had been struck by two sledge hammers! Strangely, the water seemed not much warmer when summer arrived and I helped Dave set up the operation.

Although these large storage jars and 4-m (13-ft) long iron anchors at Sadana Island, Egypt, identify this site as a shipwreck, only its excavation revealed traces of the tons of coffee, coconuts, and incense the ship carried.

The *Defence* had provided my first experience of diving with only a few inches of visibility. The visibility was even less in Virginia's York River. There, John Broadwater, who had been with me on INA's 1973 survey of the Turkish coast, instigated serious work on the ships scuttled by General Charles Cornwallis just before his 1781 surrender, which gave independence to the colonies. Soon I was invited by Ivor Noel Hume of Colonial Williamsburg to undertake the excavation of the "Cornwallis Cave Wreck," so named due to its proximity to a landmark near the river. Having solved many of the problems of excavating in clear but deep water in the Mediterranean, I was intrigued by how one might overcome the obstacles of virtually zero visibility and a strong current, and tried building a cofferdam around the site to block the current and allow the water inside to be clarified by industrial filters. John worked with me on those problems during the partial excavation off Cornwallis Cave, and here describes how he vastly improved on that experience during his full-scale excavation of the better-preserved *Betsy*.

We end this section once more in clear water, this time in the Caribbean. Margaret Leshikar-Denton tells us how she located and studied the remains of "the most famous maritime disaster in Cayman Islands history": the Wreck of the Ten Sail in 1794. By combining archaeology, conservation, oral history, and archival research, she has woven a tale that has been commemorated by stamps, a book, a coin, a museum display, and the Wreck of the Ten Sail Park, which overlooks the reefs that sank the ships, and which was dedicated by Queen Elizabeth II during the bicentennial anniversary of the event.

Above **From the cold, murky water of Maine's Penobscot Bay divers raise a rack, still holding cannonballs, that had rested on the deck of the American privateer** *Defence.*
Below **Places mentioned in this section, with the featured wrecks in bold.**

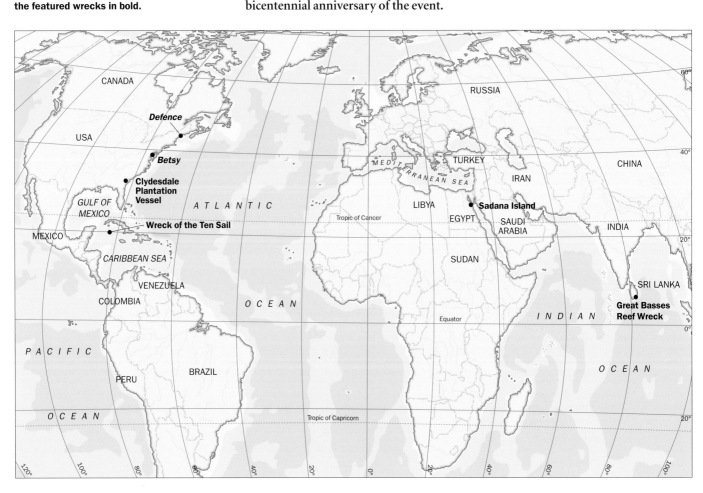

Revisiting the Great Basses Reef, Sri Lanka

JEREMY GREEN

JEREMY GREEN

Great Basses Reef Wreck

Date early 18th century
Dated by over 10,000 coins
Found by Mike Wilson, Bobby Kriegel, and Mark Smith, 1961
Nationality unknown

The Great Basses Lighthouse. Designed by Sir J.N. Douglass, the engineer for Trinity House who also built the Eddystone Light, it was prefabricated in Scotland, sent out to Sri Lanka, and erected in 1873 on a small reef top about 200 m (660 ft) from the Great Basses Wreck.

The Great Basses Reef lies 20 nautical miles (37 km) off Kirinda on the southeast coast of Sri Lanka. A long and dangerous reef, situated on the direct route between the East and the West, it surely caused countless shipwrecks over the ages. The most famous of the wrecks is the Great Basses Wreck discovered on 22 March 1961 by Mike Wilson, Bobby Kriegel, and Mark Smith. A subsequent expedition, led by Arthur C. Clarke in 1963, included Mike Wilson, Rodney Jonklaas, and Peter Throckmorton.

In Clarke's 1964 book, *The Treasure of the Great Reef*, Throckmorton describes the wreck in his notes as lying in a natural north–south gully, perhaps 9 m (30 ft) wide, between two seabed ridges. He notes that the site is about 18 m (60 ft) long, with two large iron anchors at one end and a series of cannons, jumbled like matchsticks, in the middle. "At about twenty or thirty feet [6–9 m] to the west of the cannons" he continues, "is a smaller brass cannon, about four feet [1.2 m] long by a foot [0.3 m] in diameter – perhaps smaller…and where the brass cannon lies, the bottom is a mass of concreted corrosion products of iron, bits of silver coins, musket balls and so forth, and lying just above the muzzle of the cannon – which lies in [a] north and south direction with its muzzle disappearing into the overgrowth of coral…are two or three pieces of iron, and a mass of generalized corroded mess. I picked out of it the wooden stock of a pistol – still in fairly good condition although just broken off. I tagged the brass cannon. It's got the number 3 on it now. I tagged a couple of the others also."

Clarke's book goes on to tell of the trials and tribulations of that early work, where Peter Throckmorton, fresh from his exploits in the Mediterranean, helped excavate and survey the site. Finds included two small bronze cannon, some copper bars, 20 musket balls, and about 10,000 coins, weighing approximately 160 kg (350 lb), all dated 1113 (Arabic) which equates to AD 1702, except for one dated 1685.

Galle

In 1993 I was in Sri Lanka with a team of maritime archaeologists, mainly from my department at the Western Australian Maritime Museum, conducting a training program for the Sri Lankan Department of Archaeology. The Sri Lankan Government, over the years following the Clarke discoveries, had become concerned about the possibilities of looting and the growing interest from various treasure-hunter groups who wanted to operate in Sri Lanka. Our program, one of many that we had instigated in the Asian region, was designed to train Sri Lankan archaeologists in the techniques of maritime archaeology. To do this it is necessary to make the training practical and apply it to the conditions in the country concerned. The Post Graduate Institute for Archaeology (PGIR) under the direction of Professor Senake

183

Bandaranayake was our lead institution. Senake had suggested we conduct our training in the World Heritage-listed port city of Galle, and there we set up operations for the program. We found 28 sites, including two 17th-century Dutch East Indiamen, and what is thought to be a pre-European site.

During this exciting and hectic time I was approached by the Department of Archaeology and asked if we could carry out an inspection of the Great Basses Wreck. We were more than happy to take a break from the murky waters of Galle for what we knew to be the crystal clear waters of the Basses.

The Site in 1993

Overnight accommodation was at a rest house at Kataragama. On our first morning we chartered an 8-m (26-ft) fishing boat and a small 5-m (16.5-ft) dingy from the fishing village of Kirinda, following in the footsteps of Clarke and Throckmorton. The trip to the Great Basses took 90 minutes. We anchored our boat on the southern

Below **Archaeologists survey the Great Basses site. The large anchor in the foreground lies alongside an iron cannon. Other iron cannon can be seen in the distance.**

side of the reef, to the west of the lighthouse, the reef running from the lighthouse almost WSW. The site is located against the southern side of the reef between the "Shark's Tooth" rock and a large, flat rock closer to the lighthouse. We found it essentially as described by Clarke and Throckmorton, although there are some discrepancies, the most obvious difference being that there are now only two of the four anchors described by Throckmorton. We assume that the other two have been looted. The main coin area, described by Clarke, is now unrecognizable. Our 1993 team raised a total of 613 coins from this general area together with 56 concretions containing an indeterminate number of coins. We also made a brief tape survey of the site in order to construct a sketch plan.

Obviously the identification of the site is important. The loss of a vessel of this size, carrying such a large cargo of silver, is unlikely to have passed without comment by the colonial administrators. Present indications from the artifacts suggest that the vessel was possibly European. It is thought not to be a Dutch East India Company ship since there were none of the distinctive VOC markings, and since it carried stone ballast rather than the usual brick; the only positive suggestion is the word "Batavia" on a bronze gun said to have been raised from the site later. The vessel could possibly be British from the evidence of guns and ballast. The clustering of the guns strongly suggests that they were in the hold as ballast. This is reinforced by the lack of solid shot on the site. Thus these iron guns could either have been old guns used as permanent ballast, or else they were temporarily placed in the hold as ballast for this trip and the ship was supplied with a small amount of solid iron shot. It is interesting that more grenades were found than solid shot.

The wreck on the Great Basses reef has still a great deal of archaeological potential, although there is now only a small proportion of what was originally on the site. A further archaeological excavation would serve two purposes: to remove the remaining coins and thus make the site reasonably secure; and to recover the remaining artifacts that could help to identify the site. It would be possible, although difficult, to raise one or two of the iron guns; the difficulty being not so much in the recovery operation, but in the ensuing logistical and management problems of conservation.

Chinese Porcelain for the Ottoman Court: Sadana Island, Egypt

CHERYL WARD

Sadana Island Shipwreck

Date *c* 1765
Depth 30 m (99 ft)
Excavation 1995–1998
Number of dives Over 3,000
Hull 50 m (165 ft) long,
18 m (59 ft) wide
Tonnage *c* 900

Over a decade before I directed the first Institute of Nautical Archaeology survey in Egypt, George Bass told a group of new graduate students assisting in the Uluburun ship excavation that the easiest way to find a wreck was to have someone show you where it is. Now I was spending months meeting people who dived for much of each year in the Red Sea, talking to them about our intention to do scientific archaeology on underwater sites and to improve the world's knowledge of Egypt's rich maritime heritage. I began to hear about historic ships around the Sinai Peninsula, some visited by archaeologist Avner Raban in the early 1970s, others where visiting sport divers were taken to see pockets of artifacts in the sand.

First Impressions

Our survey began in July of 1994, with Texas A&M nautical archaeology graduate students Peter van Alfen, Elizabeth Greene, and Colin O'Bannon joining Douglas Haldane, Mohamed Mustafa, Mohamed abd el Hamid, Ashraf Hanna, and me in Egypt.

"Land Rovers!" Peter exclaimed as he looked at the two vintage examples Doug had resurrected from junk with the aid of "mechanics alley" in Giza. They carried our tents, water, food, compressors and dive gear, an Egyptian cook, an antiquities inspector, and a representative from the Egyptian Navy. We began at our most southerly point, near the Roman and medieval port of Quseir, and planned to reach Ras Mohamed National Park near Sharm el-Sheikh in the Sinai by mid-August. I checked in with the American Research Center in Egypt one day, and got a phone message: Dr Cheryl was to call a number in Sharm el-Sheikh. No name was attached to the message. As I dialed, I had no inkling of how my life would change in just a few short minutes.

"Hello, this is Dr Cheryl. I have a message to call this number."

"Ah, Dr Cheryl," said a mature male voice with an Egyptian accent. "Sadana Island." Click. And the buzz of an open line was all that remained.

Sadana Island? I remembered seeing the name somewhere, so I consulted our geological survey maps, and my heartbeat quickened. Sadana Island was located in the area that several informants had told me held a huge ship, sunk at the base of a reef and still loaded with a cargo of Chinese porcelain. I had seen several pieces from the wreck, and knew that a dive safari company had spent time at a site like this, but I had not been told exactly where to find it.

After a drive across a bumpy desert road, we arrived at a scooped-out *wadi* where Sadana Island could be seen about 500 m (1650 ft) off shore, but still connected to

Sadana Island probably seemed like an ideal haven, but anchors spread on the seabed northwest of the wreck suggest the ship broke free of a mooring and slammed against the reef edge, here spanned by a metal platform built to move divers and artifacts safely over its razor-sharp topography.

Each morning, as the sun lit up our camp, yawning archaeologists emerged from tents to plan the day's dives to the shipwreck stretching more than 50 m (165 ft) along the base of a vibrantly colored coral reef.

land by a fringing reef. We set up our tents, laid out the dive gear, and paired off for the afternoon's explorations.

Peter and I walked out to the island and began our dive by swimming around its outer edge, continuing to the inner side of the fringing reef, seeing only the explosive beauty of sponges, corals, fish, and even sea turtles that accompanied us. As we looked for a convenient place to mark the extent of our survey, we turned to each other at the same time, eyes wide with excitement, because there below us, stretching more than 50 m (165 ft) along the base of the reef, lay the wreck. The next dive team quickly replaced us. They established the parameters of the wreck, noting a stack of giant iron anchors, hundreds of clay pitchers, and brilliant white, blue, and blue-and-white pieces of broken Chinese porcelain scattered along the ship's massive timbers.

The Historical Setting

The ship and its cargo fascinated me from the outset, in part because it was clear that the ship was built in a fashion unlike any I had seen in years of studying ancient ship construction. We knew that the porcelain from the site dated to the 18th century, but it wasn't until the end of 1996, after two seasons of excavation with an international team of archaeologists, students, and skilled volunteers, that Arabic inscriptions on copper cooking pots proved that the ship could not have sunk before 1765.

The ship sank at a time when Ottoman Turks ruled Egypt. The Ottoman Empire, based in Istanbul, had controlled shipping in the Red Sea and Indian Ocean for centuries, but the arrival of Europeans in search of luxury wares from the Far East created a volatile situation. For millennia, Alexandria's warehouses had stocked European and Mediterranean cabinets with spices and luxuries from the East. In the late 1500s, unhappy with paying premium prices and able to reach the Indian Ocean in their own ships, Europeans began trading directly for cinnamon, nutmeg, cloves, and mace. The Dutch take-over of spice-producing islands in about 1600 forever changed world trade. The Ottoman Empire withdrew from the Indian Ocean, and Egypt lost its monopoly on "fine spices" and instead focused on becoming the coffee supplier to Europe and the Ottoman world.

Egypt dominated the coffee market through the 17th century, and even in the later 18th century coffee made up two-thirds of the value of Egypt's imports from the Red Sea. About half of the coffee that reached Cairo was re-exported to the Ottoman world, and this stimulating, and some said, sinful drink, made waves wherever it went. Ottoman sultans periodically ordered all coffee houses shut and trade in coffee halted to prevent the rise of places filled with people doing nothing but sitting about, drinking this dark, bitter beverage and talking to one another, often about politics and government.

When it sank, the Sadana ship was heavily laden with coffee. Longer than the Statue of Liberty is tall and capable of carrying about 900 tons of cargo, this immense ship was sailing north toward Suez when it struck a coral reef and plunged more than 30 m (99 ft) beneath the sea. Its cargo – low-volume, high-value goods – originated in markets stocked with the luxuries of Africa, India, and the Far East. Stacks of porcelain, copper cooking pots and trays, and several thousand large and small clay jars occupied only about a quarter of the site. Egyptian archaeologists cried "Luban!"

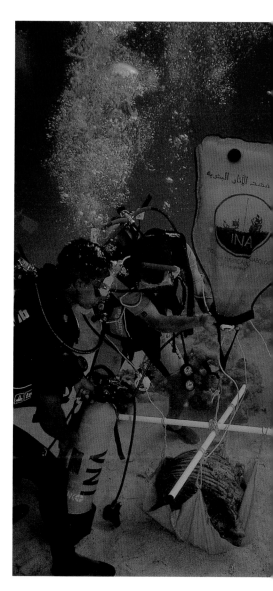

when they smelled lumps of the golden aromatic resin we call frankincense. In addition to these expensive exotics, we recovered stacks of black-lipped pearl oyster shells, spices, packing materials, foodstuffs, and about a hundred coconuts, originally stuffed into every possible nook and cranny of the ship.

The products of China and other ports remained highly esteemed by the wealthy upper classes of Egypt and other parts of the Ottoman Empire, and reached those customers through an elaborate network of trade contacts across thousands of miles. Near journey's end, one of the last stages of sea transport stretched from Jeddah in Saudi Arabia to Suez, where goods were unloaded from ships like the one resting at the base of the Sadana reef.

Goods like these fed the coffers of the Ottoman Empire through assessed customs duties and also found ready buyers in major cities like Istanbul. The Sultan's palace at Topkapi in Istanbul exhibits one of the world's finest collections of Chinese export porcelain designed for the Middle Eastern market, many pieces from crates that remained unpacked for hundreds of years after arrival. Chinese porcelain factories catered to Muslim customers just as they created special shapes and designs for European or American markets. Cultural injunctions against the representation of human and animal figures meant that most porcelain sold in Islamic markets featured floral or geometric designs. When I first visited the converted kitchens of Topkapi Palace, where 18th-century wares were displayed, it was like looking at a catalogue of some of the finest pieces from our site. The trade was so profitable that even a ship as large as that at Sadana paid for itself after only three voyages between Suez and Jeddah.

The Porcelain

Europeans trading at Mocha in Yemen knew they could bring porcelain from Chinese kilns to trade for coffee. Mocha traders often took the porcelain north to Jeddah with their coffee cargoes, and we suspect that is where the merchants who stocked the Sadana ship obtained the thousands of dishes, cups, and platters originally stowed in the lowest levels of the hull. A quarter of the Sadana porcelain relies on carefully painted underglaze blue designs. The rest, however, is of a popular type called Chinese Imari, which imitates a Japanese style of decoration using red, gold, and other colored enamels over previously fired cobalt blue underglaze patterns. Enameled wares cost at least twice as much as pieces decorated with blue alone. We also excavated dishes, plates, and platters that appeared to be white, but that we suspected had once been highly colored. Our problem lay in discovering the original decoration schemes for the Sadana porcelain because almost all of it had lost its brilliant enamel colors to the unrelenting effects of submersion in the sea.

Luckily, longtime INA artist Netia Piercy possessed the imagination, patience, and recognition of the positive effects of raking light to work wonders. Because the enamel colors lasted long enough to protect the fired white surface beneath them slightly from the effects of salt water, she could trace the designs long vanished from the porcelain.

In addition to beautiful lidded bowls featuring day lilies and chrysanthemums in a framework of underglaze blue leaves with flowering grasses and standard lozenges, Netia's work showed us that we had large bowls with grape-leaf-shaped medallions and spiraling blue panels originally glowing with emerald green, scarlet, and gold like examples at Topkapi. The most brilliant may have been some shallow dishes and plates of three sizes, dull white when excavated. Netia's painstaking work revealed on them a delicate scrolling shell and floral border around a nosegay of spring flowers that originally were hot pink, green, and yellow. In addition to the many enameled bowls and plates, the ship carried thousands of coffee cups, some an intense cobalt blue with now invisible patterns of intricate gilt flowers. Rich brown, pale green, and many blue, red, and gold examples complete the catalogue.

The Ship

The ship, the largest and most technologically informative artifact on the site, has yielded its secrets slowly. Despite a long history of contact between Europeans,

Above **Cheryl Ward and Peter Hitchcock excavate the remains of the largest artifact at the site – the ship itself. Although this ship never left the Red Sea, it probably was built near Suez of oak and pine imported from Mediterranean forests such as those on Rhodes.**

Left **Coffee cups glazed green, brown, or deep blue, bowls once blazing with scarlet and gold enamel over cobalt blue underglaze, and blue-and-white dishes sold well in Muslim markets if they featured geometric and floral themes.**

Egyptians, and others who sailed the western Indian Ocean and Red Sea, separate shipbuilding traditions continued. The Sadana Island ship is an example of a type that is non-European, non-Arab, and non-Mediterranean. Ribs (frames and floor timbers) joined by iron fastenings are spaced more widely apart than in other contemporary traditions, while stringers that stretch from one end of the hull to the other above the lowest of three decks are unusually robust. Because these timbers are primarily oak for framing and pine for planking, we look to the Mediterranean as their source. But the way the ship is built suggests that it represents an indigenous Red Sea adaptation to working with raw materials that had to be brought to Alexandria, up the Nile to Cairo, and carried 150 km (90 miles) by camel to the shipyards at Suez.

Curiously, there are no cannon on the ship, which tells me that its voyages probably were confined to the Red Sea, within the boundaries of the Ottoman Empire, and its owners had no need to defend themselves from pirates or from European merchant ships with few compunctions against appropriating goods from other vessels in the southern Red Sea. A small gunpowder flask removed by a casual visitor to the site in the early 1990s and fewer than a dozen 1-cm-diameter lead musket balls that couldn't even be loaded into a gun because their casting sprues are still intact comprise the entire armament of this massive ship with its valuable cargo.

The ship, owned and operated by Arabic speakers, carried a crew of 75 men who owned little more than the clothes they wore, but its cargo would have made the owners rich men had it reached port. The north end of the Red Sea was an Ottoman lake in the later 18th century, and the Sadana ship reveals a mini-history of Red Sea trade that dovetails into the greater scheme of international commerce between East and West. Although the last of our 3,000 dives at Sadana Island was in 1998, I sometimes still see the ship in my mind, exposed to the tape measures and cameras of archaeologists, requiring us all to look much closer before it shares its secrets.

The *Clydesdale Plantation Vessel:* Savannah River, South Carolina

FRED HOCKER

The lightning stopped and the thunderclouds moved off down the river. We loaded the boat with our shovels, notebooks, and cameras and prepared to go home. Everyone clambered in, I put the motor down and turned the key, and was greeted by silence. Not even a click or buzz. The downpour had shorted the electrical system. Our mechanical wizard, Charlie Harris, tried every trick he knew, but the motor was dead. I hate outboards.

If we did not want to spend the night in the swamp, we had to walk down the river to the nearest road, about a mile away. So, with the sun setting and the tide rising, we half-walked and half-swam in the chest-deep water until we could climb out of the river. We were held up near the end by a pair of alligators that disappeared into the sawgrass just ahead of us, but as darkness fell we had reached civilization again and were glad to be out of the mud. The next day, we returned to the boat, pushed it into the water, changed the battery, and started it on the first try. I really hate outboards.

We were excavating a small sailing vessel that had been buried to stabilize a levee near Savannah, Georgia, sometime around 1800. The man-made bank was part of Clydesdale, one of the rice plantations that had dominated the lower Savannah River before the Civil War, and had suffered a blow-out. The hole had to be plugged quickly, or the river would tear away the bank, destroying the valuable rice fields behind. To save the bank, an old boat had been sunk in the gap, and gangs of slaves had shovelled heavy clay into and around the boat until the bank had been built up again.

The boat lay there until the US Army Corps of Engineers changed the flow of the river as a means of naturally dredging the port of Savannah. The boat began to erode out of the bank and was discovered during a survey of the river in 1991. Judy Wood, the Corps archaeologist, invited me to take a look, and after a survey with Kevin Crisman in the winter of 1992, I returned with a crew of six that summer to excavate, document and re-bury the boat.

The Savannah area was developed for rice farming because the Atlantic tide reaches well up the river, with a range of up to 3 m (10 ft). Plantation owners could use the tide to flood and drain the fields, which made rice culture practical, but complicates archaeology. Our choice was to dive at high tide, in zero visibility and with a current, or to dig with shovels at low tide. Either way, we would only have a short window in which we could reach the site by boat. We decided to dig, and so each day we shovelled clay like demons for four hours, then came home to process the day's finds, write up field notes, and rest.

The clay was initially firm, but as we walked around in it, it quickly became softer, until we sank to our hips in the black goo. It had, however, preserved the timbers of

Clydesdale
Plantation Vessel

Burial 1780–1810
Excavation 1992
Tons of clay excavated by hand 90
Alligator sightings average 4 per day
Hull 13.4 m (44 ft) long,
5.1 m (16.7 ft) wide
Tonnage 20 tons burthen

Above left **Standing in waist-deep mud, Noreen Doyle clears the port side of the Clydesdale sloop's heavy keel. Not what she expected after years of studying Egyptology!**

Above **Despite its small size, the sloop shows elegant lines and sophisticated craftsmanship. Here excavators clean the remains for photography and begin to record the structure.**

the boat beautifully. It took three weeks to clear a meter (over 3 ft) of clay off the remains, and when we were finished recording, we had to shovel the same 90 tons of clay back into the hole, to protect the boat.

The reward for those sweaty days out in the swamp was a glimpse of an early high point in American shipbuilding. The boat we had excavated was only 13.4 m (44 ft) long, but it had been built with a heavy keel and a sharp bottom, to sail fast under a large press of canvas. It may have been built as a pilot boat, but such vessels were also used for carrying cargoes, and cleared southern ports bound for the Caribbean, Bermuda, and New England. These southern sloops and schooners were popular for high-value cargoes, both legal and illegal, and their reputation for speed and sailing qualities reached across the Atlantic. The little Clydesdale Plantation sloop was an early member of the larger family that included the Baltimore clippers, War of 1812 privateers, slavers, and revenue cutters.

Excavating the Colonial Privateer
Defence: Penobscot Bay, Maine

DAVID C. SWITZER

Defence

Built 1779, Beverly, Massachusetts
Scuttled 14 August 1779
Depth 8 m (25 ft)
Found by Maine Maritime Academy,
Castine, 1973
Excavation 1975–1981
Weaponry 16 guns
Crew 100

What were the chances that an archaeological undertaking could at least soften the memory of a failed military and naval operation during the American Revolution? An archaeological postscript to the ill-fated Penobscot Expedition of 1779 provided the answer.

The American Revolution was in its third year when that expedition set forth from Massachusetts bound for Maine's Penobscot Bay. It consisted of a fleet of more than 40 vessels, representing the largest American military and naval operation of the Revolution. About half the vessels were warships drafted from the Continental and state navies. A privateer contingent numbered 13. The remainder included unarmed

The arrival of the British Squadron. In the background the vessels of the Penobscot Expedition are retreating towards the Penobscot River where they were soon scuttled to avoid capture.

transports carrying 900 militiamen and a unit of US Marines. The expedition mission was to dislodge a British force from the present-day town of Castine. The arrival of a Royal Navy five-ship squadron, however, put the American armada to flight. By the evening of 14 August the Penobscot River was ablaze with burning and scuttled vessels – a naval disaster rarely mentioned in general histories of the American War of Independence.

Unforeseen Results

One Massachusetts-built privateer mounting 16 guns was not among the self-destructed vessels in the river. Under the command of Captain John Edwards, *Defence* sought to escape by hiding in a small inlet, but was tracked down by a British man-of-war. To avoid certain capture, Captain Edwards issued orders to set explosive charges to sink his ship. Officers and crew, leaving possessions behind, reached the nearby shore. On board the pursuing HMS *Camilla*, the commanding officer noted the explosion in the ship's log. *Defence* had disappeared from history – or had it?

She was indeed forgotten, like the ill-fated Penobscot Expedition – until 1973. That summer students and faculty of Maine Maritime Academy at Castine built a makeshift sonar and tested it across Penobscot Bay, the very inlet where *Defence* was scuttled 193 years earlier. The sonar recorded "something" projecting above the seabed. Exploratory dives by Academy students revealed it was the top of a brick galley stove; test trenches turned up pulleys, bottles, barrel staves, and cannonballs. Later two cannons were recovered.

By the time the discovery was reported to the Maine State Museum, research by Maritime Academy history professor Dean Mayhew had identified the site as that of *Defence*. In 1975, on the eve of the Bicentennial of the Revolution's beginning, the Museum initiated the *Defence* Project, or Project Heritage Restored, which resulted in a seven-summer archaeological excavation. When Captain Edwards saw *Defence* disappear beneath the waters of Stockton Harbor, he could not have realized that he was burying a time capsule.

George Bass asked me to direct the *Defence* Project, which was to last from 1975 to 1981. We were both introduced to the wreck site during a dive on a cold and snowy day in January 1975. As chunks of ice clustered around us, the adrenalin surge counteracted the frigid conditions as I saw the galley stove, the eroded stump of the foremast, and the pristine condition of the inner hull planking.

Opening the Time Capsule

The initial field season of the *Defence* Project in 1975 was a trial period for the task force created by the State Museum. Logistical support was provided by the Maritime Academy, whose Dave Wyman served as associate project director. The recently formed Institute of Nautical Archaeology was given responsibility for conducting the archaeology through field schools. By the end of the seven summers more than 40 students, 25 Earthwatch volunteers, and many non-affiliated assistants had participated. The Museum took responsibility for the conservation and eventual display of artifacts.

The remains of *Defence*, at a depth of 8 m (25 ft), were embedded in a flat, featureless, non-reflective seabed covered by a deep layer of silt, a combination that

A diver/excavator rests on the grid frame above the brick galley cook stove.

sometimes caused blackout conditions; even on the best of days, it was impossible to see more than a few feet. Diver orientation was achieved by means of grids of white PVC pipe, but it was not until we produced a site plan that we could really understand or "see" the entire site.

As we dug, largely by feel, airlifts emptied into constantly monitored floating sieve boxes on the surface.

During that first summer Maritime Academy support included a floating work platform; dormitory living and dining facilities; and our own boat, skippered by Dave Wyman, for the hour-long passage between Castine and the site. During the bicentennial summer of 1976, we were provided with the tugboat *Dirigo* as a research vessel.

At the beginning, we had dreams of raising and preserving the "capsule's" largest artifact, the hull, in the fashion of the Kyrenia ship, dreams quickly dashed for lack of funds, lack of an adequate conservation facility, and lack of interest in a memorial to a naval disaster! The alternate became our motto: preservation through documentation.

Thanks to excellent preservation in the anaerobic environment, fully 40 percent of the hull remained intact, extending some 21 m (70 ft) from bow to stern. This provided a rare opportunity to record the work of the Massachusetts shipwrights. Structural details were photographed when visibility permitted; recorded through the artistic ability of Peter Hentschel; and superbly drafted by Dave Wyman. From the resultant plans and detailed drawings, we concluded that *Defence*'s designer had been innovative in producing a hull configuration similar to that of the fast clipper ships of a later era.

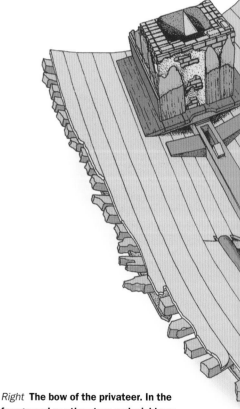

Right **The bow of the privateer. In the foreground are the stem and wishbone-shaped breasthook; farther aft is the brick galley stove with its copper cauldron; just before it stood the foremast.**

Opposite left **An excavator descends to the grid frame and the square in which the airlift would be put to work removing bottom sediments.**

Opposite **As the airlift brings sediments up to the sieve box, a "tender" watches for finds that may have been missed by the excavator below.**

Right **The leather sail maker's palm was used to push a needle through heavy canvas.**
Far right **The stave-built mess kid or bucket was used to carry portions of food from the galley to groups of seamen or mess sections who ate their shares from wooden bowls.**
Below right **What every archaeologist hopes to find at a nautical site, an artifact bearing the initials of a crew member and confirmation of the date of the site, "JL 1779"!**

As someone who had studied and taught American maritime history, I was thrilled by the ability to touch evidence from the past instead of only reading about it. Rather than the usual museum displays of well-known maritime instruments and other accessories, from *Defence* came the everyday items used by seamen and officers, representing aspects of life and work at sea that were unique.

The contents of a trench across the hull illustrated the variety of items we registered and catalogued daily, ranging from leather shoes, a fragile hat ribbon, and cannon wadding, to the carpenter's and boatswain's tools. Interspersed were artifacts related to the distribution of the daily fare of salt beef or pork. They included wooden bowls, a wooden trencher or plate, ceramic cups, and small wooden buckets or mess kids. Various bottle types suggested that a fair amount of wine and gin was consumed.

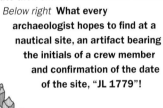

Excavating the Colonial Privateer Defence: *Penobscot Bay, Maine* **197**

Left **Sixteen wooden "tags" (one for each cannon of** *Defence***) were recovered from the galley area, designating portions of boiled meat destined for a "mess section," a gun crew of four to eight seamen. The wooden spoon (** *right* **) was probably whittled by a seaman, although the trencher may have been used by the ship's officers. The mug is of a style attributable to a Massachusetts potter by the name of Bagley.**

Below **The pewter military button was a unique find; all the other buttons were "civilian" and either handmade of wood, bone, or leather or manufactured of metal.**

Bottom **Soft pewter spoons with a lead content of 80 percent were recovered from the galley area. Wear marks on their bowls indicated the "handedness" of the users; initials identified the owners. The distorted spoon is evidence of the heat of the scuttling fire.**

In the galley the cook made edible the salt pork and beef found stored in provision barrels. Portions of meat designated for a group of six or eight seamen, a mess section, were boiled in the copper cauldron to remove the salt. Each portion was identified by a small wooden tag bearing initials or symbols. Matching initials on the mess kids probably identified the "mess captains" who were responsible for doling out the rations.

The seamen ate from wooden trenchers with pewter spoons on which the users or owners had scratched their initials. Tooth marks on the edges of the bowls told us whether each user was right- or left-handed.

A divider in the cauldron suggested that the officers may have been fed a better fare. While eating from pewter plates, officers may have quaffed their drinks from the stave-built tankards. Their items of personal adornment reflected their status: they wore better shoes with fancy buckles, and fastened their coats with metal buttons. One pewter button had the embossed letters USA. One or two officers, perhaps Captain Edwards, drank tea from a fine English Whieldonware tea service.

Traditionally, the captain was responsible for navigating his vessel. *Defence* may also have had a mate with navigation skills. In the galley area where many of the "life and work at sea" items were recovered, navigational instruments included an intact Gunter scale, a rarity among finds from shipwrecks. Made of rosewood, 90 cm (3 ft) long and looking like a yardstick, it was used to solve time and distance problems. Evidence of another instrument was limited to three pieces of a wooden Davis quadrant. A fragment of a slate inscribed with faint lines suggesting navigational use also came to light.

The seamen and the gunners who supervised the operation of six-pounder cannons were well equipped. Wooden tompions sealed the muzzles watertight and wooden crowbars or heavers were used to lever the cannon tubes or wheeled gun carriages. Copper ladles loaded powder, and rammers sent home cannonballs and wadding. To damage enemy rigging or clear his decks, *Defence*'s ammunition stores included both

Left **Cannonballs recovered on the shot rack that held them on the deck between the cannons. Once each ball weighed six pounds, but they have lost most of their iron content and now weigh only a fraction of that.**

Below **Another form of cannon projectile was grapeshot that consisted of a bag of lead balls packed around a wooden spindle. When fired the balls spread out and were a deadly antipersonnel weapon.**

grape shot and langrage, in addition to cannonballs in "ready racks" on the deck. Both types of ammunition are described in the works of C.S. Forester and Patrick O'Brien, but intact stands of grape shot or scrap metal fragments that made up langrage are seldom found in museum displays.

Of the 16 guns *Defence* carried on her deck, only two were recovered when the site was discovered. What of the remaining 14? Had they been salvaged sometime after she sank? The historical record is silent. There is the possibility that they rest deeply buried outside the hull structure. Believing that the recording of structural details was a major goal, we did not excavate outside the hull for fear of disturbing the integrity of the site's major artifact.

The fact that the mystery of the missing cannon was not solved did not trouble me. While we know a great deal about cannons – their calibers and techniques of casting – the variety of artifacts we did recover represented life and work at sea in the 18th century as strikingly as their excellent condition. And the proveniences of these finds showed where they were stored or used on board.

The Legacy of Defence

It is time to return to the question posed at the beginning of this account: could the results of an archaeological endeavor expiate a military and naval disaster? I believe the answer is that it could, and has!

From the first moment we first delved into the hull of *Defence* it seemed that we were present at that chaotic moment when the crew were fleeing the privateer, with no time to save either personal items or equipment. Many Revolutionary War battlefields and encampments have been investigated by historical archaeologists, but the "time capsule" aspect has never been as literally evident as was the case with *Defence*.

Maine and national periodicals provided excellent coverage of our seven summers of excavation, never failing to make some analogy between the *Defence* project and the 1779 Penobscot Expedition, stating how present events were offsetting those of the past.

There has been another legacy of the *Defence* excavation. Influenced by their field-school experiences, a number of students and volunteers went on to follow careers in nautical archaeology. In this light, the "second Penobscot Expedition" has indeed overshadowed its predecessor.

From Collier to Troop Transport: The Betsy, Yorktown, Virginia

JOHN D. BROADWATER

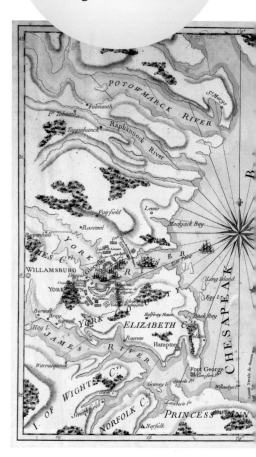

The Betsy

Built 1772, Whitehaven,
Cumbria, England
Sunk October 1781
Depth 7 m (23 ft)
Excavation 1982–1988
Hull 23 m (75 ft) long
Tonnage 176 tons burthen

Events leading to the discovery and excavation of the *Betsy* began in late October 1975, as I sat in a small Yorktown restaurant overlooking the cold, turbid waters of the York River. With me, studiously examining several damp sketches on Mylar, were William Kelso, Virginia State Archaeologist; Gordon Watts, North Carolina State Underwater Archaeologist; and John Sands, Director for Collections at The Mariners' Museum. Gordon and I were explaining the sketches from our day's dive just offshore from where we sat. Gordon reported, "We have a large wooden shipwreck, more than 30 m (99 ft) long. There's every reason to believe that it dates to the American Revolution."

"And there's evidence it's being pilfered by recreational divers," I added.

John Sands was aware of the artifact removal. His recently completed Masters' thesis examined the history of British ships sunk during the Battle of Yorktown, the last major battle of the American War of Independence. He had learned that a shipwreck at Yorktown was being looted and had alerted the Commonwealth of Virginia. Sands reminded the state that this area of the York River had been designated a Historic District on the National Register of Historic Places – the first underwater site to receive this distinction. The state's response was not encouraging, so John and I resolved to organize our own Yorktown survey. The North Carolina Division of Archives and History allowed Watts to assist us, and Bill Kelso, with a limited budget and no nautical archaeologists on his staff, granted us access to the site and provided staff support.

The survey report we submitted to the state verified that a significant 18th-century shipwreck lay in state-owned waters off Yorktown and was threatened both by looting and shoreline erosion. We recommended an intensive assessment of the site along with its protection from further unauthorized disturbance. Press coverage of our survey had an unexpected result. The Virginia General Assembly, concerned about the looting, passed an emergency bill that resulted in the Virginia Underwater Historic Properties Act of 1976. With no formal state support and no funds, our private survey team had done all it could. At that time, archaeology was an avocation for me, and I could volunteer only during weekends and annual leave.

Not long after we submitted our report, the Virginia Historic Landmarks Commission invited George Bass to conduct a formal investigation of the shipwreck. George, in the process of relocating his Institute of Nautical Archaeology to new quarters at Texas A&M University, agreed to organize a Yorktown field school for the following summer. I was elated. I had worked as sonar operator and diver with George in Turkey in 1973, on INA's very first survey, and thought that Virginia could do no better than to collaborate with the Institute.

Opposite **Major General Charles Cornwallis, commander of the Southern British Army, in a portrait by Thomas Gainsborough. Shortly before he surrendered his forces at Yorktown on 19 October, 1781, he scuttled at least a dozen vessels in the York River as beach obstructions to thwart a French amphibious attack.**

1976: The "Cornwallis Cave Shipwreck"

Thus, in July 1976, the bicentenary of the American Revolution, excavation began on the "Cornwallis Cave Shipwreck," named after a local landmark on the adjacent Yorktown shore. The site proved to be the lower hull of a large wooden ship whose nautical and military artifacts confirmed that it was a British vessel of the late 18th century – almost guaranteeing that it was associated with the British fleet sunk during the Battle of Yorktown in 1781. There was ample evidence of recent disturbance and artifact removal, but George converted and enlisted the help of some of the local divers who had been collecting souvenirs. The local press became fascinated with the wreck and the historic artifacts brought daily to the surface.

While the field school continued, George and Bill Kelso prepared a grant application requesting funds from the National Endowment for the Humanities (NEH) for additional research at Yorktown. His field school concluded that the "Cornwallis Cave Shipwreck" was historically and archaeologically significant and should be documented before divers and erosion destroyed it. I was certain the proposal would be funded, but for a variety of reasons George had to return to Turkey in order to concentrate on other promising projects for his fledgling INA. Bill Kelso then turned to me. Would I consider being designated project director for the Yorktown grant application? As project director, I could apply my expertise in marine survey to the location of additional shipwrecks while Kelso, as principal investigator, would provide his academic skills for a detailed archaeological plan. I was overwhelmed by the offer and asked for time to consider the opportunity. The first person I consulted was my wife, the second was George Bass. George said that if I accepted the position, he would continue to mentor me as he had done since 1973.

The 1978 Shipwreck Survey

I accepted the state's offer, recommending that we amend the grant application to propose a one-year survey to locate and assess as many Yorktown wrecks as possible. Sands' research had revealed that 26 British ships were unaccounted for after the Battle of Yorktown. Thus, if successful, our survey would allow us to evaluate numerous shipwrecks before committing to a full-scale excavation. The grant was approved in May 1978 and I was hired as Virginia's first underwater archaeologist. Kelso immediately assigned a member of his staff to the Yorktown Project on a temporary basis. But we needed a larger team. Turning to INA, I hired two of their recent M.A. graduates to assist me.

The 1978 survey was more successful than we dared hope. We located nine shipwrecks from the Battle of Yorktown, seven along the Yorktown shore and two on the opposite bank. With these results, we were granted NEH funds for survey, assessment, and excavation planning.

The 1980 HMS Charon Field School

In 1980, with excavation planning still underway, INA again collaborated with Virginia for a Yorktown field school, this time investigating a wreck on the north shore, at Gloucester Point, believed to be the remains of HMS *Charon*, the largest British warship at Yorktown. The team, directed by Dick Steffy, confirmed the

Below **A French map, published soon after the Battle of Yorktown, depicts several events that took place in September–October 1781, including the "Battle of the Virginia Capes," the subsequent French blockade of the mouth of the Chesapeake Bay, followed by the entrapment of British forces at Yorktown (far left).**

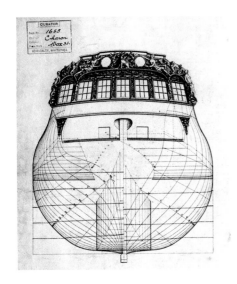

Above **A stern plan of HMS *Charon*, the largest British warship at Yorktown. *Charon*, set afire by red-hot shot from a French battery, sank on the night of 10 October, 1781, the first major casualty of the French-American siege of the British position.**

Below The cofferdam built to facilitate the excavation of the *Betsy* at Yorktown.

identity of *Charon* while recovering a variety of artifacts. I had the pleasure of sharing office space with Dick Steffy while he assimilated the daily site data and compared them to surviving plans of the *Charon*. One day I heard Dick chuckling to himself which meant, I had learned, that he had discovered something interesting in the data. Curious, I went to his drafting table. He glanced up with a satisfied grin and said, "Just look at what that shipwright did during the construction of *Charon*. See these site drawings from yesterday? There's a mortise in the keelson that's been plugged and there are three stanchions – instead of two, as shown on the plans – to support the capstan. That shipwright said to himself, 'I don't care what those fancy Admiralty architects drew, I know that capstan needs three stanchions to support it!' And three stanchions he installed!" Although an electrical engineer by training, Dick could get into the minds of long-dead shipwrights better than any anthropologist I've ever met.

The Betsy *Cofferdam Excavation*

Our survey results, the INA excavations, and the resultant press coverage helped us obtain federal, state, and private funds for the excavation of the Yorktown shipwreck that offered the most research potential, a well-preserved wreck known only by its official site number, 44YO88. Although the vessel was buried, we could tell that it sat on an even keel and that approximately half of its hull was intact.

Because the visibility in the York River rarely exceeded a few inches, and because strong currents and choppy waves made diving difficult, we built a steel enclosure, or cofferdam, around the wreck to eliminate currents, and then filtered the enclosed water to improve visibility. Usually, water is pumped out of cofferdams, but we proposed retaining the water to protect the ship's fragile timbers and artifacts from exposure to air, which would accelerate decomposition. This idea had been proposed previously but never implemented.

The cofferdam was completed in 1982. A pier between the cofferdam and shore provided access for staff and utilities – and allowed thousands of visitors to watch our excavation in progress, possibly the world's first publicly accessible underwater archaeology project. The filtration system improved visibility to an average 7.6–9.1 m (25–30 ft), increasing excavation efficiency and allowing us to document the site photographically. Excavation continued through 1988, providing training opportunities for scores of students; more than a dozen field schools and an equal number of internships were conducted at the cofferdam.

Research and Analysis

As excavation progressed, we developed a better picture of 44YO88: she was relatively small, approximately 23 m (75 ft) from stem to stern and a maximum beam of 7.3 m (24 ft); her hull was boxlike, suggesting a merchant ship; she had two masts; she had a large central cargo hold, with a bulkhead well forward and another aft. In the stern we recovered cabin furnishings and personal effects, several of which provided important clues. The head of a small barrel was carved with the initials "JY" and there were several uniform buttons from the British 43rd Regiment of Foot. The bow contained an assortment of boatswain's stores

Above **Archaeologists encountered a variety of cooperage in the *Betsy*'s hold, including many with markings identifying contents and packing locations.**

Below **The *Betsy* yielded an assortment of buttons, including several from the 43rd Regiment of Foot; regimental records eventually led to the identification of the *Betsy*.**

and large and small barrels, many with markings identifying contents and shipping points. Amidships, on the starboard side, we learned how the ship sank. A hole had been cut through her hull, just below the waterline. The barrels, buttons, and hole supported our hypothesis that 44YO88 was serving as a British transport when she was purposely scuttled during the Battle of Yorktown.

As we had hoped, the buttons proved to be critical clues. John William Morris III and I learned that soldiers from the 43rd Regiment were transported to Yorktown aboard three vessels, one of which, the *Betsy*, was the same size as 44YO88.

Investigating further, we found a listing for a *Betsy* of the same size and same type of rig – and its captain and owner was Joseph Younghusband, whose initials matched those on the barrel. Over a period of several years, this identity was confirmed and a detailed picture of *Betsy* began to form.

An Image of the Betsy

Betsy was built in 1772 in Whitehaven on the northwest coast of England. We feel certain that Younghusband, the captain and owner, named *Betsy* for his wife, Elizabeth. *Betsy* was a collier, a vessel built to carry coal. English colliers were known for their sturdy, bluff-bowed hulls, ideally suited to the transport of bulk cargo. Like the majority of her contemporaries, *Betsy* was rigged as a brig. While colliers were not noted for speed or beauty, their reliability and strength were legendary. Captain James Cook, one of England's greatest explorers, chose British colliers for his round-the-world voyages. Bligh's *Bounty* was a collier.

Every six to eight weeks during spring through fall, *Betsy* delivered coal from Whitehaven to Dublin, Ireland. Then, in 1780, she was leased to the Royal Navy for use as a transport in the war in America. Late the following summer *Betsy*, with her original captain and crew, joined a fleet of nearly 60 warships and transports under the command of General Cornwallis, who moved the fleet to Yorktown, Virginia, along with his army of about 10,000 men. In September, he found his army surrounded by French and American troops, with French warships blocking his escape to the sea.

Above **The *Betsy*'s bow proved to be unique, without a traditional apron structure; the horizontal interior bow framing and radial cant frames suggest possible Dutch influence.**

Left **A wooden gun carriage, intact but for a missing truck, was discovered in *Betsy*'s hold. Examination showed that the carriage had never been used.**

To prevent a French assault from the river, Cornwallis ordered more than a dozen transports, including *Betsy*, scuttled as beach obstructions. Not long afterward, surrounded, outnumbered, and with no hope of reinforcements, Cornwallis asked for terms of surrender. After the British surrender on 19 October 1781 the French conducted limited salvage operations, soon abandoned. The Yorktown ships passed out of memory as they settled into the protective riverbed sediments.

The End and a New Beginning

As the excavation was ending and efforts were shifting to conservation and analysis, Virginia's governor cancelled the underwater archaeology program and abolished our jobs. I could not, however, abandon this ship. Throughout the Yorktown Project I received much good advice from George Bass, including: "Always remember, an unpublished site is a looted site!" After several years, with the assistance of another NEH grant and nearly a dozen collaborators, I was able to produce a final project report.

I made numerous trips to England, frequently at my own expense, where new discoveries provided tremendous personal satisfaction. In Whitehaven, I stood before the tombstone of Joseph and Elizabeth Younghusband, and later held the family Bible bearing an entry describing Joseph's death in Charleston, South Carolina, in 1782, presumably from disease while in a prison camp. *Betsy* taught us a great deal about the construction of 18th-century British merchant vessels, but there is more to be learned. Research never seems to end on a project of this scale.

Top **The *Betsy* was purposely sunk by a single hole cut in her starboard side, amidships.**

Above **The hole that scuttled the *Betsy* had been cut below the main deck by someone who chiseled a neat opening in an inner starboard plank, as if he knew his work would someday be inspected.**

Tracing the Wreck of the Ten Sail: Grand Cayman, Cayman Islands

MARGARET LESHIKAR-DENTON

Wreck of the Ten Sail

Date 8 February 1794
Ships lost HMS *Convert*, Captain John Lawford; *William and Elizabeth*, Goodwin; *Moorhall*, Nicholson; *Ludlow*, McLure; *Britannia*, Martin; *Richard*, Hughes; *Nancy*, Leary; *Eagle*, Ainsworth; *Sally*, Watson; and *Fortune*, Love

A cannon shot roared from the darkness. "Breakers ahead! Close to us!" cried a seaman from a topsail yard of His Majesty's Ship *Convert*, on an 18th-century passage to Europe from the Caribbean. Captain Lawford bounded up on deck as Grand Cayman's jagged eastern reefs appeared in every direction. To his surprise and dismay, the ship firing distress was ahead of its escort, as were several others – not collected, as they should have been, with the Jamaica fleet sailing under *Convert*'s protection. Fifty-eight merchant ships were in peril – but not from the French, from whom *Convert*, formerly *l'Inconstante*, was a recent prize. Royal Navy gunners signaled the convoy, laden with West Indian wood, cotton, sugar, and rum, to disperse and save themselves. A merchantman on the opposite tack crashed into *Convert*'s bow, foiling her escape. As the crews of the two wooden ships disentangled their rigging, *Convert* struck and bilged. It was three o'clock in the morning, 8 February 1794.

"The dawning of the day presented a most melancholy scene. Seven ships and two Brigs on the same reef with the *Convert*, a heavy sea running and the wind blowing directly on shore," wrote John Lawford in a dispatch to the Admiralty. Eight people drowned. The loss of the well-armed frigate during wartime – the French

Below **HMS *Convert* and nine merchant ships sailing under the frigate's protection wrecked on 8 February 1794, on the windward reefs of Grand Cayman. A 20th-century wreck attests to the ever-present danger of this fringing coral barrier.**

Revolutionary Wars (1792–1802) – presented a hardship to Great Britain and agony to her newly appointed captain, though he was honorably acquitted by court martial. So did the catastrophic loss of nine merchant ships, returning to Europe with much-needed supplies from the colonies. The small island population, for its part, recovering from an October hurricane, had much to gain in salvageable goods.

Archives

Details of this remarkable tale were revealed in original documents that I discovered in the early 1990s. Clues emerged from the ink on weathered pages in English, French, and Jamaican archives. *L'Inconstante*'s papers and those of her first commander, Captain Riouffe, are in various national and military archives in France. Engravings of frigates and official cannon regulations are in French naval scholar Jean Boudriot's collection. In Jamaica, the Public Archives and National Library hold *l'Inconstante*'s prize papers, Council of Jamaica Minutes on the convoy and impressment of seamen, and periodicals containing advertisements for convoy ships. David Lyon helped acquire draughts of *l'Unité*, *Convert*'s sister ship, at London's National Maritime Museum. Lloyd's Register of Shipping provided merchant ship details, while the College of Arms illuminated a chronology of Captain Lawford's career. The Public Record Office (PRO) in Kew, London, houses the greatest wealth of documents: Admiralty and Secretariat Papers, Captain Lawford's letters and court-martial proceedings, convoy registers and instructions, *Convert*'s muster table and salvage account, related captains' and masters' logs, merchant ship registers, periodicals, and miscellaneous original correspondence.

There was a remarkable moment at the PRO when new discoveries had become infrequent. I found the *Royal Gazette* of early 1794; no prior volumes were listed, and none again until 1813. I turned the pages, hardly breathing, until I read, "Thursday night arrived from the Grand Caymanas, Lieutenant Bogue, of His Majesty's Ship

Above **Captain Lawford survived the Wreck of the Ten Sail, which occurred when he was 38 years old, without any major effect on his reputation. He went on commanding ships until 1811. With a career spanning the American War of Independence, the French Revolutionary Wars and the Napoleonic Wars, Lawford attained the rank of Admiral by the time of his death in 1842, aged 86.**

Above **A General Post Office notice regarding HMS *Convert* appeared in the Jamaica Royal Gazette of 18–25 January 1794, only days before *Convert*'s loss.**

Right **HMS *Convert*, formerly *l'Inconstante*, was a French-built 12-pounder frigate, as illustrated by Pierre Ozanne in an 18th-century engraving, "view of a frigate seen from abeam close-hauled on the port tack."**

Tracing the Wreck of the Ten Sail: Grand Cayman, Cayman Islands   **207**

Convert, with the melancholy intelligence of the loss of that frigate, with nine vessels of the fleet under her convoy, on the North-east end of that island…names of the merchant vessels lost are the *William and Elizabeth*, Goodwin; *Moorhall*, Nicholson; *Ludlow*, McLure; *Britannia*, Martin; *Richard*, Hughes; *Nancy*, Leary; *Eagle*, Ainsworth; *Sally*, Watson; and *Fortune*, Love." This discovery alone was worth the trip to England. Suddenly I knew the precise wreck location, and the name of every ship and captain.

Oral History

The Wreck of the Ten Sail is the most famous maritime disaster in Cayman Islands history. R. Tulloh Coe remembered a story – correct in many details – told by his grandfather, who assisted the survivors. Upon hearing Coe's account, Cayman Islands Commissioner George Hirst, writing in 1910, dismissed hearsay that cannons on the Gun Bay reef were remains of a fort and affirmed that "on this spot, the 'wreck of the ten sail' took place." Hirst was on target, but his words, like the names of the wrecked ships, faded. The Wreck of the Ten Sail became a legend.

Archaeology

I had seen artifacts, thought to be from the Wreck of the Ten Sail, on the seabed in 1980 while participating in an INA shipwreck survey with Roger Smith. Ten years later, as an INA research associate, funded in part by a Texas A&M dissertation fellowship and the Cayman Islands National Museum, I combined archaeology, archival research, and oral history to piece together the truth. The strategy was to locate, document, and assess sites associated with the *Convert* convoy, to make recommendations for further investigation and future management, and to recover, conserve, and analyze samples of artifacts.

A search for cannons adorning public and private places on land was a priority. My team of volunteers documented over 30 guns; ten had come from a sandbar inside the East End reef. They are 12-pounder cannons cast in 1781 at Forge-Neuve, an ironworks near Angoulême in Charente, France. The long-pattern cannons, cast according to the French Navy's "Regulations of 1778–1779", are part of the original ordnance placed on board *l'Inconstante*, which was lost when *Convert* wrecked.

Offshore work relied on visual survey with metal detectors over a 3-mile (5-km) tropical reef zone. This method is effective in the clear waters off Grand Cayman, especially in shallow areas that are inaccessible to boats. Test-excavations on the sandbar where the French cannon had been found suggest that 13 cannons remain buried here, most likely the final resting place of *Convert*'s gundeck, carried up and over the reef.

Crumpled copper sheathing at the nearby Frigate Spillage Site testifies to the *Convert*'s grinding over the reef, while 12-pounder cannonballs and barshot match

Below left **Ten *Convert* cannons, raised to adorn public and private places years before our project, were located and documented. This gun, like most antiquities raised by non-archaeologists, has suffered from corrosion due to lack of professional conservation.**

Below **Inscriptions on one of HMS *Convert*'s cannons reveal that it was a 12-pounder cast in 1781 at Forge-Neuve, a French ironworks.**

the calibre of the French guns. Pig-iron ballast, standing rigging, and ship's fittings lie encrusted but exposed on the seabed. The trained eye will recognize their shapes, so we mapped their locations over a 12,000-square-meter area, leaving most *in situ*. We mapped and collected copper ships' nails, galley bricks, ceramics, glass, cutlery, personal items, and samples of shingle ballast.

Anchors, ships' fittings, and concentrations of ballast mark sites along the reefline where hulls of the merchantmen once appeared. Directly ashore is the Salvage Campsite, containing many 18th-century artifact fragments. On this spot, near a place where fresh water percolates into shallow seawater, Captain Lawford camped for six weeks with his officers and 30 chosen seamen, salvaging what they could from the wrecked frigate while they waited for a Royal Navy ship to carry them back to Jamaica.

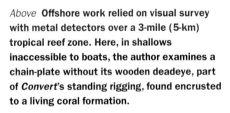

Above Offshore work relied on visual survey with metal detectors over a 3-mile (5-km) tropical reef zone. Here, in shallows inaccessible to boats, the author examines a chain-plate without its wooden deadeye, part of *Convert*'s standing rigging, found encrusted to a living coral formation.

Above right Wreck of the Ten Sail artifacts, including ships' equipment like this 18th-century anchor, lie encrusted but exposed on the seabed.

Right The author explains a 1994 exhibition commemorating the 200th anniversary of the Wreck of the Ten Sail, in the Cayman Islands National Museum, to Britain's Queen Elizabeth II and Prince Philip. During her visit, the Queen dedicated the Wreck of the Ten Sail Park, which includes a view of Grand Cayman's windward reefs.

Tracing the Wreck of the Ten Sail: Grand Cayman, Cayman Islands   **209**

WRECKS OF MODERN TIMES

O ur coverage of modern times, from the beginning of the 19th century, begins with the rather bizarre story of the first deepwater yacht built in the United States, a yacht sold in 1820 to King Kamehameha II of Hawaii. Paul Johnston describes the history of the yacht and his excavation of its remains.

We then move to boats that were not propelled by wind or steam, but by horses. This might seem like the lead-in to a joke about how many horse-power any given boat had, but horse-powered ferries were surprisingly common in North America in the early decades of the 19th century, at the very time that steam propulsion was gaining popularity. Kevin Crisman had the good fortune to excavate what today would be considered a most exotic craft. As this is written, Kevin is excavating the earliest known steam-powered western riverboat yet found in the United States, the *Heroine*, which sank in 1838 in the Red River, which now separates Oklahoma from Texas.

It is little appreciated that when the mass production of large steamboats began, they had a more profound effect on the western movement of people across North America than did the railroad – my great-grandfather, as a young man, wrote letters home about his trip from Virginia to Texas by river steamers in the 1850s.

Within a quarter century of the *Heroine's* sinking, steamships were serving other purposes in North America. The battle between the famed Civil War ironclads *Merrimack* and *Monitor* may have marked, according to Winston Churchill, "the greatest change in sea-fighting since cannon fired by gunpowder had been mounted on ships," but fast, wooden steamships that evaded the blockade of the Confederate States proclaimed by President Lincoln were equally important at the time. Barto Arnold describes his work on one of the most successful of these blockade-runners, the *Denbigh*.

Art Cohn, who calls canal boats "the 19th-century equivalent of the modern tractor-trailer," describes the discovery of a type of canal boat that was not thought to have existed in North America. Such discoveries keep nautical archaeology constantly exciting.

At last we enter the 20th century. I crossed the Atlantic Ocean 28 times by ship before ever I flew across, something I now do several times a year. Three times I passed through hurricanes, and once traveled from France to New York in a full December gale on the *Queen Mary*, before she was stabilized, in waves the size of mountains. These were unforgettable experiences. There were daily sailings from New York. "Do you want to go to northern Europe or to the Mediterranean on Tuesday?" the agent would ask. It is hard to realize, then, that to future historians of

One of *Titanic's* huge bronze propellers, more than 7 m (23 ft) in diameter, rests in a bed of rusticles that have fallen from the ship's deteriorating hull.

211

Above **J. Barto Arnold with the 250-kg (550-lb) connecting rod of the blockade-runner** *Denbigh*'**s port engine before it was cleaned of encrustation.**

Below **Places mentioned in this section, with the featured wrecks in bold.**

seafaring, the entire history of transoceanic passenger steamships will be but a tiny blip, only slightly more pronounced than the history of transoceanic travel by propeller-driven airplanes, which lasted only decades. Transatlantic passenger steamships operated regularly for but a century and a half after their introduction in 1830. That is not much time to an ancient historian.

Yet that short era produced the most famous ship, and the most famous shipwreck, in history – the *Titanic*. Even before the blockbuster film "Titanic," the story of the "unsinkable" ship, the iceberg, and how 1,500 people died in freezing water in April of 1912 was known around the world. Certainly, no other wreck could have tempted me to descend two and a half miles below the surface of the North Atlantic. What nautical archaeologist could resist? Would you have done it?

World War II saw the most powerful military fleets ever assembled. Yet the military vessels that are the subjects of the last two contributions to this book were not victims of giant naval battles between warships. All of the losses date to 1944. The Japanese ships that now make Truk Lagoon one of the most favored diving spots in the world were sunk by American warplanes while at anchor. Jeremy Green describes how he located one that had earlier escaped detection, and the immediate aftermath of his discovery.

The American vessels studied by Brett Phaneuf off the coast of Normandy were not battleships, cruisers, or destroyers, but the more modest landing craft that ferried thousands of troops across the English Channel to Normandy on 6 June 1944 – modest in size, perhaps, but not in their monumental contribution to eventual allied victory in Europe.

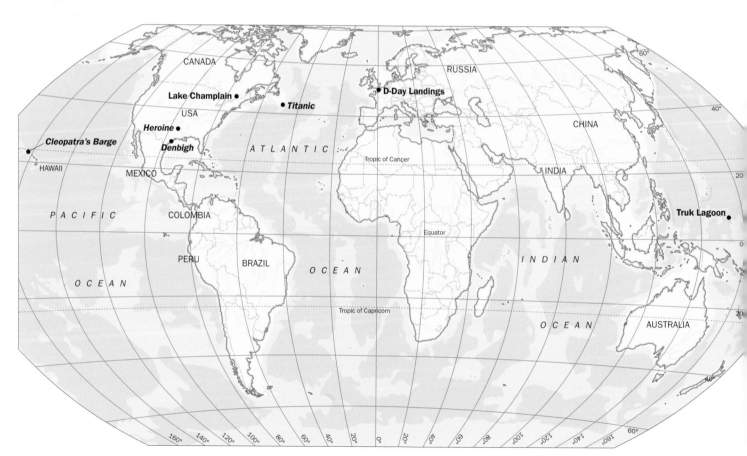

Cleopatra's Barge

Built 1816, Salem,
Massachusetts
Builder Retire Becket
Renamed Ha'aheo o Hawai'i
Sunk 6 April 1824
Excavation 1995–2000
Hull 30.5 m (100 ft) long

Cleopatra's Barge:
Kauai, Hawaii

PAUL F. JOHNSTON

Below **The eldest of five sons, George Crowninshield Jr worked for his family's shipping company in Salem, Massachusetts. By the age of 20, he had served as a ship captain, but he preferred shore duty and took over the construction, fitting out, and maintenance of his family's sizable fleet of merchant ships.**

Below right **Deaf-and-dumb artist George Ropes painted this extraordinary portrait of *Cleopatra's Barge* in August 1818, the same month the famous yacht was auctioned after her owner's death. Every sail is bent, and the hermaphrodite brig is tearing along in a stiff breeze.**

I first heard the story of *Cleopatra's Barge*, America's first ocean-going yacht, on the first day of my first real job after graduate school. Newly hired as Maritime Curator at the Peabody Museum in Salem, Massachusetts, I was ushered into a small period room decorated with exotic woods, red velvet, and gold leaf. Cabinets were filled with ancient curiosities, and the room itself was a replica of the main salon of the *Barge*, based upon descriptions contemporary with the vessel's construction in 1816 in Salem. Adjacent rooms held ship models, rare furniture, log books from old ships, memorabilia, and watercolor portraits of those same ships – all related to George Crowninshield Jr (1766–1817) of Salem, owner of the fabled yacht.

Objects from the *Barge* had been removed before the ship's public auction in 1818, then passed down to family members or sold off. Over the next 163 years they made their way into the Peabody's collections, helped largely by two proud Crowninshield descendants who had cleared out their attics, browbeaten relatives, and followed marine art auctions for more than 50 years, snatching up anything to do with their famous ancestors and their large fleet of deepwater trading ships.

As I learned the story of the famous ship – one of the most bizarre in America's maritime heritage – it sent chills down my spine. It seemed an authentic tall tale, but

it was true, involving such diverse elements as an American president, a pair of Emperor Napoleon's boots, seven lines of Shakespeare, British explorer Captain James Cook's entrails, the respective kings of England and Hawaii, and the first elephant in America.

But although much was published about the first half of the ship's life, mostly in and out of New England, the second half of her short, eight-year career prior to her violent loss in 1824 was totally unknown.

It was this uncharted and unexplored later phase, which took place in the Pacific island kingdom of Hawaii, that appealed so strongly to me. Almost nothing is preserved from early 19th-century Hawaii (or earlier periods), due to both the tropical environment and the organic origins of most objects prior to the "discovery" of the Sandwich Islands by British Captain James Cook in 1778. What might be left of the wreck of the famous ship, and what could it tell us about the material culture of the early Hawaiian monarchy – America's only authentic royalty?

Research revealed that a pipe was the only surviving possession of the Hawaiian king who had bought *Cleopatra's Barge*: Kamehameha II, nicknamed Liholiho. Son of Kamehameha the Great, who had united the Hawaiian Islands, Liholiho was responsible for the breakup of the royal system of taboos in Hawaii, and for allowing Christian missionaries in, changing Old Hawaiian culture forever.

Purchased from Boston China traders for $80,000-worth of sandalwood only ten days after her arrival in Hawaii in 1820, Liholiho's royal yacht and her contents promised to amplify the sparse story of his brief, five-year reign, a story written almost exclusively by *haoles*, or foreigners.

Search and Discovery

I contacted the State of Hawaii regarding a survey for the wreck of *Cleopatra's Barge* in early 1994. On the basis of experience elsewhere, I expected to obtain a permit through the State Historic Preservation Office and begin diving that summer in Hanalei Bay, where the *Barge* had sunk. But my permit application was the first ever

Above **King Kamehameha II inherited both a love of western ships from his father, as well as an appreciation for their social and political value. In an 1821 letter, local American merchant Charles Bullard wrote, "All sects are tolerated but the King worships the *Barge*." He always captained the ship when aboard.**

Below **Hanalei Bay, Kauai, where the royal yacht sank in 1824. On the ship's first visit to this island in 1821, King Kamehameha II used her to kidnap the local ruler, thus cementing his rule over all Hawaii. The wreck site is in the water to the right, very near the shoreline.**

Below **The "W&G" stamp on the corner of this piece of copper hull sheathing refers to Williams & Grenfell, the early 19th-century Liverpool copper merchants. The "G24" represents 24-gauge copper, which weighed 24 oz per sq. ft.**

received by the state for a scientific underwater archaeological survey, and consequently there was no process for such an application. As a result, I needed to submit a formal Environmental Assessment for review by 26 state and federal agencies as well as the general public, and found out that a separate permit would be required by the US Army Corps of Engineers. Moreover, one of the state agencies reserved a year's review period "after receipt of a complete application," and informed me that there were 60–70 applications ahead of mine!

A year later I held five different state and federal permits, one non-permit, and a total of 44 discrete conditions for the survey. And this was only for permission to *search* for the wreck – what might be required if we actually *found* something and it warranted fuller investigation?

Written in May 1824, Boston missionary Hiram Bingham's eyewitness account of the *Barge*'s partial salvage by Kauai islanders stated that she had struck a shallow reef and sunk off the mouth of the Waioli River, near the beach in Hanalei Bay, on 6 April 1824. The wreck had occurred as the result of a storm, a parted anchor cable, and an intoxicated crew. This information, combined with the use of a magnetometer and metal detector, resulted in test trenches that quickly yielded early 19th-century artifacts. A piece of copper hull sheathing stamped "W&G/G 24" was traced to the early 19th-century British copper dealers Williams & Grenfell. Other 1995 finds verified the wreck's identity and indicated that there was enough left to justify excavation before storm-driven waves finally destroyed what remained.

Finds

Over the next four excavation seasons, more than 1,250 artifacts were found on the site, including a 12.2-m (40-ft) section of the stern nestled against the reef that had wrecked the ship. Among the most significant small finds were 18 fragments of olive-green square case bottles, so-called because they packed easily into wooden cases. The presence of these alcoholic spirit containers aboard the royal yacht lent weight to

Below **These fragmentary square-sided case bottles from the early 19th century most commonly held alcoholic spirits, such as gin. Their presence aboard the royal yacht supports contemporary accounts that alcoholic beverages were a factor in the ship's loss.**

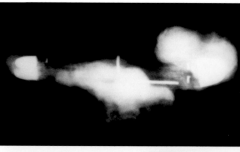

contemporary missionary accounts that one of the reasons the ship had sunk was due to an inebriated native Hawaiian crew.

The discovery of five human bones was unexpected. Historical accounts indicated that no one was injured during the 1824 wrecking, much less killed. The distribution of bone types and ages from the site did not match the bodies of unrecovered victims of recorded drownings in Hanalei Bay. Stronger possibilities were bones washed out of a Japanese cemetery just up the Waioli River, or bones from shallow Hawaiian beach burials from the pre-contact period. However, there is no Hawaiian DNA database from which to derive concrete answers, so a definitive source for the bones remains a mystery.

Personal items included unfinished carved sperm whale teeth, an ivory finger ring, a pair of nail scissors, a pen (folding) knife, and a table knife and fork. Among maritime tools were a leather belt holster containing a sailmaker's heaver; a sail needle; a sand glass for measuring the speed of the boat; and a meat fork whose identical twin was illustrated in a late 18th-century marine dictionary.

In October 1822, King Liholiho sold ten cannon from his yacht – now renamed *Haʻaheo o Hawaiʻi* (*Pride of Hawaii*) – in exchange for the timber from a condemned ship; according to contemporary missionary accounts, he retained at least one as a signal gun to announce his comings and goings from local ports. Two guns were recovered in an 1857 salvage of the yacht's wreck, but we found none. Nevertheless, evidence for their presence was recovered, in the form of a lead cannon apron; part of a wooden gun carriage wheel; a wooden tompion (plug for a gun muzzle to prevent moisture or contamination); and a large, hollow iron shell that would have been packed with powder and plugged with a fuse before firing. Other firearms were confirmed by a wooden musket forestock; three sizes of lead shot; a small patent powder flask made of copper; and remains of a small powder keg filled to the brim with gunpowder.

Hawaiian Finds

Relatively few native Hawaiian objects appeared, but the highlight was a *pu*, or conch shell horn, complete with a tonal hole knocked into its side. In Old Hawaii, these were

Above left **Tom Ormsby and Rick Rogers record details of the royal yacht's teredo-ridden bow timbers, found hard against the reef that sank the ship.**

Above **Artifacts containing iron bond with the surrounding sand and form shapeless lumps, called concretions, as they deteriorate over time underwater. Here, an X-ray of such a concretion reveals a folding knife, which has then been partly exposed as the hard crust is carefully removed in the conservation process.**

Below **A copper musket (or "pocket") powder flask attests to the presence of modern western weapons aboard King Liholiho's yacht. The type was patented in 1814 by Briton Thomas Sykes; this example may be an American copy of the English patent.**

used as horns signaling an event or arrival, not as musical instruments. Dozens of iron adze heads, made from sections of straight and slightly curved barrel hooping, were paralleled by two Hawaiian stone examples. Iron adzes were highly prized in the early contact period, and the royal yacht has yielded the largest known hoard, dated far later than historical sources would indicate. Pointed tools included two picks or awls of bone, and two made from copper hull spikes. Two large, heavy grindstones served to sharpen a variety of Hawaiian tools; they are joined by a remarkable French or English copper furniture mount, originally gilded, depicting a cupid sharpening his arrow on a foot-treadle-operated circular grindstone. Two large pounders and a small oil lamp made of local, rough-surfaced lava are relatively crude, not what one would expect aboard the yacht of a monarch. A few other stone tools for sharpening or burnishing complete the Hawaiian tool kit left behind by the vessel's original salvors. Thin-walled gourd fragments attested to organic liquid containers aboard the vessel; these and two cowrie shells pierced for octopus lures were the only evidence for Hawaiian food gathering, preparation, or consumption.

Three large, ovoid lava stones, with grooves cut around their short sides for ropes, were known as canoe breakers, swung and flung at enemy canoes, and then hauled back for another broadside. With Western firearms, powder, and ammunition on board, it is hard to believe that they were anything but anachronisms – or perhaps a nod to tradition.

What was not found is as telling as what we recovered. Of course, delicate organic objects had not survived the dynamic surf zone in which the ship had been cradled. However, not a sherd of Chinese export porcelain was found, nor remnants of any other luxury items that would be expected to adorn a king's yacht. The overall picture that emerges from the five-year archaeological investigations of the vessel that served as the royal Hawaiian yacht from 1820 to 1824 is one of extreme modesty, excepting only parts of the hardware that were almost certainly part of the original Crowninshield fitting out.

Aftermath

Perhaps the absence of any royal trappings can be explained by their removal and storage when the king left the islands in November 1823 to meet and consult with King George IV in England. Whatever was left aboard could also have been removed during the 1824 salvage, broken up in the surf-lashed reef environment, consumed by voracious teredo worms, or further broken down during the 1857 salvage. These sorts of unknowns embody the old adage that archaeology always poses more questions than it answers.

King Kamehameha never learned of *Ha'aheo*'s loss. He and his favorite queen were still at sea when the ship wrecked in Hanalei Bay. Before news of the tragedy could reach him, they both died in London, on the other side of the world, victims of measles, a western disease to which their Pacific island kingdom had never been exposed. Today, around a quarter of *Ha'aheo*'s hull structure below the water line remains buried in the shallow sands of Hanalei Bay, one of the most beautiful spots in Hawaii. It and the artifacts recovered from five seasons of excavations are all that remain of the fabled ship, one New Englander's dream and a Hawaiian king's most cherished possession.

A Horse-Powered Ferry: Burlington Bay, Lake Champlain

KEVIN CRISMAN

Horse Ferry

Built	1820–1840
Sunk	1840s
Depth	15 m (50 ft)
Hull	18 m (59 ft) long, 4.6 m (15 ft) wide
Deck	7.2 m (23.5 ft) wide
Crew	2–4 men, 2 horses

There's an old saying: "You can lead a horse to water but you cannot make him drink." True, perhaps, but you could make him walk on water if you lived in the 19th century and owned the latest in maritime technology: a horse-powered boat. Hundreds of these ingenious craft once plied ferry crossings throughout the North American continent, whisking people, livestock, and wagons over the rivers and lakes that were a barrier to overland travel. In their day "horseboats" (also known as "teamboats") were a common sight, but their story was largely forgotten until the discovery of a horseboat wreck in Burlington Bay, Lake Champlain.

The wreck first appeared on a side-scan sonar printout, sitting upright in 15 m (50 ft) of water, listing over slightly to port, its deck extending out beyond the sides of the hull in the manner of a steamboat. A pair of sidewheels were visible slightly forward of amidships. Only 18 m (59 ft) long, the wreck looked like a small steamboat, but when my colleague Arthur Cohn and I dived into the cold, greenish depths, we saw no signs of a boiler or steam engine. There was machinery, however: a giant spoked wheel beneath the after deck, connected to the sidewheel axle by iron gear wheels and an iron transmission shaft. This was surely one of the lake's mysterious horse-powered ferries, but how did it work?

Answering that question and many others took four years of measuring timbers and digging out the fine mud that filled the wreck. Inside the bow were artifacts that told part of the story: broken horse shoes (for relatively small horses); pieces of discarded leather horse harness; gear wheels and a bearing from the machinery, all heavily worn; a shattered, cheaply made teapot; a caulking iron; and the extensively repaired rudder. The ferry had obviously seen many years of service on the lake and was scuttled in Burlington Bay when no longer worthy of repair.

The other part of the story was found in libraries and archives, where much time was spent researching the history and technology of horseboats. We learned that the idea of harnessing animals to simple machines and to power boats went back as far as the Roman era, and that working versions were made in the 17th and 18th centuries. The idea really caught on when steamboats began paddling over North American waters after 1807. Paddle-wheel propulsion was a gigantic leap forward in transportation, but steam engines and boilers were not always economical for smaller craft like ferryboats. Horses were a cheaper alternative, and unlike early boilers, they did not explode. The first teamboat ferry began service in New York City in 1814, starting a craze for these boats that continued for many decades.

Horse machinery changed over time. The earliest type forced the horses to walk in a circle, much like an animated merry-go-round. It worked, but the contraption took

Above **Texas A&M University graduate students Gail Erwin and Joseph Cozzi record the horse ferry wreck's heavily repaired rudder.**

Below **A photomosaic of the wreck as it was found on the bottom of the lake. The fore deck was missing, and the planking of the after deck was in sad shape, but the hull and its unusual machinery were nearly complete.**

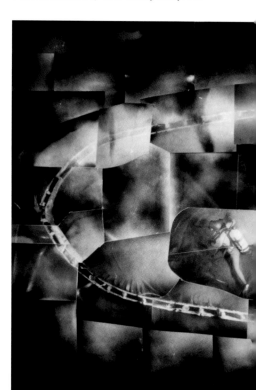

up too much deck space and the horses got dizzy. The second type, patented in 1819 and widely employed over the next two decades, had a flat treadwheel under the after deck with openings cut through on each side to allow the horses to walk in place on the wheel. The third and final type, the treadmill, looked and worked much like the modern version used for exercising people: the horse stood in a narrow stall and walked upon an "endless floor" that revolved under its hooves. This machinery, having the advantage of being lightweight and easily repaired, caught on in the 1840s. The wreck in Burlington Bay was outfitted with a horizontal treadwheel, and was therefore built sometime between 1820 and 1840 when this mechanism was popular.

Historical records suggested that Lake Champlain entered the horse ferry era in the mid-1820s, and that about ten such ferries were employed over the next 40 years. *Experiment* was the first horseboat on the lake. *Eagle* rescued the crew of a sinking steamboat in 1841 and was in service for at least 12 years. *Eclipse* was a six-horse boat that also enjoyed a long career, but had to be abandoned after a heavy cargo of cattle collapsed the deck onto the treadwheel. *Gypsey*, a treadmill-equipped boat, was probably the last horse ferry on the lake.

And what was the name of the vessel sunk in Burlington Bay? Neither the wreck nor the historical record could tell us. What is certain is that the ferry had a long and honorable career carrying people and goods over the waters of Lake Champlain. Listen closely and you may still hear the clop of hooves, the splash of paddle wheels, and the snorts of the ferry's engines.

Above **A diver inspects the corroded but intact gear shift system of the Lake Champlain horse ferry.**

Below **An interior profile view of the horse-powered ferry, reconstructed to show one of the horses on the treadwheel. The ferry was equipped with hinged ramps at the bow and stern (not shown) to facilitate loading and unloading passengers, livestock, and wagons.**

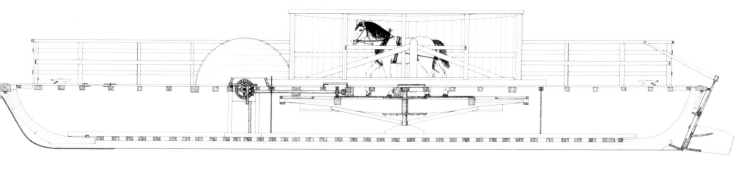

The Sidewheel Steamer Heroine: Red River, Oklahoma

KEVIN CRISMAN

In March, 1838, the river steamboat *Heroine* loaded provisions and stores in Vicksburg, Mississippi, to supply the US Army garrison at Fort Towson in the Oklahoma Territory. Shortly after leaving Vicksburg, *Heroine* began the hazardous 600-mile (965-km) voyage up the winding Red River. Submerged logs – "snags" – lurked beneath the surface and had already sunk two steamers that spring, but *Heroine*'s pilot was skilled – or perhaps just lucky. Near the fort, however, the luck ran out, and with a crash the boat ran headlong into a snag. Water poured in and the steamboat settled to the bottom. No lives were endangered – the upper decks still protruded above the river – but *Heroine*'s career was over. Much of the cargo was ruined, but the crew unbolted the engine and loaded it onto a steamboat bound for New Orleans. A sudden rise in the river a few days later filled the hold with sand and ended salvage operations. Abandoned by all, the steamboat was forgotten for the next 150 years.

"They don't call it the Red River for nothing." The words of INA President Donny Hamilton came back to me as, in September 2002, I dipped my face into the river for a first "look" at the unknown steamboat below. Once on the wreck I could feel the structure around me, but its timbers were nearly invisible in the swirls of reddish-brown water. However, if the river was turbid, the wreck's potential was clear.

Amidships, a center-mounted flywheel for a single piston poked above the surface of the water. Single-piston sidewheelers were largely obsolete by the 1840s, making this vessel the earliest western river steamboat yet discovered. Test excavations inside the hull in 2001 and 2002 turned up tools and barrels of provisions, while probing in 2002 showed that the hull was complete to the main deck and stretched for 43 m

Heroine

Sunk May 1838
Excavation 2001–present
Cargo military provisions and stores for Fort Towson
Hull 42.7 m (140 ft) long, 7.3 m (24 ft) wide
Tonnage 160 tons
Crew *c* 20
Casualties none

Below left **A contemporary watercolor of the steamboat *Ouishita* on the Red River, similar to *Heroine* in its age and tonnage. Cargo, livestock, and steerage passengers occupied the main deck, while cabins on the upper deck provided comfort for first-class passengers.**

Below **The iron hub and support timbers for *Heroine*'s flywheel protrude from the river during a time of low water. The cast iron used for the machinery shattered easily, as evidenced by signs of both damage and repairs on *Heroine*'s surviving sidewheel.**

(140 ft) under the sand. All in all, it was a spectacular discovery in an unusual location – the only known historical shipwreck in the state of Oklahoma.

In 2003 and 2004, we were back to excavate the steamboat's stern, braving strong currents in the shallowest and most exposed part of the wreck. With small headlamps to illuminate the area directly in front of our masks, it was just possible to read measuring tapes. Despite the buffeting, three teams excavating with dredges recovered scores of artifacts and exposed the hull structure.

One of our first discoveries was a small hatchway through the main deck at the stern, an opening once secured by a long iron hasp. Digging under the deck revealed a cramped space filled with mundane objects: a giant C-clamp, a pair of can hooks for lifting barrels, a broken iron fire grating, and personal possessions such as a boot and shoes, an iron stirrup, and a silver spoon handle with the owner's initials scratched into the surface. The compartment, we later learned, was known as the "run" and commonly held the crew's belongings. On this vessel it was also a catch-all for tools, ship's stores, and worn-out equipment.

The adjacent cargo hold held barrels of pickled pork intended to feed the garrison at Fort Towson. Several barrels were recovered for treatment at Texas A&M University's Conservation Research Laboratory. The pork flesh had congealed – "saponified" is the technical term – into waxy, pungent blocks of fat and bones that included halved pig skulls. From an 1830s perspective, modern military rations look quite appetizing.

The largest artifact yet recovered is the steamboat's rudder. A massive assembly of oak timbers, the rudder had many cracks and repairs. These and other clues suggested that the steamboat had seen much service before it was fatally snagged – a suggestion that was proved when the steamboat was later identified.

For a time the name of the wreck eluded us, although we were able to narrow the likely date of its sinking to the late 1830s. Research turned up letters from Fort Towson's commander describing the loss of an unnamed supply boat in May of 1838. New Orleans newspapers finally provided the name: *Heroine*. Western river steamers fundamentally changed concepts of time and distance, and forever changed the interior of North America, yet our knowledge of their architecture and steam machinery has been sketchy at best. The *Heroine* is helping to reveal these secrets, while its equipment, personal effects, and cargo tell us about river navigation, river life, and river trade. More exciting discoveries surely lie ahead.

Above left **Rafts and boats moored over the steamboat *Heroine* support divers studying the wreck. The placid surface of the Red River belies the turbulent conditions encountered by divers beneath its waters.**

Above **Pierre Laroque, Arthur Cohn, and Jim Lee remove lifting slings used to recover the rudder of the *Heroine*. Despite 165 years under water the rudder still retained traces of its original paint.**

Below **A computer-generated image of *Heroine*'s stern as it appears today. A shallow draft hull was necessary for successful navigation of the western rivers, and *Heroine* was therefore lightly built in comparison with seagoing ships.**

The Denbigh, *A Civil War Blockade Runner: Galveston, Texas*

J. BARTO ARNOLD III

Denbigh

Built 1860 in Birkenhead, England
Sunk 23 or 24 May 1865
Excavation 1998–2002
Hull 55.5 m (182 ft) long,
6.7 m (22 ft) wide
Trips as runner 13 successful
round trips
Cargo capacity c 500 bales, or
225,000 lb cotton
Crew 21

I looked at Tom Oertling, he looked at me, and we both looked back at the buoy we had just dropped. "Oh, no," I said, "somebody sank a shrimp boat in the middle of our search area." The buoy floated just 10 m (33 ft) from the large iron wreckage that barely broke the surface of Galveston Bay's entrance from the Gulf of Mexico.

We were in a small boat with four dedicated avocational archaeologists from the Southwest Underwater Archaeological Society (SUAS). Our purpose on that December day in 1997 was to scout the general area where the famous and successful Civil War blockade runner *Denbigh* had been sunk. On a dark night in May 1865, this speedy and elusive vessel was sneaking through the Union Navy's cordon around the bay entrance. The vessel was carrying military supplies and manufactured goods urgently needed by the Confederate Department of the Trans-Mississippi, where Rebels still held out after General Robert E. Lee's surrender at Appomattox in April – and even after President Lincoln's assassination. In fact, the next morning, as the *Denbigh* burned furiously after being shelled by the blockading fleet, Sherman's army was holding a victory parade down Pennsylvania Avenue in Washington, DC.

Surely, we thought, modern wreckage was the most likely identity of the debris the INA preliminary survey party viewed that day, since, in Texas waters as in most

Below **Thomas C. Healy's portrait of the *Denbigh* dated 29 July, 1864, at Mobile, Alabama. The painting shows the *Denbigh* running out of Mobile with a full cargo of cotton.**

Above **High-resolution side-scan sonar image of the portions of the *Denbigh* that protrude above the bottom of the bay. The twin paddle-wheel frames of iron appear at top and bottom, the boiler at the right, and, in the center, the eccentrics and disconnecting mechanisms on the axle or shaft.**

Below **The covered paddle wheel with its feathering mechanism was mounted outboard of the hull, supported by the sponson on which the man stands. This computer-generated reconstruction shows the feathering paddle wheel that greatly increased efficiency by keeping the wooden paddle blades near vertical while in the water.**

places, historic wrecks are usually buried in the muddy bottom. We continued to circle the debris lying exactly where the *Denbigh* appeared on an 1880s map Tom had turned up by chance in the course of other research. Slowly it dawned on me that the cluster of broken pipes exposed by an unusually low tide combined with the effects of strong offshore winds must be steam machinery! Tom and I snorkeled the next day in the frigid but clearer than normal water, locating the paddle wheels and measuring what we later learned was the ship's boiler. The *Denbigh* was found, though we said to ourselves: "This can't be it. It's never this easy!"

The Paddler

The *Denbigh* was a distinctive type of ship known as a British coastal paddle steamer. She served for a few years as a passenger ship plying the short run from Liverpool to Rhyl, a resort in Wales. At the time the *Denbigh* was built, at a cost of £10,250 (approximately $1 million today), the coastal paddle steamer was something of a test case for the development of maritime technology.

In building this type of vessel, the prominent shipyards experimented, participating in a virtual race to improve speed and efficiency. At her launch and time trials in 1860, the *Denbigh* was recognized as a shining example of her kind, and she became one of the most successful blockade runners of the Civil War.

Running military supplies and manufactured goods into the South and, especially, running cotton out was an astoundingly lucrative trade. Just one round trip would buy the ship outright, pay for inbound and outbound cargo, handsomely pay the crew – and still turn a profit. The average runner survived four trips, but the *Denbigh*, capable of carrying approximately 500 bales, or 102,273 kg (225,000 lb) of cotton at a speed of 13.7 knots (15.75 mph), racked up a near-record 13 successful round trips.

Skillful and daring masters and pilots were indispensable in a blockade-runner's success. Captain Godfrey of the *Denbigh* had these qualities. He earned a small fortune, and after the war bought the finest hotel in Mobile, Alabama, the port that was the *Denbigh*'s first Confederate terminus. Sadly, Captain Godfrey then promptly drank himself to death.

Not only were coastal paddle steamers perhaps the most successful vessels used for blockade running, the Union Navy similarly found that captured runners of this type were the most effective cruisers for offshore patrol against blockade running.

The more general type, the side-wheel steamer, was the progenitor of modern marine engineering. Although paddles were eventually replaced by screw propulsion, and reciprocating engines were replaced by steam turbines and then internal combustion engines, the story of marine engineering began with the paddle wheel. All of which underscores the importance of the *Denbigh* as a rare surviving example of a side-wheel coastal steamer.

Speed was the overriding consideration for a blockade-runner. Shallow draft was also important in order that runners could use secondary shore channels for entering Southern ports, and in keeping their distance from deeper-drafted Union vessels. Improving speed by increasing length in proportion to the beam of a vessel reduced cargo space, as did shallow drafts, but for cargo of sufficiently high value, the ability simply to get through outweighed the reduction in cargo-carrying ability.

Despite its shallow-draft advantages, the *Denbigh* ran aground at the entrance of Galveston Bay, and was then shelled and burned by the Union blockading fleet.

INA's **Denbigh** *Shipwreck Project*

The goals of the INA *Denbigh* Project are research, education, and public outreach. Archaeological research at the *Denbigh* site is particularly important because, although there is historical evidence for her operations, the historic record preserves almost nothing of her construction details. For example, plans of the ship have not survived, although descriptive information on the dimensions, cargo capacity, operational history, and other aspects of the vessel exist.

Below **Computer reconstruction of the ship's boiler based on details recorded under water in near zero visibility, and on plans for a similar Laird's boiler from archival sources.**

The 1998 field season's pre-excavation mapping of the *Denbigh* included recording the remains of the vessel's machinery that protruded above the 2-m (6.6-ft) deep floor of the bay to a height usually just below the water surface. In addition to mapping exposed remains, the first season's working phase included remote sensing surveys using magnetometer, side-scan sonar, sub-bottom sonar, and fathometer. The exposed remains consisted of portions of the *Denbigh*'s boiler, paddle wheels, and the very upper parts of the twin steam engines. The deck level was just below the muddy sand bottom.

The 1999 season consisted of three units of test excavations: one centrally located in the engine room, one in the forward area thought to be a cargo hold, and one toward the stern in an area thought to lie beneath the crew quarters. The engine room revealed that the major components of the *Denbigh*'s machinery were intact. This was a welcome but somewhat unexpected discovery, since engines and other machinery were often salvaged. The finding was particularly important because the ship's technology was a major aspect of interest for further investigation. The test excavation unit in the forward area found the port side of the

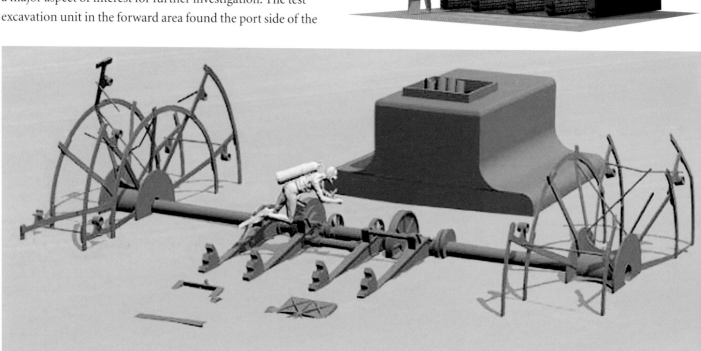

ship had broken and collapsed outward. The aft test excavation unit found the stern area of the hull intact. Beneath about 3 m (10 ft) of overburden, a few artifacts were found, hinting at the presence of cargo and crew possessions. Only the first 60 cm (2 ft) above the hull's bottom yielded relatively undisturbed archaeological deposits, a pattern that seems to be usual at this site.

Three summers of full-scale excavation from 2000 to 2002 allowed us to record the hull construction, the complex paddlewheel and drive train, and the port engine together with the condenser, air pump, hot well, and boiler. Another excavation unit in the stern half of the hull helped confirm the location of the crew quarters, but excavations were mainly concentrated in the engine room and just outboard of the engine room.

Small artifacts were generally scarce, but a remote corner of the engine room contained a storage area for engineering department tools and a private stash of liquor. Some bottles were sealed with intact contents, which we will soon analyze and identify.

Our excavation strategy was to study the wreck in place rather than raise the hull. The cost of completely excavating, recovering, and then conserving, restoring, and exhibiting a 55.5-m (182-ft) long by 6.7-m (22-ft) wide iron hull are beyond practical contemplation. The expense would run into many tens of millions of dollars.

The *Denbigh* Project now enters a phase of conservation, analysis, and publication. We plan at least two more books to join W. Watson's *The Civil War Adventures of a Blockade Runner* (2001) in a series: first, the main excavation report and history of the ship, and second, a collection of documentary sources about the *Denbigh*. Historical research continues, and the archaeological potential of the site is far from exhausted. The bow and the stern need attention as the next areas for excavation and study. Very likely there are further areas in the hull where important and intact archaeological deposits remain. When the present reporting phase is complete, INA's *Denbigh* Project excavations will continue.

Above **Computer generated reconstruction of the *Denbigh*'s engine room and machinery without the iron hull plates and wooden deck. The stern and the twin inclined engines are to the left. Each engine had a single 40-inch-diameter cylinder and a high-tech cutoff valve.**

Opposite **Exposed remains of the *Denbigh*'s machinery in a computer-generated image. The ship's buried deck level is just inches below the paddle shaft. Beyond the boiler at top right, the bow lies buried.**

Far right **Helen Dewolf and Amy Borgens prepare *Denbigh*'s calcareous encrusted superheater top for X-ray at Texas A&M University's Conservation Research Laboratory where the *Denbigh* artifacts are being cleaned and preserved. The X-ray (*right*) reveals the construction details of its connection to the pipes through which smoke and hot air from the burning coal entered the smoke stack. Steam surrounded the pipes after exiting the boiler, gaining heat and expansive force. The superheater was an advanced feature helping produce superior speed and efficiency.**

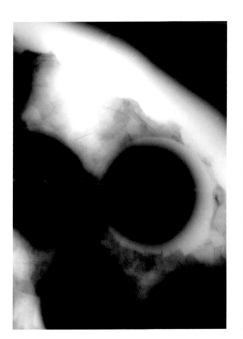

The Sailing Canal Boats of Lake Champlain

ARTHUR COHN

After three decades working in Lake Champlain's cold, dark waters, it may have been the most extraordinary sight I had ever seen. The Lake Champlain Maritime Museum's side-sonar survey team of Fred Fayette, Peter Barranco, and Tom and Pat Manley of Middlebury College had located an intriguing anomaly in the lake's deep water. Our instruments told us the object rose more than 9 m (30 ft) off the bottom, far too tall for any of Lake Champlain's wooden shipwrecks. It must be geological, perhaps an oddly shaped boulder dropped 10,000 years ago by a receding glacier, we agreed. Although it did not look like a shipwreck, we still needed to identify what lay more than 30 m (100 ft) below us. As I descended slowly into darkness I was left with only my dive light to illuminate a narrow channel of water in front of me. I could scarcely believe it as the sodden timbers of a boat's transom appeared, towering above the lake bottom. At that moment I knew I had solved a 175-year-old tragic mystery with the discovery of the canal schooner *Troy of Westport*.

To some observers Lake Champlain may seem an unlikely place to study shipwrecks. The lake lies far from the ocean, nestled between Vermont's Green Mountains and New York's Adirondacks. However, geography favored this inland lake as it provided a 193-km (120-mile) long north–south navigable waterway. During the historic period when roads were awful, if they existed at all, travel by water was the best option. Today, the lake's collection of some 300 shipwrecks (and still counting) attest to the rich and layered history that took place around and over Lake Champlain.

Sailing Canal Boats

The disappearance of the *Troy* is wrapped within a larger mystery that began with the discovery in 1980 of the *General Butler*, an intact shipwreck a stone's throw from the shoreline of Burlington, Vermont. Old timers had told me about a boat that sank in 1876 after running headlong into Burlington's massive timber-cribbed, stone-filled breakwater. When the *General Butler* was discovered its dimensions suggested it was one of the region's typical wooden canal boats. Canal boats were the 19th-century equivalent of the modern tractor-trailer, carrying freight throughout the communities located along the region's waterways. The canal boom engulfed Lake Champlain in 1823 when the Champlain Canal opened. The canal connected Lake Champlain to the Hudson River, and in 1825 to the Erie Canal; commercial shipping on Lake Champlain prospered like never before. Canal boats had a distinctive long, narrow shape designed to maximize their cargo capacity while still allowing them to fit through the canal locks. They were towed by steamboats or tugboats when in open

Below **The canal schooner *General Butler* as she looks on the bottom of Lake Champlain.**

water, such as Lake Champlain, or pulled by horses or mules when in the canals. As we examined the remarkably intact remains of the *General Butler* we noted rigging elements and two mast tabernacles, three-sided boxes used for stepping a mast on the deck, all suggesting that this canal boat was designed to sail.

"Not so!" was the universal response from canal historians we approached for information. According to these experts, while sailing barges had been part of European maritime history, they had never been built in North America. Never. Happily, we can now report that the discovery of the *General Butler* has opened up a new branch on the North American naval architecture tree. Research over the past two decades with my partner, INA's Kevin Crisman, has determined that sailing canal boats appeared on Lake Champlain simultaneously with the opening of the Champlain Canal in 1823. The very first boat to transit the new canal was the *Gleaner* from St. Albans Bay, Vermont. The *Gleaner* was celebrated at Hudson River ports all the way to New York City where she received a 24-gun salute. In the New York newspaper *Mercantile Advertiser*, she was described as a vessel "built as an experiment and is found to all the uses intended. She sails as fast and bears the changes in weather in the lake and river as well as ordinary sloops and is constructed properly for passing through the canal." The *Gleaner* was a Lake Champlain sailing canal boat!

Sailing canal boats were the practical response of Lake Champlain merchants and mariners who wanted a vessel that could be loaded with cargo and then have the independent ability to sail to the canal entrance at Whitehall, New York. Once arrived, they lowered their masts, which stepped on the deck, and raised their centerboards for the trip by mule through the canal. Once on the Hudson River, they would raise their masts, lower their centerboards and sail south, all without having to handle their cargo until they reached their final destinations. As the 19th century progressed, steam towboats on the Hudson River became more reliable, so few sailing canal boat captains found it economical to sail on the Hudson. Most left their masts and sails in storage at Whitehall to be re-stepped on the northbound journey.

Lake Champlain's sailing canal boats evolved over time. The first generation of sailing canal boats, known as the 1823-class, were 24 m (79 ft) long and 4.1 m (13.5 ft) wide. The earliest boats of the 1823-class were built as experiments, and it was not until 1841 that a more standardized design was adopted by the region's shipwrights. In 1862, the first expansion of the Champlain Canal locks was

Above left **Rigging elements such as this deadeye on the *General Butler*'s bow were the first clues that this was no ordinary canal boat.**

Above center **The *General Butler* was lost, in part, because its steering mechanism broke. The captain rigged the rudderpost with a makeshift tiller, but it was still not enough to save the boat.**

Above **Toy model of a sloop-rigged sailing canal boat found aboard the *General Butler*.**

Below **Sailing canal boat *P.E. Havens*, circa 1900.**

Above **The still intact wheel of the *O.J. Walker* attests to the excellent shipwreck preservation conditions in Lake Champlain.**

Above right **The stock of an anchor hangs over the *O.J. Walker*'s bow.**

Below **Drawing of the canal schooner *Troy* as it looks today.**

completed giving rise to the 1862-class of boats. These were 26.8 m (88 ft) long and 4.4 m (14.5 ft) in beam. The 1873 expansion of the canal gave rise to boats that were 29.6 m (97 ft) long and 5.3 m (17.5 ft) in beam. These 97-footers were the last of the line. The sailing canal boat was becoming obsolete, a victim to the year-round and expanding railroads.

Historian Scott McLaughlin estimates that only 250 sailing canal boats were built on Lake Champlain during their century of operations as compared to 4,000 towed canal boats. During our sonar surveys we have located more than 50 standard canal boat shipwrecks, as compared to only five intact sailing canal boat shipwrecks. The *General Butler*, built in 1862 in Essex, New York, lies within a half-mile of the *O.J. Walker*, built in Burlington, also in 1862. The *Butler* carries marble blocks and the *Walker* bricks and tile. Two intact but still nameless 1841-class sailing canal boats have been located, one with a load of marble and one with a load of iron ore. Both have the standardized look expected of boats built in the 1840s or later. Missing from this collection was an archaeological example of an early experimental 1823-class vessel – until the discovery of the *Troy*.

Troy of Westport

We knew from historical research that the canal schooner *Troy of Westport* had been lost in 1825 in a November gale. Her crew of five young men and boys were never found and her loss devastated the community. Details of the tragedy became evident as I descended along the hull. Unbelievably, the transom hung in the water, while the rest of the hull plummeted perilously downward. As I reached the bow, a tangle of spars and cargo lay strewn before me on the otherwise featureless bottom. It was clear

that the heavy cargo of iron ore had rushed into the bow as the boat sank, pulling it rapidly toward the bottom. The steep descent was halted when the bow slammed into the soft mud of the bottom, those tons of iron ore acting as a massive anchor, which ensured that the rest of the hulk would continue to hang in the water column, precariously reaching for the surface.

An Underwater Preserve and the Canal Schooner Lois McClure

We left the *Troy* exactly as we found it, as the Lake Champlain Maritime Museum has done with the vast majority of Lake Champlain's shipwrecks. Its deep-water location and the probability that it contains human remains make management of the site a complicated matter. The sailing canal boats *O.J. Walker* and *General Butler*, however, are seasonally visited by hundreds of recreational divers. These vessels are part of the Lake Champlain Underwater Historic Preserve – a program that began in 1985 as a tool for giving recreational divers reasonable access to appropriate shipwreck sites. Of course, most of the public does not dive, so the Lake Champlain Maritime Museum was founded, in part to allow the public access to Lake Champlain's extraordinary shipwreck collection. As a museum, we are always looking for new and effective ways to share the shipwrecks and their stories. In the 1980s we built, launched and operated a Colonial era bateau (1758) and a replica of the *Philadelphia*, one of Benedict Arnold's gunboats at the Battle of Valcour Island (1776). On 3 July 2004 we launched a full-sized, working reproduction of an 1862-class sailing Lake Champlain canal boat. The new schooner, christened *Lois McClure*, will serve as an ambassador from her time and to the fragile and irreplaceable shipwrecks on the bottom of Lake Champlain.

Mapping the "Unsinkable" Titanic

GEORGE F. BASS

Titanic

Sunk   14 April 1912
Depth   3,798 m (12,460 ft)
Length   269 m (882.5 ft)
Displacement   66,000 tons
Speed   24–25 knots
Passengers and crew   2,207
Survivors   705

Many events in my career as a nautical archaeologist have resulted from a single piece of mail. It was a letter from Peter Throckmorton to the University of Pennsylvania Museum in 1959 that led to my even learning to dive. Forty-four years later, on 22 May 2003, another letter arrived, this one by e-mail from Captain Craig McLean, Director of the Office of Ocean Exploration for the National Oceanic and Atmospheric Administration (NOAA):

Below **For a brief few days, until sent to a watery grave two-and-a-half miles deep by an iceberg, RMS *Titanic* was the largest and most luxurious liner on the Atlantic Ocean.**

"Hello George.

"I have an opportunity for you, if I can tear you away from Turkey. NOAA's exploration program is using the Russian vessel *Keldysh* and the two *Mir* submersibles to visit some mid-Atlantic ridge areas for biological and geological inventory. Shortly thereafter, we are able to make some dives on *Titanic*....We will make a brief excursion for some photomosaic work....Would you like to join us and make a dive? Your views and expertise on the matter would render a respected voice to be heard as this subject further develops. Craig"

Above **At the very tip of the bow, one of** *Titanic*'s **spare anchors rests under the anchor crane, still secured to the deck. Rusticles on the railing were produced by iron-eating microbes.**

Anyone, nautical archaeologist or not, would jump at the opportunity of visiting the most famous shipwreck anywhere – and since I had designed the first method of making shipwreck photomosaics from a submersible back in 1964, I might be helpful. But I was hesitant. It was not just that the deepest I had ever been was 90 m (300 ft), and *Titanic* lies two-and-a-half miles – that's 12,460 ft or almost 4 km – beneath the North Atlantic. I'm a little superstitious. In 2003, after more than four decades of fieldwork, being responsible for tens of thousands of deep decompression dives, and dives in various types of experimental submersibles, I had just decided to end it, without announcement, to simply stop while I was ahead – the news item about an aging stuntman who was killed when making one last jump with his car, after announcing his plan to retire, has long stayed with me.

Why would I go to a place where rescue was out of the question if any piece of equipment failed? What if a spark started an electrical fire? Or my *Mir* became trapped by wreckage? The pressure on the submersible at that depth would be 3 tons per square inch! Small wonder that more people have been in outer space than have ever visited *Titanic*. In fact, more people have been to the top of Mount Everest in a single month than have ever seen first hand those spectacular remains.

I turned to the ultimate authorities: my family. In less than 24 hours my writer son, Gordon, e-mailed me in Turkey: "Come on, you HAVE to do it!" Alan, my younger son, said by telephone that I'd be crazy not to go. I assumed that my wife, Ann, would talk me out of it. I was wrong.

R/V Akademik Mstislav Keldysh

With no more excuses, I sailed out of St. John's, Newfoundland, on 20 June, aboard the Russian *R/V Akademik Mstislav Keldysh*, the world's largest research ship. Icebergs in the distance reminded me of why I was there.

I represented INA among a seven-person team headed by NOAA marine archaeologist Jeremy Weirich. Others were National Park Service archaeologist Larry Murphy, whose continuing study of the battleship *Arizona* at Pearl Harbor has made him especially knowledgeable about the long-term stability of iron hulls, and Drs. Roy Cullimore and Lori Johnston, microbiologists who specialize in the study of the microbes that eat iron and form, at *Titanic*'s depth, huge brown things like stalactites that were dubbed "rusticles" by Robert Ballard when he located the wreck. Both Roy and Lori were returning to *Titanic*, Lori for her fifth visit. Rounding out the team were NOAA's Laura Rear, who had taken care of the logistics of the mission, and Craig McLean himself, whose impressive background includes not only degrees in zoology and law, but two years as a professional helmet diver.

The *Keldysh* carries *Mir 1* and *Mir 2*, two of only four submersibles in the world capable of diving as deep as *Titanic*, the subs used by James Cameron in his epic film "Titanic." Each cost $20 million. They usually dive together, about an hour apart. No one said it explicitly, but I think part of the reason for this is safety, for one sub, with its manipulators, could help untangle the other should it become snared by cables or twisted metal.

Dr Anatoly Sagalevitch is the driving force behind *Keldysh* and the *Mirs*. Since the collapse of the Soviet Union, under which all three vessels were built, he has had to depend on private sources to fund their operation – indeed, to fund all of the

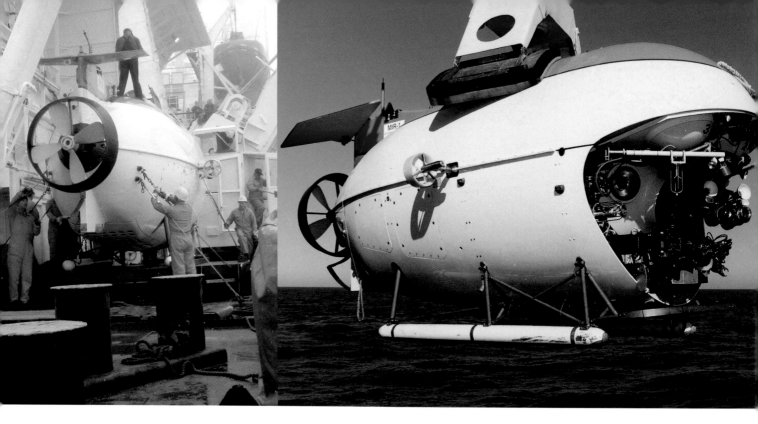

Above **The crew of R/V *Akademik Mstislav Keldysh* unloosen the restraining cables of *Mir 2* in preparation for the submersible's dive. The great protective hangar for the two *Mirs* has already been raised up and out of the way on its hinges.**

Above right **Mir 2 is lowered into the sea from the deck of R/V *Akademik Mstislav Keldysh*. Once in the water, it will be towed farther to sea by a launch before beginning its descent.**

Opposite above **During the dive, the two submersibles took turns at the widely separated parts of *Titanic*. Here, in this reconstruction painting, those in *Mir 2* map the bow section while those in *Mir 1*, in the distance, study rusticles at the stern.**

oceanographic research conducted from *Keldysh*. He thus often uses them for projects like the one I was on, or for filming, or even for taking paying passengers to *Titanic* for $36,000 a dive. I became highly impressed by Anatoly's entrepreneurship and his humanity.

On our first morning over the wreck, the crew of *Keldysh*, using GPS coordinates, dropped four transponders around *Titanic*. Every other day for the next ten days the *Mir*s dived and navigated with seeming ease within this "sonic box." I was scheduled to be on the last dive.

There were many books and videos about *Titanic* on board, so I spent the time before my dive becoming completely familiar with the story of the ship and what has happened to her since she was discovered. Early one morning I stood alone on deck, staring at the calm sea, thinking about the fact that one night in 1912, exactly at this place, over 1,500 people in life jackets were calling for help, drowning, or freezing to death.

Down in Mir 2

On the day of my dive, 29 June, I felt like an astronaut as I walked the corridor to the *Mir* laboratory in my blue, fireproof jump suit. Then, up the ladder, off with shoes, and down inside a steel sphere about 2 m (7 ft) in diameter.

Craig McLean had preceded me into *Mir 2*. I was followed by Victor Nischcheta, our Russian pilot. A technician closed the hatch, which would soon be held tight by mounting pressure, and we were attached to the ship's crane and lowered over the side, all 18 tons of us, barely swinging from side to side. We were blessed by smooth seas for the entire voyage, as today, when it was calm but foggy. The instant we hit the water, a Russian "cowboy" leapt from a Zodiac onto the top of the *Mir* to unhook us from the crane and hook us to a launch, which towed us clear of the *Keldysh*. We were

in a near dead calm, but I have seen films of these cowboys performing the same maneuver in large waves that washed completely over them as they held on for dear life like aquatic broncobusters.

Mir 1, with Anatoly Sagalevitch at the controls, had descended about an hour earlier. Now we began our two-and-a-half-hour descent. I glanced often at our depth gauge. Two miles down, Victor pulled out box lunches for the three of us. When we eventually reached 3,790 m (12,434 ft), the incredibly bright exterior lights went on, flooding the seabed. Almost immediately I spotted a large soup tureen, and then dozens or hundreds of wine bottles in the positions they had held in wooden cases

Below **INA's George Bass, Russian pilot Victor Nischcheta, and Captain Craig McLean, Director of the National Oceanic and Atmospheric Administration's Office of Ocean Exploration, assemble in front of *Mir 2* just before it takes them down to *Titanic*.**

nine decades ago, followed by a bathtub. I was moved emotionally when I saw a woman's lonely, high-topped shoe.

Our exact position within the four seabed transponders was being carefully monitored in the navigation room on *Keldysh*, which remained in contact with Victor over transceivers, so we knew that we would soon reach *Titanic*'s badly mangled stern. Once there, we began a four-hour program of videotaping the wreckage for a photomosaic that should serve as a database against which future damage from age, visitors, and remotely operated salvage equipment can be measured. Kneeling before a central port about 20 cm (8 in) in diameter, Victor operated the *Mir* with intense concentration, often glancing quickly at a compass to be sure we were on line. Craig, using coordinates from the sonic transponder "box" in which we operated, guided

Below left **Titanic**'s great bow remains an awe-inspiring sight, approached either from below or, as here, from above. Without the dangling rusticles, the railing would appear as new.
Below A photomosaic shows **Titanic**'s anchor crane extending up and over the bow. A spare anchor, still secured to the deck, rests at the crane's base, and the port anchor is seen in the lower right corner of the image.
Bottom Looking from port to starboard, this photomosaic of **Titanic**'s bow depicts the aft portion of the forecastle where the forward mast had fallen back, collapsing over deck winches and the #1 hold.

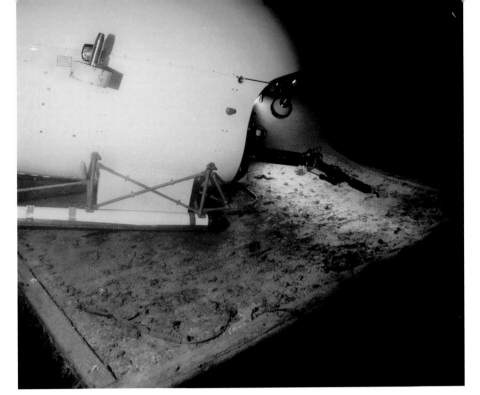

Victor to the starting point for each of the 16 parallel passes, and then, reading from a digital monitor, recorded on paper at timed intervals our exact position. Similarly, so that Victor would not be distracted by keeping track of too many gauges, Craig routinely read aloud our depth from another monitor, letting us know that we were staying exactly 3,783 m (12,411 ft) deep. Sometimes I relieved Craig by reading our depth aloud. At other times I lay on my stomach on my bench to follow our progress, occasionally photographing through my smaller, starboard port.

After nearly four hours, we saw a startling sight: traffic! Two-and-a-half miles down in the sea! *Mir 1*, with Lori Johnston and Jeremy Weirich inside, was coming to take our place at the stern. Although I often could not identify what I was seeing on the wreck, Roy and Lori must have had a field day studying the rusticles. They estimate, I believe, that the ship is disintegrating more quickly than previously supposed.

It was time for us to move about 600 m (2,000 ft) to *Titanic*'s better-preserved bow. The great ship broke into two immense pieces, which landed nearly half a mile apart. The vast debris field between the two halves of *Titanic* has been legally picked over by RMST Inc., which holds salvage rights to the ship, and which has raised and conserved several thousand artifacts that have been seen by millions of people. Still, many plates and other objects remain in this area. The salvors are forbidden by law to sell anything, I am told, or to take anything from inside the ship, itself.

14 April 1912

Then we arrived at the bow, which is magnificent, stunning – and unimaginably huge. More than 15 m (50 ft) of it are buried in the seabed into which the ship plowed with tremendous force when it landed, but its towering height remains awesome.

We rose slowly until we reached the railing. Here the ship is so well preserved I wondered if I would see Jack and Rose standing at the rail, with Jack proclaiming himself "King of the World." We soon began to move slowly over the seemingly solid

Far left **A massive anchor chain still lies by one of *Titanic*'s great capstans. The top of the capstan, being of bronze, has deteriorated less than the iron.**

Left **The mast from which lookout Frederick Fleet spotted the iceberg has now collapsed backward, its crow's nest fallen away.**

Below ***Titanic*'s bronze telemotor, on which the ship's wooden wheel was once mounted, still stands on the bridge where First Officer Murdock made his fatal mistake. Modern memorial plaques have been placed at its base by previous submersible visitors.**

deck in controlled and carefully navigated passes, at a fixed depth, making a mosaic of the shipwreck from above with the submersible's external video camera. Deck winches looked as if they could be oiled and put back to work. I spotted a davit from which one of the far-too-few lifeboats was lowered.

We reached the mast, which has toppled backward. As we moved along its length, we saw clearly the opening through which lookout Frederick Fleet stepped out into the crow's nest from which, not long before midnight on 14 April 1912, he rang the warning bell three times and called down to the bridge those immortal words, "Iceberg, right ahead!" The crow's nest was still in place when Robert Ballard found the *Titanic* in 1985, but we saw no sign of it. There are rumors of illegal and clandestine salvors visiting the wreck during winter months, with remotely operated vehicles to remove more objects, but we do not know if the crow's nest has simply fallen.

On the bridge, First Officer William Murdock made a fatal mistake when he received Fleet's warning. He ordered the ship turned hard to port, which meant *Titanic* scraped the iceberg, tearing a long gash in her starboard side that allowed too many watertight compartments to flood. A head-on collision would not have been so devastating.

The ship's brass telemotor, on which the great wooden wheel was mounted, stands as a silent reminder of the moment the helmsman spun it as far as he could. Memorial plaques have been placed at its base by past submersible visits.

But we did not linger. There was more work ahead. We began to make a video mosaic of the starboard side of this part of the wreck, often drifting with the current at a fixed depth. The lights of the submersible were so bright I could see from the top of the ship to the seabed far below, and could imagine passengers promenading just inside on some of the open-air decks. Most of the portholes still have their glass in place. Several were open. Did a passenger look out of that open window, nearly a century ago, to see what all the commotion was about?

As excited as we were by our dive, we knew that on a cold night just over 90 years before, more than 1,500 passengers and crew perished in this ship or in the sea around it. There were only 705 survivors. Stories of bravery and cowardice have become legend. It is true that all the members of the ship's band played until the end, and all perished. One of the objects raised by the salvors is a clarinet. It is true that Captain Smith went down with his ship, and it is true that Mrs Isador Straus, on being urged to climb into a lifeboat, returned to her husband's side, saying: "We have been living together for many years. Where you go, I go." When offered space in a lifeboat so he could accompany his wife, Straus refused, saying there were still women

to be saved. They were last seen sitting side by side in deck chairs. Benjamin Guggenheim and his valet went below and returned in their evening clothes, prepared, as Guggenheim said, to "go down like gentlemen."

Ascent

We had been in *Mir 2* for seven-and-a-half hours, with two-and-a-half hours of ascent still ahead. It was time to leave *Titanic*. Victor had been deep in concentration for every second during our mapping program. Now he could relax. As we started up, he offered Craig and me hot tea and biscuits. Later, in various positions, the three of us used the large plastic bottles that were under Craig's seat for their special purpose.

We came up after dark in a dense fog. After ten hours in the *Mir*, we flopped around for about half an hour more before we felt that we were being towed back to *Keldysh* by the launch. Soon the cowboy, balanced like a circus bareback rider, attached the crane's heavy lifting cable, which would bring us back on board *Keldysh*. Then he leapt back onto his Zodiac. We were quickly on deck and outside our *Mir*, with hugs all around (especially from Anatoly, who had preceded us up in *Mir 1*), followed by dinner that had been saved for Craig and me in the dining room. With most of the NOAA team around us, we toasted with Russian vodka our successful dives.

Then two full days back to St. Pierre (how many people know that there are two tiny, tiny French islands only a few miles south of Newfoundland?), an overnight stay, and on to St. John's by small charter jet.

On our way back from Turkey in August 2003, Ann and I visited Cobh, Ireland, *Titanic*'s last port of call – then called Queenstown – on the great ship's only voyage. In just one summer I had been to the beginning and end of one of the most famous ocean trips in history.

The Japanese Fleet in Truk Lagoon, Micronesia

JEREMY GREEN

Sapporo Maru

Built 1930, Japan
Sunk April 1944
Original use deep-sea fishing trawler
Wartime use auxiliary provisions storeship
Tonnage 361 tons
Casualties unknown

Following World War I, Japan was awarded German Micronesia, including the Truk Islands, and secured a mandate from the League of Nations following the Treaty of Versailles. In the inter-war years Japanese interest was to make the South Sea Islands profitable, and in the late 1930s the base at Truk was expanded with new airfields and military installations. By 1941, the Japanese, aware of the looming prospect of war with the United States, started to fortify the islands. After the outbreak of the war, the island maintained its strategic position, but by late 1943 the writing was on the wall that the Americans were coming.

Truk in World War II

In February 1944 two Catalina photo-reconnaissance aircraft overflew Truk and photographed the assembled Japanese fleet of over 60 vessels, including the fabled *Musashi* and *Yamato* battleships. The Americans had been planning a naval offensive against Truk, and this was an opportune moment. The ensuing operation, designated "Hailstone," was under the command of Pacific Fleet Commander Admiral Chester Nimitz, with Task Force 50 totalling over 53 vessels, including nine aircraft carriers able to send up over 500 combat aircraft that included fighters, bombers, and torpedo aircraft.

On 17 February the task force approached Truk undetected. The attack that followed caught the Japanese completely unaware. The first wave of fighter aircraft began what has been described as the greatest all-fighter-plane battle of history. The initial waves destroyed most of the Japanese air opposition. Then installations and

Below left **Marine reconnaissance photograph taken prior to the first attack on Truk. The photograph shows numerous warships and merchantmen at anchor. Etan Island is in the center with Dublon Island to the left and Fefan Island in the lower right.**

Below **Dublon Island during an attack on 17 February 1944 by aircraft from USS *Enterprise*. The crippled *Seiko Maru* is on fire and sinking at the center. To the right is the undamaged *Hokuyo Maru*. Two attacking aircraft can be seen above center.**

Right **Inside the Betty bomber lying in shallow water off Etan Island. The view looks forward toward the now missing cockpit, which was probably demolished in the crash. The aluminum fuselage is slowly corroding, as seen at the upper left.**

shipping were targeted. Luckily for the Japanese, the earlier reconnaissance aircraft had been spotted and some of the fleet had already escaped, but the Americans still found over 60 vessels within the lagoon and managed to sink 45 of them, including two light cruisers, four destroyers, and 26 naval and army auxiliaries, totalling over 220,000 tons. During the two-day operation, 270 aircraft were destroyed. A second strike, on 29 and 30 April, further reduced the effectiveness of Truk as a Japanese base. For the rest of the war Truk was effectively bypassed and neutralized, and a land-based invasion became unnecessary as Truk was no longer a threat. This was probably a relief to the Americans, as landing on islands with considerable elevation and heavily fortified gun emplacements would have been costly.

By October 1944, Truk was so irrelevant it was being used as a training area by the Allies to provide battle experience to new units; aircraft used the island for bombing exercises and fleets stood off to sea and bombarded the island as they passed on their way to Japan.

Side-Scan Sonar Survey

In late 2001, I was involved with a local documentary company to produce three television programs about the work of my Department of Maritime Archaeology at the Western Australian Maritime Museum. The series, called *Shipwreck Detectives*, was being produced by Ed Punchard, a colleague and former student of mine. We were having problems with a program about remote sensing, for the story simply was not interesting enough. Ed was wringing his hands and wondering aloud what else we might film. A few months earlier I had been asked by another old colleague, Bill Jeffery, if I could help with a project he was undertaking for the Federated States of Micronesia, providing a management plan for the ships and aircraft lost in Truk Lagoon. He wanted me to bring our side-scan sonar to accurately pinpoint known sites and to look for some missing sites, but there were money problems and it looked impossible for him.

I said to Ed: "How about Truk Lagoon?"

"Fantastic! When can we go?"

So in February 2002 we joined Bill Jeffery in Truk.

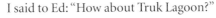

These sites are now a major tourist destination and the Government of the Federated States of Micronesia is concerned that they are properly managed and preserved. The objective of the survey was to relocate as many of the known wrecks as possible and produce detailed sonar images that could be placed on a GIS (Geographical Information System) plan of Chuuk, the modern name for Truk. Most of the sites are known to dive tour operators, but their precise locations are not recorded, nor are their orientations, sizes and conditions. For two weeks we steamed around the atoll locating sites and creating side-scan sonar images of the wrecks. With these images Bill was able to list and record all the sites known only anecdotally.

The Sapporo Maru

In addition Bill wanted us to find one of the last undiscovered shipwrecks in Truk Lagoon, the *Sapporo Maru*. Dan Bailey's definitive book *World War II Wrecks of the Truk Lagoon* provides a background to the vessel: "The *Sapporo Maru* had been built in 1930 as a trawler…[in] January 1944, the *Sapporo Maru* was attached to the 4th Fleet at Truk as part of the Replenishment Force and categorized as an Auxiliary Transport (provision ship) or Special Transport (provision)….Japanese sources indicated that the vessel went down north of Fefan Island….The wreck of the *Sapporo Maru* is one of the few that have not been located at Truk."

So the *Sapporo Maru* was not one of the great warships of Truk. It was an ordinary small supply vessel – but, at 361 tons, one of the last of the larger vessels yet to be found there.

We searched with side-scan for several days, confirming known vessels in the general area, but as with all searches there were hours of frustrating steaming up and down in a systematic search pattern over the area thought to contain the site. The survey for the *Sapporo Maru* was planned to end on 13 February. On the last day on the very last run I saw a target. It was worth going back to for re-examination. On the return run we obtained a stunning image of a vessel lying upright on a sandy seabed with reefs all around. Incredible! Examination of the sonar target showed that we had a vessel with two masts, a central bridge "island," and a length of about 115 m (377 ft). Not only was the *Sapporo Maru* 113 m (371 ft) long, according to Bailey's book, but his published image corresponded almost exactly to the sonar image. There was no doubt we had found the *Sapporo Maru*.

We returned to our base at Moen, one of the islands in the lagoon, where Dan Bailey was staying. We told him that we were pretty sure we had found the last of the big missing ships of Truk. He was delighted and we planned to visit the site the next day. Diving on a new site is always exciting, even if one is an archaeologist, and this site was no exception. I swam around the bridge, looked in the holds, and saw the engine, while making the basic measurements and photographs to confirm that this was indeed the *Sapporo Maru*. One of our team found the ship's bell. Bill was particularly pleased because he had a site that no one had dived on before and it would be possible to use the site, once we made its location public, as a measure of the impact that sport diving or "eco-tourism" had on these sites. It was a unique and fascinating opportunity. Little did we realize how soon the impact would occur! While we worked, some people in the area had been interested in what we were doing. "What are you looking for?" was the usual question, but others generally kept their

Above **Corioli Souter, Bill Jeffery, and Glen Dillon, left to right, lower the 70-kg (154-lb) side-scan sonar fish carefully into the water, always a tricky operation. Working with big iron wrecks also posed a problem: note the nose of the fish has hit some major objects.**

Below **The side-scan trace of the *Sapporo Maru* lying on a sandy seabed between two reefs. Clearly visible are two masts, the forepeak, the bridge, and the engine room and funnel. Because the sonar is linked to a GPS (global positioning system) it is possible to measure the size of the vessel and to accurately plot its position.**

Right **Inside the wheelhouse of the *Sapporo Maru* on the first dive to the site. The wood of the ship's wheel has rotted away, leaving just the boss that can be seen at center right.**

Below right **A recent picture of the *Sapporo Maru*'s bell that was removed from the site less than 24 hours after its discovery.**

distance. I was told later that on the day we dived on the site a local dive boat passed us, but it neither stopped nor aroused any particular interest.

The next day we advised the Government that we had found a new site, and invited the Governor to dive on it. On the same day we arranged for a team to revisit the site to further record it with photographs. To our surprise, the team returned with news that the ship's bell was missing – not 24 hours after the discovery! We were stunned. Who could have done such a thing? It was only then that someone remembered the boat passing nonchalantly by while we were diving on the site. With modern GPS (Global Positioning System) devices they could have returned to the site easily, in late evening or early morning, and removed the bell. Imagine our chagrin, having spent so much time searching for the site, to have the bell stolen so quickly. Should we not have dived on the site? Was the work worth it, with such an iconic item stolen in such a short time? These are unanswerable questions. It shows however, the very real problems of managing sites such as Truk, a place visited by over 6,000 divers every year. There are anecdotal stories of other World War II souvenirs being taken from the lagoon, and artifacts said to be from Truk are sometimes sold on online auction sites such as Ebay. It was a long time after the discovery of the *Sapporo Maru* that I heard from Dan Bailey that the bell had been removed by a guide from a local dive shop. He recovered the bell to prevent it from being "stolen" by unscrupulous divers, and it is now apparently kept under lock and key by the dive shop. This is not really the way heritage should be managed. All we know is that if the wrecks of Truk Lagoon are going to survive for future generations, some serious management plans are needed – and quickly.

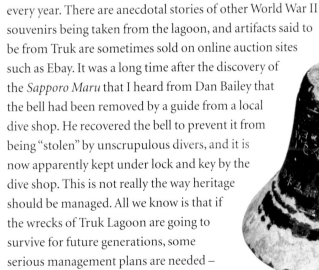

Exploring D-Day Landing Craft: Normandy, France

BRETT PHANEUF

D-Day Landings

Date 6 June 1944
Number of ships c 5,000
Number of landing craft over 3,000
Number of men over 150,000
Number of vehicles 30,000
Number of "DD" tanks 128

D-Day – 6 June 1944 – marked the long-anticipated Allied invasion of Nazi-held Europe. Operation Overlord had begun the day before with Operation Neptune, the most massive naval action in the history of warfare, aptly described by Cornelius Ryan in his moving work, *The Longest Day*: "They came, rank after relentless rank, ten lanes wide, twenty miles across, five thousand ships of every description."

In addition to the 5,000 ships were as many as 8,000 support aircraft, ranging from fighter planes to bombers, gliders, and paratroop transports. Essentially, anything that could float or fly was pressed into service and sent across the English Channel.

My involvement with this moment in history began in 1997 when I was in France with Robert Neyland, Head of the US Naval Historical Center Underwater Archaeology Branch, to collect sonar images of a 19th-century American shipwreck. A weather delay gave me time to tour the American D-Day landing sectors. Standing at Point du Hoc, or on Utah and Omaha Beaches, I found it impossible not to wonder what remains of the invasion fleet lay beneath the waves. I began planning for a survey of the area in collaboration with the Naval Historical Center.

Project Neptune 2K

Although more than 50 years of historical research had been conducted on the landings, and although modern navigation charts mark numerous wrecks and obstructions, there had been no archaeological investigation to correlate underwater remains with the historical record. Faced with the continued loss of the

Left **INA team members prepare to launch the *Oceaneering* remotely operated vehicle offshore of Omaha Beach, May 2001.**

Above **Side-scan sonar image of a "landing barge" in an exceptional state of preservation located off Utah.**

Below **Side-scan sonar image of a "DD" Sherman tank from the 741st Tank Battalion lost off Omaha Beach on D-Day. The tank sits upright on the seafloor with its front facing right. Its circular turret lies on the seafloor above the tank, likely dislodged by a fisherman's trawl.**

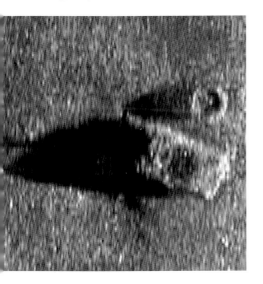

archaeological remains of Operation Neptune to erosion and the clearing of navigational hazards, the Institute of Nautical Archaeology (INA) at Texas A&M University, in cooperation with Naval Historical Center's Underwater Archaeology Branch, embarked upon an underwater archaeological reconnaissance: Project Neptune 2K.

After noting on French nautical charts the shipwrecks and other obstructions littering the seafloor, we began work in 2000 with a side-scan sonar and magnetometer survey off Utah Beach to the west and Omaha Beach to the east, with Point du Hoc between, utilizing a boat provided by INA director George Robb. Initially we eschewed consultation with local wreck divers as our intent was to compile a comprehensive archaeological map not only of shipwrecks, but also of artificial harbor-works, vehicles, artillery, ordnance, personal effects, and defensive obstacles and structures, without bias from persons who were actively disturbing them. These last vestiges of the largest invasion fleet ever assembled warrant the legal protection provided by the French government, but more exploration and interpretation are needed so that diving tourists can visit these sites with the same reverence they would show at the American Cemetery on the bluff nearby.

We incorporated into a master database and map the remains of landing craft, artillery, ships, ordnance, and any other equipment. Analysis of the data provided me with more than 800 targets that deserved inspection by a remotely operated vehicle – an expensive proposition. Fortuitously, the Discovery Channel and the BBC offered to fund the 2001 field season in exchange for exclusive rights to film our efforts for a documentary (*D-Day: Beneath the Waves*).

Of concern was the difficulty of crafting a coherent story for viewers; we could not investigate all potential targets on the seafloor in 2001, or 2002, or even during the next decade.

However, during the course of data analysis, we recognized near the eastern end of the Omaha Beach survey area several clusters of what I identified as tanks, most probably from the 741st Tank Battalion. Cursory research revealed that many of the personnel who served in the amphibious, or "DD (Duplex Drive)" Sherman tanks of that battalion were alive and willing to talk with us. The focus of our research and the film quickly became their harrowing ordeal when they were launched into the sea from landing craft-tanks (LCTs). Of the 32 amphibious tanks, only two managed the "swim" to the beach; three were taken directly to shore by LCT and the rest were lost at sea.

"DD" Amphibious Tanks

Shifting the focus of Project Neptune 2K to the loss of the 741st Tank Battalion not only allowed for the telling of a single, coherent story, but also for an exacting analysis of what was responsible for the failure of the "DD" tanks on D-Day. It was at this point that INA opted to embark on a separate program of research from that of the Naval Historical Center.

In May 2001 the INA team returned to Normandy. With the assistance of Oceaneering International we deployed a remotely operated vehicle (ROV) offshore of Omaha Beach to collect detailed photographs of the objects believed to be tanks from the 741st Tank Battalion. After nearly a month, all of the sonar anomalies

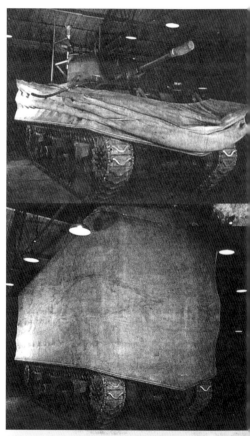

believed to be tanks had been identified, and further research in Britain at the Tank Museum in Bovington, as well as in the United States, was required. In Bovington, that research included my learning to drive a World War II vintage Sherman tank! I had driven M60A3 main battle tanks in the National Guard and jumped at the chance, especially since my instructor was the very person, now in his 80s, who had trained many of the servicemen from the UK and US Armies in Sherman tank operation for Operation Overlord.

"DD" (Duplex Drive) Sherman tanks were invented by a Hungarian-born engineer, Nicholas Straussler, working for the British Ministry of Defence. A veteran of the 741st Tank Battalion described one to me as a "large canvas bucket with a 35-ton iron bottom." A large rubberized canvas skirt around the tank, reinforced with metal hoops, could be raised by means of 36 rubber bladders attached to the tank and inflated by compressed air cylinders. The commander stood behind the turret and steered by means of a tiller attached to dual propellers that were driven by the rear track idler sprocket, so while the tank "swam" the tracks were turning. Once the driver, always inside, felt the tank touch bottom, the screen could be lowered and the tank was ready for action. From the shore, "DD" tanks looked like small rubber boats that, by design, would attract little enemy fire. Once ashore, they were to assist infantry and take out pillboxes. But it was not to be. The tanks were not seaworthy and foundered in the rough weather of D-Day.

After my trip to Bovington, I traveled to the National D-Day Memorial in Bedford, Virginia, to meet with survivors of the 741st Tank Battalion both to discuss my findings and to ask many questions. Immediately thereafter I returned to France to finalize fieldwork with a set of dives at selected sites to capture high-resolution images of several "DD" tanks for use in the Discovery Channel/BBC film.

Loss of the 741st Tank Battalion on D-Day

On the morning of 6 June 1944 the flotilla carrying the 741st and 743rd Tank Battalions arrived off Omaha Beach and prepared for their assault. Orders were to

launch at 5:30 in the morning about 5,500 m (6,000 yds) offshore, in order to arrive ten minutes before the infantry from the 1st and 29th Divisions. In perfect weather the "DD" Tanks could have made it.

The Naval Commander of the flotilla of 16 LCTs, in consultation with the Army commander of the two battalions, decided not to launch but instead to take the "DD" tanks directly to shore. Unfortunately, the commanding officers of the LCTs carrying the tanks, or the commanding officer of the 741st Tank Battalion, either never received the message, or ignored it; whether the Army or Navy ordered the launching of the tanks is still a point of contention. LCT600 launched the first tank and it swam only a short distance before succumbing to the high seas. During that launch the LCT lurched violently, ripping the flotation screens still onboard, and so carried its three remaining tanks directly to shore. However, the rest of the LCTs commenced launching and the tanks foundered one by one, some swimming only a short distance, others lasting for some time before sinking.

The tanks sank mainly because of weather conditions. Flotation skirts collapsed under the strain from the waves, and bilge pumps inside the tanks were too small to keep up with the influx of seawater. In addition, with a tide running at nearly 3 knots, the LCTs were being swept east along the coast, as were the tanks once they were in the water. To counteract this the crews steered a heading that was increasingly westward, which put the waves on the "beam" of their amphibious tanks, the weakest part of the flotation skirts. Canvas collapsed and the tanks sank from sight. Fortunately, the crews were equipped with life rafts and underwater breathing apparatus and most escaped drowning.

Two of the floating tanks made it to shore. Interviews with the families of their commanders revealed that both were avid boaters and fishermen who had turned their tanks' "sterns" into the waves to "surf" in on the swell. Once ashore they linked up with the three tanks carried directly in by LCT600, and with elements of the 743rd Tank Battalion, and served with distinction assisting in clearing German defenses and opening exits from the beach.

Above Two "DD" Sherman tanks from the 741st Tank Battalion that made it to shore. Of 32 "DDs," only 5 reached the beach, two swimming and three taken directly ashore by the landing craft tank that carried them.

Below Tank crewman demonstrating the Advanced Tank Escape Apparatus. Because the ATEA could not actually fit through a Sherman hatch, the driver was instructed to "ride" a sinking tank to the seafloor, remove the ATEA, exit the tank, re-don the ATEA, and then make an ascent. Remarkably, several men of the 741st Tank Battalion accomplished this feat on D-Day!

Further Reading

Past and future adventures of the Institute of Nautical Archaeology have been and will be described in the *INA Quarterly* (formerly the *INA Newsletter*), published by the Institute of Nautical Archaeology, P.O. Drawer HG, College Station, Texas 77841-5137, USA.

INTRODUCTION AND GENERAL SOURCES

Bass, G.F., *Archaeology Beneath the Sea* (New York, 1975)
——*Archaeology Under Water* (London & New York, 1966)
——(ed.), *A History of Seafaring Based on Underwater Archaeology* (London & New York, 1972)
——"A Plea for Historical Particularism in Nautical Archaeology," in R.A. Gould (ed.), *Shipwreck Anthropology* (Albuquerque, 1983), 91–104.
——(ed.), *Ships and Shipwrecks of the Americas* (London & New York, 1988)
Cousteau, J.-Y. with F. Dumas, *The Silent World* (London, 1953; New York, 1956)
Delgado, J.P. (ed.), *Encyclopaedia of Underwater and Maritime Archaeology* (London & New Haven, 1997)
Diolé, P., *4000 Years Under the Sea, Excursions in Underwater Archaeology* (London, 1954)
Franzén, A., *The Warship Vasa* (Stockholm, 1960)
Gianfrotta, P.A. & P. Pomey, *Archeologia subacquea, storia, tecniche, scoperte e relitti* (Milan, 1981)
Oeland, G., "The H.L. *Hunley*: Secret Weapon of the Confederacy," *National Geographic* 200.7 (July 2002), 82–101
Pomey, P. (ed.), *La navigation dans l'antiquité* (Aix-en-Provence, 1997)
Steffy, J.R., *Wooden Ship Building and the Interpretation of Shipwrecks* (College Station, 1994)
Throckmorton, P., *The Sea Remembers: Shipwrecks and Archaeology* (London, 1987; New York, 1991)
Uceli, G., *Le navi di Nemi* (Rome, 1950)
Wheeler, R.C., W.A. Kenyon, A.R. Woolworth & D.A. Birk, *Voices from the Rapids: An Underwater Search for Fur Trade Artifacts 1960–1973* (St. Paul, 1975)

ŞEYTAN DERESI

Bass, G.F., *Archaeology Beneath the Sea* (New York, 1975), 207–221
——"The Wreck at Sheytan Deresi," *Oceans* 10.1 (1977), 34–39
——"Sheytan Deresi: Preliminary Report," *International Journal of Nautical Archaeology* 5 (1976), 293–303

ULUBURUN

G.F. Bass, "A Bronze Age Shipwreck at Ulu Burun (Kaş): 1984 Campaign," *American Journal of Archaeology* 90 (1986), 269–96
——"Oldest Known Shipwreck Reveals Splendors of the Bronze Age," *National Geographic* 172.6 (December 1987), 692–733
——, C. Pulak, D. Collon, and J. Weinstein, "The Bronze Age Shipwreck at Ulu Burun: 1986 Campaign," *American Journal of Archaeology* 93 (1989), 1–29
C. Pulak, "The Bronze Age Shipwreck at Ulu Burun, Turkey: 1985 Campaign," *American Journal of Archaeology* 92 (1988), 1–37
——"The Uluburun Hull Remains," in H.E. Tzalas (ed.), *Tropis VII. Proceedings of the 7th International Symposium on Ship Construction in Antiquity (27–31 August, Pylos)* (Athens 2002), 615–36
——"Evidence from the Uluburun Shipwreck for Cypriot Trade with the Aegean and Beyond," in L. Bonfante and V. Karageorghis (eds.), *Italy and Cyprus in Antiquity, 1500–450 BCE* (Nicosia, Cyprus 2001), 13–60
——"The Cargo of Copper and Tin Ingots from the Late Bronze Age Shipwreck at Uluburun," in Ünsal Yalçın (ed.), *International Symposium 'Anatolian Metal I'*, (Der Anschnitt, Bochum, Beiheft 13, 2000), 137–57
——"The Uluburun Shipwreck: An Overview," *International Journal of Nautical Archaeology* 27 (1998), 188–224

CAPE GELIDONYA

Bass, G.F., *Cape Gelidonya: A Bronze Age Shipwreck*, Transactions of the American Philosophical Society 57 no. 8 (Philadelphia, 1967)
——*Archaeology Beneath the Sea* (New York, 1975), 1–59
——"Beneath the Wine Dark Sea: Nautical Archaeology and the Phoenicians of the *Odyssey*, in J. Coleman & C. Walz (eds.), *Greeks and Barbarians: Essays on the Interactions between Greeks and Non-Greeks in Antiquity and the Consequences for Eurocentrism* (Ithaca, 1997), 71–101
——"Sailing Between the Aegean and the Orient in the Second Millennium BC," in E.H. Cline & D. Harris-Cline (eds.), *The Aegean and the Orient in the Second Millennium: Proceedings of the 50th Anniversary Symposium, Cincinnati, 18-20 April 1997* (Liège & Austin, 1998), 183–91
——"The Hull and Anchor of the Cape Gelidonya Ship," in Betancourt, P.P. *et al* (eds.), *Meletemata* (Liège & Austin, 1999), 21–24
Throckmorton P., "Oldest Known Shipwreck Yields Bronze Age Cargo," *National Geographic* 121.5 (May 1962), 696–711
——*The Lost Ships: An Adventure in Underwater Archaeology* (Boston & Toronto, 1964)

PABUÇ BURNU

Casson, L., *Ships and Seamanship in the Ancient World* (Princeton, 1971)
Cook, R.M. & P. Dupont, *East Greek Pottery* (London, 1998)
Horden, P. & N. Purcell, *The Corrupting Sea: A Study of Mediterranean History* (Oxford, 2000)
Mark, S., "*Odyssey* 5.234-53 and Homeric Ship Construction: A Reappraisal," *American Journal of Archaeology* 95 (1991), 441-445
Pomey, P. (ed.), *La navigation dans l'antiquité* (Aix-en-Provence, 1997)
Roebuck, C., *Ionian Trade and Colonization* (New York, 1959)

TEKTAŞ BURNU

Bass, G.F., "Golden Age Treasures," *National Geographic* 201.3 (March 2002), 102–17
Carlson, D.N., "The Classical Greek Shipwreck at Tektaş Burnu, Turkey," *American Journal of Archaeology* 107 (2003), 581–600
Green, J., S. Matthews & T. Turanlı, "Underwater Archaeological Surveying Using PhotoModeler, VirtualMapper: Different Applications for Different Problems," *International Journal of Nautical Archaeology* 31 (2002), 283–92
Nowak, T.J., "A Preliminary Report on *Ophthalmoi* from the Tektaş Burnu Shipwreck," *International Journal of Nautical Archaeology* 30 (2001), 86–94
Trethewey, K., "Lead Anchor Stock Cores from Tektaş Burnu, Turkey," *International Journal of Nautical Archaeology* 30 (2001), 109–14

KYRENIA

Berthold, R.M., *Rhodes in the Hellenistic Age* (Ithaca & London, 1984)
Katzev, M.L., "Resurrecting the Oldest Known Greek Ship", *National Geographic* 137.6 (June 1970), 840–57
——and Katzev, S.W., "Last Harbor for the Oldest Ship", *National Geographic* 146.5 (November 1974), 618–25
Ormerod, H.A., *Piracy in the Ancient World* (Chicago, 1967)
Steffy, J.R, *Wooden Shipbuilding and the Interpretation of Shipwrecks* (College Station, 1994), 42–59

LA SECCA DI CAPISTELLO

Frey, D., "Deepwater Archaeology," *Sea Frontiers* 25 no.4 (1979), 194–203
——, F.D. Hentschel & D.H. Keith, "Deepwater Archaeology. The Capistello Wreck Excavation, Lipari, Aeolian Islands," *International Journal of Nautical Archaeology and Underwater Exploration* 7 (1978), 279–300
Keith, D.H. & D.A. Frey, "Saturation Diving in Nautical Archaeology," *Archaeology* 32 no. 4 (1979), 24–33

SERÇE LIMANI HELLENISTIC WRECK

C. Pulak & R. F. Townsend, "The Hellenistic Shipwreck at Serçe Limanı, Turkey: Preliminary Report," *American Journal of Archaeology* 91 (1987), 31–57

SEA OF GALILEE BOAT

Wachsmann, S. "The Galilee Boat: 2,000-Year-Old Hull Recovered Intact," *Biblical Archaeology Review* 14 no. 5 (1988), 18–33

——, et al., *The Excavation of an Ancient Boat in the Sea of Galilee (Lake Kinneret)*, 'Atiqot 19, English Series (Jerusalem, 1990)

——*The Sea of Galilee Boat: An Extraordinary 2000 Year Old Discovery* (New York & London, 1995)

YASSIADA 7TH-CENTURY WRECK

Bass, G.F. & F.H. van Doorninck Jr (eds.), *Yassi Ada, vol. 1: A Seventh-Century Byzantine Shipwreck* (College Station, 1982)

Pevny, T., "Shipbuilding Traditions: Building the Yassıada Exhibit," *INA Quarterly* 24 no.3 (1997), 4–11

van Alfen, P.G., "New Light on the 7th-c. Yassı Ada Shipwreck: Capacities and Standard Sizes of LRA1 Amphoras," *Journal of Roman Archaeology* 9 (1996), 189–213

van Doorninck, F.H. Jr, "The Cargo Amphoras on the 7th Century Yassi Ada and 11th Century Serçe Limanı Shipwrecks: Two Examples of a Reuse of Byzantine Amphoras as Transport Jars," in V. Déroche & J.-M. Spieser (eds.), *Recherches sur la céramique byzantine*, Bulletin de Correspondance Hellénique Supplément 18 (Paris, 1989), 247–57

TANTURA LAGOON

Kahanov, Y., "The Byzantine Shipwreck (Tantura A) in the Tantura Lagoon, Israel: Hull Construction Report," in *Tropis VI. Sixth International Symposium on Ship Construction in Antiquity (Athens, 28–30 August 1996)* (Athens, 2001), 265–71

——"The Tantura B Shipwreck. Tantura Lagoon, Israel: Preliminary Hull Construction Report," in J. Litwin (ed.), *Down the River to the Sea,* Proceedings of the Eighth International Symposium on Boat and Ship Archaeology, Gdansk 1997 (Gdansk, 2000), 151–54

Royal, J. & Y. Kahanov, "An Arab Period Merchant Vessel at Tantura Lagoon, Israel," *International Journal of Nautical Archaeology* 29 (2000), 151–53

Wachsmann, S., "Technology Before its Time: A Byzantine Shipwreck from Tantura Lagoon," *The Explorers Journal* 74 no. 1 (1996), 19–23

——and K. Raveh, "A Concise Nautical History of Dor/Tantura," *International Journal of Nautical Archaeology* 13 (1984), 223–41

BOZBURUN

Hocker, F.M., "Cargo Stowage, Jettison and Wreck Formation Processes: Information on Middle Byzantine Commerce from the Ninth-Century Bozburun Shipwreck," *Archeologia delle acque* I no. 2 (1999), 28–38

Treadgold, W., *The Byzantine Revival 780–842* (Stanford, California, 1988)

SERÇE LIMANI 11TH-CENTURY WRECK

Bass, G.F., "The Nature of the Serçe Limani Glass," *Journal of Glass Studies* 26 (1984), 64–9.

——, S.D. Matthews, J.R. Steffy, & F.H. van Doorninck Jr, *Serçe Limani: An Eleventh-Century Shipwreck* (College Station, 2004)

Lledó, B., "Mold Siblings in the 11th-Century Cullet from Serçe Limanı," *Journal of Glass Studies* 39 (1997), 43–55

van Doorninck, F.H. Jr, "The Medieval Shipwreck at Serçe Limani: An Early 11th-Century Fatimid-Byzantine Commercial Voyage," *Graeco-Arabica* 4 (1991), 45–52

——"The Byzantine Ship at Serçe Limanı: An Example of Small-Scale Maritime Commerce with Fatimid Syria in the Early Eleventh Century," in R. Macrides (ed.), *Travel in the Byzantine World* (Aldershot and Burlington, 2002), 137–48

Steffy, J.R., *Wooden Ship Building and the Interpretation of Shipwrecks* (College Station, 1994), 85–91

ÇAMALTI BURNU

Günsenin, N., "From Ganos to Serçe Limanı: Social and Economic Activities in the Propontis during Medieval Times, Illuminated by Recent Archaeological and Historical Discoveries," *The INA Quarterly* 26 no. 3 (1999), 18–23

——"L'épave de Çamaltı Burnu I (île de Marmara, Proconnèse): résultats des années 1998–2000," *Anatolia Antiqua* 9 (2001), 117–33

——"L'épave de Çamaltı Burnu I (île de Marmara, Proconnèse): résultats des années 2001–2002," *Anatolia Antiqua* 11 (2003), 361–76

——"Underwater Archaeological Research in the Sea of Marmara," in T. Akal, R.D. Ballard, & G.F. Bass (eds.), *The Application of Recent Advances in Underwater Detection and Survey Techniques to Underwater Archaeology* (Istanbul, 2004), 31–38

For the ongoing project please refer to Nergis Günsenin's website: www.nautarch.org

BLACK SEA DEEP-WATER PROJECT

Ballard, R.D. & W. Hively, *The Eternal Darkness: A Personal History of Deep-Sea Exploration* (Princeton, 2000)

——"Deep Black Sea," *National Geographic* 199.5 (May 2001), 52–69

——, et al., "Deepwater Archaeology of the Black Sea: The 2000 Season at Sinop, Turkey," *American Journal of Archaeology* 105 (2001), 607–23

De Jonge, P., "Being Bob Ballard," *National Geographic* 205.5 (May 2004), 112–29

Ward, C. & R.D. Ballard, "Black Sea Shipwreck Survey 2000," *International Journal of Nautical Archaeology* 33 (2004), 2–13

SHINAN WRECK

Green, J., "The Shinan Excavation, Korea: An Interim Report on the Hull Structure," *International Journal of Nautical Archaeology* 12 (1983), 293–301

——& Z.G. Kim, "The Shinan and Wando Sites, Korea: Further Information," *International Journal of Nautical Archaeology* 18 (1989), 33–41

Keith, D.H., "A Fourteenth-Century Cargo Makes Port at Last," *National Geographic* 156.2 (August 1979), 230–43

——"A Fourteenth Century Shipwreck at Sinan-gun," *Archaeology* 33 no. 2 (1980), 33–43

——& C.J. Buys, "New Light on Medieval Chinese Seagoing Ship Construction," *International Journal of Nautical Archaeology* 10 (1981), 119–32

ALMERE COG

Hocker, F.M., "Cogge en Coggeschip: Late Trends in Cog Development," in R. Reinders (ed.), *Bouwtraditie en Scheepstype* (Groningen, 1991), 25–32

——"Bottom-Based Shipbuilding in Northwestern Europe," in F.M. Hocker and C. Ward (eds.), *The Philosophy of Shipbuilding: Conceptual Approaches to the Study of Wooden Ships* (College Station, 2004), 65–93

——& K. Vlierman, *A Small Cog Wrecked on the Zuiderzee in the Early Fifteenth Century*. NISA Excavation Report 19/Flevobericht 408 (Lelystad, 1997)

KO SI CHANG

Green, J.N., "Maritime Archaeology in Southeast and East Asia," *Antiquity* 64 (1990), 347–63

——& R.Harper, "The Ko Si Chang Excavation Report 1983," *Bulletin of the Australian Institute for Maritime Archaeology* 7. 2 (1983), 9–37

——, R. Harper & V. Intakosi, "The Ko Si Chang One Shipwreck Excavation 1983–1985," *International Journal of Nautical Archaeology* 15 (1986), 105–22

——*The Maritime Archaeology of Shipwrecks and Ceramics in Southeast Asia and the Ko Si Chang Three Shipwreck Excavation,* Institute for Maritime Archaeology, Special Publication No. 4 (Fremantle, 1987)

——, R. Harper & S. Prishanchittara, *The Excavation of the Ko Kradat Wreck Site, Thailand 1979–1980*, Western Australian Museum Special Publication (Fremantle, 1981)

YASSIADA OTTOMAN WRECK

Beeching, J., *The Galleys at Lepanto* (New York, 1982)

Brummett, P., *Ottoman Seapower and Levantine Diplomacy in the Age of Discovery* (New York, 1994)

"SHIP IN A HAY FIELD", ZUIDERSEE

McLaughlin-Neyland, K. & R.S. Neyland, *Two Prams Wrecked on the Zuiderzee in the Late Eighteenth-Century*, Nederlands Instituut voor Scheeps- en onderwaterArcheologie Reports 15 and 16 (Lelystad, 1993)

Neyland, R.S., "The Preliminary Hull Analysis of Two Eighteenth-Century Dutch Prams", in J.C. Broadwater, (ed.), *Underwater Archaeology Proceedings from the Society for Historical Archaeology Conference, Richmond* (Richmond, Virginia, 1991), 111–4

—— & B. Schröder, *A Late Seventeenth Century Dutch Freighter Wrecked on the Zuiderzee*, Nederlands Instituut voor Scheeps- en onderwaterArcheologie Report 20 (Lelystad, 1996)

NOSSA SENHORA DOS MÁRTIRES

Afonso, S.L. (ed.), *Nossa Senhora dos Mártires: The Last Voyage* (Lisbon, 1998)

Castro, F., "The Remains of a Portuguese Indiaman at Tagus Mouth, Lisbon, Portugal (Nossa Senhora dos Mártires, 1606?)" in Alves, F. (ed.), *Proceedings of the International Symposium "Archaeology of Medieval and Modern Ships of Iberian-Atlantic Tradition", Lisbon, 1998* (Lisbon, 2001), 381–404

——"The Pepper Wreck", *Archaeology* (March/April 2003), 30–35

—— "The Pepper Wreck", *International Journal of Nautical Archaeology* 32 (2003), 6–23

——*The Pepper Wreck* (College Station, 2005)

—— "Rigging the Pepper Wreck. Part I: Masts and Yards", *International Journal of Nautical Archaeology* 34 (2005), 112–124

MONTE CRISTI PIPE WRECK

De Roever, M., "The Fort Orange 'EB' Pipe Bowls: An Investigation of the Origin of American Objects in Dutch Seventeenth-Century Documents," in *New World Dutch Studies: Dutch Arts and Culture in Colonial America 1609–1776* (Albany Institute of History and Art, 1987)

Duco, D.H., "*De Kleipijp in de Zeentiende Eeuwse Nederlanden* (The Clay Pipe in Seventeenth-Century Netherlands)," in P. Davey (ed.), *The Archaeology of the Clay Tobacco Pipe V, Europe* (BAR International Series, 1981)

Hall, J.L., *A Seventeenth-Century Northern European Merchant Shipwreck in Monte Cristi Bay, Dominican Republic* (unpublished Ph.D. dissertation, Texas A&M University, 1996)

Lessman, A.W., *The Rhenish Stoneware From the Monte Cristi Shipwreck, Dominican Republic* (unpublished M.A. thesis, Texas A&M University, 1997)

LA BELLE

Arnold, J.B. III, "Magnetometer Survey of La Salle's Ship the *Belle*," *International Journal of Nautical Archaeology* 25 (1996), 243–49

——"The Texas Historical Commission's Underwater Archaeological Survey of 1995 and the Preliminary Report on the *Belle*, La Salle's Shipwreck of 1686," *Historical Archaeology* 30 (1996), 66–87

Bruseth, J.E., T. S. Turner, M.P. Kelsey, & R.B. Hutchison, *From A Watery Grave: The Discovery And Excavation Of La Salle's Shipwreck,* La Belle (College Station, Texas, 2005)

Weddle, Robert S., *The Wreck of the Belle, the Ruin of La Salle* (College Station, Texas, 2001)

PORT ROYAL

Donachie, M.J., *Household Ceramics at Port Royal, Jamaica, 1655–1692*, BAR International Series 1195 (Oxford, 2003)

Fox, G.L., *The Kaolin Clay Tobacco Pipe Collection from Port Royal, Jamaica.* BAR International Series 809 (Oxford, 1999)

Hamilton, D.L., "Simon Benning, Pewterer of Port Royal," in B.J. Little (ed.), *Text-Aided Archaeology* (Boca Raton, 1992), 39–53

——"The City Under the Sea," in *Science Year, 1986*, The World Book Science Annual (Chicago, 1986), 92–109

——"Port Royal Revisited," in C.R. Cummings (ed.), *Underwater Archaeology: The Proceedings of the Fourteenth Conference on Underwater Archaeology* (San Marino, California, 1986), 73–81

——"Preliminary Report on the Archaeological Investigations of the Submerged Remains of Port Royal, Jamaica, 1981–1982," *The International Journal of Nautical Archaeology and Underwater Exploration* 13 no. 1 (1984), 11–25

——and R. Woodward, "A Sunken 17th-Century City: Port Royal, Jamaica," *Archaeology* 37 no. 1 (1984), 38–45

Link, M.C., "Exploring the Drowned City of Port Royal," *National Geographic* 117.2 (1960), 151–182

Marx, R.F., *Pirate Port* (Cleveland, 1967)

——*Port Royal Rediscovered* (New York, 1973)

Pawson, M. & D. Buisseret, *Port Royal, Jamaica* (Kingston, Jamaica, 2000)

Smith, W.C., *The Final Analysis of Weights from Port Royal, Jamaica*, BAR International Series 675 (Oxford, 1997)

SANTO ANTONIO DE TANNA

Boxer, C. R. & C. de Azevedo, *Fort Jesus and the Portuguese in Mombasa* (London, 1960)

Kirkman, J.S., *Fort Jesus: A Portuguese Fortress on the East African Coast* (Oxford, 1974)

——*Men and Monuments on the East African Coast* (London, 1964)

——"A Portuguese Wreck off Mombasa," *International Journal of Nautical Archaeology* 1 (1972), 153–57

Piercy, R.C.M., "Mombasa Wreck Excavation Reports" *International Journal of Nautical Archaeology* 6 (1977), 331–47; 7 (1978), 301–19; 8 (1979), 303–09; 10 (1981), 109–18

Sassoon, H., "Ceramics from the Wreck of a Portuguese Ship at Mombasa," *Azania* 16 (1981), 98–130

GREAT BASSES REEF

Clarke, A.C., *The Treasure of the Great Reef* (rev. ed., New York, 1974)

Green, J.N., *The Australian-Sri-Lanka-Netherlands Galle Harbour Project 1992–1998*, Report of Maritime Archaeology, Western Australian Maritime Museum, No. 1 (Fremantle, 1998)

——and S. Devendra, "Interim Report on the Joint Sri Lanka–Australian Maritime Archaeology Training and Research Programme, 1992–3," *International Journal of Nautical Archaeology* 22 (1993), 331–43

SADANA ISLAND, EGYPT

Krahl, R. & J. Ayers (eds.), *Chinese Ceramics in the Topkapi Saray Museum, Istanbul III, Qing Dynasty Porcelains* (London, 1986)

Niebuhr, C., *Travels through Arabia, and Other Countries in the East, Performed by M. Niebuhr,* I & II, translated by R. Heron (Reading, 1994 reprint of 1792 edition)

Panzac, D., "International and Domestic Maritime Trade in the Ottoman Empire During the 18th Century," *International Journal of Middle East Studies* 24 (1992), 189–206

Pearson, M.N., *Pious Passengers: The Haj in Earlier Times* (New Delhi, 1994)

Raban, A., "The Shipwreck off Sharm-el-Sheikh," *Archaeology,* 24 no. 2 (1971), 146–55

Tuchscherer, M., "Production et commerce du café en Mer Rouge au XVIe siècle," in M. Tuchscherer (ed.), *Le Café avant l'ère des plantations coloniales: espaces, réseaux, sociétés (XVe-XVIIIe siécle)* (Cairo, 2001), 69–90

Ward, C., "The Sadana Island Shipwreck," in U. Baram & L. Carroll (eds.), *A Historical Archaeology of the Ottoman Empire* (New York 2000), 185–202

——"The Sadana Island Shipwreck: An Eighteenth-Century AD Merchantman off the Red Sea Coast of Egypt," *World Archaeology* 32 (2001), 371–85

CLYDESDALE PLANTATION VESSEL

Amer, C.F. & F.M. Hocker, "A Comparative Analysis of Three Sailing Merchant Vessels From the Carolina Coast," in W.C. Fleetwood, Jr, *Tidecraft: The Boats of South Carolina, Georgia and Northeastern Florida, 1550–1950* (Tybee Island, Georgia, 1995), 295–303

Footner, G.M., *Tidewater Triumph: The Development and World-Wide Success of the Chesapeake Bay Pilot Schooner* (Mystic Seaport Museum, 1998)

Hocker, F.M., "The Clydesdale Plantation Vessel Project: 1992 Field Report," *INA Quarterly* 19 no. 4 (1992), 12–16

Smith, J.F., *Slavery and Rice Culture in Low Country Georgia 1750–1860* (Knoxville, 1985)

DEFENCE

Allen, G., *Naval History in the Revolution*, 2 vols. (New York, 1962)

Leamon, J.S., *Revolution Downeast: The War For Independence in Maine* (Amherst, 1993)

Switzer, D.C., "Nautical Archaeology in Penobscot Bay: The Revolutionary War Privateer *Defence*," in C. Symonds (ed.), *Aspects of Naval History* (Annapolis, 1981), 90–101

——"The Excavation of the Privateer *Defence*," Symposium on the Archaeology of the Revolutionary War Period, *Northeast Historical Archaeology* 12 (1983), 43–50

——"Excavations of the Wreck of the Privateer *Defence*," in W. Swanson (ed.), *National Geographic Society Research Reports* 18 (1983), 719–31

——"The *Defence* Project," in M. Bound (ed.), *The Archaeology of the Warship* (Ostwestry, 1985), 183–91

——with B. Ford, *Underwater Dig: The Excavation of a Revolutionary War Privateer* (New York, 1982)

BETSY

Broadwater, J.D., "Secrets of a Yorktown Shipwreck," *National Geographic* 173.6 (June 1988), 804–23

——"Shipwreck in a Swimming Pool: An Assessment of the Methodology and Technology Utilized on the Yorktown Shipwreck Archaeological Project," in J.B. Arnold, III (ed.), *Historical Archaeology* 26 no. 4 (1992), 36–46

——"In the Shadow of Wooden Walls: Naval Transports During the American War of Independence," in M. Bound (ed.), *The Archaeology of Ships of War* (Oswestry, UK, 1995)

——, R.M. Adams, & M.A. Renner, "The Yorktown Shipwreck Archaeological Project: An Interim Report on the Excavation of Shipwreck 44YO88," *The International Journal of Nautical Archaeology and Underwater Exploration* 14 (1985), 301–14

Johnston, P.F, J.O. Sands, & J.R. Steffy, "The Cornwallis Cave Shipwreck, Yorktown, Virginia," *The International Journal of Nautical Archaeology and Underwater Exploration* 7 (1978), 205–26

Sands, J.O., *Yorktown's Captive Fleet* (Charlottesville, VA, 1983)

WRECK OF THE TEN SAIL

Leshikar, M.E., *The 1794 Wreck of the Ten Sail, Cayman Islands, British West Indies: A Historical Study and Archaeological Survey.* Ph.D. dissertation, Texas A&M University, 1993 (University Microfilms, Ann Arbor, Michigan)

Leshikar-Denton, M.E., *Our Islands' Past, Vol. 2, The Wreck of the Ten Sails* (Grand Cayman, 1994)

——"Caribbean, Cayman Islands, and Ten Sail," in J.P. Delgado (ed.), *Encyclopaedia of Underwater and Maritime Archaeology* (London, 1997), 86–9

——"Problems and Progress in the Caribbean," in C. Ruppé, & J. Barstad (eds.), *International Handbook of Underwater Archaeology* (New York, 2002), 279–98

Smith, R.C., *The Maritime Heritage of the Cayman Islands* (Gainesville, 2000)

CLEOPATRA'S BARGE

Crowninshield, F.B., *The Story of George Crowninshield's Yacht* Cleopatra's Barge *on a Voyage of Pleasure to the Western Islands and the Mediterranean 1816–1817* (Boston, 1913)

Ferguson, D.L., *Cleopatra's Barge: The Crowninshield Story* (Boston, 1976)

Johnston, P. F., "Preliminary Report on the 1998 Excavations of the 1824 Wreck of the Royal Hawaiian Yacht *Ha'aheo o Hawaii* (ex-*Cleopatra's Barge*)", in A.A. Askins and M.W. Russell (eds.), *Underwater Archaeology 1999* (Tucson: Society for Historical Archaeology, 1999), 107–114

HORSE FERRY

Crisman, K.J. & A.B. Cohn, *When Horses Walked on Water: Horse-Powered Ferries in Nineteenth-Century America* (Washington and London, 1998)

Shomette, D., "Heyday of the Horse Ferry," *National Geographic* 176, no. 4 (October, 1989), 548–556

HEROINE

Bates, A.L., *The Western Rivers Steamboat Cyclopedium* (Leonia, NJ, 1968)

Hunter, L.C., *Steamboats on Western Rivers, An Economic and Technological History* (New York, 1969)

Kane, A.I., *The Western River Steamboat* (College Station, 2004)

DENBIGH

Arnold, J. B., T.J. Oertling & A.W. Hall, "The Denbigh Project: Initial Observations on a Civil War Blockade-Runner and its Wreck-Site," *International Journal of Nautical Archaeology* 28 (1999), 126–44

——"The Denbigh Project: Excavation of a Civil War Blockade-Runner," *International Journal of Nautical Archaeology* 30 (2001), 231–49

Griffiths, D., "Marine Engineering Development in the 19th Century," in R. Gardiner (ed.), The Advent of Steam: The Merchant Steamship Before 1900 (London, 1993)

Watson, W., *The Civil War Adventures of a Blockade Runner* (College Station, 2001)

Wise, S., *Lifeline of the Confederacy: Blockade Running during the Civil War* (Columbia, SC, 1988)

LAKE CHAMPLAIN SAILING CANAL BOATS

Cohn, A.B., *Lake Champlain's Sailing Canal Boat: An Illustrated Journey From Burlington Bay to the Hudson River* (Lake Champlain Maritime Museum, 2003)

——& M.M. True, "The Wreck of the General Butler and the Mystery of Lake Champlain's Sailing Canal Boats," *Vermont History* 60 no. 1 (1992), 29–45

TITANIC

Ballard, R.D., *The Discovery of the Titanic* (Toronto, 1987)

Lord, W., *A Night to Remember* (New York, 1955)

Lynch, D. & K. Marschall, *Ghosts of the Abyss: A Journey into the Heart of the Titanic* (Toronto, 2003)

Wels, S., *Titanic: Legacy of the World's Greatest Ocean Liner* (Alexandria, Virginia, 1997)

Winocour, J. (ed.), *The Story of the Titanic as Told by its Survivors* (New York, 1960)

TRUK LAGOON

Bailey, D.E., *World War II Wrecks of the Truk Lagoon* (Redding, California, 2000)

D-DAY LANDINGS

Harris, G., *Cross Channel Attack* (1951)

Hunnicutt, R.P., *Sherman: History of the American Medium Tank* (1994)

Lewis, A., *Omaha Beach, A Flawed Victory* (2001)

Messenger, C., *The D-Day Atlas: Anatomy of the Normandy Campaign* (London & New York, 2004)

Morison, S.E., *History of the United States Naval Operations in World War II, volume XI: The Invasion of France and Germany, 1944-1945* (Boston, 1957)

Ryan, C., *The Longest Day: June 6, 1944* (New York, 1959)

Winser, J., *The D-Day Ships – Neptune* (Kendal, England, 1994)

Acknowledgments and Sponsors

When great discoveries are made, archaeologists bask in the limelight. But equally important are those who pay for the archaeologists' research. Without the generous but modest Directors of INA, little in this book could have occurred. Those on the Board who contributed substantially and annually, a few for only one or two years, but most for decades, are:

Oren E. Atkins, Oŷuz Aydemir, John H. Baird, Joe Ballew, George F. Bass, Harry W. Bass Jr, Richard D. Bass, Duncan Boeckman, Edward O. Boshell Jr, Elizabeth L. Bruni, Allan Campbell, John Cassils, Charles Collins, Gregory M. Cook, John Brown Cook, Marian Miner Cook, Harlan Crow, William C. Culp, Frank Darden, Lucy Darden, Thomas F. Darden, John De Lapa, Claude Duthuit, Harrison Eiteljorg II, Danielle J. Feeney, Donald G. Geddes III, Sumner Gerard, Nixon Griffis, Harry C. Kahn II, Selçuk Kolay, David C. Langworthy, Norma Langworthy, Francine LeFrak-Friedberg, Samuel J. Le Frak, Frederick R. Mayer, Charles McWhirter, Alex G. Nason, George E. Robb Jr, W.F. Searle Jr, Lynn Baird Shaw, J. Richard Steffy, William T. Sturgis, Frederick H. van Doorninck Jr, Peter M. Way, Garry A. Weber, Elizabeth A. Whitehead, Martin A. Wilcox, and George O. Yamini.

Because he was the first to make a pledge of financial support, when INA was more dream than reality, I dedicate this book to Jack W. Kelley and to his fellow Tulsa, Oklahoma, businessmen who joined him on the Board of Directors: John A. Brock, Ronnie Chamness, Robert E. Lorton, L. Francis Rooney, Ray H. Siegfried II, T. Hastings Siegfried, Richard A. Williford, and Lew O. Ward from nearby Enid.

INA Associate Directors, who also contribute annually, have included Raynette Boshell, Nicholas Griffis, Robin P. Hartmann, Faith D. Hentschel, Susan Katzev, William C. Klein, George Lodge, Thomas McCasland Jr, Dana F. McGinnis, Michael Plank, Molly Reily, Betsey Boshell Todd, Casidy Ward, William Ward, and Robyn Woodward.

Those who have endowed professorships or fellowships in INA or the affiliated Texas A&M University Nautical Archaeology Program include the Abell-Hanger Foundation, John H. Baird, Marian Miner Cook, Donald G. Geddes III, Frederick Mayer, Meadows Foundation, Ray H. Siegfried II, Mary Ausplund Tooze, and George O. Yamini.

And there are those whose generous patronage for specific or general purposes has meant so much to the Institute over the years: Archaeological Institute of America, Fred B. Aurin, Edward Bader, Toni & Maria Pia Bassani, Baroline & Richard Bienia, Mimi & Gerald Branower, Ron Bural, Joy Campanaro, Frederick Campbell, Stanley Chase, J.E.R. Chilton, Peter Clark, Anna & Oliver Colburn, Charles W. Consolvo, Donna & Bob Dales, P.S. de Beaumont, Maurice Duca, Bruce Dunlevie, Cynthia & James Eiseman, Roger H. Gesswein Jr, Griffis Foundation, Theodor Halpern, Chatten Hayes, Michael Hitchcock, Institute for Aegean Prehistory, Jean B. James, Erik Jonsson, the Joukowsky Family, Norma & Rubin Kershaw, Richard MacDonald, Hillary Magowan, Mark Mathesen, Roy Matthews, Anna Maguerite McCann, John Merwin, Drew Morris, Marjorie & Isaac A. Morris, Nason Foundation, National Endowment for the Humanities, Ernestine O'Connell, Jenniffer & David Perlman, Alice & Howard Rankin, Leon Riebman, Sanford Robertson, Margaret Rogers, Mary & Richard Rosenberg, Robert Rubenstein, Billings Ruddock, L.J. Skaggs and Mary C. Skaggs Foundation, Peter Skinner, Patricia Stephens, Ellie & John Stern, Stephen Susman, Hazel & Ronald Vandehey, Shelby White & Leon Levy, James Wikert, the Northwest Friends of INA in Portland, Oregon, anonymous donors, and all INA members.

MAJOR PROJECT SPONSORS:

Abbreviations: NEH: National Endowment for the Humanities; NGS: National Geographic Society; NSF: National Science Foundation; TAMU: Texas A&M University

ŞEYTAN DERESI, TURKEY: INA; NGS; SCM Corporation; Alcoa Foundation; Triopian Foundation; F. Alex Nason; Harrison Eiteljorg, Sr

ULUBURUN, TURKEY: INA; NEH; NGS; NSF; TAMU; Institute for Aegean Prehistory; Shell; Cressi-sub

CAPE GELIDONYA, TURKEY: University of Pennsylvania Museum; American Philosophical Society; Nixon Griffis; John Huston of the Council of Underwater Archaeology; Lucius N. Littauer Foundation; British Academy and the Craven Fund; US Divers Co.; La Spirotechnique; Wellcome Foundation; British School at Athens; Bauer Kompressoren; Nikon Company; Polaroid Corporation; INA; TAMU

PABUÇ BURNU, TURKEY: INA; NGS; TAMU; Smothers-Bruni Foundation; Eugene McDermott Foundation; Claude Duthuit; Wellesley College

TEKTAŞ BURNU, TURKEY: INA; TAMU; NGS; NEH; Turkish Airlines

KYRENIA, CYPRUS: Cyprus Department of Antiquities; Oberlin College; University Museum of the University of Pennsylvania; Cook Foundation; National Geographic Society; Cyprus Mines Corporation; National Endowment for the Humanities; UNESCO; Dietrich Foundation; Ford Foundation; Houghton-Carpenter Foundation; Louise Taft Semple Foundation; INA; HIPNT; and generous individual donors

LA SECCA DI CAPISTELLO, ITALY: Sub Sea Oil Services of Milan; INA; TAMU

SERÇE LIMANI HELLENISTIC WRECK, TURKEY: INA; NGS; TAMU

SEA OF GALILEE BOAT, ISRAEL: Model built at TAMU under graduate assistantship funded by the Meadows Foundation

YASSIADA 7TH-CENTURY WRECK, TURKEY: University of Pennsylvania Museum; NGS; Catherwood Foundation; American Philosophical Society; Littauer Foundation through Colgate University; Bauer Kompressoren of Munich; Main Line Divers Club of Philadelphia; Corning Museum of Glass; Nixon Griffis; Ruth and James Magill; Bodrum Museum of Underwater Archaeology; INA; TAMU; NSF; William van Alen

TANTURA LAGOON, ISRAEL: NGS; L.J. Skaggs & Mary C. Skaggs Foundation; Mr & Mrs Harry Kahn II; INA; TAMU College of Liberal Arts; and numerous other supporters

BOZBURUN, TURKEY: INA; NEH; TAMU; Smothers Foundation; Türk Hava Yoları (Turkish Airlines); Efes Brewing; MARES Diving Equipment; Paradise Scuba; Feyyaz Subay & Fey Diving; Mary & Richard Rosenberg; Hazel & Ron Vandehey; Cem Boyner; Jon Faucher; John DeLapa; Danielle Feeney; George Robb; the Muhtar and people of Selimiye; and numerous others, including INA members who contributed to the 1998 annual appeal

SERÇE LIMANI 11TH-CENTURY WRECK, TURKEY: NEH; INA; NGS; TAMU; NSF; Corning Glass Works Foundation; F. Alex Nason; Ashland Oil Company

ÇAMALTI BURNU, TURKEY: Istanbul University Research Fund; Turkish Ministry of Culture; Turkish Foundation of Underwater Archaeology (TINA); French Institute of Anatolian Studies (IFEA); the Turkish Army; NGS; INA; and many generous individuals

BLACK SEA DEEP-WATER PROJECT
NSF; NGS; Florida State University; INA; IFE

SHINAN WRECK, KOREA: South Korean Cultural Property Preservation Bureau; South Korean Navy; National Maritime Museum at Mokpo; and NGS for Donald Keith's visits to the site

ALMERE COG, ZUIDERSEE, NETHERLANDS: Museum voor Scheepsarcheologie; Ketelhaven International Association for the Exchange of Students for Technical Experience; INA; TAMU

KO SI CHANG, THAILAND: Western Australian Museum; Australian Research Council

YASSIADA OTTOMAN WRECK, TURKEY: INA; TAMU; Bodrum Museum

"SHIP IN A HAY FIELD, ZUIDERSEE, NETHERLANDS: Nederlands Instituut voor Scheeps- en OnderwaterArcheologie (Netherlands Institute for Ship and Underwater Archaeology); TAMU

NOSSA SENHORA DOS MÁRTIRES, PORTUGAL: Instituto Portugues de Arqueologia; and the Portuguese Navy and MARCASACAIS for docking facilities

MONTE CRISTI PIPE WRECK, DOMINICAN REPUBLIC: RPM Nautical Foundation; Ronald Halbert; Neil Blaine Fisher; Don Pedro Borrell Bentz; Marvin Omar Hall; Malinda Mary Hall; Francis Soto Tejeda; Earthwatch; INA; TAMU

LA BELLE, TEXAS, USA: The survey was sponsored by the Texas Historical Commission, Trull Foundation, Kathryn O'Connor Foundation, and Texas Department of Transportation's Intermodal Surface Transportation Efficiency Act program; with equipment donations by Trimble Navigation, Inc. and Compaq Computer Corporation. Conservation is sponsored by the Texas Historical Commission; TAMU; Baldor Electric; Dow Chemical Company; Dow Corning Corporation; Dynacon, Inc.; Fibergrate Composite Structures, Inc.; Fuji NDT Systems; Huntsman Chemicals; Mallinckrodt-Baker, Inc.; INA; and donations of equipment and supplies by over 250 other generous firms and individuals

PORT ROYAL, JAMAICA: TAMU; INA; Jamaica Defense Force; Kaiser Aluminum Corporation; Port Royal Brotherhood

SANTO ANTONIO DE TANNA, KENYA: NGS; INA; Charles Consolvo; Harry Kahn; National Museums of Kenya; Kenya Navy; Gulbenkian Foundation; Western Australian Maritime Museum; elements of the Royal Navy, Royal Air Force, and British Army particularly the Royal Engineers Diving Unit; Kenya Port Authority; Bamburi Cement Co.; Hamo Sassoon; DiveCon; Portuguese Navy; TAMU; British School in Eastern Africa; East African Marine Engineering Ltd; Mombasa Club Ltd; Frederick Mayer; Conway Plough; the Hinawy Family; Fort Jesus Museum; the people of Mombasa and generous individuals who gave donations or gifts in kind.

GREAT BASSES REEF, SRI LANKA: Western Australian Museum; Australian Research Council

SADANA ISLAND, EGYPT: Amoco Foundation; Billings Ruddock; NGS; INA; John & Donnie Brock Foundation; Harry & Joan Kahn; George & Marilyn Lodge; Richard & Mary Rosenberg; Danielle Feeney. And the generous assistance of the Supreme Council of Antiquities of Egypt, the American Research Center in Egypt, and many individuals and organizations described on http://www.adventurecorps.com/sadana/inasponsors.html

CLYDESDALE PLANTATION VESSEL, SOUTH CAROLINA, USA: INA; South Carolina Institute of Archeology and Anthropology; Rusty Fleetwood and the Coastal Heritage Society, Savannah; 24th Infantry Division (Mechanized) Museum, Ft. Stewart, Georgia; Judy Wood and the US Army Corps of Engineers, Savannah District; Craig and Stanley Lester

DEFENCE, PENOBSCOT BAY, MAINE, USA: INA; TAMU; NGS; Maine Bicentennial Commission; Maine State Museum; Maine Maritime Academy; Maine Historic Preservation Commission; Earthwatch

BETSY, YORKTOWN, VIRGINIA, USA: Yorktown Shipwreck Archaeological Project; Commonwealth of Virginia; County of York; East Carolina University Maritime Studies Program; NGS; INA; NEH; TAMU Nautical Archaeology Program; US Dept. of the Interior; HCRS Maritime Grants Program; Yorktown Maritime Heritage Foundation; Amoco Foundation; Max and Victoria Dreyfus Foundation; Norfolk Foundation; Virginia Institute of Marine Science; The College of William and Mary

WRECK OF THE TEN SAIL, CAYMAN ISLANDS: TAMU College of Liberal Arts dissertation award; Cayman Islands National Museum; and equipment and services donated by INA, Atlantis Research Submersibles, Morritts Tortuga Club, Tortuga Divers, Keith Moorehead of NGS, and the yacht Platinum

CLEOPATRA'S BARGE, KAUAI, USA: Ship Plans Fund; National Museum of American History; Smithsonian Research Opportunities Fund; Salem Marine Society, Salem, MA; and, in Hawaii, The Princeville Corporation and Hotel, Princeville; Bay Island Watersports, Princeville; Save Our Seas and Bali Hai Realty, Inc., Hanalei; Sunrise Diving Adventures, Kapa'a; Ship Stores Gallery of Kapa'a

HORSE FERRY, LAKE CHAMPLAIN, USA: Lake Champlain Maritime Museum; Vermont Division for Historic Preservation; TAMU; INA; Ray Siegfried II; John & Ellie Stern; Harry Kahn

HEROINE, RED RIVER, OKLAHOMA, USA: Oklahoma Historical Society; TAMU; Oklahoma Department of Transportation; INA; Harry Kahn; Carrington Weems; and a "Creative and Scholarly Activities" grant provided by the TAMU Office of the Vice President for Research

DENBIGH, GALVESTON, TEXAS, USA: Albert & Ethel Herzstein Charitable Foundation of Houston; Anchorage Foundation of New Braunfels; Communities Foundation of Texas; Brown Foundation, Houston; Ed Rachal Foundation of Corpus Christi; Hillcrest Foundation of Dallas, founded by Mrs. W.W. Caruth, Sr.; Horlock Foundation, Houston; Houston Endowment, Inc.; Strake Foundation of Houston; Summerfield G. Roberts Foundation of Dallas; Summerlee Foundation of Dallas; TAMU-Galveston; Joseph Ballard Archeology Fund of the Texas Historical Foundation of Austin; Trull Foundation of Palacios

LAKE CHAMPLAIN SAILING CANAL BOATS, USA: City of Burlington, Vermont; Freeman Foundation; Champlain Basin Program; Lake Champlain Maritime Museum; Lintilhac Foundation; Lois & J. Warren McClure; INA; TAMU; University of Vermont; Vermont Division for Historic Preservation; Waterfront Diving Center

TITANIC, ATLANTIC OCEAN: National Oceanic and Atmospheric Administration

TRUK LAGOON, PACIFIC OCEAN: Western Australian Museum; Australian Research Council; Prospero Productions

D-DAY LANDINGS, NORMANDY, FRANCE: US Naval Historical Center Underwater Archaeology Branch; Discovery Channel; British Broadcasting Corporation; Oceaneering International; INA; TAMU

Of course we are all most grateful to those national and state governments who permitted our research in their waters, and to the local museums that curate and display our finds for the public.

Sources of Illustrations

a: above; b: below; c: center; l: left; r: right

The following abbreviations are used to identify sources: CP – Courtney Platt; DAF – Donald A. Frey; IFE/IAO – Institute for Exploration, Mystic, CT/Institute for Archaeological Oceanography, URI/GSO; INA – Institute of Nautical Archaeology; JDB – John D. Broadwater; JG – Jeremy Green; LCMMC – Lake Champlain Maritime Museum Collection; ML – ML Design © Thames & Hudson Ltd, London; MSM – Maine State Museum; NAP – Nautical Archaeological Program, TAMU; NISA – Netherlands Institute for Ship- and Underwater Archaeology; PB – Peter Bull Art Studio © Thames & Hudson Ltd, London; PT – Peter Throckmorton; R/V AMK – Courtesy of R/V *Akademik Mstislav Keldysh*; S/NMAH – Courtesy of the Smithsonian/National Museum of American History – Transportation; SWK – Susan Womer Katzev

1 DAF; 2–3 Alexander Mustard; 5c DAF; 5b SWK; 6a DAF; 6c H. Edward Kim/National Geographic; 6b José Pessoa (CNANS archives); 7a Elizabeth Greene; 7c S/NMAH; 7b INA; 10–11a JDB; 11b Robin Piercy; 12 PT; 13al DAF; 13br Davis Meltzer; 14 PT; 15 DAF; 16al Waldemar Illing; 16–17b DAF; 17a Charles R. Nicklin, Jr; 18–19a University of Pennsylvania Museum; 18bl Tony Boegeman; 18–19b DAF; 20 Robin Piercy; 21a JDB; 21br JDB; 22 JDB; 23bl Friends of *Hunley*; 23br Friends of *Hunley*; 24 Tufan Turanlı; 25c Library of Congress, Washington D.C.; 25b US Navy, NOAA *Monitor* Collection; 26l Xu hai bin; 26-27a Larry LePage; 26-27b Dennis Denton; 28 DAF; 30a DAF; 30b ML; 31cl JDB; 31b JDB; 32a INA; 32b Robin Piercy; 33a John Cassils; 33c John Cassils; 34bl DAF; 34–35a INA; 35bl INA; 36 Cemal Pulak and Wendy Van-Duivenvoorde; 37a DAF; 37b DAF; 38al DAF; 38–39a Shih-Han Samuel Lin; 39b DAF; 40l DAF; 40r DAF; 41a DAF; 41b DAF; 42a DAF; 42c DAF; 42b DAF; 43a DAF; 43b DAF; 44a PB after Cemal Pulak; 44b DAF; 45 DAF; 46a DAF; 46b Egypt Exploration Society; 47a DAF; 47b DAF; 48–49 PT; 49r Herb Greer; 50a Herb Greer; 50b PT; 51cl DAF; 51ac DAF; 51ar DAF; 51c DAF; 51cr DAF; 51br DAF; 52–53a PT; 52b DAF; 53ar from *The Tomb of Huy* by Nina de Garis Davis & Alan H. Gardiner, Egypt Exploration Society, 1926; 54l DAF; 54–55 DAF; 55r DAF; 56 DAF; 58a John Veltri; 58b ML; 59 DAF; 60a Sheila Matthews; 60cr DAF; 60b DAF; 61 Sheila Matthews; 62l Sheila Matthews; 62r Volkan Kaya; 63a PB after Mark Polzer; 63b British Museum, London; 64–65b CP; 65a British Museum, London; 65br CP; 66a CP; 66–67b CP; 67a CP; 67br DAF; 68a DAF; 68c DAF; 69al DAF; 69ar CP; 69bl PB after Robert La Pointe; 69br CP; 70–71a JG and Sheila Matthews; 70b INA; 71ar Donald Demers; 72–73 Bates Littlehales; 73ar Michael L. Katzev; 74al Michael L. Katzev; 74ar SWK; 74–75b SWK; 75ac SWK; 75ar SWK; 76a SWK; 76b SWK; 77ar SWK; 77b Richard Schlecht; 78al Ira Block; 78ar SWK; 78–79b Yiannis Vichos, HIPNT; 80 Donald H. Keith; 81a Donald H. Keith; 81b DAF; 82–83 INA; 83r DAF; 84 DAF; 85al DAF; 85bl DAF; 85r DAF; 86 DAF; 88a DAF; 88b ML; 89 Shelley Wachsmann; 90a William H. Charlton Jr; 90b William H. Charlton Jr; 91a Danny Syon; 91bl Jim Lyle; 91br Jim Lyle; 92ar Robert Goodman; 92–93b Charles R. Nicklin, Jr; 93br University of Pennsylvania Museum; 94al Robert Goodman; 94ar DAF; 94cl DAF; 94bl Donald M. Rosencrantz; 95 DAF; 96al DAF; 96–97b Bobbe Baker; 97al Oğuz Hamza; 97ar Bodrum Museum of Underwater Archaeology; 98bl Shelley Wachsmann; 98ar Shelley Wachsmann; 98–99b Shelley Wachsmann; 99ar Arik Baltinester; 100–101 DAF; 101cr DAF; 101br DAF; 102 INA; 103 INA; 104a INA; 104bl DAF; 104bc DAF; 105a DAF; 105b DAF; 106–107 Donald H. Keith; 107br Jonathan Blair; 108–109 Jonathan Blair; 109ar DAF; 110 DAF; 111 DAF; 112a DAF; 112b DAF; 113a Cemal Pulak; 113b DAF; 114a PB after J. Richard Steffy; 114b DAF; 115al DAF; 115ar DAF; 115cr DAF; 115b DAF; 116al DAF; 116ar DAF; 116cr DAF; 117a DAF; 117b DAF; 118–119 Engin Aygün; 119r Engin Aygün; 120 Recep Dönmez; 121 Recep Dönmez; 122a Nergis Günsenin; 122b Recep Dönmez; 123a Recep Dönmez; 123c Nergis Gunsenin; 123b Ufuk Kocobaş; 124–125 Cheryl Ward; 125bl IFE/IAO; 125br IFE/IAO; 126a IFE/IAO; 126b Dave Wright; 127a Aurora Photos, Photo David McLain; 127b IFE/IAO; 128 JG, Department of Maritime Archaeology, WA Maritime Museum; 130a DAF; 130b ML; 131 H. Edward Kim/National Geographic; 132–133 H. Edward Kim/National Geographic; 133ar British Library, London; 133br H. Edward Kim/National Geographic; 134l NISA/ROB; 134r NISA/ROB; 135a NISA/ROB; 135b NISA/ROB; 136bl Brian Richards; 136ar Brian Richards; 137al Brian Richards; 137ar Brian Richards; 137br Private Collection; 138–139 DAF; 139ar INA; 140 DAF; 141al DAF; 141ar PB after Jay Rosloff; 141b Cemal Pulak; 142 JG; 144a INA; 144b ML; 145 Robert S. Neyland; 146a Robert S. Neyland; 146b Robert S. Neyland; 147 Robert S. Neyland; 148bl Pinto, Maria Helena Mendes, Biombos Namban, Lisbon: Museu Nacional de Arte Antiga, 1993; 148ar Memoria das Armadas, Biblioteca da Academia das Ciências de Lisboa; 149a Guilherme Garcia (CNANS archives); 149b Pedro Gonçalves (CNANS archives); 150 Pedro Gonçalves (CNANS archives); 151a José Pessoa (CNANS archives); 151cr Pedro Gonçalves (CNANS archives); 151br PB after Filipe Castro; 152l Jerome Lynn Hall; 152–153 Jerome Lynn Hall; 153bl Jerome Lynn Hall; 153ar Tinken Museum of Art, San Diego, CA; 154al Courtesy of PIMA Archives; 154cl Jillian Nelson; 154bl Pedro Borrell Bentz; 155a Larry Sanders; 155b Len Tantillo; 156 Center for American History, The University of Texas at Austin; 157a NAP; 157c Clif Bosler; 157b Texas Historical Commission; 158al Texas Historical Commission; 158bl Texas Historical Commission; 159 Texas Historical Commission; 160a NAP; 160c NAP; 160bl NAP; 160–161b NAP; 161a NAP; 162a NAP; 162b NAP; 163al NAP; 163ar NAP; 163br Denis Lee; 164ar Science Year, The World Book Science Annual 1982; 164b Dennis Denton; 165ar INA; 165b INA; 166al Oliver Cox; 166ar Luis Marden; 166bl INA; 167a Broadside, London, 1692; 167b W.D. Vaughn; 168al INA; 168ar INA; 168bl INA; 168br INA; 169 INA; 170al INA; 170–171a INA; 170bl INA; 171cl INA; 171bl INA; 172–173 Noel Jones; 173a From *Descripçam da Fortaleza de Sofala, e das mais da Índia com uma Rellaçam das Religiões todas q há no mesmo Estado, pelo Cosmógrafo Mor António de Mariz Carneiro*, 1639; 174 Hamo Sassoon; 175a Noel Jones; 175b Robert K. Vincent; 176a Robert K. Vincent; 176b Hamo Sassoon; 177ac Robert K. Vincent; 177ar Robert K. Vincent; 177br Robert K. Vincent; 178a JG; 178–179b Netia Piercy; 179a PB after Caroline Sassoon; 180 Udo Kefrig; 182a Philip Voss; 182b ML; 183 Patrick Baker, Department of Maritime Archaeology, WA Maritime Museum; 184–185 Patrick Baker, Department of Maritime Archaeology, WA Maritime Museum; 185a Patrick Baker, Department of Maritime Archaeology, WA Maritime Museum; 186–187b Netia Piercy; 187a Lyman Labry; 188al Meredith Kato; 188bl Netia Piercy; 188br Meredith Kato; 189a Meredith Kato; 189br Alan Flanigan; 190b Netia Piercy; 190–191a Alan Flanigan; 191a From *Travels through Arabia, and Other Countries in the East*, Niebuhr, C.,1792; 191br Howard Wellman; 192 Fred Hocker; 193 Fred Hocker; 194 Courtesy of the Mariner's Museum, Newport News, VA; 195 Philip Voss; 196al Roger Smith; 196ar David Switzer; 196-197b PB after Peter Hentschel; 197cl David Switzer; 197cr MSM; 197br David Switzer; 198al MSM; 198ar MSM; 198cl MSM; 198bl MSM; 199al David Switzer; 199cr MSM; 200–201 Courtesy of the Mariner's Museum, Newport News, VA; 201bl National Portrait Gallery, London; 202a National Maritime Museum, London; 202b Bates Littlehales; 203a JDB, courtesy Virginia Department of Historic Resources; 203b Bates Littlehales; 204bl Bates Littlehales; 204–205a JDB, courtesy Virginia Department of Historic Resources; 205ar JDB, courtesy Virginia Department of Historic Resources; 205cr Roy Anderson; 206 Margaret Leshikar-Denton; 207ar from *One Hundred Silhouette Portraits from the Collection of Francis Wellesley*, Oxford University Press, 1912; 207bl Royal Gazette XVI, no. 4, 18–25 January 1794, Jamaica, from the Public Record Office, Kew, London; 207br Collection Jean Boudriot, France; 208bl Margaret Leshikar-Denton; 208br Indiana University SRD; 208–209a Dennis Denton; 209ar Mike Guderian; 209br Photo courtesy of Lennon Christian, Cayman Islands Government Information Services; 210 R/V AMK; 212a Amy Borgens; 212b ML; 213l Peabody Essex Museum; 213r Photo Courtesy Peabody Essex Museum M8255; 214a Courtesy of the Bernice Pauahi Bishop Museum; 214b S/NMAH; 215a Painting by Richard W. Rogers, S/NMAH; 215cr S/NMAH; 215br S/NMAH; 216al S/NMAH; 216ar Photo by Conservation Research Laboratory, TAMU; 216br S/NMAH; 217a S/NMAH; 217b S/NMAH; 218cr John Butler; 218–219b Vermont Division for Historic Preservation; 219ar John Butler; 219c Kevin Crisman; 220bl Amon Carter Museum, Fort Worth, Texas; 220br Kevin Crisman; 220–221a Carrie Sowden; 221ar Carrie Sowden; 221br Steven Wilson; 222 Private Collection; 223a Brett Phaneuf/Barto Arnold; 223b Andy Hall; 224cr Andy Hall; 224b Andy Hall; 225a Andy Hall; 225bc Helen Dewolf/Barto Arnold; 225br Barto Arnold; 226 Kevin Crisman; 227al LCMMC; 227ac LCMMC; 227ar LCMMC; 227br LCMMC; 228al Pierre LaRocque, LCMMC; 228ar LCMMC; 228bl Kevin Crisman; 229ar Nick Lavecchia, LCMMC; 229bl Eric Bessette, LCMMC; 230–231b Courtesy of the Mariner's Museum, Newport News, VA; 231a R/V AMK; 232al Jeremy Weirich; 232ar R/V AMK; 233a Sergei Gyduk, courtesy Anatoly Sagalevitch; 233b R/V AMK; 234l R/V AMK; 234r Produced by Yuri Rzhanov for the National Oceanic and Atmospheric Administration and the University of New Hampshire's Center for Coastal Ocean Mapping; 235l R/V AMK; 235r George F. Bass; 236al R/V AMK; 236ac R/V AMK; 236bl Courtesy of National Oceanic and Atmospheric Administration; 237ar R/V AMK; 237bl Jeremy Weirich; 238l US National Archives and Records Administration; 238–239 US National Archives and Records Administration; 239ar JG; 240ar JG; 240–241b JG; 241a JG; 241br Brian Beltz; 242 INA; 243a INA; 243b INA; 244al Courtesy of the BBC and Discovery Channel; 244br Tank Museum, Bovington; 245a Photo © Robert Capa Magnum Photos; 246br Tank Museum, Bovington

Index

Page numbers in *italic* refer to illustrations and in **bold** to main entries